Springer Texts in Statistics

Springer Texts in Statistics (STS) includes advanced textbooks from 3rd- to 4th-year undergraduate levels to 1st- to 2nd-year graduate levels. Exercise sets should be included. The series editors are currently Genevera I. Allen, Richard D. De Veaux, and Rebecca Nugent. Stephen Fienberg, George Casella, and Ingram Olkin were editors of the series for many years.

Gareth James • Daniela Witten • Trevor Hastie
Robert Tibshirani • Jonathan Taylor

An Introduction to Statistical Learning

with Applications in Python

Springer

Gareth James
Goizueta Business School
Emory University
Atlanta, GA, USA

Trevor Hastie
Departments of Statistics
and Biomedical Data Science
Stanford University
Stanford, CA, USA

Jonathan Taylor
Department of Statistics
Stanford University
Stanford, CA, USA

Daniela Witten
Departments of Statistics
and Biostatistics
University of Washington
Seattle, WA, USA

Robert Tibshirani
Departments of Biomedical
Data Science and Statistics
Stanford University
Stanford, CA, USA

ISSN 1431-875X ISSN 2197-4136 (electronic)
Springer Texts in Statistics
https://doi.org/10.1007/978-3-031-38747-0

This Springer imprint is published by the registered company Springer Nature Switzerland AG
The registered company address is: Gewerbestrasse 11, 6330 Cham, Switzerland

To our parents:

Alison and Michael James

Chiara Nappi and Edward Witten

Valerie and Patrick Hastie

Vera and Sami Tibshirani

John and Brenda Taylor

and to our families:

Michael, Daniel, and Catherine

Tessa, Theo, Otto, and Ari

Samantha, Timothy, and Lynda

Charlie, Ryan, Julie, and Cheryl

Lee-Ann and Isobel

Preface

Statistical learning refers to a set of tools for *making sense of complex datasets*. In recent years, we have seen a staggering increase in the scale and scope of data collection across virtually all areas of science and industry. As a result, statistical learning has become a critical toolkit for anyone who wishes to understand data — and as more and more of today's jobs involve data, this means that statistical learning is fast becoming a critical toolkit for *everyone*.

One of the first books on statistical learning — *The Elements of Statistical Learning* (ESL, by Hastie, Tibshirani, and Friedman) — was published in 2001, with a second edition in 2009. ESL has become a popular text not only in statistics but also in related fields. One of the reasons for ESL's popularity is its relatively accessible style. But ESL is best-suited for individuals with advanced training in the mathematical sciences.

An Introduction to Statistical Learning, With Applications in R (ISLR) — first published in 2013, with a second edition in 2021 — arose from the clear need for a broader and less technical treatment of the key topics in statistical learning. In addition to a review of linear regression, ISLR covers many of today's most important statistical and machine learning approaches, including resampling, sparse methods for classification and regression, generalized additive models, tree-based methods, support vector machines, deep learning, survival analysis, clustering, and multiple testing.

Since it was published in 2013, ISLR has become a mainstay of undergraduate and graduate classrooms worldwide, as well as an important reference book for data scientists. One of the keys to its success has been that, beginning with Chapter 2, each chapter contains an `R` lab illustrating how to implement the statistical learning methods seen in that chapter, providing the reader with valuable hands-on experience.

However, in recent years `Python` has become an increasingly popular language for data science, and there has been increasing demand for a `Python`-

based alternative to ISLR. Hence, this book, *An Introduction to Statistical Learning, With Applications in Python* (ISLP), covers the same materials as ISLR but with labs implemented in `Python` — a feat accomplished by the addition of a new co-author, Jonathan Taylor. Several of the labs make use of the `ISLP` `Python` package, which we have written to facilitate carrying out the statistical learning methods covered in each chapter in `Python`. These labs will be useful both for `Python` novices, as well as experienced users.

The intention behind ISLP (and ISLR) is to concentrate more on the applications of the methods and less on the mathematical details, so it is appropriate for advanced undergraduates or master's students in statistics or related quantitative fields, or for individuals in other disciplines who wish to use statistical learning tools to analyze their data. It can be used as a textbook for a course spanning two semesters.

We are grateful to these readers for providing valuable comments on the first edition of ISLR: Pallavi Basu, Alexandra Chouldechova, Patrick Danaher, Will Fithian, Luella Fu, Sam Gross, Max Grazier G'Sell, Courtney Paulson, Xinghao Qiao, Elisa Sheng, Noah Simon, Kean Ming Tan, Xin Lu Tan. We thank these readers for helpful input on the second edition of ISLR: Alan Agresti, Iain Carmichael, Yiqun Chen, Erin Craig, Daisy Ding, Lucy Gao, Ismael Lemhadri, Bryan Martin, Anna Neufeld, Geoff Tims, Carsten Voelkmann, Steve Yadlowsky, and James Zou. We are immensely grateful to Balasubramanian "Naras" Narasimhan for his assistance on both ISLR and ISLP.

It has been an honor and a privilege for us to see the considerable impact that ISLR has had on the way in which statistical learning is practiced, both in and out of the academic setting. We hope that this new `Python` edition will continue to give today's and tomorrow's applied statisticians and data scientists the tools they need for success in a data-driven world.

It's tough to make predictions, especially about the future.

-Yogi Berra

Contents

1
Introduction

An Overview of Statistical Learning

Statistical learning refers to a vast set of tools for *understanding data.* These tools can be classified as *supervised* or *unsupervised.* Broadly speaking, supervised statistical learning involves building a statistical model for predicting, or estimating, an *output* based on one or more *inputs.* Problems of this nature occur in fields as diverse as business, medicine, astrophysics, and public policy. With unsupervised statistical learning, there are inputs but no supervising output; nevertheless we can learn relationships and structure from such data. To provide an illustration of some applications of statistical learning, we briefly discuss three real-world data sets that are considered in this book.

Wage Data

In this application (which we refer to as the `Wage` data set throughout this book), we examine a number of factors that relate to wages for a group of men from the Atlantic region of the United States. In particular, we wish to understand the association between an employee's `age` and `education`, as well as the calendar `year`, on his `wage`. Consider, for example, the left-hand panel of Figure 1.1, which displays `wage` versus `age` for each of the individuals in the data set. There is evidence that `wage` increases with `age` but then decreases again after approximately age 60. The blue line, which provides an estimate of the average `wage` for a given `age`, makes this trend clearer. Given an employee's `age`, we can use this curve to *predict* his `wage`. However, it is also clear from Figure 1.1 that there is a significant amount of variability associated with this average value, and so `age` alone is unlikely to provide an accurate prediction of a particular man's `wage`.

G. James et al., *An Introduction to Statistical Learning*, Springer Texts in Statistics,
https://doi.org/10.1007/978-3-031-38747-0_1

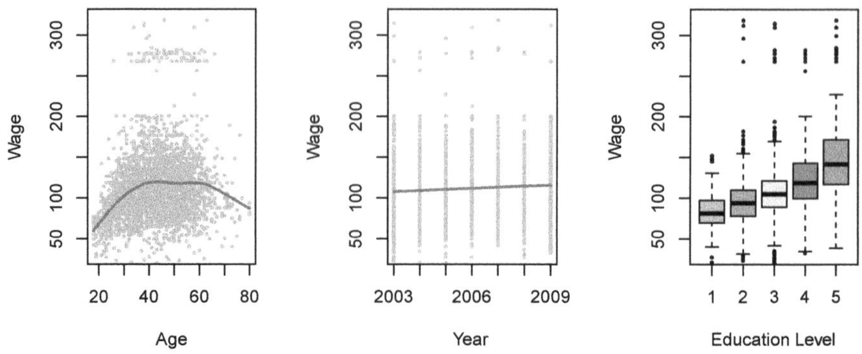

FIGURE 1.1. Wage *data, which contains income survey information for men from the central Atlantic region of the United States.* Left: wage *as a function of* age*. On average,* wage *increases with* age *until about* 60 *years of age, at which point it begins to decline.* Center: wage *as a function of* year*. There is a slow but steady increase of approximately* $10,000 *in the average* wage *between* 2003 *and* 2009. Right: *Boxplots displaying* wage *as a function of* education*, with* 1 *indicating the lowest level (no high school diploma) and* 5 *the highest level (an advanced graduate degree). On average,* wage *increases with the level of education.*

We also have information regarding each employee's education level and the year in which the wage was earned. The center and right-hand panels of Figure 1.1, which display wage as a function of both year and education, indicate that both of these factors are associated with wage. Wages increase by approximately $10,000, in a roughly linear (or straight-line) fashion, between 2003 and 2009, though this rise is very slight relative to the variability in the data. Wages are also typically greater for individuals with higher education levels: men with the lowest education level (1) tend to have substantially lower wages than those with the highest education level (5). Clearly, the most accurate prediction of a given man's wage will be obtained by combining his age, his education, and the year. In Chapter 3, we discuss linear regression, which can be used to predict wage from this data set. Ideally, we should predict wage in a way that accounts for the non-linear relationship between wage and age. In Chapter 7, we discuss a class of approaches for addressing this problem.

Stock Market Data

The Wage data involves predicting a *continuous* or *quantitative* output value. This is often referred to as a *regression* problem. However, in certain cases we may instead wish to predict a non-numerical value—that is, a *categorical* or *qualitative* output. For example, in Chapter 4 we examine a stock market data set that contains the daily movements in the Standard & Poor's 500 (S&P) stock index over a 5-year period between 2001 and 2005. We refer to this as the Smarket data. The goal is to predict whether the index will *increase* or *decrease* on a given day, using the past 5 days' percentage changes in the index. Here the statistical learning problem does not involve predicting a numerical value. Instead it involves predicting whether a given

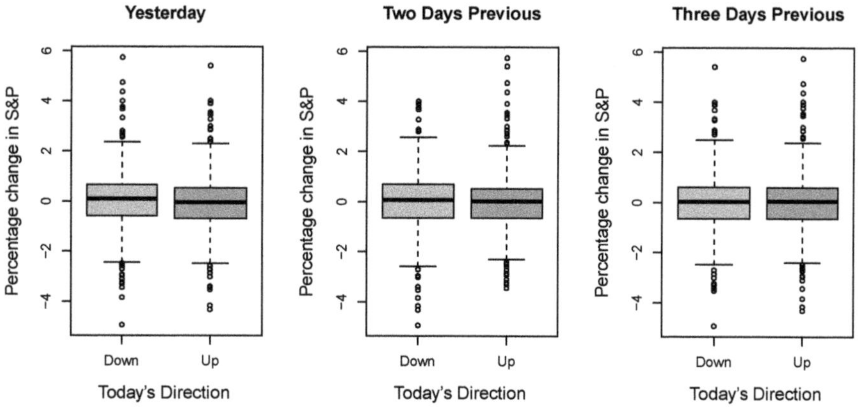

FIGURE 1.2. Left: *Boxplots of the previous day's percentage change in the S&P index for the days for which the market increased or decreased, obtained from the* `Smarket` *data.* Center and Right: *Same as left panel, but the percentage changes for 2 and 3 days previous are shown.*

day's stock market performance will fall into the `Up` bucket or the `Down` bucket. This is known as a *classification* problem. A model that could accurately predict the direction in which the market will move would be very useful!

The left-hand panel of Figure 1.2 displays two boxplots of the previous day's percentage changes in the stock index: one for the 648 days for which the market increased on the subsequent day, and one for the 602 days for which the market decreased. The two plots look almost identical, suggesting that there is no simple strategy for using yesterday's movement in the S&P to predict today's returns. The remaining panels, which display boxplots for the percentage changes 2 and 3 days previous to today, similarly indicate little association between past and present returns. Of course, this lack of pattern is to be expected: in the presence of strong correlations between successive days' returns, one could adopt a simple trading strategy to generate profits from the market. Nevertheless, in Chapter 4, we explore these data using several different statistical learning methods. Interestingly, there are hints of some weak trends in the data that suggest that, at least for this 5-year period, it is possible to correctly predict the direction of movement in the market approximately 60% of the time (Figure 1.3).

Gene Expression Data

The previous two applications illustrate data sets with both input and output variables. However, another important class of problems involves situations in which we only observe input variables, with no corresponding output. For example, in a marketing setting, we might have demographic information for a number of current or potential customers. We may wish to understand which types of customers are similar to each other by grouping individuals according to their observed characteristics. This is known as a

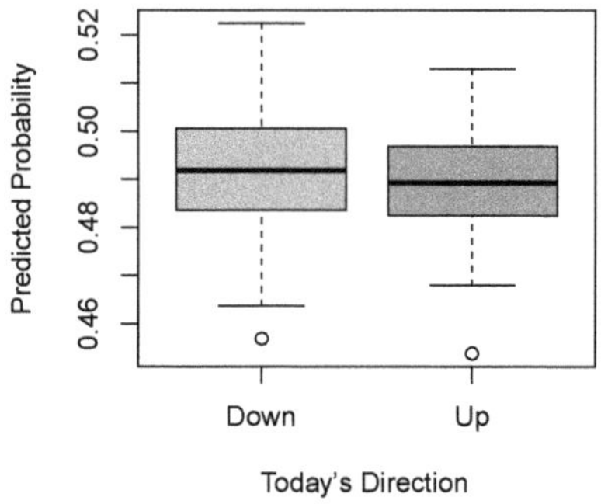

FIGURE 1.3. *We fit a quadratic discriminant analysis model to the subset of the* `Smarket` *data corresponding to the 2001–2004 time period, and predicted the probability of a stock market decrease using the 2005 data. On average, the predicted probability of decrease is higher for the days in which the market does decrease. Based on these results, we are able to correctly predict the direction of movement in the market 60% of the time.*

clustering problem. Unlike in the previous examples, here we are not trying to predict an output variable.

We devote Chapter 12 to a discussion of statistical learning methods for problems in which no natural output variable is available. We consider the `NCI60` data set, which consists of 6,830 gene expression measurements for each of 64 cancer cell lines. Instead of predicting a particular output variable, we are interested in determining whether there are groups, or clusters, among the cell lines based on their gene expression measurements. This is a difficult question to address, in part because there are thousands of gene expression measurements per cell line, making it hard to visualize the data.

The left-hand panel of Figure 1.4 addresses this problem by representing each of the 64 cell lines using just two numbers, Z_1 and Z_2. These are the first two *principal components* of the data, which summarize the 6,830 expression measurements for each cell line down to two numbers or *dimensions*. While it is likely that this dimension reduction has resulted in some loss of information, it is now possible to visually examine the data for evidence of clustering. Deciding on the number of clusters is often a difficult problem. But the left-hand panel of Figure 1.4 suggests at least four groups of cell lines, which we have represented using separate colors.

In this particular data set, it turns out that the cell lines correspond to 14 different types of cancer. (However, this information was not used to create the left-hand panel of Figure 1.4.) The right-hand panel of Figure 1.4 is identical to the left-hand panel, except that the 14 cancer types are shown using distinct colored symbols. There is clear evidence that cell lines with the same cancer type tend to be located near each other in this two-dimensional representation. In addition, even though the cancer information was not used to produce the left-hand panel, the clustering obtained does bear some resemblance to some of the actual cancer types observed in the right-hand panel. This provides some independent verification of the accuracy of our clustering analysis.

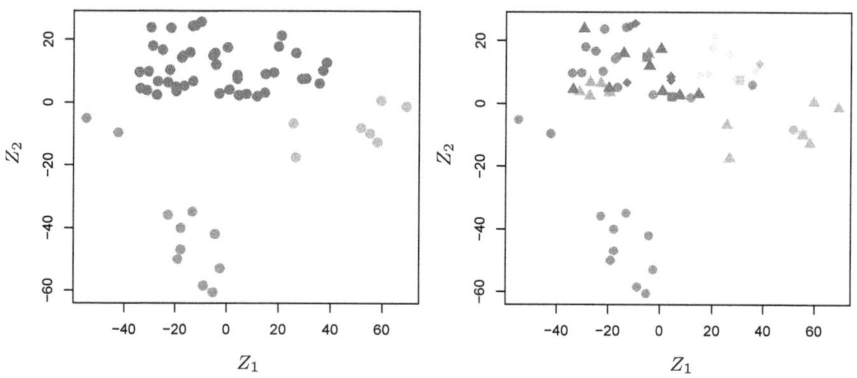

FIGURE 1.4. Left: *Representation of the* NCI60 *gene expression data set in a two-dimensional space,* Z_1 *and* Z_2*. Each point corresponds to one of the* 64 *cell lines. There appear to be four groups of cell lines, which we have represented using different colors.* Right: *Same as left panel except that we have represented each of the* 14 *different types of cancer using a different colored symbol. Cell lines corresponding to the same cancer type tend to be nearby in the two-dimensional space.*

A Brief History of Statistical Learning

Though the term *statistical learning* is fairly new, many of the concepts that underlie the field were developed long ago. At the beginning of the nineteenth century, the method of *least squares* was developed, implementing the earliest form of what is now known as *linear regression*. The approach was first successfully applied to problems in astronomy. Linear regression is used for predicting quantitative values, such as an individual's salary. In order to predict qualitative values, such as whether a patient survives or dies, or whether the stock market increases or decreases, *linear discriminant analysis* was proposed in 1936. In the 1940s, various authors put forth an alternative approach, *logistic regression*. In the early 1970s, the term *generalized linear model* was developed to describe an entire class of statistical learning methods that include both linear and logistic regression as special cases.

By the end of the 1970s, many more techniques for learning from data were available. However, they were almost exclusively *linear* methods because fitting *non-linear* relationships was computationally difficult at the time. By the 1980s, computing technology had finally improved sufficiently that non-linear methods were no longer computationally prohibitive. In the mid 1980s, *classification and regression trees* were developed, followed shortly by *generalized additive models*. *Neural networks* gained popularity in the 1980s, and *support vector machines* arose in the 1990s.

Since that time, statistical learning has emerged as a new subfield in statistics, focused on supervised and unsupervised modeling and prediction. In recent years, progress in statistical learning has been marked by the increasing availability of powerful and relatively user-friendly software, such as the popular and freely available `Python` system. This has the potential to continue the transformation of the field from a set of techniques used and developed by statisticians and computer scientists to an essential toolkit for a much broader community.

This Book

The Elements of Statistical Learning (ESL) by Hastie, Tibshirani, and Friedman was first published in 2001. Since that time, it has become an important reference on the fundamentals of statistical machine learning. Its success derives from its comprehensive and detailed treatment of many important topics in statistical learning, as well as the fact that (relative to many upper-level statistics textbooks) it is accessible to a wide audience. However, the greatest factor behind the success of ESL has been its topical nature. At the time of its publication, interest in the field of statistical learning was starting to explode. ESL provided one of the first accessible and comprehensive introductions to the topic.

Since ESL was first published, the field of statistical learning has continued to flourish. The field's expansion has taken two forms. The most obvious growth has involved the development of new and improved statistical learning approaches aimed at answering a range of scientific questions across a number of fields. However, the field of statistical learning has also expanded its audience. In the 1990s, increases in computational power generated a surge of interest in the field from non-statisticians who were eager to use cutting-edge statistical tools to analyze their data. Unfortunately, the highly technical nature of these approaches meant that the user community remained primarily restricted to experts in statistics, computer science, and related fields with the training (and time) to understand and implement them.

In recent years, new and improved software packages have significantly eased the implementation burden for many statistical learning methods. At the same time, there has been growing recognition across a number of fields, from business to health care to genetics to the social sciences and beyond, that statistical learning is a powerful tool with important practical applications. As a result, the field has moved from one of primarily academic interest to a mainstream discipline, with an enormous potential audience. This trend will surely continue with the increasing availability of enormous quantities of data and the software to analyze it.

The purpose of *An Introduction to Statistical Learning* (ISL) is to facilitate the transition of statistical learning from an academic to a mainstream field. ISL is not intended to replace ESL, which is a far more comprehensive text both in terms of the number of approaches considered and the depth to which they are explored. We consider ESL to be an important companion for professionals (with graduate degrees in statistics, machine learning, or related fields) who need to understand the technical details behind statistical learning approaches. However, the community of users of statistical learning techniques has expanded to include individuals with a wider range of interests and backgrounds. Therefore, there is a place for a less technical and more accessible version of ESL.

In teaching these topics over the years, we have discovered that they are of interest to master's and PhD students in fields as disparate as business administration, biology, and computer science, as well as to quantitatively-oriented upper-division undergraduates. It is important for this diverse group to be able to understand the models, intuitions, and strengths and weaknesses of the various approaches. But for this audience, many of the technical details behind statistical learning methods, such as optimization algorithms and theoretical properties, are not of primary interest. We believe that these students do not need a deep understanding of these aspects in order to become informed users of the various methodologies, and in order to contribute to their chosen fields through the use of statistical learning tools.

ISL is based on the following four premises.

1. *Many statistical learning methods are relevant and useful in a wide range of academic and non-academic disciplines, beyond just the statistical sciences.* We believe that many contemporary statistical learning procedures should, and will, become as widely available and used as is currently the case for classical methods such as linear regression. As a result, rather than attempting to consider every possible approach (an impossible task), we have concentrated on presenting the methods that we believe are most widely applicable.

2. *Statistical learning should not be viewed as a series of black boxes.* No single approach will perform well in all possible applications. Without understanding all of the cogs inside the box, or the interaction between those cogs, it is impossible to select the best box. Hence, we have attempted to carefully describe the model, intuition, assumptions, and trade-offs behind each of the methods that we consider.

3. *While it is important to know what job is performed by each cog, it is not necessary to have the skills to construct the machine inside the box!* Thus, we have minimized discussion of technical details related to fitting procedures and theoretical properties. We assume that the reader is comfortable with basic mathematical concepts, but we do not assume a graduate degree in the mathematical sciences. For instance, we have almost completely avoided the use of matrix algebra, and it is possible to understand the entire book without a detailed knowledge of matrices and vectors.

4. *We presume that the reader is interested in applying statistical learning methods to real-world problems.* In order to facilitate this, as well as to motivate the techniques discussed, we have devoted a section within each chapter to computer labs. In each lab, we walk the reader through a realistic application of the methods considered in that chapter. When we have taught this material in our courses, we have allocated roughly one-third of classroom time to working through the labs, and we have found them to be extremely useful. Many of the less computationally-oriented students who were initially intimidated by the labs got the hang of things over the course of the quarter or semester. This book originally appeared (2013, second edition 2021)

with computer labs written in the R language. Since then, there has been increasing demand for Python implementations of the important techniques in statistical learning. Consequently, this version has labs in Python. There are a rapidly growing number of Python packages available, and by examination of the imports at the beginning of each lab, readers will see that we have carefully selected and used the most appropriate. We have also supplied some additional code and functionality in our package ISLP. However, the labs in ISL are self-contained, and can be skipped if the reader wishes to use a different software package or does not wish to apply the methods discussed to real-world problems.

Who Should Read This Book?

This book is intended for anyone who is interested in using modern statistical methods for modeling and prediction from data. This group includes scientists, engineers, data analysts, data scientists, and quants, but also less technical individuals with degrees in non-quantitative fields such as the social sciences or business. We expect that the reader will have had at least one elementary course in statistics. Background in linear regression is also useful, though not required, since we review the key concepts behind linear regression in Chapter 3. The mathematical level of this book is modest, and a detailed knowledge of matrix operations is not required. This book provides an introduction to Python. Previous exposure to a programming language, such as MATLAB or R, is useful but not required.

The first edition of this textbook has been used to teach master's and PhD students in business, economics, computer science, biology, earth sciences, psychology, and many other areas of the physical and social sciences. It has also been used to teach advanced undergraduates who have already taken a course on linear regression. In the context of a more mathematically rigorous course in which ESL serves as the primary textbook, ISL could be used as a supplementary text for teaching computational aspects of the various approaches.

Notation and Simple Matrix Algebra

Choosing notation for a textbook is always a difficult task. For the most part we adopt the same notational conventions as ESL.

We will use n to represent the number of distinct data points, or observations, in our sample. We will let p denote the number of variables that are available for use in making predictions. For example, the Wage data set consists of 11 variables for 3,000 people, so we have $n = 3{,}000$ observations and $p = 11$ variables (such as year, age, race, and more). Note that throughout this book, we indicate variable names using colored font: Variable Name.

In some examples, p might be quite large, such as on the order of thousands or even millions; this situation arises quite often, for example, in the analysis of modern biological data or web-based advertising data.

In general, we will let x_{ij} represent the value of the jth variable for the ith observation, where $i = 1, 2, \ldots, n$ and $j = 1, 2, \ldots, p$. Throughout this book, i will be used to index the samples or observations (from 1 to n) and j will be used to index the variables (from 1 to p). We let $\mathbf{X}$ denote an $n \times p$ matrix whose (i, j)th element is x_{ij}. That is,

$$\mathbf{X} = \begin{pmatrix} x_{11} & x_{12} & \ldots & x_{1p} \\ x_{21} & x_{22} & \ldots & x_{2p} \\ \vdots & \vdots & \ddots & \vdots \\ x_{n1} & x_{n2} & \ldots & x_{np} \end{pmatrix}.$$

For readers who are unfamiliar with matrices, it is useful to visualize $\mathbf{X}$ as a spreadsheet of numbers with n rows and p columns.

At times we will be interested in the rows of $\mathbf{X}$, which we write as $x_1, x_2, \ldots, x_n$. Here x_i is a vector of length p, containing the p variable measurements for the ith observation. That is,

$$x_i = \begin{pmatrix} x_{i1} \\ x_{i2} \\ \vdots \\ x_{ip} \end{pmatrix}. \tag{1.1}$$

(Vectors are by default represented as columns.) For example, for the `Wage` data, x_i is a vector of length 11, consisting of `year`, `age`, `race`, and other values for the ith individual. At other times we will instead be interested in the columns of $\mathbf{X}$, which we write as $\mathbf{x}_1, \mathbf{x}_2, \ldots, \mathbf{x}_p$. Each is a vector of length n. That is,

$$\mathbf{x}_j = \begin{pmatrix} x_{1j} \\ x_{2j} \\ \vdots \\ x_{nj} \end{pmatrix}.$$

For example, for the `Wage` data, $\mathbf{x}_1$ contains the $n = 3{,}000$ values for `year`.

Using this notation, the matrix $\mathbf{X}$ can be written as

$$\mathbf{X} = \begin{pmatrix} \mathbf{x}_1 & \mathbf{x}_2 & \cdots & \mathbf{x}_p \end{pmatrix},$$

or

$$\mathbf{X} = \begin{pmatrix} x_1^T \\ x_2^T \\ \vdots \\ x_n^T \end{pmatrix}.$$

The ^{T} notation denotes the *transpose* of a matrix or vector. So, for example,

$$\mathbf{X}^T = \begin{pmatrix} x_{11} & x_{21} & \ldots & x_{n1} \\ x_{12} & x_{22} & \ldots & x_{n2} \\ \vdots & \vdots & & \vdots \\ x_{1p} & x_{2p} & \ldots & x_{np} \end{pmatrix},$$

while

$$x_i^T = \begin{pmatrix} x_{i1} & x_{i2} & \cdots & x_{ip} \end{pmatrix}.$$

We use y_i to denote the ith observation of the variable on which we wish to make predictions, such as `wage`. Hence, we write the set of all n observations in vector form as

$$\mathbf{y} = \begin{pmatrix} y_1 \\ y_2 \\ \vdots \\ y_n \end{pmatrix}.$$

Then our observed data consists of $\{(x_1, y_1), (x_2, y_2), \ldots, (x_n, y_n)\}$, where each x_i is a vector of length p. (If $p = 1$, then x_i is simply a scalar.)

In this text, a vector of length n will always be denoted in *lower case bold*; e.g.

$$\mathbf{a} = \begin{pmatrix} a_1 \\ a_2 \\ \vdots \\ a_n \end{pmatrix}.$$

However, vectors that are not of length n (such as feature vectors of length p, as in (1.1)) will be denoted in *lower case normal font*, e.g. a. Scalars will also be denoted in *lower case normal font*, e.g. a. In the rare cases in which these two uses for lower case normal font lead to ambiguity, we will clarify which use is intended. Matrices will be denoted using *bold capitals*, such as $\mathbf{A}$. Random variables will be denoted using *capital normal font*, e.g. A, regardless of their dimensions.

Occasionally we will want to indicate the dimension of a particular object. To indicate that an object is a scalar, we will use the notation $a \in \mathbb{R}$. To indicate that it is a vector of length k, we will use $a \in \mathbb{R}^k$ (or $\mathbf{a} \in \mathbb{R}^n$ if it is of length n). We will indicate that an object is an $r \times s$ matrix using $\mathbf{A} \in \mathbb{R}^{r \times s}$.

We have avoided using matrix algebra whenever possible. However, in a few instances it becomes too cumbersome to avoid it entirely. In these rare instances it is important to understand the concept of multiplying two matrices. Suppose that $\mathbf{A} \in \mathbb{R}^{r \times d}$ and $\mathbf{B} \in \mathbb{R}^{d \times s}$. Then the product of $\mathbf{A}$ and $\mathbf{B}$ is denoted $\mathbf{AB}$. The (i,j)th element of $\mathbf{AB}$ is computed by multiplying each element of the ith row of $\mathbf{A}$ by the corresponding element of the jth column of $\mathbf{B}$. That is, $(\mathbf{AB})_{ij} = \sum_{k=1}^{d} a_{ik} b_{kj}$. As an example, consider

$$\mathbf{A} = \begin{pmatrix} 1 & 2 \\ 3 & 4 \end{pmatrix} \quad \text{and} \quad \mathbf{B} = \begin{pmatrix} 5 & 6 \\ 7 & 8 \end{pmatrix}.$$

Then

$$\mathbf{AB} = \begin{pmatrix} 1 & 2 \\ 3 & 4 \end{pmatrix} \begin{pmatrix} 5 & 6 \\ 7 & 8 \end{pmatrix} = \begin{pmatrix} 1 \times 5 + 2 \times 7 & 1 \times 6 + 2 \times 8 \\ 3 \times 5 + 4 \times 7 & 3 \times 6 + 4 \times 8 \end{pmatrix} = \begin{pmatrix} 19 & 22 \\ 43 & 50 \end{pmatrix}.$$

Note that this operation produces an $r \times s$ matrix. It is only possible to compute $\mathbf{AB}$ if the number of columns of $\mathbf{A}$ is the same as the number of rows of $\mathbf{B}$.

Organization of This Book

Chapter 2 introduces the basic terminology and concepts behind statistical learning. This chapter also presents the *K-nearest neighbor* classifier, a very simple method that works surprisingly well on many problems. Chapters 3 and 4 cover classical linear methods for regression and classification. In particular, Chapter 3 reviews *linear regression*, the fundamental starting point for all regression methods. In Chapter 4 we discuss two of the most important classical classification methods, *logistic regression* and *linear discriminant analysis.*

A central problem in all statistical learning situations involves choosing the best method for a given application. Hence, in Chapter 5 we introduce *cross-validation* and the *bootstrap*, which can be used to estimate the accuracy of a number of different methods in order to choose the best one.

Much of the recent research in statistical learning has concentrated on non-linear methods. However, linear methods often have advantages over their non-linear competitors in terms of interpretability and sometimes also accuracy. Hence, in Chapter 6 we consider a host of linear methods, both classical and more modern, which offer potential improvements over standard linear regression. These include *stepwise selection*, *ridge regression*, *principal components regression*, and the *lasso.*

The remaining chapters move into the world of non-linear statistical learning. We first introduce in Chapter 7 a number of non-linear methods that work well for problems with a single input variable. We then show how these methods can be used to fit non-linear *additive* models for which there is more than one input. In Chapter 8, we investigate *tree*-based methods, including *bagging*, *boosting*, and *random forests. Support vector machines*, a set of approaches for performing both linear and non-linear classification, are discussed in Chapter 9. We cover *deep learning*, an approach for non-linear regression and classification that has received a lot of attention in recent years, in Chapter 10. Chapter 11 explores *survival analysis*, a regression approach that is specialized to the setting in which the output variable is *censored*, i.e. not fully observed.

In Chapter 12, we consider the *unsupervised* setting in which we have input variables but no output variable. In particular, we present *principal components analysis*, *K-means clustering*, and *hierarchical clustering.* Finally, in Chapter 13 we cover the very important topic of multiple hypothesis testing.

At the end of each chapter, we present one or more `Python` lab sections in which we systematically work through applications of the various methods discussed in that chapter. These labs demonstrate the strengths and weaknesses of the various approaches, and also provide a useful reference for the syntax required to implement the various methods. The reader may choose to work through the labs at their own pace, or the labs may be the focus of group sessions as part of a classroom environment. Within each `Python` lab, we present the results that we obtained when we performed the lab at the time of writing this book. However, new versions of `Python` are continuously released, and over time, the packages called in the labs will be updated. Therefore, in the future, it is possible that the results shown in

Name	Description
`Auto`	Gas mileage, horsepower, and other information for cars.
`Bikeshare`	Hourly usage of a bike sharing program in Washington, DC.
`Boston`	Housing values and other information about Boston census tracts.
`BrainCancer`	Survival times for patients diagnosed with brain cancer.
`Caravan`	Information about individuals offered caravan insurance.
`Carseats`	Information about car seat sales in 400 stores.
`College`	Demographic characteristics, tuition, and more for USA colleges.
`Credit`	Information about credit card debt for 400 customers.
`Default`	Customer default records for a credit card company.
`Fund`	Returns of 2,000 hedge fund managers over 50 months.
`Hitters`	Records and salaries for baseball players.
`Khan`	Gene expression measurements for four cancer types.
`NCI60`	Gene expression measurements for 64 cancer cell lines.
`NYSE`	Returns, volatility, and volume for the New York Stock Exchange.
`OJ`	Sales information for Citrus Hill and Minute Maid orange juice.
`Portfolio`	Past values of financial assets, for use in portfolio allocation.
`Publication`	Time to publication for 244 clinical trials.
`Smarket`	Daily percentage returns for S&P 500 over a 5-year period.
`USArrests`	Crime statistics per 100,000 residents in 50 states of USA.
`Wage`	Income survey data for men in central Atlantic region of USA.
`Weekly`	1,089 weekly stock market returns for 21 years.

TABLE 1.1. *A list of data sets needed to perform the labs and exercises in this textbook. All data sets are available in the* `ISLP` *package, with the exception of* `USArrests`*, which is part of the base* `R` *distribution, but accessible from* `Python`.

the lab sections may no longer correspond precisely to the results obtained by the reader who performs the labs. As necessary, we will post updates to the labs on the book website.

We use the symbol to denote sections or exercises that contain more challenging concepts. These can be easily skipped by readers who do not wish to delve as deeply into the material, or who lack the mathematical background.

Data Sets Used in Labs and Exercises

In this textbook, we illustrate statistical learning methods using applications from marketing, finance, biology, and other areas. The `ISLP` package contains a number of data sets that are required in order to perform the labs and exercises associated with this book. One other data set is part of the base `R` distribution (the `USArrests` data), and we show how to access it from `Python` in Section 12.5.1. Table 1.1 contains a summary of the data sets required to perform the labs and exercises. A couple of these data sets are also available as text files on the book website, for use in Chapter 2.

Book Website

The website for this book is located at

`www.statlearning.com`

It contains a number of resources, including the `Python` package associated with this book, and some additional data sets.

Acknowledgements

A few of the plots in this book were taken from ESL: Figures 6.7, 8.3, and 12.14. All other plots were produced for the `R` version of ISL, except for Figure 13.10 which differs because of the `Python` software supporting the plot.

2
Statistical Learning

2.1 What Is Statistical Learning?

In order to motivate our study of statistical learning, we begin with a simple example. Suppose that we are statistical consultants hired by a client to investigate the association between advertising and sales of a particular product. The `Advertising` data set consists of the `sales` of that product in 200 different markets, along with advertising budgets for the product in each of those markets for three different media: `TV`, `radio`, and `newspaper`. The data are displayed in Figure 2.1. It is not possible for our client to directly increase sales of the product. On the other hand, they can control the advertising expenditure in each of the three media. Therefore, if we determine that there is an association between advertising and sales, then we can instruct our client to adjust advertising budgets, thereby indirectly increasing sales. In other words, our goal is to develop an accurate model that can be used to predict sales on the basis of the three media budgets.

In this setting, the advertising budgets are *input variables* while `sales` is an *output variable*. The input variables are typically denoted using the symbol X, with a subscript to distinguish them. So X_1 might be the `TV` budget, X_2 the `radio` budget, and X_3 the `newspaper` budget. The inputs go by different names, such as *predictors*, *independent variables*, *features*, or sometimes just *variables*. The output variable—in this case, `sales`—is often called the *response* or *dependent variable*, and is typically denoted using the symbol Y. Throughout this book, we will use all of these terms interchangeably.

input variable
output variable
predictor
independent variable
feature
variable
response
dependent variable

More generally, suppose that we observe a quantitative response Y and p different predictors, $X_1, X_2, \ldots, X_p$. We assume that there is some relationship between Y and $X = (X_1, X_2, \ldots, X_p)$, which can be written in the very general form

$$Y = f(X) + \epsilon. \tag{2.1}$$

G. James et al., *An Introduction to Statistical Learning*, Springer Texts in Statistics,
https://doi.org/10.1007/978-3-031-38747-0_2

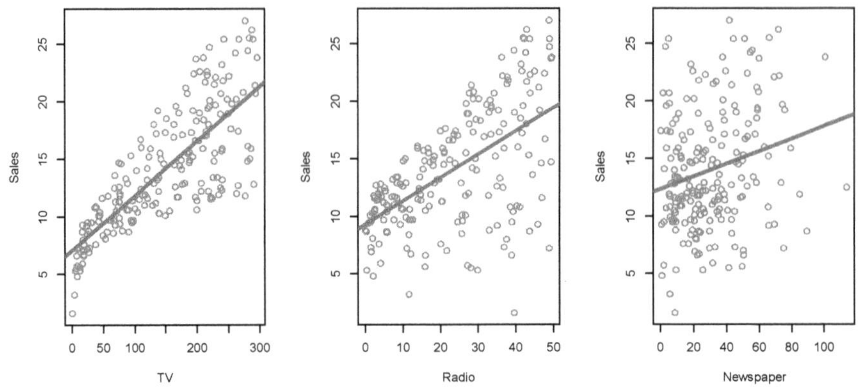

FIGURE 2.1. *The* `Advertising` *data set. The plot displays* `sales`*, in thousands of units, as a function of* `TV`*,* `radio`*, and* `newspaper` *budgets, in thousands of dollars, for* 200 *different markets. In each plot we show the simple least squares fit of* `sales` *to that variable, as described in Chapter 3. In other words, each blue line represents a simple model that can be used to predict* `sales` *using* `TV`*,* `radio`*, and* `newspaper`*, respectively.*

Here f is some fixed but unknown function of $X_1, \ldots, X_p$, and ϵ is a random *error term*, which is independent of X and has mean zero. In this formulation, f represents the *systematic* information that X provides about Y.

error term

systematic

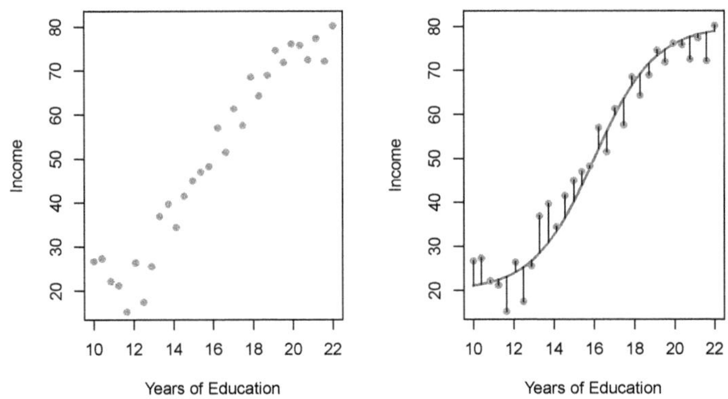

FIGURE 2.2. *The* `Income` *data set.* Left: *The red dots are the observed values of* `income` *(in thousands of dollars) and* `years of education` *for* 30 *individuals.* Right: *The blue curve represents the true underlying relationship between* `income` *and* `years of education`*, which is generally unknown (but is known in this case because the data were simulated). The black lines represent the error associated with each observation. Note that some errors are positive (if an observation lies above the blue curve) and some are negative (if an observation lies below the curve). Overall, these errors have approximately mean zero.*

As another example, consider the left-hand panel of Figure 2.2, a plot of `income` versus `years of education` for 30 individuals in the `Income` data set. The plot suggests that one might be able to predict `income` using `years of education`. However, the function f that connects the input variable to the output variable is in general unknown. In this situation one must estimate f based on the observed points. Since `Income` is a simulated data set, f is known and is shown by the blue curve in the right-hand panel of Figure 2.2. The vertical lines represent the error terms ϵ. We note that some of the 30 observations lie above the blue curve and some lie below it; overall, the errors have approximately mean zero.

In general, the function f may involve more than one input variable. In Figure 2.3 we plot `income` as a function of `years of education` and `seniority`. Here f is a two-dimensional surface that must be estimated based on the observed data.

In essence, statistical learning refers to a set of approaches for estimating f. In this chapter we outline some of the key theoretical concepts that arise in estimating f, as well as tools for evaluating the estimates obtained.

2.1.1 Why Estimate f?

There are two main reasons that we may wish to estimate f: *prediction* and *inference*. We discuss each in turn.

Prediction

In many situations, a set of inputs X are readily available, but the output Y cannot be easily obtained. In this setting, since the error term averages to zero, we can predict Y using

$$\hat{Y} = \hat{f}(X), \tag{2.2}$$

where $\hat{f}$ represents our estimate for f, and $\hat{Y}$ represents the resulting prediction for Y. In this setting, $\hat{f}$ is often treated as a *black box*, in the sense that one is not typically concerned with the exact form of $\hat{f}$, provided that it yields accurate predictions for Y.

As an example, suppose that $X_1, \ldots, X_p$ are characteristics of a patient's blood sample that can be easily measured in a lab, and Y is a variable encoding the patient's risk for a severe adverse reaction to a particular drug. It is natural to seek to predict Y using X, since we can then avoid giving the drug in question to patients who are at high risk of an adverse reaction—that is, patients for whom the estimate of Y is high.

The accuracy of $\hat{Y}$ as a prediction for Y depends on two quantities, which we will call the *reducible error* and the *irreducible error*. In general, $\hat{f}$ will not be a perfect estimate for f, and this inaccuracy will introduce some error. This error is *reducible* because we can potentially improve the accuracy of $\hat{f}$ by using the most appropriate statistical learning technique to estimate f. However, even if it were possible to form a perfect estimate for f, so that our estimated response took the form $\hat{Y} = f(X)$, our prediction would still have some error in it! This is because Y is also a function of ϵ, which, by definition, cannot be predicted using X. Therefore, variability associated with ϵ also affects the accuracy of our predictions. This is known as the *irreducible* error, because no matter how well we estimate f, we cannot reduce the error introduced by ϵ.

reducible error

irreducible error

Why is the irreducible error larger than zero? The quantity ϵ may contain unmeasured variables that are useful in predicting Y: since we don't

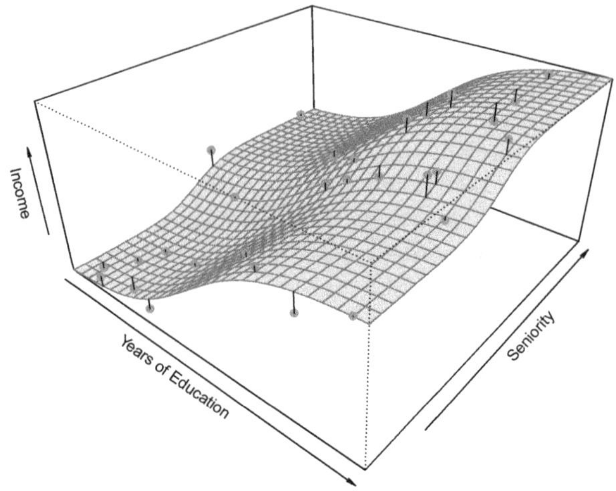

FIGURE 2.3. *The plot displays* `income` *as a function of* `years of education` *and* `seniority` *in the* `Income` *data set. The blue surface represents the true underlying relationship between* `income` *and* `years of education` *and* `seniority`*, which is known since the data are simulated. The red dots indicate the observed values of these quantities for* 30 *individuals.*

measure them, f cannot use them for its prediction. The quantity ϵ may also contain unmeasurable variation. For example, the risk of an adverse reaction might vary for a given patient on a given day, depending on manufacturing variation in the drug itself or the patient's general feeling of well-being on that day.

Consider a given estimate $\hat{f}$ and a set of predictors X, which yields the prediction $\hat{Y} = \hat{f}(X)$. Assume for a moment that both $\hat{f}$ and X are fixed, so that the only variability comes from ϵ. Then, it is easy to show that

$$\begin{aligned} \mathrm{E}(Y - \hat{Y})^2 &= \mathrm{E}[f(X) + \epsilon - \hat{f}(X)]^2 \\ &= \underbrace{[f(X) - \hat{f}(X)]^2}_{\text{Reducible}} + \underbrace{\mathrm{Var}(\epsilon)}_{\text{Irreducible}} , \end{aligned} \tag{2.3}$$

where $\mathrm{E}(Y - \hat{Y})^2$ represents the average, or *expected value*, of the squared difference between the predicted and actual value of Y, and $\mathrm{Var}(\epsilon)$ represents the *variance* associated with the error term ϵ.

expected value

variance

The focus of this book is on techniques for estimating f with the aim of minimizing the reducible error. It is important to keep in mind that the irreducible error will always provide an upper bound on the accuracy of our prediction for Y. This bound is almost always unknown in practice.

Inference

We are often interested in understanding the association between Y and $X_1, \ldots, X_p$. In this situation we wish to estimate f, but our goal is not necessarily to make predictions for Y. Now $\hat{f}$ cannot be treated as a black box, because we need to know its exact form. In this setting, one may be interested in answering the following questions:

- *Which predictors are associated with the response?* It is often the case that only a small fraction of the available predictors are substantially associated with Y. Identifying the few *important* predictors among a large set of possible variables can be extremely useful, depending on the application.
- *What is the relationship between the response and each predictor?* Some predictors may have a positive relationship with Y, in the sense that larger values of the predictor are associated with larger values of Y. Other predictors may have the opposite relationship. Depending on the complexity of f, the relationship between the response and a given predictor may also depend on the values of the other predictors.
- *Can the relationship between Y and each predictor be adequately summarized using a linear equation, or is the relationship more complicated?* Historically, most methods for estimating f have taken a linear form. In some situations, such an assumption is reasonable or even desirable. But often the true relationship is more complicated, in which case a linear model may not provide an accurate representation of the relationship between the input and output variables.

In this book, we will see a number of examples that fall into the prediction setting, the inference setting, or a combination of the two.

For instance, consider a company that is interested in conducting a direct-marketing campaign. The goal is to identify individuals who are likely to respond positively to a mailing, based on observations of demographic variables measured on each individual. In this case, the demographic variables serve as predictors, and response to the marketing campaign (either positive or negative) serves as the outcome. The company is not interested in obtaining a deep understanding of the relationships between each individual predictor and the response; instead, the company simply wants to accurately predict the response using the predictors. This is an example of modeling for prediction.

In contrast, consider the `Advertising` data illustrated in Figure 2.1. One may be interested in answering questions such as:

- *Which media are associated with sales?*
- *Which media generate the biggest boost in sales?* or
- *How large of an increase in sales is associated with a given increase in TV advertising?*

This situation falls into the inference paradigm. Another example involves modeling the brand of a product that a customer might purchase based on variables such as price, store location, discount levels, competition price, and so forth. In this situation one might really be most interested in the association between each variable and the probability of purchase. For instance, *to what extent is the product's price associated with sales?* This is an example of modeling for inference.

Finally, some modeling could be conducted both for prediction and inference. For example, in a real estate setting, one may seek to relate values of homes to inputs such as crime rate, zoning, distance from a river, air quality, schools, income level of community, size of houses, and so forth. In this case one might be interested in the association between each individual input variable and housing price—for instance, *how much extra will a house be worth if it has a view of the river?* This is an inference problem. Alternatively, one may simply be interested in predicting the value of a home given its characteristics: *is this house under- or over-valued?* This is a prediction problem.

Depending on whether our ultimate goal is prediction, inference, or a combination of the two, different methods for estimating f may be appropriate. For example, *linear models* allow for relatively simple and interpretable inference, but may not yield as accurate predictions as some other approaches. In contrast, some of the highly non-linear approaches that we discuss in the later chapters of this book can potentially provide quite accurate predictions for Y, but this comes at the expense of a less interpretable model for which inference is more challenging.

linear model

2.1.2 How Do We Estimate f?

Throughout this book, we explore many linear and non-linear approaches for estimating f. However, these methods generally share certain characteristics. We provide an overview of these shared characteristics in this section. We will always assume that we have observed a set of n different data points. For example in Figure 2.2 we observed $n = 30$ data points. These observations are called the *training data* because we will use these observations to train, or teach, our method how to estimate f. Let x_{ij} represent the value of the jth predictor, or input, for observation i, where $i = 1, 2, \ldots, n$ and $j = 1, 2, \ldots, p$. Correspondingly, let y_i represent the response variable for the ith observation. Then our training data consist of $\{(x_1, y_1), (x_2, y_2), \ldots, (x_n, y_n)\}$ where $x_i = (x_{i1}, x_{i2}, \ldots, x_{ip})^T$.

training data

Our goal is to apply a statistical learning method to the training data in order to estimate the unknown function f. In other words, we want to find a function $\hat{f}$ such that $Y \approx \hat{f}(X)$ for any observation (X, Y). Broadly speaking, most statistical learning methods for this task can be characterized as either *parametric* or *non-parametric*. We now briefly discuss these two types of approaches.

parametric

non-parametric

Parametric Methods

Parametric methods involve a two-step model-based approach.

1. First, we make an assumption about the functional form, or shape, of f. For example, one very simple assumption is that f is linear in X:

$$f(X) = \beta_0 + \beta_1 X_1 + \beta_2 X_2 + \cdots + \beta_p X_p. \quad (2.4)$$

   This is a *linear model*, which will be discussed extensively in Chapter 3. Once we have assumed that f is linear, the problem of estimating f is greatly simplified. Instead of having to estimate an entirely arbitrary p-dimensional function $f(X)$, one only needs to estimate the $p + 1$ coefficients $\beta_0, \beta_1, \ldots, \beta_p$.

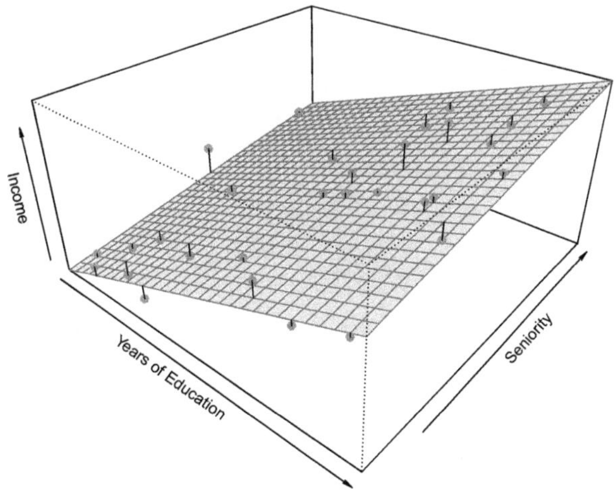

FIGURE 2.4. *A linear model fit by least squares to the* `Income` *data from Figure 2.3. The observations are shown in red, and the yellow plane indicates the least squares fit to the data.*

2. After a model has been selected, we need a procedure that uses the training data to *fit* or *train* the model. In the case of the linear model (2.4), we need to estimate the parameters $\beta_0, \beta_1, \ldots, \beta_p$. That is, we want to find values of these parameters such that fit train

$$Y \approx \beta_0 + \beta_1 X_1 + \beta_2 X_2 + \cdots + \beta_p X_p.$$

The most common approach to fitting the model (2.4) is referred to as *(ordinary) least squares*, which we discuss in Chapter 3. However, least squares is one of many possible ways to fit the linear model. In Chapter 6, we discuss other approaches for estimating the parameters in (2.4). least squares

The model-based approach just described is referred to as *parametric*; it reduces the problem of estimating f down to one of estimating a set of parameters. Assuming a parametric form for f simplifies the problem of estimating f because it is generally much easier to estimate a set of parameters, such as $\beta_0, \beta_1, \ldots, \beta_p$ in the linear model (2.4), than it is to fit an entirely arbitrary function f. The potential disadvantage of a parametric approach is that the model we choose will usually not match the true unknown form of f. If the chosen model is too far from the true f, then our estimate will be poor. We can try to address this problem by choosing *flexible* models that can fit many different possible functional forms for f. But in general, fitting a more flexible model requires estimating a greater number of parameters. These more complex models can lead to a phenomenon known as *overfitting* the data, which essentially means they follow the errors, or *noise*, too closely. These issues are discussed throughout this book. flexible overfitting noise

Figure 2.4 shows an example of the parametric approach applied to the `Income` data from Figure 2.3. We have fit a linear model of the form

$$\texttt{income} \approx \beta_0 + \beta_1 \times \texttt{education} + \beta_2 \times \texttt{seniority}.$$

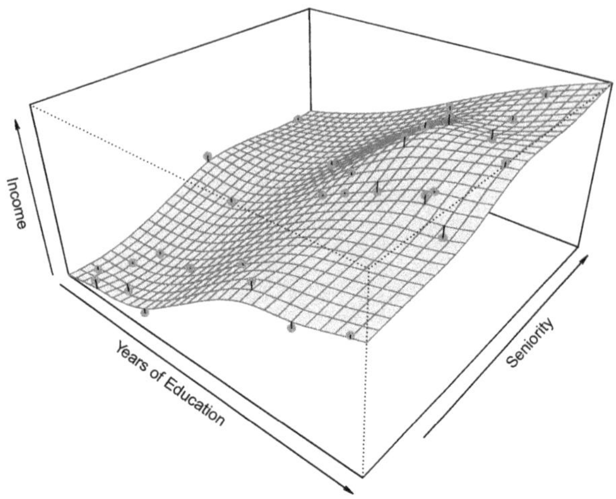

FIGURE 2.5. *A smooth thin-plate spline fit to the* `Income` *data from Figure 2.3 is shown in yellow; the observations are displayed in red. Splines are discussed in Chapter 7.*

Since we have assumed a linear relationship between the response and the two predictors, the entire fitting problem reduces to estimating β_0, β_1, and β_2, which we do using least squares linear regression. Comparing Figure 2.3 to Figure 2.4, we can see that the linear fit given in Figure 2.4 is not quite right: the true f has some curvature that is not captured in the linear fit. However, the linear fit still appears to do a reasonable job of capturing the positive relationship between `years of education` and `income`, as well as the slightly less positive relationship between `seniority` and `income`. It may be that with such a small number of observations, this is the best we can do.

Non-Parametric Methods

Non-parametric methods do not make explicit assumptions about the functional form of f. Instead they seek an estimate of f that gets as close to the data points as possible without being too rough or wiggly. Such approaches can have a major advantage over parametric approaches: by avoiding the assumption of a particular functional form for f, they have the potential to accurately fit a wider range of possible shapes for f. Any parametric approach brings with it the possibility that the functional form used to estimate f is very different from the true f, in which case the resulting model will not fit the data well. In contrast, non-parametric approaches completely avoid this danger, since essentially no assumption about the form of f is made. But non-parametric approaches do suffer from a major disadvantage: since they do not reduce the problem of estimating f to a small number of parameters, a very large number of observations (far more than is typically needed for a parametric approach) is required in order to obtain an accurate estimate for f.

An example of a non-parametric approach to fitting the `Income` data is shown in Figure 2.5. A *thin-plate spline* is used to estimate f. This approach does not impose any pre-specified model on f. It instead attempts thin-plate spline

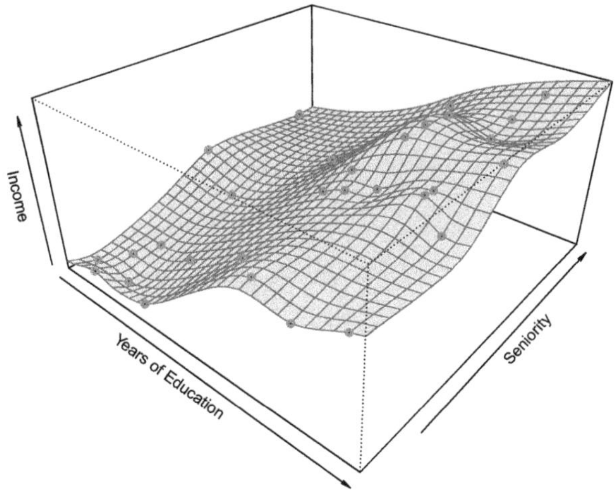

FIGURE 2.6. *A rough thin-plate spline fit to the* `Income` *data from Figure 2.3. This fit makes zero errors on the training data.*

to produce an estimate for f that is as close as possible to the observed data, subject to the fit—that is, the yellow surface in Figure 2.5—being *smooth*. In this case, the non-parametric fit has produced a remarkably accurate estimate of the true f shown in Figure 2.3. In order to fit a thin-plate spline, the data analyst must select a level of smoothness. Figure 2.6 shows the same thin-plate spline fit using a lower level of smoothness, allowing for a rougher fit. The resulting estimate fits the observed data perfectly! However, the spline fit shown in Figure 2.6 is far more variable than the true function f, from Figure 2.3. This is an example of overfitting the data, which we discussed previously. It is an undesirable situation because the fit obtained will not yield accurate estimates of the response on new observations that were not part of the original training data set. We discuss methods for choosing the *correct* amount of smoothness in Chapter 5. Splines are discussed in Chapter 7.

As we have seen, there are advantages and disadvantages to parametric and non-parametric methods for statistical learning. We explore both types of methods throughout this book.

2.1.3 The Trade-Off Between Prediction Accuracy and Model Interpretability

Of the many methods that we examine in this book, some are less flexible, or more restrictive, in the sense that they can produce just a relatively small range of shapes to estimate f. For example, linear regression is a relatively inflexible approach, because it can only generate linear functions such as the lines shown in Figure 2.1 or the plane shown in Figure 2.4. Other methods, such as the thin plate splines shown in Figures 2.5 and 2.6, are considerably more flexible because they can generate a much wider range of possible shapes to estimate f.

FIGURE 2.7. *A representation of the tradeoff between flexibility and interpretability, using different statistical learning methods. In general, as the flexibility of a method increases, its interpretability decreases.*

One might reasonably ask the following question: *why would we ever choose to use a more restrictive method instead of a very flexible approach?* There are several reasons that we might prefer a more restrictive model. If we are mainly interested in inference, then restrictive models are much more interpretable. For instance, when inference is the goal, the linear model may be a good choice since it will be quite easy to understand the relationship between Y and $X_1, X_2, \ldots, X_p$. In contrast, very flexible approaches, such as the splines discussed in Chapter 7 and displayed in Figures 2.5 and 2.6, and the boosting methods discussed in Chapter 8, can lead to such complicated estimates of f that it is difficult to understand how any individual predictor is associated with the response.

Figure 2.7 provides an illustration of the trade-off between flexibility and interpretability for some of the methods that we cover in this book. Least squares linear regression, discussed in Chapter 3, is relatively inflexible but is quite interpretable. The *lasso*, discussed in Chapter 6, relies upon the linear model (2.4) but uses an alternative fitting procedure for estimating the coefficients $\beta_0, \beta_1, \ldots, \beta_p$. The new procedure is more restrictive in estimating the coefficients, and sets a number of them to exactly zero. Hence in this sense the lasso is a less flexible approach than linear regression. It is also more interpretable than linear regression, because in the final model the response variable will only be related to a small subset of the predictors—namely, those with nonzero coefficient estimates. *Generalized additive models* (GAMs), discussed in Chapter 7, instead extend the linear model (2.4) to allow for certain non-linear relationships. Consequently, GAMs are more flexible than linear regression. They are also somewhat less interpretable than linear regression, because the relationship between each predictor and the response is now modeled using a curve. Finally, fully non-linear methods such as *bagging*, *boosting*, *support vector machines* with non-linear kernels, and *neural networks* (deep learning), discussed in Chapters 8, 9, and 10, are highly flexible approaches that are harder to interpret.

lasso

generalized additive model

bagging boosting support vector machine

We have established that when inference is the goal, there are clear advantages to using simple and relatively inflexible statistical learning methods. In some settings, however, we are only interested in prediction, and the interpretability of the predictive model is simply not of interest. For instance, if we seek to develop an algorithm to predict the price of a stock, our sole requirement for the algorithm is that it predict accurately—interpretability is not a concern. In this setting, we might expect that it will be best to use the most flexible model available. Surprisingly, this is not always the case! We will often obtain more accurate predictions using a less flexible method. This phenomenon, which may seem counterintuitive at first glance, has to do with the potential for overfitting in highly flexible methods. We saw an example of overfitting in Figure 2.6. We will discuss this very important concept further in Section 2.2 and throughout this book.

2.1.4 Supervised Versus Unsupervised Learning

Most statistical learning problems fall into one of two categories: ***supervised*** or ***unsupervised***. The examples that we have discussed so far in this chapter all fall into the supervised learning domain. For each observation of the predictor measurement(s) x_i, $i = 1, \ldots, n$ there is an associated response measurement y_i. We wish to fit a model that relates the response to the predictors, with the aim of accurately predicting the response for future observations (prediction) or better understanding the relationship between the response and the predictors (inference). Many classical statistical learning methods such as linear regression and ***logistic regression*** (Chapter 4), as well as more modern approaches such as GAM, boosting, and support vector machines, operate in the supervised learning domain. The vast majority of this book is devoted to this setting.

supervised

unsupervised

logistic regression

By contrast, unsupervised learning describes the somewhat more challenging situation in which for every observation $i = 1, \ldots, n$, we observe a vector of measurements x_i but no associated response y_i. It is not possible to fit a linear regression model, since there is no response variable to predict. In this setting, we are in some sense working blind; the situation is referred to as *unsupervised* because we lack a response variable that can supervise our analysis. What sort of statistical analysis is possible? We can seek to understand the relationships between the variables or between the observations. One statistical learning tool that we may use in this setting is ***cluster analysis***, or clustering. The goal of cluster analysis is to ascertain, on the basis of $x_1, \ldots, x_n$, whether the observations fall into relatively distinct groups. For example, in a market segmentation study we might observe multiple characteristics (variables) for potential customers, such as zip code, family income, and shopping habits. We might believe that the customers fall into different groups, such as big spenders versus low spenders. If the information about each customer's spending patterns were available, then a supervised analysis would be possible. However, this information is not available—that is, we do not know whether each potential customer is a big spender or not. In this setting, we can try to cluster the customers on the basis of the variables measured, in order to identify

cluster analysis

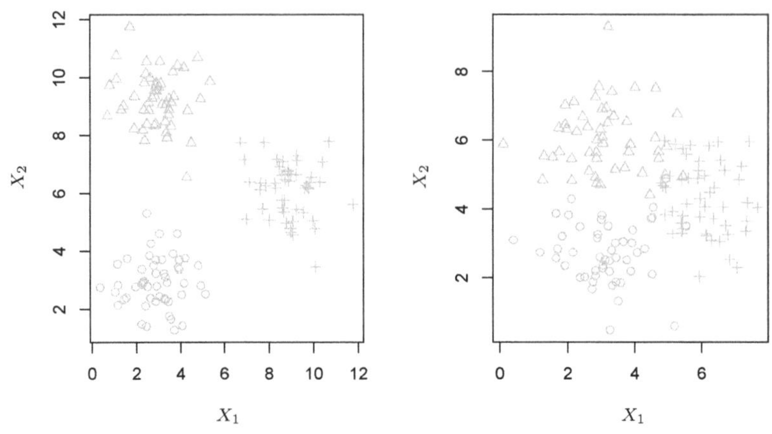

FIGURE 2.8. *A clustering data set involving three groups. Each group is shown using a different colored symbol.* Left: *The three groups are well-separated. In this setting, a clustering approach should successfully identify the three groups.* Right: *There is some overlap among the groups. Now the clustering task is more challenging.*

distinct groups of potential customers. Identifying such groups can be of interest because it might be that the groups differ with respect to some property of interest, such as spending habits.

Figure 2.8 provides a simple illustration of the clustering problem. We have plotted 150 observations with measurements on two variables, X_1 and X_2. Each observation corresponds to one of three distinct groups. For illustrative purposes, we have plotted the members of each group using different colors and symbols. However, in practice the group memberships are unknown, and the goal is to determine the group to which each observation belongs. In the left-hand panel of Figure 2.8, this is a relatively easy task because the groups are well-separated. By contrast, the right-hand panel illustrates a more challenging setting in which there is some overlap between the groups. A clustering method could not be expected to assign all of the overlapping points to their correct group (blue, green, or orange).

In the examples shown in Figure 2.8, there are only two variables, and so one can simply visually inspect the scatterplots of the observations in order to identify clusters. However, in practice, we often encounter data sets that contain many more than two variables. In this case, we cannot easily plot the observations. For instance, if there are p variables in our data set, then $p(p-1)/2$ distinct scatterplots can be made, and visual inspection is simply not a viable way to identify clusters. For this reason, automated clustering methods are important. We discuss clustering and other unsupervised learning approaches in Chapter 12.

Many problems fall naturally into the supervised or unsupervised learning paradigms. However, sometimes the question of whether an analysis should be considered supervised or unsupervised is less clear-cut. For instance, suppose that we have a set of n observations. For m of the observations, where $m < n$, we have both predictor measurements and a response measurement. For the remaining $n - m$ observations, we have predictor measurements but no response measurement. Such a scenario can arise if the predictors can be measured relatively cheaply but the corresponding responses are much more expensive to collect. We refer to this setting as a *semi-supervised learning* problem. In this setting, we wish to use a statistical learning method that can incorporate the m observations for which response measurements are available as well as the $n - m$ observations for which they are not. Although this is an interesting topic, it is beyond the scope of this book.

semi-supervised learning

2.1.5 Regression Versus Classification Problems

Variables can be characterized as either *quantitative* or *qualitative* (also known as *categorical*). Quantitative variables take on numerical values. Examples include a person's age, height, or income, the value of a house, and the price of a stock. In contrast, qualitative variables take on values in one of K different *classes*, or categories. Examples of qualitative variables include a person's marital status (married or not), the brand of product purchased (brand A, B, or C), whether a person defaults on a debt (yes or no), or a cancer diagnosis (Acute Myelogenous Leukemia, Acute Lymphoblastic Leukemia, or No Leukemia). We tend to refer to problems with a quantitative response as *regression* problems, while those involving a qualitative response are often referred to as *classification* problems. However, the distinction is not always that crisp. Least squares linear regression (Chapter 3) is used with a quantitative response, whereas logistic regression (Chapter 4) is typically used with a qualitative (two-class, or *binary*) response. Thus, despite its name, logistic regression is a classification method. But since it estimates class probabilities, it can be thought of as a regression method as well. Some statistical methods, such as K-nearest neighbors (Chapters 2 and 4) and boosting (Chapter 8), can be used in the case of either quantitative or qualitative responses.

quantitative
qualitative
categorical
class
regression
classification
binary

We tend to select statistical learning methods on the basis of whether the response is quantitative or qualitative; i.e. we might use linear regression when quantitative and logistic regression when qualitative. However, whether the *predictors* are qualitative or quantitative is generally considered less important. Most of the statistical learning methods discussed in this book can be applied regardless of the predictor variable type, provided that any qualitative predictors are properly *coded* before the analysis is performed. This is discussed in Chapter 3.

2.2 Assessing Model Accuracy

One of the key aims of this book is to introduce the reader to a wide range of statistical learning methods that extend far beyond the standard linear regression approach. Why is it necessary to introduce so many different statistical learning approaches, rather than just a single *best* method? *There is no free lunch in statistics:* no one method dominates all others over all possible data sets. On a particular data set, one specific method may work best, but some other method may work better on a similar but different data set. Hence it is an important task to decide for any given set of data which method produces the best results. Selecting the best approach can be one of the most challenging parts of performing statistical learning in practice.

In this section, we discuss some of the most important concepts that arise in selecting a statistical learning procedure for a specific data set. As the book progresses, we will explain how the concepts presented here can be applied in practice.

2.2.1 Measuring the Quality of Fit

In order to evaluate the performance of a statistical learning method on a given data set, we need some way to measure how well its predictions actually match the observed data. That is, we need to quantify the extent to which the predicted response value for a given observation is close to the true response value for that observation. In the regression setting, the most commonly-used measure is the *mean squared error* (MSE), given by

mean squared error

$$\text{MSE} = \frac{1}{n}\sum_{i=1}^{n}(y_i - \hat{f}(x_i))^2, \tag{2.5}$$

where $\hat{f}(x_i)$ is the prediction that $\hat{f}$ gives for the ith observation. The MSE will be small if the predicted responses are very close to the true responses, and will be large if for some of the observations, the predicted and true responses differ substantially.

The MSE in (2.5) is computed using the training data that was used to fit the model, and so should more accurately be referred to as the *training MSE*. But in general, we do not really care how well the method works on the training data. Rather, *we are interested in the accuracy of the predictions that we obtain when we apply our method to previously unseen test data.* Why is this what we care about? Suppose that we are interested in developing an algorithm to predict a stock's price based on previous stock returns. We can train the method using stock returns from the past 6 months. But we don't really care how well our method predicts last week's stock price. We instead care about how well it will predict tomorrow's price or next month's price. On a similar note, suppose that we have clinical measurements (e.g. weight, blood pressure, height, age, family history of disease) for a number of patients, as well as information about whether each patient has diabetes. We can use these patients to train a statistical learning method to predict risk of diabetes based on clinical measurements. In practice, we want this method to accurately predict diabetes risk for *future patients* based on their clinical measurements. We are not very interested in whether or not the method accurately predicts diabetes risk for patients used to train the model, since we already know which of those patients have diabetes.

training MSE

test data

To state it more mathematically, suppose that we fit our statistical learning method on our training observations $\{(x_1, y_1), (x_2, y_2), \ldots, (x_n, y_n)\}$, and we obtain the estimate $\hat{f}$. We can then compute $\hat{f}(x_1), \hat{f}(x_2), \ldots, \hat{f}(x_n)$.

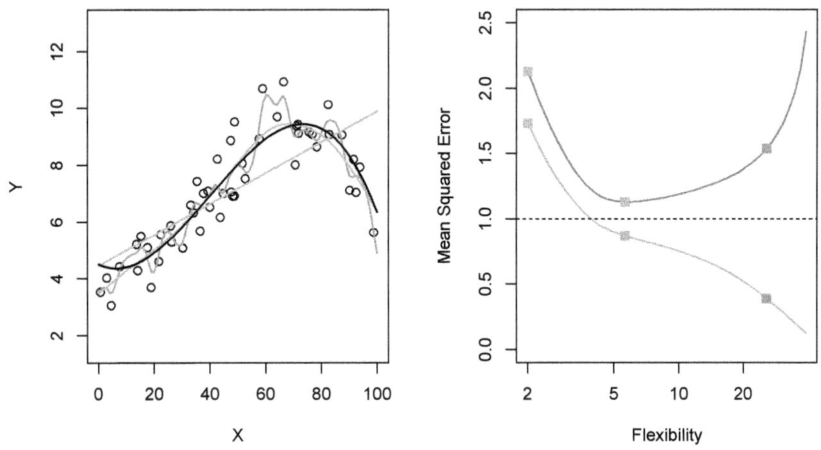

FIGURE 2.9. Left: *Data simulated from* f*, shown in black. Three estimates of* f *are shown: the linear regression line (orange curve), and two smoothing spline fits (blue and green curves).* Right: *Training MSE (grey curve), test MSE (red curve), and minimum possible test MSE over all methods (dashed line). Squares represent the training and test MSEs for the three fits shown in the left-hand panel.*

If these are approximately equal to $y_1, y_2, \ldots, y_n$, then the training MSE given by (2.5) is small. However, we are really not interested in whether $\hat{f}(x_i) \approx y_i$; instead, we want to know whether $\hat{f}(x_0)$ is approximately equal to y_0, where (x_0, y_0) is a *previously unseen test observation not used to train the statistical learning method.* We want to choose the method that gives the lowest *test MSE*, as opposed to the lowest training MSE. In other words, if we had a large number of test observations, we could compute test MSE

$$\text{Ave}(y_0 - \hat{f}(x_0))^2, \tag{2.6}$$

the average squared prediction error for these test observations (x_0, y_0). We'd like to select the model for which this quantity is as small as possible.

How can we go about trying to select a method that minimizes the test MSE? In some settings, we may have a test data set available—that is, we may have access to a set of observations that were not used to train the statistical learning method. We can then simply evaluate (2.6) on the test observations, and select the learning method for which the test MSE is smallest. But what if no test observations are available? In that case, one might imagine simply selecting a statistical learning method that minimizes the training MSE (2.5). This seems like it might be a sensible approach, since the training MSE and the test MSE appear to be closely related. Unfortunately, there is a fundamental problem with this strategy: there is no guarantee that the method with the lowest training MSE will also have the lowest test MSE. Roughly speaking, the problem is that many statistical methods specifically estimate coefficients so as to minimize the training set MSE. For these methods, the training set MSE can be quite small, but the test MSE is often much larger.

Figure 2.9 illustrates this phenomenon on a simple example. In the left-hand panel of Figure 2.9, we have generated observations from (2.1) with the true f given by the black curve. The orange, blue and green curves illustrate three possible estimates for f obtained using methods with increasing levels of flexibility. The orange line is the linear regression fit, which is relatively inflexible. The blue and green curves were produced using *smoothing splines*, discussed in Chapter 7, with different levels of smoothness. It is clear that as the level of flexibility increases, the curves fit the observed data more closely. The green curve is the most flexible and matches the data very well; however, we observe that it fits the true f (shown in black) poorly because it is too wiggly. By adjusting the level of flexibility of the smoothing spline fit, we can produce many different fits to this data.

smoothing spline

We now move on to the right-hand panel of Figure 2.9. The grey curve displays the average training MSE as a function of flexibility, or more formally the *degrees of freedom*, for a number of smoothing splines. The degrees of freedom is a quantity that summarizes the flexibility of a curve; it is discussed more fully in Chapter 7. The orange, blue and green squares indicate the MSEs associated with the corresponding curves in the left-hand panel. A more restricted and hence smoother curve has fewer degrees of freedom than a wiggly curve—note that in Figure 2.9, linear regression is at the most restrictive end, with two degrees of freedom. The training MSE declines monotonically as flexibility increases. In this example the true f is non-linear, and so the orange linear fit is not flexible enough to estimate f well. The green curve has the lowest training MSE of all three methods, since it corresponds to the most flexible of the three curves fit in the left-hand panel.

degrees of freedom

In this example, we know the true function f, and so we can also compute the test MSE over a very large test set, as a function of flexibility. (Of course, in general f is unknown, so this will not be possible.) The test MSE is displayed using the red curve in the right-hand panel of Figure 2.9. As with the training MSE, the test MSE initially declines as the level of flexibility increases. However, at some point the test MSE levels off and then starts to increase again. Consequently, the orange and green curves both have high test MSE. The blue curve minimizes the test MSE, which should not be surprising given that visually it appears to estimate f the best in the left-hand panel of Figure 2.9. The horizontal dashed line indicates $\text{Var}(\epsilon)$, the irreducible error in (2.3), which corresponds to the lowest achievable test MSE among all possible methods. Hence, the smoothing spline represented by the blue curve is close to optimal.

In the right-hand panel of Figure 2.9, as the flexibility of the statistical learning method increases, we observe a monotone decrease in the training MSE and a *U-shape* in the test MSE. This is a fundamental property of statistical learning that holds regardless of the particular data set at hand and regardless of the statistical method being used. As model flexibility increases, the training MSE will decrease, but the test MSE may not. When a given method yields a small training MSE but a large test MSE, we are said to be *overfitting* the data. This happens because our statistical learning procedure is working too hard to find patterns in the training data, and may be picking up some patterns that are just caused by random chance rather than by true properties of the unknown function f. When we overfit the training data, the test MSE will be very large because the supposed

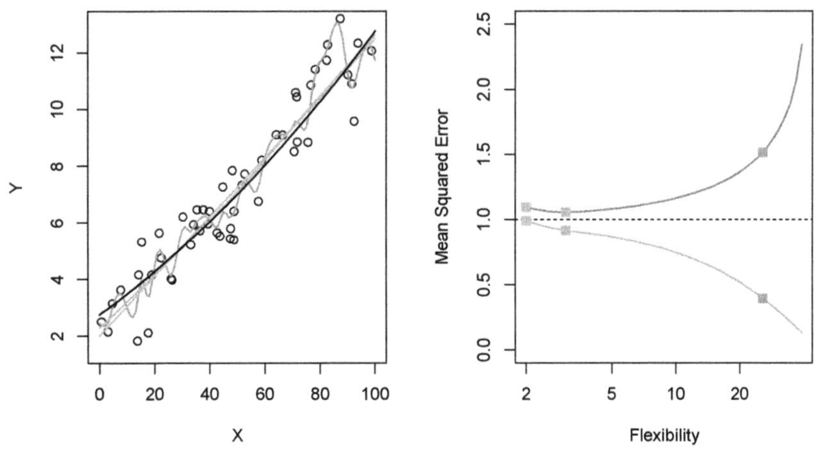

FIGURE 2.10. *Details are as in Figure 2.9, using a different true f that is much closer to linear. In this setting, linear regression provides a very good fit to the data.*

patterns that the method found in the training data simply don't exist in the test data. Note that regardless of whether or not overfitting has occurred, we almost always expect the training MSE to be smaller than the test MSE because most statistical learning methods either directly or indirectly seek to minimize the training MSE. Overfitting refers specifically to the case in which a less flexible model would have yielded a smaller test MSE.

Figure 2.10 provides another example in which the true f is approximately linear. Again we observe that the training MSE decreases monotonically as the model flexibility increases, and that there is a U-shape in the test MSE. However, because the truth is close to linear, the test MSE only decreases slightly before increasing again, so that the orange least squares fit is substantially better than the highly flexible green curve. Finally, Figure 2.11 displays an example in which f is highly non-linear. The training and test MSE curves still exhibit the same general patterns, but now there is a rapid decrease in both curves before the test MSE starts to increase slowly.

In practice, one can usually compute the training MSE with relative ease, but estimating the test MSE is considerably more difficult because usually no test data are available. As the previous three examples illustrate, the flexibility level corresponding to the model with the minimal test MSE can vary considerably among data sets. Throughout this book, we discuss a variety of approaches that can be used in practice to estimate this minimum point. One important method is *cross-validation* (Chapter 5), which is a method for estimating the test MSE using the training data. cross-validation

2.2.2 The Bias-Variance Trade-Off

The U-shape observed in the test MSE curves (Figures 2.9–2.11) turns out to be the result of two competing properties of statistical learning methods.

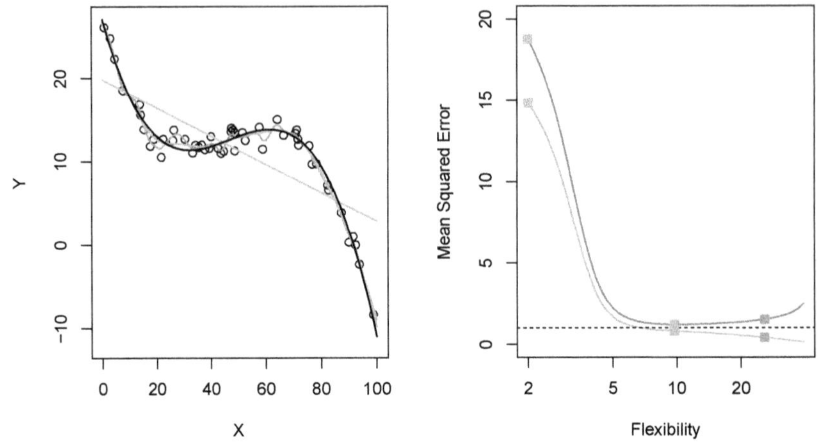

FIGURE 2.11. *Details are as in Figure 2.9, using a different f that is far from linear. In this setting, linear regression provides a very poor fit to the data.*

Though the mathematical proof is beyond the scope of this book, it is possible to show that the expected test MSE, for a given value x_0, can always be decomposed into the sum of three fundamental quantities: the *variance* of $\hat{f}(x_0)$, the squared *bias* of $\hat{f}(x_0)$ and the variance of the error terms ϵ. That is,

variance

bias

$$E\left(y_0 - \hat{f}(x_0)\right)^2 = \text{Var}(\hat{f}(x_0)) + [\text{Bias}(\hat{f}(x_0))]^2 + \text{Var}(\epsilon). \tag{2.7}$$

Here the notation $E\left(y_0 - \hat{f}(x_0)\right)^2$ defines the *expected test MSE* at x_0, and refers to the average test MSE that we would obtain if we repeatedly estimated f using a large number of training sets, and tested each at x_0. The overall expected test MSE can be computed by averaging $E\left(y_0 - \hat{f}(x_0)\right)^2$ over all possible values of x_0 in the test set.

expected test MSE

Equation 2.7 tells us that in order to minimize the expected test error, we need to select a statistical learning method that simultaneously achieves *low variance* and *low bias*. Note that variance is inherently a nonnegative quantity, and squared bias is also nonnegative. Hence, we see that the expected test MSE can never lie below $\text{Var}(\epsilon)$, the irreducible error from (2.3).

What do we mean by the *variance* and *bias* of a statistical learning method? *Variance* refers to the amount by which $\hat{f}$ would change if we estimated it using a different training data set. Since the training data are used to fit the statistical learning method, different training data sets will result in a different $\hat{f}$. But ideally the estimate for f should not vary too much between training sets. However, if a method has high variance then small changes in the training data can result in large changes in $\hat{f}$. In general, more flexible statistical methods have higher variance. Consider the green and orange curves in Figure 2.9. The flexible green curve is following the observations very closely. It has high variance because changing any one of these data points may cause the estimate $\hat{f}$ to change considerably.

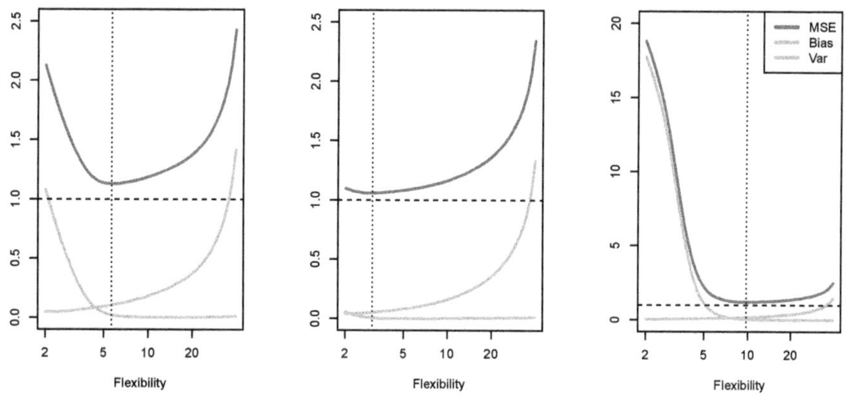

FIGURE 2.12. *Squared bias (blue curve), variance (orange curve), Var(ϵ) (dashed line), and test MSE (red curve) for the three data sets in Figures 2.9–2.11. The vertical dotted line indicates the flexibility level corresponding to the smallest test MSE.*

In contrast, the orange least squares line is relatively inflexible and has low variance, because moving any single observation will likely cause only a small shift in the position of the line.

On the other hand, *bias* refers to the error that is introduced by approximating a real-life problem, which may be extremely complicated, by a much simpler model. For example, linear regression assumes that there is a linear relationship between Y and $X_1, X_2, \ldots, X_p$. It is unlikely that any real-life problem truly has such a simple linear relationship, and so performing linear regression will undoubtedly result in some bias in the estimate of f. In Figure 2.11, the true f is substantially non-linear, so no matter how many training observations we are given, it will not be possible to produce an accurate estimate using linear regression. In other words, linear regression results in high bias in this example. However, in Figure 2.10 the true f is very close to linear, and so given enough data, it should be possible for linear regression to produce an accurate estimate. Generally, more flexible methods result in less bias.

As a general rule, as we use more flexible methods, the variance will increase and the bias will decrease. The relative rate of change of these two quantities determines whether the test MSE increases or decreases. As we increase the flexibility of a class of methods, the bias tends to initially decrease faster than the variance increases. Consequently, the expected test MSE declines. However, at some point increasing flexibility has little impact on the bias but starts to significantly increase the variance. When this happens the test MSE increases. Note that we observed this pattern of decreasing test MSE followed by increasing test MSE in the right-hand panels of Figures 2.9–2.11.

The three plots in Figure 2.12 illustrate Equation 2.7 for the examples in Figures 2.9–2.11. In each case the blue solid curve represents the squared bias, for different levels of flexibility, while the orange curve corresponds to the variance. The horizontal dashed line represents Var(ϵ), the irreducible error. Finally, the red curve, corresponding to the test set MSE, is the sum of these three quantities. In all three cases, the variance increases and the bias decreases as the method's flexibility increases. However, the flexibility level corresponding to the optimal test MSE differs considerably among the three data sets, because the squared bias and variance change at different rates in each of the data sets. In the left-hand panel of Figure 2.12, the bias initially decreases rapidly, resulting in an initial sharp decrease in the expected test MSE. On the other hand, in the center panel of Figure 2.12 the true f is close to linear, so there is only a small decrease in bias as flexibility increases, and the test MSE only declines slightly before increasing rapidly as the variance increases. Finally, in the right-hand panel of Figure 2.12, as flexibility increases, there is a dramatic decline in bias because the true f is very non-linear. There is also very little increase in variance as flexibility increases. Consequently, the test MSE declines substantially before experiencing a small increase as model flexibility increases.

The relationship between bias, variance, and test set MSE given in Equation 2.7 and displayed in Figure 2.12 is referred to as the *bias-variance trade-off*. Good test set performance of a statistical learning method requires low variance as well as low squared bias. This is referred to as a trade-off because it is easy to obtain a method with extremely low bias but high variance (for instance, by drawing a curve that passes through every single training observation) or a method with very low variance but high bias (by fitting a horizontal line to the data). The challenge lies in finding a method for which both the variance and the squared bias are low. This trade-off is one of the most important recurring themes in this book. bias-variance trade-off

In a real-life situation in which f is unobserved, it is generally not possible to explicitly compute the test MSE, bias, or variance for a statistical learning method. Nevertheless, one should always keep the bias-variance trade-off in mind. In this book we explore methods that are extremely flexible and hence can essentially eliminate bias. However, this does not guarantee that they will outperform a much simpler method such as linear regression. To take an extreme example, suppose that the true f is linear. In this situation linear regression will have no bias, making it very hard for a more flexible method to compete. In contrast, if the true f is highly non-linear and we have an ample number of training observations, then we may do better using a highly flexible approach, as in Figure 2.11. In Chapter 5 we discuss cross-validation, which is a way to estimate the test MSE using the training data.

2.2.3 The Classification Setting

Thus far, our discussion of model accuracy has been focused on the regression setting. But many of the concepts that we have encountered, such as the bias-variance trade-off, transfer over to the classification setting with only some modifications due to the fact that y_i is no longer quantitative. Suppose that we seek to estimate f on the basis of training observations $\{(x_1, y_1), \ldots, (x_n, y_n)\}$, where now $y_1, \ldots, y_n$ are qualitative. The most common approach for quantifying the accuracy of our estimate $\hat{f}$ is the training *error rate*, the proportion of mistakes that are made if we apply error rate our estimate $\hat{f}$ to the training observations:

$$\frac{1}{n}\sum_{i=1}^{n} I(y_i \neq \hat{y}_i). \tag{2.8}$$

Here $\hat{y}_i$ is the predicted class label for the ith observation using $\hat{f}$. And $I(y_i \neq \hat{y}_i)$ is an *indicator variable* that equals 1 if $y_i \neq \hat{y}_i$ and zero if $y_i = \hat{y}_i$. If $I(y_i \neq \hat{y}_i) = 0$ then the ith observation was classified correctly by our classification method; otherwise it was misclassified. Hence Equation 2.8 computes the fraction of incorrect classifications.

indicator variable

Equation 2.8 is referred to as the *training error* rate because it is computed based on the data that was used to train our classifier. As in the regression setting, we are most interested in the error rates that result from applying our classifier to test observations that were not used in training. The *test error* rate associated with a set of test observations of the form (x_0, y_0) is given by

training error

test error

$$\text{Ave}\left(I(y_0 \neq \hat{y}_0)\right), \tag{2.9}$$

where $\hat{y}_0$ is the predicted class label that results from applying the classifier to the test observation with predictor x_0. A *good* classifier is one for which the test error (2.9) is smallest.

The Bayes Classifier

It is possible to show (though the proof is outside of the scope of this book) that the test error rate given in (2.9) is minimized, on average, by a very simple classifier that *assigns each observation to the most likely class, given its predictor values*. In other words, we should simply assign a test observation with predictor vector x_0 to the class j for which

$$\Pr(Y = j|X = x_0) \tag{2.10}$$

is largest. Note that (2.10) is a *conditional probability*: it is the probability that $Y = j$, given the observed predictor vector x_0. This very simple classifier is called the *Bayes classifier*. In a two-class problem where there are only two possible response values, say *class 1* or *class 2*, the Bayes classifier corresponds to predicting class one if $\Pr(Y = 1|X = x_0) > 0.5$, and class two otherwise.

conditional probability

Bayes classifier

Figure 2.13 provides an example using a simulated data set in a two-dimensional space consisting of predictors X_1 and X_2. The orange and blue circles correspond to training observations that belong to two different classes. For each value of X_1 and X_2, there is a different probability of the response being orange or blue. Since this is simulated data, we know how the data were generated and we can calculate the conditional probabilities for each value of X_1 and X_2. The orange shaded region reflects the set of points for which $\Pr(Y = \text{orange}|X)$ is greater than 50 %, while the blue shaded region indicates the set of points for which the probability is below 50 %. The purple dashed line represents the points where the probability is exactly 50 %. This is called the *Bayes decision boundary*. The Bayes classifier's prediction is determined by the Bayes decision boundary; an observation that falls on the orange side of the boundary will be assigned

Bayes decision boundary

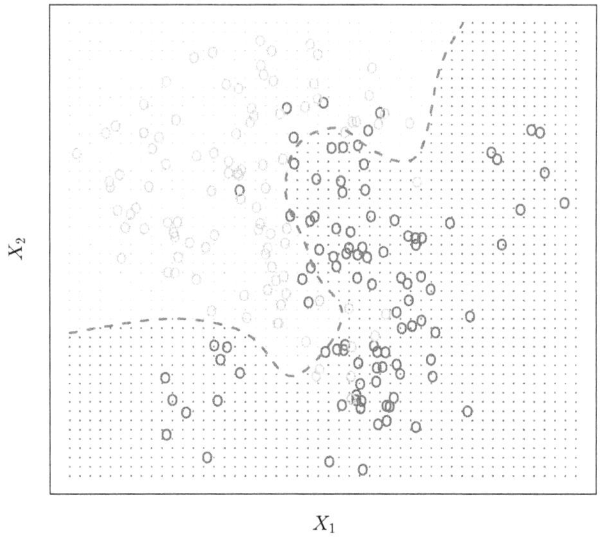

FIGURE 2.13. *A simulated data set consisting of* 100 *observations in each of two groups, indicated in blue and in orange. The purple dashed line represents the Bayes decision boundary. The orange background grid indicates the region in which a test observation will be assigned to the orange class, and the blue background grid indicates the region in which a test observation will be assigned to the blue class.*

to the orange class, and similarly an observation on the blue side of the boundary will be assigned to the blue class.

The Bayes classifier produces the lowest possible test error rate, called the *Bayes error rate*. Since the Bayes classifier will always choose the class for which (2.10) is largest, the error rate will be $1-\max_j \Pr(Y=j|X=x_0)$ at $X=x_0$. In general, the overall Bayes error rate is given by

Bayes error rate

$$1 - E\left(\max_j \Pr(Y=j|X)\right), \tag{2.11}$$

where the expectation averages the probability over all possible values of X. For our simulated data, the Bayes error rate is 0.133. It is greater than zero, because the classes overlap in the true population, which implies that $\max_j \Pr(Y=j|X=x_0) < 1$ for some values of x_0. The Bayes error rate is analogous to the irreducible error, discussed earlier.

K-Nearest Neighbors

In theory we would always like to predict qualitative responses using the Bayes classifier. But for real data, we do not know the conditional distribution of Y given X, and so computing the Bayes classifier is impossible. Therefore, the Bayes classifier serves as an unattainable gold standard against which to compare other methods. Many approaches attempt to estimate the conditional distribution of Y given X, and then classify a given observation to the class with highest *estimated* probability. One such method is the *K-nearest neighbors* (KNN) classifier. Given a positive in-

K-nearest neighbors

teger K and a test observation x_0, the KNN classifier first identifies the K points in the training data that are closest to x_0, represented by $\mathcal{N}_0$. It then estimates the conditional probability for class j as the fraction of points in $\mathcal{N}_0$ whose response values equal j:

$$\Pr(Y = j|X = x_0) = \frac{1}{K} \sum_{i \in \mathcal{N}_0} I(y_i = j). \tag{2.12}$$

Finally, KNN classifies the test observation x_0 to the class with the largest probability from (2.12).

Figure 2.14 provides an illustrative example of the KNN approach. In the left-hand panel, we have plotted a small training data set consisting of six blue and six orange observations. Our goal is to make a prediction for the point labeled by the black cross. Suppose that we choose $K = 3$. Then KNN will first identify the three observations that are closest to the cross. This neighborhood is shown as a circle. It consists of two blue points and one orange point, resulting in estimated probabilities of 2/3 for the blue class and 1/3 for the orange class. Hence KNN will predict that the black cross belongs to the blue class. In the right-hand panel of Figure 2.14 we have applied the KNN approach with $K = 3$ at all of the possible values for X_1 and X_2, and have drawn in the corresponding KNN decision boundary.

Despite the fact that it is a very simple approach, KNN can often produce classifiers that are surprisingly close to the optimal Bayes classifier. Figure 2.15 displays the KNN decision boundary, using $K = 10$, when applied to the larger simulated data set from Figure 2.13. Notice that even though the true distribution is not known by the KNN classifier, the KNN decision boundary is very close to that of the Bayes classifier. The test error rate using KNN is 0.1363, which is close to the Bayes error rate of 0.1304.

The choice of K has a drastic effect on the KNN classifier obtained. Figure 2.16 displays two KNN fits to the simulated data from Figure 2.13, using $K = 1$ and $K = 100$. When $K = 1$, the decision boundary is overly flexible and finds patterns in the data that don't correspond to the Bayes decision boundary. This corresponds to a classifier that has low bias but very high variance. As K grows, the method becomes less flexible and produces a decision boundary that is close to linear. This corresponds to a low-variance but high-bias classifier. On this simulated data set, neither $K = 1$ nor $K = 100$ give good predictions: they have test error rates of 0.1695 and 0.1925, respectively.

Just as in the regression setting, there is not a strong relationship between the training error rate and the test error rate. With $K = 1$, the KNN training error rate is 0, but the test error rate may be quite high. In general, as we use more flexible classification methods, the training error rate will decline but the test error rate may not. In Figure 2.17, we have plotted the KNN test and training errors as a function of $1/K$. As $1/K$ increases, the method becomes more flexible. As in the regression setting, the training error rate consistently declines as the flexibility increases. However, the test error exhibits a characteristic U-shape, declining at first (with a minimum at approximately $K = 10$) before increasing again when the method becomes excessively flexible and overfits.

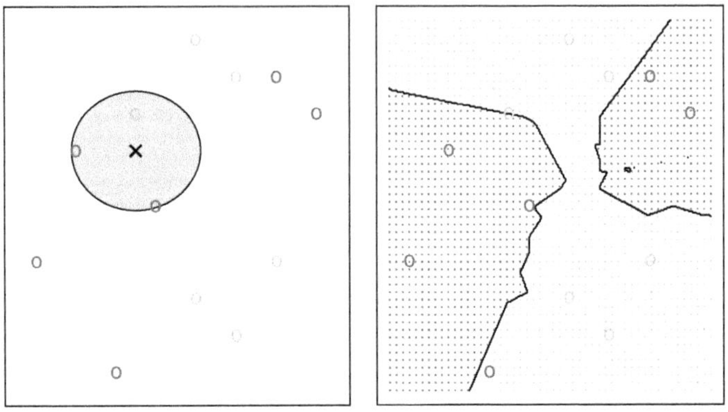

FIGURE 2.14. *The KNN approach, using $K = 3$, is illustrated in a simple situation with six blue observations and six orange observations.* Left: *a test observation at which a predicted class label is desired is shown as a black cross. The three closest points to the test observation are identified, and it is predicted that the test observation belongs to the most commonly-occurring class, in this case blue.* Right: *The KNN decision boundary for this example is shown in black. The blue grid indicates the region in which a test observation will be assigned to the blue class, and the orange grid indicates the region in which it will be assigned to the orange class.*

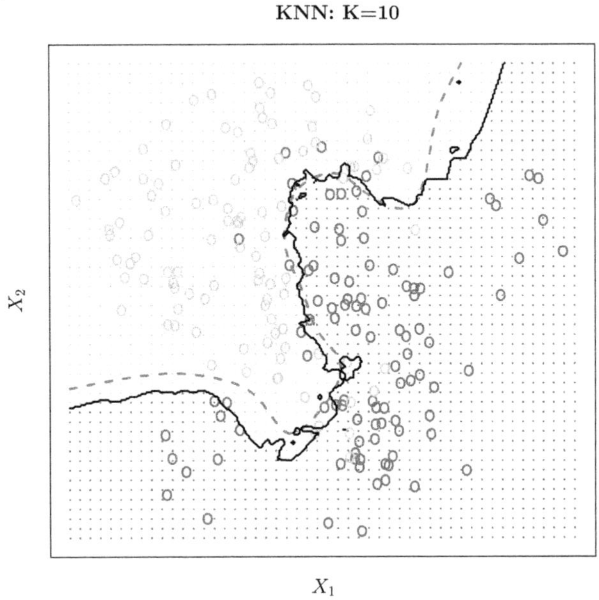

FIGURE 2.15. *The black curve indicates the KNN decision boundary on the data from Figure 2.13, using $K = 10$. The Bayes decision boundary is shown as a purple dashed line. The KNN and Bayes decision boundaries are very similar.*

In both the regression and classification settings, choosing the correct level of flexibility is critical to the success of any statistical learning method. The bias-variance tradeoff, and the resulting U-shape in the test error, can make this a difficult task. In Chapter 5, we return to this topic and discuss

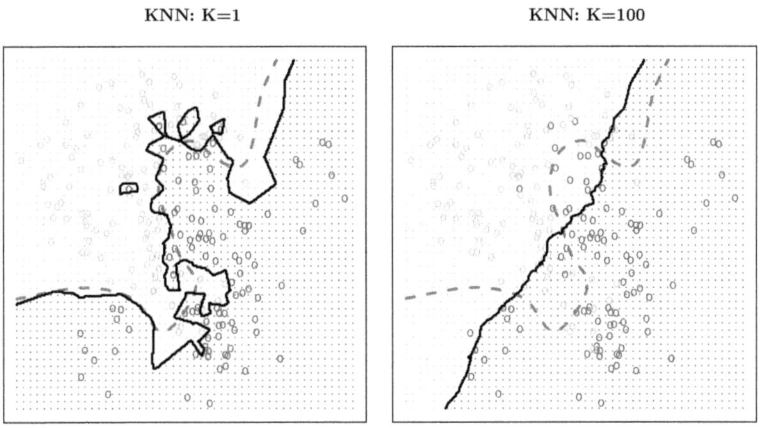

FIGURE 2.16. *A comparison of the KNN decision boundaries (solid black curves) obtained using $K = 1$ and $K = 100$ on the data from Figure 2.13. With $K = 1$, the decision boundary is overly flexible, while with $K = 100$ it is not sufficiently flexible. The Bayes decision boundary is shown as a purple dashed line.*

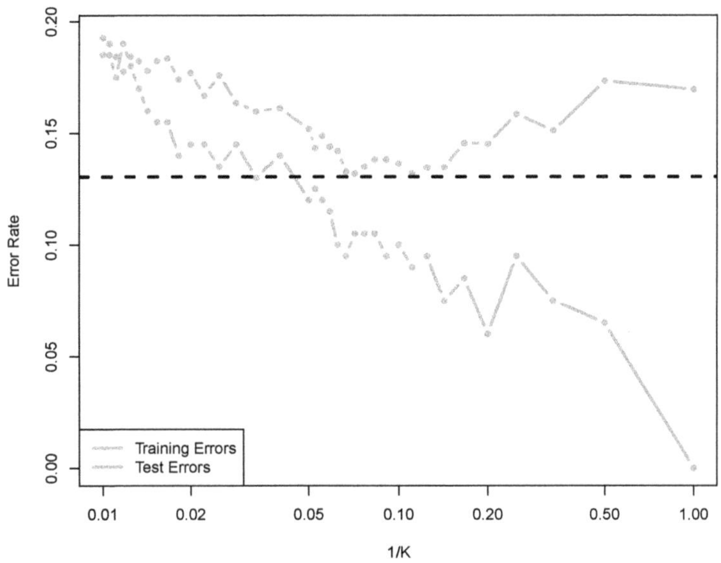

FIGURE 2.17. *The KNN training error rate (blue, 200 observations) and test error rate (orange, 5,000 observations) on the data from Figure 2.13, as the level of flexibility (assessed using $1/K$ on the log scale) increases, or equivalently as the number of neighbors K decreases. The black dashed line indicates the Bayes error rate. The jumpiness of the curves is due to the small size of the training data set.*

various methods for estimating test error rates and thereby choosing the optimal level of flexibility for a given statistical learning method.

2.3 Lab: Introduction to Python

2.3.1 Getting Started

To run the labs in this book, you will need two things:

1. An installation of `Python3`, which is the specific version of `Python` used in the labs.

2. Access to `Jupyter`, a very popular `Python` interface that runs code through a file called a *notebook*. notebook

You can download and install `Python3` by following the instructions available at anaconda.com.

There are a number of ways to get access to `Jupyter`. Here are just a few:

1. Using Google's `Colaboratory` service: colab.research.google.com/.

2. Using `JupyterHub`, available at jupyter.org/hub.

3. Using your own `jupyter` installation. Installation instructions are available at jupyter.org/install.

Please see the `Python` resources page on the book website statlearning.com for up-to-date information about getting `Python` and `Jupyter` working on your computer.

You will need to install the `ISLP` package, which provides access to the datasets and custom-built functions that we provide. Inside a macOS or Linux terminal type `pip install ISLP`; this also installs most other packages needed in the labs. The `Python` resources page has a link to the `ISLP` documentation website.

To run this lab, download the file `Ch2-statlearn-lab.ipynb` from the `Python` resources page. Now run the following code at the command line: `jupyter lab Ch2-statlearn-lab.ipynb`.

If you're using Windows, you can use the `start menu` to access `anaconda`, and follow the links. For example, to install `ISLP` and run this lab, you can run the same code above in an `anaconda` shell.

2.3.2 Basic Commands

In this lab, we will introduce some simple `Python` commands. For more resources about `Python` in general, readers may want to consult the tutorial at docs.python.org/3/tutorial/.

Like most programming languages, `Python` uses *functions* to perform operations. To run a function called `fun`, we type `fun(input1,input2)`, where the inputs (or *arguments*) `input1` and `input2` tell `Python` how to run the function. A function can have any number of inputs. For example, the `print()` function outputs a text representation of all of its arguments to the console.

function

argument

`print()`

```
In [1]: print('fit a model with', 11, 'variables')
```

```
fit a model with 11 variables
```

The following command will provide information about the `print()` function.

In [2]:
```
print?
```

Adding two integers in `Python` is pretty intuitive.

In [3]:
```
3 + 5
```

Out[3]: 8

In `Python`, textual data is handled using *strings*. For instance, `"hello"` and `'hello'` are strings. We can concatenate them using the addition `+` symbol.

string

In [4]:
```
"hello" + " " + "world"
```

Out[4]: 'hello world'

A string is actually a type of *sequence*: this is a generic term for an ordered list. The three most important types of sequences are lists, tuples, and strings. We introduce lists now.

sequence

The following command instructs `Python` to join together the numbers 3, 4, and 5, and to save them as a *list* named `x`. When we type `x`, it gives us back the list.

list

In [5]:
```
x = [3, 4, 5]
x
```

Out[5]: [3, 4, 5]

Note that we used the brackets `[]` to construct this list.

We will often want to add two sets of numbers together. It is reasonable to try the following code, though it will not produce the desired results.

In [6]:
```
y = [4, 9, 7]
x + y
```

Out[6]: [3, 4, 5, 4, 9, 7]

The result may appear slightly counterintuitive: why did `Python` not add the entries of the lists element-by-element? In `Python`, lists hold *arbitrary* objects, and are added using *concatenation*. In fact, concatenation is the behavior that we saw earlier when we entered `"hello" + " " + "world"`.

concatenation

This example reflects the fact that `Python` is a general-purpose programming language. Much of `Python`'s data-specific functionality comes from other packages, notably `numpy` and `pandas`. In the next section, we will introduce the `numpy` package. See docs.scipy.org/doc/numpy/user/quickstart.html for more information about `numpy`.

2.3.3 Introduction to Numerical Python

As mentioned earlier, this book makes use of functionality that is contained in the `numpy` *library*, or *package*. A package is a collection of modules that are not necessarily included in the base `Python` distribution. The name `numpy` is an abbreviation for *numerical Python*. numpy package

To access `numpy`, we must first `import` it. import

In [7]:
```
import numpy as np
```

In the previous line, we named the `numpy` *module* `np`; an abbreviation for easier referencing. module

In `numpy`, an *array* is a generic term for a multidimensional set of numbers. We use the `np.array()` function to define `x` and `y`, which are one-dimensional arrays, i.e. vectors. array np.array()

In [8]:
```
x = np.array([3, 4, 5])
y = np.array([4, 9, 7])
```

Note that if you forgot to run the `import numpy as np` command earlier, then you will encounter an error in calling the `np.array()` function in the previous line. The syntax `np.array()` indicates that the function being called is part of the `numpy` package, which we have abbreviated as `np`.

Since `x` and `y` have been defined using `np.array()`, we get a sensible result when we add them together. Compare this to our results in the previous section, when we tried to add two lists without using `numpy`.

In [9]:
```
x + y
```

Out[9]:
```
array([ 7, 13, 12])
```

In `numpy`, matrices are typically represented as two-dimensional arrays, and vectors as one-dimensional arrays.[1] We can create a two-dimensional array as follows.

In [10]:
```
x = np.array([[1, 2], [3, 4]])
x
```

Out[10]:
```
array([[1, 2],
       [3, 4]])
```

The object `x` has several *attributes*, or associated objects. To access an attribute of `x`, we type `x.attribute`, where we replace `attribute` with the name of the attribute. For instance, we can access the `ndim` attribute of `x` as follows. attribute ndim

In [11]:
```
x.ndim
```

Out[11]:
```
2
```

The output indicates that `x` is a two-dimensional array. Similarly, `x.dtype` is the *data type* attribute of the object `x`. This indicates that `x` is comprised of 64-bit integers: data type

---

[1]While it is also possible to create matrices using `np.matrix()`, we will use `np.array()` throughout the labs in this book.

```
In [12]: x.dtype
```

```
Out[12]: dtype('int64')
```

Why is `x` comprised of integers? This is because we created `x` by passing in exclusively integers to the `np.array()` function. If we had passed in any decimals, then we would have obtained an array of *floating point numbers* (i.e. real-valued numbers).

floating point

```
In [13]: np.array([[1, 2], [3.0, 4]]).dtype
```

```
Out[13]: dtype('float64')
```

Typing `fun?` will cause `Python` to display documentation associated with the function `fun`, if it exists. We can try this for `np.array()`.

```
In [14]: np.array?
```

This documentation indicates that we could create a floating point array by passing a `dtype` argument into `np.array()`.

`dtype`

```
In [15]: np.array([[1, 2], [3, 4]], float).dtype
```

```
Out[15]: dtype('float64')
```

The array `x` is two-dimensional. We can find out the number of rows and columns by looking at its `shape` attribute.

`shape`

```
In [16]: x.shape
```

```
Out[16]: (2, 2)
```

A *method* is a function that is associated with an object. For instance, given an array `x`, the expression `x.sum()` sums all of its elements, using the `sum()` method for arrays. The call `x.sum()` automatically provides `x` as the first argument to its `sum()` method.

method

`.sum()`

```
In [17]: x = np.array([1, 2, 3, 4])
         x.sum()
```

```
Out[17]: 10
```

We could also sum the elements of `x` by passing in `x` as an argument to the `np.sum()` function.

`np.sum()`

```
In [18]: x = np.array([1, 2, 3, 4])
         np.sum(x)
```

```
Out[18]: 10
```

As another example, the `reshape()` method returns a new array with the same elements as `x`, but a different shape. We do this by passing in a `tuple`

`.reshape()`

`tuple`

in our call to `reshape()`, in this case `(2, 3)`. This tuple specifies that we would like to create a two-dimensional array with 2 rows and 3 columns.[2]

In what follows, the `\n` character creates a *new line*.

In [19]:
```
x = np.array([1, 2, 3, 4, 5, 6])
print('beginning x:\n', x)
x_reshape = x.reshape((2, 3))
print('reshaped x:\n', x_reshape)
```

```
beginning x:
 [1 2 3 4 5 6]
reshaped x:
 [[1 2 3]
 [4 5 6]]
```

The previous output reveals that `numpy` arrays are specified as a sequence of *rows*. This is called *row-major ordering*, as opposed to *column-major ordering*.

`Python` (and hence `numpy`) uses 0-based indexing. This means that to access the top left element of `x_reshape`, we type in `x_reshape[0,0]`.

In [20]:
```
x_reshape[0, 0]
```

Out[20]: 1

Similarly, `x_reshape[1,2]` yields the element in the second row and the third column of `x_reshape`.

In [21]:
```
x_reshape[1, 2]
```

Out[21]: 6

Similarly, `x[2]` yields the third entry of `x`.

Now, let's modify the top left element of `x_reshape`. To our surprise, we discover that the first element of `x` has been modified as well!

In [22]:
```
print('x before we modify x_reshape:\n', x)
print('x_reshape before we modify x_reshape:\n', x_reshape)
x_reshape[0, 0] = 5
print('x_reshape after we modify its top left element:\n',
    x_reshape)
print('x after we modify top left element of x_reshape:\n', x)
```

Out[22]:
```
x before we modify x_reshape:
 [1 2 3 4 5 6]
x_reshape before we modify x_reshape:
 [[1 2 3]
 [4 5 6]]
x_reshape after we modify its top left element:
 [[5 2 3]
```

[2]Like lists, tuples represent a sequence of objects. Why do we need more than one way to create a sequence? There are a few differences between tuples and lists, but perhaps the most important is that elements of a tuple cannot be modified, whereas elements of a list can be.

```
 [4 5 6]]
x after we modify top left element of x_reshape:
 [5 2 3 4 5 6]
```

Modifying `x_reshape` also modified `x` because the two objects occupy the same space in memory.

We just saw that we can modify an element of an array. Can we also modify a tuple? It turns out that we cannot — and trying to do so introduces an *exception*, or error.

exception

```
In [23]: my_tuple = (3, 4, 5)
         my_tuple[0] = 2
```

```
TypeError: 'tuple' object does not support item assignment
```

We now briefly mention some attributes of arrays that will come in handy. An array's `shape` attribute contains its dimension; this is always a tuple. The `ndim` attribute yields the number of dimensions, and `T` provides its transpose.

```
In [24]: x_reshape.shape, x_reshape.ndim, x_reshape.T
```

```
Out[24]: ((2, 3),
          2,
          array([[5, 4],
                 [2, 5],
                 [3, 6]]))
```

Notice that the three individual outputs `(2,3)`, `2`, and `array([[5, 4],[2, 5], [3,6]])` are themselves output as a tuple.

We will often want to apply functions to arrays. For instance, we can compute the square root of the entries using the `np.sqrt()` function:

np.sqrt()

```
In [25]: np.sqrt(x)
```

```
Out[25]: array([2.24, 1.41, 1.73, 2., 2.24, 2.45])
```

We can also square the elements:

```
In [26]: x**2
```

```
Out[26]: array([25, 4, 9, 16, 25, 36])
```

We can compute the square roots using the same notation, raising to the power of 1/2 instead of 2.

```
In [27]: x**0.5
```

```
Out[27]: array([2.24, 1.41, 1.73, 2., 2.24, 2.45])
```

Throughout this book, we will often want to generate random data. The `np.random.normal()` function generates a vector of random normal variables. We can learn more about this function by looking at the help page, via a call to `np.random.normal?`. The first line of the help page reads `normal(loc=0.0, scale=1.0, size=None)`. This *signature* line tells us that the function's ar-

np.random.normal()

signature

guments are loc, scale, and size. These are *keyword* arguments, which means that when they are passed into the function, they can be referred to by name (in any order).[3] By default, this function will generate random normal variable(s) with mean (loc) 0 and standard deviation (scale) 1; furthermore, a single random variable will be generated unless the argument to size is changed. keyword

We now generate 50 independent random variables from a $N(0,1)$ distribution.

```
In [28]: x = np.random.normal(size=50)
         x

Out[28]: array([-1.19,  0.41,  0.9 , -0.44, -0.9 , -0.38,  0.13,  1.87,
                -0.35,  1.16,  0.79, -0.97, -1.21,  0.06, -1.62, -0.6 ,
                -0.77, -2.12,  0.38, -1.22, -0.06, -1.97, -1.74, -0.56,
                 1.7 , -0.95,  0.56,  0.35,  0.87,  0.88, -1.66, -0.32,
                -0.3 , -1.36,  0.92, -0.31,  1.28, -1.94,  1.07,  0.07,
                 0.79, -0.46,  2.19, -0.27, -0.64,  0.85,  0.13,  0.46,
                -0.09,  0.7 ])
```

We create an array y by adding an independent $N(50,1)$ random variable to each element of x.

```
In [29]: y = x + np.random.normal(loc=50, scale=1, size=50)
```

The np.corrcoef() function computes the correlation matrix between x and y. The off-diagonal elements give the correlation between x and y. np.corrcoef

```
In [30]: np.corrcoef(x, y)

Out[30]: array([[1.  , 0.69],
                [0.69, 1.  ]])
```

If you're following along in your own Jupyter notebook, then you probably noticed that you got a different set of results when you ran the past few commands. In particular, each time we call np.random.normal(), we will get a different answer, as shown in the following example.

```
In [31]: print(np.random.normal(scale=5, size=2))
         print(np.random.normal(scale=5, size=2))

Out[31]: [4.28 2.59]
         [4.62 -2.54]
```

In order to ensure that our code provides exactly the same results each time it is run, we can set a *random seed* using the np.random.default_rng() function. This function takes an arbitrary, user-specified integer argument. If we set a random seed before generating random data, then re-running our code will yield the same results. The object rng has essentially all the random seed np.random.default_rng

[3]Python also uses *positional* arguments. Positional arguments do not need to use a keyword. To see an example, type in np.sum?. We see that a is a positional argument, i.e. this function assumes that the first unnamed argument that it receives is the array to be summed. By contrast, axis and dtype are keyword arguments: the position in which these arguments are entered into np.sum() does not matter.

random number generating methods found in `np.random`. Hence, to generate normal data we use `rng.normal()`.

```
In [32]: rng = np.random.default_rng(1303)
         print(rng.normal(scale=5, size=2))
         rng2 = np.random.default_rng(1303)
         print(rng2.normal(scale=5, size=2))
```

```
Out[32]: [4.09  -1.07 ]
         [4.09  -1.07 ]
```

Throughout the labs in this book, we use `np.random.default_rng()` whenever we perform calculations involving random quantities within `numpy`. In principle, this should enable the reader to exactly reproduce the stated results. However, as new versions of `numpy` become available, it is possible that some small discrepancies may occur between the output in the labs and the output from `numpy`.

The `np.mean()`, `np.var()`, and `np.std()` functions can be used to compute the mean, variance, and standard deviation of arrays. These functions are also available as methods on the arrays.

`np.mean()`
`np.var()`
`np.std()`

```
In [33]: rng = np.random.default_rng(3)
         y = rng.standard_normal(10)
         np.mean(y), y.mean()
```

```
Out[33]: (-0.11, -0.11)
```

```
In [34]: np.var(y), y.var(), np.mean((y - y.mean())**2)
```

```
Out[34]: (2.72, 2.72, 2.72)
```

Notice that by default `np.var()` divides by the sample size n rather than $n-1$; see the `ddof` argument in `np.var?`.

```
In [35]: np.sqrt(np.var(y)), np.std(y)
```

```
Out[35]: (1.65, 1.65)
```

The `np.mean()`, `np.var()`, and `np.std()` functions can also be applied to the rows and columns of a matrix. To see this, we construct a 10×3 matrix of $N(0,1)$ random variables, and consider computing its row sums.

```
In [36]: X = rng.standard_normal((10, 3))
         X
```

```
Out[36]: array([[ 0.23, -0.35, -0.28],
                [-0.67, -1.06, -0.39],
                [ 0.48, -0.24,  0.96],
                [-0.2 ,  0.02,  1.55],
                [ 0.55, -0.51, -0.18],
                [ 0.54,  1.94, -0.27],
                [-0.24,  1.  , -0.89],
                [-0.29,  0.88,  0.58],
                [ 0.09,  0.67, -2.83],
                [ 1.02, -0.96, -1.67]])
```

Since arrays are row-major ordered, the first axis, i.e. `axis=0`, refers to its rows. We pass this argument into the `mean()` method for the object `X`.

`.mean()`

```
In [37]: X.mean(axis=0)
```

```
Out[37]: array([0.15, 0.14, -0.34])
```

The following yields the same result.

```
In [38]: X.mean(0)
```

```
Out[38]: array([0.15, 0.14, -0.34])
```

2.3.4 Graphics

In `Python`, common practice is to use the library `matplotlib` for graphics. However, since `Python` was not written with data analysis in mind, the notion of plotting is not intrinsic to the language. We will use the `subplots()` function from `matplotlib.pyplot` to create a figure and the axes onto which we plot our data. For many more examples of how to make plots in `Python`, readers are encouraged to visit matplotlib.org/stable/gallery/.

`matplotlib`

In `matplotlib`, a plot consists of a *figure* and one or more *axes*. You can think of the figure as the blank canvas upon which one or more plots will be displayed: it is the entire plotting window. The *axes* contain important information about each plot, such as its x- and y-axis labels, title, and more. (Note that in `matplotlib`, the word *axes* is not the plural of *axis*: a plot's *axes* contains much more information than just the x-axis and the y-axis.)

figure
axes

We begin by importing the `subplots()` function from `matplotlib`. We use this function throughout when creating figures. The function returns a tuple of length two: a figure object as well as the relevant axes object. We will typically pass `figsize` as a keyword argument. Having created our axes, we attempt our first plot using its `plot()` method. To learn more about it, type `ax.plot?`.

`subplots()`
`.plot()`

```
In [39]: from matplotlib.pyplot import subplots
         fig, ax = subplots(figsize=(8, 8))
         x = rng.standard_normal(100)
         y = rng.standard_normal(100)
         ax.plot(x, y);
```

We pause here to note that we have *unpacked* the tuple of length two returned by `subplots()` into the two distinct variables `fig` and `ax`. Unpacking is typically preferred to the following equivalent but slightly more verbose code:

```
In [40]: output = subplots(figsize=(8, 8))
         fig = output[0]
         ax = output[1]
```

We see that our earlier cell produced a line plot, which is the default. To create a scatterplot, we provide an additional argument to `ax.plot()`, indicating that circles should be displayed.

```
In [41]: fig, ax = subplots(figsize=(8, 8))
         ax.plot(x, y, 'o');
```

Different values of this additional argument can be used to produce different colored lines as well as different linestyles.

As an alternative, we could use the ax.scatter() function to create a scatterplot. .scatter()

```
In [42]: fig, ax = subplots(figsize=(8, 8))
         ax.scatter(x, y, marker='o');
```

Notice that in the code blocks above, we have ended the last line with a semicolon. This prevents ax.plot(x, y) from printing text to the notebook. However, it does not prevent a plot from being produced. If we omit the trailing semi-colon, then we obtain the following output:

```
In [43]: fig, ax = subplots(figsize=(8, 8))
         ax.scatter(x, y, marker='o')

Out[43]: <matplotlib.collections.PathCollection at 0x7fb3d9c8f310>
         Figure(432x288)
```

In what follows, we will use trailing semicolons whenever the text that would be output is not germane to the discussion at hand.

To label our plot, we make use of the set_xlabel(), set_ylabel(), and set_title() methods of ax. .set_xlabel() .set_ylabel() .set_title()

```
In [44]: fig, ax = subplots(figsize=(8, 8))
         ax.scatter(x, y, marker='o')
         ax.set_xlabel("this is the x-axis")
         ax.set_ylabel("this is the y-axis")
         ax.set_title("Plot of X vs Y");
```

Having access to the figure object fig itself means that we can go in and change some aspects and then redisplay it. Here, we change the size from (8, 8) to (12, 3).

```
fig.set_size_inches(12,3)
fig
```

Occasionally we will want to create several plots within a figure. This can be achieved by passing additional arguments to subplots(). Below, we create a 2×3 grid of plots in a figure of size determined by the figsize argument. In such situations, there is often a relationship between the axes in the plots. For example, all plots may have a common x-axis. The subplots() function can automatically handle this situation when passed the keyword argument sharex=True. The axes object below is an array pointing to different plots in the figure.

```
In [45]: fig, axes = subplots(nrows=2,
                              ncols=3,
                              figsize=(15, 5))
```

We now produce a scatter plot with 'o' in the second column of the first row and a scatter plot with '+' in the third column of the second row.

In [46]:
```
axes[0,1].plot(x, y, 'o')
axes[1,2].scatter(x, y, marker='+')
fig
```

Type `subplots?` to learn more about `subplots()`.

To save the output of `fig`, we call its `savefig()` method. The argument `dpi` is the dots per inch, used to determine how large the figure will be in pixels.

`.savefig()`

In [47]:
```
fig.savefig("Figure.png", dpi=400)
fig.savefig("Figure.pdf", dpi=200);
```

We can continue to modify `fig` using step-by-step updates; for example, we can modify the range of the x-axis, re-save the figure, and even re-display it.

In [48]:
```
axes[0,1].set_xlim([-1,1])
fig.savefig("Figure_updated.jpg")
fig
```

We now create some more sophisticated plots. The `ax.contour()` method produces a *contour plot* in order to represent three-dimensional data, similar to a topographical map. It takes three arguments:

`.contour()`

contour plot

- A vector of `x` values (the first dimension),
- A vector of `y` values (the second dimension), and
- A matrix whose elements correspond to the `z` value (the third dimension) for each pair of `(x,y)` coordinates.

To create `x` and `y`, we'll use the command `np.linspace(a, b, n)`, which returns a vector of `n` numbers starting at `a` and ending at `b`.

`np.linspace`

In [49]:
```
fig, ax = subplots(figsize=(8, 8))
x = np.linspace(-np.pi, np.pi, 50)
y = x
f = np.multiply.outer(np.cos(y), 1 / (1 + x**2))
ax.contour(x, y, f);
```

We can increase the resolution by adding more levels to the image.

In [50]:
```
fig, ax = subplots(figsize=(8, 8))
ax.contour(x, y, f, levels=45);
```

To fine-tune the output of the `ax.contour()` function, take a look at the help file by typing `?plt.contour`.

The `ax.imshow()` method is similar to `ax.contour()`, except that it produces a color-coded plot whose colors depend on the `z` value. This is known as a *heatmap*, and is sometimes used to plot temperature in weather forecasts.

`.imshow()`

heatmap

In [51]:
```
fig, ax = subplots(figsize=(8, 8))
ax.imshow(f);
```

2.3.5 Sequences and Slice Notation

As seen above, the function `np.linspace()` can be used to create a sequence of numbers.

```
In [52]: seq1 = np.linspace(0, 10, 11)
         seq1
```

```
Out[52]: array([ 0.,  1.,  2.,  3.,  4.,  5.,  6.,  7.,  8.,  9., 10.])
```

The function `np.arange()` returns a sequence of numbers spaced out by `step`. If `step` is not specified, then a default value of 1 is used. Let's create a sequence that starts at 0 and ends at 10. `np.arange()`

```
In [53]: seq2 = np.arange(0, 10)
         seq2
```

```
Out[53]: array([0, 1, 2, 3, 4, 5, 6, 7, 8, 9])
```

Why isn't 10 output above? This has to do with *slice* notation in `Python`. Slice notation is used to index sequences such as lists, tuples and arrays. Suppose we want to retrieve the fourth through sixth (inclusive) entries of a string. We obtain a slice of the string using the indexing notation `[3:6]`. slice

```
In [54]: "hello world"[3:6]
```

```
Out[54]: 'lo '
```

In the code block above, the notation `3:6` is shorthand for `slice(3,6)` when used inside `[]`.

```
In [55]: "hello world"[slice(3,6)]
```

```
Out[55]: 'lo '
```

You might have expected `slice(3,6)` to output the fourth through seventh characters in the text string (recalling that `Python` begins its indexing at zero), but instead it output the fourth through sixth. This also explains why the earlier `np.arange(0, 10)` command output only the integers from 0 to 9. See the documentation `slice?` for useful options in creating slices.

2.3.6 Indexing Data

To begin, we create a two-dimensional `numpy` array.

```
In [56]: A = np.array(np.arange(16)).reshape((4, 4))
         A
```

```
Out[56]: array([[ 0,  1,  2,  3],
                [ 4,  5,  6,  7],
                [ 8,  9, 10, 11],
                [12, 13, 14, 15]])
```

Typing `A[1,2]` retrieves the element corresponding to the second row and third column. (As usual, `Python` indexes from 0.)

```
In [57]: A[1,2]
```

```
Out[57]: 6
```

The first number after the open-bracket symbol `[` refers to the row, and the second number refers to the column.

Indexing Rows, Columns, and Submatrices

To select multiple rows at a time, we can pass in a list specifying our selection. For instance, `[1,3]` will retrieve the second and fourth rows:

```
In [58]: A[[1,3]]
```

```
Out[58]: array([[ 4,  5,  6,  7],
                [12, 13, 14, 15]])
```

To select the first and third columns, we pass in `[0,2]` as the second argument in the square brackets. In this case we need to supply the first argument `:` which selects all rows.

```
In [59]: A[:,[0,2]]
```

```
Out[59]: array([[ 0,  2],
                [ 4,  6],
                [ 8, 10],
                [12, 14]])
```

Now, suppose that we want to select the submatrix made up of the second and fourth rows as well as the first and third columns. This is where indexing gets slightly tricky. It is natural to try to use lists to retrieve the rows and columns:

```
In [60]: A[[1,3],[0,2]]
```

```
Out[60]: array([ 4, 14])
```

Oops — what happened? We got a one-dimensional array of length two identical to

```
In [61]: np.array([A[1,0],A[3,2]])
```

```
Out[61]: array([ 4, 14])
```

Similarly, the following code fails to extract the submatrix comprised of the second and fourth rows and the first, third, and fourth columns:

```
In [62]: A[[1,3],[0,2,3]]
```

```
IndexError: shape mismatch: indexing arrays could not be broadcast
    together with shapes (2,) (3,)
```

We can see what has gone wrong here. When supplied with two indexing lists, the numpy interpretation is that these provide pairs of i, j indices for a series of entries. That is why the pair of lists must have the same length. However, that was not our intent, since we are looking for a submatrix.

One easy way to do this is as follows. We first create a submatrix by subsetting the rows of A, and then on the fly we make a further submatrix by subsetting its columns.

```
In [63]: A[[1,3]][:,[0,2]]
```

```
Out[63]: array([[ 4,  6],
                [12, 14]])
```

There are more efficient ways of achieving the same result.

The *convenience function* np.ix_() allows us to extract a submatrix using lists, by creating an intermediate *mesh* object.

convenience function

np.ix_()

mesh

```
In [64]: idx = np.ix_([1,3],[0,2,3])
         A[idx]
```

```
Out[64]: array([[ 4,  6,  7],
                [12, 14, 15]])
```

Alternatively, we can subset matrices efficiently using slices. The slice 1:4:2 captures the second and fourth items of a sequence, while the slice 0:3:2 captures the first and third items (the third element in a slice sequence is the step size).

```
In [65]: A[1:4:2,0:3:2]
```

```
Out[65]: array([[ 4,  6],
                [12, 14]])
```

Why are we able to retrieve a submatrix directly using slices but not using lists? Its because they are different Python types, and are treated differently by numpy. Slices can be used to extract objects from arbitrary sequences, such as strings, lists, and tuples, while the use of lists for indexing is more limited.

Boolean Indexing

In numpy, a *Boolean* is a type that equals either True or False (also represented as 1 and 0, respectively). The next line creates a vector of 0's, represented as Booleans, of length equal to the first dimension of A.

Boolean

```
In [66]: keep_rows = np.zeros(A.shape[0], bool)
         keep_rows
```

```
Out[66]: array([False, False, False, False])
```

We now set two of the elements to True.

```
In [67]: keep_rows[[1,3]] = True
         keep_rows
```

```
Out[67]: array([False,  True, False,  True])
```

Note that the elements of `keep_rows`, when viewed as integers, are the same as the values of `np.array([0,1,0,1])`. Below, we use `==` to verify their equality. When applied to two arrays, the `==` operation is applied elementwise.

```
In [68]: np.all(keep_rows == np.array([0,1,0,1]))
```

```
Out[68]: True
```

(Here, the function `np.all()` has checked whether all entries of an array are `True`. A similar function, `np.any()`, can be used to check whether any entries of an array are `True`.) `np.all()` `np.any()`

However, even though `np.array([0,1,0,1])` and `keep_rows` are equal according to `==`, they index different sets of rows! The former retrieves the first, second, first, and second rows of `A`.

```
In [69]: A[np.array([0,1,0,1])]
```

```
Out[69]: array([[0, 1, 2, 3],
                [4, 5, 6, 7],
                [0, 1, 2, 3],
                [4, 5, 6, 7]])
```

By contrast, `keep_rows` retrieves only the second and fourth rows of `A` — i.e. the rows for which the Boolean equals `TRUE`.

```
In [70]: A[keep_rows]
```

```
Out[70]: array([[ 4,  5,  6,  7],
                [12, 13, 14, 15]])
```

This example shows that Booleans and integers are treated differently by `numpy`.

We again make use of the `np.ix_()` function to create a mesh containing the second and fourth rows, and the first, third, and fourth columns. This time, we apply the function to Booleans, rather than lists.

```
In [71]: keep_cols = np.zeros(A.shape[1], bool)
         keep_cols[[0, 2, 3]] = True
         idx_bool = np.ix_(keep_rows, keep_cols)
         A[idx_bool]
```

```
Out[71]: array([[ 4,  6,  7],
                [12, 14, 15]])
```

We can also mix a list with an array of Booleans in the arguments to `np.ix_()`:

```
In [72]: idx_mixed = np.ix_([1,3], keep_cols)
         A[idx_mixed]
```

```
Out[72]: array([[ 4,  6,  7],
                [12, 14, 15]])
```

For more details on indexing in `numpy`, readers are referred to the `numpy` tutorial mentioned earlier.

2.3.7 Loading Data

Data sets often contain different types of data, and may have names associated with the rows or columns. For these reasons, they typically are best accommodated using a *data frame*. We can think of a data frame as a sequence of arrays of identical length; these are the columns. Entries in the different arrays can be combined to form a row. The `pandas` library can be used to create and work with data frame objects.

data frame

Reading in a Data Set

The first step of most analyses involves importing a data set into `Python`. Before attempting to load a data set, we must make sure that `Python` knows where to find the file containing it. If the file is in the same location as this notebook file, then we are all set. Otherwise, the command `os.chdir()` can be used to *change directory*. (You will need to call `import os` before calling `os.chdir()`.)

os.chdir()

We will begin by reading in `Auto.csv`, available on the book website. This is a comma-separated file, and can be read in using `pd.read_csv()`:

pd.read_csv()

In [73]:
```
import pandas as pd
Auto = pd.read_csv('Auto.csv')
Auto
```

The book website also has a whitespace-delimited version of this data, called `Auto.data`. This can be read in as follows:

In [74]:
```
Auto = pd.read_csv('Auto.data', delim_whitespace=True)
```

Both `Auto.csv` and `Auto.data` are simply text files. Before loading data into `Python`, it is a good idea to view it using a text editor or other software, such as Microsoft Excel.

We now take a look at the column of `Auto` corresponding to the variable `horsepower`:

In [75]:
```
Auto['horsepower']
```

Out[75]:
```
0       130.0
1       165.0
2       150.0
3       150.0
4       140.0
        ...
392     86.00
393     52.00
394     84.00
395     79.00
396     82.00
Name: horsepower, Length: 397, dtype: object
```

We see that the `dtype` of this column is `object`. It turns out that all values of the `horsepower` column were interpreted as strings when reading in the data. We can find out why by looking at the unique values.

In [76]:
```
np.unique(Auto['horsepower'])
```

To save space, we have omitted the output of the previous code block. We see the culprit is the value `?`, which is being used to encode missing values.

To fix the problem, we must provide `pd.read_csv()` with an argument called `na_values`. Now, each instance of `?` in the file is replaced with the value `np.nan`, which means *not a number*:

```
In [77]: Auto = pd.read_csv('Auto.data',
                            na_values=['?'],
                            delim_whitespace=True)
         Auto['horsepower'].sum()
```

```
Out[77]: 40952.0
```

The `Auto.shape` attribute tells us that the data has 397 observations, or rows, and nine variables, or columns.

```
In [78]: Auto.shape
```

```
Out[78]: (397, 9)
```

There are various ways to deal with missing data. In this case, since only five of the rows contain missing observations, we choose to use the `Auto.dropna()` method to simply remove these rows. `.dropna()`

```
In [79]: Auto_new = Auto.dropna()
         Auto_new.shape
```

```
Out[79]: (392, 9)
```

Basics of Selecting Rows and Columns

We can use `Auto.columns` to check the variable names.

```
In [80]: Auto = Auto_new # overwrite the previous value
         Auto.columns
```

```
Out[80]: Index(['mpg', 'cylinders', 'displacement', 'horsepower',
                'weight', 'acceleration', 'year', 'origin', 'name'],
                dtype='object')
```

Accessing the rows and columns of a data frame is similar, but not identical, to accessing the rows and columns of an array. Recall that the first argument to the `[]` method is always applied to the rows of the array. Similarly, passing in a slice to the `[]` method creates a data frame whose *rows* are determined by the slice:

```
In [81]: Auto[:3]
```

```
Out[81]:     mpg   cylinders   displacement   horsepower   weight   ...
         0   18.0          8          307.0        130.0   3504.0   ...
         1   15.0          8          350.0        165.0   3693.0   ...
         2   18.0          8          318.0        150.0   3436.0   ...
```

Similarly, an array of Booleans can be used to subset the rows:

```
In [82]: idx_80 = Auto['year'] > 80
         Auto[idx_80]
```

However, if we pass in a list of strings to the `[]` method, then we obtain a data frame containing the corresponding set of *columns*.

```
In [83]: Auto[['mpg', 'horsepower']]
```

```
Out[83]:        mpg     horsepower
         0      18.0    130.0
         1      15.0    165.0
         2      18.0    150.0
         3      16.0    150.0
         4      17.0    140.0
         ...    ...     ...
         392    27.0    86.0
         393    44.0    52.0
         394    32.0    84.0
         395    28.0    79.0
         396    31.0    82.0
         392 rows x 2 columns
```

Since we did not specify an *index* column when we loaded our data frame, the rows are labeled using integers 0 to 396.

```
In [84]: Auto.index
```

```
Out[84]: Int64Index([  0,   1,   2,   3,   4,   5,   6,   7,   8,   9,
                     ...
                     387, 388, 389, 390, 391, 392, 393, 394, 395, 396],
                    dtype='int64', length=392)
```

We can use the `set_index()` method to re-name the rows using the contents of `Auto['name']`. .set_index()

```
In [85]: Auto_re = Auto.set_index('name')
         Auto_re
```

```
Out[85]:                          mpg   cylinders   displacement   ...
                         name

         chevrolet chevelle malibu   18.0           8          307.0   ...
                 buick skylark 32   15.0           8          350.0   ...
               plymouth satellite   18.0           8          318.0   ...
                    amc rebel sst   16.0           8          304.0   ...
```

```
In [86]: Auto_re.columns
```

```
Out[86]: Index(['mpg', 'cylinders', 'displacement', 'horsepower',
                'weight', 'acceleration', 'year', 'origin'],
               dtype='object')
```

We see that the column `'name'` is no longer there.

Now that the index has been set to `name`, we can access rows of the data frame by `name` using the `loc[]` method of `Auto`: .loc[]

```
In [87]: rows = ['amc rebel sst', 'ford torino']
         Auto_re.loc[rows]
```

```
Out[87]:                mpg  cylinders  displacement horsepower  ...
               name
      amc rebel sst    16.0          8         304.0      150.0  ...
        ford torino    17.0          8         302.0      140.0  ...
```

As an alternative to using the index name, we could retrieve the 4th and 5th rows of `Auto` using the `iloc[]` method:

.iloc[]

```
In [88]: Auto_re.iloc[[3,4]]
```

We can also use it to retrieve the 1st, 3rd and and 4th columns of `Auto_re`:

```
In [89]: Auto_re.iloc[:,[0,2,3]]
```

We can extract the 4th and 5th rows, as well as the 1st, 3rd and 4th columns, using a single call to `iloc[]`:

```
In [90]: Auto_re.iloc[[3,4],[0,2,3]]
```

```
Out[90]:                mpg  displacement  horsepower
               name
      amc rebel sst    16.0         304.0       150.0
        ford torino    17.0         302.0       140.0
```

Index entries need not be unique: there are several cars in the data frame named `ford galaxie 500`.

```
In [91]: Auto_re.loc['ford galaxie 500', ['mpg', 'origin']]
```

```
Out[91]:                   mpg   origin
                  name
      ford galaxie 500    15.0        1
      ford galaxie 500    14.0        1
      ford galaxie 500    14.0        1
```

More on Selecting Rows and Columns

Suppose now that we want to create a data frame consisting of the `weight` and `origin` of the subset of cars with `year` greater than 80 — i.e. those built after 1980. To do this, we first create a Boolean array that indexes the rows. The `loc[]` method allows for Boolean entries as well as strings:

```
In [92]: idx_80 = Auto_re['year'] > 80
         Auto_re.loc[idx_80, ['weight', 'origin']]
```

To do this more concisely, we can use an anonymous function called a `lambda`:

lambda

```
In [93]: Auto_re.loc[lambda df: df['year'] > 80, ['weight', 'origin']]
```

The `lambda` call creates a function that takes a single argument, here `df`, and returns `df['year']>80`. Since it is created inside the `loc[]` method for the dataframe Auto_re, that dataframe will be the argument supplied. As another example of using a lambda, suppose that we want all cars built after 1980 that achieve greater than 30 miles per gallon:

In [94]:
```
Auto_re.loc[lambda df: (df['year'] > 80) & (df['mpg'] > 30),
            ['weight', 'origin']
           ]
```

The symbol & computes an element-wise *and* operation. As another example, suppose that we want to retrieve all Ford and Datsun cars with displacement less than 300. We check whether each name entry contains either the string ford or datsun using the str.contains() method of the index attribute of of the dataframe:

.str.contains()

In [95]:
```
Auto_re.loc[lambda df: (df['displacement'] < 300)
                       & (df.index.str.contains('ford')
                       | df.index.str.contains('datsun')),
            ['weight', 'origin']
           ]
```

Here, the symbol | computes an element-wise *or* operation.

In summary, a powerful set of operations is available to index the rows and columns of data frames. For integer based queries, use the iloc[] method. For string and Boolean selections, use the loc[] method. For functional queries that filter rows, use the loc[] method with a function (typically a lambda) in the rows argument.

2.3.8 For Loops

A for loop is a standard tool in many languages that repeatedly evaluates some chunk of code while varying different values inside the code. For example, suppose we loop over elements of a list and compute their sum.

for

In [96]:
```
total = 0
for value in [3,2,19]:
    total += value
print('Total is: {0}'.format(total))
```

```
Total is: 24
```

The indented code beneath the line with the for statement is run for each value in the sequence specified in the for statement. The loop ends either when the cell ends or when code is indented at the same level as the original for statement. We see that the final line above which prints the total is executed only once after the for loop has terminated. Loops can be nested by additional indentation.

In [97]:
```
total = 0
for value in [2,3,19]:
    for weight in [3, 2, 1]:
        total += value * weight
print('Total is: {0}'.format(total))
```

```
Total is: 144
```

Above, we summed over each combination of `value` and `weight`. We also took advantage of the *increment* notation in `Python`: the expression `a += b` is equivalent to `a = a + b`. Besides being a convenient notation, this can save time in computationally heavy tasks in which the intermediate value of `a+b` need not be explicitly created.

increment

Perhaps a more common task would be to sum over `(value, weight)` pairs. For instance, to compute the average value of a random variable that takes on possible values 2, 3 or 19 with probability 0.2, 0.3, 0.5 respectively we would compute the weighted sum. Tasks such as this can often be accomplished using the `zip()` function that loops over a sequence of tuples.

zip()

In [98]:
```
total = 0
for value, weight in zip([2,3,19],
                         [0.2,0.3,0.5]):
    total += weight * value
print('Weighted average is: {0}'.format(total))
```

```
Weighted average is: 10.8
```

String Formatting

In the code chunk above we also printed a string displaying the total. However, the object `total` is an integer and not a string. Inserting the value of something into a string is a common task, made simple using some of the powerful string formatting tools in `Python`. Many data cleaning tasks involve manipulating and programmatically producing strings.

For example we may want to loop over the columns of a data frame and print the percent missing in each column. Let's create a data frame `D` with columns in which 20% of the entries are missing i.e. set to `np.nan`. We'll create the values in `D` from a normal distribution with mean 0 and variance 1 using `rng.standard_normal()` and then overwrite some random entries using `rng.choice()`.

np.nan

In [99]:
```
rng = np.random.default_rng(1)
A = rng.standard_normal((127, 5))
M = rng.choice([0, np.nan], p=[0.8,0.2], size=A.shape)
A += M
D = pd.DataFrame(A, columns=['food',
                             'bar',
                             'pickle',
                             'snack',
                             'popcorn'])
D[:3]
```

Out[99]:

	food	bar	pickle	snack	popcorn
0	0.345584	0.821618	0.330437	-1.303157	NaN
1	NaN	-0.536953	0.581118	0.364572	0.294132
2	NaN	0.546713	NaN	-0.162910	-0.482119

In [100]:
```
for col in D.columns:
    template = 'Column "{0}" has {1:.2%} missing values'
    print(template.format(col,
          np.isnan(D[col]).mean()))
```

```
Column "food" has 16.54% missing values
Column "bar" has 25.98% missing values
Column "pickle" has 29.13% missing values
Column "snack" has 21.26% missing values
Column "popcorn" has 22.83% missing values
```

We see that the `template.format()` method expects two arguments `{0}` and `{1:.2%}`, and the latter includes some formatting information. In particular, it specifies that the second argument should be expressed as a percent with two decimal digits.

The reference docs.python.org/3/library/string.html includes many helpful and more complex examples.

2.3.9 Additional Graphical and Numerical Summaries

We can use the `ax.plot()` or `ax.scatter()` functions to display the quantitative variables. However, simply typing the variable names will produce an error message, because `Python` does not know to look in the `Auto` data set for those variables.

```
In [101]: fig, ax = subplots(figsize=(8, 8))
          ax.plot(horsepower, mpg, 'o');
```

```
NameError: name 'horsepower' is not defined
```

We can address this by accessing the columns directly:

```
In [102]: fig, ax = subplots(figsize=(8, 8))
          ax.plot(Auto['horsepower'], Auto['mpg'], 'o');
```

Alternatively, we can use the `plot()` method with the call `Auto.plot()`. Using this method, the variables can be accessed by name. The plot methods of a data frame return a familiar object: an axes. We can use it to update the plot as we did previously: `.plot()`

```
In [103]: ax = Auto.plot.scatter('horsepower', 'mpg');
          ax.set_title('Horsepower vs. MPG')
```

If we want to save the figure that contains a given axes, we can find the relevant figure by accessing the `figure` attribute:

```
In [104]: fig = ax.figure
          fig.savefig('horsepower_mpg.png');
```

We can further instruct the data frame to plot to a particular axes object. In this case the corresponding `plot()` method will return the modified axes we passed in as an argument. Note that when we request a one-dimensional grid of plots, the object `axes` is similarly one-dimensional. We place our scatter plot in the middle plot of a row of three plots within a figure.

```
In [105]: fig, axes = subplots(ncols=3, figsize=(15, 5))
          Auto.plot.scatter('horsepower', 'mpg', ax=axes[1]);
```

Note also that the columns of a data frame can be accessed as attributes: try typing in `Auto.horsepower`.

We now consider the `cylinders` variable. Typing in `Auto.cylinders.dtype` reveals that it is being treated as a quantitative variable. However, since there is only a small number of possible values for this variable, we may wish to treat it as qualitative. Below, we replace the `cylinders` column with a categorical version of `Auto.cylinders`. The function `pd.Series()` owes its name to the fact that `pandas` is often used in time series applications.

`pd.Series()`

```
In [106]: Auto.cylinders = pd.Series(Auto.cylinders, dtype='category')
          Auto.cylinders.dtype
```

Now that `cylinders` is qualitative, we can display it using the `boxplot()` method.

`.boxplot()`

```
In [107]: fig, ax = subplots(figsize=(8, 8))
          Auto.boxplot('mpg', by='cylinders', ax=ax);
```

The `hist()` method can be used to plot a *histogram*.

`.hist()`

```
In [108]: fig, ax = subplots(figsize=(8, 8))
          Auto.hist('mpg', ax=ax);
```

The color of the bars and the number of bins can be changed:

```
In [109]: fig, ax = subplots(figsize=(8, 8))
          Auto.hist('mpg', color='red', bins=12, ax=ax);
```

See `Auto.hist?` for more plotting options.

We can use the `pd.plotting.scatter_matrix()` function to create a *scatterplot matrix* to visualize all of the pairwise relationships between the columns in a data frame.

`pd.plotting. scatter_ matrix()`

```
In [110]: pd.plotting.scatter_matrix(Auto);
```

We can also produce scatterplots for a subset of the variables.

```
In [111]: pd.plotting.scatter_matrix(Auto[['mpg',
                                           'displacement',
                                           'weight']]);
```

The `describe()` method produces a numerical summary of each column in a data frame.

`.describe()`

```
In [112]: Auto[['mpg', 'weight']].describe()
```

We can also produce a summary of just a single column.

```
In [113]: Auto['cylinders'].describe()
          Auto['mpg'].describe()
```

To exit `Jupyter`, select `File / Close and Halt`.

2.4 Exercises

Conceptual

1. For each of parts (a) through (d), indicate whether we would generally expect the performance of a flexible statistical learning method to be better or worse than an inflexible method. Justify your answer.

   (a) The sample size n is extremely large, and the number of predictors p is small.

   (b) The number of predictors p is extremely large, and the number of observations n is small.

   (c) The relationship between the predictors and response is highly non-linear.

   (d) The variance of the error terms, i.e. $\sigma^2 = \text{Var}(\epsilon)$, is extremely high.

2. Explain whether each scenario is a classification or regression problem, and indicate whether we are most interested in inference or prediction. Finally, provide n and p.

   (a) We collect a set of data on the top 500 firms in the US. For each firm we record profit, number of employees, industry and the CEO salary. We are interested in understanding which factors affect CEO salary.

   (b) We are considering launching a new product and wish to know whether it will be a *success* or a *failure*. We collect data on 20 similar products that were previously launched. For each product we have recorded whether it was a success or failure, price charged for the product, marketing budget, competition price, and ten other variables.

   (c) We are interested in predicting the % change in the USD/Euro exchange rate in relation to the weekly changes in the world stock markets. Hence we collect weekly data for all of 2012. For each week we record the % change in the USD/Euro, the % change in the US market, the % change in the British market, and the % change in the German market.

3. We now revisit the bias-variance decomposition.

   (a) Provide a sketch of typical (squared) bias, variance, training error, test error, and Bayes (or irreducible) error curves, on a single plot, as we go from less flexible statistical learning methods towards more flexible approaches. The x-axis should represent the amount of flexibility in the method, and the y-axis should represent the values for each curve. There should be five curves. Make sure to label each one.

   (b) Explain why each of the five curves has the shape displayed in part (a).

4. You will now think of some real-life applications for statistical learning.

   (a) Describe three real-life applications in which *classification* might be useful. Describe the response, as well as the predictors. Is the goal of each application inference or prediction? Explain your answer.

   (b) Describe three real-life applications in which *regression* might be useful. Describe the response, as well as the predictors. Is the goal of each application inference or prediction? Explain your answer.

   (c) Describe three real-life applications in which *cluster analysis* might be useful.

5. What are the advantages and disadvantages of a very flexible (versus a less flexible) approach for regression or classification? Under what circumstances might a more flexible approach be preferred to a less flexible approach? When might a less flexible approach be preferred?

6. Describe the differences between a parametric and a non-parametric statistical learning approach. What are the advantages of a parametric approach to regression or classification (as opposed to a non-parametric approach)? What are its disadvantages?

7. The table below provides a training data set containing six observations, three predictors, and one qualitative response variable.

Obs.	X_1	X_2	X_3	Y
1	0	3	0	Red
2	2	0	0	Red
3	0	1	3	Red
4	0	1	2	Green
5	−1	0	1	Green
6	1	1	1	Red

   Suppose we wish to use this data set to make a prediction for Y when $X_1 = X_2 = X_3 = 0$ using K-nearest neighbors.

   (a) Compute the Euclidean distance between each observation and the test point, $X_1 = X_2 = X_3 = 0$.

   (b) What is our prediction with $K = 1$? Why?

   (c) What is our prediction with $K = 3$? Why?

   (d) If the Bayes decision boundary in this problem is highly nonlinear, then would we expect the *best* value for K to be large or small? Why?

Applied

8. This exercise relates to the `College` data set, which can be found in the file `College.csv` on the book website. It contains a number of variables for 777 different universities and colleges in the US. The variables are

   - `Private` : Public/private indicator
   - `Apps` : Number of applications received
   - `Accept` : Number of applicants accepted
   - `Enroll` : Number of new students enrolled
   - `Top10perc` : New students from top 10 % of high school class
   - `Top25perc` : New students from top 25 % of high school class
   - `F.Undergrad` : Number of full-time undergraduates
   - `P.Undergrad` : Number of part-time undergraduates
   - `Outstate` : Out-of-state tuition
   - `Room.Board` : Room and board costs
   - `Books` : Estimated book costs
   - `Personal` : Estimated personal spending
   - `PhD` : Percent of faculty with Ph.D.s
   - `Terminal` : Percent of faculty with terminal degree
   - `S.F.Ratio` : Student/faculty ratio
   - `perc.alumni` : Percent of alumni who donate
   - `Expend` : Instructional expenditure per student
   - `Grad.Rate` : Graduation rate

   Before reading the data into `Python`, it can be viewed in Excel or a text editor.

   (a) Use the `pd.read_csv()` function to read the data into `Python`. Call the loaded data `college`. Make sure that you have the directory set to the correct location for the data.

   (b) Look at the data used in the notebook by creating and running a new cell with just the code `college` in it. You should notice that the first column is just the name of each university in a column named something like `Unnamed: 0`. We don't really want `pandas` to treat this as data. However, it may be handy to have these names for later. Try the following commands and similarly look at the resulting data frames:

```
college2 = pd.read_csv('College.csv', index_col=0)
college3 = college.rename({'Unnamed: 0': 'College'},
                          axis=1)
college3 = college3.set_index('College')
```

This has used the first column in the file as an `index` for the data frame. This means that `pandas` has given each row a name corresponding to the appropriate university. Now you should see that the first data column is `Private`. Note that the names of the colleges appear on the left of the table. We also introduced a new python object above: a *dictionary*, which is specified by `(key, value)` pairs. Keep your modified version of the data with the following: dictionary

```
college = college3
```

(c) Use the `describe()` method of to produce a numerical summary of the variables in the data set.

(d) Use the `pd.plotting.scatter_matrix()` function to produce a scatterplot matrix of the first columns `[Top10perc, Apps, Enroll]`. Recall that you can reference a list `C` of columns of a data frame `A` using `A[C]`.

(e) Use the `boxplot()` method of `college` to produce side-by-side boxplots of `Outstate` versus `Private`.

(f) Create a new qualitative variable, called `Elite`, by *binning* the `Top10perc` variable into two groups based on whether or not the proportion of students coming from the top 10% of their high school classes exceeds 50%.

```
college['Elite'] = pd.cut(college['Top10perc'],
                          [0,0.5,1],
                          labels=['No', 'Yes'])
```

Use the `value_counts()` method of `college['Elite']` to see how many elite universities there are. Finally, use the `boxplot()` method again to produce side-by-side boxplots of `Outstate` versus `Elite`.

(g) Use the `plot.hist()` method of `college` to produce some histograms with differing numbers of bins for a few of the quantitative variables. The command `plt.subplots(2, 2)` may be useful: it will divide the plot window into four regions so that four plots can be made simultaneously. By changing the arguments you can divide the screen up in other combinations.

(h) Continue exploring the data, and provide a brief summary of what you discover.

9. This exercise involves the `Auto` data set studied in the lab. Make sure that the missing values have been removed from the data.

(a) Which of the predictors are quantitative, and which are qualitative?

(b) What is the *range* of each quantitative predictor? You can answer this using the `min()` and `max()` methods in `numpy`. `.min()`

(c) What is the mean and standard deviation of each quantitative predictor? `.max()`

(d) Now remove the 10th through 85th observations. What is the range, mean, and standard deviation of each predictor in the subset of the data that remains?

(e) Using the full data set, investigate the predictors graphically, using scatterplots or other tools of your choice. Create some plots highlighting the relationships among the predictors. Comment on your findings.

(f) Suppose that we wish to predict gas mileage (`mpg`) on the basis of the other variables. Do your plots suggest that any of the other variables might be useful in predicting `mpg`? Justify your answer.

10. This exercise involves the `Boston` housing data set.

(a) To begin, load in the `Boston` data set, which is part of the `ISLP` library.

(b) How many rows are in this data set? How many columns? What do the rows and columns represent?

(c) Make some pairwise scatterplots of the predictors (columns) in this data set. Describe your findings.

(d) Are any of the predictors associated with per capita crime rate? If so, explain the relationship.

(e) Do any of the suburbs of Boston appear to have particularly high crime rates? Tax rates? Pupil-teacher ratios? Comment on the range of each predictor.

(f) How many of the suburbs in this data set bound the Charles river?

(g) What is the median pupil-teacher ratio among the towns in this data set?

(h) Which suburb of Boston has lowest median value of owner-occupied homes? What are the values of the other predictors for that suburb, and how do those values compare to the overall ranges for those predictors? Comment on your findings.

(i) In this data set, how many of the suburbs average more than seven rooms per dwelling? More than eight rooms per dwelling? Comment on the suburbs that average more than eight rooms per dwelling.

3
Linear Regression

This chapter is about *linear regression*, a very simple approach for supervised learning. In particular, linear regression is a useful tool for predicting a quantitative response. It has been around for a long time and is the topic of innumerable textbooks. Though it may seem somewhat dull compared to some of the more modern statistical learning approaches described in later chapters of this book, linear regression is still a useful and widely used statistical learning method. Moreover, it serves as a good jumping-off point for newer approaches: as we will see in later chapters, many fancy statistical learning approaches can be seen as generalizations or extensions of linear regression. Consequently, the importance of having a good understanding of linear regression before studying more complex learning methods cannot be overstated. In this chapter, we review some of the key ideas underlying the linear regression model, as well as the least squares approach that is most commonly used to fit this model.

Recall the `Advertising` data from Chapter 2. Figure 2.1 displays `sales` (in thousands of units) for a particular product as a function of advertising budgets (in thousands of dollars) for `TV`, `radio`, and `newspaper` media. Suppose that in our role as statistical consultants we are asked to suggest, on the basis of this data, a marketing plan for next year that will result in high product sales. What information would be useful in order to provide such a recommendation? Here are a few important questions that we might seek to address:

1. *Is there a relationship between advertising budget and sales?*
   Our first goal should be to determine whether the data provide evidence of an association between advertising expenditure and sales. If the evidence is weak, then one might argue that no money should be spent on advertising!

G. James et al., *An Introduction to Statistical Learning*, Springer Texts in Statistics,
https://doi.org/10.1007/978-3-031-38747-0_3

2. *How strong is the relationship between advertising budget and sales?* Assuming that there is a relationship between advertising and sales, we would like to know the strength of this relationship. Does knowledge of the advertising budget provide a lot of information about product sales?

3. *Which media are associated with sales?* Are all three media—TV, radio, and newspaper—associated with sales, or are just one or two of the media associated? To answer this question, we must find a way to separate out the individual contribution of each medium to sales when we have spent money on all three media.

4. *How large is the association between each medium and sales?* For every dollar spent on advertising in a particular medium, by what amount will sales increase? How accurately can we predict this amount of increase?

5. *How accurately can we predict future sales?* For any given level of television, radio, or newspaper advertising, what is our prediction for sales, and what is the accuracy of this prediction?

6. *Is the relationship linear?* If there is approximately a straight-line relationship between advertising expenditure in the various media and sales, then linear regression is an appropriate tool. If not, then it may still be possible to transform the predictor or the response so that linear regression can be used.

7. *Is there synergy among the advertising media?* Perhaps spending \$50,000 on television advertising and \$50,000 on radio advertising is associated with higher sales than allocating \$100,000 to either television or radio individually. In marketing, this is known as a *synergy* effect, while in statistics it is called an *interaction* effect. synergy interaction

It turns out that linear regression can be used to answer each of these questions. We will first discuss all of these questions in a general context, and then return to them in this specific context in Section 3.4.

3.1 Simple Linear Regression

Simple linear regression lives up to its name: it is a very straightforward approach for predicting a quantitative response Y on the basis of a single predictor variable X. It assumes that there is approximately a linear relationship between X and Y. Mathematically, we can write this linear relationship as simple linear regression

$$Y \approx \beta_0 + \beta_1 X. \tag{3.1}$$

You might read "$\approx$" as *"is approximately modeled as"*. We will sometimes describe (3.1) by saying that we are *regressing Y on X* (or *Y onto X*).

For example, X may represent `TV` advertising and Y may represent `sales`. Then we can regress `sales` onto `TV` by fitting the model

$$\texttt{sales} \approx \beta_0 + \beta_1 \times \texttt{TV}.$$

In Equation 3.1, β_0 and β_1 are two unknown constants that represent the *intercept* and *slope* terms in the linear model. Together, β_0 and β_1 are known as the model *coefficients* or *parameters*. Once we have used our training data to produce estimates $\hat{\beta}_0$ and $\hat{\beta}_1$ for the model coefficients, we can predict future sales on the basis of a particular value of TV advertising by computing

intercept

slope

coefficient

parameter

$$\hat{y} = \hat{\beta}_0 + \hat{\beta}_1 x, \tag{3.2}$$

where $\hat{y}$ indicates a prediction of Y on the basis of $X = x$. Here we use a *hat* symbol, $\hat{}$, to denote the estimated value for an unknown parameter or coefficient, or to denote the predicted value of the response.

3.1.1 Estimating the Coefficients

In practice, β_0 and β_1 are unknown. So before we can use (3.1) to make predictions, we must use data to estimate the coefficients. Let

$$(x_1, y_1),\ (x_2, y_2), \ldots,\ (x_n, y_n)$$

represent n observation pairs, each of which consists of a measurement of X and a measurement of Y. In the `Advertising` example, this data set consists of the TV advertising budget and product sales in $n = 200$ different markets. (Recall that the data are displayed in Figure 2.1.) Our goal is to obtain coefficient estimates $\hat{\beta}_0$ and $\hat{\beta}_1$ such that the linear model (3.1) fits the available data well—that is, so that $y_i \approx \hat{\beta}_0 + \hat{\beta}_1 x_i$ for $i = 1, \ldots, n$. In other words, we want to find an intercept $\hat{\beta}_0$ and a slope $\hat{\beta}_1$ such that the resulting line is as close as possible to the $n = 200$ data points. There are a number of ways of measuring *closeness*. However, by far the most common approach involves minimizing the *least squares* criterion, and we take that approach in this chapter. Alternative approaches will be considered in Chapter 6.

least squares

Let $\hat{y}_i = \hat{\beta}_0 + \hat{\beta}_1 x_i$ be the prediction for Y based on the ith value of X. Then $e_i = y_i - \hat{y}_i$ represents the ith *residual*—this is the difference between the ith observed response value and the ith response value that is predicted by our linear model. We define the *residual sum of squares* (RSS) as

residual

residual sum of squares

$$\text{RSS} = e_1^2 + e_2^2 + \cdots + e_n^2,$$

or equivalently as

$$\text{RSS} = (y_1 - \hat{\beta}_0 - \hat{\beta}_1 x_1)^2 + (y_2 - \hat{\beta}_0 - \hat{\beta}_1 x_2)^2 + \cdots + (y_n - \hat{\beta}_0 - \hat{\beta}_1 x_n)^2. \tag{3.3}$$

The least squares approach chooses $\hat{\beta}_0$ and $\hat{\beta}_1$ to minimize the RSS. Using some calculus, one can show that the minimizers are

$$\begin{aligned} \hat{\beta}_1 &= \frac{\sum_{i=1}^{n}(x_i - \bar{x})(y_i - \bar{y})}{\sum_{i=1}^{n}(x_i - \bar{x})^2}, \\ \hat{\beta}_0 &= \bar{y} - \hat{\beta}_1 \bar{x}, \end{aligned} \tag{3.4}$$

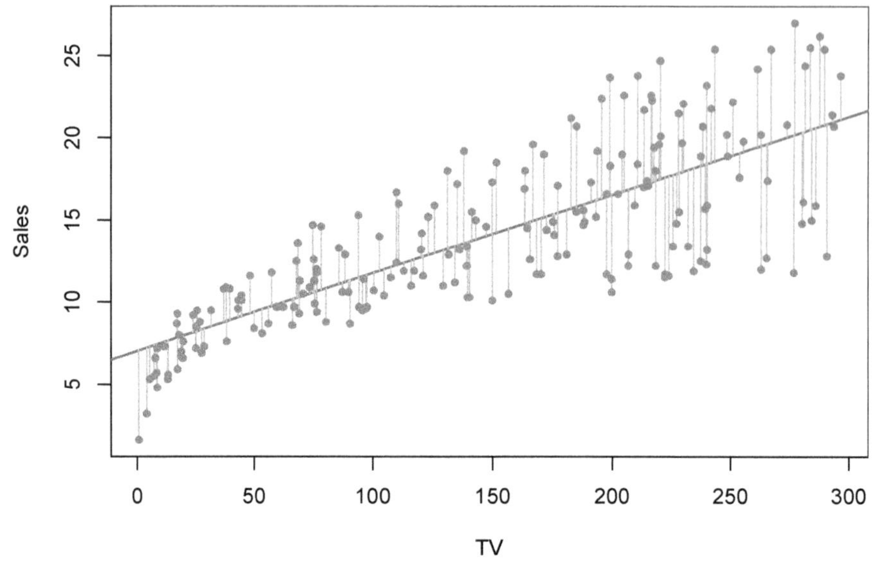

FIGURE 3.1. *For the* Advertising *data, the least squares fit for the regression of* sales *onto* TV *is shown. The fit is found by minimizing the residual sum of squares. Each grey line segment represents a residual. In this case a linear fit captures the essence of the relationship, although it overestimates the trend in the left of the plot.*

where $\bar{y} \equiv \frac{1}{n}\sum_{i=1}^{n} y_i$ and $\bar{x} \equiv \frac{1}{n}\sum_{i=1}^{n} x_i$ are the sample means. In other words, (3.4) defines the *least squares coefficient estimates* for simple linear regression.

Figure 3.1 displays the simple linear regression fit to the Advertising data, where $\hat{\beta}_0 = 7.03$ and $\hat{\beta}_1 = 0.0475$. In other words, according to this approximation, an additional $1,000 spent on TV advertising is associated with selling approximately 47.5 additional units of the product. In Figure 3.2, we have computed RSS for a number of values of β_0 and β_1, using the advertising data with sales as the response and TV as the predictor. In each plot, the red dot represents the pair of least squares estimates $(\hat{\beta}_0, \hat{\beta}_1)$ given by (3.4). These values clearly minimize the RSS.

3.1.2 Assessing the Accuracy of the Coefficient Estimates

Recall from (2.1) that we assume that the *true* relationship between X and Y takes the form $Y = f(X) + \epsilon$ for some unknown function f, where ϵ is a mean-zero random error term. If f is to be approximated by a linear function, then we can write this relationship as

$$Y = \beta_0 + \beta_1 X + \epsilon. \tag{3.5}$$

Here β_0 is the intercept term—that is, the expected value of Y when $X = 0$, and β_1 is the slope—the average increase in Y associated with a one-unit increase in X. The error term is a catch-all for what we miss with this simple model: the true relationship is probably not linear, there may be other variables that cause variation in Y, and there may be measurement error. We typically assume that the error term is independent of X.

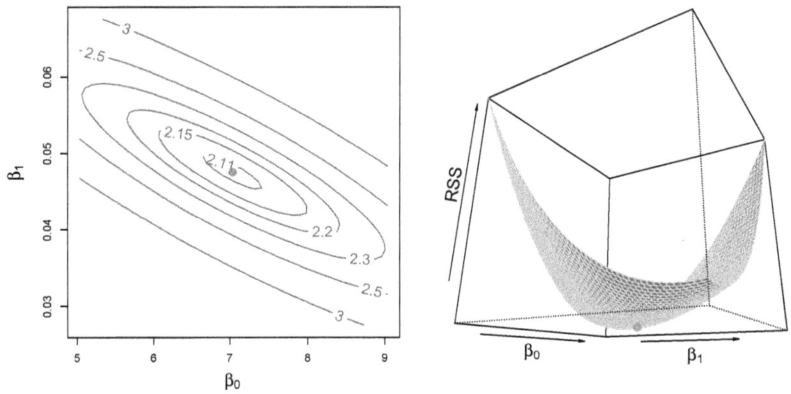

FIGURE 3.2. *Contour and three-dimensional plots of the RSS on the* `Advertising` *data, using* `sales` *as the response and* `TV` *as the predictor. The red dots correspond to the least squares estimates $\hat{\beta}_0$ and $\hat{\beta}_1$, given by (3.4).*

The model given by (3.5) defines the *population regression line*, which is the best linear approximation to the true relationship between X and Y.[1] The least squares regression coefficient estimates (3.4) characterize the *least squares line* (3.2). The left-hand panel of Figure 3.3 displays these two lines in a simple simulated example. We created 100 random Xs, and generated 100 corresponding Ys from the model

population regression line

least squares line

$$Y = 2 + 3X + \epsilon, \tag{3.6}$$

where ϵ was generated from a normal distribution with mean zero. The red line in the left-hand panel of Figure 3.3 displays the *true* relationship, $f(X) = 2 + 3X$, while the blue line is the least squares estimate based on the observed data. The true relationship is generally not known for real data, but the least squares line can always be computed using the coefficient estimates given in (3.4). In other words, in real applications, we have access to a set of observations from which we can compute the least squares line; however, the population regression line is unobserved. In the right-hand panel of Figure 3.3 we have generated ten different data sets from the model given by (3.6) and plotted the corresponding ten least squares lines. Notice that different data sets generated from the same true model result in slightly different least squares lines, but the unobserved population regression line does not change.

At first glance, the difference between the population regression line and the least squares line may seem subtle and confusing. We only have one data set, and so what does it mean that two different lines describe the relationship between the predictor and the response? Fundamentally, the concept of these two lines is a natural extension of the standard statistical approach of using information from a sample to estimate characteristics of a large population. For example, suppose that we are interested in knowing

[1]The assumption of linearity is often a useful working model. However, despite what many textbooks might tell us, we seldom believe that the true relationship is linear.

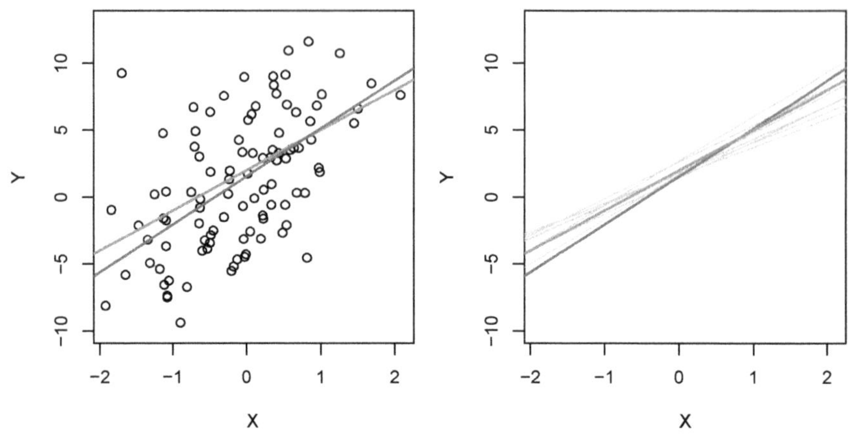

FIGURE 3.3. *A simulated data set.* Left: *The red line represents the true relationship, $f(X) = 2 + 3X$, which is known as the population regression line. The blue line is the least squares line; it is the least squares estimate for $f(X)$ based on the observed data, shown in black.* Right: *The population regression line is again shown in red, and the least squares line in dark blue. In light blue, ten least squares lines are shown, each computed on the basis of a separate random set of observations. Each least squares line is different, but on average, the least squares lines are quite close to the population regression line.*

the population mean μ of some random variable Y. Unfortunately, μ is unknown, but we do have access to n observations from Y, $y_1, \ldots, y_n$, which we can use to estimate μ. A reasonable estimate is $\hat{\mu} = \bar{y}$, where $\bar{y} = \frac{1}{n}\sum_{i=1}^{n} y_i$ is the sample mean. The sample mean and the population mean are different, but in general the sample mean will provide a good estimate of the population mean. In the same way, the unknown coefficients β_0 and β_1 in linear regression define the population regression line. We seek to estimate these unknown coefficients using $\hat{\beta}_0$ and $\hat{\beta}_1$ given in (3.4). These coefficient estimates define the least squares line.

The analogy between linear regression and estimation of the mean of a random variable is an apt one based on the concept of *bias*. If we use the sample mean $\hat{\mu}$ to estimate μ, this estimate is *unbiased*, in the sense that on average, we expect $\hat{\mu}$ to equal μ. What exactly does this mean? It means that on the basis of one particular set of observations $y_1, \ldots, y_n$, $\hat{\mu}$ might overestimate μ, and on the basis of another set of observations, $\hat{\mu}$ might underestimate μ. But if we could average a huge number of estimates of μ obtained from a huge number of sets of observations, then this average would *exactly* equal μ. Hence, an unbiased estimator does not *systematically* over- or under-estimate the true parameter. The property of unbiasedness holds for the least squares coefficient estimates given by (3.4) as well: if we estimate β_0 and β_1 on the basis of a particular data set, then our estimates won't be exactly equal to β_0 and β_1. But if we could average the estimates obtained over a huge number of data sets, then the average of these estimates would be spot on! In fact, we can see from the right-hand panel of Figure 3.3 that the average of many least squares lines, each

bias

unbiased

estimated from a separate data set, is pretty close to the true population regression line.

We continue the analogy with the estimation of the population mean μ of a random variable Y. A natural question is as follows: how accurate is the sample mean $\hat{\mu}$ as an estimate of μ? We have established that the average of $\hat{\mu}$'s over many data sets will be very close to μ, but that a single estimate $\hat{\mu}$ may be a substantial underestimate or overestimate of μ. How far off will that single estimate of $\hat{\mu}$ be? In general, we answer this question by computing the *standard error* of $\hat{\mu}$, written as $\mathrm{SE}(\hat{\mu})$. We have the well-known formula

standard error

$$\mathrm{Var}(\hat{\mu}) = \mathrm{SE}(\hat{\mu})^2 = \frac{\sigma^2}{n}, \tag{3.7}$$

where σ is the standard deviation of each of the realizations y_i of Y.[2] Roughly speaking, the standard error tells us the average amount that this estimate $\hat{\mu}$ differs from the actual value of μ. Equation 3.7 also tells us how this deviation shrinks with n—the more observations we have, the smaller the standard error of $\hat{\mu}$. In a similar vein, we can wonder how close $\hat{\beta}_0$ and $\hat{\beta}_1$ are to the true values β_0 and β_1. To compute the standard errors associated with $\hat{\beta}_0$ and $\hat{\beta}_1$, we use the following formulas:

$$\mathrm{SE}(\hat{\beta}_0)^2 = \sigma^2 \left[\frac{1}{n} + \frac{\bar{x}^2}{\sum_{i=1}^{n}(x_i - \bar{x})^2}\right], \quad \mathrm{SE}(\hat{\beta}_1)^2 = \frac{\sigma^2}{\sum_{i=1}^{n}(x_i - \bar{x})^2}, \tag{3.8}$$

where $\sigma^2 = \mathrm{Var}(\epsilon)$. For these formulas to be strictly valid, we need to assume that the errors ϵ_i for each observation have common variance σ^2 and are uncorrelated. This is clearly not true in Figure 3.1, but the formula still turns out to be a good approximation. Notice in the formula that $\mathrm{SE}(\hat{\beta}_1)$ is smaller when the x_i are more spread out; intuitively we have more *leverage* to estimate a slope when this is the case. We also see that $\mathrm{SE}(\hat{\beta}_0)$ would be the same as $\mathrm{SE}(\hat{\mu})$ if $\bar{x}$ were zero (in which case $\hat{\beta}_0$ would be equal to $\bar{y}$). In general, σ^2 is not known, but can be estimated from the data. This estimate of σ is known as the *residual standard error*, and is given by the formula $\mathrm{RSE} = \sqrt{\mathrm{RSS}/(n-2)}$. Strictly speaking, when σ^2 is estimated from the data we should write $\widehat{\mathrm{SE}}(\hat{\beta}_1)$ to indicate that an estimate has been made, but for simplicity of notation we will drop this extra "hat".

residual standard error

Standard errors can be used to compute *confidence intervals*. A 95 % confidence interval is defined as a range of values such that with 95 % probability, the range will contain the true unknown value of the parameter. The range is defined in terms of lower and upper limits computed from the sample of data. A 95% confidence interval has the following property: if we take repeated samples and construct the confidence interval for each sample, 95% of the intervals will contain the true unknown value of the parameter. For linear regression, the 95 % confidence interval for β_1 approximately takes the form

confidence interval

$$\hat{\beta}_1 \pm 2 \cdot \mathrm{SE}(\hat{\beta}_1). \tag{3.9}$$

[2]This formula holds provided that the n observations are uncorrelated.

That is, there is approximately a 95 % chance that the interval

$$\left[\hat{\beta}_1 - 2 \cdot \mathrm{SE}(\hat{\beta}_1),\ \hat{\beta}_1 + 2 \cdot \mathrm{SE}(\hat{\beta}_1)\right] \tag{3.10}$$

will contain the true value of β_1.[3] Similarly, a confidence interval for β_0 approximately takes the form

$$\hat{\beta}_0 \pm 2 \cdot \mathrm{SE}(\hat{\beta}_0). \tag{3.11}$$

In the case of the advertising data, the 95 % confidence interval for β_0 is $[6.130, 7.935]$ and the 95 % confidence interval for β_1 is $[0.042, 0.053]$. Therefore, we can conclude that in the absence of any advertising, sales will, on average, fall somewhere between 6,130 and 7,935 units. Furthermore, for each \$1,000 increase in television advertising, there will be an average increase in sales of between 42 and 53 units.

Standard errors can also be used to perform *hypothesis tests* on the coefficients. The most common hypothesis test involves testing the *null hypothesis* of

hypothesis test

null hypothesis

$$H_0 : \text{There is no relationship between } X \text{ and } Y \tag{3.12}$$

versus the *alternative hypothesis*

alternative hypothesis

$$H_a : \text{There is some relationship between } X \text{ and } Y. \tag{3.13}$$

Mathematically, this corresponds to testing

$$H_0 : \beta_1 = 0$$

versus

$$H_a : \beta_1 \neq 0,$$

since if $\beta_1 = 0$ then the model (3.5) reduces to $Y = \beta_0 + \epsilon$, and X is not associated with Y. To test the null hypothesis, we need to determine whether $\hat{\beta}_1$, our estimate for β_1, is sufficiently far from zero that we can be confident that β_1 is non-zero. How far is far enough? This of course depends on the accuracy of $\hat{\beta}_1$—that is, it depends on $\mathrm{SE}(\hat{\beta}_1)$. If $\mathrm{SE}(\hat{\beta}_1)$ is small, then even relatively small values of $\hat{\beta}_1$ may provide strong evidence that $\beta_1 \neq 0$, and hence that there is a relationship between X and Y. In contrast, if $\mathrm{SE}(\hat{\beta}_1)$ is large, then $\hat{\beta}_1$ must be large in absolute value in order for us to reject the null hypothesis. In practice, we compute a *t-statistic*, given by

t-statistic

$$t = \frac{\hat{\beta}_1 - 0}{\mathrm{SE}(\hat{\beta}_1)}, \tag{3.14}$$

[3] *Approximately* for several reasons. Equation 3.10 relies on the assumption that the errors are Gaussian. Also, the factor of 2 in front of the $\mathrm{SE}(\hat{\beta}_1)$ term will vary slightly depending on the number of observations n in the linear regression. To be precise, rather than the number 2, (3.10) should contain the 97.5 % quantile of a t-distribution with $n-2$ degrees of freedom. Details of how to compute the 95 % confidence interval precisely in R will be provided later in this chapter.

	Coefficient	Std. error	t-statistic	p-value
Intercept	7.0325	0.4578	15.36	< 0.0001
TV	0.0475	0.0027	17.67	< 0.0001

TABLE 3.1. *For the* Advertising *data, coefficients of the least squares model for the regression of number of units sold on TV advertising budget. An increase of* \$1,000 *in the TV advertising budget is associated with an increase in sales by around 50 units. (Recall that the* sales *variable is in thousands of units, and the* TV *variable is in thousands of dollars.)*

which measures the number of standard deviations that $\hat{\beta}_1$ is away from 0. If there really is no relationship between X and Y, then we expect that (3.14) will have a t-distribution with $n-2$ degrees of freedom. The t-distribution has a bell shape and for values of n greater than approximately 30 it is quite similar to the standard normal distribution. Consequently, it is a simple matter to compute the probability of observing any number equal to $|t|$ or larger in absolute value, assuming $\beta_1 = 0$. We call this probability the *p-value*. Roughly speaking, we interpret the p-value as follows: a small p-value indicates that it is unlikely to observe such a substantial association between the predictor and the response due to chance, in the absence of any real association between the predictor and the response. Hence, if we see a small p-value, then we can infer that there is an association between the predictor and the response. We *reject the null hypothesis*—that is, we declare a relationship to exist between X and Y—if the p-value is small enough. Typical p-value cutoffs for rejecting the null hypothesis are 5% or 1%, although this topic will be explored in much greater detail in Chapter 13. When $n = 30$, these correspond to t-statistics (3.14) of around 2 and 2.75, respectively.

p-value

Table 3.1 provides details of the least squares model for the regression of number of units sold on TV advertising budget for the Advertising data. Notice that the coefficients for $\hat{\beta}_0$ and $\hat{\beta}_1$ are very large relative to their standard errors, so the t-statistics are also large; the probabilities of seeing such values if H_0 is true are virtually zero. Hence we can conclude that $\beta_0 \neq 0$ and $\beta_1 \neq 0$.[4]

3.1.3 Assessing the Accuracy of the Model

Once we have rejected the null hypothesis (3.12) in favor of the alternative hypothesis (3.13), it is natural to want to quantify *the extent to which the model fits the data.* The quality of a linear regression fit is typically assessed using two related quantities: the *residual standard error* (RSE) and the R^2 statistic.

R^2

[4]In Table 3.1, a small p-value for the intercept indicates that we can reject the null hypothesis that $\beta_0 = 0$, and a small p-value for TV indicates that we can reject the null hypothesis that $\beta_1 = 0$. Rejecting the latter null hypothesis allows us to conclude that there is a relationship between TV and sales. Rejecting the former allows us to conclude that in the absence of TV expenditure, sales are non-zero.

Quantity	Value
Residual standard error	3.26
R^2	0.612
F-statistic	312.1

TABLE 3.2. *For the* `Advertising` *data, more information about the least squares model for the regression of number of units sold on TV advertising budget.*

Table 3.2 displays the RSE, the R^2 statistic, and the F-statistic (to be described in Section 3.2.2) for the linear regression of number of units sold on TV advertising budget.

Residual Standard Error

Recall from the model (3.5) that associated with each observation is an error term ϵ. Due to the presence of these error terms, even if we knew the true regression line (i.e. even if β_0 and β_1 were known), we would not be able to perfectly predict Y from X. The RSE is an estimate of the standard deviation of ϵ. Roughly speaking, it is the average amount that the response will deviate from the true regression line. It is computed using the formula

$$\text{RSE} = \sqrt{\frac{1}{n-2}\text{RSS}} = \sqrt{\frac{1}{n-2}\sum_{i=1}^{n}(y_i - \hat{y}_i)^2}. \tag{3.15}$$

Note that RSS was defined in Section 3.1.1, and is given by the formula

$$\text{RSS} = \sum_{i=1}^{n}(y_i - \hat{y}_i)^2. \tag{3.16}$$

In the case of the advertising data, we see from the linear regression output in Table 3.2 that the RSE is 3.26. In other words, actual sales in each market deviate from the true regression line by approximately 3,260 units, on average. Another way to think about this is that even if the model were correct and the true values of the unknown coefficients β_0 and β_1 were known exactly, any prediction of sales on the basis of TV advertising would still be off by about 3,260 units on average. Of course, whether or not 3,260 units is an acceptable prediction error depends on the problem context. In the advertising data set, the mean value of `sales` over all markets is approximately 14,000 units, and so the percentage error is $3{,}260/14{,}000 = 23\,\%$.

The RSE is considered a measure of the *lack of fit* of the model (3.5) to the data. If the predictions obtained using the model are very close to the true outcome values—that is, if $\hat{y}_i \approx y_i$ for $i = 1, \ldots, n$—then (3.15) will be small, and we can conclude that the model fits the data very well. On the other hand, if $\hat{y}_i$ is very far from y_i for one or more observations, then the RSE may be quite large, indicating that the model doesn't fit the data well.

R^2 Statistic

The RSE provides an absolute measure of lack of fit of the model (3.5) to the data. But since it is measured in the units of Y, it is not always clear what constitutes a good RSE. The R^2 statistic provides an alternative measure of fit. It takes the form of a *proportion*—the proportion of variance explained—and so it always takes on a value between 0 and 1, and is independent of the scale of Y.

To calculate R^2, we use the formula

$$R^2 = \frac{\text{TSS} - \text{RSS}}{\text{TSS}} = 1 - \frac{\text{RSS}}{\text{TSS}} \tag{3.17}$$

where $\text{TSS} = \sum(y_i - \bar{y})^2$ is the *total sum of squares*, and RSS is defined in (3.16). TSS measures the total variance in the response Y, and can be thought of as the amount of variability inherent in the response before the regression is performed. In contrast, RSS measures the amount of variability that is left unexplained after performing the regression. Hence, TSS − RSS measures the amount of variability in the response that is explained (or removed) by performing the regression, and R^2 measures the *proportion of variability in Y that can be explained using X*. An R^2 statistic that is close to 1 indicates that a large proportion of the variability in the response is explained by the regression. A number near 0 indicates that the regression does not explain much of the variability in the response; this might occur because the linear model is wrong, or the error variance σ^2 is high, or both. In Table 3.2, the R^2 was 0.61, and so just under two-thirds of the variability in `sales` is explained by a linear regression on `TV`.

total sum of squares

The R^2 statistic (3.17) has an interpretational advantage over the RSE (3.15), since unlike the RSE, it always lies between 0 and 1. However, it can still be challenging to determine what is a *good* R^2 value, and in general, this will depend on the application. For instance, in certain problems in physics, we may know that the data truly comes from a linear model with a small residual error. In this case, we would expect to see an R^2 value that is extremely close to 1, and a substantially smaller R^2 value might indicate a serious problem with the experiment in which the data were generated. On the other hand, in typical applications in biology, psychology, marketing, and other domains, the linear model (3.5) is at best an extremely rough approximation to the data, and residual errors due to other unmeasured factors are often very large. In this setting, we would expect only a very small proportion of the variance in the response to be explained by the predictor, and an R^2 value well below 0.1 might be more realistic!

The R^2 statistic is a measure of the linear relationship between X and Y. Recall that *correlation*, defined as

correlation

$$\text{Cor}(X, Y) = \frac{\sum_{i=1}^n (x_i - \bar{x})(y_i - \bar{y})}{\sqrt{\sum_{i=1}^n (x_i - \bar{x})^2}\sqrt{\sum_{i=1}^n (y_i - \bar{y})^2}}, \tag{3.18}$$

is also a measure of the linear relationship between X and Y.[5] This suggests that we might be able to use $r = \text{Cor}(X, Y)$ instead of R^2 in order to assess the fit of the linear model. In fact, it can be shown that in the simple

[5]We note that in fact, the right-hand side of (3.18) is the sample correlation; thus, it would be more correct to write $\widehat{\text{Cor}(X, Y)}$; however, we omit the "hat" for ease of notation.

Simple regression of `sales` on `radio`

	Coefficient	Std. error	t-statistic	p-value
`Intercept`	9.312	0.563	16.54	< 0.0001
`radio`	0.203	0.020	9.92	< 0.0001

Simple regression of `sales` on `newspaper`

	Coefficient	Std. error	t-statistic	p-value
`Intercept`	12.351	0.621	19.88	< 0.0001
`newspaper`	0.055	0.017	3.30	0.00115

TABLE 3.3. *More simple linear regression models for the* `Advertising` *data. Coefficients of the simple linear regression model for number of units sold on* Top: *radio advertising budget and* Bottom: *newspaper advertising budget. A \$1,000 increase in spending on radio advertising is associated with an average increase in sales by around 203 units, while the same increase in spending on newspaper advertising is associated with an average increase in sales by around 55 units. (Note that the* `sales` *variable is in thousands of units, and the* `radio` *and* `newspaper` *variables are in thousands of dollars.)*

linear regression setting, $R^2 = r^2$. In other words, the squared correlation and the R^2 statistic are identical. However, in the next section we will discuss the multiple linear regression problem, in which we use several predictors simultaneously to predict the response. The concept of correlation between the predictors and the response does not extend automatically to this setting, since correlation quantifies the association between a single pair of variables rather than between a larger number of variables. We will see that R^2 fills this role.

3.2 Multiple Linear Regression

Simple linear regression is a useful approach for predicting a response on the basis of a single predictor variable. However, in practice we often have more than one predictor. For example, in the `Advertising` data, we have examined the relationship between sales and TV advertising. We also have data for the amount of money spent advertising on the radio and in newspapers, and we may want to know whether either of these two media is associated with sales. How can we extend our analysis of the advertising data in order to accommodate these two additional predictors?

One option is to run three separate simple linear regressions, each of which uses a different advertising medium as a predictor. For instance, we can fit a simple linear regression to predict sales on the basis of the amount spent on radio advertisements. Results are shown in Table 3.3 (top table). We find that a \$1,000 increase in spending on radio advertising is associated with an increase in sales of around 203 units. Table 3.3 (bottom table) contains the least squares coefficients for a simple linear regression of sales onto newspaper advertising budget. A \$1,000 increase in newspaper advertising budget is associated with an increase in sales of approximately 55 units.

However, the approach of fitting a separate simple linear regression model for each predictor is not entirely satisfactory. First of all, it is unclear how to make a single prediction of sales given the three advertising media budgets, since each of the budgets is associated with a separate regression equation. Second, each of the three regression equations ignores the other two media in forming estimates for the regression coefficients. We will see shortly that if the media budgets are correlated with each other in the 200 markets in our data set, then this can lead to very misleading estimates of the association between each media budget and sales.

Instead of fitting a separate simple linear regression model for each predictor, a better approach is to extend the simple linear regression model (3.5) so that it can directly accommodate multiple predictors. We can do this by giving each predictor a separate slope coefficient in a single model. In general, suppose that we have p distinct predictors. Then the multiple linear regression model takes the form

$$Y = \beta_0 + \beta_1 X_1 + \beta_2 X_2 + \cdots + \beta_p X_p + \epsilon, \tag{3.19}$$

where X_j represents the jth predictor and β_j quantifies the association between that variable and the response. We interpret β_j as the *average* effect on Y of a one unit increase in X_j, *holding all other predictors fixed.* In the advertising example, (3.19) becomes

$$\texttt{sales} = \beta_0 + \beta_1 \times \texttt{TV} + \beta_2 \times \texttt{radio} + \beta_3 \times \texttt{newspaper} + \epsilon. \tag{3.20}$$

3.2.1 Estimating the Regression Coefficients

As was the case in the simple linear regression setting, the regression coefficients $\beta_0, \beta_1, \ldots, \beta_p$ in (3.19) are unknown, and must be estimated. Given estimates $\hat{\beta}_0, \hat{\beta}_1, \ldots, \hat{\beta}_p$, we can make predictions using the formula

$$\hat{y} = \hat{\beta}_0 + \hat{\beta}_1 x_1 + \hat{\beta}_2 x_2 + \cdots + \hat{\beta}_p x_p. \tag{3.21}$$

The parameters are estimated using the same least squares approach that we saw in the context of simple linear regression. We choose $\beta_0, \beta_1, \ldots, \beta_p$ to minimize the sum of squared residuals

$$\begin{aligned} \text{RSS} &= \sum_{i=1}^{n} (y_i - \hat{y}_i)^2 \\ &= \sum_{i=1}^{n} (y_i - \hat{\beta}_0 - \hat{\beta}_1 x_{i1} - \hat{\beta}_2 x_{i2} - \cdots - \hat{\beta}_p x_{ip})^2. \end{aligned} \tag{3.22}$$

The values $\hat{\beta}_0, \hat{\beta}_1, \ldots, \hat{\beta}_p$ that minimize (3.22) are the multiple least squares regression coefficient estimates. Unlike the simple linear regression estimates given in (3.4), the multiple regression coefficient estimates have somewhat complicated forms that are most easily represented using matrix algebra. For this reason, we do not provide them here. Any statistical software package can be used to compute these coefficient estimates, and later in this chapter we will show how this can be done in `R`. Figure 3.4

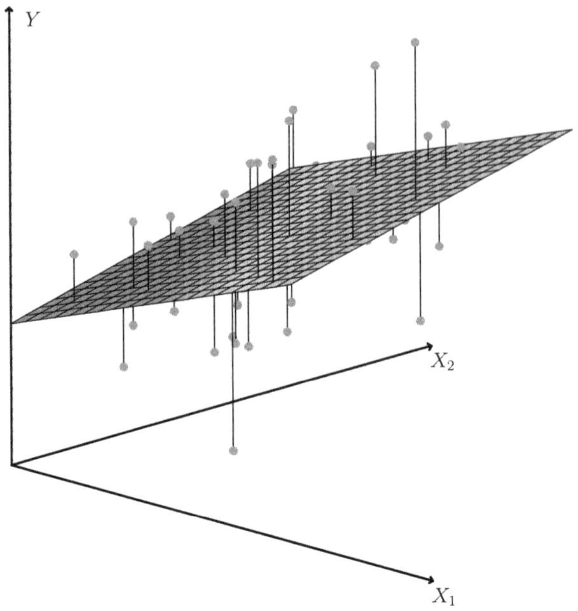

FIGURE 3.4. *In a three-dimensional setting, with two predictors and one response, the least squares regression line becomes a plane. The plane is chosen to minimize the sum of the squared vertical distances between each observation (shown in red) and the plane.*

illustrates an example of the least squares fit to a toy data set with $p = 2$ predictors.

Table 3.4 displays the multiple regression coefficient estimates when TV, radio, and newspaper advertising budgets are used to predict product sales using the `Advertising` data. We interpret these results as follows: for a given amount of TV and newspaper advertising, spending an additional \$1,000 on radio advertising is associated with approximately 189 units of additional sales. Comparing these coefficient estimates to those displayed in Tables 3.1 and 3.3, we notice that the multiple regression coefficient estimates for `TV` and `radio` are pretty similar to the simple linear regression coefficient estimates. However, while the `newspaper` regression coefficient estimate in Table 3.3 was significantly non-zero, the coefficient estimate for `newspaper` in the multiple regression model is close to zero, and the corresponding p-value is no longer significant, with a value around 0.86. This illustrates that the simple and multiple regression coefficients can be quite different. This difference stems from the fact that in the simple regression case, the slope term represents the average increase in product sales associated with a \$1,000 increase in newspaper advertising, ignoring other predictors such as `TV` and `radio`. By contrast, in the multiple regression setting, the coefficient for `newspaper` represents the average increase in product sales associated with increasing newspaper spending by \$1,000 while holding `TV` and `radio` fixed.

Does it make sense for the multiple regression to suggest no relationship between `sales` and `newspaper` while the simple linear regression implies the

	Coefficient	Std. error	t-statistic	p-value
Intercept	2.939	0.3119	9.42	< 0.0001
TV	0.046	0.0014	32.81	< 0.0001
radio	0.189	0.0086	21.89	< 0.0001
newspaper	−0.001	0.0059	−0.18	0.8599

TABLE 3.4. *For the* Advertising *data, least squares coefficient estimates of the multiple linear regression of number of units sold on TV, radio, and newspaper advertising budgets.*

	TV	radio	newspaper	sales
TV	1.0000	0.0548	0.0567	0.7822
radio		1.0000	0.3541	0.5762
newspaper			1.0000	0.2283
sales				1.0000

TABLE 3.5. *Correlation matrix for* TV, radio, newspaper, *and* sales *for the* Advertising *data.*

opposite? In fact it does. Consider the correlation matrix for the three predictor variables and response variable, displayed in Table 3.5. Notice that the correlation between radio and newspaper is 0.35. This indicates that markets with high newspaper advertising tend to also have high radio advertising. Now suppose that the multiple regression is correct and newspaper advertising is not associated with sales, but radio advertising is associated with sales. Then in markets where we spend more on radio our sales will tend to be higher, and as our correlation matrix shows, we also tend to spend more on newspaper advertising in those same markets. Hence, in a simple linear regression which only examines sales versus newspaper, we will observe that higher values of newspaper tend to be associated with higher values of sales, even though newspaper advertising is not directly associated with sales. So newspaper advertising is a surrogate for radio advertising; newspaper gets "credit" for the association between radio on sales.

This slightly counterintuitive result is very common in many real life situations. Consider an absurd example to illustrate the point. Running a regression of shark attacks versus ice cream sales for data collected at a given beach community over a period of time would show a positive relationship, similar to that seen between sales and newspaper. Of course no one has (yet) suggested that ice creams should be banned at beaches to reduce shark attacks. In reality, higher temperatures cause more people to visit the beach, which in turn results in more ice cream sales and more shark attacks. A multiple regression of shark attacks onto ice cream sales and temperature reveals that, as intuition implies, ice cream sales is no longer a significant predictor after adjusting for temperature.

3.2.2 Some Important Questions

When we perform multiple linear regression, we usually are interested in answering a few important questions.

1. *Is at least one of the predictors $X_1, X_2, \ldots, X_p$ useful in predicting the response?*

2. *Do all the predictors help to explain Y, or is only a subset of the predictors useful?*

3. *How well does the model fit the data?*

4. *Given a set of predictor values, what response value should we predict, and how accurate is our prediction?*

We now address each of these questions in turn.

One: Is There a Relationship Between the Response and Predictors?

Recall that in the simple linear regression setting, in order to determine whether there is a relationship between the response and the predictor we can simply check whether $\beta_1 = 0$. In the multiple regression setting with p predictors, we need to ask whether all of the regression coefficients are zero, i.e. whether $\beta_1 = \beta_2 = \cdots = \beta_p = 0$. As in the simple linear regression setting, we use a hypothesis test to answer this question. We test the null hypothesis,

$$H_0 : \beta_1 = \beta_2 = \cdots = \beta_p = 0$$

versus the alternative

$$H_a : \text{ at least one } \beta_j \text{ is non-zero.}$$

This hypothesis test is performed by computing the *F-statistic*,

F-statistic

$$F = \frac{(\text{TSS} - \text{RSS})/p}{\text{RSS}/(n-p-1)}, \tag{3.23}$$

where, as with simple linear regression, $\text{TSS} = \sum(y_i - \bar{y})^2$ and $\text{RSS} = \sum(y_i - \hat{y}_i)^2$. If the linear model assumptions are correct, one can show that

$$E\{\text{RSS}/(n-p-1)\} = \sigma^2$$

and that, provided H_0 is true,

$$E\{(\text{TSS} - \text{RSS})/p\} = \sigma^2.$$

Hence, when there is no relationship between the response and predictors, one would expect the F-statistic to take on a value close to 1. On the other hand, if H_a is true, then $E\{(\text{TSS} - \text{RSS})/p\} > \sigma^2$, so we expect F to be greater than 1.

The F-statistic for the multiple linear regression model obtained by regressing `sales` onto `radio`, `TV`, and `newspaper` is shown in Table 3.6. In this example the F-statistic is 570. Since this is far larger than 1, it provides compelling evidence against the null hypothesis H_0. In other words, the large F-statistic suggests that at least one of the advertising media must be related to `sales`. However, what if the F-statistic had been closer to 1? How large does the F-statistic need to be before we can reject H_0 and

Quantity	Value
Residual standard error	1.69
R^2	0.897
F-statistic	570

TABLE 3.6. *More information about the least squares model for the regression of number of units sold on TV, newspaper, and radio advertising budgets in the* Advertising *data. Other information about this model was displayed in Table 3.4.*

conclude that there is a relationship? It turns out that the answer depends on the values of n and p. When n is large, an F-statistic that is just a little larger than 1 might still provide evidence against H_0. In contrast, a larger F-statistic is needed to reject H_0 if n is small. When H_0 is true and the errors ϵ_i have a normal distribution, the F-statistic follows an F-distribution.[6] For any given value of n and p, any statistical software package can be used to compute the p-value associated with the F-statistic using this distribution. Based on this p-value, we can determine whether or not to reject H_0. For the advertising data, the p-value associated with the F-statistic in Table 3.6 is essentially zero, so we have extremely strong evidence that at least one of the media is associated with increased sales.

In (3.23) we are testing H_0 that all the coefficients are zero. Sometimes we want to test that a particular subset of q of the coefficients are zero. This corresponds to a null hypothesis

$$H_0: \quad \beta_{p-q+1} = \beta_{p-q+2} = \cdots = \beta_p = 0,$$

where for convenience we have put the variables chosen for omission at the end of the list. In this case we fit a second model that uses all the variables *except* those last q. Suppose that the residual sum of squares for that model is RSS_0. Then the appropriate F-statistic is

$$F = \frac{(\text{RSS}_0 - \text{RSS})/q}{\text{RSS}/(n-p-1)}. \tag{3.24}$$

Notice that in Table 3.4, for each individual predictor a t-statistic and a p-value were reported. These provide information about whether each individual predictor is related to the response, after adjusting for the other predictors. It turns out that each of these is exactly equivalent[7] to the F-test that omits that single variable from the model, leaving all the others in—i.e. q=1 in (3.24). So it reports the *partial effect* of adding that variable to the model. For instance, as we discussed earlier, these p-values indicate that TV and radio are related to sales, but that there is no evidence that newspaper is associated with sales, when TV and radio are held fixed.

Given these individual p-values for each variable, why do we need to look at the overall F-statistic? After all, it seems likely that if any one of the p-values for the individual variables is very small, then *at least one of the predictors is related to the response*. However, this logic is flawed, especially when the number of predictors p is large.

[6]Even if the errors are not normally-distributed, the F-statistic approximately follows an F-distribution provided that the sample size n is large.

[7]The square of each t-statistic is the corresponding F-statistic.

For instance, consider an example in which $p = 100$ and $H_0 : \beta_1 = \beta_2 = \cdots = \beta_p = 0$ is true, so no variable is truly associated with the response. In this situation, about 5 % of the p-values associated with each variable (of the type shown in Table 3.4) will be below 0.05 by chance. In other words, we expect to see approximately five *small* p-values even in the absence of any true association between the predictors and the response.[8] In fact, it is likely that we will observe at least one p-value below 0.05 by chance! Hence, if we use the individual t-statistics and associated p-values in order to decide whether or not there is any association between the variables and the response, there is a very high chance that we will incorrectly conclude that there is a relationship. However, the F-statistic does not suffer from this problem because it adjusts for the number of predictors. Hence, if H_0 is true, there is only a 5 % chance that the F-statistic will result in a p-value below 0.05, regardless of the number of predictors or the number of observations.

The approach of using an F-statistic to test for any association between the predictors and the response works when p is relatively small, and certainly small compared to n. However, sometimes we have a very large number of variables. If $p > n$ then there are more coefficients β_j to estimate than observations from which to estimate them. In this case we cannot even fit the multiple linear regression model using least squares, so the F-statistic cannot be used, and neither can most of the other concepts that we have seen so far in this chapter. When p is large, some of the approaches discussed in the next section, such as *forward selection*, can be used. This *high-dimensional* setting is discussed in greater detail in Chapter 6.

high-dimensional

Two: Deciding on Important Variables

As discussed in the previous section, the first step in a multiple regression analysis is to compute the F-statistic and to examine the associated p-value. If we conclude on the basis of that p-value that at least one of the predictors is related to the response, then it is natural to wonder *which* are the guilty ones! We could look at the individual p-values as in Table 3.4, but as discussed (and as further explored in Chapter 13), if p is large we are likely to make some false discoveries.

It is possible that all of the predictors are associated with the response, but it is more often the case that the response is only associated with a subset of the predictors. The task of determining which predictors are associated with the response, in order to fit a single model involving only those predictors, is referred to as *variable selection*. The variable selection problem is studied extensively in Chapter 6, and so here we will provide only a brief outline of some classical approaches.

variable selection

Ideally, we would like to perform variable selection by trying out a lot of different models, each containing a different subset of the predictors. For instance, if $p = 2$, then we can consider four models: (1) a model containing no variables, (2) a model containing X_1 only, (3) a model containing

[8]This is related to the important concept of *multiple testing*, which is the focus of Chapter 13.

X_2 only, and (4) a model containing both X_1 and X_2. We can then select the *best* model out of all of the models that we have considered. How do we determine which model is best? Various statistics can be used to judge the quality of a model. These include *Mallow's C_p*, *Akaike information criterion* (AIC), *Bayesian information criterion* (BIC), and *adjusted R^2*. These are discussed in more detail in Chapter 6. We can also determine which model is best by plotting various model outputs, such as the residuals, in order to search for patterns.

Mallow's C_p
Akaike information criterion
Bayesian information criterion
adjusted R^2

Unfortunately, there are a total of 2^p models that contain subsets of p variables. This means that even for moderate p, trying out every possible subset of the predictors is infeasible. For instance, we saw that if $p = 2$, then there are $2^2 = 4$ models to consider. But if $p = 30$, then we must consider $2^{30} = 1{,}073{,}741{,}824$ models! This is not practical. Therefore, unless p is very small, we cannot consider all 2^p models, and instead we need an automated and efficient approach to choose a smaller set of models to consider. There are three classical approaches for this task:

- *Forward selection*. We begin with the *null model*—a model that contains an intercept but no predictors. We then fit p simple linear regressions and add to the null model the variable that results in the lowest RSS. We then add to that model the variable that results in the lowest RSS for the new two-variable model. This approach is continued until some stopping rule is satisfied.

forward selection
null model

- *Backward selection*. We start with all variables in the model, and remove the variable with the largest p-value—that is, the variable that is the least statistically significant. The new $(p - 1)$-variable model is fit, and the variable with the largest p-value is removed. This procedure continues until a stopping rule is reached. For instance, we may stop when all remaining variables have a p-value below some threshold.

backward selection

- *Mixed selection*. This is a combination of forward and backward selection. We start with no variables in the model, and as with forward selection, we add the variable that provides the best fit. We continue to add variables one-by-one. Of course, as we noted with the `Advertising` example, the p-values for variables can become larger as new predictors are added to the model. Hence, if at any point the p-value for one of the variables in the model rises above a certain threshold, then we remove that variable from the model. We continue to perform these forward and backward steps until all variables in the model have a sufficiently low p-value, and all variables outside the model would have a large p-value if added to the model.

mixed selection

Backward selection cannot be used if $p > n$, while forward selection can always be used. Forward selection is a greedy approach, and might include variables early that later become redundant. Mixed selection can remedy this.

Three: Model Fit

Two of the most common numerical measures of model fit are the RSE and R^2, the fraction of variance explained. These quantities are computed and interpreted in the same fashion as for simple linear regression.

Recall that in simple regression, R^2 is the square of the correlation of the response and the variable. In multiple linear regression, it turns out that it equals $\text{Cor}(Y, \hat{Y})^2$, the square of the correlation between the response and the fitted linear model; in fact one property of the fitted linear model is that it maximizes this correlation among all possible linear models.

An R^2 value close to 1 indicates that the model explains a large portion of the variance in the response variable. As an example, we saw in Table 3.6 that for the `Advertising` data, the model that uses all three advertising media to predict `sales` has an R^2 of 0.8972. On the other hand, the model that uses only `TV` and `radio` to predict `sales` has an R^2 value of 0.89719. In other words, there is a *small* increase in R^2 if we include newspaper advertising in the model that already contains TV and radio advertising, even though we saw earlier that the p-value for newspaper advertising in Table 3.4 is not significant. It turns out that R^2 will always increase when more variables are added to the model, even if those variables are only weakly associated with the response. This is due to the fact that adding another variable always results in a decrease in the residual sum of squares on the training data (though not necessarily the testing data). Thus, the R^2 statistic, which is also computed on the training data, must increase. The fact that adding newspaper advertising to the model containing only TV and radio advertising leads to just a tiny increase in R^2 provides additional evidence that `newspaper` can be dropped from the model. Essentially, `newspaper` provides no real improvement in the model fit to the training samples, and its inclusion will likely lead to poor results on independent test samples due to overfitting.

By contrast, the model containing only `TV` as a predictor had an R^2 of 0.61 (Table 3.2). Adding `radio` to the model leads to a substantial improvement in R^2. This implies that a model that uses TV and radio expenditures to predict sales is substantially better than one that uses only TV advertising. We could further quantify this improvement by looking at the p-value for the `radio` coefficient in a model that contains only `TV` and `radio` as predictors.

The model that contains only `TV` and `radio` as predictors has an RSE of 1.681, and the model that also contains `newspaper` as a predictor has an RSE of 1.686 (Table 3.6). In contrast, the model that contains only `TV` has an RSE of 3.26 (Table 3.2). This corroborates our previous conclusion that a model that uses TV and radio expenditures to predict sales is much more accurate (on the training data) than one that only uses TV spending. Furthermore, given that TV and radio expenditures are used as predictors, there is no point in also using newspaper spending as a predictor in the model. The observant reader may wonder how RSE can increase when `newspaper` is added to the model given that RSS must decrease. In general RSE is defined as

$$\text{RSE} = \sqrt{\frac{1}{n-p-1}\text{RSS}}, \tag{3.25}$$

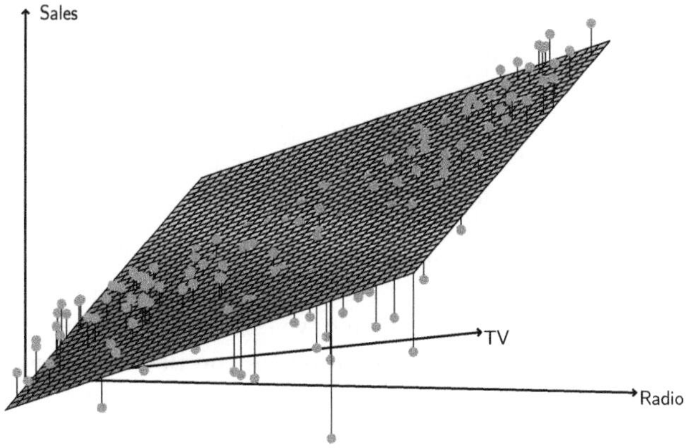

FIGURE 3.5. *For the* Advertising *data, a linear regression fit to* sales *using* TV *and* radio *as predictors. From the pattern of the residuals, we can see that there is a pronounced non-linear relationship in the data. The positive residuals (those visible above the surface), tend to lie along the 45-degree line, where TV and Radio budgets are split evenly. The negative residuals (most not visible), tend to lie away from this line, where budgets are more lopsided.*

which simplifies to (3.15) for a simple linear regression. Thus, models with more variables can have higher RSE if the decrease in RSS is small relative to the increase in p.

In addition to looking at the RSE and R^2 statistics just discussed, it can be useful to plot the data. Graphical summaries can reveal problems with a model that are not visible from numerical statistics. For example, Figure 3.5 displays a three-dimensional plot of TV and radio versus sales. We see that some observations lie above and some observations lie below the least squares regression plane. In particular, the linear model seems to overestimate sales for instances in which most of the advertising money was spent exclusively on either TV or radio. It underestimates sales for instances where the budget was split between the two media. This pronounced non-linear pattern suggests a *synergy* or *interaction* effect between the advertising media, whereby combining the media together results in a bigger boost to sales than using any single medium. In Section 3.3.2, we will discuss extending the linear model to accommodate such synergistic effects through the use of interaction terms. interaction

Four: Predictions

Once we have fit the multiple regression model, it is straightforward to apply (3.21) in order to predict the response Y on the basis of a set of values for the predictors $X_1, X_2, \ldots, X_p$. However, there are three sorts of uncertainty associated with this prediction.

1. The coefficient estimates $\hat{\beta}_0, \hat{\beta}_1, \ldots, \hat{\beta}_p$ are estimates for $\beta_0, \beta_1, \ldots, \beta_p$. That is, the *least squares plane*

$$\hat{Y} = \hat{\beta}_0 + \hat{\beta}_1 X_1 + \cdots + \hat{\beta}_p X_p$$

is only an estimate for the *true population regression plane*

$$f(X) = \beta_0 + \beta_1 X_1 + \cdots + \beta_p X_p.$$

The inaccuracy in the coefficient estimates is related to the *reducible error* from Chapter 2. We can compute a *confidence interval* in order to determine how close $\hat{Y}$ will be to $f(X)$.

2. Of course, in practice assuming a linear model for $f(X)$ is almost always an approximation of reality, so there is an additional source of potentially reducible error which we call *model bias*. So when we use a linear model, we are in fact estimating the best linear approximation to the true surface. However, here we will ignore this discrepancy, and operate as if the linear model were correct.

3. Even if we knew $f(X)$—that is, even if we knew the true values for $\beta_0, \beta_1, \ldots, \beta_p$—the response value cannot be predicted perfectly because of the random error ϵ in the model (3.20). In Chapter 2, we referred to this as the *irreducible error*. How much will Y vary from $\hat{Y}$? We use *prediction intervals* to answer this question. Prediction intervals are always wider than confidence intervals, because they incorporate both the error in the estimate for $f(X)$ (the reducible error) and the uncertainty as to how much an individual point will differ from the population regression plane (the irreducible error).

We use a *confidence interval* to quantify the uncertainty surrounding the *average* `sales` over a large number of cities. For example, given that \$100,000 is spent on `TV` advertising and \$20,000 is spent on `radio` advertising in each city, the 95 % confidence interval is [10,985, 11,528]. We interpret this to mean that 95 % of intervals of this form will contain the true value of $f(X)$.[9] On the other hand, a *prediction interval* can be used to quantify the uncertainty surrounding `sales` for a *particular* city. Given that \$100,000 is spent on `TV` advertising and \$20,000 is spent on `radio` advertising in that city the 95 % prediction interval is [7,930, 14,580]. We interpret this to mean that 95 % of intervals of this form will contain the true value of Y for this city. Note that both intervals are centered at 11,256, but that the prediction interval is substantially wider than the confidence interval, reflecting the increased uncertainty about `sales` for a given city in comparison to the average `sales` over many locations.

confidence interval

prediction interval

[9]In other words, if we collect a large number of data sets like the `Advertising` data set, and we construct a confidence interval for the average `sales` on the basis of each data set (given \$100,000 in `TV` and \$20,000 in `radio` advertising), then 95 % of these confidence intervals will contain the true value of average `sales`.

3.3 Other Considerations in the Regression Model

3.3.1 Qualitative Predictors

In our discussion so far, we have assumed that all variables in our linear regression model are *quantitative*. But in practice, this is not necessarily the case; often some predictors are *qualitative*.

For example, the `Credit` data set displayed in Figure 3.6 records variables for a number of credit card holders. The response is `balance` (average credit card debt for each individual) and there are several quantitative predictors: `age`, `cards` (number of credit cards), `education` (years of education), `income` (in thousands of dollars), `limit` (credit limit), and `rating` (credit rating). Each panel of Figure 3.6 is a scatterplot for a pair of variables whose identities are given by the corresponding row and column labels. For example, the scatterplot directly to the right of the word "Balance" depicts `balance` versus `age`, while the plot directly to the right of "Age" corresponds to `age` versus `cards`. In addition to these quantitative variables, we also have four qualitative variables: `own` (house ownership), `student` (student status), `status` (marital status), and `region` (East, West or South).

Predictors with Only Two Levels

Suppose that we wish to investigate differences in credit card balance between those who own a house and those who don't, ignoring the other variables for the moment. If a qualitative predictor (also known as a *factor*) only has two *levels*, or possible values, then incorporating it into a regression model is very simple. We simply create an indicator or *dummy variable* that takes on two possible numerical values.[10] For example, based on the `own` variable, we can create a new variable that takes the form

factor
level
dummy variable

$$x_i = \begin{cases} 1 & \text{if } i\text{th person owns a house} \\ 0 & \text{if } i\text{th person does not own a house,} \end{cases} \tag{3.26}$$

and use this variable as a predictor in the regression equation. This results in the model

$$y_i = \beta_0 + \beta_1 x_i + \epsilon_i = \begin{cases} \beta_0 + \beta_1 + \epsilon_i & \text{if } i\text{th person owns a house} \\ \beta_0 + \epsilon_i & \text{if } i\text{th person does not.} \end{cases} \tag{3.27}$$

Now β_0 can be interpreted as the average credit card balance among those who do not own, $\beta_0 + \beta_1$ as the average credit card balance among those who do own their house, and β_1 as the average difference in credit card balance between owners and non-owners.

Table 3.7 displays the coefficient estimates and other information associated with the model (3.27). The average credit card debt for non-owners is estimated to be \$509.80, whereas owners are estimated to carry \$19.73 in additional debt for a total of \$509.80 + \$19.73 = \$529.53. However, we

[10] In the machine learning community, the creation of dummy variables to handle qualitative predictors is known as "one-hot encoding".

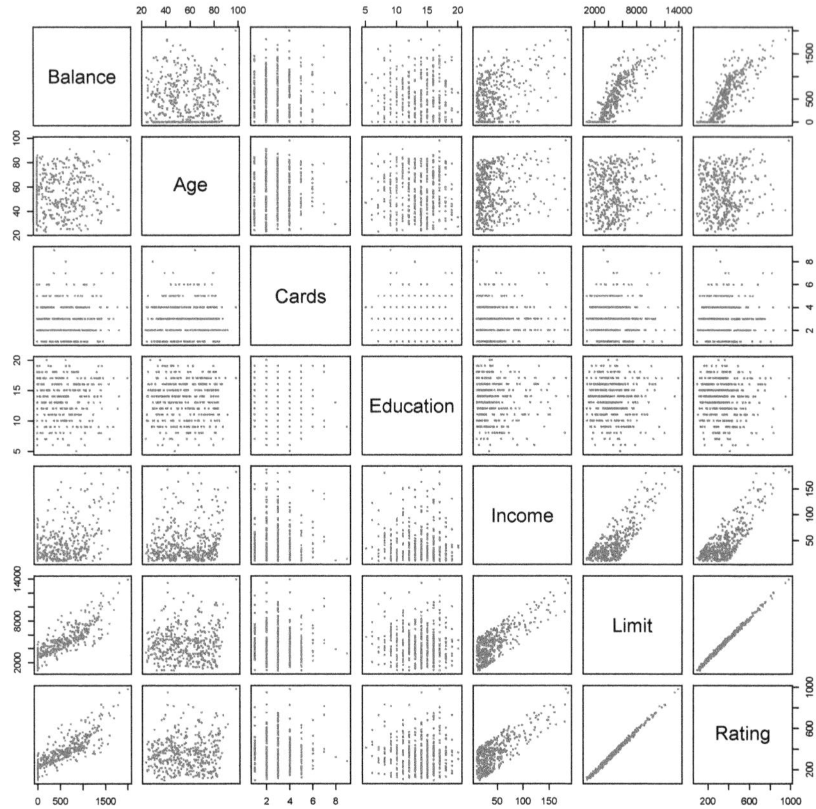

FIGURE 3.6. *The* `Credit` *data set contains information about* `balance`, `age`, `cards`, `education`, `income`, `limit`, *and* `rating` *for a number of potential customers.*

notice that the p-value for the dummy variable is very high. This indicates that there is no statistical evidence of a difference in average credit card balance based on house ownership.

The decision to code owners as 1 and non-owners as 0 in (3.27) is arbitrary, and has no effect on the regression fit, but does alter the interpretation of the coefficients. If we had coded non-owners as 1 and owners as 0, then the estimates for β_0 and β_1 would have been 529.53 and -19.73, respectively, leading once again to a prediction of credit card debt of \$529.53 − \$19.73 = \$509.80 for non-owners and a prediction of \$529.53 for owners. Alternatively, instead of a 0/1 coding scheme, we could create a dummy variable

$$x_i = \begin{cases} 1 & \text{if } i\text{th person owns a house} \\ -1 & \text{if } i\text{th person does not own a house} \end{cases}$$

and use this variable in the regression equation. This results in the model

$$y_i = \beta_0 + \beta_1 x_i + \epsilon_i = \begin{cases} \beta_0 + \beta_1 + \epsilon_i & \text{if } i\text{th person owns a house} \\ \beta_0 - \beta_1 + \epsilon_i & \text{if } i\text{th person does not own a house.} \end{cases}$$

	Coefficient	Std. error	t-statistic	p-value
`Intercept`	509.80	33.13	15.389	< 0.0001
`own[Yes]`	19.73	46.05	0.429	0.6690

TABLE 3.7. *Least squares coefficient estimates associated with the regression of* `balance` *onto* `own` *in the* `Credit` *data set. The linear model is given in (3.27). That is, ownership is encoded as a dummy variable, as in (3.26).*

Now β_0 can be interpreted as the overall average credit card balance (ignoring the house ownership effect), and β_1 is the amount by which house owners and non-owners have credit card balances that are above and below the average, respectively.[11] In this example, the estimate for β_0 is \$519.665, halfway between the non-owner and owner averages of \$509.80 and \$529.53. The estimate for β_1 is \$9.865, which is half of \$19.73, the average difference between owners and non-owners. It is important to note that the final predictions for the credit balances of owners and non-owners will be identical regardless of the coding scheme used. The only difference is in the way that the coefficients are interpreted.

Qualitative Predictors with More than Two Levels

When a qualitative predictor has more than two levels, a single dummy variable cannot represent all possible values. In this situation, we can create additional dummy variables. For example, for the `region` variable we create two dummy variables. The first could be

$$x_{i1} = \begin{cases} 1 & \text{if } i\text{th person is from the South} \\ 0 & \text{if } i\text{th person is not from the South,} \end{cases} \tag{3.28}$$

and the second could be

$$x_{i2} = \begin{cases} 1 & \text{if } i\text{th person is from the West} \\ 0 & \text{if } i\text{th person is not from the West.} \end{cases} \tag{3.29}$$

Then both of these variables can be used in the regression equation, in order to obtain the model

$$y_i = \beta_0 + \beta_1 x_{i1} + \beta_2 x_{i2} + \epsilon_i = \begin{cases} \beta_0 + \beta_1 + \epsilon_i & \text{if } i\text{th person is from the South} \\ \beta_0 + \beta_2 + \epsilon_i & \text{if } i\text{th person is from the West} \\ \beta_0 + \epsilon_i & \text{if } i\text{th person is from the East.} \end{cases} \tag{3.30}$$

Now β_0 can be interpreted as the average credit card balance for individuals from the East, β_1 can be interpreted as the difference in the average balance between people from the South versus the East, and β_2 can be interpreted as the difference in the average balance between those from the West versus the East. There will always be one fewer dummy variable than the number of levels. The level with no dummy variable—East in this example—is known as the *baseline*.

baseline

[11]Technically β_0 is half the sum of the average debt for house owners and the average debt for non-house owners. Hence, β_0 is exactly equal to the overall average only if the two groups have an equal number of members.

	Coefficient	Std. error	t-statistic	p-value
`Intercept`	531.00	46.32	11.464	< 0.0001
`region[South]`	−12.50	56.68	−0.221	0.8260
`region[West]`	−18.69	65.02	−0.287	0.7740

TABLE 3.8. *Least squares coefficient estimates associated with the regression of* `balance` *onto* `region` *in the* `Credit` *data set. The linear model is given in (3.30). That is, region is encoded via two dummy variables (3.28) and (3.29).*

From Table 3.8, we see that the estimated `balance` for the baseline, East, is \$531.00. It is estimated that those in the South will have \$18.69 less debt than those in the East, and that those in the West will have \$12.50 less debt than those in the East. However, the p-values associated with the coefficient estimates for the two dummy variables are very large, suggesting no statistical evidence of a real difference in average credit card balance between South and East or between West and East.[12] Once again, the level selected as the baseline category is arbitrary, and the final predictions for each group will be the same regardless of this choice. However, the coefficients and their p-values do depend on the choice of dummy variable coding. Rather than rely on the individual coefficients, we can use an F-test to test $H_0 : \beta_1 = \beta_2 = 0$; this does not depend on the coding. This F-test has a p-value of 0.96, indicating that we cannot reject the null hypothesis that there is no relationship between `balance` and `region`.

Using this dummy variable approach presents no difficulties when incorporating both quantitative and qualitative predictors. For example, to regress `balance` on both a quantitative variable such as `income` and a qualitative variable such as `student`, we must simply create a dummy variable for `student` and then fit a multiple regression model using `income` and the dummy variable as predictors for credit card balance.

There are many different ways of coding qualitative variables besides the dummy variable approach taken here. All of these approaches lead to equivalent model fits, but the coefficients are different and have different interpretations, and are designed to measure particular *contrasts*. This topic is beyond the scope of the book. contrast

3.3.2 Extensions of the Linear Model

The standard linear regression model (3.19) provides interpretable results and works quite well on many real-world problems. However, it makes several highly restrictive assumptions that are often violated in practice. Two of the most important assumptions state that the relationship between the predictors and response are *additive* and *linear*. The additivity assumption means that the association between a predictor X_j and the response Y does not depend on the values of the other predictors. The linearity assumption states that the change in the response Y associated with a one-unit change in X_j is constant, regardless of the value of X_j. In later chapters of this book, we examine a number of sophisticated methods that relax these two

additive

linear

[12]There could still in theory be a difference between South and West, although the data here does not suggest any difference.

assumptions. Here, we briefly examine some common classical approaches for extending the linear model.

Removing the Additive Assumption

In our previous analysis of the `Advertising` data, we concluded that both `TV` and `radio` seem to be associated with `sales`. The linear models that formed the basis for this conclusion assumed that the effect on `sales` of increasing one advertising medium is independent of the amount spent on the other media. For example, the linear model (3.20) states that the average increase in `sales` associated with a one-unit increase in `TV` is always β_1, regardless of the amount spent on `radio`.

However, this simple model may be incorrect. Suppose that spending money on radio advertising actually increases the effectiveness of TV advertising, so that the slope term for `TV` should increase as `radio` increases. In this situation, given a fixed budget of \$100,000, spending half on `radio` and half on `TV` may increase `sales` more than allocating the entire amount to either `TV` or to `radio`. In marketing, this is known as a *synergy* effect, and in statistics it is referred to as an *interaction* effect. Figure 3.5 suggests that such an effect may be present in the advertising data. Notice that when levels of either `TV` or `radio` are low, then the true `sales` are lower than predicted by the linear model. But when advertising is split between the two media, then the model tends to underestimate `sales`.

Consider the standard linear regression model with two variables,

$$Y = \beta_0 + \beta_1 X_1 + \beta_2 X_2 + \epsilon.$$

According to this model, a one-unit increase in X_1 is associated with an average increase in Y of β_1 units. Notice that the presence of X_2 does not alter this statement—that is, regardless of the value of X_2, a one-unit increase in X_1 is associated with a β_1-unit increase in Y. One way of extending this model is to include a third predictor, called an *interaction term*, which is constructed by computing the product of X_1 and X_2. This results in the model

$$Y = \beta_0 + \beta_1 X_1 + \beta_2 X_2 + \beta_3 X_1 X_2 + \epsilon. \tag{3.31}$$

How does inclusion of this interaction term relax the additive assumption? Notice that (3.31) can be rewritten as

$$\begin{aligned} Y &= \beta_0 + (\beta_1 + \beta_3 X_2) X_1 + \beta_2 X_2 + \epsilon \\ &= \beta_0 + \tilde{\beta}_1 X_1 + \beta_2 X_2 + \epsilon \end{aligned} \tag{3.32}$$

where $\tilde{\beta}_1 = \beta_1 + \beta_3 X_2$. Since $\tilde{\beta}_1$ is now a function of X_2, the association between X_1 and Y is no longer constant: a change in the value of X_2 will change the association between X_1 and Y. A similar argument shows that a change in the value of X_1 changes the association between X_2 and Y.

For example, suppose that we are interested in studying the productivity of a factory. We wish to predict the number of `units` produced on the basis of the number of production `lines` and the total number of `workers`. It seems likely that the effect of increasing the number of production lines

	Coefficient	Std. error	t-statistic	p-value
Intercept	6.7502	0.248	27.23	< 0.0001
TV	0.0191	0.002	12.70	< 0.0001
radio	0.0289	0.009	3.24	0.0014
TV×radio	0.0011	0.000	20.73	< 0.0001

TABLE 3.9. *For the* Advertising *data, least squares coefficient estimates associated with the regression of* sales *onto* TV *and* radio*, with an interaction term, as in (3.33).*

will depend on the number of workers, since if no workers are available to operate the lines, then increasing the number of lines will not increase production. This suggests that it would be appropriate to include an interaction term between lines and workers in a linear model to predict units. Suppose that when we fit the model, we obtain

$$\begin{aligned} \texttt{units} &\approx 1.2 + 3.4 \times \texttt{lines} + 0.22 \times \texttt{workers} + 1.4 \times (\texttt{lines} \times \texttt{workers}) \\ &= 1.2 + (3.4 + 1.4 \times \texttt{workers}) \times \texttt{lines} + 0.22 \times \texttt{workers}. \end{aligned}$$

In other words, adding an additional line will increase the number of units produced by $3.4 + 1.4 \times$ workers. Hence the more workers we have, the stronger will be the effect of lines.

We now return to the Advertising example. A linear model that uses radio, TV, and an interaction between the two to predict sales takes the form

$$\begin{aligned} \texttt{sales} &= \beta_0 + \beta_1 \times \texttt{TV} + \beta_2 \times \texttt{radio} + \beta_3 \times (\texttt{radio} \times \texttt{TV}) + \epsilon \\ &= \beta_0 + (\beta_1 + \beta_3 \times \texttt{radio}) \times \texttt{TV} + \beta_2 \times \texttt{radio} + \epsilon. \end{aligned} \quad (3.33)$$

We can interpret β_3 as the increase in the effectiveness of TV advertising associated with a one-unit increase in radio advertising (or vice-versa). The coefficients that result from fitting the model (3.33) are given in Table 3.9.

The results in Table 3.9 strongly suggest that the model that includes the interaction term is superior to the model that contains only *main effects*. The p-value for the interaction term, TV×radio, is extremely low, indicating that there is strong evidence for $H_a : \beta_3 \neq 0$. In other words, it is clear that the true relationship is not additive. The R^2 for the model (3.33) is 96.8 %, compared to only 89.7 % for the model that predicts sales using TV and radio without an interaction term. This means that $(96.8 - 89.7)/(100 - 89.7) = 69\,\%$ of the variability in sales that remains after fitting the additive model has been explained by the interaction term. The coefficient estimates in Table 3.9 suggest that an increase in TV advertising of \$1,000 is associated with increased sales of $(\hat{\beta}_1 + \hat{\beta}_3 \times \texttt{radio}) \times 1{,}000 = 19 + 1.1 \times \texttt{radio}$ units. And an increase in radio advertising of \$1,000 will be associated with an increase in sales of $(\hat{\beta}_2 + \hat{\beta}_3 \times \texttt{TV}) \times 1{,}000 = 29 + 1.1 \times \texttt{TV}$ units.

main effect

In this example, the p-values associated with TV, radio, and the interaction term all are statistically significant (Table 3.9), and so it is obvious that all three variables should be included in the model. However, it is sometimes the case that an interaction term has a very small p-value, but the associated main effects (in this case, TV and radio) do not. The *hierarchical principle* states that *if we include an interaction in a model, we*

hierarchical principle

should also include the main effects, even if the p-values associated with their coefficients are not significant. In other words, if the interaction between X_1 and X_2 seems important, then we should include both X_1 and X_2 in the model even if their coefficient estimates have large p-values. The rationale for this principle is that if $X_1 \times X_2$ is related to the response, then whether or not the coefficients of X_1 or X_2 are exactly zero is of little interest. Also $X_1 \times X_2$ is typically correlated with X_1 and X_2, and so leaving them out tends to alter the meaning of the interaction.

In the previous example, we considered an interaction between `TV` and `radio`, both of which are quantitative variables. However, the concept of interactions applies just as well to qualitative variables, or to a combination of quantitative and qualitative variables. In fact, an interaction between a qualitative variable and a quantitative variable has a particularly nice interpretation. Consider the `Credit` data set from Section 3.3.1, and suppose that we wish to predict `balance` using the `income` (quantitative) and `student` (qualitative) variables. In the absence of an interaction term, the model takes the form

$$\begin{aligned} \texttt{balance}_i &\approx \beta_0 + \beta_1 \times \texttt{income}_i + \begin{cases} \beta_2 & \text{if } i\text{th person is a student} \\ 0 & \text{if } i\text{th person is not a student} \end{cases} \\ &= \beta_1 \times \texttt{income}_i + \begin{cases} \beta_0 + \beta_2 & \text{if } i\text{th person is a student} \\ \beta_0 & \text{if } i\text{th person is not a student.} \end{cases} \end{aligned} \tag{3.34}$$

Notice that this amounts to fitting two parallel lines to the data, one for students and one for non-students. The lines for students and non-students have different intercepts, $\beta_0 + \beta_2$ versus β_0, but the same slope, β_1. This is illustrated in the left-hand panel of Figure 3.7. The fact that the lines are parallel means that the average effect on `balance` of a one-unit increase in `income` does not depend on whether or not the individual is a student. This represents a potentially serious limitation of the model, since in fact a change in `income` may have a very different effect on the credit card balance of a student versus a non-student.

This limitation can be addressed by adding an interaction variable, created by multiplying `income` with the dummy variable for `student`. Our model now becomes

$$\begin{aligned} \texttt{balance}_i &\approx \beta_0 + \beta_1 \times \texttt{income}_i + \begin{cases} \beta_2 + \beta_3 \times \texttt{income}_i & \text{if student} \\ 0 & \text{if not student} \end{cases} \\ &= \begin{cases} (\beta_0 + \beta_2) + (\beta_1 + \beta_3) \times \texttt{income}_i & \text{if student} \\ \beta_0 + \beta_1 \times \texttt{income}_i & \text{if not student.} \end{cases} \end{aligned} \tag{3.35}$$

Once again, we have two different regression lines for the students and the non-students. But now those regression lines have different intercepts, $\beta_0+\beta_2$ versus β_0, as well as different slopes, $\beta_1+\beta_3$ versus β_1. This allows for the possibility that changes in income may affect the credit card balances of students and non-students differently. The right-hand panel of Figure 3.7

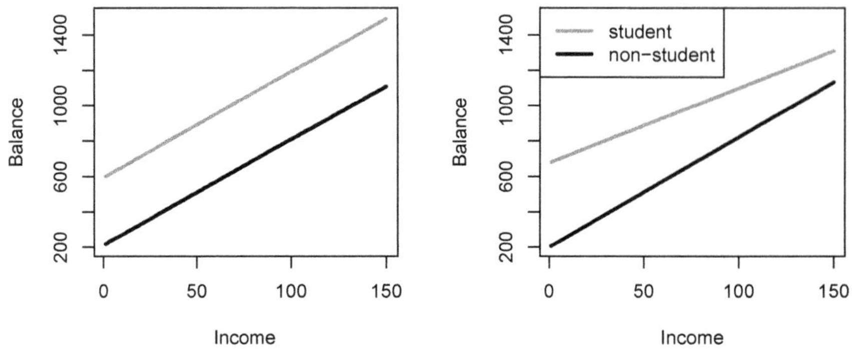

FIGURE 3.7. *For the* Credit *data, the least squares lines are shown for prediction of* balance *from* income *for students and non-students.* Left: *The model (3.34) was fit. There is no interaction between* income *and* student. Right: *The model (3.35) was fit. There is an interaction term between* income *and* student.

shows the estimated relationships between income and balance for students and non-students in the model (3.35). We note that the slope for students is lower than the slope for non-students. This suggests that increases in income are associated with smaller increases in credit card balance among students as compared to non-students.

Non-linear Relationships

As discussed previously, the linear regression model (3.19) assumes a linear relationship between the response and predictors. But in some cases, the true relationship between the response and the predictors may be non-linear. Here we present a very simple way to directly extend the linear model to accommodate non-linear relationships, using *polynomial regression.* In later chapters, we will present more complex approaches for performing non-linear fits in more general settings.

polynomial regression

Consider Figure 3.8, in which the mpg (gas mileage in miles per gallon) versus horsepower is shown for a number of cars in the Auto data set. The orange line represents the linear regression fit. There is a pronounced relationship between mpg and horsepower, but it seems clear that this relationship is in fact non-linear: the data suggest a curved relationship. A simple approach for incorporating non-linear associations in a linear model is to include transformed versions of the predictors. For example, the points in Figure 3.8 seem to have a *quadratic* shape, suggesting that a model of the form

quadratic

$$\texttt{mpg} = \beta_0 + \beta_1 \times \texttt{horsepower} + \beta_2 \times \texttt{horsepower}^2 + \epsilon \quad (3.36)$$

may provide a better fit. Equation 3.36 involves predicting mpg using a non-linear function of horsepower. *But it is still a linear model!* That is, (3.36) is simply a multiple linear regression model with $X_1 = \texttt{horsepower}$ and $X_2 = \texttt{horsepower}^2$. So we can use standard linear regression software to estimate β_0, β_1, and β_2 in order to produce a non-linear fit. The blue curve in Figure 3.8 shows the resulting quadratic fit to the data. The quadratic

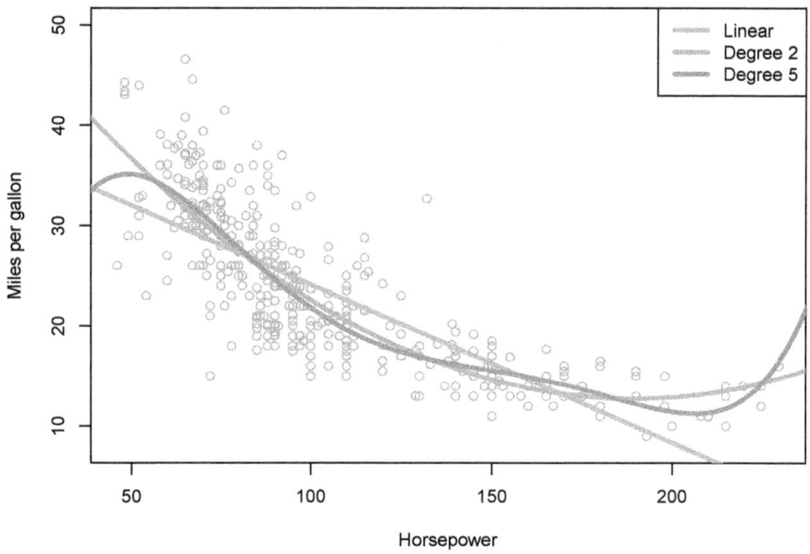

FIGURE 3.8. *The* Auto *data set. For a number of cars,* mpg *and* horsepower *are shown. The linear regression fit is shown in orange. The linear regression fit for a model that includes* horsepower^2 *is shown as a blue curve. The linear regression fit for a model that includes all polynomials of* horsepower *up to fifth-degree is shown in green.*

	Coefficient	Std. error	t-statistic	p-value
Intercept	56.9001	1.8004	31.6	< 0.0001
horsepower	-0.4662	0.0311	-15.0	< 0.0001
horsepower^2	0.0012	0.0001	10.1	< 0.0001

TABLE 3.10. *For the* Auto *data set, least squares coefficient estimates associated with the regression of* mpg *onto* horsepower *and* horsepower^2.

fit appears to be substantially better than the fit obtained when just the linear term is included. The R^2 of the quadratic fit is 0.688, compared to 0.606 for the linear fit, and the p-value in Table 3.10 for the quadratic term is highly significant.

If including horsepower^2 led to such a big improvement in the model, why not include horsepower^3, horsepower^4, or even horsepower^5? The green curve in Figure 3.8 displays the fit that results from including all polynomials up to fifth degree in the model (3.36). The resulting fit seems unnecessarily wiggly—that is, it is unclear that including the additional terms really has led to a better fit to the data.

The approach that we have just described for extending the linear model to accommodate non-linear relationships is known as *polynomial regression*, since we have included polynomial functions of the predictors in the regression model. We further explore this approach and other non-linear extensions of the linear model in Chapter 7.

3.3.3 Potential Problems

When we fit a linear regression model to a particular data set, many problems may occur. Most common among these are the following:

1. *Non-linearity of the response-predictor relationships.*
2. *Correlation of error terms.*
3. *Non-constant variance of error terms.*
4. *Outliers.*
5. *High-leverage points.*
6. *Collinearity.*

In practice, identifying and overcoming these problems is as much an art as a science. Many pages in countless books have been written on this topic. Since the linear regression model is not our primary focus here, we will provide only a brief summary of some key points.

1. Non-linearity of the Data

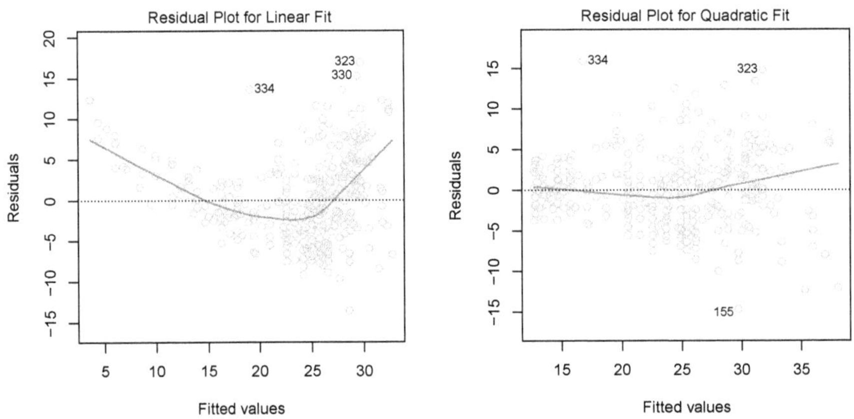

FIGURE 3.9. *Plots of residuals versus predicted (or fitted) values for the* Auto *data set. In each plot, the red line is a smooth fit to the residuals, intended to make it easier to identify a trend.* Left: *A linear regression of* mpg *on* horsepower. *A strong pattern in the residuals indicates non-linearity in the data.* Right: *A linear regression of* mpg *on* horsepower *and* horsepower^2. *There is little pattern in the residuals.*

The linear regression model assumes that there is a straight-line relationship between the predictors and the response. If the true relationship is far from linear, then virtually all of the conclusions that we draw from the fit are suspect. In addition, the prediction accuracy of the model can be significantly reduced.

Residual plots are a useful graphical tool for identifying non-linearity. Given a simple linear regression model, we can plot the residuals, $e_i =$ residual plot

$y_i - \hat{y}_i$, versus the predictor x_i. In the case of a multiple regression model, since there are multiple predictors, we instead plot the residuals versus the predicted (or *fitted*) values $\hat{y}_i$. Ideally, the residual plot will show no discernible pattern. The presence of a pattern may indicate a problem with some aspect of the linear model.

fitted

The left panel of Figure 3.9 displays a residual plot from the linear regression of `mpg` onto `horsepower` on the `Auto` data set that was illustrated in Figure 3.8. The red line is a smooth fit to the residuals, which is displayed in order to make it easier to identify any trends. The residuals exhibit a clear U-shape, which provides a strong indication of non-linearity in the data. In contrast, the right-hand panel of Figure 3.9 displays the residual plot that results from the model (3.36), which contains a quadratic term. There appears to be little pattern in the residuals, suggesting that the quadratic term improves the fit to the data.

If the residual plot indicates that there are non-linear associations in the data, then a simple approach is to use non-linear transformations of the predictors, such as $\log X$, $\sqrt{X}$, and X^2, in the regression model. In the later chapters of this book, we will discuss other more advanced non-linear approaches for addressing this issue.

2. Correlation of Error Terms

An important assumption of the linear regression model is that the error terms, $\epsilon_1, \epsilon_2, \ldots, \epsilon_n$, are uncorrelated. What does this mean? For instance, if the errors are uncorrelated, then the fact that ϵ_i is positive provides little or no information about the sign of ϵ_{i+1}. The standard errors that are computed for the estimated regression coefficients or the fitted values are based on the assumption of uncorrelated error terms. If in fact there is correlation among the error terms, then the estimated standard errors will tend to underestimate the true standard errors. As a result, confidence and prediction intervals will be narrower than they should be. For example, a 95 % confidence interval may in reality have a much lower probability than 0.95 of containing the true value of the parameter. In addition, *p*-values associated with the model will be lower than they should be; this could cause us to erroneously conclude that a parameter is statistically significant. In short, if the error terms are correlated, we may have an unwarranted sense of confidence in our model.

As an extreme example, suppose we accidentally doubled our data, leading to observations and error terms identical in pairs. If we ignored this, our standard error calculations would be as if we had a sample of size $2n$, when in fact we have only n samples. Our estimated parameters would be the same for the $2n$ samples as for the n samples, but the confidence intervals would be narrower by a factor of $\sqrt{2}$!

Why might correlations among the error terms occur? Such correlations frequently occur in the context of *time series* data, which consists of observations for which measurements are obtained at discrete points in time. In many cases, observations that are obtained at adjacent time points will have positively correlated errors. In order to determine if this is the case for a given data set, we can plot the residuals from our model as a function of time. If the errors are uncorrelated, then there should be no discernible pat-

time series

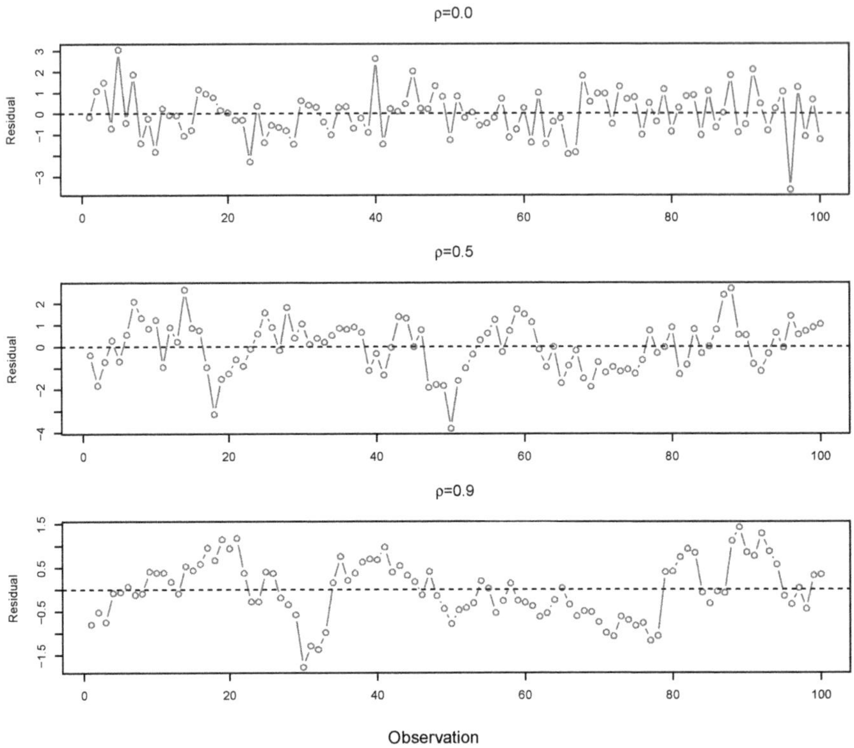

FIGURE 3.10. *Plots of residuals from simulated time series data sets generated with differing levels of correlation ρ between error terms for adjacent time points.*

tern. On the other hand, if the error terms are positively correlated, then we may see *tracking* in the residuals—that is, adjacent residuals may have similar values. Figure 3.10 provides an illustration. In the top panel, we see the residuals from a linear regression fit to data generated with uncorrelated errors. There is no evidence of a time-related trend in the residuals. In contrast, the residuals in the bottom panel are from a data set in which adjacent errors had a correlation of 0.9. Now there is a clear pattern in the residuals—adjacent residuals tend to take on similar values. Finally, the center panel illustrates a more moderate case in which the residuals had a correlation of 0.5. There is still evidence of tracking, but the pattern is less clear.

tracking

Many methods have been developed to properly take account of correlations in the error terms in time series data. Correlation among the error terms can also occur outside of time series data. For instance, consider a study in which individuals' heights are predicted from their weights. The assumption of uncorrelated errors could be violated if some of the individuals in the study are members of the same family, eat the same diet, or have been exposed to the same environmental factors. In general, the assumption of uncorrelated errors is extremely important for linear regression as well as for other statistical methods, and good experimental design is crucial in order to mitigate the risk of such correlations.

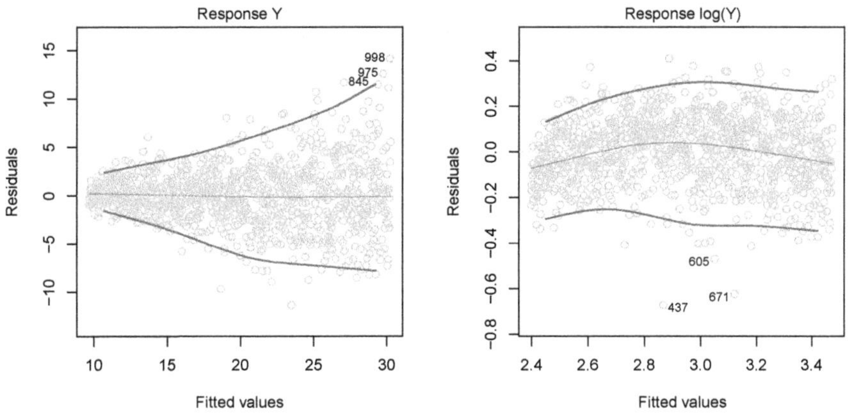

FIGURE 3.11. *Residual plots. In each plot, the red line is a smooth fit to the residuals, intended to make it easier to identify a trend. The blue lines track the outer quantiles of the residuals, and emphasize patterns.* Left: *The funnel shape indicates heteroscedasticity.* Right: *The response has been log transformed, and there is now no evidence of heteroscedasticity.*

3. Non-constant Variance of Error Terms

Another important assumption of the linear regression model is that the error terms have a constant variance, $\mathrm{Var}(\epsilon_i) = \sigma^2$. The standard errors, confidence intervals, and hypothesis tests associated with the linear model rely upon this assumption.

Unfortunately, it is often the case that the variances of the error terms are non-constant. For instance, the variances of the error terms may increase with the value of the response. One can identify non-constant variances in the errors, or *heteroscedasticity*, from the presence of a *funnel shape* in the residual plot. An example is shown in the left-hand panel of Figure 3.11, in which the magnitude of the residuals tends to increase with the fitted values. When faced with this problem, one possible solution is to transform the response Y using a concave function such as $\log Y$ or $\sqrt{Y}$. Such a transformation results in a greater amount of shrinkage of the larger responses, leading to a reduction in heteroscedasticity. The right-hand panel of Figure 3.11 displays the residual plot after transforming the response using $\log Y$. The residuals now appear to have constant variance, though there is some evidence of a slight non-linear relationship in the data.

hetero-scedasticity

Sometimes we have a good idea of the variance of each response. For example, the ith response could be an average of n_i raw observations. If each of these raw observations is uncorrelated with variance σ^2, then their average has variance $\sigma_i^2 = \sigma^2/n_i$. In this case a simple remedy is to fit our model by *weighted least squares*, with weights proportional to the inverse variances—i.e. $w_i = n_i$ in this case. Most linear regression software allows for observation weights.

weighted least squares

4. Outliers

An *outlier* is a point for which y_i is far from the value predicted by the

outlier

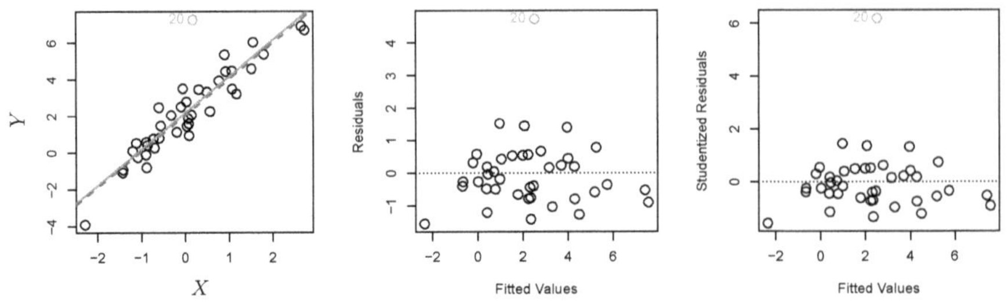

FIGURE 3.12. Left: *The least squares regression line is shown in red, and the regression line after removing the outlier is shown in blue.* Center: *The residual plot clearly identifies the outlier.* Right: *The outlier has a studentized residual of 6; typically we expect values between* -3 *and* 3.

model. Outliers can arise for a variety of reasons, such as incorrect recording of an observation during data collection.

The red point (observation 20) in the left-hand panel of Figure 3.12 illustrates a typical outlier. The red solid line is the least squares regression fit, while the blue dashed line is the least squares fit after removal of the outlier. In this case, removing the outlier has little effect on the least squares line: it leads to almost no change in the slope, and a miniscule reduction in the intercept. It is typical for an outlier that does not have an unusual predictor value to have little effect on the least squares fit. However, even if an outlier does not have much effect on the least squares fit, it can cause other problems. For instance, in this example, the RSE is 1.09 when the outlier is included in the regression, but it is only 0.77 when the outlier is removed. Since the RSE is used to compute all confidence intervals and p-values, such a dramatic increase caused by a single data point can have implications for the interpretation of the fit. Similarly, inclusion of the outlier causes the R^2 to decline from 0.892 to 0.805.

Residual plots can be used to identify outliers. In this example, the outlier is clearly visible in the residual plot illustrated in the center panel of Figure 3.12. But in practice, it can be difficult to decide how large a residual needs to be before we consider the point to be an outlier. To address this problem, instead of plotting the residuals, we can plot the *studentized residuals*, computed by dividing each residual e_i by its estimated standard error. Observations whose studentized residuals are greater than 3 in absolute value are possible outliers. In the right-hand panel of Figure 3.12, the outlier's studentized residual exceeds 6, while all other observations have studentized residuals between -2 and 2.

studentized residual

If we believe that an outlier has occurred due to an error in data collection or recording, then one solution is to simply remove the observation. However, care should be taken, since an outlier may instead indicate a deficiency with the model, such as a missing predictor.

5. High Leverage Points

We just saw that outliers are observations for which the response y_i is unusual given the predictor x_i. In contrast, observations with *high leverage* have an unusual value for x_i. For example, observation 41 in the left-hand

high leverage

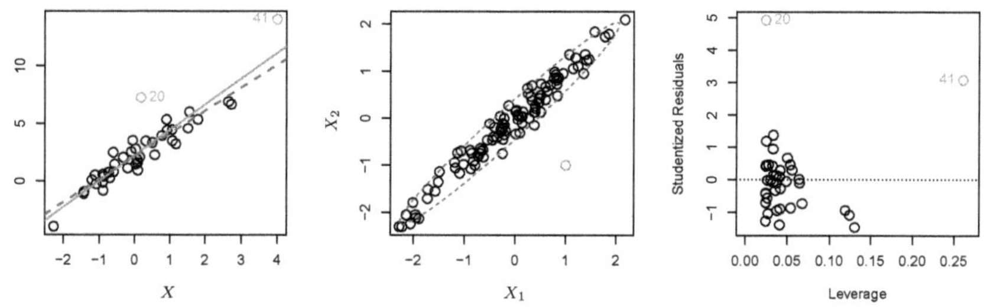

FIGURE 3.13. Left: *Observation 41 is a high leverage point, while 20 is not. The red line is the fit to all the data, and the blue line is the fit with observation 41 removed.* Center: *The red observation is not unusual in terms of its X_1 value or its X_2 value, but still falls outside the bulk of the data, and hence has high leverage.* Right: *Observation* 41 *has a high leverage and a high residual.*

panel of Figure 3.13 has high leverage, in that the predictor value for this observation is large relative to the other observations. (Note that the data displayed in Figure 3.13 are the same as the data displayed in Figure 3.12, but with the addition of a single high leverage observation.) The red solid line is the least squares fit to the data, while the blue dashed line is the fit produced when observation 41 is removed. Comparing the left-hand panels of Figures 3.12 and 3.13, we observe that removing the high leverage observation has a much more substantial impact on the least squares line than removing the outlier. In fact, high leverage observations tend to have a sizable impact on the estimated regression line. It is cause for concern if the least squares line is heavily affected by just a couple of observations, because any problems with these points may invalidate the entire fit. For this reason, it is important to identify high leverage observations.

In a simple linear regression, high leverage observations are fairly easy to identify, since we can simply look for observations for which the predictor value is outside of the normal range of the observations. But in a multiple linear regression with many predictors, it is possible to have an observation that is well within the range of each individual predictor's values, but that is unusual in terms of the full set of predictors. An example is shown in the center panel of Figure 3.13, for a data set with two predictors, X_1 and X_2. Most of the observations' predictor values fall within the blue dashed ellipse, but the red observation is well outside of this range. But neither its value for X_1 nor its value for X_2 is unusual. So if we examine just X_1 or just X_2, we will fail to notice this high leverage point. This problem is more pronounced in multiple regression settings with more than two predictors, because then there is no simple way to plot all dimensions of the data simultaneously.

In order to quantify an observation's leverage, we compute the *leverage statistic*. A large value of this statistic indicates an observation with high leverage. For a simple linear regression,

leverage statistic

$$h_i = \frac{1}{n} + \frac{(x_i - \bar{x})^2}{\sum_{i'=1}^{n}(x_{i'} - \bar{x})^2}. \tag{3.37}$$

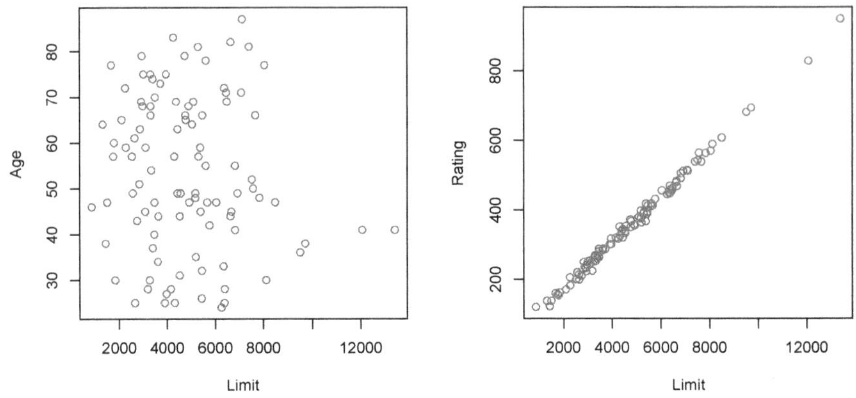

FIGURE 3.14. *Scatterplots of the observations from the* `Credit` *data set.* Left: *A plot of* `age` *versus* `limit`*. These two variables are not collinear.* Right: *A plot of* `rating` *versus* `limit`*. There is high collinearity.*

It is clear from this equation that h_i increases with the distance of x_i from $\bar{x}$. There is a simple extension of h_i to the case of multiple predictors, though we do not provide the formula here. The leverage statistic h_i is always between $1/n$ and 1, and the average leverage for all the observations is always equal to $(p+1)/n$. So if a given observation has a leverage statistic that greatly exceeds $(p+1)/n$, then we may suspect that the corresponding point has high leverage.

The right-hand panel of Figure 3.13 provides a plot of the studentized residuals versus h_i for the data in the left-hand panel of Figure 3.13. Observation 41 stands out as having a very high leverage statistic as well as a high studentized residual. In other words, it is an outlier as well as a high leverage observation. This is a particularly dangerous combination! This plot also reveals the reason that observation 20 had relatively little effect on the least squares fit in Figure 3.12: it has low leverage.

6. Collinearity

Collinearity refers to the situation in which two or more predictor variables are closely related to one another. The concept of collinearity is illustrated in Figure 3.14 using the `Credit` data set. In the left-hand panel of Figure 3.14, the two predictors `limit` and `age` appear to have no obvious relationship. In contrast, in the right-hand panel of Figure 3.14, the predictors `limit` and `rating` are very highly correlated with each other, and we say that they are *collinear*. The presence of collinearity can pose problems in the regression context, since it can be difficult to separate out the individual effects of collinear variables on the response. In other words, since `limit` and `rating` tend to increase or decrease together, it can be difficult to determine how each one separately is associated with the response, `balance`. collinearity

Figure 3.15 illustrates some of the difficulties that can result from collinearity. The left-hand panel of Figure 3.15 is a contour plot of the RSS (3.22) associated with different possible coefficient estimates for the regression of `balance` on `limit` and `age`. Each ellipse represents a set of coefficients

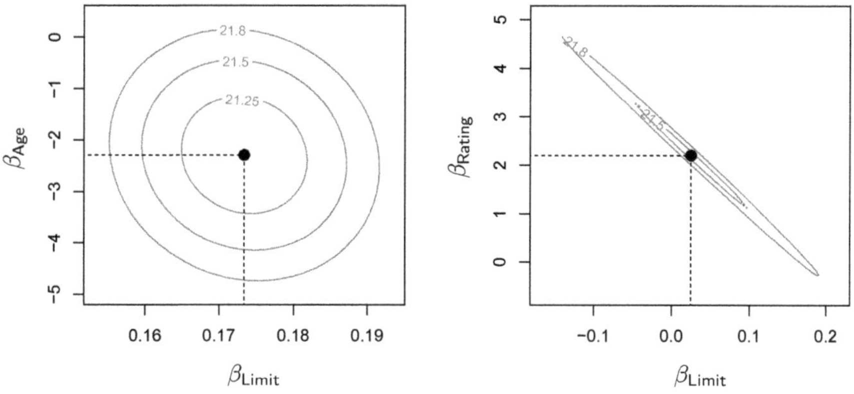

FIGURE 3.15. *Contour plots for the RSS values as a function of the parameters β for various regressions involving the* `Credit` *data set. In each plot, the black dots represent the coefficient values corresponding to the minimum RSS.* Left: *A contour plot of RSS for the regression of* `balance` *onto* `age` *and* `limit`*. The minimum value is well defined.* Right: *A contour plot of RSS for the regression of* `balance` *onto* `rating` *and* `limit`*. Because of the collinearity, there are many pairs ($\beta_{\text{Limit}}, \beta_{\text{Rating}}$) with a similar value for RSS.*

that correspond to the same RSS, with ellipses nearest to the center taking on the lowest values of RSS. The black dots and associated dashed lines represent the coefficient estimates that result in the smallest possible RSS—in other words, these are the least squares estimates. The axes for `limit` and `age` have been scaled so that the plot includes possible coefficient estimates that are up to four standard errors on either side of the least squares estimates. Thus the plot includes all plausible values for the coefficients. For example, we see that the true `limit` coefficient is almost certainly somewhere between 0.15 and 0.20.

In contrast, the right-hand panel of Figure 3.15 displays contour plots of the RSS associated with possible coefficient estimates for the regression of `balance` onto `limit` and `rating`, which we know to be highly collinear. Now the contours run along a narrow valley; there is a broad range of values for the coefficient estimates that result in equal values for RSS. Hence a small change in the data could cause the pair of coefficient values that yield the smallest RSS—that is, the least squares estimates—to move anywhere along this valley. This results in a great deal of uncertainty in the coefficient estimates. Notice that the scale for the `limit` coefficient now runs from roughly -0.2 to 0.2; this is an eight-fold increase over the plausible range of the `limit` coefficient in the regression with `age`. Interestingly, even though the `limit` and `rating` coefficients now have much more individual uncertainty, they will almost certainly lie somewhere in this contour valley. For example, we would not expect the true value of the `limit` and `rating` coefficients to be -0.1 and 1 respectively, even though such a value is plausible for each coefficient individually.

Since collinearity reduces the accuracy of the estimates of the regression coefficients, it causes the standard error for $\hat{\beta}_j$ to grow. Recall that the t-statistic for each predictor is calculated by dividing $\hat{\beta}_j$ by its standard

		Coefficient	Std. error	t-statistic	p-value
Model 1	`Intercept`	−173.411	43.828	−3.957	< 0.0001
	`age`	−2.292	0.672	−3.407	0.0007
	`limit`	0.173	0.005	34.496	< 0.0001
Model 2	`Intercept`	−377.537	45.254	−8.343	< 0.0001
	`rating`	2.202	0.952	2.312	0.0213
	`limit`	0.025	0.064	0.384	0.7012

TABLE 3.11. *The results for two multiple regression models involving the* `Credit` *data set are shown. Model 1 is a regression of* `balance` *on* `age` *and* `limit`*, and Model 2 a regression of* `balance` *on* `rating` *and* `limit`*. The standard error of* $\hat{\beta}_{\text{limit}}$ *increases 12-fold in the second regression, due to collinearity.*

error. Consequently, collinearity results in a decline in the t-statistic. As a result, in the presence of collinearity, we may fail to reject $H_0 : \beta_j = 0$. This means that the *power* of the hypothesis test—the probability of correctly detecting a *non-zero* coefficient—is reduced by collinearity. power

Table 3.11 compares the coefficient estimates obtained from two separate multiple regression models. The first is a regression of `balance` on `age` and `limit`, and the second is a regression of `balance` on `rating` and `limit`. In the first regression, both `age` and `limit` are highly significant with very small p-values. In the second, the collinearity between `limit` and `rating` has caused the standard error for the `limit` coefficient estimate to increase by a factor of 12 and the p-value to increase to 0.701. In other words, the importance of the `limit` variable has been masked due to the presence of collinearity. To avoid such a situation, it is desirable to identify and address potential collinearity problems while fitting the model.

A simple way to detect collinearity is to look at the correlation matrix of the predictors. An element of this matrix that is large in absolute value indicates a pair of highly correlated variables, and therefore a collinearity problem in the data. Unfortunately, not all collinearity problems can be detected by inspection of the correlation matrix: it is possible for collinearity to exist between three or more variables even if no pair of variables has a particularly high correlation. We call this situation *multicollinearity*. Instead of inspecting the correlation matrix, a better way to assess multicollinearity is to compute the *variance inflation factor* (VIF). The VIF is the ratio of the variance of $\hat{\beta}_j$ when fitting the full model divided by the variance of $\hat{\beta}_j$ if fit on its own. The smallest possible value for VIF is 1, which indicates the complete absence of collinearity. Typically in practice there is a small amount of collinearity among the predictors. As a rule of thumb, a VIF value that exceeds 5 or 10 indicates a problematic amount of collinearity. The VIF for each variable can be computed using the formula multi-collinearity variance inflation factor

$$\text{VIF}(\hat{\beta}_j) = \frac{1}{1 - R^2_{X_j|X_{-j}}},$$

where $R^2_{X_j|X_{-j}}$ is the R^2 from a regression of X_j onto all of the other predictors. If $R^2_{X_j|X_{-j}}$ is close to one, then collinearity is present, and so the VIF will be large.

In the `Credit` data, a regression of `balance` on `age`, `rating`, and `limit` indicates that the predictors have VIF values of 1.01, 160.67, and 160.59. As we suspected, there is considerable collinearity in the data!

When faced with the problem of collinearity, there are two simple solutions. The first is to drop one of the problematic variables from the regression. This can usually be done without much compromise to the regression fit, since the presence of collinearity implies that the information that this variable provides about the response is redundant in the presence of the other variables. For instance, if we regress `balance` onto `age` and `limit`, without the `rating` predictor, then the resulting VIF values are close to the minimum possible value of 1, and the R^2 drops from 0.754 to 0.75. So dropping `rating` from the set of predictors has effectively solved the collinearity problem without compromising the fit. The second solution is to combine the collinear variables together into a single predictor. For instance, we might take the average of standardized versions of `limit` and `rating` in order to create a new variable that measures *credit worthiness*.

3.4 The Marketing Plan

We now briefly return to the seven questions about the `Advertising` data that we set out to answer at the beginning of this chapter.

1. *Is there a relationship between sales and advertising budget?*
   This question can be answered by fitting a multiple regression model of `sales` onto `TV`, `radio`, and `newspaper`, as in (3.20), and testing the hypothesis $H_0 : \beta_{\texttt{TV}} = \beta_{\texttt{radio}} = \beta_{\texttt{newspaper}} = 0$. In Section 3.2.2, we showed that the F-statistic can be used to determine whether or not we should reject this null hypothesis. In this case the p-value corresponding to the F-statistic in Table 3.6 is very low, indicating clear evidence of a relationship between advertising and sales.

2. *How strong is the relationship?*
   We discussed two measures of model accuracy in Section 3.1.3. First, the RSE estimates the standard deviation of the response from the population regression line. For the `Advertising` data, the RSE is 1.69 units while the mean value for the response is 14.022, indicating a percentage error of roughly 12 %. Second, the R^2 statistic records the percentage of variability in the response that is explained by the predictors. The predictors explain almost 90 % of the variance in `sales`. The RSE and R^2 statistics are displayed in Table 3.6.

3. *Which media are associated with sales?*
   To answer this question, we can examine the p-values associated with each predictor's t-statistic (Section 3.1.2). In the multiple linear regression displayed in Table 3.4, the p-values for `TV` and `radio` are low, but the p-value for `newspaper` is not. This suggests that only `TV` and `radio` are related to `sales`. In Chapter 6 we explore this question in greater detail.

4. *How large is the association between each medium and sales?*
We saw in Section 3.1.2 that the standard error of $\hat{\beta}_j$ can be used to construct confidence intervals for β_j. For the Advertising data, we can use the results in Table 3.4 to compute the 95 % confidence intervals for the coefficients in a multiple regression model using all three media budgets as predictors. The confidence intervals are as follows: $(0.043, 0.049)$ for TV, $(0.172, 0.206)$ for radio, and $(-0.013, 0.011)$ for newspaper. The confidence intervals for TV and radio are narrow and far from zero, providing evidence that these media are related to sales. But the interval for newspaper includes zero, indicating that the variable is not statistically significant given the values of TV and radio.

   We saw in Section 3.3.3 that collinearity can result in very wide standard errors. Could collinearity be the reason that the confidence interval associated with newspaper is so wide? The VIF scores are 1.005, 1.145, and 1.145 for TV, radio, and newspaper, suggesting no evidence of collinearity.

   In order to assess the association of each medium individually on sales, we can perform three separate simple linear regressions. Results are shown in Tables 3.1 and 3.3. There is evidence of an extremely strong association between TV and sales and between radio and sales. There is evidence of a mild association between newspaper and sales, when the values of TV and radio are ignored.

5. *How accurately can we predict future sales?*
The response can be predicted using (3.21). The accuracy associated with this estimate depends on whether we wish to predict an individual response, $Y = f(X) + \epsilon$, or the average response, $f(X)$ (Section 3.2.2). If the former, we use a prediction interval, and if the latter, we use a confidence interval. Prediction intervals will always be wider than confidence intervals because they account for the uncertainty associated with ϵ, the irreducible error.

6. *Is the relationship linear?*
In Section 3.3.3, we saw that residual plots can be used in order to identify non-linearity. If the relationships are linear, then the residual plots should display no pattern. In the case of the Advertising data, we observe a non-linear effect in Figure 3.5, though this effect could also be observed in a residual plot. In Section 3.3.2, we discussed the inclusion of transformations of the predictors in the linear regression model in order to accommodate non-linear relationships.

7. *Is there synergy among the advertising media?*
The standard linear regression model assumes an additive relationship between the predictors and the response. An additive model is easy to interpret because the association between each predictor and the response is unrelated to the values of the other predictors. However, the additive assumption may be unrealistic for certain data sets. In Section 3.3.2, we showed how to include an interaction term

in the regression model in order to accommodate non-additive relationships. A small p-value associated with the interaction term indicates the presence of such relationships. Figure 3.5 suggested that the `Advertising` data may not be additive. Including an interaction term in the model results in a substantial increase in R^2, from around 90 % to almost 97 %.

3.5 Comparison of Linear Regression with K-Nearest Neighbors

As discussed in Chapter 2, linear regression is an example of a *parametric* approach because it assumes a linear functional form for $f(X)$. Parametric methods have several advantages. They are often easy to fit, because one need estimate only a small number of coefficients. In the case of linear regression, the coefficients have simple interpretations, and tests of statistical significance can be easily performed. But parametric methods do have a disadvantage: by construction, they make strong assumptions about the form of $f(X)$. If the specified functional form is far from the truth, and prediction accuracy is our goal, then the parametric method will perform poorly. For instance, if we assume a linear relationship between X and Y but the true relationship is far from linear, then the resulting model will provide a poor fit to the data, and any conclusions drawn from it will be suspect.

In contrast, *non-parametric* methods do not explicitly assume a parametric form for $f(X)$, and thereby provide an alternative and more flexible approach for performing regression. We discuss various non-parametric methods in this book. Here we consider one of the simplest and best-known non-parametric methods, *K-nearest neighbors regression* (KNN regression). The KNN regression method is closely related to the KNN classifier discussed in Chapter 2. Given a value for K and a prediction point x_0, KNN regression first identifies the K training observations that are closest to x_0, represented by $\mathcal{N}_0$. It then estimates $f(x_0)$ using the average of all the training responses in $\mathcal{N}_0$. In other words,

K-nearest neighbors regression

$$\hat{f}(x_0) = \frac{1}{K} \sum_{x_i \in \mathcal{N}_0} y_i.$$

Figure 3.16 illustrates two KNN fits on a data set with $p = 2$ predictors. The fit with $K = 1$ is shown in the left-hand panel, while the right-hand panel corresponds to $K = 9$. We see that when $K = 1$, the KNN fit perfectly interpolates the training observations, and consequently takes the form of a step function. When $K = 9$, the KNN fit still is a step function, but averaging over nine observations results in much smaller regions of constant prediction, and consequently a smoother fit. In general, the optimal value for K will depend on the *bias-variance tradeoff*, which we introduced in Chapter 2. A small value for K provides the most flexible fit, which will have low bias but high variance. This variance is due to the fact that the prediction in a given region is entirely dependent on just one observation.

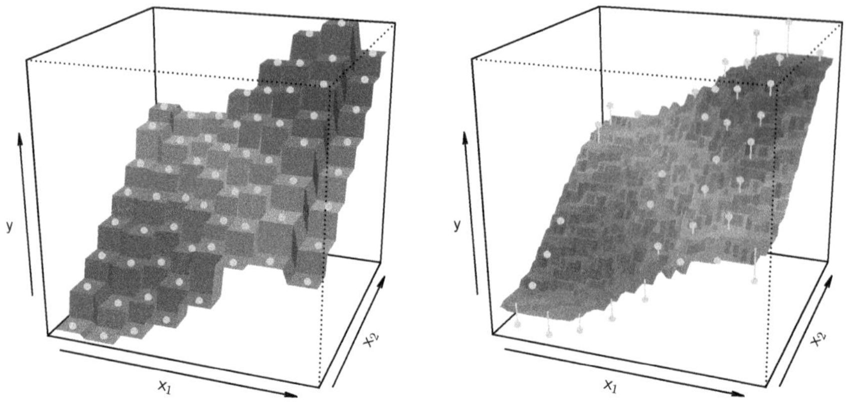

FIGURE 3.16. *Plots of* $\hat{f}(X)$ *using KNN regression on a two-dimensional data set with* 64 *observations (orange dots).* Left: $K = 1$ *results in a rough step function fit.* Right: $K = 9$ *produces a much smoother fit.*

In contrast, larger values of K provide a smoother and less variable fit; the prediction in a region is an average of several points, and so changing one observation has a smaller effect. However, the smoothing may cause bias by masking some of the structure in $f(X)$. In Chapter 5, we introduce several approaches for estimating test error rates. These methods can be used to identify the optimal value of K in KNN regression.

In what setting will a parametric approach such as least squares linear regression outperform a non-parametric approach such as KNN regression? The answer is simple: *the parametric approach will outperform the non-parametric approach if the parametric form that has been selected is close to the true form of* f. Figure 3.17 provides an example with data generated from a one-dimensional linear regression model. The black solid lines represent $f(X)$, while the blue curves correspond to the KNN fits using $K = 1$ and $K = 9$. In this case, the $K = 1$ predictions are far too variable, while the smoother $K = 9$ fit is much closer to $f(X)$. However, since the true relationship is linear, it is hard for a non-parametric approach to compete with linear regression: a non-parametric approach incurs a cost in variance that is not offset by a reduction in bias. The blue dashed line in the left-hand panel of Figure 3.18 represents the linear regression fit to the same data. It is almost perfect. The right-hand panel of Figure 3.18 reveals that linear regression outperforms KNN for this data. The green solid line, plotted as a function of $1/K$, represents the test set mean squared error (MSE) for KNN. The KNN errors are well above the black dashed line, which is the test MSE for linear regression. When the value of K is large, then KNN performs only a little worse than least squares regression in terms of MSE. It performs far worse when K is small.

In practice, the true relationship between X and Y is rarely exactly linear. Figure 3.19 examines the relative performances of least squares regression and KNN under increasing levels of non-linearity in the relationship between X and Y. In the top row, the true relationship is nearly linear. In this case we see that the test MSE for linear regression is still superior

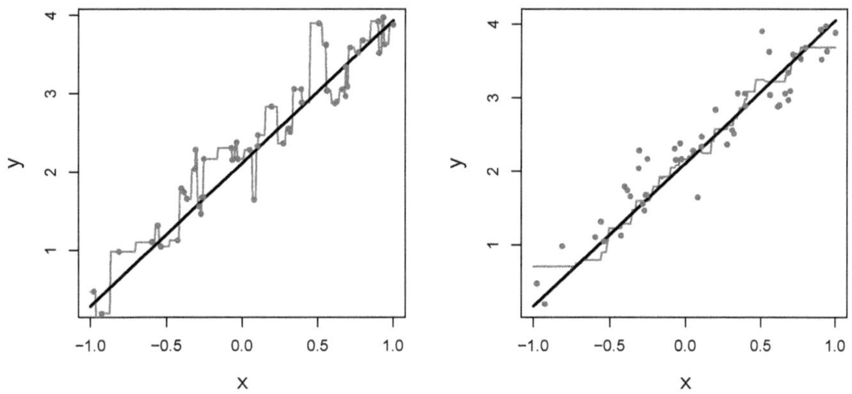

FIGURE 3.17. *Plots of* $\hat{f}(X)$ *using KNN regression on a one-dimensional data set with* 50 *observations. The true relationship is given by the black solid line.* Left: *The blue curve corresponds to* $K = 1$ *and interpolates (i.e. passes directly through) the training data.* Right: *The blue curve corresponds to* $K = 9$, *and represents a smoother fit.*

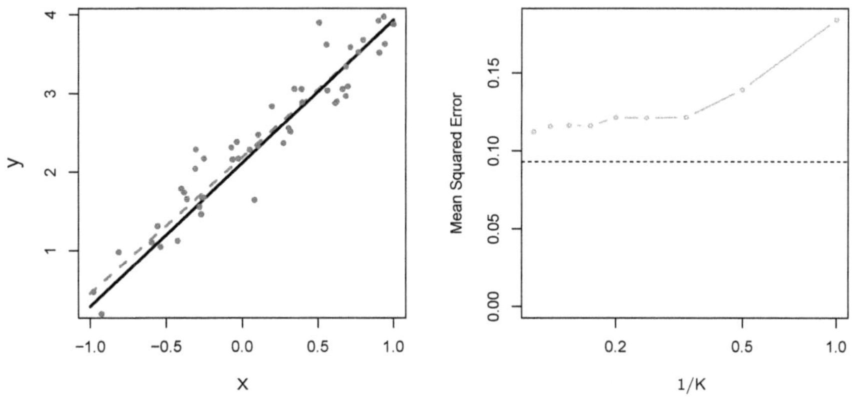

FIGURE 3.18. *The same data set shown in Figure 3.17 is investigated further.* Left: *The blue dashed line is the least squares fit to the data. Since* $f(X)$ *is in fact linear (displayed as the black line), the least squares regression line provides a very good estimate of* $f(X)$. Right: *The dashed horizontal line represents the least squares test set MSE, while the green solid line corresponds to the MSE for KNN as a function of* $1/K$ *(on the log scale). Linear regression achieves a lower test MSE than does KNN regression, since* $f(X)$ *is in fact linear. For KNN regression, the best results occur with a very large value of* K, *corresponding to a small value of* $1/K$.

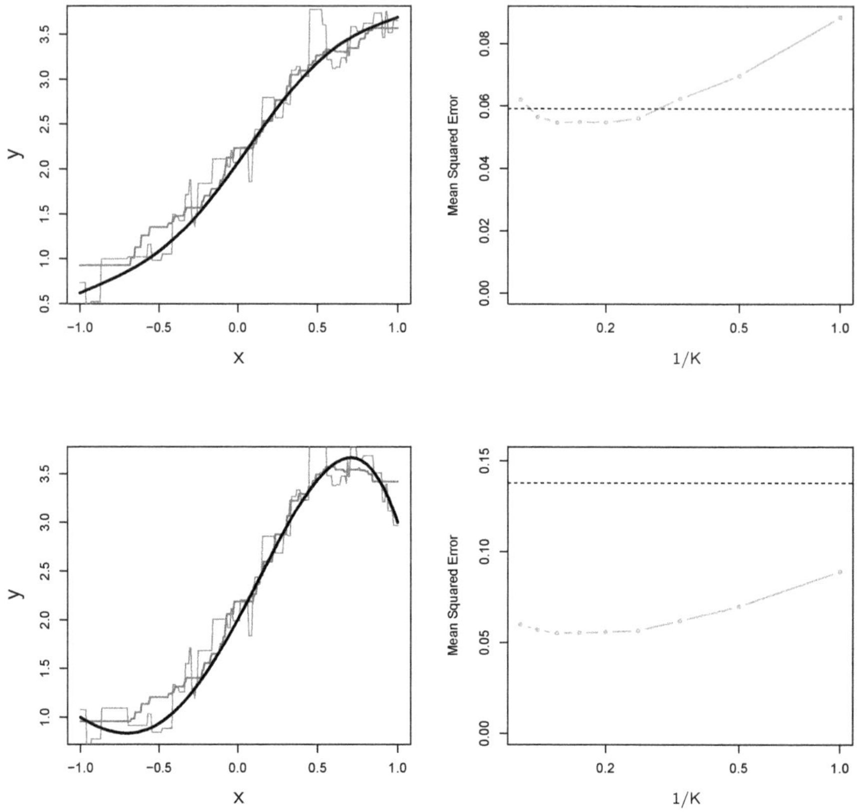

FIGURE 3.19. Top Left: *In a setting with a slightly non-linear relationship between X and Y (solid black line), the KNN fits with $K = 1$ (blue) and $K = 9$ (red) are displayed.* Top Right: *For the slightly non-linear data, the test set MSE for least squares regression (horizontal black) and KNN with various values of $1/K$ (green) are displayed.* Bottom Left and Bottom Right: *As in the top panel, but with a strongly non-linear relationship between X and Y.*

to that of KNN for low values of K. However, for $K \geq 4$, KNN outperforms linear regression. The second row illustrates a more substantial deviation from linearity. In this situation, KNN substantially outperforms linear regression for all values of K. Note that as the extent of non-linearity increases, there is little change in the test set MSE for the non-parametric KNN method, but there is a large increase in the test set MSE of linear regression.

Figures 3.18 and 3.19 display situations in which KNN performs slightly worse than linear regression when the relationship is linear, but much better than linear regression for nonlinear situations. In a real life situation in which the true relationship is unknown, one might suspect that KNN should be favored over linear regression because it will at worst be slightly inferior to linear regression if the true relationship is linear, and may give substantially better results if the true relationship is non-linear. But in reality, even when the true relationship is highly non-linear, KNN may still provide inferior results to linear regression. In particular, both Figures 3.18

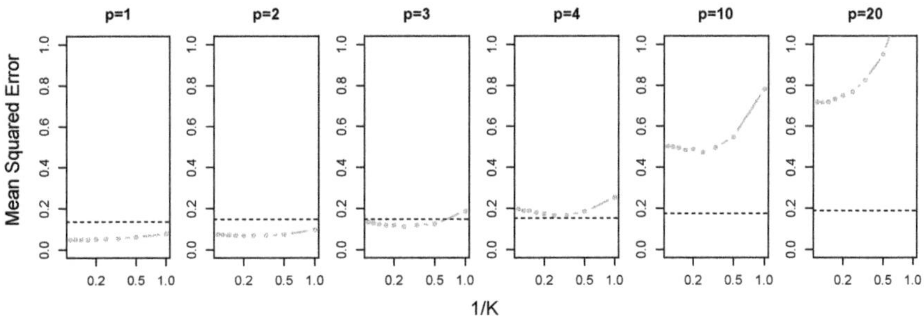

FIGURE 3.20. *Test MSE for linear regression (black dashed lines) and KNN (green curves) as the number of variables p increases. The true function is non-linear in the first variable, as in the lower panel in Figure 3.19, and does not depend on the additional variables. The performance of linear regression deteriorates slowly in the presence of these additional noise variables, whereas KNN's performance degrades much more quickly as p increases.*

and 3.19 illustrate settings with $p = 1$ predictor. But in higher dimensions, KNN often performs worse than linear regression.

Figure 3.20 considers the same strongly non-linear situation as in the second row of Figure 3.19, except that we have added additional *noise* predictors that are not associated with the response. When $p = 1$ or $p = 2$, KNN outperforms linear regression. But for $p = 3$ the results are mixed, and for $p \geq 4$ linear regression is superior to KNN. In fact, the increase in dimension has only caused a small deterioration in the linear regression test set MSE, but it has caused more than a ten-fold increase in the MSE for KNN. This decrease in performance as the dimension increases is a common problem for KNN, and results from the fact that in higher dimensions there is effectively a reduction in sample size. In this data set there are 50 training observations; when $p = 1$, this provides enough information to accurately estimate $f(X)$. However, spreading 50 observations over $p = 20$ dimensions results in a phenomenon in which a given observation has no *nearby neighbors*—this is the so-called *curse of dimensionality*. That is, the K observations that are nearest to a given test observation x_0 may be very far away from x_0 in p-dimensional space when p is large, leading to a very poor prediction of $f(x_0)$ and hence a poor KNN fit. As a general rule, parametric methods will tend to outperform non-parametric approaches when there is a small number of observations per predictor.

curse of dimensionality

Even when the dimension is small, we might prefer linear regression to KNN from an interpretability standpoint. If the test MSE of KNN is only slightly lower than that of linear regression, we might be willing to forego a little bit of prediction accuracy for the sake of a simple model that can be described in terms of just a few coefficients, and for which p-values are available.

3.6 Lab: Linear Regression

3.6.1 Importing packages

We import our standard libraries at this top level.

In [1]:
```
import numpy as np
import pandas as pd
from matplotlib.pyplot import subplots
```

New imports

Throughout this lab we will introduce new functions and libraries. However, we will import them here to emphasize these are the new code objects in this lab. Keeping imports near the top of a notebook makes the code more readable, since scanning the first few lines tells us what libraries are used.

In [2]:
```
import statsmodels.api as sm
```

We will provide relevant details about the functions below as they are needed.

Besides importing whole modules, it is also possible to import only a few items from a given module. This will help keep the *namespace* clean. We will use a few specific objects from the `statsmodels` package which we import here.

namespace

`statsmodels`

In [3]:
```
from statsmodels.stats.outliers_influence \
     import variance_inflation_factor as VIF
from statsmodels.stats.anova import anova_lm
```

As one of the import statements above is quite a long line, we inserted a line break \ to ease readability.

We will also use some functions written for the labs in this book in the `ISLP` package.

In [4]:
```
from ISLP import load_data
from ISLP.models import (ModelSpec as MS,
                         summarize,
                         poly)
```

Inspecting Objects and Namespaces

The function `dir()` provides a list of objects in a namespace.

`dir()`

In [5]:
```
dir()
```

Out[5]:
```
['In',
 'MS',
 '_',
 '__',
 '___',
 '__builtin__',
 '__builtins__',
 ...
```

```
 'poly',
 'quit',
 'sm',
 'summarize']
```

This shows you everything that Python can find at the top level. There are certain objects like `__builtins__` that contain references to built-in functions like `print()`.

Every python object has its own notion of namespace, also accessible with `dir()`. This will include both the attributes of the object as well as any methods associated with it. For instance, we see `'sum'` in the listing for an array.

```
In [6]: A = np.array([3,5,11])
        dir(A)
```

```
Out[6]:  ...
 'strides',
 'sum',
 'swapaxes',
 ...
```

This indicates that the object `A.sum` exists. In this case it is a method that can be used to compute the sum of the array `A` as can be seen by typing `A.sum?`.

```
In [7]: A.sum()
```

```
Out[7]: 19
```

3.6.2 Simple Linear Regression

In this section we will construct model matrices (also called design matrices) using the `ModelSpec()` transform from `ISLP.models`.

We will use the `Boston` housing data set, which is contained in the `ISLP` package. The `Boston` dataset records `medv` (median house value) for 506 neighborhoods around Boston. We will build a regression model to predict `medv` using 13 predictors such as `rmvar` (average number of rooms per house), `age` (proportion of owner-occupied units built prior to 1940), and `lstat` (percent of households with low socioeconomic status). We will use `statsmodels` for this task, a `Python` package that implements several commonly used regression methods.

We have included a simple loading function `load_data()` in the `ISLP` package: `load_data()`

```
In [8]: Boston = load_data("Boston")
        Boston.columns
```

```
Out[8]: Index(['crim', 'zn', 'indus', 'chas', 'nox', 'rm', 'age', 'dis',
               'rad', 'tax', 'ptratio', 'black', 'lstat', 'medv'],
              dtype='object')
```

Type `Boston?` to find out more about these data.

We start by using the `sm.OLS()` function to fit a simple linear regression model. Our response will be `medv` and `lstat` will be the single predictor. For this model, we can create the model matrix by hand. `sm.OLS()`

In [9]:
```
X = pd.DataFrame({'intercept': np.ones(Boston.shape[0]),
                  'lstat': Boston['lstat']})
X[:4]
```

Out[9]:
```
   intercept  lstat
0        1.0   4.98
1        1.0   9.14
2        1.0   4.03
3        1.0   2.94
```

We extract the response, and fit the model.

In [10]:
```
y = Boston['medv']
model = sm.OLS(y, X)
results = model.fit()
```

Note that `sm.OLS()` does not fit the model; it specifies the model, and then `model.fit()` does the actual fitting.

Our `ISLP` function `summarize()` produces a simple table of the parameter estimates, their standard errors, t-statistics and p-values. The function takes a single argument, such as the object `results` returned here by the `fit` method, and returns such a summary. `summarize()`

In [11]:
```
summarize(results)
```

Out[11]:
```
              coef  std err        t  P>|t|
intercept  34.5538    0.563   61.415    0.0
lstat      -0.9500    0.039  -24.528    0.0
```

Before we describe other methods for working with fitted models, we outline a more useful and general framework for constructing a model matrix `X`.

Using Transformations: Fit and Transform

Our model above has a single predictor, and constructing `X` was straightforward. In practice we often fit models with more than one predictor, typically selected from an array or data frame. We may wish to introduce transformations to the variables before fitting the model, specify interactions between variables, and expand some particular variables into sets of variables (e.g. polynomials). The `sklearn` package has a particular notion for this type of task: a *transform*. A transform is an object that is created with some parameters as arguments. The object has two main methods: `fit()` and `transform()`. `sklearn`

We provide a general approach for specifying models and constructing the model matrix through the transform `ModelSpec()` in the `ISLP` library. `ModelSpec()` (renamed `MS()` in the preamble) creates a transform object, and then a pair of methods `transform()` and `fit()` are used to construct a corresponding model matrix. `.fit()` `.transform()` `ModelSpec()`

We first describe this process for our simple regression model using a single predictor `lstat` in the `Boston` data frame, but will use it repeatedly in more complex tasks in this and other labs in this book. In our case the transform is created by the expression `design = MS(['lstat'])`.

The `fit()` method takes the original array and may do some initial computations on it, as specified in the transform object. For example, it may compute means and standard deviations for centering and scaling. The `transform()` method applies the fitted transformation to the array of data, and produces the model matrix.

```
In [12]: design = MS(['lstat'])
         design = design.fit(Boston)
         X = design.transform(Boston)
         X[:4]
```

```
Out[12]:    intercept  lstat
         0        1.0   4.98
         1        1.0   9.14
         2        1.0   4.03
         3        1.0   2.94
```

In this simple case, the `fit()` method does very little; it simply checks that the variable `'lstat'` specified in `design` exists in `Boston`. Then `transform()` constructs the model matrix with two columns: an `intercept` and the variable `lstat`.

These two operations can be combined with the `fit_transform()` method.

.fit_
transform()

```
In [13]: design = MS(['lstat'])
         X = design.fit_transform(Boston)
         X[:4]
```

```
Out[13]:    intercept  lstat
         0        1.0   4.98
         1        1.0   9.14
         2        1.0   4.03
         3        1.0   2.94
```

Note that, as in the previous code chunk when the two steps were done separately, the `design` object is changed as a result of the `fit()` operation. The power of this pipeline will become clearer when we fit more complex models that involve interactions and transformations.

Let's return to our fitted regression model. The object `results` has several methods that can be used for inference. We already presented a function `summarize()` for showing the essentials of the fit. For a full and somewhat exhaustive summary of the fit, we can use the `summary()` method (output not shown).

```
In [14]: results.summary()
```

The fitted coefficients can also be retrieved as the `params` attribute of `results`.

```
In [15]: results.params
```

```
Out[15]: intercept    34.553841
         lstat        -0.950049
         dtype: float64
```

The `get_prediction()` method can be used to obtain predictions, and produce confidence intervals and prediction intervals for the prediction of `medv` for given values of `lstat`.

.get_
prediction()

We first create a new data frame, in this case containing only the variable `lstat`, with the values for this variable at which we wish to make predictions. We then use the `transform()` method of `design` to create the corresponding model matrix.

```
In [16]: new_df = pd.DataFrame({'lstat':[5, 10, 15]})
         newX = design.transform(new_df)
         newX
```

```
Out[16]:   intercept  lstat
         0       1.0      5
         1       1.0     10
         2       1.0     15
```

Next we compute the predictions at `newX`, and view them by extracting the `predicted_mean` attribute.

```
In [17]: new_predictions = results.get_prediction(newX);
         new_predictions.predicted_mean
```

```
Out[17]: array([29.80359411, 25.05334734, 20.30310057])
```

We can produce confidence intervals for the predicted values.

```
In [18]: new_predictions.conf_int(alpha=0.05)
```

```
Out[18]: array([[29.00741194, 30.59977628],
                [24.47413202, 25.63256267],
                [19.73158815, 20.87461299]])
```

Prediction intervals are computing by setting `obs=True`:

```
In [19]: new_predictions.conf_int(obs=True, alpha=0.05)
```

```
Out[19]: array([[17.56567478, 42.04151344],
                [12.82762635, 37.27906833],
                [ 8.0777421 , 32.52845905]])
```

For instance, the 95% confidence interval associated with an `lstat` value of 10 is (24.47, 25.63), and the 95% prediction interval is (12.82, 37.28). As expected, the confidence and prediction intervals are centered around the same point (a predicted value of 25.05 for `medv` when `lstat` equals 10), but the latter are substantially wider.

Next we will plot `medv` and `lstat` using `DataFrame.plot.scatter()`, and wish to add the regression line to the resulting plot.

.plot.
scatter()

Defining Functions

While there is a function within the ISLP package that adds a line to an existing plot, we take this opportunity to define our first function to do so. def

In [20]:
```
def abline(ax, b, m):
    "Add a line with slope m and intercept b to ax"
    xlim = ax.get_xlim()
    ylim = [m * xlim[0] + b, m * xlim[1] + b]
    ax.plot(xlim, ylim)
```

A few things are illustrated above. First we see the syntax for defining a function: `def funcname(...)`. The function has arguments `ax, b, m` where `ax` is an axis object for an exisiting plot, `b` is the intercept and `m` is the slope of the desired line. Other plotting options can be passed on to `ax.plot` by including additional optional arguments as follows:

In [21]:
```
def abline(ax, b, m, *args, **kwargs):
    "Add a line with slope m and intercept b to ax"
    xlim = ax.get_xlim()
    ylim = [m * xlim[0] + b, m * xlim[1] + b]
    ax.plot(xlim, ylim, *args, **kwargs)
```

The addition of `*args` allows any number of non-named arguments to `abline`, while `*kwargs` allows any number of named arguments (such as `linewidth=3`) to `abline`. In our function, we pass these arguments verbatim to `ax.plot` above. Readers interested in learning more about functions are referred to the section on defining functions in docs.python.org/tutorial.

Let's use our new function to add this regression line to a plot of `medv` vs. `lstat`.

In [22]:
```
ax = Boston.plot.scatter('lstat', 'medv')
abline(ax,
       results.params[0],
       results.params[1],
       'r--',
       linewidth=3)
```

Thus, the final call to `ax.plot()` is `ax.plot(xlim, ylim, 'r--', linewidth=3)`. We have used the argument `'r--'` to produce a red dashed line, and added an argument to make it of width 3. There is some evidence for non-linearity in the relationship between `lstat` and `medv`. We will explore this issue later in this lab.

As mentioned above, there is an existing function to add a line to a plot — `ax.axline()` — but knowing how to write such functions empowers us to create more expressive displays.

Next we examine some diagnostic plots, several of which were discussed in Section 3.3.3. We can find the fitted values and residuals of the fit as attributes of the `results` object. Various influence measures describing the regression model are computed with the `get_influence()` method. As we will not use the `fig` component returned as the first value from `subplots()`, we simply capture the second returned value in `ax` below. .get_influence()

In [23]:
```
ax = subplots(figsize=(8,8))[1]
```

```
ax.scatter(results.fittedvalues, results.resid)
ax.set_xlabel('Fitted value')
ax.set_ylabel('Residual')
ax.axhline(0, c='k', ls='--');
```

We add a horizontal line at 0 for reference using the `ax.axhline()` method, indicating it should be black (`c='k'`) and have a dashed linestyle (`ls='--'`).

.axhline()

On the basis of the residual plot (not shown), there is some evidence of non-linearity. Leverage statistics can be computed for any number of predictors using the `hat_matrix_diag` attribute of the value returned by the `get_influence()` method.

In [24]:
```
infl = results.get_influence()
ax = subplots(figsize=(8,8))[1]
ax.scatter(np.arange(X.shape[0]), infl.hat_matrix_diag)
ax.set_xlabel('Index')
ax.set_ylabel('Leverage')
np.argmax(infl.hat_matrix_diag)
```

Out[24]: 374

The `np.argmax()` function identifies the index of the largest element of an array, optionally computed over an axis of the array. In this case, we maximized over the entire array to determine which observation has the largest leverage statistic.

np.argmax()

3.6.3 *Multiple Linear Regression*

In order to fit a multiple linear regression model using least squares, we again use the `ModelSpec()` transform to construct the required model matrix and response. The arguments to `ModelSpec()` can be quite general, but in this case a list of column names suffice. We consider a fit here with the two variables `lstat` and `age`.

In [25]:
```
X = MS(['lstat', 'age']).fit_transform(Boston)
model1 = sm.OLS(y, X)
results1 = model1.fit()
summarize(results1)
```

Out[25]:

	coef	std err	t	P>|t|
intercept	33.2228	0.731	45.458	0.000
lstat	-1.0321	0.048	-21.416	0.000
age	0.0345	0.012	2.826	0.005

Notice how we have compacted the first line into a succinct expression describing the construction of `X`.

The `Boston` data set contains 12 variables, and so it would be cumbersome to have to type all of these in order to perform a regression using all of the predictors. Instead, we can use the following short-hand:

.columns.drop()

In [26]:
```
terms = Boston.columns.drop('medv')
terms
```

```
Out[26]: Index(['crim', 'zn', 'indus', 'chas', 'nox', 'rm', 'age', 'dis',
               'rad', 'tax', 'ptratio', 'lstat'],
              dtype='object')
```

We can now fit the model with all the variables in `terms` using the same model matrix builder.

```
In [27]: X = MS(terms).fit_transform(Boston)
         model = sm.OLS(y, X)
         results = model.fit()
         summarize(results)
```

```
Out[27]:
                coef  std err       t  P>|t|
intercept    41.6173    4.936   8.431  0.000
crim         -0.1214    0.033  -3.678  0.000
zn            0.0470    0.014   3.384  0.001
indus         0.0135    0.062   0.217  0.829
chas          2.8400    0.870   3.264  0.001
nox         -18.7580    3.851  -4.870  0.000
rm            3.6581    0.420   8.705  0.000
age           0.0036    0.013   0.271  0.787
dis          -1.4908    0.202  -7.394  0.000
rad           0.2894    0.067   4.325  0.000
tax          -0.0127    0.004  -3.337  0.001
ptratio      -0.9375    0.132  -7.091  0.000
lstat        -0.5520    0.051 -10.897  0.000
```

What if we would like to perform a regression using all of the variables but one? For example, in the above regression output, `age` has a high p-value. So we may wish to run a regression excluding this predictor. The following syntax results in a regression using all predictors except `age` (output not shown).

```
In [28]: minus_age = Boston.columns.drop(['medv', 'age'])
         Xma = MS(minus_age).fit_transform(Boston)
         model1 = sm.OLS(y, Xma)
         summarize(model1.fit())
```

3.6.4 *Multivariate Goodness of Fit*

We can access the individual components of `results` by name (`dir(results)` shows us what is available). Hence `results.rsquared` gives us the R^2, and `np.sqrt(results.scale)` gives us the RSE.

Variance inflation factors (section 3.3.3) are sometimes useful to assess the effect of collinearity in the model matrix of a regression model. We will compute the VIFs in our multiple regression fit, and use the opportunity to introduce the idea of *list comprehension*.

list comprehension

List Comprehension

Often we encounter a sequence of objects which we would like to transform for some other task. Below, we compute the VIF for each feature in our `X` matrix and produce a data frame whose index agrees with the columns of `X`. The notion of list comprehension can often make such a task easier.

List comprehensions are simple and powerful ways to form lists of Python objects. The language also supports dictionary and *generator* comprehension, though these are beyond our scope here. Let's look at an example. We compute the VIF for each of the variables in the model matrix X, using the function variance_inflation_factor().

variance_
inflation_
factor()

In [29]:
```
vals = [VIF(X, i)
        for i in range(1, X.shape[1])]
vif = pd.DataFrame({'vif':vals},
                   index=X.columns[1:])
vif
```

Out[29]:
```
            vif
crim      1.767
zn        2.298
indus     3.987
chas      1.071
nox       4.369
rm        1.913
age       3.088
dis       3.954
rad       7.445
tax       9.002
ptratio 1.797
lstat     2.871
```

The function VIF() takes two arguments: a dataframe or array, and a variable column index. In the code above we call VIF() on the fly for all columns in X. We have excluded column 0 above (the intercept), which is not of interest. In this case the VIFs are not that exciting.

The object vals above could have been constructed with the following for loop:

In [30]:
```
vals = []
for i in range(1, X.values.shape[1]):
    vals.append(VIF(X.values, i))
```

List comprehension allows us to perform such repetitive operations in a more straightforward way.

3.6.5 Interaction Terms

It is easy to include interaction terms in a linear model using ModelSpec(). Including a tuple ("lstat","age") tells the model matrix builder to include an interaction term between lstat and age.

In [31]:
```
X = MS(['lstat',
        'age',
        ('lstat', 'age')]).fit_transform(Boston)
model2 = sm.OLS(y, X)
summarize(model2.fit())
```

Out[31]:
```
                coef   std err        t   P>|t|
intercept    36.0885     1.470   24.553   0.000
    lstat    -1.3921     0.167   -8.313   0.000
```

```
      age    -0.0007     0.020    -0.036    0.971
lstat:age     0.0042     0.002     2.244    0.025
```

3.6.6 Non-linear Transformations of the Predictors

The model matrix builder can include terms beyond just column names and interactions. For instance, the `poly()` function supplied in `ISLP` specifies that columns representing polynomial functions of its first argument are added to the model matrix. `poly()`

In [32]:
```
X = MS([poly('lstat', degree=2), 'age']).fit_transform(Boston)
model3 = sm.OLS(y, X)
results3 = model3.fit()
summarize(results3)
```

Out[32]:
```
                            coef    std err          t     P>|t|
              intercept  17.7151      0.781     22.681     0.000
poly(lstat, degree=2)[0] -179.2279    6.733    -26.620     0.000
poly(lstat, degree=2)[1]  72.9908     5.482     13.315     0.000
                    age   0.0703      0.011      6.471     0.000
```

The effectively zero *p*-value associated with the quadratic term (i.e. the third row above) suggests that it leads to an improved model.

By default, `poly()` creates a basis matrix for inclusion in the model matrix whose columns are *orthogonal polynomials*, which are designed for stable least squares computations.[13] Alternatively, had we included an argument `raw=True` in the above call to `poly()`, the basis matrix would consist simply of `lstat` and `lstat**2`. Since either of these bases represent quadratic polynomials, the fitted values would not change in this case, just the polynomial coefficients. Also by default, the columns created by `poly()` do not include an intercept column as that is automatically added by `MS()`. orthogonal polynomial

We use the `anova_lm()` function to further quantify the extent to which the quadratic fit is superior to the linear fit. `anova_lm()`

In [33]:
```
anova_lm(results1, results3)
```

Out[33]:
```
   df_resid        ssr  df_diff   ss_diff       F      Pr(>F)
0     503.0   19168.13      0.0       NaN     NaN         NaN
1     502.0   14165.61      1.0   5002.52  177.28    7.47e-35
```

Here `results1` represents the linear submodel containing predictors `lstat` and `age`, while `results3` corresponds to the larger model above with a quadratic term in `lstat`. The `anova_lm()` function performs a hypothesis test comparing the two models. The null hypothesis is that the quadratic term in the bigger model is not needed, and the alternative hypothesis is that the bigger model is superior. Here the *F*-statistic is 177.28 and the associated *p*-value is zero. In this case the *F*-statistic is the square of the *t*-statistic for the quadratic term in the linear model summary for `results3` — a consequence of the fact that these nested models differ by one degree of

[13] Actually, `poly()` is a wrapper for the workhorse and standalone function `Poly()` that does the work in building the model matrix.

freedom. This provides very clear evidence that the quadratic polynomial in lstat improves the linear model. This is not surprising, since earlier we saw evidence for non-linearity in the relationship between medv and lstat.

The function anova_lm() can take more than two nested models as input, in which case it compares every successive pair of models. That also explains why their are NaNs in the first row above, since there is no previous model with which to compare the first.

In [34]:
```
ax = subplots(figsize=(8,8))[1]
ax.scatter(results3.fittedvalues, results3.resid)
ax.set_xlabel('Fitted value')
ax.set_ylabel('Residual')
ax.axhline(0, c='k', ls='--')
```

We see that when the quadratic term is included in the model, there is little discernible pattern in the residuals. In order to create a cubic or higher-degree polynomial fit, we can simply change the degree argument to poly().

3.6.7 *Qualitative Predictors*

Here we use the Carseats data, which is included in the ISLP package. We will attempt to predict Sales (child car seat sales) in 400 locations based on a number of predictors.

In [35]:
```
Carseats = load_data('Carseats')
Carseats.columns
```

Out[35]:
```
Index(['Sales', 'CompPrice', 'Income', 'Advertising',
       'Population', 'Price', 'ShelveLoc', 'Age', 'Education',
       'Urban', 'US'],
      dtype='object')
```

The Carseats data includes qualitative predictors such as ShelveLoc, an indicator of the quality of the shelving location — that is, the space within a store in which the car seat is displayed. The predictor ShelveLoc takes on three possible values, Bad, Medium, and Good. Given a qualitative variable such as ShelveLoc, ModelSpec() generates dummy variables automatically. These variables are often referred to as a *one-hot encoding* of the categorical feature. Their columns sum to one, so to avoid collinearity with an intercept, the first column is dropped. Below we see the column ShelveLoc[Bad] has been dropped, since Bad is the first level of ShelveLoc. Below we fit a multiple regression model that includes some interaction terms.

one-hot encoding

In [36]:
```
allvars = list(Carseats.columns.drop('Sales'))
y = Carseats['Sales']
final = allvars + [('Income', 'Advertising'),
                   ('Price', 'Age')]
X = MS(final).fit_transform(Carseats)
model = sm.OLS(y, X)
summarize(model.fit())
```

Out[36]:
```
                      coef   std err        t    P>|t|
         intercept  6.5756     1.009    6.519    0.000
```

CompPrice	0.0929	0.004	22.567	0.000
Income	0.0109	0.003	4.183	0.000
Advertising	0.0702	0.023	3.107	0.002
Population	0.0002	0.000	0.433	0.665
Price	-0.1008	0.007	-13.549	0.000
ShelveLoc[Good]	4.8487	0.153	31.724	0.000
ShelveLoc[Medium]	1.9533	0.126	15.531	0.000
Age	-0.0579	0.016	-3.633	0.000
Education	-0.0209	0.020	-1.063	0.288
Urban[Yes]	0.1402	0.112	1.247	0.213
US[Yes]	-0.1576	0.149	-1.058	0.291
Income:Advertising	0.0008	0.000	2.698	0.007
Price:Age	0.0001	0.000	0.801	0.424

In the first line above, we made `allvars` a list, so that we could add the interaction terms two lines down. Our model-matrix builder has created a `ShelveLoc[Good]` dummy variable that takes on a value of 1 if the shelving location is good, and 0 otherwise. It has also created a `ShelveLoc[Medium]` dummy variable that equals 1 if the shelving location is medium, and 0 otherwise. A bad shelving location corresponds to a zero for each of the two dummy variables. The fact that the coefficient for `ShelveLoc[Good]` in the regression output is positive indicates that a good shelving location is associated with high sales (relative to a bad location). And `ShelveLoc[Medium]` has a smaller positive coefficient, indicating that a medium shelving location leads to higher sales than a bad shelving location, but lower sales than a good shelving location.

3.7 Exercises

Conceptual

1. Describe the null hypotheses to which the p-values given in Table 3.4 correspond. Explain what conclusions you can draw based on these p-values. Your explanation should be phrased in terms of `sales`, `TV`, `radio`, and `newspaper`, rather than in terms of the coefficients of the linear model.

2. Carefully explain the differences between the KNN classifier and KNN regression methods.

3. Suppose we have a data set with five predictors, X_1 = GPA, X_2 = IQ, X_3 = Level (1 for College and 0 for High School), X_4 = Interaction between GPA and IQ, and X_5 = Interaction between GPA and Level. The response is starting salary after graduation (in thousands of dollars). Suppose we use least squares to fit the model, and get $\hat{\beta}_0 = 50, \hat{\beta}_1 = 20, \hat{\beta}_2 = 0.07, \hat{\beta}_3 = 35, \hat{\beta}_4 = 0.01, \hat{\beta}_5 = -10$.

   (a) Which answer is correct, and why?

      i. For a fixed value of IQ and GPA, high school graduates earn more, on average, than college graduates.

      ii. For a fixed value of IQ and GPA, college graduates earn more, on average, than high school graduates.

iii. For a fixed value of IQ and GPA, high school graduates earn more, on average, than college graduates provided that the GPA is high enough.

iv. For a fixed value of IQ and GPA, college graduates earn more, on average, than high school graduates provided that the GPA is high enough.

(b) Predict the salary of a college graduate with IQ of 110 and a GPA of 4.0.

(c) True or false: Since the coefficient for the GPA/IQ interaction term is very small, there is very little evidence of an interaction effect. Justify your answer.

4. I collect a set of data ($n = 100$ observations) containing a single predictor and a quantitative response. I then fit a linear regression model to the data, as well as a separate cubic regression, i.e. $Y = \beta_0 + \beta_1 X + \beta_2 X^2 + \beta_3 X^3 + \epsilon$.

(a) Suppose that the true relationship between X and Y is linear, i.e. $Y = \beta_0 + \beta_1 X + \epsilon$. Consider the training residual sum of squares (RSS) for the linear regression, and also the training RSS for the cubic regression. Would we expect one to be lower than the other, would we expect them to be the same, or is there not enough information to tell? Justify your answer.

(b) Answer (a) using test rather than training RSS.

(c) Suppose that the true relationship between X and Y is not linear, but we don't know how far it is from linear. Consider the training RSS for the linear regression, and also the training RSS for the cubic regression. Would we expect one to be lower than the other, would we expect them to be the same, or is there not enough information to tell? Justify your answer.

(d) Answer (c) using test rather than training RSS.

5. Consider the fitted values that result from performing linear regression without an intercept. In this setting, the ith fitted value takes the form

$$\hat{y}_i = x_i \hat{\beta},$$

where

$$\hat{\beta} = \left(\sum_{i=1}^{n} x_i y_i \right) \Bigg/ \left(\sum_{i'=1}^{n} x_{i'}^2 \right). \tag{3.38}$$

Show that we can write

$$\hat{y}_i = \sum_{i'=1}^{n} a_{i'} y_{i'}.$$

What is $a_{i'}$?

Note: We interpret this result by saying that the fitted values from linear regression are linear combinations *of the response values.*

6. Using (3.4), argue that in the case of simple linear regression, the least squares line always passes through the point $(\bar{x}, \bar{y})$.

7. It is claimed in the text that in the case of simple linear regression of Y onto X, the R^2 statistic (3.17) is equal to the square of the correlation between X and Y (3.18). Prove that this is the case. For simplicity, you may assume that $\bar{x} = \bar{y} = 0$.

Applied

8. This question involves the use of simple linear regression on the `Auto` data set.

   (a) Use the `sm.OLS()` function to perform a simple linear regression with `mpg` as the response and `horsepower` as the predictor. Use the `summarize()` function to print the results. Comment on the output. For example:

      i. Is there a relationship between the predictor and the response?

      ii. How strong is the relationship between the predictor and the response?

      iii. Is the relationship between the predictor and the response positive or negative?

      iv. What is the predicted `mpg` associated with a `horsepower` of 98? What are the associated 95 % confidence and prediction intervals?

   (b) Plot the response and the predictor in a new set of axes `ax`. Use the `ax.axline()` method or the `abline()` function defined in the lab to display the least squares regression line.

   (c) Produce some of diagnostic plots of the least squares regression fit as described in the lab. Comment on any problems you see with the fit.

9. This question involves the use of multiple linear regression on the `Auto` data set.

   (a) Produce a scatterplot matrix which includes all of the variables in the data set.

   (b) Compute the matrix of correlations between the variables using the `DataFrame.corr()` method.

   `.corr()`

   (c) Use the `sm.OLS()` function to perform a multiple linear regression with `mpg` as the response and all other variables except `name` as the predictors. Use the `summarize()` function to print the results. Comment on the output. For instance:

      i. Is there a relationship between the predictors and the response? Use the `anova_lm()` function from `statsmodels` to answer this question.

ii. Which predictors appear to have a statistically significant relationship to the response?

iii. What does the coefficient for the `year` variable suggest?

(d) Produce some of diagnostic plots of the linear regression fit as described in the lab. Comment on any problems you see with the fit. Do the residual plots suggest any unusually large outliers? Does the leverage plot identify any observations with unusually high leverage?

(e) Fit some models with interactions as described in the lab. Do any interactions appear to be statistically significant?

(f) Try a few different transformations of the variables, such as $\log(X)$, $\sqrt{X}$, X^2. Comment on your findings.

10. This question should be answered using the `Carseats` data set.

(a) Fit a multiple regression model to predict `Sales` using `Price`, `Urban`, and `US`.

(b) Provide an interpretation of each coefficient in the model. Be careful—some of the variables in the model are qualitative!

(c) Write out the model in equation form, being careful to handle the qualitative variables properly.

(d) For which of the predictors can you reject the null hypothesis $H_0 : \beta_j = 0$?

(e) On the basis of your response to the previous question, fit a smaller model that only uses the predictors for which there is evidence of association with the outcome.

(f) How well do the models in (a) and (e) fit the data?

(g) Using the model from (e), obtain 95 % confidence intervals for the coefficient(s).

(h) Is there evidence of outliers or high leverage observations in the model from (e)?

11. In this problem we will investigate the t-statistic for the null hypothesis $H_0 : \beta = 0$ in simple linear regression without an intercept. To begin, we generate a predictor `x` and a response `y` as follows.

```
rng = np.random.default_rng(1)
x = rng.normal(size=100)
y = 2 * x + rng.normal(size=100)
```

(a) Perform a simple linear regression of `y` onto `x`, *without* an intercept. Report the coefficient estimate $\hat{\beta}$, the standard error of this coefficient estimate, and the t-statistic and p-value associated with the null hypothesis $H_0 : \beta = 0$. Comment on these results. (You can perform regression without an intercept using the keywords argument `intercept=False` to `ModelSpec()`.)

(b) Now perform a simple linear regression of `x` onto `y` without an intercept, and report the coefficient estimate, its standard error, and the corresponding t-statistic and p-values associated with the null hypothesis $H_0 : \beta = 0$. Comment on these results.

(c) What is the relationship between the results obtained in (a) and (b)?

(d) For the regression of Y onto X without an intercept, the t-statistic for $H_0 : \beta = 0$ takes the form $\hat{\beta}/\text{SE}(\hat{\beta})$, where $\hat{\beta}$ is given by (3.38), and where

$$\text{SE}(\hat{\beta}) = \sqrt{\frac{\sum_{i=1}^{n}(y_i - x_i\hat{\beta})^2}{(n-1)\sum_{i'=1}^{n} x_{i'}^2}}.$$

(These formulas are slightly different from those given in Sections 3.1.1 and 3.1.2, since here we are performing regression without an intercept.) Show algebraically, and confirm numerically in `R`, that the t-statistic can be written as

$$\frac{(\sqrt{n-1})\sum_{i=1}^{n} x_i y_i}{\sqrt{(\sum_{i=1}^{n} x_i^2)(\sum_{i'=1}^{n} y_{i'}^2) - (\sum_{i'=1}^{n} x_{i'} y_{i'})^2}}.$$

(e) Using the results from (d), argue that the t-statistic for the regression of `y` onto `x` is the same as the t-statistic for the regression of `x` onto `y`.

(f) In `R`, show that when regression is performed *with* an intercept, the t-statistic for $H_0 : \beta_1 = 0$ is the same for the regression of `y` onto `x` as it is for the regression of `x` onto `y`.

12. This problem involves simple linear regression without an intercept.

(a) Recall that the coefficient estimate $\hat{\beta}$ for the linear regression of Y onto X without an intercept is given by (3.38). Under what circumstance is the coefficient estimate for the regression of X onto Y the same as the coefficient estimate for the regression of Y onto X?

(b) Generate an example in `Python` with $n = 100$ observations in which the coefficient estimate for the regression of X onto Y is *different from* the coefficient estimate for the regression of Y onto X.

(c) Generate an example in `Python` with $n = 100$ observations in which the coefficient estimate for the regression of X onto Y is *the same as* the coefficient estimate for the regression of Y onto X.

13. In this exercise you will create some simulated data and will fit simple linear regression models to it. Make sure to use the default random number generator with seed set to 1 prior to starting part (a) to ensure consistent results.

(a) Using the `normal()` method of your random number generator, create a vector, `x`, containing 100 observations drawn from a $N(0, 1)$ distribution. This represents a feature, X.

(b) Using the `normal()` method, create a vector, `eps`, containing 100 observations drawn from a $N(0, 0.25)$ distribution—a normal distribution with mean zero and variance 0.25.

(c) Using `x` and `eps`, generate a vector `y` according to the model

$$Y = -1 + 0.5X + \epsilon. \tag{3.39}$$

What is the length of the vector `y`? What are the values of β_0 and β_1 in this linear model?

(d) Create a scatterplot displaying the relationship between `x` and `y`. Comment on what you observe.

(e) Fit a least squares linear model to predict `y` using `x`. Comment on the model obtained. How do $\hat{\beta}_0$ and $\hat{\beta}_1$ compare to β_0 and β_1?

(f) Display the least squares line on the scatterplot obtained in (d). Draw the population regression line on the plot, in a different color. Use the `legend()` method of the axes to create an appropriate legend.

(g) Now fit a polynomial regression model that predicts `y` using `x` and `x`^{2}. Is there evidence that the quadratic term improves the model fit? Explain your answer.

(h) Repeat (a)–(f) after modifying the data generation process in such a way that there is *less* noise in the data. The model (3.39) should remain the same. You can do this by decreasing the variance of the normal distribution used to generate the error term ϵ in (b). Describe your results.

(i) Repeat (a)–(f) after modifying the data generation process in such a way that there is *more* noise in the data. The model (3.39) should remain the same. You can do this by increasing the variance of the normal distribution used to generate the error term ϵ in (b). Describe your results.

(j) What are the confidence intervals for β_0 and β_1 based on the original data set, the noisier data set, and the less noisy data set? Comment on your results.

14. This problem focuses on the *collinearity* problem.

(a) Perform the following commands in `Python`:

```
rng = np.random.default_rng(10)
x1 = rng.uniform(0, 1, size=100)
x2 = 0.5 * x1 + rng.normal(size=100) / 10
y = 2 + 2 * x1 + 0.3 * x2 + rng.normal(size=100)
```

The last line corresponds to creating a linear model in which `y` is a function of `x1` and `x2`. Write out the form of the linear model. What are the regression coefficients?

(b) What is the correlation between `x1` and `x2`? Create a scatterplot displaying the relationship between the variables.

(c) Using this data, fit a least squares regression to predict `y` using `x1` and `x2`. Describe the results obtained. What are $\hat{\beta}_0$, $\hat{\beta}_1$, and $\hat{\beta}_2$? How do these relate to the true β_0, β_1, and β_2? Can you reject the null hypothesis $H_0 : \beta_1 = 0$? How about the null hypothesis $H_0 : \beta_2 = 0$?

(d) Now fit a least squares regression to predict `y` using only `x1`. Comment on your results. Can you reject the null hypothesis $H_0 : \beta_1 = 0$?

(e) Now fit a least squares regression to predict `y` using only `x2`. Comment on your results. Can you reject the null hypothesis $H_0 : \beta_1 = 0$?

(f) Do the results obtained in (c)–(e) contradict each other? Explain your answer.

(g) Suppose we obtain one additional observation, which was unfortunately mismeasured. We use the function `np.concatenate()` to add this additional observation to each of `x1`, `x2` and `y`.

`np.concatenate()`

```
x1 = np.concatenate([x1, [0.1]])
x2 = np.concatenate([x2, [0.8]])
y = np.concatenate([y, [6]])
```

Re-fit the linear models from (c) to (e) using this new data. What effect does this new observation have on the each of the models? In each model, is this observation an outlier? A high-leverage point? Both? Explain your answers.

15. This problem involves the `Boston` data set, which we saw in the lab for this chapter. We will now try to predict per capita crime rate using the other variables in this data set. In other words, per capita crime rate is the response, and the other variables are the predictors.

(a) For each predictor, fit a simple linear regression model to predict the response. Describe your results. In which of the models is there a statistically significant association between the predictor and the response? Create some plots to back up your assertions.

(b) Fit a multiple regression model to predict the response using all of the predictors. Describe your results. For which predictors can we reject the null hypothesis $H_0 : \beta_j = 0$?

(c) How do your results from (a) compare to your results from (b)? Create a plot displaying the univariate regression coefficients from (a) on the x-axis, and the multiple regression coefficients from (b) on the y-axis. That is, each predictor is displayed as a single point in the plot. Its coefficient in a simple linear regression model is shown on the x-axis, and its coefficient estimate in the multiple linear regression model is shown on the y-axis.

(d) Is there evidence of non-linear association between any of the predictors and the response? To answer this question, for each predictor X, fit a model of the form

$$Y = \beta_0 + \beta_1 X + \beta_2 X^2 + \beta_3 X^3 + \epsilon.$$

4
Classification

The linear regression model discussed in Chapter 3 assumes that the response variable Y is quantitative. But in many situations, the response variable is instead *qualitative*. For example, eye color is qualitative. Often qualitative variables are referred to as *categorical*; we will use these terms interchangeably. In this chapter, we study approaches for predicting qualitative responses, a process that is known as *classification*. Predicting a qualitative response for an observation can be referred to as *classifying* that observation, since it involves assigning the observation to a category, or class. On the other hand, often the methods used for classification first predict the probability that the observation belongs to each of the categories of a qualitative variable, as the basis for making the classification. In this sense they also behave like regression methods.

qualitative

classification

There are many possible classification techniques, or *classifiers*, that one might use to predict a qualitative response. We touched on some of these in Sections 2.1.5 and 2.2.3. In this chapter we discuss some widely-used classifiers: *logistic regression*, *linear discriminant analysis*, *quadratic discriminant analysis*, *naive Bayes*, and *K-nearest neighbors*. The discussion of logistic regression is used as a jumping-off point for a discussion of *generalized linear models*, and in particular, *Poisson regression*. We discuss more computer-intensive classification methods in later chapters: these include generalized additive models (Chapter 7); trees, random forests, and boosting (Chapter 8); and support vector machines (Chapter 9).

classifier

logistic regression

linear discriminant analysis

quadratic discriminant analysis

naive Bayes

K-nearest neighbors

generalized linear models

Poisson regression

4.1 An Overview of Classification

Classification problems occur often, perhaps even more so than regression problems. Some examples include:

G. James et al., *An Introduction to Statistical Learning*, Springer Texts in Statistics,
https://doi.org/10.1007/978-3-031-38747-0_4

1. A person arrives at the emergency room with a set of symptoms that could possibly be attributed to one of three medical conditions. Which of the three conditions does the individual have?

2. An online banking service must be able to determine whether or not a transaction being performed on the site is fraudulent, on the basis of the user's IP address, past transaction history, and so forth.

3. On the basis of DNA sequence data for a number of patients with and without a given disease, a biologist would like to figure out which DNA mutations are deleterious (disease-causing) and which are not.

Just as in the regression setting, in the classification setting we have a set of training observations $(x_1, y_1), \ldots, (x_n, y_n)$ that we can use to build a classifier. We want our classifier to perform well not only on the training data, but also on test observations that were not used to train the classifier.

In this chapter, we will illustrate the concept of classification using the simulated `Default` data set. We are interested in predicting whether an individual will default on his or her credit card payment, on the basis of annual income and monthly credit card balance. The data set is displayed in Figure 4.1. In the left-hand panel of Figure 4.1, we have plotted annual `income` and monthly credit card `balance` for a subset of 10,000 individuals. The individuals who defaulted in a given month are shown in orange, and those who did not in blue. (The overall default rate is about 3%, so we have plotted only a fraction of the individuals who did not default.) It appears that individuals who defaulted tended to have higher credit card balances than those who did not. In the center and right-hand panels of Figure 4.1, two pairs of boxplots are shown. The first shows the distribution of `balance` split by the binary `default` variable; the second is a similar plot for `income`. In this chapter, we learn how to build a model to predict `default` (Y) for any given value of `balance` (X_1) and `income` (X_2). Since Y is not quantitative, the simple linear regression model of Chapter 3 is not a good choice: we will elaborate on this further in Section 4.2.

It is worth noting that Figure 4.1 displays a very pronounced relationship between the predictor `balance` and the response `default`. In most real applications, the relationship between the predictor and the response will not be nearly so strong. However, for the sake of illustrating the classification procedures discussed in this chapter, we use an example in which the relationship between the predictor and the response is somewhat exaggerated.

4.2 Why Not Linear Regression?

We have stated that linear regression is not appropriate in the case of a qualitative response. Why not?

Suppose that we are trying to predict the medical condition of a patient in the emergency room on the basis of her symptoms. In this simplified example, there are three possible diagnoses: `stroke`, `drug overdose`, and

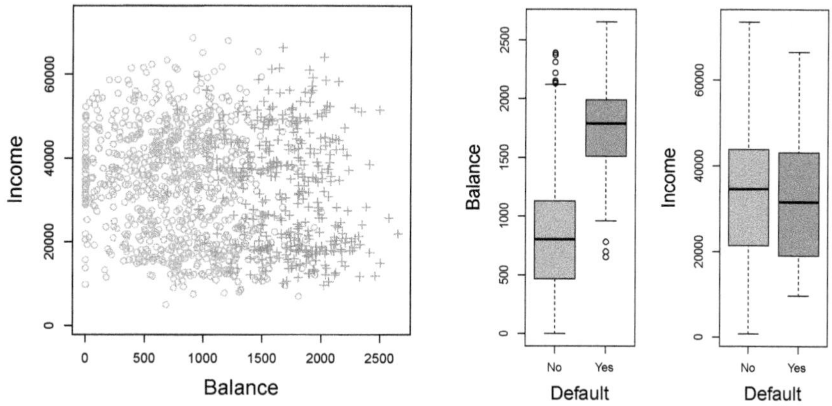

FIGURE 4.1. *The* `Default` *data set.* Left: *The annual incomes and monthly credit card balances of a number of individuals. The individuals who defaulted on their credit card payments are shown in orange, and those who did not are shown in blue.* Center: *Boxplots of* `balance` *as a function of* `default` *status.* Right: *Boxplots of* `income` *as a function of* `default` *status.*

`epileptic seizure`. We could consider encoding these values as a quantitative response variable, Y, as follows:

$$Y = \begin{cases} 1 & \text{if } \texttt{stroke}; \\ 2 & \text{if } \texttt{drug overdose}; \\ 3 & \text{if } \texttt{epileptic seizure}. \end{cases}$$

Using this coding, least squares could be used to fit a linear regression model to predict Y on the basis of a set of predictors $X_1, \ldots, X_p$. Unfortunately, this coding implies an ordering on the outcomes, putting `drug overdose` in between `stroke` and `epileptic seizure`, and insisting that the difference between `stroke` and `drug overdose` is the same as the difference between `drug overdose` and `epileptic seizure`. In practice there is no particular reason that this needs to be the case. For instance, one could choose an equally reasonable coding,

$$Y = \begin{cases} 1 & \text{if } \texttt{epileptic seizure}; \\ 2 & \text{if } \texttt{stroke}; \\ 3 & \text{if } \texttt{drug overdose}, \end{cases}$$

which would imply a totally different relationship among the three conditions. Each of these codings would produce fundamentally different linear models that would ultimately lead to different sets of predictions on test observations.

If the response variable's values did take on a natural ordering, such as *mild*, *moderate*, and *severe*, and we felt the gap between mild and moderate was similar to the gap between moderate and severe, then a 1, 2, 3 coding would be reasonable. Unfortunately, in general there is no natural way to convert a qualitative response variable with more than two levels into a quantitative response that is ready for linear regression.

For a *binary* (two level) qualitative response, the situation is better. For instance, perhaps there are only two possibilities for the patient's medical condition: `stroke` and `drug overdose`. We could then potentially use the *dummy variable* approach from Section 3.3.1 to code the response as follows: binary

$$Y = \begin{cases} 0 & \text{if } \texttt{stroke}; \\ 1 & \text{if } \texttt{drug overdose}. \end{cases}$$

We could then fit a linear regression to this binary response, and predict `drug overdose` if $\hat{Y} > 0.5$ and `stroke` otherwise. In the binary case it is not hard to show that even if we flip the above coding, linear regression will produce the same final predictions.

For a binary response with a 0/1 coding as above, regression by least squares is not completely unreasonable: it can be shown that the $X\hat{\beta}$ obtained using linear regression is in fact an estimate of $\Pr(\texttt{drug overdose}|X)$ in this special case. However, if we use linear regression, some of our estimates might be outside the $[0, 1]$ interval (see Figure 4.2), making them hard to interpret as probabilities! Nevertheless, the predictions provide an ordering and can be interpreted as crude probability estimates. Curiously, it turns out that the classifications that we get if we use linear regression to predict a binary response will be the same as for the linear discriminant analysis (LDA) procedure we discuss in Section 4.4.

To summarize, there are at least two reasons not to perform classification using a regression method: (a) a regression method cannot accommodate a qualitative response with more than two classes; (b) a regression method will not provide meaningful estimates of $\Pr(Y|X)$, even with just two classes. Thus, it is preferable to use a classification method that is truly suited for qualitative response values. In the next section, we present logistic regression, which is well-suited for the case of a binary qualitative response; in later sections we will cover classification methods that are appropriate when the qualitative response has two or more classes.

4.3 Logistic Regression

Consider again the `Default` data set, where the response `default` falls into one of two categories, `Yes` or `No`. Rather than modeling this response Y directly, logistic regression models the *probability* that Y belongs to a particular category.

For the `Default` data, logistic regression models the probability of default. For example, the probability of default given `balance` can be written as

$$\Pr(\texttt{default} = \texttt{Yes}|\texttt{balance}).$$

The values of $\Pr(\texttt{default} = \texttt{Yes}|\texttt{balance})$, which we abbreviate $p(\texttt{balance})$, will range between 0 and 1. Then for any given value of `balance`, a prediction can be made for `default`. For example, one might predict `default` = `Yes`

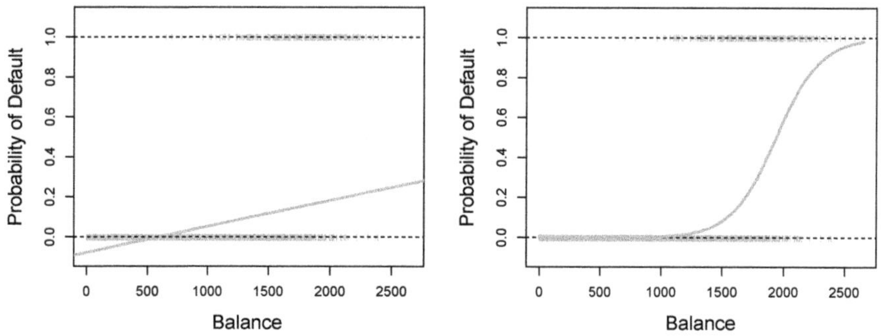

FIGURE 4.2. *Classification using the* `Default` *data.* Left: *Estimated probability of* `default` *using linear regression. Some estimated probabilities are negative! The orange ticks indicate the 0/1 values coded for* `default` *(*`No` *or* `Yes`*).* Right: *Predicted probabilities of* `default` *using logistic regression. All probabilities lie between* 0 *and* 1.

for any individual for whom $p($`balance`$) > 0.5$. Alternatively, if a company wishes to be conservative in predicting individuals who are at risk for default, then they may choose to use a lower threshold, such as $p($`balance`$) > 0.1$.

4.3.1 The Logistic Model

How should we model the relationship between $p(X) = \Pr(Y = 1|X)$ and X? (For convenience we are using the generic 0/1 coding for the response.) In Section 4.2 we considered using a linear regression model to represent these probabilities:

$$p(X) = \beta_0 + \beta_1 X. \tag{4.1}$$

If we use this approach to predict `default=Yes` using `balance`, then we obtain the model shown in the left-hand panel of Figure 4.2. Here we see the problem with this approach: for balances close to zero we predict a negative probability of default; if we were to predict for very large balances, we would get values bigger than 1. These predictions are not sensible, since of course the true probability of default, regardless of credit card balance, must fall between 0 and 1. This problem is not unique to the credit default data. Any time a straight line is fit to a binary response that is coded as 0 or 1, in principle we can always predict $p(X) < 0$ for some values of X and $p(X) > 1$ for others (unless the range of X is limited).

To avoid this problem, we must model $p(X)$ using a function that gives outputs between 0 and 1 for all values of X. Many functions meet this description. In logistic regression, we use the *logistic function*,

logistic function

$$p(X) = \frac{e^{\beta_0 + \beta_1 X}}{1 + e^{\beta_0 + \beta_1 X}}. \tag{4.2}$$

To fit the model (4.2), we use a method called *maximum likelihood*, which we discuss in the next section. The right-hand panel of Figure 4.2 illustrates the fit of the logistic regression model to the `Default` data. Notice that for

maximum likelihood

low balances we now predict the probability of default as close to, but never below, zero. Likewise, for high balances we predict a default probability close to, but never above, one. The logistic function will always produce an *S-shaped* curve of this form, and so regardless of the value of X, we will obtain a sensible prediction. We also see that the logistic model is better able to capture the range of probabilities than is the linear regression model in the left-hand plot. The average fitted probability in both cases is 0.0333 (averaged over the training data), which is the same as the overall proportion of defaulters in the data set.

After a bit of manipulation of (4.2), we find that

$$\frac{p(X)}{1 - p(X)} = e^{\beta_0 + \beta_1 X}. \tag{4.3}$$

The quantity $p(X)/[1-p(X)]$ is called the *odds*, and can take on any value between 0 and ∞. Values of the odds close to 0 and ∞ indicate very low and very high probabilities of default, respectively. For example, on average 1 in 5 people with an odds of 1/4 will default, since $p(X) = 0.2$ implies an odds of $\frac{0.2}{1-0.2} = 1/4$. Likewise, on average nine out of every ten people with an odds of 9 will default, since $p(X) = 0.9$ implies an odds of $\frac{0.9}{1-0.9} = 9$. Odds are traditionally used instead of probabilities in horse-racing, since they relate more naturally to the correct betting strategy. odds

By taking the logarithm of both sides of (4.3), we arrive at

$$\log\left(\frac{p(X)}{1 - p(X)}\right) = \beta_0 + \beta_1 X. \tag{4.4}$$

The left-hand side is called the *log odds* or *logit*. We see that the logistic regression model (4.2) has a logit that is linear in X. log odds logit

Recall from Chapter 3 that in a linear regression model, β_1 gives the average change in Y associated with a one-unit increase in X. By contrast, in a logistic regression model, increasing X by one unit changes the log odds by β_1 (4.4). Equivalently, it multiplies the odds by e^{β_1} (4.3). However, because the relationship between $p(X)$ and X in (4.2) is not a straight line, β_1 does *not* correspond to the change in $p(X)$ associated with a one-unit increase in X. The amount that $p(X)$ changes due to a one-unit change in X depends on the current value of X. But regardless of the value of X, if β_1 is positive then increasing X will be associated with increasing $p(X)$, and if β_1 is negative then increasing X will be associated with decreasing $p(X)$. The fact that there is not a straight-line relationship between $p(X)$ and X, and the fact that the rate of change in $p(X)$ per unit change in X depends on the current value of X, can also be seen by inspection of the right-hand panel of Figure 4.2.

4.3.2 Estimating the Regression Coefficients

The coefficients β_0 and β_1 in (4.2) are unknown, and must be estimated based on the available training data. In Chapter 3, we used the least squares approach to estimate the unknown linear regression coefficients. Although we could use (non-linear) least squares to fit the model (4.4), the more general method of *maximum likelihood* is preferred, since it has better statistical properties. The basic intuition behind using maximum likelihood to fit a logistic regression model is as follows: we seek estimates for β_0 and β_1 such that the predicted probability $\hat{p}(x_i)$ of default for each individual, using (4.2), corresponds as closely as possible to the individual's observed default status. In other words, we try to find $\hat{\beta}_0$ and $\hat{\beta}_1$ such that plugging these estimates into the model for $p(X)$, given in (4.2), yields a number close to one for all individuals who defaulted, and a number close to zero for all individuals who did not. This intuition can be formalized using a mathematical equation called a *likelihood function*:

likelihood function

$$\ell(\beta_0, \beta_1) = \prod_{i:y_i=1} p(x_i) \prod_{i':y_{i'}=0} (1 - p(x_{i'})). \tag{4.5}$$

The estimates $\hat{\beta}_0$ and $\hat{\beta}_1$ are chosen to *maximize* this likelihood function.

Maximum likelihood is a very general approach that is used to fit many of the non-linear models that we examine throughout this book. In the linear regression setting, the least squares approach is in fact a special case of maximum likelihood. The mathematical details of maximum likelihood are beyond the scope of this book. However, in general, logistic regression and other models can be easily fit using statistical software such as `R`, and so we do not need to concern ourselves with the details of the maximum likelihood fitting procedure.

Table 4.1 shows the coefficient estimates and related information that result from fitting a logistic regression model on the `Default` data in order to predict the probability of `default=Yes` using `balance`. We see that $\hat{\beta}_1 =$ 0.0055; this indicates that an increase in `balance` is associated with an increase in the probability of `default`. To be precise, a one-unit increase in `balance` is associated with an increase in the log odds of `default` by 0.0055 units.

Many aspects of the logistic regression output shown in Table 4.1 are similar to the linear regression output of Chapter 3. For example, we can measure the accuracy of the coefficient estimates by computing their standard errors. The z-statistic in Table 4.1 plays the same role as the t-statistic in the linear regression output, for example in Table 3.1 on page 77. For instance, the z-statistic associated with β_1 is equal to $\hat{\beta}_1/\text{SE}(\hat{\beta}_1)$, and so a large (absolute) value of the z-statistic indicates evidence against the null hypothesis $H_0 : \beta_1 = 0$. This null hypothesis implies that $p(X) = \frac{e^{\beta_0}}{1+e^{\beta_0}}$: in other words, that the probability of `default` does not depend on `balance`. Since the p-value associated with `balance` in Table 4.1 is tiny, we can reject H_0. In other words, we conclude that there is indeed an association between `balance` and probability of `default`. The estimated intercept in Table 4.1 is typically not of interest; its main purpose is to adjust the average fitted probabilities to the proportion of ones in the data (in this case, the overall default rate).

4.3.3 Making Predictions

Once the coefficients have been estimated, we can compute the probability of `default` for any given credit card balance. For example, using the coefficient estimates given in Table 4.1, we predict that the default probability

	Coefficient	Std. error	z-statistic	p-value
`Intercept`	−10.6513	0.3612	−29.5	<0.0001
`balance`	0.0055	0.0002	24.9	<0.0001

TABLE 4.1. *For the* `Default` *data, estimated coefficients of the logistic regression model that predicts the probability of* `default` *using* `balance`*. A one-unit increase in* `balance` *is associated with an increase in the log odds of* `default` *by* 0.0055 *units.*

	Coefficient	Std. error	z-statistic	p-value
`Intercept`	−3.5041	0.0707	−49.55	<0.0001
`student[Yes]`	0.4049	0.1150	3.52	0.0004

TABLE 4.2. *For the* `Default` *data, estimated coefficients of the logistic regression model that predicts the probability of* `default` *using student status. Student status is encoded as a dummy variable, with a value of* 1 *for a student and a value of* 0 *for a non-student, and represented by the variable* `student[Yes]` *in the table.*

for an individual with a `balance` of $1,000 is

$$\hat{p}(X) = \frac{e^{\hat{\beta}_0+\hat{\beta}_1 X}}{1+e^{\hat{\beta}_0+\hat{\beta}_1 X}} = \frac{e^{-10.6513+0.0055\times 1,000}}{1+e^{-10.6513+0.0055\times 1,000}} = 0.00576,$$

which is below 1 %. In contrast, the predicted probability of default for an individual with a balance of $2,000 is much higher, and equals 0.586 or 58.6 %.

One can use qualitative predictors with the logistic regression model using the dummy variable approach from Section 3.3.1. As an example, the `Default` data set contains the qualitative variable `student`. To fit a model that uses student status as a predictor variable, we simply create a dummy variable that takes on a value of 1 for students and 0 for non-students. The logistic regression model that results from predicting probability of default from student status can be seen in Table 4.2. The coefficient associated with the dummy variable is positive, and the associated p-value is statistically significant. This indicates that students tend to have higher default probabilities than non-students:

$$\widehat{\Pr}(\texttt{default=Yes}|\texttt{student=Yes}) = \frac{e^{-3.5041+0.4049\times 1}}{1+e^{-3.5041+0.4049\times 1}} = 0.0431,$$
$$\widehat{\Pr}(\texttt{default=Yes}|\texttt{student=No}) = \frac{e^{-3.5041+0.4049\times 0}}{1+e^{-3.5041+0.4049\times 0}} = 0.0292.$$

4.3.4 Multiple Logistic Regression

We now consider the problem of predicting a binary response using multiple predictors. By analogy with the extension from simple to multiple linear regression in Chapter 3, we can generalize (4.4) as follows:

$$\log\left(\frac{p(X)}{1-p(X)}\right) = \beta_0 + \beta_1 X_1 + \cdots + \beta_p X_p, \tag{4.6}$$

where $X = (X_1, \ldots, X_p)$ are p predictors. Equation 4.6 can be rewritten as

$$p(X) = \frac{e^{\beta_0+\beta_1 X_1+\cdots+\beta_p X_p}}{1+e^{\beta_0+\beta_1 X_1+\cdots+\beta_p X_p}}. \tag{4.7}$$

	Coefficient	Std. error	z-statistic	p-value
`Intercept`	−10.8690	0.4923	−22.08	<0.0001
`balance`	0.0057	0.0002	24.74	<0.0001
`income`	0.0030	0.0082	0.37	0.7115
`student[Yes]`	−0.6468	0.2362	−2.74	0.0062

TABLE 4.3. *For the* `Default` *data, estimated coefficients of the logistic regression model that predicts the probability of* `default` *using* `balance`, `income`, *and student status. Student status is encoded as a dummy variable* `student[Yes]`, *with a value of* 1 *for a student and a value of* 0 *for a non-student. In fitting this model,* `income` *was measured in thousands of dollars.*

Just as in Section 4.3.2, we use the maximum likelihood method to estimate $\beta_0, \beta_1, \ldots, \beta_p$.

Table 4.3 shows the coefficient estimates for a logistic regression model that uses `balance`, `income` (in thousands of dollars), and `student` status to predict probability of `default`. There is a surprising result here. The p-values associated with `balance` and the dummy variable for `student` status are very small, indicating that each of these variables is associated with the probability of `default`. However, the coefficient for the dummy variable is negative, indicating that students are less likely to default than non-students. In contrast, the coefficient for the dummy variable is positive in Table 4.2. How is it possible for student status to be associated with an *increase* in probability of default in Table 4.2 and a *decrease* in probability of default in Table 4.3? The left-hand panel of Figure 4.3 provides a graphical illustration of this apparent paradox. The orange and blue solid lines show the average default rates for students and non-students, respectively, as a function of credit card balance. The negative coefficient for `student` in the multiple logistic regression indicates that *for a fixed value of* `balance` *and* `income`, a student is less likely to default than a non-student. Indeed, we observe from the left-hand panel of Figure 4.3 that the student default rate is at or below that of the non-student default rate for every value of `balance`. But the horizontal broken lines near the base of the plot, which show the default rates for students and non-students averaged over all values of `balance` and `income`, suggest the opposite effect: the overall student default rate is higher than the non-student default rate. Consequently, there is a positive coefficient for `student` in the single variable logistic regression output shown in Table 4.2.

The right-hand panel of Figure 4.3 provides an explanation for this discrepancy. The variables `student` and `balance` are correlated. Students tend to hold higher levels of debt, which is in turn associated with higher probability of default. In other words, students are more likely to have large credit card balances, which, as we know from the left-hand panel of Figure 4.3, tend to be associated with high default rates. Thus, even though an individual student with a given credit card balance will tend to have a lower probability of default than a non-student with the same credit card balance, the fact that students on the whole tend to have higher credit card balances means that overall, students tend to default at a higher rate than non-students. This is an important distinction for a credit card company that is trying to determine to whom they should offer credit. A student is riskier than a non-student if no information about the student's credit card

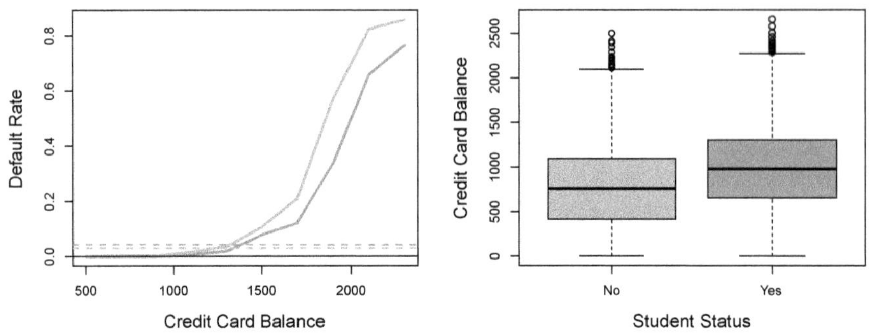

FIGURE 4.3. *Confounding in the* `Default` *data.* Left: *Default rates are shown for students (orange) and non-students (blue). The solid lines display default rate as a function of* `balance`*, while the horizontal broken lines display the overall default rates.* Right: *Boxplots of* `balance` *for students (orange) and non-students (blue) are shown.*

balance is available. However, that student is less risky than a non-student *with the same credit card balance*!

This simple example illustrates the dangers and subtleties associated with performing regressions involving only a single predictor when other predictors may also be relevant. As in the linear regression setting, the results obtained using one predictor may be quite different from those obtained using multiple predictors, especially when there is correlation among the predictors. In general, the phenomenon seen in Figure 4.3 is known as *confounding*. confounding

By substituting estimates for the regression coefficients from Table 4.3 into (4.7), we can make predictions. For example, a student with a credit card balance of \$1,500 and an income of \$40,000 has an estimated probability of default of

$$\hat{p}(X) = \frac{e^{-10.869+0.00574\times 1{,}500+0.003\times 40-0.6468\times 1}}{1+e^{-10.869+0.00574\times 1{,}500+0.003\times 40-0.6468\times 1}} = 0.058. \qquad (4.8)$$

A non-student with the same balance and income has an estimated probability of default of

$$\hat{p}(X) = \frac{e^{-10.869+0.00574\times 1{,}500+0.003\times 40-0.6468\times 0}}{1+e^{-10.869+0.00574\times 1{,}500+0.003\times 40-0.6468\times 0}} = 0.105. \qquad (4.9)$$

(Here we multiply the `income` coefficient estimate from Table 4.3 by 40, rather than by 40,000, because in that table the model was fit with `income` measured in units of \$1,000.)

4.3.5 Multinomial Logistic Regression

We sometimes wish to classify a response variable that has more than two classes. For example, in Section 4.2 we had three categories of medical condition in the emergency room: `stroke`, `drug overdose`, `epileptic seizure`. However, the logistic regression approach that we have seen in this section only allows for $K = 2$ classes for the response variable.

It turns out that it is possible to extend the two-class logistic regression approach to the setting of $K > 2$ classes. This extension is sometimes known as *multinomial logistic regression*. To do this, we first select a single class to serve as the *baseline*; without loss of generality, we select the Kth class for this role. Then we replace the model (4.7) with the model

multinomial logistic regression

$$\Pr(Y = k|X = x) = \frac{e^{\beta_{k0}+\beta_{k1}x_1+\cdots+\beta_{kp}x_p}}{1 + \sum_{l=1}^{K-1} e^{\beta_{l0}+\beta_{l1}x_1+\cdots+\beta_{lp}x_p}} \tag{4.10}$$

for $k = 1, \ldots, K-1$, and

$$\Pr(Y = K|X = x) = \frac{1}{1 + \sum_{l=1}^{K-1} e^{\beta_{l0}+\beta_{l1}x_1+\cdots+\beta_{lp}x_p}}. \tag{4.11}$$

It is not hard to show that for $k = 1, \ldots, K-1$,

$$\log\left(\frac{\Pr(Y = k|X = x)}{\Pr(Y = K|X = x)}\right) = \beta_{k0} + \beta_{k1}x_1 + \cdots + \beta_{kp}x_p. \tag{4.12}$$

Notice that (4.12) is quite similar to (4.6). Equation 4.12 indicates that once again, the log odds between any pair of classes is linear in the features.

It turns out that in (4.10)–(4.12), the decision to treat the Kth class as the baseline is unimportant. For example, when classifying emergency room visits into `stroke`, `drug overdose`, and `epileptic seizure`, suppose that we fit two multinomial logistic regression models: one treating `stroke` as the baseline, another treating `drug overdose` as the baseline. The coefficient estimates will differ between the two fitted models due to the differing choice of baseline, but the fitted values (predictions), the log odds between any pair of classes, and the other key model outputs will remain the same.

Nonetheless, interpretation of the coefficients in a multinomial logistic regression model must be done with care, since it is tied to the choice of baseline. For example, if we set `epileptic seizure` to be the baseline, then we can interpret $\beta_{\texttt{stroke}0}$ as the log odds of `stroke` versus `epileptic seizure`, given that $x_1 = \cdots = x_p = 0$. Furthermore, a one-unit increase in X_j is associated with a $\beta_{\texttt{stroke}j}$ increase in the log odds of `stroke` over `epileptic seizure`. Stated another way, if X_j increases by one unit, then

$$\frac{\Pr(Y = \texttt{stroke}|X = x)}{\Pr(Y = \texttt{epileptic seizure}|X = x)}$$

increases by $e^{\beta_{\texttt{stroke}j}}$.

We now briefly present an alternative coding for multinomial logistic regression, known as the *softmax* coding. The softmax coding is equivalent to the coding just described in the sense that the fitted values, log odds between any pair of classes, and other key model outputs will remain the same, regardless of coding. But the softmax coding is used extensively in some areas of the machine learning literature (and will appear again in Chapter 10), so it is worth being aware of it. In the softmax coding, rather than selecting a baseline class, we treat all K classes symmetrically, and assume that for $k = 1, \ldots, K$,

softmax

$$\Pr(Y = k|X = x) = \frac{e^{\beta_{k0}+\beta_{k1}x_1+\cdots+\beta_{kp}x_p}}{\sum_{l=1}^{K} e^{\beta_{l0}+\beta_{l1}x_1+\cdots+\beta_{lp}x_p}}. \tag{4.13}$$

Thus, rather than estimating coefficients for $K - 1$ classes, we actually estimate coefficients for all K classes. It is not hard to see that as a result of (4.13), the log odds ratio between the kth and k'th classes equals

$$\log\left(\frac{\Pr(Y=k|X=x)}{\Pr(Y=k'|X=x)}\right) = (\beta_{k0}-\beta_{k'0}) + (\beta_{k1}-\beta_{k'1})x_1 + \cdots + (\beta_{kp}-\beta_{k'p})x_p. \tag{4.14}$$

4.4 Generative Models for Classification

Logistic regression involves directly modeling $\Pr(Y = k|X = x)$ using the logistic function, given by (4.7) for the case of two response classes. In statistical jargon, we model the conditional distribution of the response Y, given the predictor(s) X. We now consider an alternative and less direct approach to estimating these probabilities. In this new approach, we model the distribution of the predictors X separately in each of the response classes (i.e. for each value of Y). We then use Bayes' theorem to flip these around into estimates for $\Pr(Y = k|X = x)$. When the distribution of X within each class is assumed to be normal, it turns out that the model is very similar in form to logistic regression.

Why do we need another method, when we have logistic regression? There are several reasons:

- When there is substantial separation between the two classes, the parameter estimates for the logistic regression model are surprisingly unstable. The methods that we consider in this section do not suffer from this problem.
- If the distribution of the predictors X is approximately normal in each of the classes and the sample size is small, then the approaches in this section may be more accurate than logistic regression.
- The methods in this section can be naturally extended to the case of more than two response classes. (In the case of more than two response classes, we can also use multinomial logistic regression from Section 4.3.5.)

Suppose that we wish to classify an observation into one of K classes, where $K \geq 2$. In other words, the qualitative response variable Y can take on K possible distinct and unordered values. Let π_k represent the overall or *prior* probability that a randomly chosen observation comes from the kth class. Let $f_k(X) \equiv \Pr(X|Y = k)$[1] denote the *density function* of X for an observation that comes from the kth class. In other words, $f_k(x)$ is relatively large if there is a high probability that an observation in the kth class has $X \approx x$, and $f_k(x)$ is small if it is very unlikely that an observation in the kth class has $X \approx x$. Then *Bayes' theorem* states that

prior

density function

Bayes' theorem

[1]Technically, this definition is only correct if X is a qualitative random variable. If X is quantitative, then $f_k(x)dx$ corresponds to the probability of X falling in a small region dx around x.

$$\Pr(Y = k|X = x) = \frac{\pi_k f_k(x)}{\sum_{l=1}^{K} \pi_l f_l(x)}. \tag{4.15}$$

In accordance with our earlier notation, we will use the abbreviation $p_k(x) = \Pr(Y = k|X = x)$; this is the *posterior* probability that an observation $X = x$ belongs to the kth class. That is, it is the probability that the observation belongs to the kth class, *given* the predictor value for that observation.

posterior

Equation 4.15 suggests that instead of directly computing the posterior probability $p_k(x)$ as in Section 4.3.1, we can simply plug in estimates of π_k and $f_k(x)$ into (4.15). In general, estimating π_k is easy if we have a random sample from the population: we simply compute the fraction of the training observations that belong to the kth class. However, estimating the density function $f_k(x)$ is much more challenging. As we will see, to estimate $f_k(x)$, we will typically have to make some simplifying assumptions.

We know from Chapter 2 that the Bayes classifier, which classifies an observation x to the class for which $p_k(x)$ is largest, has the lowest possible error rate out of all classifiers. (Of course, this is only true if all of the terms in (4.15) are correctly specified.) Therefore, if we can find a way to estimate $f_k(x)$, then we can plug it into (4.15) in order to approximate the Bayes classifier.

In the following sections, we discuss three classifiers that use different estimates of $f_k(x)$ in (4.15) to approximate the Bayes classifier: *linear discriminant analysis, quadratic discriminant analysis,* and *naive Bayes.*

4.4.1 Linear Discriminant Analysis for $p = 1$

For now, assume that $p = 1$—that is, we have only one predictor. We would like to obtain an estimate for $f_k(x)$ that we can plug into (4.15) in order to estimate $p_k(x)$. We will then classify an observation to the class for which $p_k(x)$ is greatest. To estimate $f_k(x)$, we will first make some assumptions about its form.

In particular, we assume that $f_k(x)$ is *normal* or *Gaussian.* In the one-dimensional setting, the normal density takes the form

normal
Gaussian

$$f_k(x) = \frac{1}{\sqrt{2\pi}\sigma_k} \exp\left(-\frac{1}{2\sigma_k^2}(x - \mu_k)^2\right), \tag{4.16}$$

where μ_k and σ_k^2 are the mean and variance parameters for the kth class. For now, let us further assume that $\sigma_1^2 = \cdots = \sigma_K^2$: that is, there is a shared variance term across all K classes, which for simplicity we can denote by σ^2. Plugging (4.16) into (4.15), we find that

$$p_k(x) = \frac{\pi_k \frac{1}{\sqrt{2\pi}\sigma} \exp\left(-\frac{1}{2\sigma^2}(x - \mu_k)^2\right)}{\sum_{l=1}^{K} \pi_l \frac{1}{\sqrt{2\pi}\sigma} \exp\left(-\frac{1}{2\sigma^2}(x - \mu_l)^2\right)}. \tag{4.17}$$

(Note that in (4.17), π_k denotes the prior probability that an observation belongs to the kth class, not to be confused with $\pi \approx 3.14159$, the mathematical constant.) The Bayes classifier[2] involves assigning an observation

[2]Recall that the *Bayes classifier* assigns an observation to the class for which $p_k(x)$ is largest. This is different from *Bayes' theorem* in (4.15), which allows us to manipulate conditional distributions.

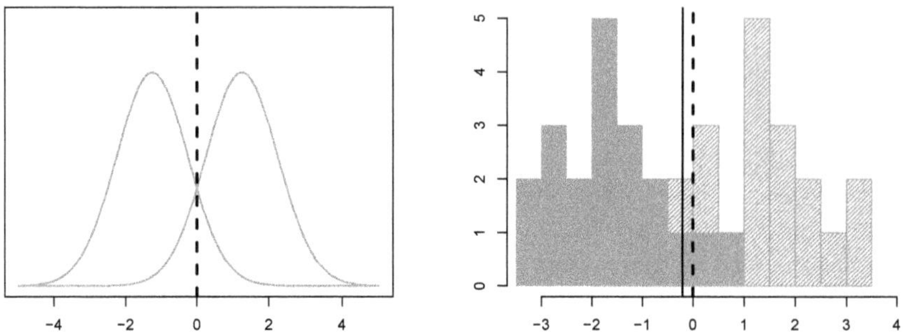

FIGURE 4.4. Left: *Two one-dimensional normal density functions are shown. The dashed vertical line represents the Bayes decision boundary.* Right: *20 observations were drawn from each of the two classes, and are shown as histograms. The Bayes decision boundary is again shown as a dashed vertical line. The solid vertical line represents the LDA decision boundary estimated from the training data.*

$X = x$ to the class for which (4.17) is largest. Taking the log of (4.17) and rearranging the terms, it is not hard to show[3] that this is equivalent to assigning the observation to the class for which

$$\delta_k(x) = x \cdot \frac{\mu_k}{\sigma^2} - \frac{\mu_k^2}{2\sigma^2} + \log(\pi_k) \tag{4.18}$$

is largest. For instance, if $K = 2$ and $\pi_1 = \pi_2$, then the Bayes classifier assigns an observation to class 1 if $2x(\mu_1 - \mu_2) > \mu_1^2 - \mu_2^2$, and to class 2 otherwise. The Bayes decision boundary is the point for which $\delta_1(x) = \delta_2(x)$; one can show that this amounts to

$$x = \frac{\mu_1^2 - \mu_2^2}{2(\mu_1 - \mu_2)} = \frac{\mu_1 + \mu_2}{2}. \tag{4.19}$$

An example is shown in the left-hand panel of Figure 4.4. The two normal density functions that are displayed, $f_1(x)$ and $f_2(x)$, represent two distinct classes. The mean and variance parameters for the two density functions are $\mu_1 = -1.25$, $\mu_2 = 1.25$, and $\sigma_1^2 = \sigma_2^2 = 1$. The two densities overlap, and so given that $X = x$, there is some uncertainty about the class to which the observation belongs. If we assume that an observation is equally likely to come from either class—that is, $\pi_1 = \pi_2 = 0.5$—then by inspection of (4.19), we see that the Bayes classifier assigns the observation to class 1 if $x < 0$ and class 2 otherwise. Note that in this case, we can compute the Bayes classifier because we know that X is drawn from a Gaussian distribution within each class, and we know all of the parameters involved. In a real-life situation, we are not able to calculate the Bayes classifier.

In practice, even if we are quite certain of our assumption that X is drawn from a Gaussian distribution within each class, to apply the Bayes classifier we still have to estimate the parameters $\mu_1, \ldots, \mu_K$, $\pi_1, \ldots, \pi_K$, and σ^2. The *linear discriminant analysis* (LDA) method approximates the Bayes classifier by plugging estimates for π_k, μ_k, and σ^2 into (4.18). In

linear discriminant analysis

[3]See Exercise 2 at the end of this chapter.

particular, the following estimates are used:

$$\hat{\mu}_k = \frac{1}{n_k}\sum_{i:y_i=k} x_i$$
$$\hat{\sigma}^2 = \frac{1}{n-K}\sum_{k=1}^{K}\sum_{i:y_i=k}(x_i-\hat{\mu}_k)^2 \quad (4.20)$$

where n is the total number of training observations, and n_k is the number of training observations in the kth class. The estimate for μ_k is simply the average of all the training observations from the kth class, while $\hat{\sigma}^2$ can be seen as a weighted average of the sample variances for each of the K classes. Sometimes we have knowledge of the class membership probabilities $\pi_1, \ldots, \pi_K$, which can be used directly. In the absence of any additional information, LDA estimates π_k using the proportion of the training observations that belong to the kth class. In other words,

$$\hat{\pi}_k = n_k/n. \quad (4.21)$$

The LDA classifier plugs the estimates given in (4.20) and (4.21) into (4.18), and assigns an observation $X = x$ to the class for which

$$\hat{\delta}_k(x) = x \cdot \frac{\hat{\mu}_k}{\hat{\sigma}^2} - \frac{\hat{\mu}_k^2}{2\hat{\sigma}^2} + \log(\hat{\pi}_k) \quad (4.22)$$

is largest. The word *linear* in the classifier's name stems from the fact that the *discriminant functions* $\hat{\delta}_k(x)$ in (4.22) are linear functions of x (as opposed to a more complex function of x).

discriminant function

The right-hand panel of Figure 4.4 displays a histogram of a random sample of 20 observations from each class. To implement LDA, we began by estimating π_k, μ_k, and σ^2 using (4.20) and (4.21). We then computed the decision boundary, shown as a black solid line, that results from assigning an observation to the class for which (4.22) is largest. All points to the left of this line will be assigned to the green class, while points to the right of this line are assigned to the purple class. In this case, since $n_1 = n_2 = 20$, we have $\hat{\pi}_1 = \hat{\pi}_2$. As a result, the decision boundary corresponds to the midpoint between the sample means for the two classes, $(\hat{\mu}_1 + \hat{\mu}_2)/2$. The figure indicates that the LDA decision boundary is slightly to the left of the optimal Bayes decision boundary, which instead equals $(\mu_1 + \mu_2)/2 = 0$. How well does the LDA classifier perform on this data? Since this is simulated data, we can generate a large number of test observations in order to compute the Bayes error rate and the LDA test error rate. These are 10.6 % and 11.1 %, respectively. In other words, the LDA classifier's error rate is only 0.5 % above the smallest possible error rate! This indicates that LDA is performing pretty well on this data set.

To reiterate, the LDA classifier results from assuming that the observations within each class come from a normal distribution with a class-specific mean and a common variance σ^2, and plugging estimates for these parameters into the Bayes classifier. In Section 4.4.3, we will consider a less stringent set of assumptions, by allowing the observations in the kth class to have a class-specific variance, σ_k^2.

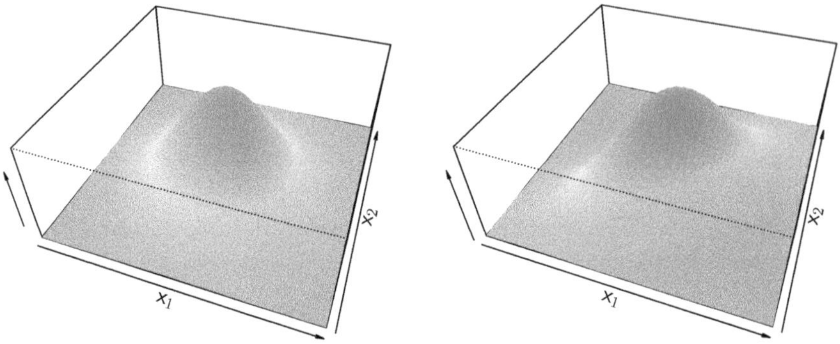

FIGURE 4.5. *Two multivariate Gaussian density functions are shown, with* $p = 2$. Left: *The two predictors are uncorrelated.* Right: *The two variables have a correlation of* 0.7.

4.4.2 Linear Discriminant Analysis for p >1

We now extend the LDA classifier to the case of multiple predictors. To do this, we will assume that $X = (X_1, X_2, \ldots, X_p)$ is drawn from a *multivariate Gaussian* (or multivariate normal) distribution, with a class-specific mean vector and a common covariance matrix. We begin with a brief review of this distribution.

multivariate Gaussian

The multivariate Gaussian distribution assumes that each individual predictor follows a one-dimensional normal distribution, as in (4.16), with some correlation between each pair of predictors. Two examples of multivariate Gaussian distributions with $p = 2$ are shown in Figure 4.5. The height of the surface at any particular point represents the probability that both X_1 and X_2 fall in a small region around that point. In either panel, if the surface is cut along the X_1 axis or along the X_2 axis, the resulting cross-section will have the shape of a one-dimensional normal distribution. The left-hand panel of Figure 4.5 illustrates an example in which $\text{Var}(X_1) = \text{Var}(X_2)$ and $\text{Cor}(X_1, X_2) = 0$; this surface has a characteristic *bell shape.* However, the bell shape will be distorted if the predictors are correlated or have unequal variances, as is illustrated in the right-hand panel of Figure 4.5. In this situation, the base of the bell will have an elliptical, rather than circular, shape. To indicate that a p-dimensional random variable X has a multivariate Gaussian distribution, we write $X \sim N(\mu, \mathbf{\Sigma})$. Here $\text{E}(X) = \mu$ is the mean of X (a vector with p components), and $\text{Cov}(X) = \mathbf{\Sigma}$ is the $p \times p$ covariance matrix of X. Formally, the multivariate Gaussian density is defined as

$$f(x) = \frac{1}{(2\pi)^{p/2}|\mathbf{\Sigma}|^{1/2}} \exp\left(-\frac{1}{2}(x-\mu)^T\mathbf{\Sigma}^{-1}(x-\mu)\right). \tag{4.23}$$

In the case of $p > 1$ predictors, the LDA classifier assumes that the observations in the kth class are drawn from a multivariate Gaussian distribution $N(\mu_k, \mathbf{\Sigma})$, where μ_k is a class-specific mean vector, and $\mathbf{\Sigma}$ is a covariance matrix that is common to all K classes. Plugging the density function for the kth class, $f_k(X = x)$, into (4.15) and performing a little bit of algebra reveals that the Bayes classifier assigns an observation $X = x$

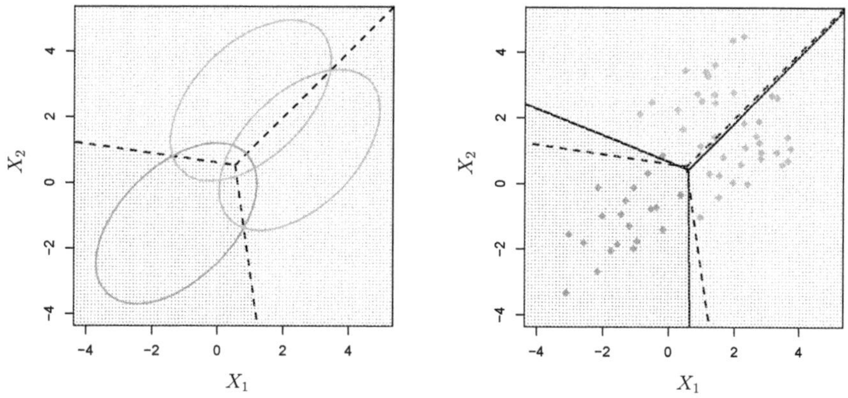

FIGURE 4.6. *An example with three classes. The observations from each class are drawn from a multivariate Gaussian distribution with* $p = 2$*, with a class-specific mean vector and a common covariance matrix.* Left: *Ellipses that contain 95 % of the probability for each of the three classes are shown. The dashed lines are the Bayes decision boundaries.* Right: 20 *observations were generated from each class, and the corresponding LDA decision boundaries are indicated using solid black lines. The Bayes decision boundaries are once again shown as dashed lines.*

to the class for which

$$\delta_k(x) = x^T \mathbf{\Sigma}^{-1} \mu_k - \frac{1}{2} \mu_k^T \mathbf{\Sigma}^{-1} \mu_k + \log \pi_k \tag{4.24}$$

is largest. This is the vector/matrix version of (4.18).

An example is shown in the left-hand panel of Figure 4.6. Three equally-sized Gaussian classes are shown with class-specific mean vectors and a common covariance matrix. The three ellipses represent regions that contain 95 % of the probability for each of the three classes. The dashed lines are the Bayes decision boundaries. In other words, they represent the set of values x for which $\delta_k(x) = \delta_\ell(x)$; i.e.

$$x^T \mathbf{\Sigma}^{-1} \mu_k - \frac{1}{2} \mu_k^T \mathbf{\Sigma}^{-1} \mu_k = x^T \mathbf{\Sigma}^{-1} \mu_l - \frac{1}{2} \mu_l^T \mathbf{\Sigma}^{-1} \mu_l \tag{4.25}$$

for $k \neq l$. (The $\log \pi_k$ term from (4.24) has disappeared because each of the three classes has the same number of training observations; i.e. π_k is the same for each class.) Note that there are three lines representing the Bayes decision boundaries because there are three *pairs of classes* among the three classes. That is, one Bayes decision boundary separates class 1 from class 2, one separates class 1 from class 3, and one separates class 2 from class 3. These three Bayes decision boundaries divide the predictor space into three regions. The Bayes classifier will classify an observation according to the region in which it is located.

Once again, we need to estimate the unknown parameters $\mu_1, \ldots, \mu_K$, $\pi_1, \ldots, \pi_K$, and $\mathbf{\Sigma}$; the formulas are similar to those used in the one-dimensional case, given in (4.20). To assign a new observation $X = x$, LDA plugs these estimates into (4.24) to obtain quantities $\hat{\delta}_k(x)$, and classifies to the class for which $\hat{\delta}_k(x)$ is largest. Note that in (4.24) $\delta_k(x)$ is a linear function of x; that is, the LDA decision rule depends on x only

		True default status		
		No	Yes	Total
Predicted	No	9644	252	9896
default status	Yes	23	81	104
	Total	9667	333	10000

TABLE 4.4. *A confusion matrix compares the LDA predictions to the true default statuses for the* 10,000 *training observations in the* `Default` *data set. Elements on the diagonal of the matrix represent individuals whose default statuses were correctly predicted, while off-diagonal elements represent individuals that were misclassified. LDA made incorrect predictions for* 23 *individuals who did not default and for* 252 *individuals who did default.*

through a linear combination of its elements. As previously discussed, this is the reason for the word *linear* in LDA.

In the right-hand panel of Figure 4.6, 20 observations drawn from each of the three classes are displayed, and the resulting LDA decision boundaries are shown as solid black lines. Overall, the LDA decision boundaries are pretty close to the Bayes decision boundaries, shown again as dashed lines. The test error rates for the Bayes and LDA classifiers are 0.0746 and 0.0770, respectively. This indicates that LDA is performing well on this data.

We can perform LDA on the `Default` data in order to predict whether or not an individual will default on the basis of credit card balance and student status.[4] The LDA model fit to the 10,000 training samples results in a *training* error rate of 2.75 %. This sounds like a low error rate, but two caveats must be noted.

- First of all, training error rates will usually be lower than test error rates, which are the real quantity of interest. In other words, we might expect this classifier to perform worse if we use it to predict whether or not a new set of individuals will default. The reason is that we specifically adjust the parameters of our model to do well on the training data. The higher the ratio of parameters p to number of samples n, the more we expect this *overfitting* to play a role. For these data we don't expect this to be a problem, since $p = 2$ and $n = 10,000$. overfitting

- Second, since only 3.33 % of the individuals in the training sample defaulted, a simple but useless classifier that always predicts that an individual will not default, regardless of his or her credit card balance and student status, will result in an error rate of 3.33 %. In other words, the trivial *null* classifier will achieve an error rate that is only a bit higher than the LDA training set error rate. null

In practice, a binary classifier such as this one can make two types of errors: it can incorrectly assign an individual who defaults to the *no default* category, or it can incorrectly assign an individual who does not default to

[4]The careful reader will notice that student status is qualitative — thus, the normality assumption made by LDA is clearly violated in this example! However, LDA is often remarkably robust to model violations, as this example shows. Naive Bayes, discussed in Section 4.4.4, provides an alternative to LDA that does not assume normally distributed predictors.

the *default* category. It is often of interest to determine which of these two types of errors are being made. A *confusion matrix*, shown for the `Default` data in Table 4.4, is a convenient way to display this information. The table reveals that LDA predicted that a total of 104 people would default. Of these people, 81 actually defaulted and 23 did not. Hence only 23 out of 9,667 of the individuals who did not default were incorrectly labeled. This looks like a pretty low error rate! However, of the 333 individuals who defaulted, 252 (or 75.7 %) were missed by LDA. So while the overall error rate is low, the error rate among individuals who defaulted is very high. From the perspective of a credit card company that is trying to identify high-risk individuals, an error rate of $252/333 = 75.7\,\%$ among individuals who default may well be unacceptable.

confusion matrix

Class-specific performance is also important in medicine and biology, where the terms *sensitivity* and *specificity* characterize the performance of a classifier or screening test. In this case the sensitivity is the percentage of true defaulters that are identified; it equals 24.3 %. The specificity is the percentage of non-defaulters that are correctly identified; it equals $(1 - 23/9667) = 99.8\,\%$.

sensitivity

specificity

Why does LDA do such a poor job of classifying the customers who default? In other words, why does it have such low sensitivity? As we have seen, LDA is trying to approximate the Bayes classifier, which has the lowest *total* error rate out of all classifiers. That is, the Bayes classifier will yield the smallest possible total number of misclassified observations, regardless of the class from which the errors stem. Some misclassifications will result from incorrectly assigning a customer who does not default to the default class, and others will result from incorrectly assigning a customer who defaults to the non-default class. In contrast, a credit card company might particularly wish to avoid incorrectly classifying an individual who will default, whereas incorrectly classifying an individual who will not default, though still to be avoided, is less problematic. We will now see that it is possible to modify LDA in order to develop a classifier that better meets the credit card company's needs.

The Bayes classifier works by assigning an observation to the class for which the posterior probability $p_k(X)$ is greatest. In the two-class case, this amounts to assigning an observation to the *default* class if

$$\Pr(\texttt{default} = \texttt{Yes}|X = x) > 0.5. \tag{4.26}$$

Thus, the Bayes classifier, and by extension LDA, uses a threshold of 50 % for the posterior probability of default in order to assign an observation to the *default* class. However, if we are concerned about incorrectly predicting the default status for individuals who default, then we can consider lowering this threshold. For instance, we might label any customer with a posterior probability of default above 20 % to the *default* class. In other words, instead of assigning an observation to the *default* class if (4.26) holds, we could instead assign an observation to this class if

$$\Pr(\texttt{default} = \texttt{Yes}|X = x) > 0.2. \tag{4.27}$$

The error rates that result from taking this approach are shown in Table 4.5. Now LDA predicts that 430 individuals will default. Of the 333 individuals who default, LDA correctly predicts all but 138, or 41.4 %. This is a vast

		True default status		
		No	Yes	Total
Predicted	No	9432	138	9570
default status	Yes	235	195	430
	Total	9667	333	10000

TABLE 4.5. *A confusion matrix compares the LDA predictions to the true default statuses for the* 10,000 *training observations in the* Default *data set, using a modified threshold value that predicts default for any individuals whose posterior default probability exceeds* 20 %.

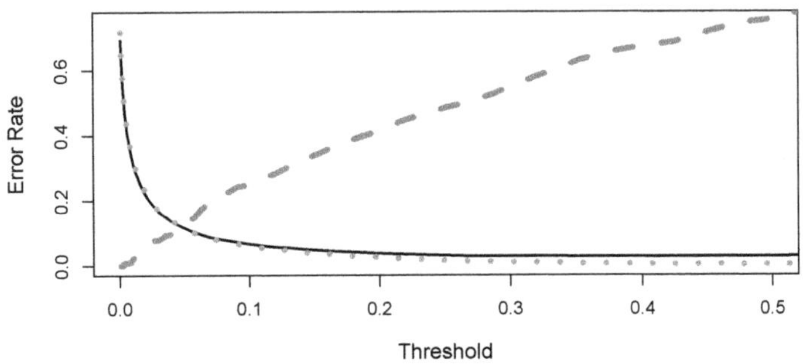

FIGURE 4.7. *For the* Default *data set, error rates are shown as a function of the threshold value for the posterior probability that is used to perform the assignment. The black solid line displays the overall error rate. The blue dashed line represents the fraction of defaulting customers that are incorrectly classified, and the orange dotted line indicates the fraction of errors among the non-defaulting customers.*

improvement over the error rate of 75.7 % that resulted from using the threshold of 50 %. However, this improvement comes at a cost: now 235 individuals who do not default are incorrectly classified. As a result, the overall error rate has increased slightly to 3.73 %. But a credit card company may consider this slight increase in the total error rate to be a small price to pay for more accurate identification of individuals who do indeed default.

Figure 4.7 illustrates the trade-off that results from modifying the threshold value for the posterior probability of default. Various error rates are shown as a function of the threshold value. Using a threshold of 0.5, as in (4.26), minimizes the overall error rate, shown as a black solid line. This is to be expected, since the Bayes classifier uses a threshold of 0.5 and is known to have the lowest overall error rate. But when a threshold of 0.5 is used, the error rate among the individuals who default is quite high (blue dashed line). As the threshold is reduced, the error rate among individuals who default decreases steadily, but the error rate among the individuals who do not default increases. How can we decide which threshold value is best? Such a decision must be based on *domain knowledge*, such as detailed information about the costs associated with default.

The *ROC curve* is a popular graphic for simultaneously displaying the two types of errors for all possible thresholds. The name "ROC" is historic, and comes from communications theory. It is an acronym for *receiver operating characteristics*. Figure 4.8 displays the ROC curve for the LDA classifier on the training data. The overall performance of a classifier, sum- ROC curve

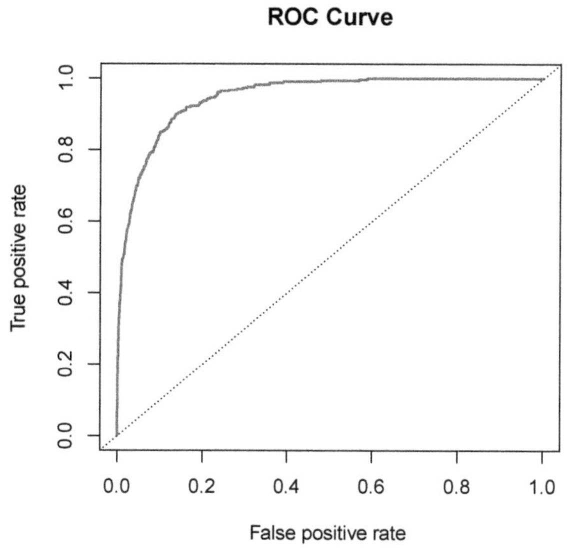

FIGURE 4.8. *A ROC curve for the LDA classifier on the* `Default` *data. It traces out two types of error as we vary the threshold value for the posterior probability of default. The actual thresholds are not shown. The true positive rate is the sensitivity: the fraction of defaulters that are correctly identified, using a given threshold value. The false positive rate is 1-specificity: the fraction of non-defaulters that we classify incorrectly as defaulters, using that same threshold value. The ideal ROC curve hugs the top left corner, indicating a high true positive rate and a low false positive rate. The dotted line represents the "no information" classifier; this is what we would expect if student status and credit card balance are not associated with probability of default.*

marized over all possible thresholds, is given by the *area under the (ROC) curve* (AUC). An ideal ROC curve will hug the top left corner, so the larger the AUC the better the classifier. For this data the AUC is 0.95, which is close to the maximum of 1.0, so would be considered very good. We expect a classifier that performs no better than chance to have an AUC of 0.5 (when evaluated on an independent test set not used in model training). ROC curves are useful for comparing different classifiers, since they take into account all possible thresholds. It turns out that the ROC curve for the logistic regression model of Section 4.3.4 fit to these data is virtually indistinguishable from this one for the LDA model, so we do not display it here.

area under the (ROC) curve

As we have seen above, varying the classifier threshold changes its true positive and false positive rate. These are also called the *sensitivity* and one minus the *specificity* of our classifier. Since there is an almost bewildering array of terms used in this context, we now give a summary. Table 4.6 shows the possible results when applying a classifier (or diagnostic test) to a population. To make the connection with the epidemiology literature, we think of "+" as the "disease" that we are trying to detect, and "−" as the "non-disease" state. To make the connection to the classical hypothesis testing literature, we think of "−" as the null hypothesis and "+" as the

sensitivity

specificity

		True class		
		− or Null	+ or Non-null	Total
Predicted	− or Null	True Neg. (TN)	False Neg. (FN)	N*
class	+ or Non-null	False Pos. (FP)	True Pos. (TP)	P*
	Total	N	P	

TABLE 4.6. *Possible results when applying a classifier or diagnostic test to a population.*

Name	Definition	Synonyms
False Pos. rate	FP/N	Type I error, 1−Specificity
True Pos. rate	TP/P	1−Type II error, power, sensitivity, recall
Pos. Pred. value	TP/P*	Precision, 1−false discovery proportion
Neg. Pred. value	TN/N*	

TABLE 4.7. *Important measures for classification and diagnostic testing, derived from quantities in Table 4.6.*

alternative (non-null) hypothesis. In the context of the `Default` data, "+" indicates an individual who defaults, and "−" indicates one who does not.

Table 4.7 lists many of the popular performance measures that are used in this context. The denominators for the false positive and true positive rates are the actual population counts in each class. In contrast, the denominators for the positive predictive value and the negative predictive value are the total predicted counts for each class.

4.4.3 Quadratic Discriminant Analysis

As we have discussed, LDA assumes that the observations within each class are drawn from a multivariate Gaussian distribution with a class-specific mean vector and a covariance matrix that is common to all K classes. *Quadratic discriminant analysis* (QDA) provides an alternative approach. Like LDA, the QDA classifier results from assuming that the observations from each class are drawn from a Gaussian distribution, and plugging estimates for the parameters into Bayes' theorem in order to perform prediction. However, unlike LDA, QDA assumes that each class has its own covariance matrix. That is, it assumes that an observation from the kth class is of the form $X \sim N(\mu_k, \mathbf{\Sigma}_k)$, where $\mathbf{\Sigma}_k$ is a covariance matrix for the kth class. Under this assumption, the Bayes classifier assigns an observation $X = x$ to the class for which

quadratic discriminant analysis

$$\begin{aligned} \delta_k(x) &= -\frac{1}{2}(x-\mu_k)^T \mathbf{\Sigma}_k^{-1}(x-\mu_k) - \frac{1}{2}\log|\mathbf{\Sigma}_k| + \log \pi_k \\ &= -\frac{1}{2}x^T\mathbf{\Sigma}_k^{-1}x + x^T\mathbf{\Sigma}_k^{-1}\mu_k - \frac{1}{2}\mu_k^T\mathbf{\Sigma}_k^{-1}\mu_k - \frac{1}{2}\log|\mathbf{\Sigma}_k| + \log \pi_k \end{aligned} \quad (4.28)$$

is largest. So the QDA classifier involves plugging estimates for $\mathbf{\Sigma}_k$, μ_k, and π_k into (4.28), and then assigning an observation $X = x$ to the class for which this quantity is largest. Unlike in (4.24), the quantity x appears as a *quadratic* function in (4.28). This is where QDA gets its name.

Why does it matter whether or not we assume that the K classes share a common covariance matrix? In other words, why would one prefer LDA to

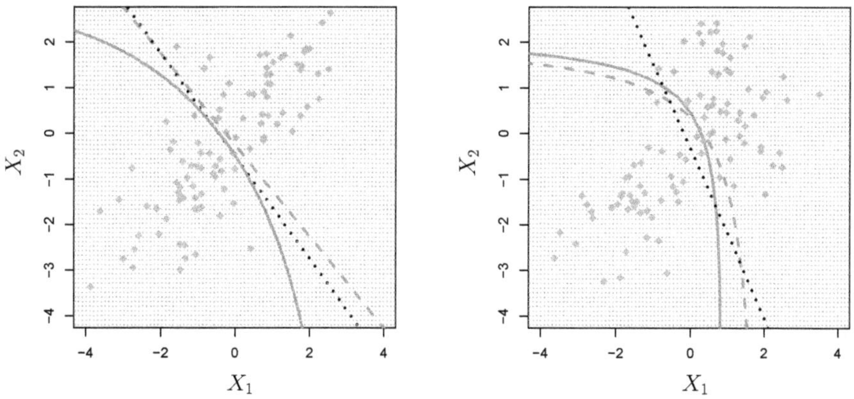

FIGURE 4.9. Left: *The Bayes (purple dashed), LDA (black dotted), and QDA (green solid) decision boundaries for a two-class problem with* $\mathbf{\Sigma}_1 = \mathbf{\Sigma}_2$. *The shading indicates the QDA decision rule. Since the Bayes decision boundary is linear, it is more accurately approximated by LDA than by QDA.* Right: *Details are as given in the left-hand panel, except that* $\mathbf{\Sigma}_1 \neq \mathbf{\Sigma}_2$. *Since the Bayes decision boundary is non-linear, it is more accurately approximated by QDA than by LDA.*

QDA, or vice-versa? The answer lies in the bias-variance trade-off. When there are p predictors, then estimating a covariance matrix requires estimating $p(p+1)/2$ parameters. QDA estimates a separate covariance matrix for each class, for a total of $Kp(p+1)/2$ parameters. With 50 predictors this is some multiple of 1,275, which is a lot of parameters. By instead assuming that the K classes share a common covariance matrix, the LDA model becomes linear in x, which means there are Kp linear coefficients to estimate. Consequently, LDA is a much less flexible classifier than QDA, and so has substantially lower variance. This can potentially lead to improved prediction performance. But there is a trade-off: if LDA's assumption that the K classes share a common covariance matrix is badly off, then LDA can suffer from high bias. Roughly speaking, LDA tends to be a better bet than QDA if there are relatively few training observations and so reducing variance is crucial. In contrast, QDA is recommended if the training set is very large, so that the variance of the classifier is not a major concern, or if the assumption of a common covariance matrix for the K classes is clearly untenable.

Figure 4.9 illustrates the performances of LDA and QDA in two scenarios. In the left-hand panel, the two Gaussian classes have a common correlation of 0.7 between X_1 and X_2. As a result, the Bayes decision boundary is linear and is accurately approximated by the LDA decision boundary. The QDA decision boundary is inferior, because it suffers from higher variance without a corresponding decrease in bias. In contrast, the right-hand panel displays a situation in which the orange class has a correlation of 0.7 between the variables and the blue class has a correlation of -0.7. Now the Bayes decision boundary is quadratic, and so QDA more accurately approximates this boundary than does LDA.

4.4.4 Naive Bayes

In previous sections, we used Bayes' theorem (4.15) to develop the LDA and QDA classifiers. Here, we use Bayes' theorem to motivate the popular *naive Bayes* classifier.

naive Bayes

Recall that Bayes' theorem (4.15) provides an expression for the posterior probability $p_k(x) = \Pr(Y = k|X = x)$ in terms of $\pi_1, \ldots, \pi_K$ and $f_1(x), \ldots, f_K(x)$. To use (4.15) in practice, we need estimates for $\pi_1, \ldots, \pi_K$ and $f_1(x), \ldots, f_K(x)$. As we saw in previous sections, estimating the prior probabilities $\pi_1, \ldots, \pi_K$ is typically straightforward: for instance, we can estimate $\hat{\pi}_k$ as the proportion of training observations belonging to the kth class, for $k = 1, \ldots, K$.

However, estimating $f_1(x), \ldots, f_K(x)$ is more subtle. Recall that $f_k(x)$ is the p-dimensional density function for an observation in the kth class, for $k = 1, \ldots, K$. In general, estimating a p-dimensional density function is challenging. In LDA, we make a very strong assumption that greatly simplifies the task: we assume that f_k is the density function for a multivariate normal random variable with class-specific mean μ_k, and shared covariance matrix $\boldsymbol{\Sigma}$. By contrast, in QDA, we assume that f_k is the density function for a multivariate normal random variable with class-specific mean μ_k, and class-specific covariance matrix $\boldsymbol{\Sigma}_k$. By making these very strong assumptions, we are able to replace the very challenging problem of estimating K p-dimensional density functions with the much simpler problem of estimating K p-dimensional mean vectors and one (in the case of LDA) or K (in the case of QDA) $(p \times p)$-dimensional covariance matrices.

The naive Bayes classifier takes a different tack for estimating $f_1(x), \ldots,$ $f_K(x)$. Instead of assuming that these functions belong to a particular family of distributions (e.g. multivariate normal), we instead make a single assumption:

Within the kth class, the p predictors are independent.

Stated mathematically, this assumption means that for $k = 1, \ldots, K$,

$$f_k(x) = f_{k1}(x_1) \times f_{k2}(x_2) \times \cdots \times f_{kp}(x_p), \tag{4.29}$$

where f_{kj} is the density function of the jth predictor among observations in the kth class.

Why is this assumption so powerful? Essentially, estimating a p-dimensional density function is challenging because we must consider not only the *marginal distribution* of each predictor — that is, the distribution of each predictor on its own — but also the *joint distribution* of the predictors — that is, the association between the different predictors. In the case of a multivariate normal distribution, the association between the different predictors is summarized by the off-diagonal elements of the covariance matrix. However, in general, this association can be very hard to characterize, and exceedingly challenging to estimate. But by assuming that the p covariates are independent within each class, we completely eliminate the need to worry about the association between the p predictors, because we have simply assumed that there is *no* association between the predictors!

marginal distribution
joint distribution

Do we really believe the naive Bayes assumption that the p covariates are independent within each class? In most settings, we do not. But even though this modeling assumption is made for convenience, it often leads to pretty decent results, especially in settings where n is not large enough relative to p for us to effectively estimate the joint distribution of the predictors within each class. In fact, since estimating a joint distribution requires such a huge amount of data, naive Bayes is a good choice in a wide range of settings. Essentially, the naive Bayes assumption introduces some bias, but reduces variance, leading to a classifier that works quite well in practice as a result of the bias-variance trade-off.

Once we have made the naive Bayes assumption, we can plug (4.29) into (4.15) to obtain an expression for the posterior probability,

$$\Pr(Y = k|X = x) = \frac{\pi_k \times f_{k1}(x_1) \times f_{k2}(x_2) \times \cdots \times f_{kp}(x_p)}{\sum_{l=1}^{K} \pi_l \times f_{l1}(x_1) \times f_{l2}(x_2) \times \cdots \times f_{lp}(x_p)} \tag{4.30}$$

for $k = 1, \ldots, K$.

To estimate the one-dimensional density function f_{kj} using training data $x_{1j}, \ldots, x_{nj}$, we have a few options.

- If X_j is quantitative, then we can assume that $X_j|Y = k \sim N(\mu_{jk}, \sigma_{jk}^2)$. In other words, we assume that within each class, the jth predictor is drawn from a (univariate) normal distribution. While this may sound a bit like QDA, there is one key difference, in that here we are assuming that the predictors are independent; this amounts to QDA with an additional assumption that the class-specific covariance matrix is diagonal.

- If X_j is quantitative, then another option is to use a non-parametric estimate for f_{kj}. A very simple way to do this is by making a histogram for the observations of the jth predictor within each class. Then we can estimate $f_{kj}(x_j)$ as the fraction of the training observations in the kth class that belong to the same histogram bin as x_j. Alternatively, we can use a *kernel density estimator*, which is essentially a smoothed version of a histogram.

kernel density estimator

- If X_j is qualitative, then we can simply count the proportion of training observations for the jth predictor corresponding to each class. For instance, suppose that $X_j \in \{1, 2, 3\}$, and we have 100 observations in the kth class. Suppose that the jth predictor takes on values of 1, 2, and 3 in 32, 55, and 13 of those observations, respectively. Then we can estimate f_{kj} as

$$\hat{f}_{kj}(x_j) = \begin{cases} 0.32 & \text{if } x_j = 1 \\ 0.55 & \text{if } x_j = 2 \\ 0.13 & \text{if } x_j = 3. \end{cases}$$

We now consider the naive Bayes classifier in a toy example with $p = 3$ predictors and $K = 2$ classes. The first two predictors are quantitative, and the third predictor is qualitative with three levels. Suppose further that $\hat{\pi}_1 = \hat{\pi}_2 = 0.5$. The estimated density functions $\hat{f}_{kj}$ for $k = 1, 2$ and $j = 1, 2, 3$ are displayed in Figure 4.10. Now suppose that we wish to classify a new observation, $x^* = (0.4, 1.5, 1)^T$. It turns out that in this

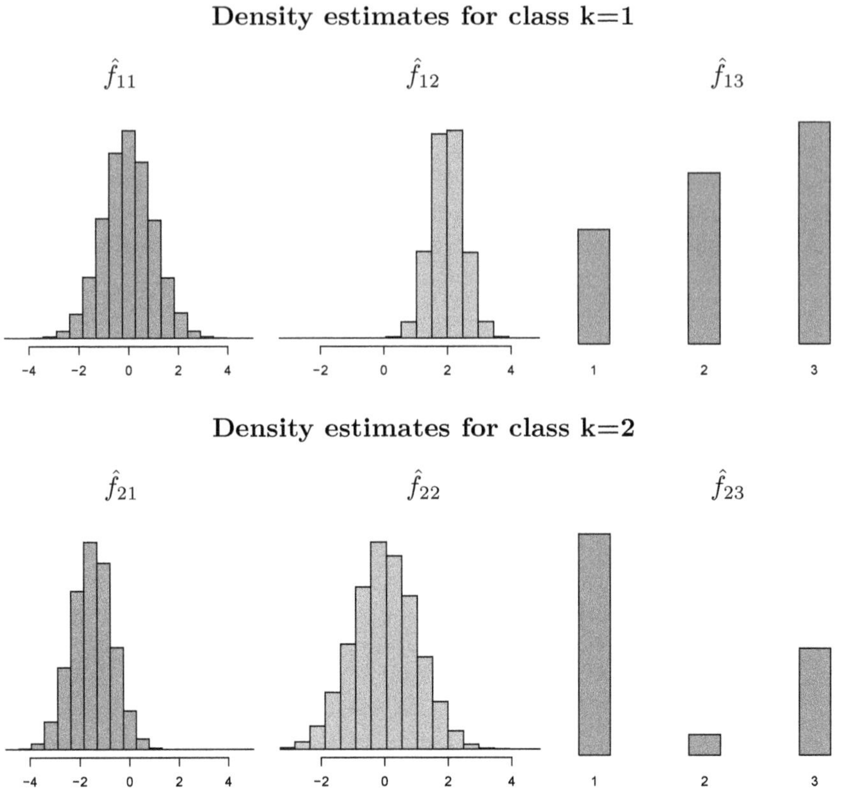

FIGURE 4.10. *In the toy example in Section 4.4.4, we generate data with* $p = 3$ *predictors and* $K = 2$ *classes. The first two predictors are quantitative, and the third predictor is qualitative with three levels. In each class, the estimated density for each of the three predictors is displayed. If the prior probabilities for the two classes are equal, then the observation* $x^* = (0.4, 1.5, 1)^T$ *has a* 94.4% *posterior probability of belonging to the first class.*

		True default status		
		No	Yes	Total
Predicted	No	9621	244	9865
default status	Yes	46	89	135
	Total	9667	333	10000

TABLE 4.8. *Comparison of the naive Bayes predictions to the true default status for the* 10,000 *training observations in the* `Default` *data set, when we predict default for any observation for which* $P(Y = \texttt{default}|X = x) > 0.5$.

example, $\hat{f}_{11}(0.4) = 0.368$, $\hat{f}_{12}(1.5) = 0.484$, $\hat{f}_{13}(1) = 0.226$, and $\hat{f}_{21}(0.4) = 0.030$, $\hat{f}_{22}(1.5) = 0.130$, $\hat{f}_{23}(1) = 0.616$. Plugging these estimates into (4.30) results in posterior probability estimates of $\Pr(Y = 1|X = x^*) = 0.944$ and $\Pr(Y = 2|X = x^*) = 0.056$.

Table 4.8 provides the confusion matrix resulting from applying the naive Bayes classifier to the `Default` data set, where we predict a default if the posterior probability of a default — that is, $P(Y = \texttt{default}|X = x)$ — exceeds 0.5. Comparing this to the results for LDA in Table 4.4, our findings are mixed. While LDA has a slightly lower overall error rate, naive Bayes

		True default status		
		No	Yes	Total
Predicted	No	9339	130	9469
default status	Yes	328	203	531
	Total	9667	333	10000

TABLE 4.9. *Comparison of the naive Bayes predictions to the true default status for the* 10,000 *training observations in the* `Default` *data set, when we predict default for any observation for which* $P(Y = \texttt{default}|X = x) > 0.2$.

correctly predicts a higher fraction of the true defaulters. In this implementation of naive Bayes, we have assumed that each quantitative predictor is drawn from a Gaussian distribution (and, of course, that within each class, each predictor is independent).

Just as with LDA, we can easily adjust the probability threshold for predicting a default. For example, Table 4.9 provides the confusion matrix resulting from predicting a default if $P(Y = \texttt{default}|X = x) > 0.2$. Again, the results are mixed relative to LDA with the same threshold (Table 4.5). Naive Bayes has a higher error rate, but correctly predicts almost two-thirds of the true defaults.

In this example, it should not be too surprising that naive Bayes does not convincingly outperform LDA: this data set has $n = 10{,}000$ and $p = 2$, and so the reduction in variance resulting from the naive Bayes assumption is not necessarily worthwhile. We expect to see a greater pay-off to using naive Bayes relative to LDA or QDA in instances where p is larger or n is smaller, so that reducing the variance is very important.

4.5 A Comparison of Classification Methods

4.5.1 An Analytical Comparison

We now perform an *analytical* (or mathematical) comparison of LDA, QDA, naive Bayes, and logistic regression. We consider these approaches in a setting with K classes, so that we assign an observation to the class that maximizes $\Pr(Y = k|X = x)$. Equivalently, we can set K as the *baseline* class and assign an observation to the class that maximizes

$$\log\left(\frac{\Pr(Y = k|X = x)}{\Pr(Y = K|X = x)}\right) \tag{4.31}$$

for $k = 1, \ldots, K$. Examining the specific form of (4.31) for each method provides a clear understanding of their similarities and differences.

First, for LDA, we can make use of Bayes' theorem (4.15) as well as the assumption that the predictors within each class are drawn from a multivariate normal density (4.23) with class-specific mean and shared covariance matrix in order to show that

$$\begin{aligned}
\log\left(\frac{\Pr(Y=k|X=x)}{\Pr(Y=K|X=x)}\right) &= \log\left(\frac{\pi_k f_k(x)}{\pi_K f_K(x)}\right)\\
&= \log\left(\frac{\pi_k \exp\left(-\frac{1}{2}(x-\mu_k)^T\boldsymbol{\Sigma}^{-1}(x-\mu_k)\right)}{\pi_K \exp\left(-\frac{1}{2}(x-\mu_K)^T\boldsymbol{\Sigma}^{-1}(x-\mu_K)\right)}\right)\\
&= \log\left(\frac{\pi_k}{\pi_K}\right) - \frac{1}{2}(x-\mu_k)^T\boldsymbol{\Sigma}^{-1}(x-\mu_k)\\
&\quad +\frac{1}{2}(x-\mu_K)^T\boldsymbol{\Sigma}^{-1}(x-\mu_K)\\
&= \log\left(\frac{\pi_k}{\pi_K}\right) - \frac{1}{2}(\mu_k+\mu_K)^T\boldsymbol{\Sigma}^{-1}(\mu_k-\mu_K)\\
&\quad + x^T\boldsymbol{\Sigma}^{-1}(\mu_k-\mu_K)\\
&= a_k + \sum_{j=1}^p b_{kj}x_j, \qquad (4.32)
\end{aligned}$$

where $a_k = \log\left(\frac{\pi_k}{\pi_K}\right) - \frac{1}{2}(\mu_k+\mu_K)^T\boldsymbol{\Sigma}^{-1}(\mu_k-\mu_K)$ and b_{kj} is the jth component of $\boldsymbol{\Sigma}^{-1}(\mu_k-\mu_K)$. Hence LDA, like logistic regression, assumes that the log odds of the posterior probabilities is linear in x.

Using similar calculations, in the QDA setting (4.31) becomes

$$\log\left(\frac{\Pr(Y=k|X=x)}{\Pr(Y=K|X=x)}\right) = a_k + \sum_{j=1}^p b_{kj}x_j + \sum_{j=1}^p\sum_{l=1}^p c_{kjl}x_jx_l, \qquad (4.33)$$

where a_k, b_{kj}, and c_{kjl} are functions of $\pi_k, \pi_K, \mu_k, \mu_K, \boldsymbol{\Sigma}_k$ and $\boldsymbol{\Sigma}_K$. Again, as the name suggests, QDA assumes that the log odds of the posterior probabilities is quadratic in x.

Finally, we examine (4.31) in the naive Bayes setting. Recall that in this setting, $f_k(x)$ is modeled as a product of p one-dimensional functions $f_{kj}(x_j)$ for $j = 1, \ldots, p$. Hence,

$$\begin{aligned}
\log\left(\frac{\Pr(Y=k|X=x)}{\Pr(Y=K|X=x)}\right) &= \log\left(\frac{\pi_k f_k(x)}{\pi_K f_K(x)}\right)\\
&= \log\left(\frac{\pi_k \prod_{j=1}^p f_{kj}(x_j)}{\pi_K \prod_{j=1}^p f_{Kj}(x_j)}\right)\\
&= \log\left(\frac{\pi_k}{\pi_K}\right) + \sum_{j=1}^p \log\left(\frac{f_{kj}(x_j)}{f_{Kj}(x_j)}\right)\\
&= a_k + \sum_{j=1}^p g_{kj}(x_j), \qquad (4.34)
\end{aligned}$$

where $a_k = \log\left(\frac{\pi_k}{\pi_K}\right)$ and $g_{kj}(x_j) = \log\left(\frac{f_{kj}(x_j)}{f_{Kj}(x_j)}\right)$. Hence, the right-hand side of (4.34) takes the form of a *generalized additive model*, a topic that is discussed further in Chapter 7.

Inspection of (4.32), (4.33), and (4.34) yields the following observations about LDA, QDA, and naive Bayes:

- LDA is a special case of QDA with $c_{kjl} = 0$ for all $j = 1, \ldots, p$, $l = 1, \ldots, p$, and $k = 1, \ldots, K$. (Of course, this is not surprising, since LDA is simply a restricted version of QDA with $\mathbf{\Sigma}_1 = \cdots = \mathbf{\Sigma}_K = \mathbf{\Sigma}$.)

- Any classifier with a linear decision boundary is a special case of naive Bayes with $g_{kj}(x_j) = b_{kj}x_j$. In particular, this means that LDA is a special case of naive Bayes! This is not at all obvious from the descriptions of LDA and naive Bayes earlier in this chapter, since each method makes very different assumptions: LDA assumes that the features are normally distributed with a common within-class covariance matrix, and naive Bayes instead assumes independence of the features.

- If we model $f_{kj}(x_j)$ in the naive Bayes classifier using a one-dimensional Gaussian distribution $N(\mu_{kj}, \sigma_j^2)$, then we end up with $g_{kj}(x_j) = b_{kj}x_j$ where $b_{kj} = (\mu_{kj} - \mu_{Kj})/\sigma_j^2$. In this case, naive Bayes is actually a special case of LDA with $\mathbf{\Sigma}$ restricted to be a diagonal matrix with jth diagonal element equal to σ_j^2.

- Neither QDA nor naive Bayes is a special case of the other. Naive Bayes can produce a more flexible fit, since any choice can be made for $g_{kj}(x_j)$. However, it is restricted to a purely *additive* fit, in the sense that in (4.34), a function of x_j is *added* to a function of x_l, for $j \neq l$; however, these terms are never multiplied. By contrast, QDA includes multiplicative terms of the form $c_{kjl}x_jx_l$. Therefore, QDA has the potential to be more accurate in settings where interactions among the predictors are important in discriminating between classes.

None of these methods uniformly dominates the others: in any setting, the choice of method will depend on the true distribution of the predictors in each of the K classes, as well as other considerations, such as the values of n and p. The latter ties into the bias-variance trade-off.

How does logistic regression tie into this story? Recall from (4.12) that multinomial logistic regression takes the form

$$\log\left(\frac{\Pr(Y = k|X = x)}{\Pr(Y = K|X = x)}\right) = \beta_{k0} + \sum_{j=1}^{p} \beta_{kj}x_j.$$

This is identical to the linear form of LDA (4.32): in both cases, $\log\left(\frac{\Pr(Y=k|X=x)}{\Pr(Y=K|X=x)}\right)$ is a linear function of the predictors. In LDA, the coefficients in this linear function are functions of estimates for π_k, π_K, μ_k, μ_K, and $\mathbf{\Sigma}$ obtained by assuming that $X_1, \ldots, X_p$ follow a normal distribution within each class. By contrast, in logistic regression, the coefficients are chosen to maximize the likelihood function (4.5). Thus, we expect LDA to outperform logistic regression when the normality assumption (approximately) holds, and we expect logistic regression to perform better when it does not.

We close with a brief discussion of *K-nearest neighbors* (KNN), introduced in Chapter 2. Recall that KNN takes a completely different approach from the classifiers seen in this chapter. In order to make a prediction for an observation $X = x$, the training observations that are closest to x are identified. Then X is assigned to the class to which the plurality of these observations belong. Hence KNN is a completely non-parametric approach: no assumptions are made about the shape of the decision boundary. We make the following observations about KNN:

- Because KNN is completely non-parametric, we can expect this approach to dominate LDA and logistic regression when the decision boundary is highly non-linear, provided that n is very large and p is small.

- In order to provide accurate classification, KNN requires *a lot* of observations relative to the number of predictors—that is, n much larger than p. This has to do with the fact that KNN is non-parametric, and thus tends to reduce the bias while incurring a lot of variance.

- In settings where the decision boundary is non-linear but n is only modest, or p is not very small, then QDA may be preferred to KNN. This is because QDA can provide a non-linear decision boundary while taking advantage of a parametric form, which means that it requires a smaller sample size for accurate classification, relative to KNN.

- Unlike logistic regression, KNN does not tell us which predictors are important: we don't get a table of coefficients as in Table 4.3.

4.5.2 An Empirical Comparison

We now compare the *empirical* (practical) performance of logistic regression, LDA, QDA, naive Bayes, and KNN. We generated data from six different scenarios, each of which involves a binary (two-class) classification problem. In three of the scenarios, the Bayes decision boundary is linear, and in the remaining scenarios it is non-linear. For each scenario, we produced 100 random training data sets. On each of these training sets, we fit each method to the data and computed the resulting test error rate on a large test set. Results for the linear scenarios are shown in Figure 4.11, and the results for the non-linear scenarios are in Figure 4.12. The KNN method requires selection of K, the number of neighbors (not to be confused with the number of classes in earlier sections of this chapter). We performed KNN with two values of K: $K = 1$, and a value of K that was chosen automatically using an approach called *cross-validation*, which we discuss further in Chapter 5. We applied naive Bayes assuming univariate Gaussian densities for the features within each class (and, of course — since this is the key characteristic of naive Bayes — assuming independence of the features).

In each of the six scenarios, there were $p = 2$ quantitative predictors. The scenarios were as follows:

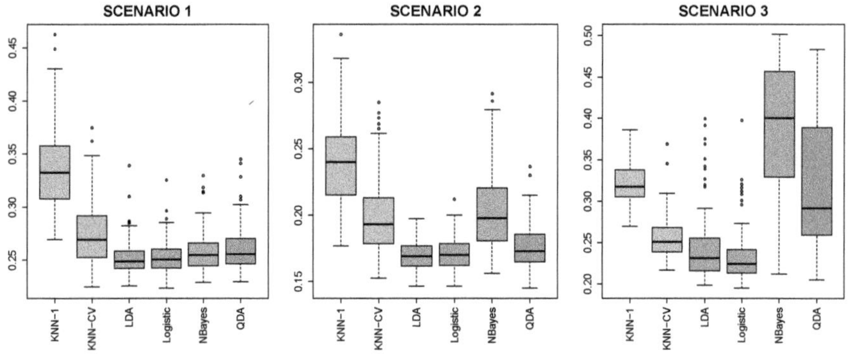

FIGURE 4.11. *Boxplots of the test error rates for each of the linear scenarios described in the main text.*

Scenario 1: There were 20 training observations in each of two classes. The observations within each class were uncorrelated random normal variables with a different mean in each class. The left-hand panel of Figure 4.11 shows that LDA performed well in this setting, as one would expect since this is the model assumed by LDA. Logistic regression also performed quite well, since it assumes a linear decision boundary. KNN performed poorly because it paid a price in terms of variance that was not offset by a reduction in bias. QDA also performed worse than LDA, since it fit a more flexible classifier than necessary. The performance of naive Bayes was slightly better than QDA, because the naive Bayes assumption of independent predictors is correct.

Scenario 2: Details are as in Scenario 1, except that within each class, the two predictors had a correlation of −0.5. The center panel of Figure 4.11 indicates that the performance of most methods is similar to the previous scenario. The notable exception is naive Bayes, which performs very poorly here, since the naive Bayes assumption of independent predictors is violated.

Scenario 3: As in the previous scenario, there is substantial negative correlation between the predictors within each class. However, this time we generated X_1 and X_2 from the ***t-distribution***, with 50 observations per class. The t-distribution has a similar shape to the normal distribution, but it has a tendency to yield more extreme points—that is, more points that are far from the mean. In this setting, the decision boundary was still linear, and so fit into the logistic regression framework. The set-up violated the assumptions of LDA, since the observations were not drawn from a normal distribution. The right-hand panel of Figure 4.11 shows that logistic regression outperformed LDA, though both methods were superior to the other approaches. In particular, the QDA results deteriorated considerably as a consequence of non-normality. Naive Bayes performed very poorly because the independence assumption is violated.

t-distribution

Scenario 4: The data were generated from a normal distribution, with a correlation of 0.5 between the predictors in the first class, and correlation of −0.5 between the predictors in the second class. This setup corresponded to the QDA assumption, and resulted in quadratic decision boundaries. The left-hand panel of Figure 4.12 shows that QDA outperformed all of the

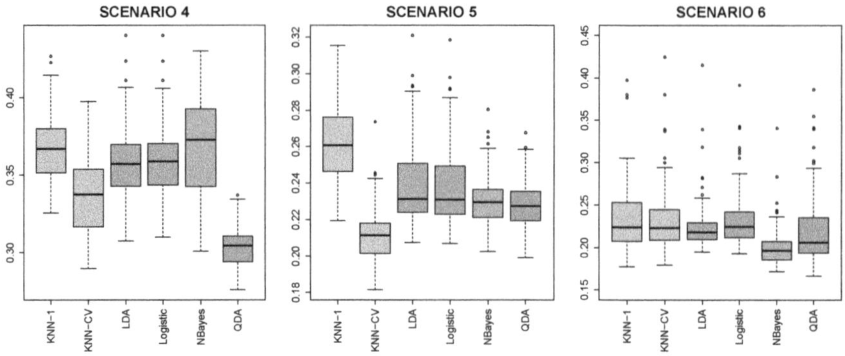

FIGURE 4.12. *Boxplots of the test error rates for each of the non-linear scenarios described in the main text.*

other approaches. The naive Bayes assumption of independent predictors is violated, so naive Bayes performs poorly.

Scenario 5: The data were generated from a normal distribution with uncorrelated predictors. Then the responses were sampled from the logistic function applied to a complicated non-linear function of the predictors. The center panel of Figure 4.12 shows that both QDA and naive Bayes gave slightly better results than the linear methods, while the much more flexible KNN-CV method gave the best results. But KNN with $K = 1$ gave the worst results out of all methods. This highlights the fact that even when the data exhibits a complex non-linear relationship, a non-parametric method such as KNN can still give poor results if the level of smoothness is not chosen correctly.

Scenario 6: The observations were generated from a normal distribution with a different diagonal covariance matrix for each class. However, the sample size was *very* small: just $n = 6$ in each class. Naive Bayes performed very well, because its assumptions are met. LDA and logistic regression performed poorly because the true decision boundary is non-linear, due to the unequal covariance matrices. QDA performed a bit worse than naive Bayes, because given the very small sample size, the former incurred too much variance in estimating the correlation between the predictors within each class. KNN's performance also suffered due to the very small sample size.

These six examples illustrate that no one method will dominate the others in every situation. When the true decision boundaries are linear, then the LDA and logistic regression approaches will tend to perform well. When the boundaries are moderately non-linear, QDA or naive Bayes may give better results. Finally, for much more complicated decision boundaries, a non-parametric approach such as KNN can be superior. But the level of smoothness for a non-parametric approach must be chosen carefully. In the next chapter we examine a number of approaches for choosing the correct level of smoothness and, in general, for selecting the best overall method.

Finally, recall from Chapter 3 that in the regression setting we can accommodate a non-linear relationship between the predictors and the response by performing regression using transformations of the predictors. A similar approach could be taken in the classification setting. For instance, we could

	Coefficient	Std. error	t-statistic	p-value
`Intercept`	73.60	5.13	14.34	0.00
`workingday`	1.27	1.78	0.71	0.48
`temp`	157.21	10.26	15.32	0.00
`weathersit[cloudy/misty]`	-12.89	1.96	-6.56	0.00
`weathersit[light rain/snow]`	-66.49	2.97	-22.43	0.00
`weathersit[heavy rain/snow]`	-109.75	76.67	-1.43	0.15

TABLE 4.10. *Results for a least squares linear model fit to predict* `bikers` *in the* `Bikeshare` *data. The predictors* `mnth` *and* `hr` *are omitted from this table due to space constraints, and can be seen in Figure 4.13. For the qualitative variable* `weathersit`*, the baseline level corresponds to clear skies.*

create a more flexible version of logistic regression by including X^2, X^3, and even X^4 as predictors. This may or may not improve logistic regression's performance, depending on whether the increase in variance due to the added flexibility is offset by a sufficiently large reduction in bias. We could do the same for LDA. If we added all possible quadratic terms and cross-products to LDA, the form of the model would be the same as the QDA model, although the parameter estimates would be different. This device allows us to move somewhere between an LDA and a QDA model.

4.6 Generalized Linear Models

In Chapter 3, we assumed that the response Y is quantitative, and explored the use of least squares linear regression to predict Y. Thus far in this chapter, we have instead assumed that Y is qualitative. However, we may sometimes be faced with situations in which Y is neither qualitative nor quantitative, and so neither linear regression from Chapter 3 nor the classification approaches covered in this chapter is applicable.

As a concrete example, we consider the `Bikeshare` data set. The response is `bikers`, the number of hourly users of a bike sharing program in Washington, DC. This response value is neither qualitative nor quantitative: instead, it takes on non-negative integer values, or *counts*. We will consider predicting `bikers` using the covariates `mnth` (month of the year), `hr` (hour of the day, from 0 to 23), `workingday` (an indicator variable that equals 1 if it is neither a weekend nor a holiday), `temp` (the normalized temperature, in Celsius), and `weathersit` (a qualitative variable that takes on one of four possible values: clear; misty or cloudy; light rain or light snow; or heavy rain or heavy snow.)

counts

In the analyses that follow, we will treat `mnth`, `hr`, and `weathersit` as qualitative variables.

4.6.1 Linear Regression on the Bikeshare Data

To begin, we consider predicting `bikers` using linear regression. The results are shown in Table 4.10.

We see, for example, that a progression of weather from clear to cloudy results in, on average, 12.89 fewer bikers per hour; however, if the weather progresses further to rain or snow, then this further results in 53.60 fewer bikers per hour. Figure 4.13 displays the coefficients associated with `mnth`

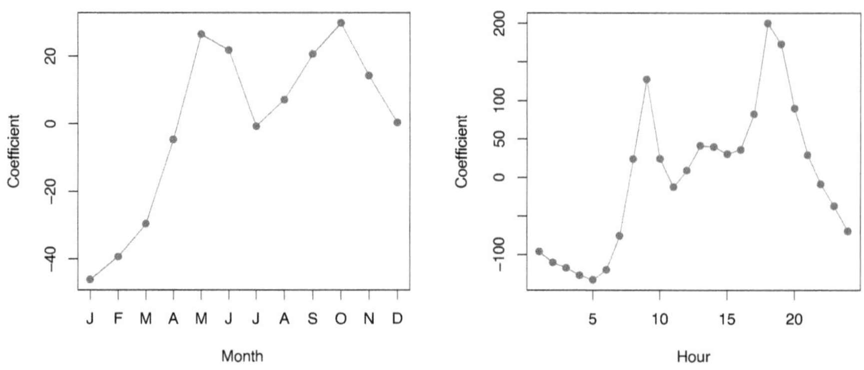

FIGURE 4.13. *A least squares linear regression model was fit to predict* `bikers` *in the* `Bikeshare` *data set.* Left: *The coefficients associated with the month of the year. Bike usage is highest in the spring and fall, and lowest in the winter.* Right: *The coefficients associated with the hour of the day. Bike usage is highest during peak commute times, and lowest overnight.*

and the coefficients associated with `hr`. We see that bike usage is highest in the spring and fall, and lowest during the winter months. Furthermore, bike usage is greatest around rush hour (9 AM and 6 PM), and lowest overnight. Thus, at first glance, fitting a linear regression model to the `Bikeshare` data set seems to provide reasonable and intuitive results.

But upon more careful inspection, some issues become apparent. For example, 9.6% of the fitted values in the `Bikeshare` data set are negative: that is, the linear regression model predicts a *negative* number of users during 9.6% of the hours in the data set. This calls into question our ability to perform meaningful predictions on the data, and it also raises concerns about the accuracy of the coefficient estimates, confidence intervals, and other outputs of the regression model.

Furthermore, it is reasonable to suspect that when the expected value of `bikers` is small, the variance of `bikers` should be small as well. For instance, at 2 AM during a heavy December snow storm, we expect that extremely few people will use a bike, and moreover that there should be little variance associated with the number of users during those conditions. This is borne out in the data: between 1 AM and 4 AM, in December, January, and February, when it is raining, there are 5.05 users, on average, with a standard deviation of 3.73. By contrast, between 7 AM and 10 AM, in April, May, and June, when skies are clear, there are 243.59 users, on average, with a standard deviation of 131.7. The mean-variance relationship is displayed in the left-hand panel of Figure 4.14. This is a major violation of the assumptions of a linear model, which state that $Y = \sum_{j=1}^{p} X_j\beta_j + \epsilon$, where ϵ is a mean-zero error term with variance σ^2 that is *constant*, and not a function of the covariates. Therefore, the heteroscedasticity of the data calls into question the suitability of a linear regression model.

Finally, the response `bikers` is integer-valued. But under a linear model, $Y = \beta_0 + \sum_{j=1}^{p} X_j\beta_j + \epsilon$, where ϵ is a continuous-valued error term. This means that in a linear model, the response Y is necessarily continuous-valued (quantitative). Thus, the integer nature of the response `bikers` suggests that a linear regression model is not entirely satisfactory for this data set.

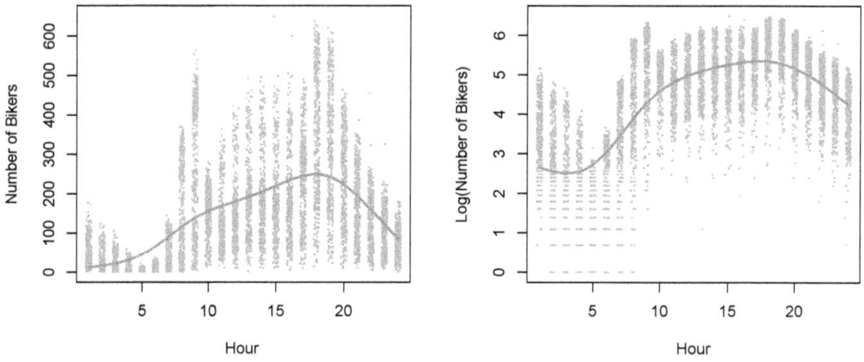

FIGURE 4.14. Left: *On the* `Bikeshare` *dataset, the number of bikers is displayed on the y-axis, and the hour of the day is displayed on the x-axis. Jitter was applied for ease of visualization. For the most part, as the mean number of bikers increases, so does the variance in the number of bikers. A smoothing spline fit is shown in green.* Right: *The log of the number of bikers is now displayed on the y-axis.*

Some of the problems that arise when fitting a linear regression model to the `Bikeshare` data can be overcome by transforming the response; for instance, we can fit the model

$$\log(Y) = \sum_{j=1}^{p} X_j\beta_j + \epsilon.$$

Transforming the response avoids the possibility of negative predictions, and it overcomes much of the heteroscedasticity in the untransformed data, as is shown in the right-hand panel of Figure 4.14. However, it is not quite a satisfactory solution, since predictions and inference are made in terms of the log of the response, rather than the response. This leads to challenges in interpretation, e.g. *"a one-unit increase in X_j is associated with an increase in the mean of the log of Y by an amount β_j"*. Furthermore, a log transformation of the response cannot be applied in settings where the response can take on a value of 0. Thus, while fitting a linear model to a transformation of the response may be an adequate approach for some count-valued data sets, it often leaves something to be desired. We will see in the next section that a Poisson regression model provides a much more natural and elegant approach for this task.

4.6.2 Poisson Regression on the Bikeshare Data

To overcome the inadequacies of linear regression for analyzing the `Bikeshare` data set, we will make use of an alternative approach, called *Poisson regression*. Before we can talk about Poisson regression, we must first introduce the *Poisson distribution*.

Poisson regression

Suppose that a random variable Y takes on nonnegative integer values, i.e. $Y \in \{0, 1, 2, \ldots\}$. If Y follows the Poisson distribution, then

Poisson distribution

$$\Pr(Y = k) = \frac{e^{-\lambda}\lambda^k}{k!} \quad \text{for } k = 0, 1, 2, \ldots. \tag{4.35}$$

Here, $\lambda > 0$ is the expected value of Y, i.e. $\text{E}(Y)$. It turns out that λ also equals the variance of Y, i.e. $\lambda = \text{E}(Y) = \text{Var}(Y)$. This means that if Y follows the Poisson distribution, then the larger the mean of Y, the larger its variance. (In (4.35), the notation $k!$, pronounced "k factorial", is defined as $k! = k \times (k-1) \times (k-2) \times \ldots \times 3 \times 2 \times 1$.)

The Poisson distribution is typically used to model *counts*; this is a natural choice for a number of reasons, including the fact that counts, like the Poisson distribution, take on nonnegative integer values. To see how we might use the Poisson distribution in practice, let Y denote the number of users of the bike sharing program during a particular hour of the day, under a particular set of weather conditions, and during a particular month of the year. We might model Y as a Poisson distribution with mean $\text{E}(Y) = \lambda = 5$. This means that the probability of no users during this particular hour is $\Pr(Y = 0) = \frac{e^{-5}5^0}{0!} = e^{-5} = 0.0067$ (where $0! = 1$ by convention). The probability that there is exactly one user is $\Pr(Y = 1) = \frac{e^{-5}5^1}{1!} = 5e^{-5} = 0.034$, the probability of two users is $\Pr(Y = 2) = \frac{e^{-5}5^2}{2!} = 0.084$, and so on.

Of course, in reality, we expect the mean number of users of the bike sharing program, $\lambda = \text{E}(Y)$, to vary as a function of the hour of the day, the month of the year, the weather conditions, and so forth. So rather than modeling the number of bikers, Y, as a Poisson distribution with a fixed mean value like $\lambda = 5$, we would like to allow the mean to vary as a function of the covariates. In particular, we consider the following model for the mean $\lambda = \text{E}(Y)$, which we now write as $\lambda(X_1, \ldots, X_p)$ to emphasize that it is a function of the covariates $X_1, \ldots, X_p$:

$$\log(\lambda(X_1, \ldots, X_p)) = \beta_0 + \beta_1 X_1 + \cdots + \beta_p X_p \tag{4.36}$$

or equivalently

$$\lambda(X_1, \ldots, X_p) = e^{\beta_0 + \beta_1 X_1 + \cdots + \beta_p X_p}. \tag{4.37}$$

Here, $\beta_0, \beta_1, \ldots, \beta_p$ are parameters to be estimated. Together, (4.35) and (4.36) define the Poisson regression model. Notice that in (4.36), we take the *log* of $\lambda(X_1, \ldots, X_p)$ to be linear in $X_1, \ldots, X_p$, rather than having $\lambda(X_1, \ldots, X_p)$ itself be linear in $X_1, \ldots, X_p$; this ensures that $\lambda(X_1, \ldots, X_p)$ takes on nonnegative values for all values of the covariates.

To estimate the coefficients $\beta_0, \beta_1, \ldots, \beta_p$, we use the same maximum likelihood approach that we adopted for logistic regression in Section 4.3.2. Specifically, given n independent observations from the Poisson regression model, the likelihood takes the form

$$\ell(\beta_0, \beta_1, \ldots, \beta_p) = \prod_{i=1}^{n} \frac{e^{-\lambda(x_i)} \lambda(x_i)^{y_i}}{y_i!}, \tag{4.38}$$

where $\lambda(x_i) = e^{\beta_0 + \beta_1 x_{i1} + \cdots + \beta_p x_{ip}}$, due to (4.37). We estimate the coefficients that maximize the likelihood $\ell(\beta_0, \beta_1, \ldots, \beta_p)$, i.e. that make the observed data as likely as possible.

We now fit a Poisson regression model to the `Bikeshare` data set. The results are shown in Table 4.11 and Figure 4.15. Qualitatively, the results are similar to those from linear regression in Section 4.6.1. We again see that bike usage is highest in the spring and fall and during rush hour,

	Coefficient	Std. error	z-statistic	p-value
`Intercept`	4.12	0.01	683.96	0.00
`workingday`	0.01	0.00	7.5	0.00
`temp`	0.79	0.01	68.43	0.00
`weathersit[cloudy/misty]`	-0.08	0.00	-34.53	0.00
`weathersit[light rain/snow]`	-0.58	0.00	-141.91	0.00
`weathersit[heavy rain/snow]`	-0.93	0.17	-5.55	0.00

TABLE 4.11. *Results for a Poisson regression model fit to predict* `bikers` *in the* `Bikeshare` *data. The predictors* `mnth` *and* `hr` *are omitted from this table due to space constraints, and can be seen in Figure 4.15. For the qualitative variable* `weathersit`*, the baseline corresponds to clear skies.*

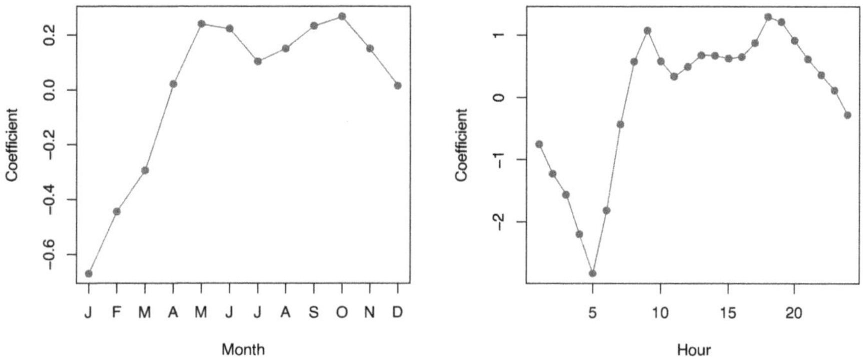

FIGURE 4.15. *A Poisson regression model was fit to predict* `bikers` *in the* `Bikeshare` *data set.* Left: *The coefficients associated with the month of the year. Bike usage is highest in the spring and fall, and lowest in the winter.* Right: *The coefficients associated with the hour of the day. Bike usage is highest during peak commute times, and lowest overnight.*

and lowest during the winter and in the early morning hours. Moreover, bike usage increases as the temperature increases, and decreases as the weather worsens. Interestingly, the coefficient associated with `workingday` is statistically significant under the Poisson regression model, but not under the linear regression model.

Some important distinctions between the Poisson regression model and the linear regression model are as follows:

- *Interpretation:* To interpret the coefficients in the Poisson regression model, we must pay close attention to (4.37), which states that an increase in X_j by one unit is associated with a change in $\text{E}(Y) = \lambda$ by a factor of $\exp(\beta_j)$. For example, a change in weather from clear to cloudy skies is associated with a change in mean bike usage by a factor of $\exp(-0.08) = 0.923$, i.e. on average, only 92.3% as many people will use bikes when it is cloudy relative to when it is clear. If the weather worsens further and it begins to rain, then the mean bike usage will further change by a factor of $\exp(-0.5) = 0.607$, i.e. on average only 60.7% as many people will use bikes when it is rainy relative to when it is cloudy.

- *Mean-variance relationship:* As mentioned earlier, under the Poisson model, $\lambda = \mathrm{E}(Y) = \mathrm{Var}(Y)$. Thus, by modeling bike usage with a Poisson regression, we implicitly assume that mean bike usage in a given hour equals the variance of bike usage during that hour. By contrast, under a linear regression model, the variance of bike usage always takes on a constant value. Recall from Figure 4.14 that in the `Bikeshare` data, when biking conditions are favorable, both the mean *and* the variance in bike usage are much higher than when conditions are unfavorable. Thus, the Poisson regression model is able to handle the mean-variance relationship seen in the `Bikeshare` data in a way that the linear regression model is not.[5]

overdispersion

- *nonnegative fitted values:* There are no negative predictions using the Poisson regression model. This is because the Poisson model itself only allows for nonnegative values; see (4.35). By contrast, when we fit a linear regression model to the `Bikeshare` data set, almost 10% of the predictions were negative.

4.6.3 Generalized Linear Models in Greater Generality

We have now discussed three types of regression models: linear, logistic and Poisson. These approaches share some common characteristics:

1. Each approach uses predictors $X_1, \ldots, X_p$ to predict a response Y. We assume that, conditional on $X_1, \ldots, X_p$, Y belongs to a certain family of distributions. For linear regression, we typically assume that Y follows a Gaussian or normal distribution. For logistic regression, we assume that Y follows a Bernoulli distribution. Finally, for Poisson regression, we assume that Y follows a Poisson distribution.

2. Each approach models the mean of Y as a function of the predictors. In linear regression, the mean of Y takes the form

$$\mathrm{E}(Y|X_1, \ldots, X_p) = \beta_0 + \beta_1 X_1 + \cdots + \beta_p X_p, \tag{4.39}$$

i.e. it is a linear function of the predictors. For logistic regression, the mean instead takes the form

$$\begin{aligned}\mathrm{E}(Y|X_1, \ldots, X_p) &= \Pr(Y = 1|X_1, \ldots, X_p) \\ &= \frac{e^{\beta_0 + \beta_1 X_1 + \cdots + \beta_p X_p}}{1 + e^{\beta_0 + \beta_1 X_1 + \cdots + \beta_p X_p}},\end{aligned} \tag{4.40}$$

while for Poisson regression it takes the form

$$\mathrm{E}(Y|X_1, \ldots, X_p) = \lambda(X_1, \ldots, X_p) = e^{\beta_0 + \beta_1 X_1 + \cdots + \beta_p X_p}. \tag{4.41}$$

Equations (4.39)–(4.41) can be expressed using a *link function*, η, which

link function

[5]In fact, the variance in the `Bikeshare` data appears to be much higher than the mean, a situation referred to as *overdispersion*. This causes the Z-values to be inflated in Table 4.11. A more careful analysis should account for this overdispersion to obtain more accurate Z-values, and there are a variety of methods for doing this. But they are beyond the scope of this book.

applies a transformation to $E(Y|X_1,\ldots,X_p)$ so that the transformed mean is a linear function of the predictors. That is,

$$\eta(E(Y|X_1,\ldots,X_p)) = \beta_0 + \beta_1 X_1 + \cdots + \beta_p X_p. \tag{4.42}$$

The link functions for linear, logistic and Poisson regression are $\eta(\mu) = \mu$, $\eta(\mu) = \log(\mu/(1-\mu))$, and $\eta(\mu) = \log(\mu)$, respectively.

The Gaussian, Bernoulli and Poisson distributions are all members of a wider class of distributions, known as the *exponential family*. Other well-known members of this family are the *exponential* distribution, the *Gamma* distribution, and the *negative binomial* distribution. In general, we can perform a regression by modeling the response Y as coming from a particular member of the exponential family, and then transforming the mean of the response so that the transformed mean is a linear function of the predictors via (4.42). Any regression approach that follows this very general recipe is known as a *generalized linear model* (GLM). Thus, linear regression, logistic regression, and Poisson regression are three examples of GLMs. Other examples not covered here include *Gamma regression* and *negative binomial regression*.

exponential family
exponential
Gamma
negative binomial
generalized linear model

4.7 Lab: Logistic Regression, LDA, QDA, and KNN

4.7.1 The Stock Market Data

In this lab we will examine the `Smarket` data, which is part of the `ISLP` library. This data set consists of percentage returns for the S&P 500 stock index over 1,250 days, from the beginning of 2001 until the end of 2005. For each date, we have recorded the percentage returns for each of the five previous trading days, `Lag1` through `Lag5`. We have also recorded `Volume` (the number of shares traded on the previous day, in billions), `Today` (the percentage return on the date in question) and `Direction` (whether the market was `Up` or `Down` on this date).

We start by importing our libraries at this top level; these are all imports we have seen in previous labs.

In [1]:
```
import numpy as np
import pandas as pd
from matplotlib.pyplot import subplots
import statsmodels.api as sm
from ISLP import load_data
from ISLP.models import (ModelSpec as MS,
                         summarize)
```

We also collect together the new imports needed for this lab.

In [2]:
```
from ISLP import confusion_table
from ISLP.models import contrast
from sklearn.discriminant_analysis import \
     (LinearDiscriminantAnalysis as LDA,
      QuadraticDiscriminantAnalysis as QDA)
from sklearn.naive_bayes import GaussianNB
from sklearn.neighbors import KNeighborsClassifier
from sklearn.preprocessing import StandardScaler
```

```
from sklearn.model_selection import train_test_split
from sklearn.linear_model import LogisticRegression
```

Now we are ready to load the Smarket data.

In [3]:
```
Smarket = load_data('Smarket')
Smarket
```

This gives a truncated listing of the data, which we do not show here. We can see what the variable names are.

In [4]:
```
Smarket.columns
```

Out[4]:
```
Index(['Year', 'Lag1', 'Lag2', 'Lag3', 'Lag4', 'Lag5', 'Volume',
       'Today', 'Direction'],
      dtype='object')
```

We compute the correlation matrix using the corr() method for data frames, which produces a matrix that contains all of the pairwise correlations among the variables. (We suppress the output here.) The pandas library does not report a correlation for the Direction variable because it is qualitative.

.corr()

In [5]:
```
Smarket.corr()
```

As one would expect, the correlations between the lagged return variables and today's return are close to zero. The only substantial correlation is between Year and Volume. By plotting the data we see that Volume is increasing over time. In other words, the average number of shares traded daily increased from 2001 to 2005.

In [6]:
```
Smarket.plot(y='Volume');
```

4.7.2 Logistic Regression

Next, we will fit a logistic regression model in order to predict Direction using Lag1 through Lag5 and Volume. The sm.GLM() function fits *generalized linear models*, a class of models that includes logistic regression. Alternatively, the function sm.Logit() fits a logistic regression model directly. The syntax of sm.GLM() is similar to that of sm.OLS(), except that we must pass in the argument family=sm.families.Binomial() in order to tell statsmodels to run a logistic regression rather than some other type of generalized linear model.

sm.GLM()
generalized linear model

In [7]:
```
allvars = Smarket.columns.drop(['Today', 'Direction', 'Year'])
design = MS(allvars)
X = design.fit_transform(Smarket)
y = Smarket.Direction == 'Up'
glm = sm.GLM(y,
             X,
             family=sm.families.Binomial())
results = glm.fit()
summarize(results)
```

```
Out[7]:             coef    std err        z    P>|z|
        intercept -0.1260    0.241   -0.523   0.601
        Lag1      -0.0731    0.050   -1.457   0.145
        Lag2      -0.0423    0.050   -0.845   0.398
        Lag3       0.0111    0.050    0.222   0.824
        Lag4       0.0094    0.050    0.187   0.851
        Lag5       0.0103    0.050    0.208   0.835
        Volume     0.1354    0.158    0.855   0.392
```

The smallest *p*-value here is associated with `Lag1`. The negative coefficient for this predictor suggests that if the market had a positive return yesterday, then it is less likely to go up today. However, at a value of 0.15, the *p*-value is still relatively large, and so there is no clear evidence of a real association between `Lag1` and `Direction`.

We use the `params` attribute of `results` in order to access just the coefficients for this fitted model.

```
In [8]: results.params
```

```
Out[8]: intercept    -0.126000
        Lag1         -0.073074
        Lag2         -0.042301
        Lag3          0.011085
        Lag4          0.009359
        Lag5          0.010313
        Volume        0.135441
        dtype: float64
```

Likewise we can use the `pvalues` attribute to access the *p*-values for the coefficients (not shown).

```
In [9]: results.pvalues
```

The `predict()` method of `results` can be used to predict the probability that the market will go up, given values of the predictors. This method returns predictions on the probability scale. If no data set is supplied to the `predict()` function, then the probabilities are computed for the training data that was used to fit the logistic regression model. As with linear regression, one can pass an optional `exog` argument consistent with a design matrix if desired. Here we have printed only the first ten probabilities.

```
In [10]: probs = results.predict()
         probs[:10]
```

```
Out[10]: array([0.5070841, 0.4814679, 0.4811388, 0.5152223, 0.5107812,
                0.5069565, 0.4926509, 0.5092292, 0.5176135, 0.4888378])
```

In order to make a prediction as to whether the market will go up or down on a particular day, we must convert these predicted probabilities into class labels, `Up` or `Down`. The following two commands create a vector of class predictions based on whether the predicted probability of a market increase is greater than or less than 0.5.

```
In [11]: labels = np.array(['Down']*1250)
         labels[probs>0.5] = "Up"
```

The `confusion_table()` function from the `ISLP` package summarizes these predictions, showing how many observations were correctly or incorrectly classified. Our function, which is adapted from a similar function in the module `sklearn.metrics`, transposes the resulting matrix and includes row and column labels. The `confusion_table()` function takes as first argument the predicted labels, and second argument the true labels.

confusion_table()

```
In [12]: confusion_table(labels, Smarket.Direction)
```

```
Out[12]:     Truth  Down   Up
         Predicted
              Down   145  141
                Up   457  507
```

The diagonal elements of the confusion matrix indicate correct predictions, while the off-diagonals represent incorrect predictions. Hence our model correctly predicted that the market would go up on 507 days and that it would go down on 145 days, for a total of 507 + 145 = 652 correct predictions. The `np.mean()` function can be used to compute the fraction of days for which the prediction was correct. In this case, logistic regression correctly predicted the movement of the market 52.2% of the time.

```
In [13]: (507+145)/1250, np.mean(labels == Smarket.Direction)
```

```
Out[13]: (0.5216, 0.5216)
```

At first glance, it appears that the logistic regression model is working a little better than random guessing. However, this result is misleading because we trained and tested the model on the same set of 1,250 observations. In other words, $100 - 52.2 = 47.8\%$ is the *training* error rate. As we have seen previously, the training error rate is often overly optimistic — it tends to underestimate the test error rate. In order to better assess the accuracy of the logistic regression model in this setting, we can fit the model using part of the data, and then examine how well it predicts the *held out* data. This will yield a more realistic error rate, in the sense that in practice we will be interested in our model's performance not on the data that we used to fit the model, but rather on days in the future for which the market's movements are unknown.

To implement this strategy, we first create a Boolean vector corresponding to the observations from 2001 through 2004. We then use this vector to create a held out data set of observations from 2005.

```
In [14]: train = (Smarket.Year < 2005)
         Smarket_train = Smarket.loc[train]
         Smarket_test = Smarket.loc[~train]
         Smarket_test.shape
```

```
Out[14]: (252, 9)
```

The object `train` is a vector of 1,250 elements, corresponding to the observations in our data set. The elements of the vector that correspond to observations that occurred before 2005 are set to `True`, whereas those that correspond to observations in 2005 are set to `False`. Hence `train` is a *boolean* array, since its elements are `True` and `False`. Boolean arrays can be used to obtain a subset of the rows or columns of a data frame using the `loc` method. For instance, the command `Smarket.loc[train]` would pick out a submatrix of the stock market data set, corresponding only to the dates before 2005, since those are the ones for which the elements of `train` are `True`. The ~ symbol can be used to negate all of the elements of a Boolean vector. That is, `~train` is a vector similar to `train`, except that the elements that are `True` in `train` get swapped to `False` in `~train`, and vice versa. Therefore, `Smarket.loc[~train]` yields a subset of the rows of the data frame of the stock market data containing only the observations for which `train` is `False`. The output above indicates that there are 252 such observations.

We now fit a logistic regression model using only the subset of the observations that correspond to dates before 2005. We then obtain predicted probabilities of the stock market going up for each of the days in our test set — that is, for the days in 2005.

In [15]:
```
X_train, X_test = X.loc[train], X.loc[~train]
y_train, y_test = y.loc[train], y.loc[~train]
glm_train = sm.GLM(y_train,
                   X_train,
                   family=sm.families.Binomial())
results = glm_train.fit()
probs = results.predict(exog=X_test)
```

Notice that we have trained and tested our model on two completely separate data sets: training was performed using only the dates before 2005, and testing was performed using only the dates in 2005.

Finally, we compare the predictions for 2005 to the actual movements of the market over that time period. We will first store the test and training labels (recall `y_test` is binary).

In [16]:
```
D = Smarket.Direction
L_train, L_test = D.loc[train], D.loc[~train]
```

Now we threshold the fitted probability at 50% to form our predicted labels.

In [17]:
```
labels = np.array(['Down']*252)
labels[probs>0.5] = 'Up'
confusion_table(labels, L_test)
```

Out[17]:
```
    Truth  Down  Up
Predicted
     Down    77  97
       Up    34  44
```

The test accuracy is about 48% while the error rate is about 52%

In [18]:
```
np.mean(labels == L_test), np.mean(labels != L_test)
```

Out[18]:
```
(0.4802, 0.5198)
```

The `!=` notation means *not equal to*, and so the last command computes the test set error rate. The results are rather disappointing: the test error rate is 52%, which is worse than random guessing! Of course this result is not all that surprising, given that one would not generally expect to be able to use previous days' returns to predict future market performance. (After all, if it were possible to do so, then the authors of this book would be out striking it rich rather than writing a statistics textbook.) `!=`

We recall that the logistic regression model had very underwhelming p-values associated with all of the predictors, and that the smallest p-value, though not very small, corresponded to Lag1. Perhaps by removing the variables that appear not to be helpful in predicting Direction, we can obtain a more effective model. After all, using predictors that have no relationship with the response tends to cause a deterioration in the test error rate (since such predictors cause an increase in variance without a corresponding decrease in bias), and so removing such predictors may in turn yield an improvement. Below we refit the logistic regression using just Lag1 and Lag2, which seemed to have the highest predictive power in the original logistic regression model.

In [19]:
```
model = MS(['Lag1', 'Lag2']).fit(Smarket)
X = model.transform(Smarket)
X_train, X_test = X.loc[train], X.loc[~train]
glm_train = sm.GLM(y_train,
                   X_train,
                   family=sm.families.Binomial())
results = glm_train.fit()
probs = results.predict(exog=X_test)
labels = np.array(['Down']*252)
labels[probs>0.5] = 'Up'
confusion_table(labels, L_test)
```

Out[19]:
```
     Truth  Down   Up
Predicted
     Down     35   35
       Up     76  106
```

Let's evaluate the overall accuracy as well as the accuracy within the days when logistic regression predicts an increase.

In [20]:
```
(35+106)/252,106/(106+76)
```

Out[20]:
```
(0.5595, 0.5824)
```

Now the results appear to be a little better: 56% of the daily movements have been correctly predicted. It is worth noting that in this case, a much simpler strategy of predicting that the market will increase every day will also be correct 56% of the time! Hence, in terms of overall error rate, the logistic regression method is no better than the naive approach. However, the confusion matrix shows that on days when logistic regression predicts an increase in the market, it has a 58% accuracy rate. This suggests a possible trading strategy of buying on days when the model predicts an increasing market, and avoiding trades on days when a decrease is predicted. Of course one would need to investigate more carefully whether this small improvement was real or just due to random chance.

Suppose that we want to predict the returns associated with particular values of Lag1 and Lag2. In particular, we want to predict Direction on a day when Lag1 and Lag2 equal 1.2 and 1.1, respectively, and on a day when they equal 1.5 and −0.8. We do this using the predict() function.

In [21]:
```
newdata = pd.DataFrame({'Lag1':[1.2, 1.5],
                        'Lag2':[1.1, -0.8]});
```

```
newX = model.transform(newdata)
results.predict(newX)
```

```
Out[21]: 0    0.4791
         1    0.4961
         dtype: float64
```

4.7.3 Linear Discriminant Analysis

We begin by performing LDA on the `Smarket` data, using the function `LinearDiscriminantAnalysis()`, which we have abbreviated `LDA()`. We fit the model using only the observations before 2005.

`Linear Discriminant Analysis()`

```
In [22]: lda = LDA(store_covariance=True)
```

Since the `LDA` estimator automatically adds an intercept, we should remove the column corresponding to the intercept in both `X_train` and `X_test`. We can also directly use the labels rather than the Boolean vectors `y_train`.

```
In [23]: X_train, X_test = [M.drop(columns=['intercept'])
                            for M in [X_train, X_test]]
         lda.fit(X_train, L_train)
```

```
Out[23]: LinearDiscriminantAnalysis(store_covariance=True)
```

Here we have used the list comprehensions introduced in Section 3.6.4. Looking at our first line above, we see that the right-hand side is a list of length two. This is because the code `for M in [X_train, X_test]` iterates over a list of length two. While here we loop over a list, the list comprehension method works when looping over any iterable object. We then apply the `drop()` method to each element in the iteration, collecting the result in a list. The left-hand side tells `Python` to unpack this list of length two, assigning its elements to the variables `X_train` and `X_test`. Of course, this overwrites the previous values of `X_train` and `X_test`.

`.drop()`

Having fit the model, we can extract the means in the two classes with the `means_` attribute. These are the average of each predictor within each class, and are used by LDA as estimates of μ_k. These suggest that there is a tendency for the previous 2 days' returns to be negative on days when the market increases, and a tendency for the previous days' returns to be positive on days when the market declines.

```
In [24]: lda.means_
```

```
Out[24]: array([[ 0.04,  0.03],
                [-0.04, -0.03]])
```

The estimated prior probabilities are stored in the `priors_` attribute. The package `sklearn` typically uses this trailing _ to denote a quantity estimated when using the `fit()` method. We can be sure of which entry corresponds to which label by looking at the `classes_` attribute.

```
In [25]: lda.classes_
```

```
Out[25]: array(['Down', 'Up'], dtype='<U4')
```

The LDA output indicates that $\hat{\pi}_{\text{Down}} = 0.492$ and $\hat{\pi}_{\text{Up}} = 0.508$.

```
In [26]: lda.priors_
```

```
Out[26]: array([0.492, 0.508])
```

The linear discriminant vectors can be found in the `scalings_` attribute:

```
In [27]: lda.scalings_
```

```
Out[27]: array([[-0.642],
                [-0.513]])
```

These values provide the linear combination of `Lag1` and `Lag2` that are used to form the LDA decision rule. In other words, these are the multipliers of the elements of $X = x$ in (4.24). If $-0.64 \times$ `Lag1` $- 0.51 \times$ `Lag2` is large, then the LDA classifier will predict a market increase, and if it is small, then the LDA classifier will predict a market decline.

```
In [28]: lda_pred = lda.predict(X_test)
```

As we observed in our comparison of classification methods (Section 4.5), the LDA and logistic regression predictions are almost identical.

```
In [29]: confusion_table(lda_pred, L_test)
```

```
Out[29]:      Truth   Down    Up
          Predicted
               Down     35    35
                 Up     76   106
```

We can also estimate the probability of each class for each point in a training set. Applying a 50% threshold to the posterior probabilities of being in class one allows us to recreate the predictions contained in `lda_pred`.

```
In [30]: lda_prob = lda.predict_proba(X_test)
         np.all(
                np.where(lda_prob[:,1] >= 0.5, 'Up','Down') == lda_pred
                )
```

```
Out[30]: True
```

Above, we used the `np.where()` function that creates an array with value `'Up'` for indices where the second column of `lda_prob` (the estimated posterior probability of `'Up'`) is greater than 0.5. For problems with more than two classes the labels are chosen as the class whose posterior probability is highest:

`np.where()`

```
In [31]: np.all(
                [lda.classes_[i] for i in np.argmax(lda_prob, 1)] ==
                    lda_pred
                )
```

```
Out[31]: True
```

If we wanted to use a posterior probability threshold other than 50% in order to make predictions, then we could easily do so. For instance, suppose that we wish to predict a market decrease only if we are very certain that the market will indeed decrease on that day — say, if the posterior probability is at least 90%. We know that the first column of `lda_prob` corresponds to the label `Down` after having checked the `classes_` attribute, hence we use the column index 0 rather than 1 as we did above.

In [32]:
```
np.sum(lda_prob[:,0] > 0.9)
```

Out[32]: 0

No days in 2005 meet that threshold! In fact, the greatest posterior probability of decrease in all of 2005 was 52.02%.

The LDA classifier above is the first classifier from the `sklearn` library. We will use several other objects from this library. The objects follow a common structure that simplifies tasks such as cross-validation, which we will see in Chapter 5. Specifically, the methods first create a generic classifier without referring to any data. This classifier is then fit to data with the `fit()` method and predictions are always produced with the `predict()` method. This pattern of first instantiating the classifier, followed by fitting it, and then producing predictions is an explicit design choice of `sklearn`. This uniformity makes it possible to cleanly copy the classifier so that it can be fit on different data; e.g. different training sets arising in cross-validation. This standard pattern also allows for a predictable formation of workflows.

4.7.4 Quadratic Discriminant Analysis

We will now fit a QDA model to the `Smarket` data. QDA is implemented via `QuadraticDiscriminantAnalysis()` in the `sklearn` package, which we abbreviate to `QDA()`. The syntax is very similar to `LDA()`.

`Quadratic Discriminant Analysis()`

In [33]:
```
qda = QDA(store_covariance=True)
qda.fit(X_train, L_train)
```

Out[33]: `QuadraticDiscriminantAnalysis(store_covariance=True)`

The `QDA()` function will again compute `means_` and `priors_`.

In [34]:
```
qda.means_, qda.priors_
```

Out[34]:
```
(array([[ 0.04279022,  0.03389409],
        [-0.03954635, -0.03132544]]),
 array([0.49198397, 0.50801603]))
```

The `QDA()` classifier will estimate one covariance per class. Here is the estimated covariance in the first class:

In [35]:
```
qda.covariance_[0]
```

Out[35]:
```
array([[ 1.50662277, -0.03924806],
       [-0.03924806,  1.53559498]])
```

The output contains the group means. But it does not contain the coefficients of the linear discriminants, because the QDA classifier involves a quadratic, rather than a linear, function of the predictors. The `predict()` function works in exactly the same fashion as for LDA.

```
In [36]: qda_pred = qda.predict(X_test)
         confusion_table(qda_pred, L_test)
```

```
Out[36]:     Truth  Down   Up
        Predicted
             Down    30   20
               Up    81  121
```

Interestingly, the QDA predictions are accurate almost 60% of the time, even though the 2005 data was not used to fit the model.

```
In [37]: np.mean(qda_pred == L_test)
```

```
Out[37]: 0.599
```

This level of accuracy is quite impressive for stock market data, which is known to be quite hard to model accurately. This suggests that the quadratic form assumed by QDA may capture the true relationship more accurately than the linear forms assumed by LDA and logistic regression. However, we recommend evaluating this method's performance on a larger test set before betting that this approach will consistently beat the market!

4.7.5 Naive Bayes

Next, we fit a naive Bayes model to the `Smarket` data. The syntax is similar to that of `LDA()` and `QDA()`. By default, this implementation `GaussianNB()` of the naive Bayes classifier models each quantitative feature using a Gaussian distribution. However, a kernel density method can also be used to estimate the distributions.

GaussianNB()

```
In [38]: NB = GaussianNB()
         NB.fit(X_train, L_train)
```

```
Out[38]: GaussianNB()
```

The classes are stored as `classes_`.

```
In [39]: NB.classes_
```

```
Out[39]: array(['Down', 'Up'], dtype='<U4')
```

The class prior probabilities are stored in the `class_prior_` attribute.

```
In [40]: NB.class_prior_
```

```
Out[40]: array([0.49, 0.51])
```

The parameters of the features can be found in the `theta_` and `var_` attributes. The number of rows is equal to the number of classes, while the number of columns is equal to the number of features. We see below that the mean for feature `Lag1` in the `Down` class is 0.043.

```
In [41]: NB.theta_
```

```
Out[41]: array([[ 0.043,  0.034],
               [-0.040, -0.031]])
```

Its variance is 1.503.

```
In [42]: NB.var_
```

```
Out[42]: array([[1.503, 1.532],
                [1.514, 1.487]])
```

How do we know the names of these attributes? We use `NB?` (or `?NB`).

We can easily verify the mean computation:

```
In [43]: X_train[L_train == 'Down'].mean()
```

```
Out[43]: Lag1     0.042790
         Lag2     0.033894
         dtype: float64
```

Similarly for the variance:

```
In [44]: X_train[L_train == 'Down'].var(ddof=0)
```

```
Out[44]: Lag1     1.503554
         Lag2     1.532467
         dtype: float64
```

The `GaussianNB()` function calculates variances using the $1/n$ formula.[6] Since `NB()` is a classifier in the `sklearn` library, making predictions uses the same syntax as for `LDA()` and `QDA()` above.

```
In [45]: nb_labels = NB.predict(X_test)
         confusion_table(nb_labels, L_test)
```

```
Out[45]:      Truth   Down   Up
         Predicted
              Down      29   20
                Up      82  121
```

Naive Bayes performs well on these data, with accurate predictions over 59% of the time. This is slightly worse than QDA, but much better than LDA.

As for `LDA`, the `predict_proba()` method estimates the probability that each observation belongs to a particular class.

```
In [46]: NB.predict_proba(X_test)[:5]
```

```
Out[46]: array([[0.4873, 0.5127],
                [0.4762, 0.5238],
                [0.4653, 0.5347],
                [0.4748, 0.5252],
                [0.4902, 0.5098]])
```

4.7.6 K-Nearest Neighbors

We will now perform KNN using the `KNeighborsClassifier()` function. This

`KNeighbors Classifier()`

---

[6]There are two formulas for computing the sample variance of n observations $x_1, \ldots, x_n$: $\frac{1}{n}\sum_{i=1}^n (x_i - \bar{x})^2$ and $\frac{1}{n-1}\sum_{i=1}^n (x_i - \bar{x})^2$ where $\bar{x}$ is the sample mean. In most cases the distinction is not important.

function works similarly to the other model-fitting functions that we have encountered thus far.

As is the case for LDA and QDA, we fit the classifier using the `fit` method. New predictions are formed using the `predict` method of the object returned by `fit()`.

In [47]:
```
knn1 = KNeighborsClassifier(n_neighbors=1)
knn1.fit(X_train, L_train)
knn1_pred = knn1.predict(X_test)
confusion_table(knn1_pred, L_test)
```

Out[47]:
```
    Truth   Down   Up
Predicted
     Down     43   58
       Up     68   83
```

The results using $K = 1$ are not very good, since only 50% of the observations are correctly predicted. Of course, it may be that $K = 1$ results in an overly-flexible fit to the data.

In [48]:
```
(83+43)/252, np.mean(knn1_pred == L_test)
```

Out[48]:
```
(0.5, 0.5)
```

We repeat the analysis below using $K = 3$.

In [49]:
```
knn3 = KNeighborsClassifier(n_neighbors=3)
knn3_pred = knn3.fit(X_train, L_train).predict(X_test)
np.mean(knn3_pred == L_test)
```

Out[49]:
```
0.532
```

The results have improved slightly. But increasing K further provides no further improvements. It appears that for these data, and this train/test split, QDA gives the best results of the methods that we have examined so far.

KNN does not perform well on the `Smarket` data, but it often does provide impressive results. As an example we will apply the KNN approach to the `Caravan` data set, which is part of the `ISLP` library. This data set includes 85 predictors that measure demographic characteristics for 5,822 individuals. The response variable is `Purchase`, which indicates whether or not a given individual purchases a caravan insurance policy. In this data set, only 6% of people purchased caravan insurance.

In [50]:
```
Caravan = load_data('Caravan')
Purchase = Caravan.Purchase
Purchase.value_counts()
```

Out[50]:
```
No     5474
Yes     348
Name: Purchase, dtype: int64
```

The method `value_counts()` takes a `pd.Series` or `pd.DataFrame` and returns a `pd.Series` with the corresponding counts for each unique element. In this case `Purchase` has only `Yes` and `No` values and returns how many values of each there are.

```
In [51]: 348 / 5822
```

```
Out[51]: 0.0598
```

Our features will include all columns except Purchase.

```
In [52]: feature_df = Caravan.drop(columns=['Purchase'])
```

Because the KNN classifier predicts the class of a given test observation by identifying the observations that are nearest to it, the scale of the variables matters. Any variables that are on a large scale will have a much larger effect on the *distance* between the observations, and hence on the KNN classifier, than variables that are on a small scale. For instance, imagine a data set that contains two variables, salary and age (measured in dollars and years, respectively). As far as KNN is concerned, a difference of 1,000 USD in salary is enormous compared to a difference of 50 years in age. Consequently, salary will drive the KNN classification results, and age will have almost no effect. This is contrary to our intuition that a salary difference of 1,000 USD is quite small compared to an age difference of 50 years. Furthermore, the importance of scale to the KNN classifier leads to another issue: if we measured salary in Japanese yen, or if we measured age in minutes, then we'd get quite different classification results from what we get if these two variables are measured in dollars and years.

A good way to handle this problem is to *standardize* the data so that all variables are given a mean of zero and a standard deviation of one. Then all variables will be on a comparable scale. This is accomplished using the StandardScaler() transformation.

standardize

Standard Scaler()

```
In [53]: scaler = StandardScaler(with_mean=True,
                                 with_std=True,
                                 copy=True)
```

The argument with_mean indicates whether or not we should subtract the mean, while with_std indicates whether or not we should scale the columns to have standard deviation of 1 or not. Finally, the argument copy=True indicates that we will always copy data, rather than trying to do calculations in place where possible.

This transformation can be fit and then applied to arbitrary data. In the first line below, the parameters for the scaling are computed and stored in scaler, while the second line actually constructs the standardized set of features.

```
In [54]: scaler.fit(feature_df)
         X_std = scaler.transform(feature_df)
```

Now every column of feature_std below has a standard deviation of one and a mean of zero.

```
In [55]: feature_std = pd.DataFrame(
                              X_std,
                              columns=feature_df.columns);
         feature_std.std()
```

```
Out[55]: MOSTYPE      1.000086
         MAANTHUI     1.000086
```

```
MGEMOMV      1.000086
MGEMLEEF     1.000086
MOSHOOFD     1.000086
                ...
AZEILPL      1.000086
APLEZIER     1.000086
AFIETS       1.000086
AINBOED      1.000086
ABYSTAND     1.000086
Length: 85, dtype: float64
```

Notice that the standard deviations are not quite 1 here; this is again due to some procedures using the $1/n$ convention for variances (in this case `scaler()`), while others use $1/(n-1)$ (the `std()` method). See the footnote on page 183. In this case it does not matter, as long as the variables are all on the same scale.

`.std()`

Using the function `train_test_split()` we now split the observations into a test set, containing 1000 observations, and a training set containing the remaining observations. The argument `random_state=0` ensures that we get the same split each time we rerun the code.

`train_test_split()`

```
In [56]: (X_train,
          X_test,
          y_train,
          y_test) = train_test_split(feature_std,
                                     Purchase,
                                     test_size=1000,
                                     random_state=0)
```

`?train_test_split` reveals that the non-keyword arguments can be `lists`, `arrays`, `pandas dataframes` etc that all have the same length (`shape[0]`) and hence are *indexable*. In this case they are the dataframe `feature_std` and the response variable `Purchase`. We fit a KNN model on the training data using $K = 1$, and evaluate its performance on the test data.

indexable

```
In [57]: knn1 = KNeighborsClassifier(n_neighbors=1)
         knn1_pred = knn1.fit(X_train, y_train).predict(X_test)
         np.mean(y_test != knn1_pred), np.mean(y_test != "No")

Out[57]: (0.111, 0.067)
```

The KNN error rate on the 1,000 test observations is about 11%. At first glance, this may appear to be fairly good. However, since just over 6% of customers purchased insurance, we could get the error rate down to almost 6% by always predicting `No` regardless of the values of the predictors! This is known as the *null rate.*

null rate

Suppose that there is some non-trivial cost to trying to sell insurance to a given individual. For instance, perhaps a salesperson must visit each potential customer. If the company tries to sell insurance to a random selection of customers, then the success rate will be only 6%, which may be far too low given the costs involved. Instead, the company would like to try to sell insurance only to customers who are likely to buy it. So the overall error rate is not of interest. Instead, the fraction of individuals that are correctly predicted to buy insurance is of interest.

```
In [58]: confusion_table(knn1_pred, y_test)
```

```
Out[58]:     Truth    No   Yes
        Predicted
               No   880    58
              Yes    53     9
```

It turns out that KNN with $K = 1$ does far better than random guessing among the customers that are predicted to buy insurance. Among 62 such customers, 9, or 14.5%, actually do purchase insurance. This is double the rate that one would obtain from random guessing.

```
In [59]: 9/(53+9)
```

```
Out[59]: 0.145
```

Tuning Parameters

The number of neighbors in KNN is referred to as a *tuning parameter*, also referred to as a *hyperparameter*. We do not know *a priori* what value to use. It is therefore of interest to see how the classifier performs on test data as we vary these parameters. This can be achieved with a `for` loop, described in Section 2.3.8. Here we use a for loop to look at the accuracy of our classifier in the group predicted to purchase insurance as we vary the number of neighbors from 1 to 5:

tuning parameter

hyper-parameter

```
In [60]: for K in range(1,6):
             knn = KNeighborsClassifier(n_neighbors=K)
             knn_pred = knn.fit(X_train, y_train).predict(X_test)
             C = confusion_table(knn_pred, y_test)
             templ = ('K={0:d}: # predicted to rent: {1:>2},' +
                     '  # who did rent {2:d}, accuracy {3:.1%}')
             pred = C.loc['Yes'].sum()
             did_rent = C.loc['Yes','Yes']
             print(templ.format(
                   K,
                   pred,
                   did_rent,
                   did_rent / pred))
```

```
K=1: # predicted to rent: 62,# who did rent 9, accuracy 14.5%
K=2: # predicted to rent:  6,# who did rent 1, accuracy 16.7%
K=3: # predicted to rent: 20,# who did rent 3, accuracy 15.0%
K=4: # predicted to rent:  3,# who did rent 0, accuracy 0.0%
K=5: # predicted to rent:  7,# who did rent 1, accuracy 14.3%
```

We see some variability — the numbers for `K=4` are very different from the rest.

Comparison to Logistic Regression

As a comparison, we can also fit a logistic regression model to the data. This can also be done with `sklearn`, though by default it fits something like the *ridge regression* version of logistic regression, which we introduce in Chapter 6. This can be modified by appropriately setting the argument `C` below. Its default value is 1 but by setting it to a very large number, the algorithm converges to the same solution as the usual (unregularized) logistic regression estimator discussed above.

Unlike the statsmodels package, sklearn focuses less on inference and more on classification. Hence, the summary methods seen in statsmodels and our simplified version seen with summarize are not generally available for the classifiers in sklearn.

```
In [61]: logit = LogisticRegression(C=1e10, solver='liblinear')
         logit.fit(X_train, y_train)
         logit_pred = logit.predict_proba(X_test)
         logit_labels = np.where(logit_pred[:,1] > 5, 'Yes', 'No')
         confusion_table(logit_labels, y_test)
```

```
Out[61]:     Truth   No  Yes
         Predicted
                No  933   67
               Yes    0    0
```

We used the argument solver='liblinear' above to avoid a warning with the default solver which would indicate that the algorithm does not converge.

If we use 0.5 as the predicted probability cut-off for the classifier, then we have a problem: none of the test observations are predicted to purchase insurance. However, we are not required to use a cut-off of 0.5. If we instead predict a purchase any time the predicted probability of purchase exceeds 0.25, we get much better results: we predict that 29 people will purchase insurance, and we are correct for about 31% of these people. This is almost five times better than random guessing!

```
In [62]: logit_labels = np.where(logit_pred[:,1]>0.25, 'Yes', 'No')
         confusion_table(logit_labels, y_test)
```

```
Out[62]:     Truth   No  Yes
         Predicted
                No  913   58
               Yes   20    9
```

```
In [63]: 9/(20+9)
```

```
Out[63]: 0.310
```

4.7.7 Linear and Poisson Regression on the Bikeshare Data

Here we fit linear and Poisson regression models to the Bikeshare data, as described in Section 4.6. The response bikers measures the number of bike rentals per hour in Washington, DC in the period 2010–2012.

```
In [64]: Bike = load_data('Bikeshare')
```

Let's have a peek at the dimensions and names of the variables in this dataframe.

```
In [65]: Bike.shape, Bike.columns
```

```
Out[65]: ((8645, 15),
         Index(['season', 'mnth', 'day', 'hr', 'holiday', 'weekday',
                'workingday', 'weathersit', 'temp', 'atemp', 'hum',
                'windspeed', 'casual', 'registered', 'bikers'],
                dtype='object'))
```

Linear Regression

We begin by fitting a linear regression model to the data.

```
In [66]: X = MS(['mnth',
                 'hr',
                 'workingday',
                 'temp',
                 'weathersit']).fit_transform(Bike)
         Y = Bike['bikers']
         M_lm = sm.OLS(Y, X).fit()
         summarize(M_lm)
```

```
Out[66]:                 coef  std err        t  P>|t|
         intercept   -68.6317    5.307  -12.932  0.000
         mnth[Feb]     6.8452    4.287    1.597  0.110
         mnth[March]  16.5514    4.301    3.848  0.000
         mnth[April]  41.4249    4.972    8.331  0.000
         mnth[May]    72.5571    5.641   12.862  0.000
         mnth[June]   67.8187    6.544   10.364  0.000
         mnth[July]   45.3245    7.081    6.401  0.000
         mnth[Aug]    53.2430    6.640    8.019  0.000
         mnth[Sept]   66.6783    5.925   11.254  0.000
         mnth[Oct]    75.8343    4.950   15.319  0.000
         mnth[Nov]    60.3100    4.610   13.083  0.000
         mnth[Dec]    46.4577    4.271   10.878  0.000
         hr[1]       -14.5793    5.699   -2.558  0.011
         hr[2]       -21.5791    5.733   -3.764  0.000
         hr[3]       -31.1408    5.778   -5.389  0.000
         .....        .......    .....    .....  .....
```

There are 24 levels in `hr` and 40 rows in all, so we have truncated the summary. In `M_lm`, the first levels `hr[0]` and `mnth[Jan]` are treated as the baseline values, and so no coefficient estimates are provided for them: implicitly, their coefficient estimates are zero, and all other levels are measured relative to these baselines. For example, the Feb coefficient of 6.845 signifies that, holding all other variables constant, there are on average about 7 more riders in February than in January. Similarly there are about 16.5 more riders in March than in January.

The results seen in Section 4.6.1 used a slightly different coding of the variables `hr` and `mnth`, as follows:

```
In [67]: hr_encode = contrast('hr', 'sum')
         mnth_encode = contrast('mnth', 'sum')
```

Refitting again:

```
In [68]: X2 = MS([mnth_encode,
                  hr_encode,
                  'workingday',
                  'temp',
```

```
            'weathersit']).fit_transform(Bike)
M2_lm = sm.OLS(Y, X2).fit()
S2 = summarize(M2_lm)
S2
```

```
Out[68]:                  coef  std err        t  P>|t|
         intercept     73.5974    5.132   14.340  0.000
         mnth[Jan]    -46.0871    4.085  -11.281  0.000
         mnth[Feb]    -39.2419    3.539  -11.088  0.000
         mnth[March]  -29.5357    3.155   -9.361  0.000
         mnth[April]   -4.6622    2.741   -1.701  0.089
         mnth[May]     26.4700    2.851    9.285  0.000
         mnth[June]    21.7317    3.465    6.272  0.000
         mnth[July]    -0.7626    3.908   -0.195  0.845
         mnth[Aug]      7.1560    3.535    2.024  0.043
         mnth[Sept]    20.5912    3.046    6.761  0.000
         mnth[Oct]     29.7472    2.700   11.019  0.000
         mnth[Nov]     14.2229    2.860    4.972  0.000
         hr[0]        -96.1420    3.955  -24.307  0.000
         hr[1]       -110.7213    3.966  -27.916  0.000
         hr[2]       -117.7212    4.016  -29.310  0.000
         .....         .......    .....   ......  .....
```

What is the difference between the two codings? In `M2_lm`, a coefficient estimate is reported for all but level `23` of `hr` and level `Dec` of `mnth`. Importantly, in `M2_lm`, the (unreported) coefficient estimate for the last level of `mnth` is not zero: instead, it equals the negative of the sum of the coefficient estimates for all of the other levels. Similarly, in `M2_lm`, the coefficient estimate for the last level of `hr` is the negative of the sum of the coefficient estimates for all of the other levels. This means that the coefficients of `hr` and `mnth` in `M2_lm` will always sum to zero, and can be interpreted as the difference from the mean level. For example, the coefficient for January of -46.087 indicates that, holding all other variables constant, there are typically 46 fewer riders in January relative to the yearly average.

It is important to realize that the choice of coding really does not matter, provided that we interpret the model output correctly in light of the coding used. For example, we see that the predictions from the linear model are the same regardless of coding:

```
In [69]: np.sum((M_lm.fittedvalues - M2_lm.fittedvalues)**2)
```

```
Out[69]: 1.53e-20
```

The sum of squared differences is zero. We can also see this using the `np.allclose()` function:

`np.allclose`

```
In [70]: np.allclose(M_lm.fittedvalues, M2_lm.fittedvalues)
```

```
Out[70]: True
```

To reproduce the left-hand side of Figure 4.13 we must first obtain the coefficient estimates associated with `mnth`. The coefficients for January through November can be obtained directly from the `M2_lm` object. The coefficient for December must be explicitly computed as the negative sum of all the other months. We first extract all the coefficients for month from the coefficients of `M2_lm`.

In [71]:
```
coef_month = S2[S2.index.str.contains('mnth')]['coef']
coef_month
```

Out[71]:
```
mnth[Jan]      -46.0871
mnth[Feb]      -39.2419
mnth[March]    -29.5357
mnth[April]     -4.6622
mnth[May]       26.4700
mnth[June]      21.7317
mnth[July]      -0.7626
mnth[Aug]        7.1560
mnth[Sept]      20.5912
mnth[Oct]       29.7472
mnth[Nov]       14.2229
Name: coef, dtype: float64
```

Next, we append `Dec` as the negative of the sum of all other months.

In [72]:
```
months = Bike['mnth'].dtype.categories
coef_month = pd.concat([
                       coef_month,
                       pd.Series([-coef_month.sum()],
                                  index=['mnth[Dec]'
                                 ])
                       ])
coef_month
```

Out[72]:
```
mnth[Jan]      -46.0871
mnth[Feb]      -39.2419
mnth[March]    -29.5357
mnth[April]     -4.6622
mnth[May]       26.4700
mnth[June]      21.7317
mnth[July]      -0.7626
mnth[Aug]        7.1560
mnth[Sept]      20.5912
mnth[Oct]       29.7472
mnth[Nov]       14.2229
mnth[Dec]        0.3705
Name: coef, dtype: float64
```

Finally, to make the plot neater, we'll just use the first letter of each month, which is the 6th entry of each of the labels in the index.

In [73]:
```
fig_month, ax_month = subplots(figsize=(8,8))
x_month = np.arange(coef_month.shape[0])
ax_month.plot(x_month, coef_month, marker='o', ms=10)
ax_month.set_xticks(x_month)
ax_month.set_xticklabels([l[5] for l in coef_month.index], fontsize
    =20)
ax_month.set_xlabel('Month', fontsize=20)
ax_month.set_ylabel('Coefficient', fontsize=20);
```

Reproducing the right-hand plot in Figure 4.13 follows a similar process.

In [74]:
```
coef_hr = S2[S2.index.str.contains('hr')]['coef']
coef_hr = coef_hr.reindex(['hr[{0}]'.format(h) for h in range(23)])
coef_hr = pd.concat([coef_hr,
```

```
                        pd.Series([-coef_hr.sum()], index=['hr[23]'])
                       ])
```

We now make the hour plot.

```
In [75]: fig_hr, ax_hr = subplots(figsize=(8,8))
         x_hr = np.arange(coef_hr.shape[0])
         ax_hr.plot(x_hr, coef_hr, marker='o', ms=10)
         ax_hr.set_xticks(x_hr[::2])
         ax_hr.set_xticklabels(range(24)[::2], fontsize=20)
         ax_hr.set_xlabel('Hour', fontsize=20)
         ax_hr.set_ylabel('Coefficient', fontsize=20);
```

Poisson Regression

Now we fit instead a Poisson regression model to the `Bikeshare` data. Very little changes, except that we now use the function `sm.GLM()` with the Poisson family specified:

```
In [76]: M_pois = sm.GLM(Y, X2, family=sm.families.Poisson()).fit()
```

We can plot the coefficients associated with `mnth` and `hr`, in order to reproduce Figure 4.15. We first complete these coefficients as before.

```
In [77]: S_pois = summarize(M_pois)
         coef_month = S_pois[S_pois.index.str.contains('mnth')]['coef']
         coef_month = pd.concat([coef_month,
                                 pd.Series([-coef_month.sum()],
                                            index=['mnth[Dec]'])])
         coef_hr = S_pois[S_pois.index.str.contains('hr')]['coef']
         coef_hr = pd.concat([coef_hr,
                              pd.Series([-coef_hr.sum()],
                              index=['hr[23]'])])
```

The plotting is as before.

```
In [78]: fig_pois, (ax_month, ax_hr) = subplots(1, 2, figsize=(16,8))
         ax_month.plot(x_month, coef_month, marker='o', ms=10)
         ax_month.set_xticks(x_month)
         ax_month.set_xticklabels([l[5] for l in coef_month.index], fontsize
             =20)
         ax_month.set_xlabel('Month', fontsize=20)
         ax_month.set_ylabel('Coefficient', fontsize=20)
         ax_hr.plot(x_hr, coef_hr, marker='o', ms=10)
         ax_hr.set_xticklabels(range(24)[::2], fontsize=20)
         ax_hr.set_xlabel('Hour', fontsize=20)
         ax_hr.set_ylabel('Coefficient', fontsize=20);
```

We compare the fitted values of the two models. The fitted values are stored in the `fittedvalues` attribute returned by the `fit()` method for both the linear regression and the Poisson fits. The linear predictors are stored as the attribute `lin_pred`.

```
In [79]: fig, ax = subplots(figsize=(8, 8))
         ax.scatter(M2_lm.fittedvalues,
                    M_pois.fittedvalues,
                    s=20)
         ax.set_xlabel('Linear Regression Fit', fontsize=20)
```

```
ax.set_ylabel('Poisson Regression Fit', fontsize=20)
ax.axline([0,0], c='black', linewidth=3,
          linestyle='--', slope=1);
```

The predictions from the Poisson regression model are correlated with those from the linear model; however, the former are non-negative. As a result the Poisson regression predictions tend to be larger than those from the linear model for either very low or very high levels of ridership.

In this section, we fit Poisson regression models using the `sm.GLM()` function with the argument `family=sm.families.Poisson()`. Earlier in this lab we used the `sm.GLM()` function with `family=sm.families.Binomial()` to perform logistic regression. Other choices for the `family` argument can be used to fit other types of GLMs. For instance, `family=sm.families.Gamma()` fits a Gamma regression model.

4.8 Exercises

Conceptual

1. Using a little bit of algebra, prove that (4.2) is equivalent to (4.3). In other words, the logistic function representation and logit representation for the logistic regression model are equivalent.

2. It was stated in the text that classifying an observation to the class for which (4.17) is largest is equivalent to classifying an observation to the class for which (4.18) is largest. Prove that this is the case. In other words, under the assumption that the observations in the kth class are drawn from a $N(\mu_k, \sigma^2)$ distribution, the Bayes classifier assigns an observation to the class for which the discriminant function is maximized.

3. This problem relates to the QDA model, in which the observations within each class are drawn from a normal distribution with a class-specific mean vector and a class specific covariance matrix. We consider the simple case where $p = 1$; i.e. there is only one feature.

   Suppose that we have K classes, and that if an observation belongs to the kth class then X comes from a one-dimensional normal distribution, $X \sim N(\mu_k, \sigma_k^2)$. Recall that the density function for the one-dimensional normal distribution is given in (4.16). Prove that in this case, the Bayes classifier is *not* linear. Argue that it is in fact quadratic.

   Hint: For this problem, you should follow the arguments laid out in Section 4.4.1, but without making the assumption that $\sigma_1^2 = \cdots = \sigma_K^2$.

4. When the number of features p is large, there tends to be a deterioration in the performance of KNN and other *local* approaches that perform prediction using only observations that are *near* the test observation for which a prediction must be made. This phenomenon is known as the *curse of dimensionality*, and it ties into the fact that non-parametric approaches often perform poorly when p is large. We will now investigate this curse.

curse of dimensionality

(a) Suppose that we have a set of observations, each with measurements on $p = 1$ feature, X. We assume that X is uniformly (evenly) distributed on $[0, 1]$. Associated with each observation is a response value. Suppose that we wish to predict a test observation's response using only observations that are within 10 % of the range of X closest to that test observation. For instance, in order to predict the response for a test observation with $X = 0.6$, we will use observations in the range $[0.55, 0.65]$. On average, what fraction of the available observations will we use to make the prediction?

(b) Now suppose that we have a set of observations, each with measurements on $p = 2$ features, X_1 and X_2. We assume that (X_1, X_2) are uniformly distributed on $[0, 1] \times [0, 1]$. We wish to predict a test observation's response using only observations that are within 10 % of the range of X_1 *and* within 10 % of the range of X_2 closest to that test observation. For instance, in order to predict the response for a test observation with $X_1 = 0.6$ and $X_2 = 0.35$, we will use observations in the range $[0.55, 0.65]$ for X_1 and in the range $[0.3, 0.4]$ for X_2. On average, what fraction of the available observations will we use to make the prediction?

(c) Now suppose that we have a set of observations on $p = 100$ features. Again the observations are uniformly distributed on each feature, and again each feature ranges in value from 0 to 1. We wish to predict a test observation's response using observations within the 10 % of each feature's range that is closest to that test observation. What fraction of the available observations will we use to make the prediction?

(d) Using your answers to parts (a)–(c), argue that a drawback of KNN when p is large is that there are very few training observations "near" any given test observation.

(e) Now suppose that we wish to make a prediction for a test observation by creating a p-dimensional hypercube centered around the test observation that contains, on average, 10 % of the training observations. For $p = 1, 2,$ and 100, what is the length of each side of the hypercube? Comment on your answer.

Note: A hypercube is a generalization of a cube to an arbitrary number of dimensions. When $p = 1$*, a hypercube is simply a line segment, when* $p = 2$ *it is a square, and when* $p = 100$ *it is a 100-dimensional cube.*

5. We now examine the differences between LDA and QDA.

(a) If the Bayes decision boundary is linear, do we expect LDA or QDA to perform better on the training set? On the test set?

(b) If the Bayes decision boundary is non-linear, do we expect LDA or QDA to perform better on the training set? On the test set?

(c) In general, as the sample size n increases, do we expect the test prediction accuracy of QDA relative to LDA to improve, decline, or be unchanged? Why?

(d) True or False: Even if the Bayes decision boundary for a given problem is linear, we will probably achieve a superior test error rate using QDA rather than LDA because QDA is flexible enough to model a linear decision boundary. Justify your answer.

6. Suppose we collect data for a group of students in a statistics class with variables $X_1 =$ hours studied, $X_2 =$ undergrad GPA, and $Y =$ receive an A. We fit a logistic regression and produce estimated coefficient, $\hat{\beta}_0 = -6, \hat{\beta}_1 = 0.05, \hat{\beta}_2 = 1$.

   (a) Estimate the probability that a student who studies for 40 h and has an undergrad GPA of 3.5 gets an A in the class.

   (b) How many hours would the student in part (a) need to study to have a 50 % chance of getting an A in the class?

7. Suppose that we wish to predict whether a given stock will issue a dividend this year ("Yes" or "No") based on X, last year's percent profit. We examine a large number of companies and discover that the mean value of X for companies that issued a dividend was $\bar{X} = 10$, while the mean for those that didn't was $\bar{X} = 0$. In addition, the variance of X for these two sets of companies was $\hat{\sigma}^2 = 36$. Finally, 80 % of companies issued dividends. Assuming that X follows a normal distribution, predict the probability that a company will issue a dividend this year given that its percentage profit was $X = 4$ last year.

   Hint: Recall that the density function for a normal random variable is $f(x) = \frac{1}{\sqrt{2\pi\sigma^2}} e^{-(x-\mu)^2/2\sigma^2}$. *You will need to use Bayes' theorem.*

8. Suppose that we take a data set, divide it into equally-sized training and test sets, and then try out two different classification procedures. First we use logistic regression and get an error rate of 20 % on the training data and 30 % on the test data. Next we use 1-nearest neighbors (i.e. $K = 1$) and get an average error rate (averaged over both test and training data sets) of 18 %. Based on these results, which method should we prefer to use for classification of new observations? Why?

9. This problem has to do with *odds*.

   (a) On average, what fraction of people with an odds of 0.37 of defaulting on their credit card payment will in fact default?

   (b) Suppose that an individual has a 16 % chance of defaulting on her credit card payment. What are the odds that she will default?

10. Equation 4.32 derived an expression for $\log\left(\frac{\Pr(Y=k|X=x)}{\Pr(Y=K|X=x)}\right)$ in the setting where $p > 1$, so that the mean for the kth class, μ_k, is a p-dimensional vector, and the shared covariance $\mathbf{\Sigma}$ is a $p \times p$ matrix. However, in the setting with $p = 1$, (4.32) takes a simpler form, since the means $\mu_1, \ldots, \mu_K$ and the variance σ^2 are scalars. In this simpler setting, repeat the calculation in (4.32), and provide expressions for a_k and b_{kj} in terms of π_k, π_K, μ_k, μ_K, and σ^2.

11. Work out the detailed forms of a_k, b_{kj}, and b_{kjl} in (4.33). Your answer should involve π_k, π_K, μ_k, μ_K, $\mathbf{\Sigma}_k$, and $\mathbf{\Sigma}_K$.

12. Suppose that you wish to classify an observation $X \in \mathbb{R}$ into `apples` and `oranges`. You fit a logistic regression model and find that

$$\widehat{\Pr}(Y = \texttt{orange}|X = x) = \frac{\exp(\hat{\beta}_0 + \hat{\beta}_1 x)}{1 + \exp(\hat{\beta}_0 + \hat{\beta}_1 x)}.$$

Your friend fits a logistic regression model to the same data using the *softmax* formulation in (4.13), and finds that

$$\widehat{\Pr}(Y = \texttt{orange}|X = x) = \frac{\exp(\hat{\alpha}_{\texttt{orange}0} + \hat{\alpha}_{\texttt{orange}1} x)}{\exp(\hat{\alpha}_{\texttt{orange}0} + \hat{\alpha}_{\texttt{orange}1} x) + \exp(\hat{\alpha}_{\texttt{apple}0} + \hat{\alpha}_{\texttt{apple}1} x)}.$$

   (a) What is the log odds of `orange` versus `apple` in your model?

   (b) What is the log odds of `orange` versus `apple` in your friend's model?

   (c) Suppose that in your model, $\hat{\beta}_0 = 2$ and $\hat{\beta}_1 = -1$. What are the coefficient estimates in your friend's model? Be as specific as possible.

   (d) Now suppose that you and your friend fit the same two models on a different data set. This time, your friend gets the coefficient estimates $\hat{\alpha}_{\texttt{orange}0} = 1.2$, $\hat{\alpha}_{\texttt{orange}1} = -2$, $\hat{\alpha}_{\texttt{orange}0} = 3$, $\hat{\alpha}_{\texttt{orange}1} = 0.6$. What are the coefficient estimates in your model?

   (e) Finally, suppose you apply both models from (d) to a data set with 2,000 test observations. What fraction of the time do you expect the predicted class labels from your model to agree with those from your friend's model? Explain your answer.

Applied

13. This question should be answered using the `Weekly` data set, which is part of the `ISLP` package. This data is similar in nature to the `Smarket` data from this chapter's lab, except that it contains 1,089 weekly returns for 21 years, from the beginning of 1990 to the end of 2010.

   (a) Produce some numerical and graphical summaries of the `Weekly` data. Do there appear to be any patterns?

(b) Use the full data set to perform a logistic regression with `Direction` as the response and the five lag variables plus `Volume` as predictors. Use the summary function to print the results. Do any of the predictors appear to be statistically significant? If so, which ones?

(c) Compute the confusion matrix and overall fraction of correct predictions. Explain what the confusion matrix is telling you about the types of mistakes made by logistic regression.

(d) Now fit the logistic regression model using a training data period from 1990 to 2008, with `Lag2` as the only predictor. Compute the confusion matrix and the overall fraction of correct predictions for the held out data (that is, the data from 2009 and 2010).

(e) Repeat (d) using LDA.

(f) Repeat (d) using QDA.

(g) Repeat (d) using KNN with $K = 1$.

(h) Repeat (d) using naive Bayes.

(i) Which of these methods appears to provide the best results on this data?

(j) Experiment with different combinations of predictors, including possible transformations and interactions, for each of the methods. Report the variables, method, and associated confusion matrix that appears to provide the best results on the held out data. Note that you should also experiment with values for K in the KNN classifier.

14. In this problem, you will develop a model to predict whether a given car gets high or low gas mileage based on the `Auto` data set.

(a) Create a binary variable, `mpg01`, that contains a 1 if `mpg` contains a value above its median, and a 0 if `mpg` contains a value below its median. You can compute the median using the `median()` method of the data frame. Note you may find it helpful to add a column `mpg01` to the data frame by assignment. Assuming you have stored the data frame as `Auto`, this can be done as follows:

```
Auto['mpg01'] = mpg01
```

(b) Explore the data graphically in order to investigate the association between `mpg01` and the other features. Which of the other features seem most likely to be useful in predicting `mpg01`? Scatterplots and boxplots may be useful tools to answer this question. Describe your findings.

(c) Split the data into a training set and a test set.

(d) Perform LDA on the training data in order to predict `mpg01` using the variables that seemed most associated with `mpg01` in (b). What is the test error of the model obtained?

(e) Perform QDA on the training data in order to predict `mpg01` using the variables that seemed most associated with `mpg01` in (b). What is the test error of the model obtained?

(f) Perform logistic regression on the training data in order to predict `mpg01` using the variables that seemed most associated with `mpg01` in (b). What is the test error of the model obtained?

(g) Perform naive Bayes on the training data in order to predict `mpg01` using the variables that seemed most associated with `mpg01` in (b). What is the test error of the model obtained?

(h) Perform KNN on the training data, with several values of K, in order to predict `mpg01`. Use only the variables that seemed most associated with `mpg01` in (b). What test errors do you obtain? Which value of K seems to perform the best on this data set?

15. This problem involves writing functions.

(a) Write a function, `Power()`, that prints out the result of raising 2 to the 3rd power. In other words, your function should compute 2^3 and print out the results.

Hint: Recall that `x**a` *raises* `x` *to the power* `a`. *Use the* `print()` *function to display the result.*

(b) Create a new function, `Power2()`, that allows you to pass *any* two numbers, `x` and `a`, and prints out the value of `x**a`. You can do this by beginning your function with the line

```
def Power2(x, a):
```

You should be able to call your function by entering, for instance,

```
Power2(3, 8)
```

on the command line. This should output the value of 3^8, namely, $6,561$.

(c) Using the `Power2()` function that you just wrote, compute 10^3, 8^{17}, and 131^3.

(d) Now create a new function, `Power3()`, that actually *returns* the result `x**a` as a `Python` object, rather than simply printing it to the screen. That is, if you store the value `x**a` in an object called `result` within your function, then you can simply `return` this result, using the following line: `return`

```
return result
```

Note that the line above should be the last line in your function, and it should be indented 4 spaces.

(e) Now using the `Power3()` function, create a plot of $f(x) = x^2$. The x-axis should display a range of integers from 1 to 10, and the y-axis should display x^2. Label the axes appropriately, and use an appropriate title for the figure. Consider displaying either the x-axis, the y-axis, or both on the log-scale. You can do this by using the `ax.set_xscale()` and `ax.set_yscale()` methods of the axes you are plotting to. `.set_xscale()` `.set_yscale()`

(f) Create a function, `PlotPower()`, that allows you to create a plot of `x` against `x**a` for a fixed `a` and a sequence of values of `x`. For instance, if you call

```
PlotPower(np.arange(1, 11), 3)
```

then a plot should be created with an x-axis taking on values $1, 2, \ldots, 10$, and a y-axis taking on values $1^3, 2^3, \ldots, 10^3$.

16. Using the `Boston` data set, fit classification models in order to predict whether a given suburb has a crime rate above or below the median. Explore logistic regression, LDA, naive Bayes, and KNN models using various subsets of the predictors. Describe your findings.

    Hint: You will have to create the response variable yourself, using the variables that are contained in the `Boston` *data set.*

5 Resampling Methods

Resampling methods are an indispensable tool in modern statistics. They involve repeatedly drawing samples from a training set and refitting a model of interest on each sample in order to obtain additional information about the fitted model. For example, in order to estimate the variability of a linear regression fit, we can repeatedly draw different samples from the training data, fit a linear regression to each new sample, and then examine the extent to which the resulting fits differ. Such an approach may allow us to obtain information that would not be available from fitting the model only once using the original training sample.

Resampling approaches can be computationally expensive, because they involve fitting the same statistical method multiple times using different subsets of the training data. However, due to recent advances in computing power, the computational requirements of resampling methods generally are not prohibitive. In this chapter, we discuss two of the most commonly used resampling methods, *cross-validation* and the *bootstrap*. Both methods are important tools in the practical application of many statistical learning procedures. For example, cross-validation can be used to estimate the test error associated with a given statistical learning method in order to evaluate its performance, or to select the appropriate level of flexibility. The process of evaluating a model's performance is known as *model assessment*, whereas the process of selecting the proper level of flexibility for a model is known as *model selection*. The bootstrap is used in several contexts, most commonly to provide a measure of accuracy of a parameter estimate or of a given statistical learning method.

model assessment

model selection

G. James et al., *An Introduction to Statistical Learning*, Springer Texts in Statistics,
https://doi.org/10.1007/978-3-031-38747-0_5

5.1 Cross-Validation

In Chapter 2 we discuss the distinction between the *test error rate* and the *training error rate*. The test error is the average error that results from using a statistical learning method to predict the response on a new observation—that is, a measurement that was not used in training the method. Given a data set, the use of a particular statistical learning method is warranted if it results in a low test error. The test error can be easily calculated if a designated test set is available. Unfortunately, this is usually not the case. In contrast, the training error can be easily calculated by applying the statistical learning method to the observations used in its training. But as we saw in Chapter 2, the training error rate often is quite different from the test error rate, and in particular the former can dramatically underestimate the latter.

In the absence of a very large designated test set that can be used to directly estimate the test error rate, a number of techniques can be used to estimate this quantity using the available training data. Some methods make a mathematical adjustment to the training error rate in order to estimate the test error rate. Such approaches are discussed in Chapter 6. In this section, we instead consider a class of methods that estimate the test error rate by *holding out* a subset of the training observations from the fitting process, and then applying the statistical learning method to those held out observations.

In Sections 5.1.1–5.1.4, for simplicity we assume that we are interested in performing regression with a quantitative response. In Section 5.1.5 we consider the case of classification with a qualitative response. As we will see, the key concepts remain the same regardless of whether the response is quantitative or qualitative.

5.1.1 The Validation Set Approach

Suppose that we would like to estimate the test error associated with fitting a particular statistical learning method on a set of observations. The *validation set approach*, displayed in Figure 5.1, is a very simple strategy for this task. It involves randomly dividing the available set of observations into two parts, a *training set* and a *validation set* or *hold-out set*. The model is fit on the training set, and the fitted model is used to predict the responses for the observations in the validation set. The resulting validation set error rate—typically assessed using MSE in the case of a quantitative response—provides an estimate of the test error rate.

validation set approach

validation set

hold-out set

We illustrate the validation set approach on the `Auto` data set. Recall from Chapter 3 that there appears to be a non-linear relationship between `mpg` and `horsepower`, and that a model that predicts `mpg` using `horsepower` and `horsepower`^{2} gives better results than a model that uses only a linear term. It is natural to wonder whether a cubic or higher-order fit might provide even better results. We answer this question in Chapter 3 by looking at the p-values associated with a cubic term and higher-order polynomial terms in a linear regression. But we could also answer this question using the validation method. We randomly split the 392 observations into two

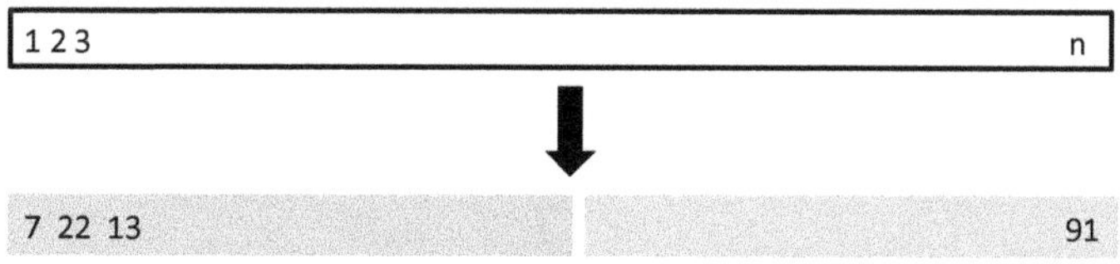

FIGURE 5.1. *A schematic display of the validation set approach. A set of n observations are randomly split into a training set (shown in blue, containing observations 7, 22, and 13, among others) and a validation set (shown in beige, and containing observation 91, among others). The statistical learning method is fit on the training set, and its performance is evaluated on the validation set.*

sets, a training set containing 196 of the data points, and a validation set containing the remaining 196 observations. The validation set error rates that result from fitting various regression models on the training sample and evaluating their performance on the validation sample, using MSE as a measure of validation set error, are shown in the left-hand panel of Figure 5.2. The validation set MSE for the quadratic fit is considerably smaller than for the linear fit. However, the validation set MSE for the cubic fit is actually slightly larger than for the quadratic fit. This implies that including a cubic term in the regression does not lead to better prediction than simply using a quadratic term.

Recall that in order to create the left-hand panel of Figure 5.2, we randomly divided the data set into two parts, a training set and a validation set. If we repeat the process of randomly splitting the sample set into two parts, we will get a somewhat different estimate for the test MSE. As an illustration, the right-hand panel of Figure 5.2 displays ten different validation set MSE curves from the `Auto` data set, produced using ten different random splits of the observations into training and validation sets. All ten curves indicate that the model with a quadratic term has a dramatically smaller validation set MSE than the model with only a linear term. Furthermore, all ten curves indicate that there is not much benefit in including cubic or higher-order polynomial terms in the model. But it is worth noting that each of the ten curves results in a different test MSE estimate for each of the ten regression models considered. And there is no consensus among the curves as to which model results in the smallest validation set MSE. Based on the variability among these curves, all that we can conclude with any confidence is that the linear fit is not adequate for this data.

The validation set approach is conceptually simple and is easy to implement. But it has two potential drawbacks:

1. As is shown in the right-hand panel of Figure 5.2, the validation estimate of the test error rate can be highly variable, depending on precisely which observations are included in the training set and which observations are included in the validation set.

2. In the validation approach, only a subset of the observations—those that are included in the training set rather than in the validation set—are used to fit the model. Since statistical methods tend to perform worse when trained on fewer observations, this suggests that the

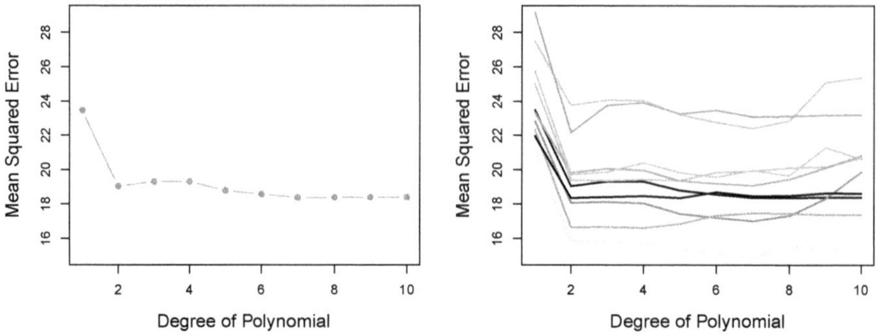

FIGURE 5.2. *The validation set approach was used on the* `Auto` *data set in order to estimate the test error that results from predicting* `mpg` *using polynomial functions of* `horsepower`. Left: *Validation error estimates for a single split into training and validation data sets.* Right: *The validation method was repeated ten times, each time using a different random split of the observations into a training set and a validation set. This illustrates the variability in the estimated test MSE that results from this approach.*

validation set error rate may tend to *overestimate* the test error rate for the model fit on the entire data set.

In the coming subsections, we will present *cross-validation*, a refinement of the validation set approach that addresses these two issues.

5.1.2 Leave-One-Out Cross-Validation

Leave-one-out cross-validation (LOOCV) is closely related to the validation set approach of Section 5.1.1, but it attempts to address that method's drawbacks.

leave-one-out cross-validation

Like the validation set approach, LOOCV involves splitting the set of observations into two parts. However, instead of creating two subsets of comparable size, a single observation (x_1, y_1) is used for the validation set, and the remaining observations $\{(x_2, y_2), \ldots, (x_n, y_n)\}$ make up the training set. The statistical learning method is fit on the $n-1$ training observations, and a prediction $\hat{y}_1$ is made for the excluded observation, using its value x_1. Since (x_1, y_1) was not used in the fitting process, $\text{MSE}_1 = (y_1 - \hat{y}_1)^2$ provides an approximately unbiased estimate for the test error. But even though MSE_1 is unbiased for the test error, it is a poor estimate because it is highly variable, since it is based upon a single observation (x_1, y_1).

We can repeat the procedure by selecting (x_2, y_2) for the validation data, training the statistical learning procedure on the $n-1$ observations $\{(x_1, y_1), (x_3, y_3), \ldots, (x_n, y_n)\}$, and computing $\text{MSE}_2 = (y_2 - \hat{y}_2)^2$. Repeating this approach n times produces n squared errors, $\text{MSE}_1, \ldots, \text{MSE}_n$. The LOOCV estimate for the test MSE is the average of these n test error estimates:

$$\text{CV}_{(n)} = \frac{1}{n}\sum_{i=1}^{n} \text{MSE}_i. \tag{5.1}$$

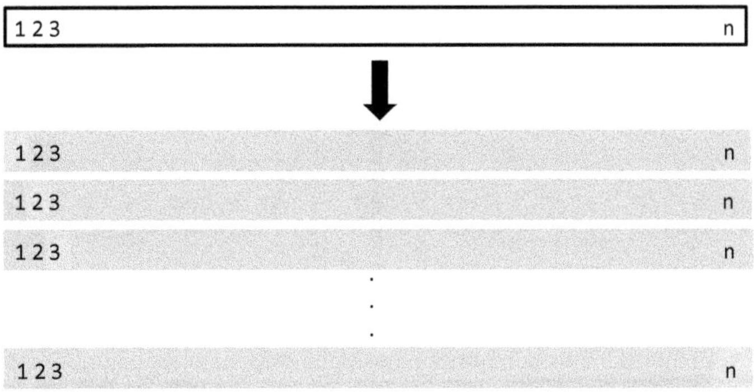

FIGURE 5.3. *A schematic display of LOOCV. A set of n data points is repeatedly split into a training set (shown in blue) containing all but one observation, and a validation set that contains only that observation (shown in beige). The test error is then estimated by averaging the n resulting MSEs. The first training set contains all but observation 1, the second training set contains all but observation 2, and so forth.*

A schematic of the LOOCV approach is illustrated in Figure 5.3.

LOOCV has a couple of major advantages over the validation set approach. First, it has far less bias. In LOOCV, we repeatedly fit the statistical learning method using training sets that contain $n - 1$ observations, almost as many as are in the entire data set. This is in contrast to the validation set approach, in which the training set is typically around half the size of the original data set. Consequently, the LOOCV approach tends not to overestimate the test error rate as much as the validation set approach does. Second, in contrast to the validation approach which will yield different results when applied repeatedly due to randomness in the training/validation set splits, performing LOOCV multiple times will always yield the same results: there is no randomness in the training/validation set splits.

We used LOOCV on the `Auto` data set in order to obtain an estimate of the test set MSE that results from fitting a linear regression model to predict `mpg` using polynomial functions of `horsepower`. The results are shown in the left-hand panel of Figure 5.4.

LOOCV has the potential to be expensive to implement, since the model has to be fit n times. This can be very time consuming if n is large, and if each individual model is slow to fit. With least squares linear or polynomial regression, an amazing shortcut makes the cost of LOOCV the same as that of a single model fit! The following formula holds:

$$\mathrm{CV}_{(n)} = \frac{1}{n}\sum_{i=1}^{n}\left(\frac{y_i - \hat{y}_i}{1 - h_i}\right)^2, \tag{5.2}$$

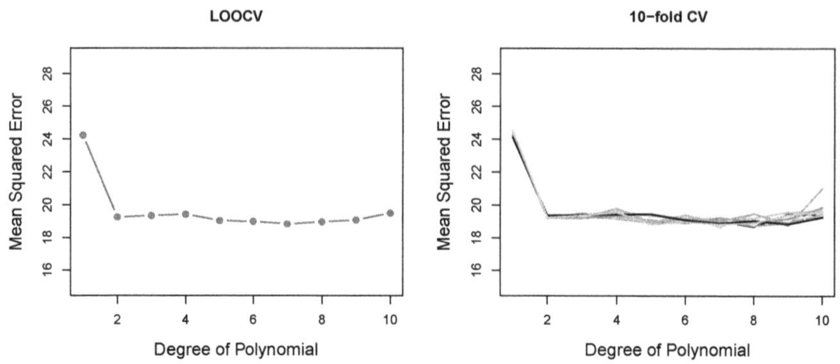

FIGURE 5.4. *Cross-validation was used on the* `Auto` *data set in order to estimate the test error that results from predicting* `mpg` *using polynomial functions of* `horsepower`. Left: *The LOOCV error curve.* Right: 10*-fold CV was run nine separate times, each with a different random split of the data into ten parts. The figure shows the nine slightly different CV error curves.*

where $\hat{y}_i$ is the ith fitted value from the original least squares fit, and h_i is the leverage defined in (3.37) on page 105.[1] This is like the ordinary MSE, except the ith residual is divided by $1 - h_i$. The leverage lies between $1/n$ and 1, and reflects the amount that an observation influences its own fit. Hence the residuals for high-leverage points are inflated in this formula by exactly the right amount for this equality to hold.

LOOCV is a very general method, and can be used with any kind of predictive modeling. For example we could use it with logistic regression or linear discriminant analysis, or any of the methods discussed in later chapters. The magic formula (5.2) does not hold in general, in which case the model has to be refit n times.

5.1.3 *k*-Fold Cross-Validation

An alternative to LOOCV is *k-fold CV*. This approach involves randomly dividing the set of observations into k groups, or *folds*, of approximately equal size. The first fold is treated as a validation set, and the method is fit on the remaining $k - 1$ folds. The mean squared error, MSE_1, is then computed on the observations in the held-out fold. This procedure is repeated k times; each time, a different group of observations is treated as a validation set. This process results in k estimates of the test error, $\text{MSE}_1, \text{MSE}_2, \ldots, \text{MSE}_k$. The k-fold CV estimate is computed by averaging these values,

k-fold CV

$$\text{CV}_{(k)} = \frac{1}{k} \sum_{i=1}^{k} \text{MSE}_i. \quad (5.3)$$

Figure 5.5 illustrates the k-fold CV approach.

[1]In the case of multiple linear regression, the leverage takes a slightly more complicated form than (3.37), but (5.2) still holds.

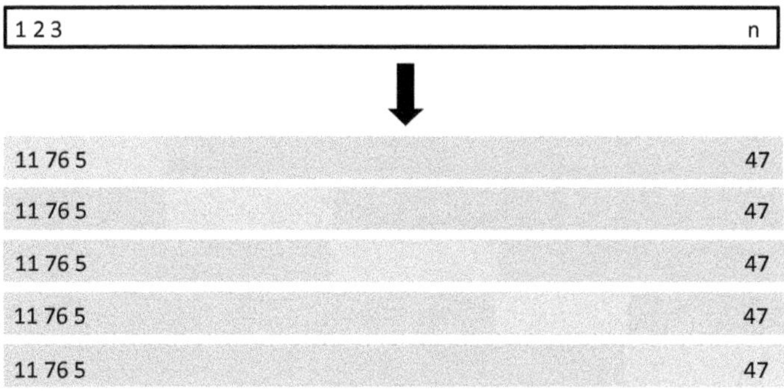

FIGURE 5.5. *A schematic display of* 5*-fold CV. A set of n observations is randomly split into five non-overlapping groups. Each of these fifths acts as a validation set (shown in beige), and the remainder as a training set (shown in blue). The test error is estimated by averaging the five resulting MSE estimates.*

It is not hard to see that LOOCV is a special case of k-fold CV in which k is set to equal n. In practice, one typically performs k-fold CV using $k = 5$ or $k = 10$. What is the advantage of using $k = 5$ or $k = 10$ rather than $k = n$? The most obvious advantage is computational. LOOCV requires fitting the statistical learning method n times. This has the potential to be computationally expensive (except for linear models fit by least squares, in which case formula (5.2) can be used). But cross-validation is a very general approach that can be applied to almost any statistical learning method. Some statistical learning methods have computationally intensive fitting procedures, and so performing LOOCV may pose computational problems, especially if n is extremely large. In contrast, performing 10-fold CV requires fitting the learning procedure only ten times, which may be much more feasible. As we see in Section 5.1.4, there also can be other non-computational advantages to performing 5-fold or 10-fold CV, which involve the bias-variance trade-off.

The right-hand panel of Figure 5.4 displays nine different 10-fold CV estimates for the `Auto` data set, each resulting from a different random split of the observations into ten folds. As we can see from the figure, there is some variability in the CV estimates as a result of the variability in how the observations are divided into ten folds. But this variability is typically much lower than the variability in the test error estimates that results from the validation set approach (right-hand panel of Figure 5.2).

When we examine real data, we do not know the *true* test MSE, and so it is difficult to determine the accuracy of the cross-validation estimate. However, if we examine simulated data, then we can compute the true test MSE, and can thereby evaluate the accuracy of our cross-validation results. In Figure 5.6, we plot the cross-validation estimates and true test error rates that result from applying smoothing splines to the simulated data sets illustrated in Figures 2.9–2.11 of Chapter 2. The true test MSE is displayed in blue. The black dashed and orange solid lines respectively show the estimated LOOCV and 10-fold CV estimates. In all three plots, the two cross-validation estimates are very similar. In the right-hand panel

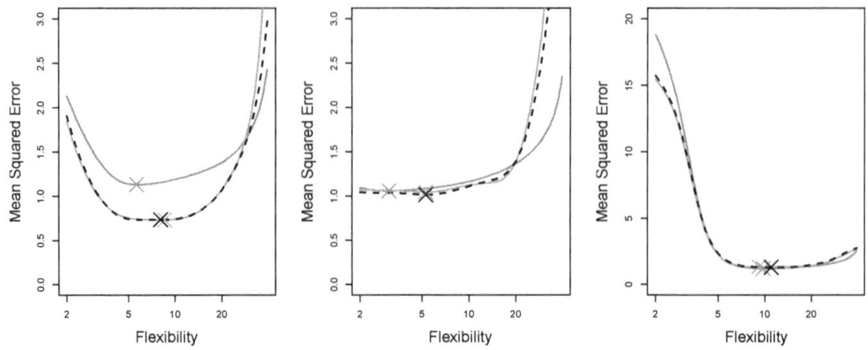

FIGURE 5.6. *True and estimated test MSE for the simulated data sets in Figures 2.9 (*left*), 2.10 (*center*), and 2.11 (*right*). The true test MSE is shown in blue, the LOOCV estimate is shown as a black dashed line, and the* 10*-fold CV estimate is shown in orange. The crosses indicate the minimum of each of the MSE curves.*

of Figure 5.6, the true test MSE and the cross-validation curves are almost identical. In the center panel of Figure 5.6, the two sets of curves are similar at the lower degrees of flexibility, while the CV curves overestimate the test set MSE for higher degrees of flexibility. In the left-hand panel of Figure 5.6, the CV curves have the correct general shape, but they underestimate the true test MSE.

When we perform cross-validation, our goal might be to determine how well a given statistical learning procedure can be expected to perform on independent data; in this case, the actual estimate of the test MSE is of interest. But at other times we are interested only in the location of the *minimum point in the estimated test MSE curve*. This is because we might be performing cross-validation on a number of statistical learning methods, or on a single method using different levels of flexibility, in order to identify the method that results in the lowest test error. For this purpose, the location of the minimum point in the estimated test MSE curve is important, but the actual value of the estimated test MSE is not. We find in Figure 5.6 that despite the fact that they sometimes underestimate the true test MSE, all of the CV curves come close to identifying the correct level of flexibility—that is, the flexibility level corresponding to the smallest test MSE.

5.1.4 Bias-Variance Trade-Off for k-Fold Cross-Validation

We mentioned in Section 5.1.3 that k-fold CV with $k < n$ has a computational advantage to LOOCV. But putting computational issues aside, a less obvious but potentially more important advantage of k-fold CV is that it often gives more accurate estimates of the test error rate than does LOOCV. This has to do with a bias-variance trade-off.

It was mentioned in Section 5.1.1 that the validation set approach can lead to overestimates of the test error rate, since in this approach the training set used to fit the statistical learning method contains only half the observations of the entire data set. Using this logic, it is not hard to see that LOOCV will give approximately unbiased estimates of the test error, since each training set contains $n-1$ observations, which is almost as many as the number of observations in the full data set. And performing k-fold CV for, say, $k = 5$ or $k = 10$ will lead to an intermediate level of bias, since each training set contains approximately $(k-1)n/k$ observations—fewer than in the LOOCV approach, but substantially more than in the validation set approach. Therefore, from the perspective of bias reduction, it is clear that LOOCV is to be preferred to k-fold CV.

However, we know that bias is not the only source for concern in an estimating procedure; we must also consider the procedure's variance. It turns out that LOOCV has higher variance than does k-fold CV with $k < n$. Why is this the case? When we perform LOOCV, we are in effect averaging the outputs of n fitted models, each of which is trained on an almost identical set of observations; therefore, these outputs are highly (positively) correlated with each other. In contrast, when we perform k-fold CV with $k < n$, we are averaging the outputs of k fitted models that are somewhat less correlated with each other, since the overlap between the training sets in each model is smaller. Since the mean of many highly correlated quantities has higher variance than does the mean of many quantities that are not as highly correlated, the test error estimate resulting from LOOCV tends to have higher variance than does the test error estimate resulting from k-fold CV.

To summarize, there is a bias-variance trade-off associated with the choice of k in k-fold cross-validation. Typically, given these considerations, one performs k-fold cross-validation using $k = 5$ or $k = 10$, as these values have been shown empirically to yield test error rate estimates that suffer neither from excessively high bias nor from very high variance.

5.1.5 Cross-Validation on Classification Problems

In this chapter so far, we have illustrated the use of cross-validation in the regression setting where the outcome Y is quantitative, and so have used MSE to quantify test error. But cross-validation can also be a very useful approach in the classification setting when Y is qualitative. In this setting, cross-validation works just as described earlier in this chapter, except that rather than using MSE to quantify test error, we instead use the number of misclassified observations. For instance, in the classification setting, the LOOCV error rate takes the form

$$\mathrm{CV}_{(n)} = \frac{1}{n}\sum_{i=1}^{n}\mathrm{Err}_i, \tag{5.4}$$

where $\mathrm{Err}_i = I(y_i \neq \hat{y}_i)$. The k-fold CV error rate and validation set error rates are defined analogously.

As an example, we fit various logistic regression models on the two-dimensional classification data displayed in Figure 2.13. In the top-left panel of Figure 5.7, the black solid line shows the estimated decision boundary resulting from fitting a standard logistic regression model to this data set. Since this is simulated data, we can compute the *true* test error rate, which takes a value of 0.201 and so is substantially larger than the Bayes

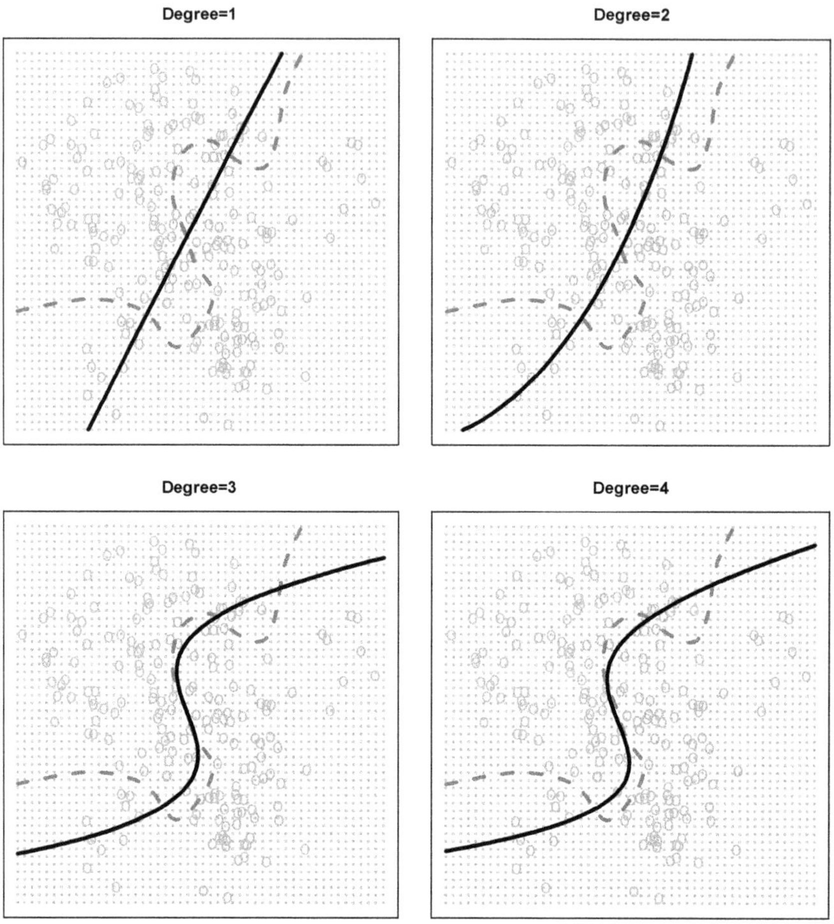

FIGURE 5.7. *Logistic regression fits on the two-dimensional classification data displayed in Figure 2.13. The Bayes decision boundary is represented using a purple dashed line. Estimated decision boundaries from linear, quadratic, cubic and quartic (degrees 1–4) logistic regressions are displayed in black. The test error rates for the four logistic regression fits are respectively* 0.201, 0.197, 0.160, *and* 0.162, *while the Bayes error rate is* 0.133.

error rate of 0.133. Clearly logistic regression does not have enough flexibility to model the Bayes decision boundary in this setting. We can easily extend logistic regression to obtain a non-linear decision boundary by using polynomial functions of the predictors, as we did in the regression setting in Section 3.3.2. For example, we can fit a *quadratic* logistic regression model, given by

$$\log\left(\frac{p}{1-p}\right) = \beta_0 + \beta_1 X_1 + \beta_2 X_1^2 + \beta_3 X_2 + \beta_4 X_2^2. \tag{5.5}$$

The top-right panel of Figure 5.7 displays the resulting decision boundary, which is now curved. However, the test error rate has improved only slightly, to 0.197. A much larger improvement is apparent in the bottom-left panel

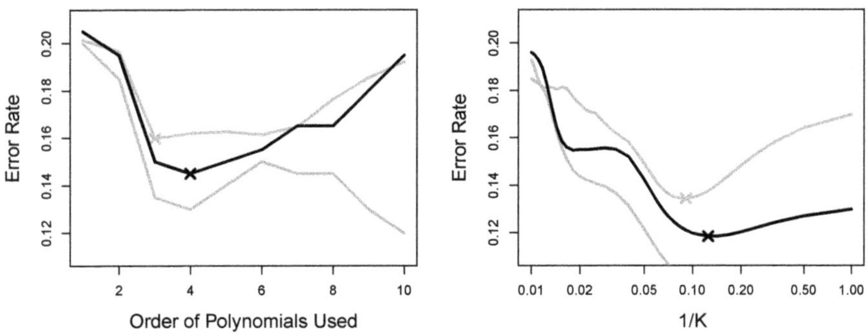

FIGURE 5.8. *Test error (brown), training error (blue), and* 10*-fold CV error (black) on the two-dimensional classification data displayed in Figure 5.7.* Left: *Logistic regression using polynomial functions of the predictors. The order of the polynomials used is displayed on the x-axis.* Right: *The KNN classifier with different values of K, the number of neighbors used in the KNN classifier.*

of Figure 5.7, in which we have fit a logistic regression model involving cubic polynomials of the predictors. Now the test error rate has decreased to 0.160. Going to a quartic polynomial (bottom-right) slightly increases the test error.

In practice, for real data, the Bayes decision boundary and the test error rates are unknown. So how might we decide between the four logistic regression models displayed in Figure 5.7? We can use cross-validation in order to make this decision. The left-hand panel of Figure 5.8 displays in black the 10-fold CV error rates that result from fitting ten logistic regression models to the data, using polynomial functions of the predictors up to tenth order. The true test errors are shown in brown, and the training errors are shown in blue. As we have seen previously, the training error tends to decrease as the flexibility of the fit increases. (The figure indicates that though the training error rate doesn't quite decrease monotonically, it tends to decrease on the whole as the model complexity increases.) In contrast, the test error displays a characteristic U-shape. The 10-fold CV error rate provides a pretty good approximation to the test error rate. While it somewhat underestimates the error rate, it reaches a minimum when fourth-order polynomials are used, which is very close to the minimum of the test curve, which occurs when third-order polynomials are used. In fact, using fourth-order polynomials would likely lead to good test set performance, as the true test error rate is approximately the same for third, fourth, fifth, and sixth-order polynomials.

The right-hand panel of Figure 5.8 displays the same three curves using the KNN approach for classification, as a function of the value of K (which in this context indicates the number of neighbors used in the KNN classifier, rather than the number of CV folds used). Again the training error rate declines as the method becomes more flexible, and so we see that the training error rate cannot be used to select the optimal value for K. Though the cross-validation error curve slightly underestimates the test error rate, it takes on a minimum very close to the best value for K.

5.2 The Bootstrap

The *bootstrap* is a widely applicable and extremely powerful statistical tool that can be used to quantify the uncertainty associated with a given estimator or statistical learning method. As a simple example, the bootstrap can be used to estimate the standard errors of the coefficients from a linear regression fit. In the specific case of linear regression, this is not particularly useful, since we saw in Chapter 3 that standard statistical software such as R outputs such standard errors automatically. However, the power of the bootstrap lies in the fact that it can be easily applied to a wide range of statistical learning methods, including some for which a measure of variability is otherwise difficult to obtain and is not automatically output by statistical software. bootstrap

In this section we illustrate the bootstrap on a toy example in which we wish to determine the best investment allocation under a simple model. In Section 5.3 we explore the use of the bootstrap to assess the variability associated with the regression coefficients in a linear model fit.

Suppose that we wish to invest a fixed sum of money in two financial assets that yield returns of X and Y, respectively, where X and Y are random quantities. We will invest a fraction α of our money in X, and will invest the remaining $1-\alpha$ in Y. Since there is variability associated with the returns on these two assets, we wish to choose α to minimize the total risk, or variance, of our investment. In other words, we want to minimize $\mathrm{Var}(\alpha X + (1-\alpha)Y)$. One can show that the value that minimizes the risk is given by

$$\alpha = \frac{\sigma_Y^2 - \sigma_{XY}}{\sigma_X^2 + \sigma_Y^2 - 2\sigma_{XY}}, \tag{5.6}$$

where $\sigma_X^2 = \mathrm{Var}(X), \sigma_Y^2 = \mathrm{Var}(Y)$, and $\sigma_{XY} = \mathrm{Cov}(X, Y)$.

In reality, the quantities σ_X^2, σ_Y^2, and σ_{XY} are unknown. We can compute estimates for these quantities, $\hat{\sigma}_X^2$, $\hat{\sigma}_Y^2$, and $\hat{\sigma}_{XY}$, using a data set that contains past measurements for X and Y. We can then estimate the value of α that minimizes the variance of our investment using

$$\hat{\alpha} = \frac{\hat{\sigma}_Y^2 - \hat{\sigma}_{XY}}{\hat{\sigma}_X^2 + \hat{\sigma}_Y^2 - 2\hat{\sigma}_{XY}}. \tag{5.7}$$

Figure 5.9 illustrates this approach for estimating α on a simulated data set. In each panel, we simulated 100 pairs of returns for the investments X and Y. We used these returns to estimate σ_X^2, σ_Y^2, and σ_{XY}, which we then substituted into (5.7) in order to obtain estimates for α. The value of $\hat{\alpha}$ resulting from each simulated data set ranges from 0.532 to 0.657.

It is natural to wish to quantify the accuracy of our estimate of α. To estimate the standard deviation of $\hat{\alpha}$, we repeated the process of simulating 100 paired observations of X and Y, and estimating α using (5.7), 1,000 times. We thereby obtained 1,000 estimates for α, which we can call $\hat{\alpha}_1, \hat{\alpha}_2, \ldots, \hat{\alpha}_{1,000}$. The left-hand panel of Figure 5.10 displays a histogram of the resulting estimates. For these simulations the parameters were set to $\sigma_X^2 = 1, \sigma_Y^2 = 1.25$, and $\sigma_{XY} = 0.5$, and so we know that the true value of α is 0.6. We indicated this value using a solid vertical line on the histogram.

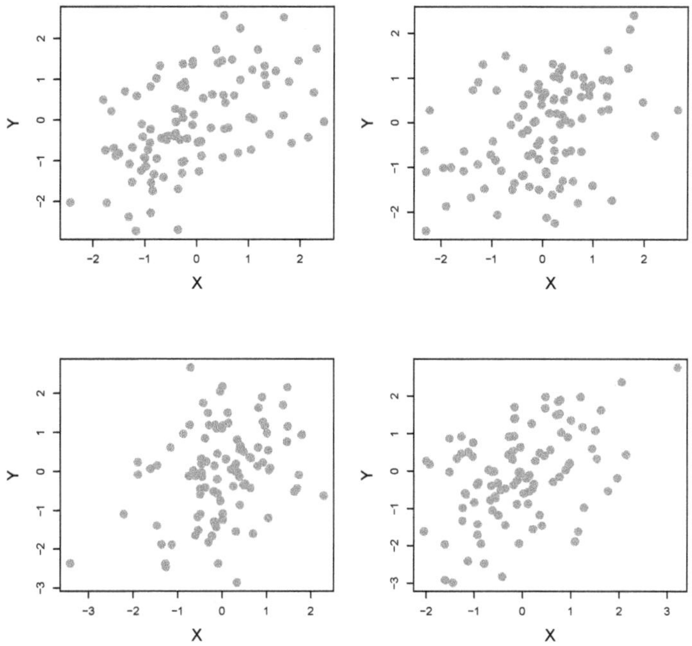

FIGURE 5.9. *Each panel displays* 100 *simulated returns for investments* X *and* Y. *From left to right and top to bottom, the resulting estimates for* α *are* 0.576, 0.532, 0.657, *and* 0.651.

The mean over all 1,000 estimates for α is

$$\bar{\alpha} = \frac{1}{1000} \sum_{r=1}^{1000} \hat{\alpha}_r = 0.5996,$$

very close to $\alpha = 0.6$, and the standard deviation of the estimates is

$$\sqrt{\frac{1}{1000 - 1} \sum_{r=1}^{1000} (\hat{\alpha}_r - \bar{\alpha})^2} = 0.083.$$

This gives us a very good idea of the accuracy of $\hat{\alpha}$: $\mathrm{SE}(\hat{\alpha}) \approx 0.083$. So roughly speaking, for a random sample from the population, we would expect $\hat{\alpha}$ to differ from α by approximately 0.08, on average.

In practice, however, the procedure for estimating $\mathrm{SE}(\hat{\alpha})$ outlined above cannot be applied, because for real data we cannot generate new samples from the original population. However, the bootstrap approach allows us to use a computer to emulate the process of obtaining new sample sets, so that we can estimate the variability of $\hat{\alpha}$ without generating additional samples. Rather than repeatedly obtaining independent data sets from the population, we instead obtain distinct data sets by repeatedly sampling observations *from the original data set.*

This approach is illustrated in Figure 5.11 on a simple data set, which we call Z, that contains only $n = 3$ observations. We randomly select n observations from the data set in order to produce a bootstrap data set,

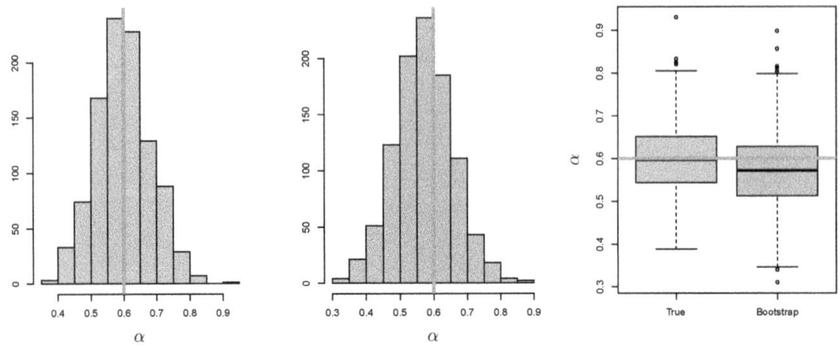

FIGURE 5.10. Left: *A histogram of the estimates of α obtained by generating 1,000 simulated data sets from the true population.* Center: *A histogram of the estimates of α obtained from 1,000 bootstrap samples from a single data set.* Right: *The estimates of α displayed in the left and center panels are shown as boxplots. In each panel, the pink line indicates the true value of α.*

Z^{*1}. The sampling is performed *with replacement*, which means that the same observation can occur more than once in the bootstrap data set. In this example, Z^{*1} contains the third observation twice, the first observation once, and no instances of the second observation. Note that if an observation is contained in Z^{*1}, then both its X and Y values are included. We can use Z^{*1} to produce a new bootstrap estimate for α, which we call $\hat{\alpha}^{*1}$. This procedure is repeated B times for some large value of B, in order to produce B different bootstrap data sets, $Z^{*1}, Z^{*2}, \ldots, Z^{*B}$, and B corresponding α estimates, $\hat{\alpha}^{*1}, \hat{\alpha}^{*2}, \ldots, \hat{\alpha}^{*B}$. We can compute the standard error of these bootstrap estimates using the formula

with replacement

$$\mathrm{SE}_B(\hat{\alpha}) = \sqrt{\frac{1}{B-1}\sum_{r=1}^{B}\left(\hat{\alpha}^{*r} - \frac{1}{B}\sum_{r'=1}^{B}\hat{\alpha}^{*r'}\right)^2}. \tag{5.8}$$

This serves as an estimate of the standard error of $\hat{\alpha}$ estimated from the original data set.

The bootstrap approach is illustrated in the center panel of Figure 5.10, which displays a histogram of 1,000 bootstrap estimates of α, each computed using a distinct bootstrap data set. This panel was constructed on the basis of a single data set, and hence could be created using real data. Note that the histogram looks very similar to the left-hand panel, which displays the idealized histogram of the estimates of α obtained by generating 1,000 simulated data sets from the true population. In particular the bootstrap estimate $\mathrm{SE}(\hat{\alpha})$ from (5.8) is 0.087, very close to the estimate of 0.083 obtained using 1,000 simulated data sets. The right-hand panel displays the information in the center and left panels in a different way, via boxplots of the estimates for α obtained by generating 1,000 simulated data sets from the true population and using the bootstrap approach. Again, the boxplots have similar spreads, indicating that the bootstrap approach can be used to effectively estimate the variability associated with $\hat{\alpha}$.

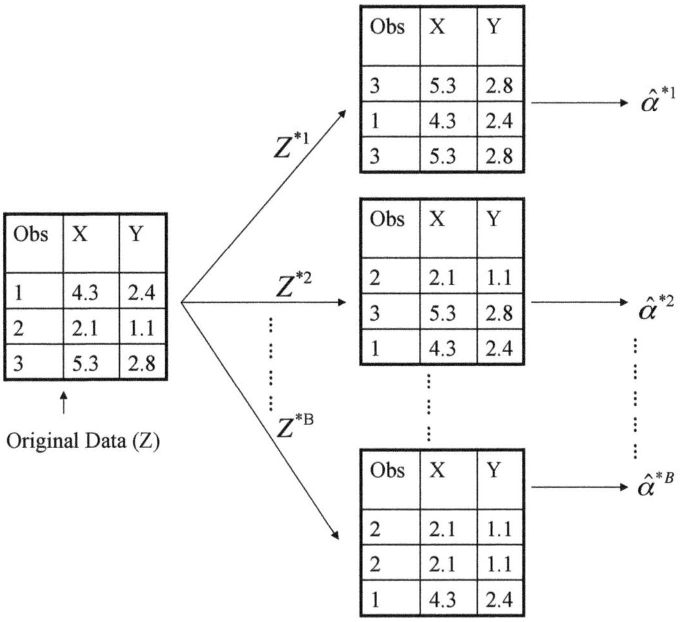

FIGURE 5.11. *A graphical illustration of the bootstrap approach on a small sample containing $n = 3$ observations. Each bootstrap data set contains n observations, sampled with replacement from the original data set. Each bootstrap data set is used to obtain an estimate of α.*

5.3 Lab: Cross-Validation and the Bootstrap

In this lab, we explore the resampling techniques covered in this chapter. Some of the commands in this lab may take a while to run on your computer.

We again begin by placing most of our imports at this top level.

In [1]:
```
import numpy as np
import statsmodels.api as sm
from ISLP import load_data
from ISLP.models import (ModelSpec as MS,
                         summarize,
                         poly)
from sklearn.model_selection import train_test_split
```

There are several new imports needed for this lab.

In [2]:
```
from functools import partial
from sklearn.model_selection import \
     (cross_validate,
      KFold,
      ShuffleSplit)
from sklearn.base import clone
from ISLP.models import sklearn_sm
```

5.3.1 The Validation Set Approach

We explore the use of the validation set approach in order to estimate the test error rates that result from fitting various linear models on the Auto data set.

We use the function train_test_split() to split the data into training and validation sets. As there are 392 observations, we split into two equal sets of size 196 using the argument test_size=196. It is generally a good idea to set a random seed when performing operations like this that contain an element of randomness, so that the results obtained can be reproduced precisely at a later time. We set the random seed of the splitter with the argument random_state=0. train_test_split()

```
In [3]: Auto = load_data('Auto')
        Auto_train, Auto_valid = train_test_split(Auto,
                                                  test_size=196,
                                                  random_state=0)
```

Now we can fit a linear regression using only the observations corresponding to the training set Auto_train.

```
In [4]: hp_mm = MS(['horsepower'])
        X_train = hp_mm.fit_transform(Auto_train)
        y_train = Auto_train['mpg']
        model = sm.OLS(y_train, X_train)
        results = model.fit()
```

We now use the predict() method of results evaluated on the model matrix for this model created using the validation data set. We also calculate the validation MSE of our model.

```
In [5]: X_valid = hp_mm.transform(Auto_valid)
        y_valid = Auto_valid['mpg']
        valid_pred = results.predict(X_valid)
        np.mean((y_valid - valid_pred)**2)
```

```
Out[5]: 23.6166
```

Hence our estimate for the validation MSE of the linear regression fit is 23.62.

We can also estimate the validation error for higher-degree polynomial regressions. We first provide a function evalMSE() that takes a model string as well as a training and test set and returns the MSE on the test set.

```
In [6]: def evalMSE(terms,
                    response,
                    train,
                    test):

           mm = MS(terms)
           X_train = mm.fit_transform(train)
           y_train = train[response]

           X_test = mm.transform(test)
           y_test = test[response]
```

```
    results = sm.OLS(y_train, X_train).fit()
    test_pred = results.predict(X_test)

    return np.mean((y_test - test_pred)**2)
```

Let's use this function to estimate the validation MSE using linear, quadratic and cubic fits. We use the `enumerate()` function here, which gives both the values and indices of objects as one iterates over a for loop.

enumerate()

```
In [7]: MSE = np.zeros(3)
        for idx, degree in enumerate(range(1, 4)):
            MSE[idx] = evalMSE([poly('horsepower', degree)],
                               'mpg',
                               Auto_train,
                               Auto_valid)
        MSE
```

```
Out[7]: array([23.62, 18.76, 18.80])
```

These error rates are $23.62, 18.76$, and 18.80, respectively. If we choose a different training/validation split instead, then we can expect somewhat different errors on the validation set.

```
In [8]: Auto_train, Auto_valid = train_test_split(Auto,
                                                  test_size=196,
                                                  random_state=3)
        MSE = np.zeros(3)
        for idx, degree in enumerate(range(1, 4)):
            MSE[idx] = evalMSE([poly('horsepower', degree)],
                               'mpg',
                               Auto_train,
                               Auto_valid)
        MSE
```

```
Out[8]: array([20.76, 16.95, 16.97])
```

Using this split of the observations into a training set and a validation set, we find that the validation set error rates for the models with linear, quadratic, and cubic terms are 20.76, 16.95, and 16.97, respectively.

These results are consistent with our previous findings: a model that predicts `mpg` using a quadratic function of `horsepower` performs better than a model that involves only a linear function of `horsepower`, and there is no evidence of an improvement in using a cubic function of `horsepower`.

5.3.2 Cross-Validation

In theory, the cross-validation estimate can be computed for any generalized linear model. In practice, however, the simplest way to cross-validate in Python is to use `sklearn`, which has a different interface or API than `statsmodels`, the code we have been using to fit GLMs.

This is a problem which often confronts data scientists: "I have a function to do task A, and need to feed it into something that performs task B, so that I can compute $B(A(D))$, where D is my data." When A and B don't naturally speak to each other, this requires the use of a *wrapper*. In the `ISLP`

wrapper

package, we provide a wrapper, `sklearn_sm()`, that enables us to easily use the cross-validation tools of `sklearn` with models fit by `statsmodels`. `sklearn_sm()`

The class `sklearn_sm()` has as its first argument a model from `statsmodels`. It can take two additional optional arguments: `model_str` which can be used to specify a formula, and `model_args` which should be a dictionary of additional arguments used when fitting the model. For example, to fit a logistic regression model we have to specify a `family` argument. This is passed as `model_args={'family':sm.families.Binomial()}`.

Here is our wrapper in action:

In [9]:
```
hp_model = sklearn_sm(sm.OLS,
                      MS(['horsepower']))
X, Y = Auto.drop(columns=['mpg']), Auto['mpg']
cv_results = cross_validate(hp_model,
                            X,
                            Y,
                            cv=Auto.shape[0])
cv_err = np.mean(cv_results['test_score'])
cv_err
```

Out[9]: 24.2315

The arguments to `cross_validate()` are as follows: an object with the appropriate `fit()`, `predict()`, and `score()` methods, an array of features `X` and a response `Y`. We also included an additional argument `cv` to `cross_validate()`; specifying an integer K results in K-fold cross-validation. We have provided a value corresponding to the total number of observations, which results in leave-one-out cross-validation (LOOCV). The `cross_validate()` function produces a dictionary with several components; we simply want the cross-validated test score here (MSE), which is estimated to be 24.23. `cross_validate()`

We can repeat this procedure for increasingly complex polynomial fits. To automate the process, we again use a for loop which iteratively fits polynomial regressions of degree 1 to 5, computes the associated cross-validation error, and stores it in the ith element of the vector `cv_error`. The variable `d` in the for loop corresponds to the degree of the polynomial. We begin by initializing the vector. This command may take a couple of seconds to run.

In [10]:
```
cv_error = np.zeros(5)
H = np.array(Auto['horsepower'])
M = sklearn_sm(sm.OLS)
for i, d in enumerate(range(1,6)):
    X = np.power.outer(H, np.arange(d+1))
    M_CV = cross_validate(M,
                          X,
                          Y,
                          cv=Auto.shape[0])
    cv_error[i] = np.mean(M_CV['test_score'])
cv_error
```

Out[10]: array([24.2315, 19.2482, 19.3350, 19.4244, 19.0332])

As in Figure 5.4, we see a sharp drop in the estimated test MSE between the linear and quadratic fits, but then no clear improvement from using higher-degree polynomials.

Above we introduced the `outer()` method of the `np.power()` function. The `outer()` method is applied to an operation that has two arguments, such as `add()`, `min()`, or `power()`. It has two arrays as arguments, and then forms a larger array where the operation is applied to each pair of elements of the two arrays.

.outer()
np.power()

```
In [11]: A = np.array([3, 5, 9])
         B = np.array([2, 4])
         np.add.outer(A, B)
```

```
Out[11]: array([[ 5,  7],
                [ 7,  9],
                [11, 13]])
```

In the CV example above, we used $K = n$, but of course we can also use $K < n$. The code is very similar to the above (and is significantly faster). Here we use `KFold()` to partition the data into $K = 10$ random groups. We use `random_state` to set a random seed and initialize a vector `cv_error` in which we will store the CV errors corresponding to the polynomial fits of degrees one to five.

KFold()

```
In [12]: cv_error = np.zeros(5)
         cv = KFold(n_splits=10,
                    shuffle=True,
                    random_state=0) # use same splits for each degree
         for i, d in enumerate(range(1,6)):
             X = np.power.outer(H, np.arange(d+1))
             M_CV = cross_validate(M,
                                   X,
                                   Y,
                                   cv=cv)
             cv_error[i] = np.mean(M_CV['test_score'])
         cv_error
```

```
Out[12]: array([24.2077, 19.1853, 19.2763, 19.4785, 19.1372])
```

Notice that the computation time is much shorter than that of LOOCV. (In principle, the computation time for LOOCV for a least squares linear model should be faster than for K-fold CV, due to the availability of the formula (5.2) for LOOCV; however, the generic `cross_validate()` function does not make use of this formula.) We still see little evidence that using cubic or higher-degree polynomial terms leads to a lower test error than simply using a quadratic fit.

The `cross_validate()` function is flexible and can take different splitting mechanisms as an argument. For instance, one can use the `ShuffleSplit()` funtion to implement the validation set approach just as easily as K-fold cross-validation.

Shuffle
Split()

```
In [13]: validation = ShuffleSplit(n_splits=1,
                                   test_size=196,
                                   random_state=0)
         results = cross_validate(hp_model,
                                  Auto.drop(['mpg'], axis=1),
                                  Auto['mpg'],
                                  cv=validation);
         results['test_score']
```

```
Out[13]: array([23.6166])
```

One can estimate the variability in the test error by running the following:

```
In [14]: validation = ShuffleSplit(n_splits=10,
                                   test_size=196,
                                   random_state=0)
         results = cross_validate(hp_model,
                                  Auto.drop(['mpg'], axis=1),
                                  Auto['mpg'],
                                  cv=validation)
         results['test_score'].mean(), results['test_score'].std()
```

```
Out[14]: (23.8022, 1.4218)
```

Note that this standard deviation is not a valid estimate of the sampling variability of the mean test score or the individual scores, since the randomly-selected training samples overlap and hence introduce correlations. But it does give an idea of the Monte Carlo variation incurred by picking different random folds.

5.3.3 The Bootstrap

We illustrate the use of the bootstrap in the simple example of Section 5.2, as well as on an example involving estimating the accuracy of the linear regression model on the `Auto` data set.

Estimating the Accuracy of a Statistic of Interest

One of the great advantages of the bootstrap approach is that it can be applied in almost all situations. No complicated mathematical calculations are required. While there are several implementations of the bootstrap in Python, its use for estimating standard error is simple enough that we write our own function below for the case when our data is stored in a dataframe.

To illustrate the bootstrap, we start with a simple example. The `Portfolio` data set in the `ISLP` package is described in Section 5.2. The goal is to estimate the sampling variance of the parameter α given in formula (5.7). We will create a function `alpha_func()`, which takes as input a dataframe `D` assumed to have columns `X` and `Y`, as well as a vector `idx` indicating which observations should be used to estimate α. The function then outputs the estimate for α based on the selected observations.

```
In [15]: Portfolio = load_data('Portfolio')
         def alpha_func(D, idx):
            cov_ = np.cov(D[['X','Y']].loc[idx], rowvar=False)
            return ((cov_[1,1] - cov_[0,1]) /
                    (cov_[0,0]+cov_[1,1]-2*cov_[0,1]))
```

This function returns an estimate for α based on applying the minimum variance formula (5.7) to the observations indexed by the argument `idx`. For instance, the following command estimates α using all 100 observations.

```
In [16]: alpha_func(Portfolio, range(100))
```

```
Out[16]: 0.5758
```

Next we randomly select 100 observations from `range(100)`, with replacement. This is equivalent to constructing a new bootstrap data set and recomputing $\hat{\alpha}$ based on the new data set.

```
In [17]: rng = np.random.default_rng(0)
         alpha_func(Portfolio,
                    rng.choice(100,
                               100,
                               replace=True))
```

```
Out[17]: 0.6074
```

This process can be generalized to create a simple function `boot_SE()` for computing the bootstrap standard error for arbitrary functions that take only a data frame as an argument.

```
In [18]: def boot_SE(func,
                     D,
                     n=None,
                     B=1000,
                     seed=0):
             rng = np.random.default_rng(seed)
             first_, second_ = 0, 0
             n = n or D.shape[0]
             for _ in range(B):
                 idx = rng.choice(D.index,
                                  n,
                                  replace=True)
                 value = func(D, idx)
                 first_ += value
                 second_ += value**2
             return np.sqrt(second_ / B - (first_ / B)**2)
```

Notice the use of `_` as a loop variable in `for _ in range(B)`. This is often used if the value of the counter is unimportant and simply makes sure the loop is executed `B` times.

Let's use our function to evaluate the accuracy of our estimate of α using $B = 1{,}000$ bootstrap replications.

```
In [19]: alpha_SE = boot_SE(alpha_func,
                            Portfolio,
                            B=1000,
                            seed=0)
         alpha_SE
```

```
Out[19]: 0.0912
```

The final output shows that the bootstrap estimate for $\mathrm{SE}(\hat{\alpha})$ is 0.0912.

Estimating the Accuracy of a Linear Regression Model

The bootstrap approach can be used to assess the variability of the coefficient estimates and predictions from a statistical learning method. Here we use the bootstrap approach in order to assess the variability of the estimates for β_0 and β_1, the intercept and slope terms for the linear regression model that uses horsepower to predict mpg in the Auto data set. We will compare the estimates obtained using the bootstrap to those obtained using the formulas for $\mathrm{SE}(\hat{\beta}_0)$ and $\mathrm{SE}(\hat{\beta}_1)$ described in Section 3.1.2.

To use our boot_SE() function, we must write a function (its first argument) that takes a data frame D and indices idx as its only arguments. But here we want to bootstrap a specific regression model, specified by a model formula and data. We show how to do this in a few simple steps.

We start by writing a generic function boot_OLS() for bootstrapping a regression model that takes a formula to define the corresponding regression. We use the clone() function to make a copy of the formula that can be refit to the new dataframe. This means that any derived features such as those defined by poly() (which we will see shortly), will be re-fit on the resampled data frame.

clone()

In [20]:
```
def boot_OLS(model_matrix, response, D, idx):
    D_ = D.loc[idx]
    Y_ = D_[response]
    X_ = clone(model_matrix).fit_transform(D_)
    return sm.OLS(Y_, X_).fit().params
```

This is not quite what is needed as the first argument to boot_SE(). The first two arguments which specify the model will not change in the bootstrap process, and we would like to *freeze* them. The function partial() from the functools module does precisely this: it takes a function as an argument, and freezes some of its arguments, starting from the left. We use it to freeze the first two model-formula arguments of boot_OLS().

partial()

In [21]:
```
hp_func = partial(boot_OLS, MS(['horsepower']), 'mpg')
```

Typing hp_func? will show that it has two arguments D and idx — it is a version of boot_OLS() with the first two arguments frozen — and hence is ideal as the first argument for boot_SE().

The hp_func() function can now be used in order to create bootstrap estimates for the intercept and slope terms by randomly sampling from among the observations with replacement. We first demonstrate its utility on 10 bootstrap samples.

In [22]:
```
rng = np.random.default_rng(0)
np.array([hp_func(Auto,
          rng.choice(392,
                     392,
                     replace=True)) for _ in range(10)])
```

Out[22]:
```
array([[39.8806, -0.1568],
       [38.733 , -0.147 ],
       [38.3173, -0.1444],
       [39.9145, -0.1578],
       [39.4335, -0.1507],
       [40.3663, -0.1591],
       [39.6233, -0.1545],
       [39.0581, -0.1495],
       [38.6669, -0.1452],
       [39.6428, -0.1556]])
```

Next, we use the `boot_SE()` function to compute the standard errors of 1,000 bootstrap estimates for the intercept and slope terms.

```
In [23]: hp_se = boot_SE(hp_func,
                         Auto,
                         B=1000,
                         seed=10)
         hp_se
```

```
Out[23]: intercept     0.8488
         horsepower    0.0074
         dtype: float64
```

This indicates that the bootstrap estimate for SE($\hat{\beta}_0$) is 0.85, and that the bootstrap estimate for SE($\hat{\beta}_1$) is 0.0074. As discussed in Section 3.1.2, standard formulas can be used to compute the standard errors for the regression coefficients in a linear model. These can be obtained using the `summarize()` function from `ISLP.sm`.

```
In [24]: hp_model.fit(Auto, Auto['mpg'])
         model_se = summarize(hp_model.results_)['std err']
         model_se
```

```
Out[24]: intercept     0.717
         horsepower    0.006
         Name: std err, dtype: float64
```

The standard error estimates for $\hat{\beta}_0$ and $\hat{\beta}_1$ obtained using the formulas from Section 3.1.2 are 0.717 for the intercept and 0.006 for the slope. Interestingly, these are somewhat different from the estimates obtained using the bootstrap. Does this indicate a problem with the bootstrap? In fact, it suggests the opposite. Recall that the standard formulas given in Equation 3.8 on page 75 rely on certain assumptions. For example, they depend on the unknown parameter σ^2, the noise variance. We then estimate σ^2 using the RSS. Now although the formula for the standard errors do not rely on the linear model being correct, the estimate for σ^2 does. We see in Figure 3.8 on page 99 that there is a non-linear relationship in the data, and so the residuals from a linear fit will be inflated, and so will $\hat{\sigma}^2$. Secondly, the standard formulas assume (somewhat unrealistically) that the x_i are fixed, and all the variability comes from the variation in the errors ϵ_i. The bootstrap approach does not rely on any of these assumptions, and so it is likely giving a more accurate estimate of the standard errors of $\hat{\beta}_0$ and $\hat{\beta}_1$ than the results from `sm.OLS`.

Below we compute the bootstrap standard error estimates and the standard linear regression estimates that result from fitting the quadratic model to the data. Since this model provides a good fit to the data (Figure 3.8), there is now a better correspondence between the bootstrap estimates and the standard estimates of SE($\hat{\beta}_0$), SE($\hat{\beta}_1$) and SE($\hat{\beta}_2$).

```
In [25]: quad_model = MS([poly('horsepower', 2, raw=True)])
         quad_func = partial(boot_OLS,
                             quad_model,
                             'mpg')
         boot_SE(quad_func, Auto, B=1000)
```

```
Out[25]: intercept                              2.067840
         poly(horsepower, 2, raw=True)[0]       0.033019
         poly(horsepower, 2, raw=True)[1]       0.000120
         dtype: float64
```

We compare the results to the standard errors computed using `sm.OLS()`.

```
In [26]: M = sm.OLS(Auto['mpg'],
                    quad_model.fit_transform(Auto))
         summarize(M.fit())['std err']
```

```
Out[26]: intercept                              1.800
         poly(horsepower, 2, raw=True)[0]       0.031
         poly(horsepower, 2, raw=True)[1]       0.000
         Name: std err, dtype: float64
```

5.4 Exercises

Conceptual

1. Using basic statistical properties of the variance, as well as single-variable calculus, derive (5.6). In other words, prove that α given by (5.6) does indeed minimize $\text{Var}(\alpha X + (1 - \alpha)Y)$.

2. We will now derive the probability that a given observation is part of a bootstrap sample. Suppose that we obtain a bootstrap sample from a set of n observations.

   (a) What is the probability that the first bootstrap observation is *not* the jth observation from the original sample? Justify your answer.

   (b) What is the probability that the second bootstrap observation is *not* the jth observation from the original sample?

   (c) Argue that the probability that the jth observation is *not* in the bootstrap sample is $(1 - 1/n)^n$.

   (d) When $n = 5$, what is the probability that the jth observation is in the bootstrap sample?

   (e) When $n = 100$, what is the probability that the jth observation is in the bootstrap sample?

   (f) When $n = 10,000$, what is the probability that the jth observation is in the bootstrap sample?

   (g) Create a plot that displays, for each integer value of n from 1 to $100,000$, the probability that the jth observation is in the bootstrap sample. Comment on what you observe.

   (h) We will now investigate numerically the probability that a bootstrap sample of size $n = 100$ contains the jth observation. Here $j = 4$. We first create an array `store` with values that will subsequently be overwritten using the function `np.empty()`. We then `np.empty()`

repeatedly create bootstrap samples, and each time we record whether or not the fifth observation is contained in the bootstrap sample.

```
rng = np.random.default_rng(10)
store = np.empty(10000)
for i in range(10000):
    store[i] = np.sum(rng.choice(100, replace=True) == 4)
        > 0
np.mean(store)
```

Comment on the results obtained.

3. We now review k-fold cross-validation.

   (a) Explain how k-fold cross-validation is implemented.

   (b) What are the advantages and disadvantages of k-fold cross-validation relative to:

      i. The validation set approach?

      ii. LOOCV?

4. Suppose that we use some statistical learning method to make a prediction for the response Y for a particular value of the predictor X. Carefully describe how we might estimate the standard deviation of our prediction.

Applied

5. In Chapter 4, we used logistic regression to predict the probability of `default` using `income` and `balance` on the `Default` data set. We will now estimate the test error of this logistic regression model using the validation set approach. Do not forget to set a random seed before beginning your analysis.

   (a) Fit a logistic regression model that uses `income` and `balance` to predict `default`.

   (b) Using the validation set approach, estimate the test error of this model. In order to do this, you must perform the following steps:

      i. Split the sample set into a training set and a validation set.

      ii. Fit a multiple logistic regression model using only the training observations.

      iii. Obtain a prediction of default status for each individual in the validation set by computing the posterior probability of default for that individual, and classifying the individual to the `default` category if the posterior probability is greater than 0.5.

      iv. Compute the validation set error, which is the fraction of the observations in the validation set that are misclassified.

   (c) Repeat the process in (b) three times, using three different splits of the observations into a training set and a validation set. Comment on the results obtained.

(d) Now consider a logistic regression model that predicts the probability of `default` using `income`, `balance`, and a dummy variable for `student`. Estimate the test error for this model using the validation set approach. Comment on whether or not including a dummy variable for `student` leads to a reduction in the test error rate.

6. We continue to consider the use of a logistic regression model to predict the probability of `default` using `income` and `balance` on the `Default` data set. In particular, we will now compute estimates for the standard errors of the `income` and `balance` logistic regression coefficients in two different ways: (1) using the bootstrap, and (2) using the standard formula for computing the standard errors in the `sm.GLM()` function. Do not forget to set a random seed before beginning your analysis.

   (a) Using the `summarize()` and `sm.GLM()` functions, determine the estimated standard errors for the coefficients associated with `income` and `balance` in a multiple logistic regression model that uses both predictors.

   (b) Write a function, `boot_fn()`, that takes as input the `Default` data set as well as an index of the observations, and that outputs the coefficient estimates for `income` and `balance` in the multiple logistic regression model.

   (c) Following the bootstrap example in the lab, use your `boot_fn()` function to estimate the standard errors of the logistic regression coefficients for `income` and `balance`.

   (d) Comment on the estimated standard errors obtained using the `sm.GLM()` function and using the bootstrap.

7. In Sections 5.1.2 and 5.1.3, we saw that the `cross_validate()` function can be used in order to compute the LOOCV test error estimate. Alternatively, one could compute those quantities using just `sm.GLM()` and the `predict()` method of the fitted model within a for loop. You will now take this approach in order to compute the LOOCV error for a simple logistic regression model on the `Weekly` data set. Recall that in the context of classification problems, the LOOCV error is given in (5.4).

   (a) Fit a logistic regression model that predicts `Direction` using `Lag1` and `Lag2`.

   (b) Fit a logistic regression model that predicts `Direction` using `Lag1` and `Lag2` *using all but the first observation.*

   (c) Use the model from (b) to predict the direction of the first observation. You can do this by predicting that the first observation will go up if $P($`Direction = "Up"`$|$`Lag1, Lag2`$) > 0.5$. Was this observation correctly classified?

   (d) Write a for loop from $i = 1$ to $i = n$, where n is the number of observations in the data set, that performs each of the following steps:

i. Fit a logistic regression model using all but the ith observation to predict `Direction` using `Lag1` and `Lag2`.

ii. Compute the posterior probability of the market moving up for the ith observation.

iii. Use the posterior probability for the ith observation in order to predict whether or not the market moves up.

iv. Determine whether or not an error was made in predicting the direction for the ith observation. If an error was made, then indicate this as a 1, and otherwise indicate it as a 0.

(e) Take the average of the n numbers obtained in (d)iv in order to obtain the LOOCV estimate for the test error. Comment on the results.

8. We will now perform cross-validation on a simulated data set.

(a) Generate a simulated data set as follows:

```
rng = np.random.default_rng(1)
x = rng.normal(size=100)
y = x - 2 * x**2 + rng.normal(size=100)
```

In this data set, what is n and what is p? Write out the model used to generate the data in equation form.

(b) Create a scatterplot of X against Y. Comment on what you find.

(c) Set a random seed, and then compute the LOOCV errors that result from fitting the following four models using least squares:

i. $Y = \beta_0 + \beta_1 X + \epsilon$

ii. $Y = \beta_0 + \beta_1 X + \beta_2 X^2 + \epsilon$

iii. $Y = \beta_0 + \beta_1 X + \beta_2 X^2 + \beta_3 X^3 + \epsilon$

iv. $Y = \beta_0 + \beta_1 X + \beta_2 X^2 + \beta_3 X^3 + \beta_4 X^4 + \epsilon$.

Note you may find it helpful to use the `data.frame()` function to create a single data set containing both X and Y.

(d) Repeat (c) using another random seed, and report your results. Are your results the same as what you got in (c)? Why?

(e) Which of the models in (c) had the smallest LOOCV error? Is this what you expected? Explain your answer.

(f) Comment on the statistical significance of the coefficient estimates that results from fitting each of the models in (c) using least squares. Do these results agree with the conclusions drawn based on the cross-validation results?

9. We will now consider the `Boston` housing data set, from the `ISLP` library.

(a) Based on this data set, provide an estimate for the population mean of `medv`. Call this estimate $\hat{\mu}$.

(b) Provide an estimate of the standard error of $\hat{\mu}$. Interpret this result.

Hint: We can compute the standard error of the sample mean by dividing the sample standard deviation by the square root of the number of observations.

(c) Now estimate the standard error of $\hat{\mu}$ using the bootstrap. How does this compare to your answer from (b)?

(d) Based on your bootstrap estimate from (c), provide a 95 % confidence interval for the mean of `medv`. Compare it to the results obtained by using `Boston['medv'].std()` and the two standard error rule (3.9).

Hint: You can approximate a 95 % confidence interval using the formula $[\hat{\mu} - 2\mathrm{SE}(\hat{\mu}), \hat{\mu} + 2\mathrm{SE}(\hat{\mu})]$.

(e) Based on this data set, provide an estimate, $\hat{\mu}_{med}$, for the median value of `medv` in the population.

(f) We now would like to estimate the standard error of $\hat{\mu}_{med}$. Unfortunately, there is no simple formula for computing the standard error of the median. Instead, estimate the standard error of the median using the bootstrap. Comment on your findings.

(g) Based on this data set, provide an estimate for the tenth percentile of `medv` in Boston census tracts. Call this quantity $\hat{\mu}_{0.1}$. (You can use the `np.percentile()` function.)

`np.percentile()`

(h) Use the bootstrap to estimate the standard error of $\hat{\mu}_{0.1}$. Comment on your findings.

6

Linear Model Selection and Regularization

In the regression setting, the standard linear model

$$Y = \beta_0 + \beta_1 X_1 + \cdots + \beta_p X_p + \epsilon \tag{6.1}$$

is commonly used to describe the relationship between a response Y and a set of variables $X_1, X_2, \ldots, X_p$. We have seen in Chapter 3 that one typically fits this model using least squares.

In the chapters that follow, we consider some approaches for extending the linear model framework. In Chapter 7 we generalize (6.1) in order to accommodate non-linear, but still additive, relationships, while in Chapters 8 and 10 we consider even more general non-linear models. However, the linear model has distinct advantages in terms of inference and, on real-world problems, is often surprisingly competitive in relation to non-linear methods. Hence, before moving to the non-linear world, we discuss in this chapter some ways in which the simple linear model can be improved, by replacing plain least squares fitting with some alternative fitting procedures.

Why might we want to use another fitting procedure instead of least squares? As we will see, alternative fitting procedures can yield better *prediction accuracy* and *model interpretability*.

- *Prediction Accuracy*: Provided that the true relationship between the response and the predictors is approximately linear, the least squares estimates will have low bias. If $n \gg p$—that is, if n, the number of observations, is much larger than p, the number of variables—then the least squares estimates tend to also have low variance, and hence will perform well on test observations. However, if n is not much larger than p, then there can be a lot of variability in the least squares fit, resulting in overfitting and consequently poor predictions on future observations not used in model training. And if $p > n$, then there is no longer a unique least squares coefficient estimate: there are infinitely

G. James et al., *An Introduction to Statistical Learning*, Springer Texts in Statistics,
https://doi.org/10.1007/978-3-031-38747-0_6

many solutions. Each of these least squares solutions gives zero error on the training data, but typically very poor test set performance due to extremely high variance.[1] By *constraining* or *shrinking* the estimated coefficients, we can often substantially reduce the variance at the cost of a negligible increase in bias. This can lead to substantial improvements in the accuracy with which we can predict the response for observations not used in model training.

- *Model Interpretability*: It is often the case that some or many of the variables used in a multiple regression model are in fact not associated with the response. Including such *irrelevant* variables leads to unnecessary complexity in the resulting model. By removing these variables—that is, by setting the corresponding coefficient estimates to zero—we can obtain a model that is more easily interpreted. Now least squares is extremely unlikely to yield any coefficient estimates that are exactly zero. In this chapter, we see some approaches for automatically performing *feature selection* or *variable selection*—that is, for excluding irrelevant variables from a multiple regression model.

feature selection

variable selection

There are many alternatives, both classical and modern, to using least squares to fit (6.1). In this chapter, we discuss three important classes of methods.

- *Subset Selection*. This approach involves identifying a subset of the p predictors that we believe to be related to the response. We then fit a model using least squares on the reduced set of variables.

- *Shrinkage*. This approach involves fitting a model involving all p predictors. However, the estimated coefficients are shrunken towards zero relative to the least squares estimates. This shrinkage (also known as *regularization*) has the effect of reducing variance. Depending on what type of shrinkage is performed, some of the coefficients may be estimated to be exactly zero. Hence, shrinkage methods can also perform variable selection.

- *Dimension Reduction*. This approach involves *projecting* the p predictors into an M-dimensional subspace, where $M < p$. This is achieved by computing M different *linear combinations*, or *projections*, of the variables. Then these M projections are used as predictors to fit a linear regression model by least squares.

In the following sections we describe each of these approaches in greater detail, along with their advantages and disadvantages. Although this chapter describes extensions and modifications to the linear model for regression seen in Chapter 3, the same concepts apply to other methods, such as the classification models seen in Chapter 4.

---

[1] When $p \gg n$, the least squares solution that has the smallest sum of squared coefficients can sometimes perform quite well. See Section 10.8 for a more detailed discussion.

6.1 Subset Selection

In this section we consider some methods for selecting subsets of predictors. These include best subset and stepwise model selection procedures.

6.1.1 Best Subset Selection

To perform ***best subset selection***, we fit a separate least squares regression for each possible combination of the p predictors. That is, we fit all p models that contain exactly one predictor, all $\binom{p}{2} = p(p-1)/2$ models that contain exactly two predictors, and so forth. We then look at all of the resulting models, with the goal of identifying the one that is *best*.

best subset selection

The problem of selecting the *best model* from among the 2^p possibilities considered by best subset selection is not trivial. This is usually broken up into two stages, as described in Algorithm 6.1.

Algorithm 6.1 *Best subset selection*

1. Let $\mathcal{M}_0$ denote the *null model*, which contains no predictors. This model simply predicts the sample mean for each observation.
2. For $k = 1, 2, \ldots p$:
   (a) Fit all $\binom{p}{k}$ models that contain exactly k predictors.
   (b) Pick the best among these $\binom{p}{k}$ models, and call it $\mathcal{M}_k$. Here *best* is defined as having the smallest RSS, or equivalently largest R^2.
3. Select a single best model from among $\mathcal{M}_0, \ldots, \mathcal{M}_p$ using using the prediction error on a validation set, C_p (AIC), BIC, or adjusted R^2. Or use the cross-validation method.

In Algorithm 6.1, Step 2 identifies the best model (on the training data) for each subset size, in order to reduce the problem from one of 2^p possible models to one of $p + 1$ possible models. In Figure 6.1, these models form the lower frontier depicted in red.

Now in order to select a single best model, we must simply choose among these $p + 1$ options. This task must be performed with care, because the RSS of these $p + 1$ models decreases monotonically, and the R^2 increases monotonically, as the number of features included in the models increases. Therefore, if we use these statistics to select the best model, then we will always end up with a model involving all of the variables. The problem is that a low RSS or a high R^2 indicates a model with a low *training* error, whereas we wish to choose a model that has a low *test* error. (As shown in Chapter 2 in Figures 2.9–2.11, training error tends to be quite a bit smaller than test error, and a low training error by no means guarantees a low test error.) Therefore, in Step 3, we use the error on a validation set, C_p, BIC, or adjusted R^2 in order to select among $\mathcal{M}_0, \mathcal{M}_1, \ldots, \mathcal{M}_p$. If cross-validation is used to select the best model, then Step 2 is repeated on each training fold, and the validation errors are averaged to select the best value of k.

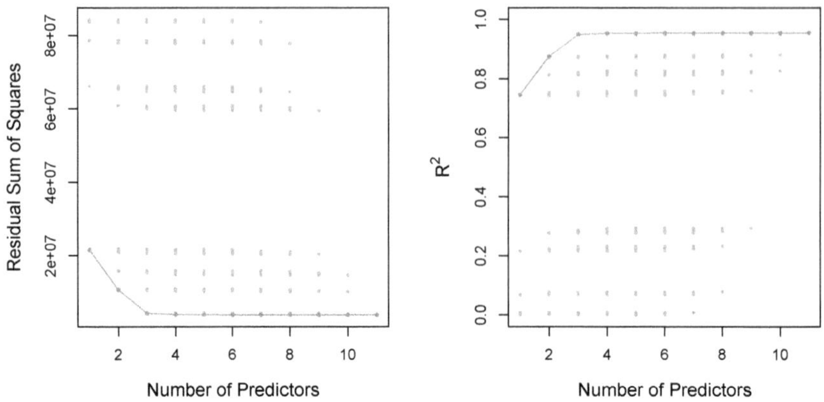

FIGURE 6.1. *For each possible model containing a subset of the ten predictors in the* `Credit` *data set, the RSS and* R^2 *are displayed. The red frontier tracks the* best *model for a given number of predictors, according to RSS and* R^2. *Though the data set contains only ten predictors, the* x*-axis ranges from* 1 *to* 11, *since one of the variables is categorical and takes on three values, leading to the creation of two dummy variables.*

Then the model $\mathcal{M}_k$ fit on the full training set is delivered for the chosen k. These approaches are discussed in Section 6.1.3.

An application of best subset selection is shown in Figure 6.1. Each plotted point corresponds to a least squares regression model fit using a different subset of the 10 predictors in the `Credit` data set, discussed in Chapter 3. Here the variable `region` is a three-level qualitative variable, and so is represented by two dummy variables, which are selected separately in this case. Hence, there are a total of 11 possible variables which can be included in the model. We have plotted the RSS and R^2 statistics for each model, as a function of the number of variables. The red curves connect the best models for each model size, according to RSS or R^2. The figure shows that, as expected, these quantities improve as the number of variables increases; however, from the three-variable model on, there is little improvement in RSS and R^2 as a result of including additional predictors.

Although we have presented best subset selection here for least squares regression, the same ideas apply to other types of models, such as logistic regression. In the case of logistic regression, instead of ordering models by RSS in Step 2 of Algorithm 6.1, we instead use the *deviance*, a measure that plays the role of RSS for a broader class of models. The deviance is negative two times the maximized log-likelihood; the smaller the deviance, the better the fit.

deviance

While best subset selection is a simple and conceptually appealing approach, it suffers from computational limitations. The number of possible models that must be considered grows rapidly as p increases. In general, there are 2^p models that involve subsets of p predictors. So if $p = 10$, then there are approximately 1,000 possible models to be considered, and if $p = 20$, then there are over one million possibilities! Consequently, best subset selection becomes computationally infeasible for values of p greater than

Algorithm 6.2 *Forward stepwise selection*

1. Let $\mathcal{M}_0$ denote the *null* model, which contains no predictors.
2. For $k = 0, \ldots, p-1$:
   (a) Consider all $p-k$ models that augment the predictors in $\mathcal{M}_k$ with one additional predictor.
   (b) Choose the *best* among these $p-k$ models, and call it $\mathcal{M}_{k+1}$. Here *best* is defined as having smallest RSS or highest R^2.
3. Select a single best model from among $\mathcal{M}_0, \ldots, \mathcal{M}_p$ using the prediction error on a validation set, C_p (AIC), BIC, or adjusted R^2. Or use the cross-validation method.

around 40, even with extremely fast modern computers. There are computational shortcuts—so called branch-and-bound techniques—for eliminating some choices, but these have their limitations as p gets large. They also only work for least squares linear regression. We present computationally efficient alternatives to best subset selection next.

6.1.2 Stepwise Selection

For computational reasons, best subset selection cannot be applied with very large p. Best subset selection may also suffer from statistical problems when p is large. The larger the search space, the higher the chance of finding models that look good on the training data, even though they might not have any predictive power on future data. Thus an enormous search space can lead to overfitting and high variance of the coefficient estimates.

For both of these reasons, *stepwise* methods, which explore a far more restricted set of models, are attractive alternatives to best subset selection.

Forward Stepwise Selection

Forward stepwise selection is a computationally efficient alternative to best subset selection. While the best subset selection procedure considers all 2^p possible models containing subsets of the p predictors, forward stepwise considers a much smaller set of models. Forward stepwise selection begins with a model containing no predictors, and then adds predictors to the model, one-at-a-time, until all of the predictors are in the model. In particular, at each step the variable that gives the greatest *additional* improvement to the fit is added to the model. More formally, the forward stepwise selection procedure is given in Algorithm 6.2.

forward stepwise selection

Unlike best subset selection, which involved fitting 2^p models, forward stepwise selection involves fitting one null model, along with $p-k$ models in the kth iteration, for $k = 0, \ldots, p-1$. This amounts to a total of $1 + \sum_{k=0}^{p-1}(p-k) = 1 + p(p+1)/2$ models. This is a substantial difference: when

# Variables	Best subset	Forward stepwise
One	`rating`	`rating`
Two	`rating, income`	`rating, income`
Three	`rating, income, student`	`rating, income, student`
Four	`cards, income` `student, limit`	`rating, income,` `student, limit`

TABLE 6.1. *The first four selected models for best subset selection and forward stepwise selection on the* `Credit` *data set. The first three models are identical but the fourth models differ.*

$p = 20$, best subset selection requires fitting 1,048,576 models, whereas forward stepwise selection requires fitting only 211 models.[2]

In Step 2(b) of Algorithm 6.2, we must identify the *best* model from among those $p-k$ that augment $\mathcal{M}_k$ with one additional predictor. We can do this by simply choosing the model with the lowest RSS or the highest R^2. However, in Step 3, we must identify the best model among a set of models with different numbers of variables. This is more challenging, and is discussed in Section 6.1.3.

Forward stepwise selection's computational advantage over best subset selection is clear. Though forward stepwise tends to do well in practice, it is not guaranteed to find the best possible model out of all 2^p models containing subsets of the p predictors. For instance, suppose that in a given data set with $p = 3$ predictors, the best possible one-variable model contains X_1, and the best possible two-variable model instead contains X_2 and X_3. Then forward stepwise selection will fail to select the best possible two-variable model, because $\mathcal{M}_1$ will contain X_1, so $\mathcal{M}_2$ must also contain X_1 together with one additional variable.

Table 6.1, which shows the first four selected models for best subset and forward stepwise selection on the `Credit` data set, illustrates this phenomenon. Both best subset selection and forward stepwise selection choose `rating` for the best one-variable model and then include `income` and `student` for the two- and three-variable models. However, best subset selection replaces `rating` by `cards` in the four-variable model, while forward stepwise selection must maintain `rating` in its four-variable model. In this example, Figure 6.1 indicates that there is not much difference between the three- and four-variable models in terms of RSS, so either of the four-variable models will likely be adequate.

Forward stepwise selection can be applied even in the high-dimensional setting where $n < p$; however, in this case, it is possible to construct submodels $\mathcal{M}_0, \ldots, \mathcal{M}_{n-1}$ only, since each submodel is fit using least squares, which will not yield a unique solution if $p \geq n$.

Backward Stepwise Selection

Like forward stepwise selection, *backward stepwise selection* provides an

backward stepwise selection

[2]Though forward stepwise selection considers $p(p+1)/2+1$ models, it performs a *guided* search over model space, and so the *effective* model space considered contains substantially more than $p(p+1)/2+1$ models.

efficient alternative to best subset selection. However, unlike forward stepwise selection, it begins with the full least squares model containing all p predictors, and then iteratively removes the least useful predictor, one-at-a-time. Details are given in Algorithm 6.3.

Algorithm 6.3 *Backward stepwise selection*

1. Let $\mathcal{M}_p$ denote the *full* model, which contains all p predictors.
2. For $k = p, p-1, \ldots, 1$:
   (a) Consider all k models that contain all but one of the predictors in $\mathcal{M}_k$, for a total of $k-1$ predictors.
   (b) Choose the *best* among these k models, and call it $\mathcal{M}_{k-1}$. Here *best* is defined as having smallest RSS or highest R^2.
3. Select a single best model from among $\mathcal{M}_0, \ldots, \mathcal{M}_p$ using the prediction error on a validation set, C_p (AIC), BIC, or adjusted R^2. Or use the cross-validation method.

Like forward stepwise selection, the backward selection approach searches through only $1+p(p+1)/2$ models, and so can be applied in settings where p is too large to apply best subset selection.[3] Also like forward stepwise selection, backward stepwise selection is not guaranteed to yield the *best* model containing a subset of the p predictors.

Backward selection requires that the number of samples n is larger than the number of variables p (so that the full model can be fit). In contrast, forward stepwise can be used even when $n < p$, and so is the only viable subset method when p is very large.

Hybrid Approaches

The best subset, forward stepwise, and backward stepwise selection approaches generally give similar but not identical models. As another alternative, hybrid versions of forward and backward stepwise selection are available, in which variables are added to the model sequentially, in analogy to forward selection. However, after adding each new variable, the method may also remove any variables that no longer provide an improvement in the model fit. Such an approach attempts to more closely mimic best subset selection while retaining the computational advantages of forward and backward stepwise selection.

6.1.3 *Choosing the Optimal Model*

Best subset selection, forward selection, and backward selection result in the creation of a set of models, each of which contains a subset of the p

[3] Like forward stepwise selection, backward stepwise selection performs a *guided* search over model space, and so effectively considers substantially more than $1+p(p+1)/2$ models.

predictors. To apply these methods, we need a way to determine which of these models is *best*. As we discussed in Section 6.1.1, the model containing all of the predictors will always have the smallest RSS and the largest R^2, since these quantities are related to the training error. Instead, we wish to choose a model with a low test error. As is evident here, and as we show in Chapter 2, the training error can be a poor estimate of the test error. Therefore, RSS and R^2 are not suitable for selecting the best model among a collection of models with different numbers of predictors.

In order to select the best model with respect to test error, we need to estimate this test error. There are two common approaches:

1. We can indirectly estimate test error by making an *adjustment* to the training error to account for the bias due to overfitting.

2. We can *directly* estimate the test error, using either a validation set approach or a cross-validation approach, as discussed in Chapter 5.

We consider both of these approaches below.

C_p, AIC, BIC, and Adjusted R^2

We show in Chapter 2 that the training set MSE is generally an under-estimate of the test MSE. (Recall that MSE = RSS/n.) This is because when we fit a model to the training data using least squares, we specifically estimate the regression coefficients such that the training RSS (but not the test RSS) is as small as possible. In particular, the training error will decrease as more variables are included in the model, but the test error may not. Therefore, training set RSS and training set R^2 cannot be used to select from among a set of models with different numbers of variables.

However, a number of techniques for *adjusting* the training error for the model size are available. These approaches can be used to select among a set of models with different numbers of variables. We now consider four such approaches: C_p, *Akaike information criterion* (AIC), *Bayesian information criterion* (BIC), and *adjusted* R^2. Figure 6.2 displays C_p, BIC, and adjusted R^2 for the best model of each size produced by best subset selection on the `Credit` data set.

C_p Akaike information criterion Bayesian information criterion adjusted R^2

For a fitted least squares model containing d predictors, the C_p estimate of test MSE is computed using the equation

$$C_p = \frac{1}{n}\left(\text{RSS} + 2d\hat{\sigma}^2\right), \tag{6.2}$$

where $\hat{\sigma}^2$ is an estimate of the variance of the error ϵ associated with each response measurement in (6.1).[4] Typically $\hat{\sigma}^2$ is estimated using the full model containing all predictors. Essentially, the C_p statistic adds a penalty of $2d\hat{\sigma}^2$ to the training RSS in order to adjust for the fact that the training error tends to underestimate the test error. Clearly, the penalty increases as the number of predictors in the model increases; this is intended to adjust

[4]Mallow's C_p is sometimes defined as $C'_p = \text{RSS}/\hat{\sigma}^2 + 2d - n$. This is equivalent to the definition given above in the sense that $C_p = \frac{1}{n}\hat{\sigma}^2(C'_p + n)$, and so the model with smallest C_p also has smallest C'_p.

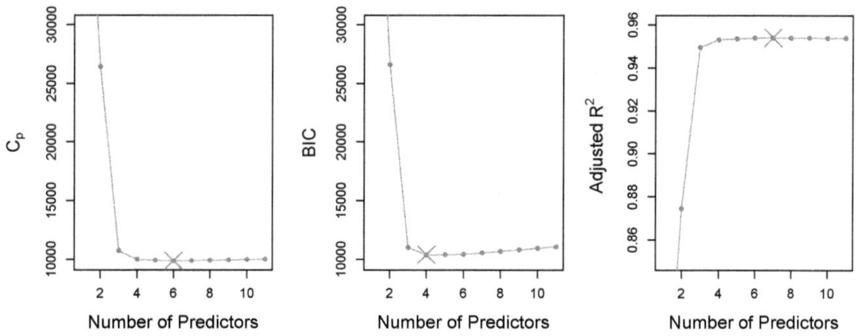

FIGURE 6.2. *C_p, BIC, and adjusted R^2 are shown for the best models of each size for the* `Credit` *data set (the lower frontier in Figure 6.1). C_p and BIC are estimates of test MSE. In the middle plot we see that the BIC estimate of test error shows an increase after four variables are selected. The other two plots are rather flat after four variables are included.*

for the corresponding decrease in training RSS. Though it is beyond the scope of this book, one can show that if $\hat{\sigma}^2$ is an unbiased estimate of σ^2 in (6.2), then C_p is an unbiased estimate of test MSE. As a consequence, the C_p statistic tends to take on a small value for models with a low test error, so when determining which of a set of models is best, we choose the model with the lowest C_p value. In Figure 6.2, C_p selects the six-variable model containing the predictors `income`, `limit`, `rating`, `cards`, `age` and `student`.

The AIC criterion is defined for a large class of models fit by maximum likelihood. In the case of the model (6.1) with Gaussian errors, maximum likelihood and least squares are the same thing. In this case AIC is given by

$$\text{AIC} = \frac{1}{n}\left(\text{RSS} + 2d\hat{\sigma}^2\right),$$

where, for simplicity, we have omitted irrelevant constants.[5] Hence for least squares models, C_p and AIC are proportional to each other, and so only C_p is displayed in Figure 6.2.

BIC is derived from a Bayesian point of view, but ends up looking similar to C_p (and AIC) as well. For the least squares model with d predictors, the BIC is, up to irrelevant constants, given by

$$\text{BIC} = \frac{1}{n}\left(\text{RSS} + \log(n)d\hat{\sigma}^2\right). \tag{6.3}$$

Like C_p, the BIC will tend to take on a small value for a model with a low test error, and so generally we select the model that has the lowest BIC value. Notice that BIC replaces the $2d\hat{\sigma}^2$ used by C_p with a $\log(n)d\hat{\sigma}^2$ term, where n is the number of observations. Since $\log n > 2$ for any $n > 7$,

[5]There are two formulas for AIC for least squares regression. The formula that we provide here requires an expression for σ^2, which we obtain using the full model containing all predictors. The second formula is appropriate when σ^2 is unknown and we do not want to explicitly estimate it; that formula has a log(RSS) term instead of an RSS term. Detailed derivations of these two formulas are outside of the scope of this book.

the BIC statistic generally places a heavier penalty on models with many variables, and hence results in the selection of smaller models than C_p. In Figure 6.2, we see that this is indeed the case for the `Credit` data set; BIC chooses a model that contains only the four predictors `income`, `limit`, `cards`, and `student`. In this case the curves are very flat and so there does not appear to be much difference in accuracy between the four-variable and six-variable models.

The adjusted R^2 statistic is another popular approach for selecting among a set of models that contain different numbers of variables. Recall from Chapter 3 that the usual R^2 is defined as $1 - \text{RSS}/\text{TSS}$, where $\text{TSS} = \sum(y_i - \overline{y})^2$ is the *total sum of squares* for the response. Since RSS always decreases as more variables are added to the model, the R^2 always increases as more variables are added. For a least squares model with d variables, the adjusted R^2 statistic is calculated as

$$\text{Adjusted } R^2 = 1 - \frac{\text{RSS}/(n-d-1)}{\text{TSS}/(n-1)}. \tag{6.4}$$

Unlike C_p, AIC, and BIC, for which a *small* value indicates a model with a low test error, a *large* value of adjusted R^2 indicates a model with a small test error. Maximizing the adjusted R^2 is equivalent to minimizing $\frac{\text{RSS}}{n-d-1}$. While RSS always decreases as the number of variables in the model increases, $\frac{\text{RSS}}{n-d-1}$ may increase or decrease, due to the presence of d in the denominator.

The intuition behind the adjusted R^2 is that once all of the correct variables have been included in the model, adding additional *noise* variables will lead to only a very small decrease in RSS. Since adding noise variables leads to an increase in d, such variables will lead to an increase in $\frac{\text{RSS}}{n-d-1}$, and consequently a decrease in the adjusted R^2. Therefore, in theory, the model with the largest adjusted R^2 will have only correct variables and no noise variables. Unlike the R^2 statistic, the adjusted R^2 statistic *pays a price* for the inclusion of unnecessary variables in the model. Figure 6.2 displays the adjusted R^2 for the `Credit` data set. Using this statistic results in the selection of a model that contains seven variables, adding `own` to the model selected by C_p and AIC.

C_p, AIC, and BIC all have rigorous theoretical justifications that are beyond the scope of this book. These justifications rely on asymptotic arguments (scenarios where the sample size n is very large). Despite its popularity, and even though it is quite intuitive, the adjusted R^2 is not as well motivated in statistical theory as AIC, BIC, and C_p. All of these measures are simple to use and compute. Here we have presented their formulas in the case of a linear model fit using least squares; however, AIC and BIC can also be defined for more general types of models.

Validation and Cross-Validation

As an alternative to the approaches just discussed, we can directly estimate the test error using the validation set and cross-validation methods discussed in Chapter 5. We can compute the validation set error or the cross-validation error for each model under consideration, and then select

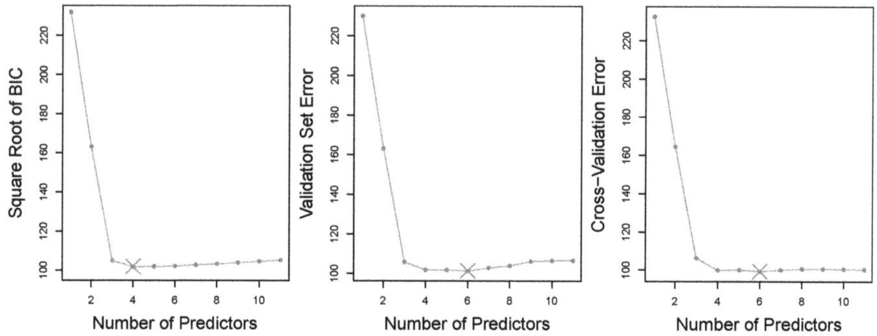

FIGURE 6.3. *For the* `Credit` *data set, three quantities are displayed for the best model containing d predictors, for d ranging from* 1 *to* 11*. The overall* best *model, based on each of these quantities, is shown as a blue cross.* Left: *Square root of BIC.* Center: *Validation set errors.* Right: *Cross-validation errors.*

the model for which the resulting estimated test error is smallest. This procedure has an advantage relative to AIC, BIC, C_p, and adjusted R^2, in that it provides a direct estimate of the test error, and makes fewer assumptions about the true underlying model. It can also be used in a wider range of model selection tasks, even in cases where it is hard to pinpoint the model degrees of freedom (e.g. the number of predictors in the model) or hard to estimate the error variance σ^2. Note that when cross-validation is used, the sequence of models $\mathcal{M}_k$ in Algorithms 6.1–6.3 is determined separately for each training fold, and the validation errors are averaged over all folds for each model size k. This means, for example with best-subset regression, that $\mathcal{M}_k$, the best subset of size k, can differ across the folds. Once the best size k is chosen, we find the best model of that size on the full data set.

In the past, performing cross-validation was computationally prohibitive for many problems with large p and/or large n, and so AIC, BIC, C_p, and adjusted R^2 were more attractive approaches for choosing among a set of models. However, nowadays with fast computers, the computations required to perform cross-validation are hardly ever an issue. Thus, cross-validation is a very attractive approach for selecting from among a number of models under consideration.

Figure 6.3 displays, as a function of d, the BIC, validation set errors, and cross-validation errors on the `Credit` data, for the best d-variable model. The validation errors were calculated by randomly selecting three-quarters of the observations as the training set, and the remainder as the validation set. The cross-validation errors were computed using $k = 10$ folds. In this case, the validation and cross-validation methods both result in a six-variable model. However, all three approaches suggest that the four-, five-, and six-variable models are roughly equivalent in terms of their test errors.

In fact, the estimated test error curves displayed in the center and right-hand panels of Figure 6.3 are quite flat. While a three-variable model clearly has lower estimated test error than a two-variable model, the estimated test errors of the 3- to 11-variable models are quite similar. Furthermore, if we repeated the validation set approach using a different split of the data into a training set and a validation set, or if we repeated cross-validation using a different set of cross-validation folds, then the precise model with the lowest estimated test error would surely change. In this setting, we can select a model using the *one-standard-error rule*. We first calculate the standard error of the estimated test MSE for each model size, and then select the smallest model for which the estimated test error is within one standard error of the lowest point on the curve. The rationale here is that if a set of models appear to be more or less equally good, then we might as well choose the simplest model—that is, the model with the smallest number of predictors. In this case, applying the one-standard-error rule to the validation set or cross-validation approach leads to selection of the three-variable model.

one-standard-error rule

6.2 Shrinkage Methods

The subset selection methods described in Section 6.1 involve using least squares to fit a linear model that contains a subset of the predictors. As an alternative, we can fit a model containing all p predictors using a technique that *constrains* or *regularizes* the coefficient estimates, or equivalently, that *shrinks* the coefficient estimates towards zero. It may not be immediately obvious why such a constraint should improve the fit, but it turns out that shrinking the coefficient estimates can significantly reduce their variance. The two best-known techniques for shrinking the regression coefficients towards zero are *ridge regression* and the *lasso*.

6.2.1 Ridge Regression

Recall from Chapter 3 that the least squares fitting procedure estimates $\beta_0, \beta_1, \ldots, \beta_p$ using the values that minimize

$$\text{RSS} = \sum_{i=1}^{n} \left(y_i - \beta_0 - \sum_{j=1}^{p} \beta_j x_{ij} \right)^2 .$$

Ridge regression is very similar to least squares, except that the coefficients are estimated by minimizing a slightly different quantity. In particular, the ridge regression coefficient estimates $\hat{\beta}^R$ are the values that minimize

ridge regression

$$\sum_{i=1}^{n} \left(y_i - \beta_0 - \sum_{j=1}^{p} \beta_j x_{ij} \right)^2 + \lambda \sum_{j=1}^{p} \beta_j^2 = \text{RSS} + \lambda \sum_{j=1}^{p} \beta_j^2, \tag{6.5}$$

where $\lambda \geq 0$ is a *tuning parameter*, to be determined separately. Equation 6.5 trades off two different criteria. As with least squares, ridge regression seeks coefficient estimates that fit the data well, by making the RSS small. However, the second term, $\lambda \sum_j \beta_j^2$, called a *shrinkage penalty*, is small when $\beta_1, \ldots, \beta_p$ are close to zero, and so it has the effect of *shrinking* the estimates of β_j towards zero. The tuning parameter λ serves to control

tuning parameter

shrinkage penalty

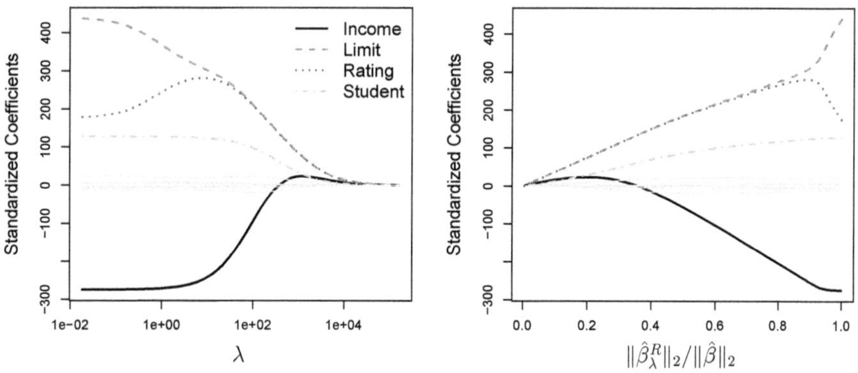

FIGURE 6.4. *The standardized ridge regression coefficients are displayed for the* `Credit` *data set, as a function of* λ *and* $\|\hat{\beta}_\lambda^R\|_2/\|\hat{\beta}\|_2$.

the relative impact of these two terms on the regression coefficient estimates. When $\lambda = 0$, the penalty term has no effect, and ridge regression will produce the least squares estimates. However, as $\lambda \to \infty$, the impact of the shrinkage penalty grows, and the ridge regression coefficient estimates will approach zero. Unlike least squares, which generates only one set of coefficient estimates, ridge regression will produce a different set of coefficient estimates, $\hat{\beta}_\lambda^R$, for each value of λ. Selecting a good value for λ is critical; we defer this discussion to Section 6.2.3, where we use cross-validation.

Note that in (6.5), the shrinkage penalty is applied to $\beta_1, \ldots, \beta_p$, but not to the intercept β_0. We want to shrink the estimated association of each variable with the response; however, we do not want to shrink the intercept, which is simply a measure of the mean value of the response when $x_{i1} = x_{i2} = \ldots = x_{ip} = 0$. If we assume that the variables—that is, the columns of the data matrix $\mathbf{X}$—have been centered to have mean zero before ridge regression is performed, then the estimated intercept will take the form $\hat{\beta}_0 = \bar{y} = \sum_{i=1}^n y_i/n$.

An Application to the Credit Data

In Figure 6.4, the ridge regression coefficient estimates for the `Credit` data set are displayed. In the left-hand panel, each curve corresponds to the ridge regression coefficient estimate for one of the ten variables, plotted as a function of λ. For example, the black solid line represents the ridge regression estimate for the `income` coefficient, as λ is varied. At the extreme left-hand side of the plot, λ is essentially zero, and so the corresponding ridge coefficient estimates are the same as the usual least squares estimates. But as λ increases, the ridge coefficient estimates shrink towards zero. When λ is extremely large, then all of the ridge coefficient estimates are basically zero; this corresponds to the *null model* that contains no predictors. In this plot, the `income`, `limit`, `rating`, and `student` variables are displayed in distinct colors, since these variables tend to have by far the largest coefficient estimates. While the ridge coefficient estimates tend to decrease in aggregate as λ increases, individual coefficients, such as `rating` and `income`, may occasionally increase as λ increases.

The right-hand panel of Figure 6.4 displays the same ridge coefficient estimates as the left-hand panel, but instead of displaying λ on the x-axis, we now display $\|\hat{\beta}_\lambda^R\|_2/\|\hat{\beta}\|_2$, where $\hat{\beta}$ denotes the vector of least squares coefficient estimates. The notation $\|\beta\|_2$ denotes the ℓ_2 *norm* (pronounced "ell 2") of a vector, and is defined as $\|\beta\|_2 = \sqrt{\sum_{j=1}^p {\beta_j}^2}$. It measures the distance of β from zero. As λ increases, the ℓ_2 norm of $\hat{\beta}_\lambda^R$ will *always* decrease, and so will $\|\hat{\beta}_\lambda^R\|_2/\|\hat{\beta}\|_2$. The latter quantity ranges from 1 (when $\lambda = 0$, in which case the ridge regression coefficient estimate is the same as the least squares estimate, and so their ℓ_2 norms are the same) to 0 (when $\lambda = \infty$, in which case the ridge regression coefficient estimate is a vector of zeros, with ℓ_2 norm equal to zero). Therefore, we can think of the x-axis in the right-hand panel of Figure 6.4 as the amount that the ridge regression coefficient estimates have been shrunken towards zero; a small value indicates that they have been shrunken very close to zero.

ℓ_2 norm

The standard least squares coefficient estimates discussed in Chapter 3 are *scale equivariant*: multiplying X_j by a constant c simply leads to a scaling of the least squares coefficient estimates by a factor of $1/c$. In other words, regardless of how the jth predictor is scaled, $X_j\hat{\beta}_j$ will remain the same. In contrast, the ridge regression coefficient estimates can change *substantially* when multiplying a given predictor by a constant. For instance, consider the `income` variable, which is measured in dollars. One could reasonably have measured income in thousands of dollars, which would result in a reduction in the observed values of `income` by a factor of 1,000. Now due to the sum of squared coefficients term in the ridge regression formulation (6.5), such a change in scale will not simply cause the ridge regression coefficient estimate for `income` to change by a factor of 1,000. In other words, $X_j\hat{\beta}_{j,\lambda}^R$ will depend not only on the value of λ, but also on the scaling of the jth predictor. In fact, the value of $X_j\hat{\beta}_{j,\lambda}^R$ may even depend on the scaling of the *other* predictors! Therefore, it is best to apply ridge regression after *standardizing the predictors*, using the formula

scale equivariant

$$\tilde{x}_{ij} = \frac{x_{ij}}{\sqrt{\frac{1}{n}\sum_{i=1}^n (x_{ij} - \overline{x}_j)^2}}, \tag{6.6}$$

so that they are all on the same scale. In (6.6), the denominator is the estimated standard deviation of the jth predictor. Consequently, all of the standardized predictors will have a standard deviation of one. As a result the final fit will not depend on the scale on which the predictors are measured. In Figure 6.4, the y-axis displays the standardized ridge regression coefficient estimates—that is, the coefficient estimates that result from performing ridge regression using standardized predictors.

Why Does Ridge Regression Improve Over Least Squares?

Ridge regression's advantage over least squares is rooted in the *bias-variance trade-off*. As λ increases, the flexibility of the ridge regression fit decreases, leading to decreased variance but increased bias. This is illustrated in the left-hand panel of Figure 6.5, using a simulated data set containing $p = 45$ predictors and $n = 50$ observations. The green curve in the left-hand panel

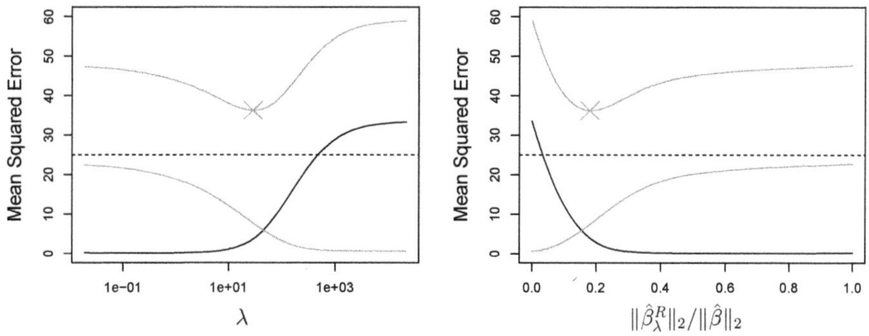

FIGURE 6.5. *Squared bias (black), variance (green), and test mean squared error (purple) for the ridge regression predictions on a simulated data set, as a function of* λ *and* $\|\hat{\beta}^R_\lambda\|_2/\|\hat{\beta}\|_2$. *The horizontal dashed lines indicate the minimum possible MSE. The purple crosses indicate the ridge regression models for which the MSE is smallest.*

of Figure 6.5 displays the variance of the ridge regression predictions as a function of λ. At the least squares coefficient estimates, which correspond to ridge regression with $\lambda = 0$, the variance is high but there is no bias. But as λ increases, the shrinkage of the ridge coefficient estimates leads to a substantial reduction in the variance of the predictions, at the expense of a slight increase in bias. Recall that the test mean squared error (MSE), plotted in purple, is closely related to the variance plus the squared bias. For values of λ up to about 10, the variance decreases rapidly, with very little increase in bias, plotted in black. Consequently, the MSE drops considerably as λ increases from 0 to 10. Beyond this point, the decrease in variance due to increasing λ slows, and the shrinkage on the coefficients causes them to be significantly underestimated, resulting in a large increase in the bias. The minimum MSE is achieved at approximately $\lambda = 30$. Interestingly, because of its high variance, the MSE associated with the least squares fit, when $\lambda = 0$, is almost as high as that of the null model for which all coefficient estimates are zero, when $\lambda = \infty$. However, for an intermediate value of λ, the MSE is considerably lower.

The right-hand panel of Figure 6.5 displays the same curves as the left-hand panel, this time plotted against the ℓ_2 norm of the ridge regression coefficient estimates divided by the ℓ_2 norm of the least squares estimates. Now as we move from left to right, the fits become more flexible, and so the bias decreases and the variance increases.

In general, in situations where the relationship between the response and the predictors is close to linear, the least squares estimates will have low bias but may have high variance. This means that a small change in the training data can cause a large change in the least squares coefficient estimates. In particular, when the number of variables p is almost as large as the number of observations n, as in the example in Figure 6.5, the least squares estimates will be extremely variable. And if $p > n$, then the least squares estimates do not even have a unique solution, whereas ridge regression can still perform well by trading off a small increase in bias for a large decrease in variance. Hence, ridge regression works best in situations where the least squares estimates have high variance.

Ridge regression also has substantial computational advantages over best subset selection, which requires searching through 2^p models. As we discussed previously, even for moderate values of p, such a search can be computationally infeasible. In contrast, for any fixed value of λ, ridge regression only fits a single model, and the model-fitting procedure can be performed quite quickly. In fact, one can show that the computations required to solve (6.5), *simultaneously for all values of* λ, are almost identical to those for fitting a model using least squares.

6.2.2 The Lasso

Ridge regression does have one obvious disadvantage. Unlike best subset, forward stepwise, and backward stepwise selection, which will generally select models that involve just a subset of the variables, ridge regression will include all p predictors in the final model. The penalty $\lambda \sum \beta_j^2$ in (6.5) will shrink all of the coefficients towards zero, but it will not set any of them exactly to zero (unless $\lambda = \infty$). This may not be a problem for prediction accuracy, but it can create a challenge in model interpretation in settings in which the number of variables p is quite large. For example, in the `Credit` data set, it appears that the most important variables are `income`, `limit`, `rating`, and `student`. So we might wish to build a model including just these predictors. However, ridge regression will always generate a model involving all ten predictors. Increasing the value of λ will tend to reduce the magnitudes of the coefficients, but will not result in exclusion of any of the variables.

The *lasso* is a relatively recent alternative to ridge regression that overcomes this disadvantage. The lasso coefficients, $\hat{\beta}_\lambda^L$, minimize the quantity lasso

$$\sum_{i=1}^{n}\left(y_i - \beta_0 - \sum_{j=1}^{p}\beta_j x_{ij}\right)^2 + \lambda\sum_{j=1}^{p}|\beta_j| = \text{RSS} + \lambda\sum_{j=1}^{p}|\beta_j|. \qquad (6.7)$$

Comparing (6.7) to (6.5), we see that the lasso and ridge regression have similar formulations. The only difference is that the β_j^2 term in the ridge regression penalty (6.5) has been replaced by $|\beta_j|$ in the lasso penalty (6.7). In statistical parlance, the lasso uses an ℓ_1 (pronounced "ell 1") penalty instead of an ℓ_2 penalty. The ℓ_1 norm of a coefficient vector β is given by $\|\beta\|_1 = \sum |\beta_j|$.

As with ridge regression, the lasso shrinks the coefficient estimates towards zero. However, in the case of the lasso, the ℓ_1 penalty has the effect of forcing some of the coefficient estimates to be exactly equal to zero when the tuning parameter λ is sufficiently large. Hence, much like best subset selection, the lasso performs *variable selection*. As a result, models generated from the lasso are generally much easier to interpret than those produced by ridge regression. We say that the lasso yields *sparse* models—that is, models that involve only a subset of the variables. As in ridge regression, selecting a good value of λ for the lasso is critical; we defer this discussion to Section 6.2.3, where we use cross-validation. sparse

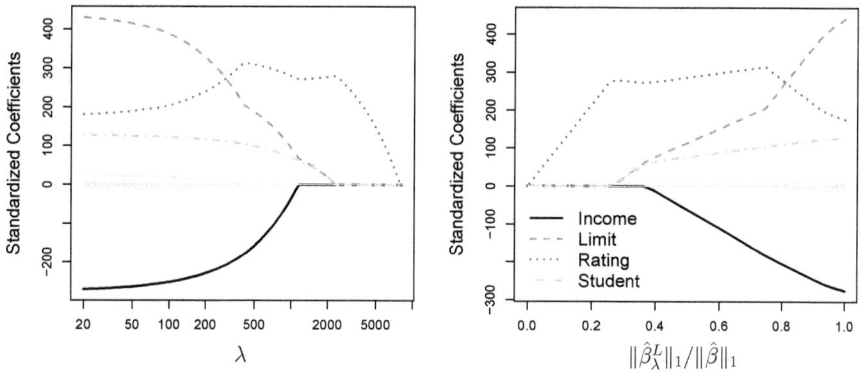

FIGURE 6.6. *The standardized lasso coefficients on the* `Credit` *data set are shown as a function of* λ *and* $\|\hat{\beta}_\lambda^L\|_1/\|\hat{\beta}\|_1$.

As an example, consider the coefficient plots in Figure 6.6, which are generated from applying the lasso to the `Credit` data set. When $\lambda = 0$, then the lasso simply gives the least squares fit, and when λ becomes sufficiently large, the lasso gives the null model in which all coefficient estimates equal zero. However, in between these two extremes, the ridge regression and lasso models are quite different from each other. Moving from left to right in the right-hand panel of Figure 6.6, we observe that at first the lasso results in a model that contains only the `rating` predictor. Then `student` and `limit` enter the model almost simultaneously, shortly followed by `income`. Eventually, the remaining variables enter the model. Hence, depending on the value of λ, the lasso can produce a model involving any number of variables. In contrast, ridge regression will always include all of the variables in the model, although the magnitude of the coefficient estimates will depend on λ.

Another Formulation for Ridge Regression and the Lasso

One can show that the lasso and ridge regression coefficient estimates solve the problems

$$\underset{\beta}{\text{minimize}} \left\{ \sum_{i=1}^{n} \left(y_i - \beta_0 - \sum_{j=1}^{p} \beta_j x_{ij} \right)^2 \right\} \quad \text{subject to} \quad \sum_{j=1}^{p} |\beta_j| \leq s \tag{6.8}$$

and

$$\underset{\beta}{\text{minimize}} \left\{ \sum_{i=1}^{n} \left(y_i - \beta_0 - \sum_{j=1}^{p} \beta_j x_{ij} \right)^2 \right\} \quad \text{subject to} \quad \sum_{j=1}^{p} \beta_j^2 \leq s, \tag{6.9}$$

respectively. In other words, for every value of λ, there is some s such that the Equations (6.7) and (6.8) will give the same lasso coefficient estimates. Similarly, for every value of λ there is a corresponding s such that Equations (6.5) and (6.9) will give the same ridge regression coefficient estimates.

When $p = 2$, then (6.8) indicates that the lasso coefficient estimates have the smallest RSS out of all points that lie within the diamond defined by $|\beta_1| + |\beta_2| \leq s$. Similarly, the ridge regression estimates have the smallest RSS out of all points that lie within the circle defined by $\beta_1^2 + \beta_2^2 \leq s$.

We can think of (6.8) as follows. When we perform the lasso we are trying to find the set of coefficient estimates that lead to the smallest RSS, subject to the constraint that there is a *budget* s for how large $\sum_{j=1}^p |\beta_j|$ can be. When s is extremely large, then this budget is not very restrictive, and so the coefficient estimates can be large. In fact, if s is large enough that the least squares solution falls within the budget, then (6.8) will simply yield the least squares solution. In contrast, if s is small, then $\sum_{j=1}^p |\beta_j|$ must be small in order to avoid violating the budget. Similarly, (6.9) indicates that when we perform ridge regression, we seek a set of coefficient estimates such that the RSS is as small as possible, subject to the requirement that $\sum_{j=1}^p \beta_j^2$ not exceed the budget s.

The formulations (6.8) and (6.9) reveal a close connection between the lasso, ridge regression, and best subset selection. Consider the problem

$$\underset{\beta}{\text{minimize}} \left\{ \sum_{i=1}^n \left(y_i - \beta_0 - \sum_{j=1}^p \beta_j x_{ij} \right)^2 \right\} \quad \text{subject to} \quad \sum_{j=1}^p I(\beta_j \neq 0) \leq s. \tag{6.10}$$

Here $I(\beta_j \neq 0)$ is an indicator variable: it takes on a value of 1 if $\beta_j \neq 0$, and equals zero otherwise. Then (6.10) amounts to finding a set of coefficient estimates such that RSS is as small as possible, subject to the constraint that no more than s coefficients can be nonzero. The problem (6.10) is equivalent to best subset selection. Unfortunately, solving (6.10) is computationally infeasible when p is large, since it requires considering all $\binom{p}{s}$ models containing s predictors. Therefore, we can interpret ridge regression and the lasso as computationally feasible alternatives to best subset selection that replace the intractable form of the budget in (6.10) with forms that are much easier to solve. Of course, the lasso is much more closely related to best subset selection, since the lasso performs feature selection for s sufficiently small in (6.8), while ridge regression does not.

The Variable Selection Property of the Lasso

Why is it that the lasso, unlike ridge regression, results in coefficient estimates that are exactly equal to zero? The formulations (6.8) and (6.9) can be used to shed light on the issue. Figure 6.7 illustrates the situation. The least squares solution is marked as $\hat{\beta}$, while the blue diamond and circle represent the lasso and ridge regression constraints in (6.8) and (6.9), respectively. If s is sufficiently large, then the constraint regions will contain $\hat{\beta}$, and so the ridge regression and lasso estimates will be the same as the least squares estimates. (Such a large value of s corresponds to $\lambda = 0$ in (6.5) and (6.7).) However, in Figure 6.7 the least squares estimates lie outside of the diamond and the circle, and so the least squares estimates are not the same as the lasso and ridge regression estimates.

Each of the ellipses centered around $\hat{\beta}$ represents a *contour*: this means that all of the points on a particular ellipse have the same RSS value. As

contour

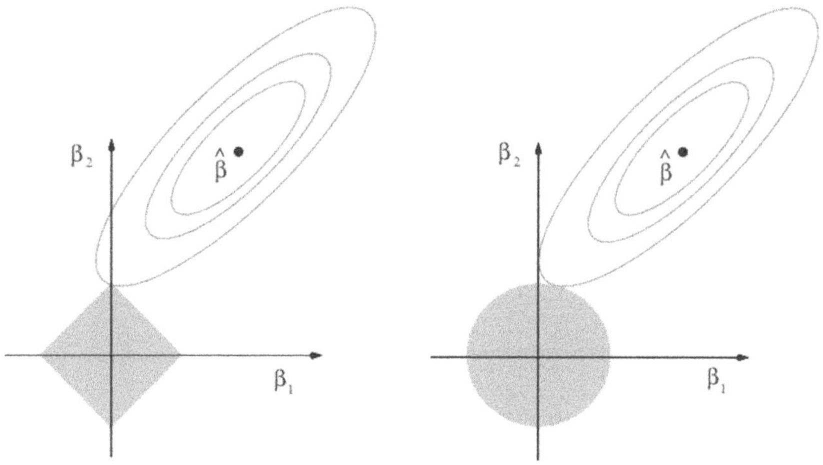

FIGURE 6.7. *Contours of the error and constraint functions for the lasso* (left) *and ridge regression* (right). *The solid blue areas are the constraint regions,* $|\beta_1| + |\beta_2| \leq s$ *and* $\beta_1^2 + \beta_2^2 \leq s$*, while the red ellipses are the contours of the RSS.*

the ellipses expand away from the least squares coefficient estimates, the RSS increases. Equations (6.8) and (6.9) indicate that the lasso and ridge regression coefficient estimates are given by the first point at which an ellipse contacts the constraint region. Since ridge regression has a circular constraint with no sharp points, this intersection will not generally occur on an axis, and so the ridge regression coefficient estimates will be exclusively non-zero. However, the lasso constraint has *corners* at each of the axes, and so the ellipse will often intersect the constraint region at an axis. When this occurs, one of the coefficients will equal zero. In higher dimensions, many of the coefficient estimates may equal zero simultaneously. In Figure 6.7, the intersection occurs at $\beta_1 = 0$, and so the resulting model will only include β_2.

In Figure 6.7, we considered the simple case of $p = 2$. When $p = 3$, then the constraint region for ridge regression becomes a sphere, and the constraint region for the lasso becomes a polyhedron. When $p > 3$, the constraint for ridge regression becomes a hypersphere, and the constraint for the lasso becomes a polytope. However, the key ideas depicted in Figure 6.7 still hold. In particular, the lasso leads to feature selection when $p > 2$ due to the sharp corners of the polyhedron or polytope.

Comparing the Lasso and Ridge Regression

It is clear that the lasso has a major advantage over ridge regression, in that it produces simpler and more interpretable models that involve only a subset of the predictors. However, which method leads to better prediction accuracy? Figure 6.8 displays the variance, squared bias, and test MSE of the lasso applied to the same simulated data as in Figure 6.5. Clearly the lasso leads to qualitatively similar behavior to ridge regression, in that as λ increases, the variance decreases and the bias increases. In the right-hand

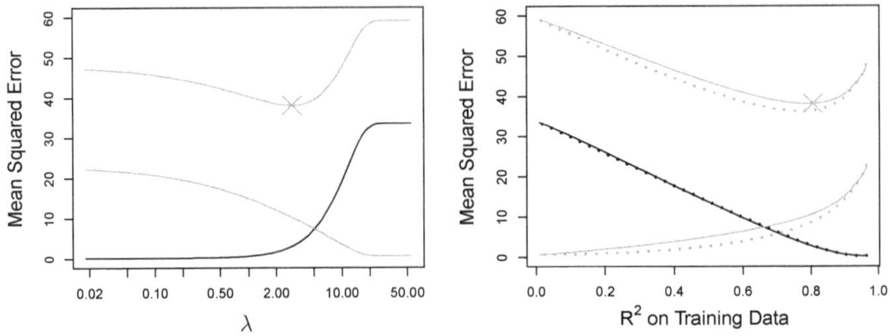

FIGURE 6.8. Left: *Plots of squared bias (black), variance (green), and test MSE (purple) for the lasso on a simulated data set.* Right: *Comparison of squared bias, variance, and test MSE between lasso (solid) and ridge (dotted). Both are plotted against their R^2 on the training data, as a common form of indexing. The crosses in both plots indicate the lasso model for which the MSE is smallest.*

panel of Figure 6.8, the dotted lines represent the ridge regression fits. Here we plot both against their R^2 on the training data. This is another useful way to index models, and can be used to compare models with different types of regularization, as is the case here. In this example, the lasso and ridge regression result in almost identical biases. However, the variance of ridge regression is slightly lower than the variance of the lasso. Consequently, the minimum MSE of ridge regression is slightly smaller than that of the lasso.

However, the data in Figure 6.8 were generated in such a way that all 45 predictors were related to the response—that is, none of the true coefficients $\beta_1, \ldots, \beta_{45}$ equaled zero. The lasso implicitly assumes that a number of the coefficients truly equal zero. Consequently, it is not surprising that ridge regression outperforms the lasso in terms of prediction error in this setting. Figure 6.9 illustrates a similar situation, except that now the response is a function of only 2 out of 45 predictors. Now the lasso tends to outperform ridge regression in terms of bias, variance, and MSE.

These two examples illustrate that neither ridge regression nor the lasso will universally dominate the other. In general, one might expect the lasso to perform better in a setting where a relatively small number of predictors have substantial coefficients, and the remaining predictors have coefficients that are very small or that equal zero. Ridge regression will perform better when the response is a function of many predictors, all with coefficients of roughly equal size. However, the number of predictors that is related to the response is never known *a priori* for real data sets. A technique such as cross-validation can be used in order to determine which approach is better on a particular data set.

As with ridge regression, when the least squares estimates have excessively high variance, the lasso solution can yield a reduction in variance at the expense of a small increase in bias, and consequently can generate more accurate predictions. Unlike ridge regression, the lasso performs variable selection, and hence results in models that are easier to interpret.

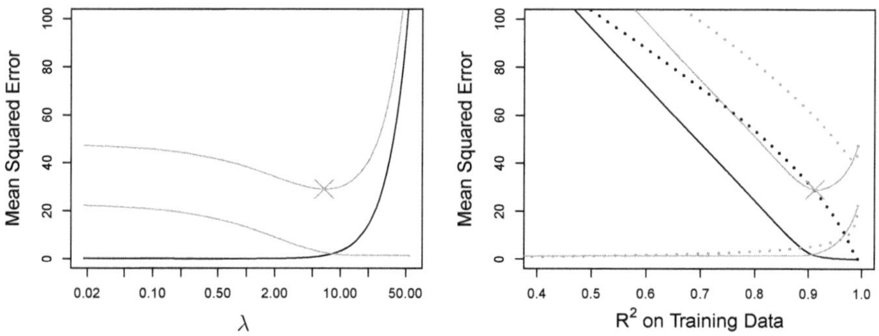

FIGURE 6.9. Left: *Plots of squared bias (black), variance (green), and test MSE (purple) for the lasso. The simulated data is similar to that in Figure 6.8, except that now only two predictors are related to the response.* Right: *Comparison of squared bias, variance, and test MSE between lasso (solid) and ridge (dotted). Both are plotted against their R^2 on the training data, as a common form of indexing. The crosses in both plots indicate the lasso model for which the MSE is smallest.*

There are very efficient algorithms for fitting both ridge and lasso models; in both cases the entire coefficient paths can be computed with about the same amount of work as a single least squares fit. We will explore this further in the lab at the end of this chapter.

A Simple Special Case for Ridge Regression and the Lasso

In order to obtain a better intuition about the behavior of ridge regression and the lasso, consider a simple special case with $n = p$, and $\mathbf{X}$ a diagonal matrix with 1's on the diagonal and 0's in all off-diagonal elements. To simplify the problem further, assume also that we are performing regression without an intercept. With these assumptions, the usual least squares problem simplifies to finding $\beta_1, \ldots, \beta_p$ that minimize

$$\sum_{j=1}^{p} (y_j - \beta_j)^2. \tag{6.11}$$

In this case, the least squares solution is given by

$$\hat{\beta}_j = y_j.$$

And in this setting, ridge regression amounts to finding $\beta_1, \ldots, \beta_p$ such that

$$\sum_{j=1}^{p} (y_j - \beta_j)^2 + \lambda \sum_{j=1}^{p} \beta_j^2 \tag{6.12}$$

is minimized, and the lasso amounts to finding the coefficients such that

$$\sum_{j=1}^{p} (y_j - \beta_j)^2 + \lambda \sum_{j=1}^{p} |\beta_j| \tag{6.13}$$

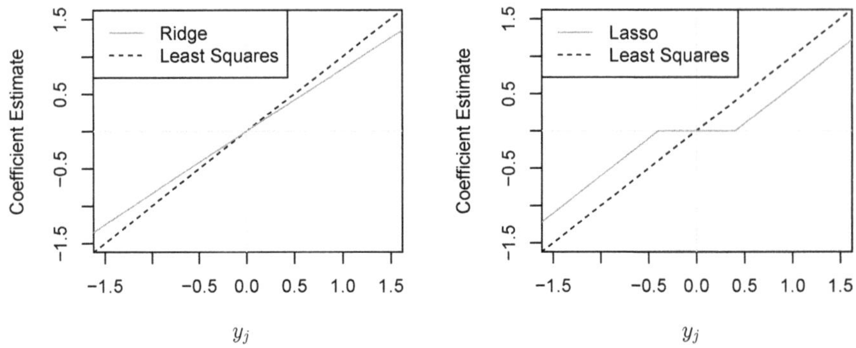

FIGURE 6.10. *The ridge regression and lasso coefficient estimates for a simple setting with $n = p$ and $\mathbf{X}$ a diagonal matrix with 1's on the diagonal.* Left: *The ridge regression coefficient estimates are shrunken proportionally towards zero, relative to the least squares estimates.* Right: *The lasso coefficient estimates are soft-thresholded towards zero.*

is minimized. One can show that in this setting, the ridge regression estimates take the form

$$\hat{\beta}_j^R = y_j/(1+\lambda), \tag{6.14}$$

and the lasso estimates take the form

$$\hat{\beta}_j^L = \begin{cases} y_j - \lambda/2 & \text{if } y_j > \lambda/2; \\ y_j + \lambda/2 & \text{if } y_j < -\lambda/2; \\ 0 & \text{if } |y_j| \leq \lambda/2. \end{cases} \tag{6.15}$$

Figure 6.10 displays the situation. We can see that ridge regression and the lasso perform two very different types of shrinkage. In ridge regression, each least squares coefficient estimate is shrunken by the same proportion. In contrast, the lasso shrinks each least squares coefficient towards zero by a constant amount, $\lambda/2$; the least squares coefficients that are less than $\lambda/2$ in absolute value are shrunken entirely to zero. The type of shrinkage performed by the lasso in this simple setting (6.15) is known as *soft-thresholding*. The fact that some lasso coefficients are shrunken entirely to zero explains why the lasso performs feature selection.

soft-thresholding

In the case of a more general data matrix $\mathbf{X}$, the story is a little more complicated than what is depicted in Figure 6.10, but the main ideas still hold approximately: ridge regression more or less shrinks every dimension of the data by the same proportion, whereas the lasso more or less shrinks all coefficients toward zero by a similar amount, and sufficiently small coefficients are shrunken all the way to zero.

Bayesian Interpretation of Ridge Regression and the Lasso

We now show that one can view ridge regression and the lasso through a Bayesian lens. A Bayesian viewpoint for regression assumes that the coefficient vector β has some *prior* distribution, say $p(\beta)$, where $\beta = (\beta_0, \beta_1, \ldots, \beta_p)^T$. The likelihood of the data can be written as $f(Y|X, \beta)$,

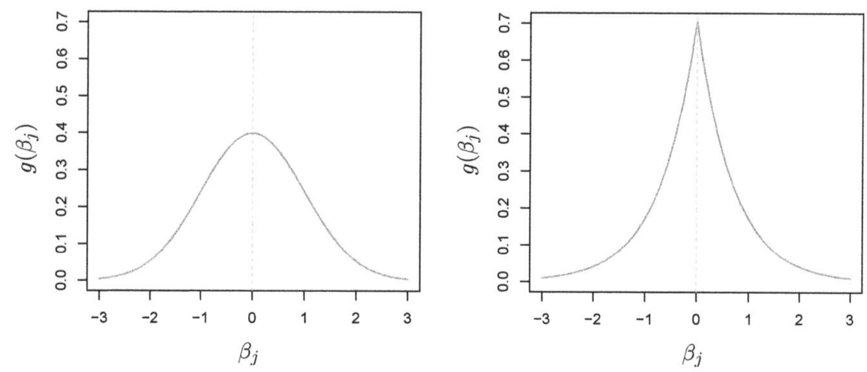

FIGURE 6.11. Left: *Ridge regression is the posterior mode for β under a Gaussian prior.* Right: *The lasso is the posterior mode for β under a double-exponential prior.*

where $X = (X_1, \dots, X_p)$. Multiplying the prior distribution by the likelihood gives us (up to a proportionality constant) the *posterior distribution*, which takes the form

posterior distribution

$$p(\beta|X, Y) \propto f(Y|X, \beta)p(\beta|X) = f(Y|X, \beta)p(\beta),$$

where the proportionality above follows from Bayes' theorem, and the equality above follows from the assumption that X is fixed.

We assume the usual linear model,

$$Y = \beta_0 + X_1\beta_1 + \cdots + X_p\beta_p + \epsilon,$$

and suppose that the errors are independent and drawn from a normal distribution. Furthermore, assume that $p(\beta) = \prod_{j=1}^{p} g(\beta_j)$, for some density function g. It turns out that ridge regression and the lasso follow naturally from two special cases of g:

- If g is a Gaussian distribution with mean zero and standard deviation a function of λ, then it follows that the *posterior mode* for β—that is, the most likely value for β, given the data—is given by the ridge regression solution. (In fact, the ridge regression solution is also the posterior mean.)

posterior mode

- If g is a double-exponential (Laplace) distribution with mean zero and scale parameter a function of λ, then it follows that the posterior mode for β is the lasso solution. (However, the lasso solution is *not* the posterior mean, and in fact, the posterior mean does not yield a sparse coefficient vector.)

The Gaussian and double-exponential priors are displayed in Figure 6.11. Therefore, from a Bayesian viewpoint, ridge regression and the lasso follow directly from assuming the usual linear model with normal errors, together with a simple prior distribution for β. Notice that the lasso prior is steeply peaked at zero, while the Gaussian is flatter and fatter at zero. Hence, the lasso expects a priori that many of the coefficients are (exactly) zero, while ridge assumes the coefficients are randomly distributed about zero.

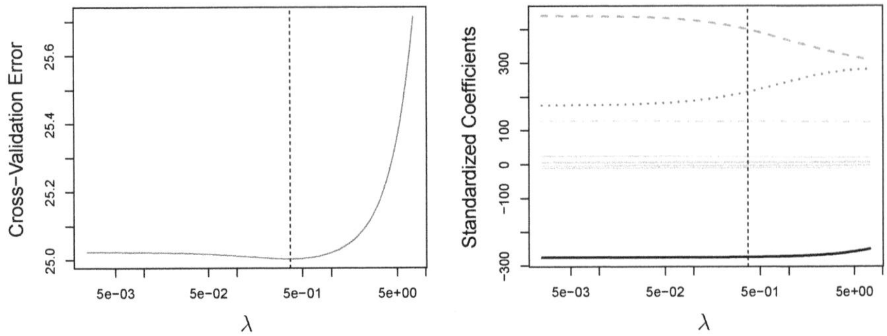

FIGURE 6.12. Left: *Cross-validation errors that result from applying ridge regression to the* `Credit` *data set with various values of* λ. Right: *The coefficient estimates as a function of* λ. *The vertical dashed lines indicate the value of* λ *selected by cross-validation.*

6.2.3 Selecting the Tuning Parameter

Just as the subset selection approaches considered in Section 6.1 require a method to determine which of the models under consideration is best, implementing ridge regression and the lasso requires a method for selecting a value for the tuning parameter λ in (6.5) and (6.7), or equivalently, the value of the constraint s in (6.9) and (6.8). Cross-validation provides a simple way to tackle this problem. We choose a grid of λ values, and compute the cross-validation error for each value of λ, as described in Chapter 5. We then select the tuning parameter value for which the cross-validation error is smallest. Finally, the model is re-fit using all of the available observations and the selected value of the tuning parameter.

Figure 6.12 displays the choice of λ that results from performing leave-one-out cross-validation on the ridge regression fits from the `Credit` data set. The dashed vertical lines indicate the selected value of λ. In this case the value is relatively small, indicating that the optimal fit only involves a small amount of shrinkage relative to the least squares solution. In addition, the dip is not very pronounced, so there is rather a wide range of values that would give a very similar error. In a case like this we might simply use the least squares solution.

Figure 6.13 provides an illustration of ten-fold cross-validation applied to the lasso fits on the sparse simulated data from Figure 6.9. The left-hand panel of Figure 6.13 displays the cross-validation error, while the right-hand panel displays the coefficient estimates. The vertical dashed lines indicate the point at which the cross-validation error is smallest. The two colored lines in the right-hand panel of Figure 6.13 represent the two predictors that are related to the response, while the grey lines represent the unrelated predictors; these are often referred to as *signal* and *noise* variables, respectively. Not only has the lasso correctly given much larger coefficient estimates to the two signal predictors, but also the minimum cross-validation error corresponds to a set of coefficient estimates for which only the signal variables are non-zero. Hence cross-validation together with the lasso has correctly identified the two signal variables in the model, even though this is a challenging setting, with $p = 45$ variables and only $n = 50$

signal

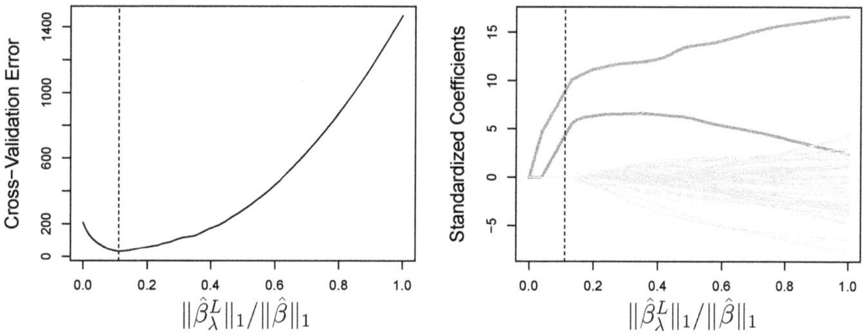

FIGURE 6.13. Left: *Ten-fold cross-validation MSE for the lasso, applied to the sparse simulated data set from Figure 6.9.* Right: *The corresponding lasso coefficient estimates are displayed. The two signal variables are shown in color, and the noise variables are in gray. The vertical dashed lines indicate the lasso fit for which the cross-validation error is smallest.*

observations. In contrast, the least squares solution—displayed on the far right of the right-hand panel of Figure 6.13—assigns a large coefficient estimate to only one of the two signal variables.

6.3 Dimension Reduction Methods

The methods that we have discussed so far in this chapter have controlled variance in two different ways, either by using a subset of the original variables, or by shrinking their coefficients toward zero. All of these methods are defined using the original predictors, $X_1, X_2, \ldots, X_p$. We now explore a class of approaches that *transform* the predictors and then fit a least squares model using the transformed variables. We will refer to these techniques as *dimension reduction* methods.

dimension reduction

linear combination

Let $Z_1, Z_2, \ldots, Z_M$ represent $M < p$ *linear combinations* of our original p predictors. That is,

$$Z_m = \sum_{j=1}^{p} \phi_{jm} X_j \tag{6.16}$$

for some constants $\phi_{1m}, \phi_{2m} \ldots, \phi_{pm}$, $m = 1, \ldots, M$. We can then fit the linear regression model

$$y_i = \theta_0 + \sum_{m=1}^{M} \theta_m z_{im} + \epsilon_i, \quad i = 1, \ldots, n, \tag{6.17}$$

using least squares. Note that in (6.17), the regression coefficients are given by $\theta_0, \theta_1, \ldots, \theta_M$. If the constants $\phi_{1m}, \phi_{2m}, \ldots, \phi_{pm}$ are chosen wisely, then such dimension reduction approaches can often outperform least squares regression. In other words, fitting (6.17) using least squares can lead to better results than fitting (6.1) using least squares.

The term *dimension reduction* comes from the fact that this approach reduces the problem of estimating the $p+1$ coefficients $\beta_0, \beta_1, \ldots, \beta_p$ to the

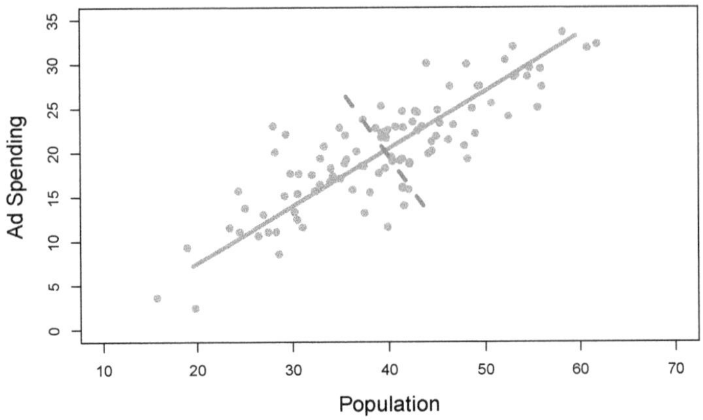

FIGURE 6.14. *The population size* (pop) *and ad spending* (ad) *for* 100 *different cities are shown as purple circles. The green solid line indicates the first principal component, and the blue dashed line indicates the second principal component.*

simpler problem of estimating the $M+1$ coefficients $\theta_0, \theta_1, \ldots, \theta_M$, where $M < p$. In other words, the dimension of the problem has been reduced from $p+1$ to $M+1$.

Notice that from (6.16),

$$\sum_{m=1}^{M} \theta_m z_{im} = \sum_{m=1}^{M} \theta_m \sum_{j=1}^{p} \phi_{jm} x_{ij} = \sum_{j=1}^{p} \sum_{m=1}^{M} \theta_m \phi_{jm} x_{ij} = \sum_{j=1}^{p} \beta_j x_{ij},$$

where

$$\beta_j = \sum_{m=1}^{M} \theta_m \phi_{jm}. \tag{6.18}$$

Hence (6.17) can be thought of as a special case of the original linear regression model given by (6.1). Dimension reduction serves to constrain the estimated β_j coefficients, since now they must take the form (6.18). This constraint on the form of the coefficients has the potential to bias the coefficient estimates. However, in situations where p is large relative to n, selecting a value of $M \ll p$ can significantly reduce the variance of the fitted coefficients. If $M = p$, and all the Z_m are linearly independent, then (6.18) poses no constraints. In this case, no dimension reduction occurs, and so fitting (6.17) is equivalent to performing least squares on the original p predictors.

All dimension reduction methods work in two steps. First, the transformed predictors $Z_1, Z_2, \ldots, Z_M$ are obtained. Second, the model is fit using these M predictors. However, the choice of $Z_1, Z_2, \ldots, Z_M$, or equivalently, the selection of the ϕ_{jm}'s, can be achieved in different ways. In this chapter, we will consider two approaches for this task: *principal components* and *partial least squares*.

6.3.1 Principal Components Regression

Principal components analysis (PCA) is a popular approach for deriving principal components analysis a low-dimensional set of features from a large set of variables. PCA is discussed in greater detail as a tool for *unsupervised learning* in Chapter 12. Here we describe its use as a dimension reduction technique for regression.

An Overview of Principal Components Analysis

PCA is a technique for reducing the dimension of an $n \times p$ data matrix $\mathbf{X}$. The *first principal component* direction of the data is that along which the observations *vary the most*. For instance, consider Figure 6.14, which shows population size (pop) in tens of thousands of people, and ad spending for a particular company (ad) in thousands of dollars, for 100 cities.[6] The green solid line represents the first principal component direction of the data. We can see by eye that this is the direction along which there is the greatest variability in the data. That is, if we *projected* the 100 observations onto this line (as shown in the left-hand panel of Figure 6.15), then the resulting projected observations would have the largest possible variance; projecting the observations onto any other line would yield projected observations with lower variance. Projecting a point onto a line simply involves finding the location on the line which is closest to the point.

The first principal component is displayed graphically in Figure 6.14, but how can it be summarized mathematically? It is given by the formula

$$Z_1 = 0.839 \times (\text{pop} - \overline{\text{pop}}) + 0.544 \times (\text{ad} - \overline{\text{ad}}). \tag{6.19}$$

Here $\phi_{11} = 0.839$ and $\phi_{21} = 0.544$ are the principal component loadings, which define the direction referred to above. In (6.19), $\overline{\text{pop}}$ indicates the mean of all pop values in this data set, and $\overline{\text{ad}}$ indicates the mean of all advertising spending. The idea is that out of every possible *linear combination* of pop and ad such that $\phi_{11}^2 + \phi_{21}^2 = 1$, this particular linear combination yields the highest variance: i.e. this is the linear combination for which $\text{Var}(\phi_{11} \times (\text{pop} - \overline{\text{pop}}) + \phi_{21} \times (\text{ad} - \overline{\text{ad}}))$ is maximized. It is necessary to consider only linear combinations of the form $\phi_{11}^2 + \phi_{21}^2 = 1$, since otherwise we could increase ϕ_{11} and ϕ_{21} arbitrarily in order to blow up the variance. In (6.19), the two loadings are both positive and have similar size, and so Z_1 is almost an *average* of the two variables.

Since $n = 100$, pop and ad are vectors of length 100, and so is Z_1 in (6.19). For instance,

$$z_{i1} = 0.839 \times (\text{pop}_i - \overline{\text{pop}}) + 0.544 \times (\text{ad}_i - \overline{\text{ad}}). \tag{6.20}$$

The values of $z_{11}, \ldots, z_{n1}$ are known as the *principal component scores*, and can be seen in the right-hand panel of Figure 6.15.

There is also another interpretation of PCA: the first principal component vector defines the line that is *as close as possible* to the data. For instance, in Figure 6.14, the first principal component line minimizes the sum of the squared perpendicular distances between each point and the line. These distances are plotted as dashed line segments in the left-hand

[6]This dataset is distinct from the `Advertising` data discussed in Chapter 3.

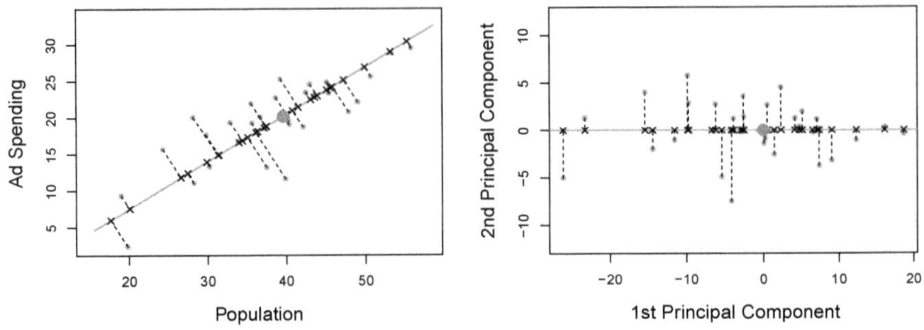

FIGURE 6.15. *A subset of the advertising data. The mean* pop *and* ad *budgets are indicated with a blue circle.* Left: *The first principal component direction is shown in green. It is the dimension along which the data vary the most, and it also defines the line that is closest to all n of the observations. The distances from each observation to the principal component are represented using the black dashed line segments. The blue dot represents* $(\overline{\text{pop}}, \overline{\text{ad}})$. Right: *The left-hand panel has been rotated so that the first principal component direction coincides with the x-axis.*

panel of Figure 6.15, in which the crosses represent the *projection* of each point onto the first principal component line. The first principal component has been chosen so that the projected observations are *as close as possible* to the original observations.

In the right-hand panel of Figure 6.15, the left-hand panel has been rotated so that the first principal component direction coincides with the x-axis. It is possible to show that the *first principal component score* for the ith observation, given in (6.20), is the distance in the x-direction of the ith cross from zero. So for example, the point in the bottom-left corner of the left-hand panel of Figure 6.15 has a large negative principal component score, $z_{i1} = -26.1$, while the point in the top-right corner has a large positive score, $z_{i1} = 18.7$. These scores can be computed directly using (6.20).

We can think of the values of the principal component Z_1 as single-number summaries of the joint pop and ad budgets for each location. In this example, if $z_{i1} = 0.839 \times (\text{pop}_i - \overline{\text{pop}}) + 0.544 \times (\text{ad}_i - \overline{\text{ad}}) < 0$, then this indicates a city with below-average population size and below-average ad spending. A positive score suggests the opposite. How well can a single number represent both pop and ad? In this case, Figure 6.14 indicates that pop and ad have approximately a linear relationship, and so we might expect that a single-number summary will work well. Figure 6.16 displays z_{i1} versus both pop and ad.[7] The plots show a strong relationship between the first principal component and the two features. In other words, the first principal component appears to capture most of the information contained in the pop and ad predictors.

So far we have concentrated on the first principal component. In general, one can construct up to p distinct principal components. The second

---

[7]The principal components were calculated after first standardizing both pop and ad, a common approach. Hence, the x-axes on Figures 6.15 and 6.16 are not on the same scale.

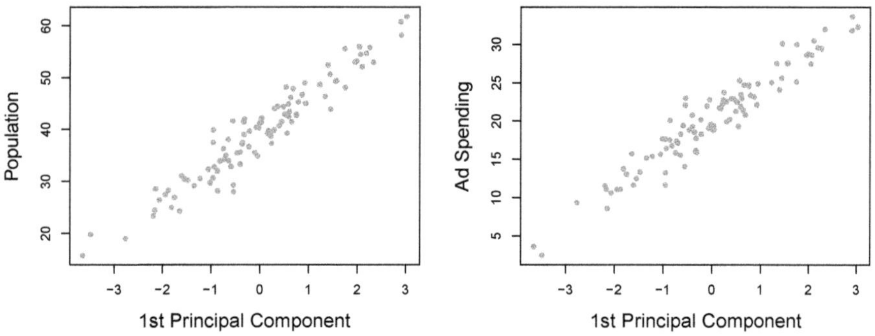

FIGURE 6.16. *Plots of the first principal component scores z_{i1} versus* pop *and* ad. *The relationships are strong.*

principal component Z_2 is a linear combination of the variables that is uncorrelated with Z_1, and has largest variance subject to this constraint. The second principal component direction is illustrated as a dashed blue line in Figure 6.14. It turns out that the zero correlation condition of Z_1 with Z_2 is equivalent to the condition that the direction must be *perpendicular*, or *orthogonal*, to the first principal component direction. The second principal component is given by the formula

perpendicular
orthogonal

$$Z_2 = 0.544 \times (\text{pop} - \overline{\text{pop}}) - 0.839 \times (\text{ad} - \overline{\text{ad}}).$$

Since the advertising data has two predictors, the first two principal components contain all of the information that is in pop and ad. However, by construction, the first component will contain the most information. Consider, for example, the much larger variability of z_{i1} (the x-axis) versus z_{i2} (the y-axis) in the right-hand panel of Figure 6.15. The fact that the second principal component scores are much closer to zero indicates that this component captures far less information. As another illustration, Figure 6.17 displays z_{i2} versus pop and ad. There is little relationship between the second principal component and these two predictors, again suggesting that in this case, one only needs the first principal component in order to accurately represent the pop and ad budgets.

With two-dimensional data, such as in our advertising example, we can construct at most two principal components. However, if we had other predictors, such as population age, income level, education, and so forth, then additional components could be constructed. They would successively maximize variance, subject to the constraint of being uncorrelated with the preceding components.

The Principal Components Regression Approach

The *principal components regression* (PCR) approach involves constructing the first M principal components, $Z_1, \ldots, Z_M$, and then using these components as the predictors in a linear regression model that is fit using least squares. The key idea is that often a small number of principal components suffice to explain most of the variability in the data, as well as the relationship with the response. In other words, we assume that *the*

principal components regression

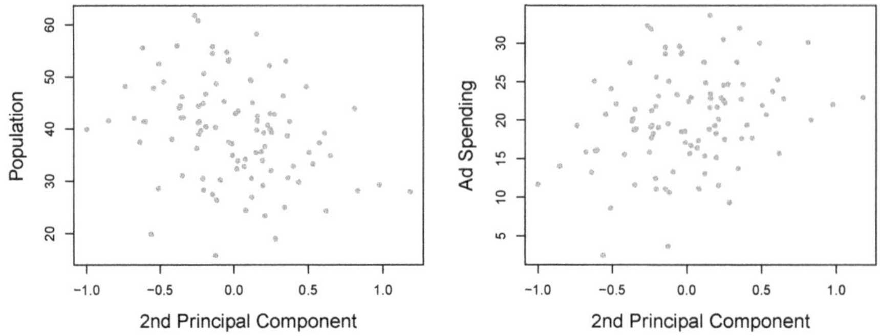

FIGURE 6.17. *Plots of the second principal component scores z_{i2} versus* pop *and* ad*. The relationships are weak.*

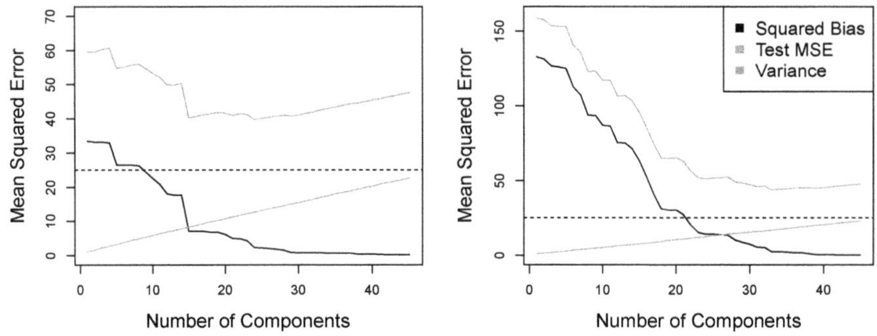

FIGURE 6.18. *PCR was applied to two simulated data sets. In each panel, the horizontal dashed line represents the irreducible error.* Left: *Simulated data from Figure 6.8.* Right: *Simulated data from Figure 6.9.*

directions in which $X_1, \ldots, X_p$ show the most variation are the directions that are associated with Y. While this assumption is not guaranteed to be true, it often turns out to be a reasonable enough approximation to give good results.

If the assumption underlying PCR holds, then fitting a least squares model to $Z_1, \ldots, Z_M$ will lead to better results than fitting a least squares model to $X_1, \ldots, X_p$, since most or all of the information in the data that relates to the response is contained in $Z_1, \ldots, Z_M$, and by estimating only $M \ll p$ coefficients we can mitigate overfitting. In the advertising data, the first principal component explains most of the variance in both pop and ad, so a principal component regression that uses this single variable to predict some response of interest, such as sales, will likely perform quite well.

Figure 6.18 displays the PCR fits on the simulated data sets from Figures 6.8 and 6.9. Recall that both data sets were generated using $n = 50$ observations and $p = 45$ predictors. However, while the response in the first data set was a function of all the predictors, the response in the second data set was generated using only two of the predictors. The curves are plotted as a function of M, the number of principal components used as predictors in the regression model. As more principal components are used

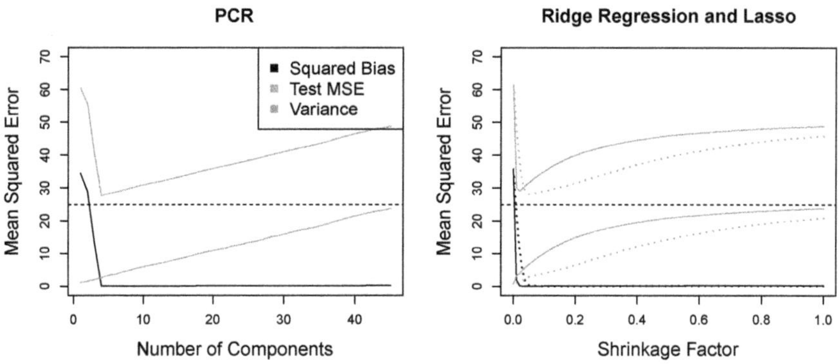

FIGURE 6.19. *PCR, ridge regression, and the lasso were applied to a simulated data set in which the first five principal components of X contain all the information about the response Y. In each panel, the irreducible error* Var(ϵ) *is shown as a horizontal dashed line.* Left: *Results for PCR.* Right: *Results for lasso (solid) and ridge regression (dotted). The x-axis displays the shrinkage factor of the coefficient estimates, defined as the ℓ_2 norm of the shrunken coefficient estimates divided by the ℓ_2 norm of the least squares estimate.*

in the regression model, the bias decreases, but the variance increases. This results in a typical U-shape for the mean squared error. When $M = p = 45$, then PCR amounts simply to a least squares fit using all of the original predictors. The figure indicates that performing PCR with an appropriate choice of M can result in a substantial improvement over least squares, especially in the left-hand panel. However, by examining the ridge regression and lasso results in Figures 6.5, 6.8, and 6.9, we see that PCR does not perform as well as the two shrinkage methods in this example.

The relatively worse performance of PCR in Figure 6.18 is a consequence of the fact that the data were generated in such a way that many principal components are required in order to adequately model the response. In contrast, PCR will tend to do well in cases when the first few principal components are sufficient to capture most of the variation in the predictors as well as the relationship with the response. The left-hand panel of Figure 6.19 illustrates the results from another simulated data set designed to be more favorable to PCR. Here the response was generated in such a way that it depends exclusively on the first five principal components. Now the bias drops to zero rapidly as M, the number of principal components used in PCR, increases. The mean squared error displays a clear minimum at $M = 5$. The right-hand panel of Figure 6.19 displays the results on these data using ridge regression and the lasso. All three methods offer a significant improvement over least squares. However, PCR and ridge regression slightly outperform the lasso.

We note that even though PCR provides a simple way to perform regression using $M < p$ predictors, it is *not* a feature selection method. This is because each of the M principal components used in the regression is a linear combination of all p of the *original* features. For instance, in (6.19), Z_1 was a linear combination of both `pop` and `ad`. Therefore, while PCR often performs quite well in many practical settings, it does not result in the

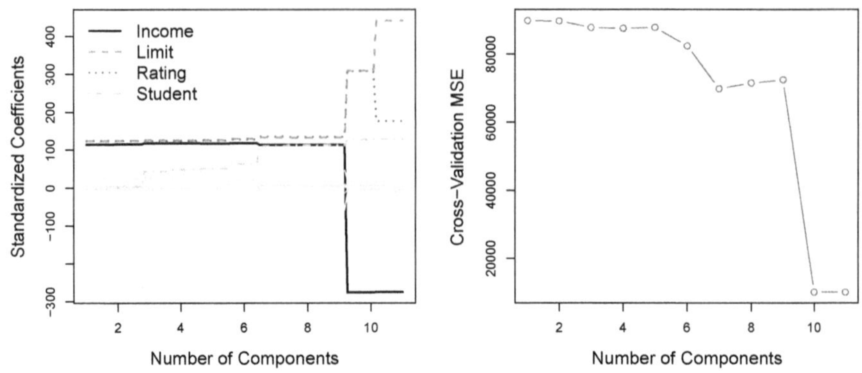

FIGURE 6.20. Left: *PCR standardized coefficient estimates on the* `Credit` *data set for different values of M.* Right: *The ten-fold cross-validation* MSE *obtained using PCR, as a function of M.*

development of a model that relies upon a small set of the original features. In this sense, PCR is more closely related to ridge regression than to the lasso. In fact, one can show that PCR and ridge regression are very closely related. One can even think of ridge regression as a continuous version of PCR![8]

In PCR, the number of principal components, M, is typically chosen by cross-validation. The results of applying PCR to the `Credit` data set are shown in Figure 6.20; the right-hand panel displays the cross-validation errors obtained, as a function of M. On these data, the lowest cross-validation error occurs when there are $M = 10$ components; this corresponds to almost no dimension reduction at all, since PCR with $M = 11$ is equivalent to simply performing least squares.

When performing PCR, we generally recommend *standardizing* each predictor, using (6.6), prior to generating the principal components. This standardization ensures that all variables are on the same scale. In the absence of standardization, the high-variance variables will tend to play a larger role in the principal components obtained, and the scale on which the variables are measured will ultimately have an effect on the final PCR model. However, if the variables are all measured in the same units (say, kilograms, or inches), then one might choose not to standardize them.

6.3.2 Partial Least Squares

The PCR approach that we just described involves identifying linear combinations, or *directions*, that best represent the predictors $X_1, \ldots, X_p$. These directions are identified in an *unsupervised* way, since the response Y is not used to help determine the principal component directions. That is, the response does not *supervise* the identification of the principal components. Consequently, PCR suffers from a drawback: there is no guarantee

[8]More details can be found in Section 3.5 of *The Elements of Statistical Learning* by Hastie, Tibshirani, and Friedman.

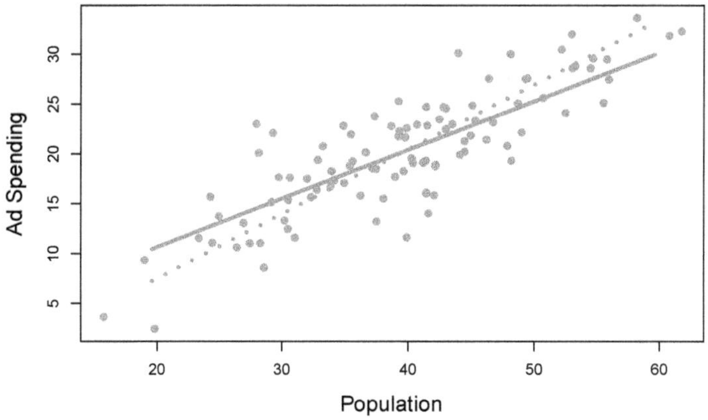

FIGURE 6.21. *For the advertising data, the first PLS direction (solid line) and first PCR direction (dotted line) are shown.*

that the directions that best explain the predictors will also be the best directions to use for predicting the response. Unsupervised methods are discussed further in Chapter 12.

We now present *partial least squares* (PLS), a *supervised* alternative to PCR. Like PCR, PLS is a dimension reduction method, which first identifies a new set of features $Z_1, \ldots, Z_M$ that are linear combinations of the original features, and then fits a linear model via least squares using these M new features. But unlike PCR, PLS identifies these new features in a supervised way—that is, it makes use of the response Y in order to identify new features that not only approximate the old features well, but also that *are related to the response*. Roughly speaking, the PLS approach attempts to find directions that help explain both the response and the predictors.

partial least squares

We now describe how the first PLS direction is computed. After standardizing the p predictors, PLS computes the first direction Z_1 by setting each ϕ_{j1} in (6.16) equal to the coefficient from the simple linear regression of Y onto X_j. One can show that this coefficient is proportional to the correlation between Y and X_j. Hence, in computing $Z_1 = \sum_{j=1}^{p} \phi_{j1} X_j$, PLS places the highest weight on the variables that are most strongly related to the response.

Figure 6.21 displays an example of PLS on a synthetic dataset with Sales in each of 100 regions as the response, and two predictors; Population Size and Advertising Spending. The solid green line indicates the first PLS direction, while the dotted line shows the first principal component direction. PLS has chosen a direction that has less change in the ad dimension per unit change in the pop dimension, relative to PCA. This suggests that pop is more highly correlated with the response than is ad. The PLS direction does not fit the predictors as closely as does PCA, but it does a better job explaining the response.

To identify the second PLS direction we first *adjust* each of the variables for Z_1, by regressing each variable on Z_1 and taking *residuals*. These residuals can be interpreted as the remaining information that has not been explained by the first PLS direction. We then compute Z_2 using this *or-*

thogonalized data in exactly the same fashion as Z_1 was computed based on the original data. This iterative approach can be repeated M times to identify multiple PLS components $Z_1, \ldots, Z_M$. Finally, at the end of this procedure, we use least squares to fit a linear model to predict Y using $Z_1, \ldots, Z_M$ in exactly the same fashion as for PCR.

As with PCR, the number M of partial least squares directions used in PLS is a tuning parameter that is typically chosen by cross-validation. We generally standardize the predictors and response before performing PLS.

PLS is popular in the field of chemometrics, where many variables arise from digitized spectrometry signals. In practice it often performs no better than ridge regression or PCR. While the supervised dimension reduction of PLS can reduce bias, it also has the potential to increase variance, so that the overall benefit of PLS relative to PCR is a wash.

6.4 Considerations in High Dimensions

6.4.1 High-Dimensional Data

Most traditional statistical techniques for regression and classification are intended for the *low-dimensional* setting in which n, the number of observations, is much greater than p, the number of features. This is due in part to the fact that throughout most of the field's history, the bulk of scientific problems requiring the use of statistics have been low-dimensional. For instance, consider the task of developing a model to predict a patient's blood pressure on the basis of his or her age, sex, and body mass index (BMI). There are three predictors, or four if an intercept is included in the model, and perhaps several thousand patients for whom blood pressure and age, sex, and BMI are available. Hence $n \gg p$, and so the problem is low-dimensional. (By dimension here we are referring to the size of p.)

low-dimensional

In the past 20 years, new technologies have changed the way that data are collected in fields as diverse as finance, marketing, and medicine. It is now commonplace to collect an almost unlimited number of feature measurements (p very large). While p can be extremely large, the number of observations n is often limited due to cost, sample availability, or other considerations. Two examples are as follows:

1. Rather than predicting blood pressure on the basis of just age, sex, and BMI, one might also collect measurements for half a million *single nucleotide polymorphisms* (SNPs; these are individual DNA mutations that are relatively common in the population) for inclusion in the predictive model. Then $n \approx 200$ and $p \approx 500{,}000$.

2. A marketing analyst interested in understanding people's online shopping patterns could treat as features all of the search terms entered by users of a search engine. This is sometimes known as the "bag-of-words" model. The same researcher might have access to the search histories of only a few hundred or a few thousand search engine users who have consented to share their information with the researcher. For a given user, each of the p search terms is scored present (0) or

absent (1), creating a large binary feature vector. Then $n \approx 1{,}000$ and p is much larger.

Data sets containing more features than observations are often referred to as *high-dimensional*. Classical approaches such as least squares linear regression are not appropriate in this setting. Many of the issues that arise in the analysis of high-dimensional data were discussed earlier in this book, since they apply also when $n > p$: these include the role of the bias-variance trade-off and the danger of overfitting. Though these issues are always relevant, they can become particularly important when the number of features is very large relative to the number of observations.

high-dimensional

We have defined the *high-dimensional setting* as the case where the number of features p is larger than the number of observations n. But the considerations that we will now discuss certainly also apply if p is slightly smaller than n, and are best always kept in mind when performing supervised learning.

6.4.2 What Goes Wrong in High Dimensions?

In order to illustrate the need for extra care and specialized techniques for regression and classification when $p > n$, we begin by examining what can go wrong if we apply a statistical technique not intended for the high-dimensional setting. For this purpose, we examine least squares regression. But the same concepts apply to logistic regression, linear discriminant analysis, and other classical statistical approaches.

When the number of features p is as large as, or larger than, the number of observations n, least squares as described in Chapter 3 cannot (or rather, *should not*) be performed. The reason is simple: regardless of whether or not there truly is a relationship between the features and the response, least squares will yield a set of coefficient estimates that result in a perfect fit to the data, such that the residuals are zero.

An example is shown in Figure 6.22 with $p = 1$ feature (plus an intercept) in two cases: when there are 20 observations, and when there are only two observations. When there are 20 observations, $n > p$ and the least squares regression line does not perfectly fit the data; instead, the regression line seeks to approximate the 20 observations as well as possible. On the other hand, when there are only two observations, then regardless of the values of those observations, the regression line will fit the data exactly. This is problematic because this perfect fit will almost certainly lead to overfitting of the data. In other words, though it is possible to perfectly fit the training data in the high-dimensional setting, the resulting linear model will perform extremely poorly on an independent test set, and therefore does not constitute a useful model. In fact, we can see that this happened in Figure 6.22: the least squares line obtained in the right-hand panel will perform very poorly on a test set comprised of the observations in the left-hand panel. The problem is simple: when $p > n$ or $p \approx n$, a simple least squares regression line is too *flexible* and hence overfits the data.

Figure 6.23 further illustrates the risk of carelessly applying least squares when the number of features p is large. Data were simulated with $n = 20$ observations, and regression was performed with between 1 and 20 features,

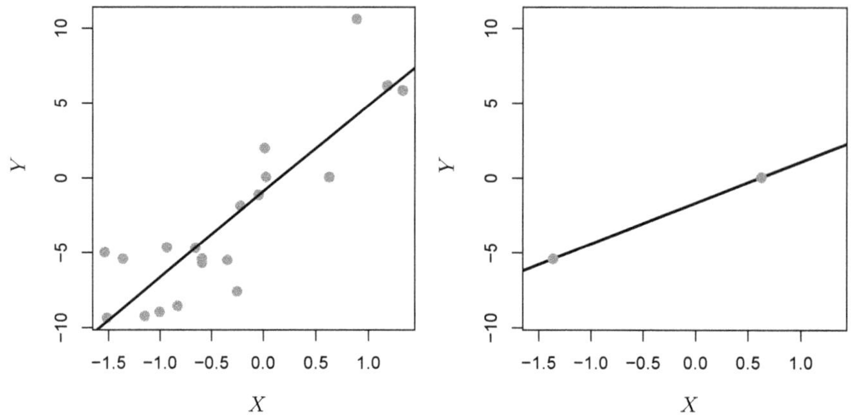

FIGURE 6.22. Left: *Least squares regression in the low-dimensional setting.* Right: *Least squares regression with* $n = 2$ *observations and two parameters to be estimated (an intercept and a coefficient).*

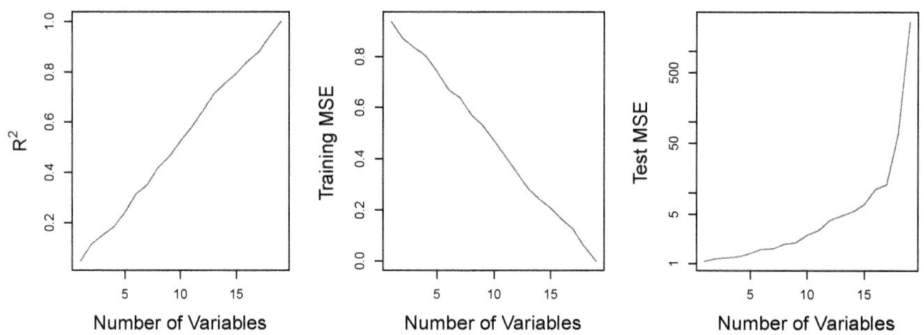

FIGURE 6.23. *On a simulated example with* $n = 20$ *training observations, features that are completely unrelated to the outcome are added to the model.* Left: *The* R^2 *increases to 1 as more features are included.* Center: *The training set MSE decreases to 0 as more features are included.* Right: *The test set MSE increases as more features are included.*

each of which was completely unrelated to the response. As shown in the figure, the model R^2 increases to 1 as the number of features included in the model increases, and correspondingly the training set MSE decreases to 0 as the number of features increases, *even though the features are completely unrelated to the response.* On the other hand, the MSE on an *independent test set* becomes extremely large as the number of features included in the model increases, because including the additional predictors leads to a vast increase in the variance of the coefficient estimates. Looking at the test set MSE, it is clear that the best model contains at most a few variables. However, someone who carelessly examines only the R^2 or the training set MSE might erroneously conclude that the model with the greatest number of variables is best. This indicates the importance of applying extra care when analyzing data sets with a large number of variables, and of always evaluating model performance on an independent test set.

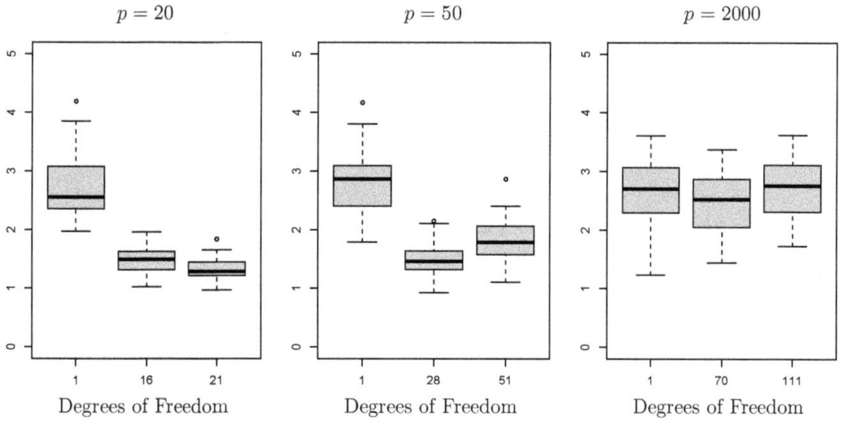

FIGURE 6.24. *The lasso was performed with $n = 100$ observations and three values of p, the number of features. Of the p features, 20 were associated with the response. The boxplots show the test MSEs that result using three different values of the tuning parameter λ in (6.7). For ease of interpretation, rather than reporting λ, the* degrees of freedom *are reported; for the lasso this turns out to be simply the number of estimated non-zero coefficients. When $p = 20$, the lowest test MSE was obtained with the smallest amount of regularization. When $p = 50$, the lowest test MSE was achieved when there is a substantial amount of regularization. When $p = 2{,}000$ the lasso performed poorly regardless of the amount of regularization, due to the fact that only 20 of the 2,000 features truly are associated with the outcome.*

In Section 6.1.3, we saw a number of approaches for adjusting the training set RSS or R^2 in order to account for the number of variables used to fit a least squares model. Unfortunately, the C_p, AIC, and BIC approaches are not appropriate in the high-dimensional setting, because estimating $\hat{\sigma}^2$ is problematic. (For instance, the formula for $\hat{\sigma}^2$ from Chapter 3 yields an estimate $\hat{\sigma}^2 = 0$ in this setting.) Similarly, problems arise in the application of adjusted R^2 in the high-dimensional setting, since one can easily obtain a model with an adjusted R^2 value of 1. Clearly, alternative approaches that are better-suited to the high-dimensional setting are required.

6.4.3 Regression in High Dimensions

It turns out that many of the methods seen in this chapter for fitting *less flexible* least squares models, such as forward stepwise selection, ridge regression, the lasso, and principal components regression, are particularly useful for performing regression in the high-dimensional setting. Essentially, these approaches avoid overfitting by using a less flexible fitting approach than least squares.

Figure 6.24 illustrates the performance of the lasso in a simple simulated example. There are $p = 20$, 50, or 2,000 features, of which 20 are truly associated with the outcome. The lasso was performed on $n = 100$ training observations, and the mean squared error was evaluated on an independent test set. As the number of features increases, the test set error increases. When $p = 20$, the lowest validation set error was achieved when λ in

(6.7) was small; however, when p was larger then the lowest validation set error was achieved using a larger value of λ. In each boxplot, rather than reporting the values of λ used, the *degrees of freedom* of the resulting lasso solution is displayed; this is simply the number of non-zero coefficient estimates in the lasso solution, and is a measure of the flexibility of the lasso fit. Figure 6.24 highlights three important points: (1) regularization or shrinkage plays a key role in high-dimensional problems, (2) appropriate tuning parameter selection is crucial for good predictive performance, and (3) the test error tends to increase as the dimensionality of the problem (i.e. the number of features or predictors) increases, unless the additional features are truly associated with the response.

The third point above is in fact a key principle in the analysis of high-dimensional data, which is known as the *curse of dimensionality*. One might think that as the number of features used to fit a model increases, the quality of the fitted model will increase as well. However, comparing the left-hand and right-hand panels in Figure 6.24, we see that this is not necessarily the case: in this example, the test set MSE almost doubles as p increases from 20 to 2,000. In general, *adding additional signal features that are truly associated with the response will improve the fitted model*, in the sense of leading to a reduction in test set error. However, adding noise features that are not truly associated with the response will lead to a deterioration in the fitted model, and consequently an increased test set error. This is because noise features increase the dimensionality of the problem, exacerbating the risk of overfitting (since noise features may be assigned nonzero coefficients due to chance associations with the response on the training set) without any potential upside in terms of improved test set error. Thus, we see that new technologies that allow for the collection of measurements for thousands or millions of features are a double-edged sword: they can lead to improved predictive models if these features are in fact relevant to the problem at hand, but will lead to worse results if the features are not relevant. Even if they are relevant, the variance incurred in fitting their coefficients may outweigh the reduction in bias that they bring.

curse of dimensionality

6.4.4 Interpreting Results in High Dimensions

When we perform the lasso, ridge regression, or other regression procedures in the high-dimensional setting, we must be quite cautious in the way that we report the results obtained. In Chapter 3, we learned about *multicollinearity*, the concept that the variables in a regression might be correlated with each other. In the high-dimensional setting, the multicollinearity problem is extreme: any variable in the model can be written as a linear combination of all of the other variables in the model. Essentially, this means that we can never know exactly which variables (if any) truly are predictive of the outcome, and we can never identify the *best* coefficients for use in the regression. At most, we can hope to assign large regression coefficients to variables that are correlated with the variables that truly are predictive of the outcome.

For instance, suppose that we are trying to predict blood pressure on the basis of half a million SNPs, and that forward stepwise selection indicates that 17 of those SNPs lead to a good predictive model on the training data. It would be incorrect to conclude that these 17 SNPs predict blood pressure more effectively than the other SNPs not included in the model. There are likely to be many sets of 17 SNPs that would predict blood pressure just as well as the selected model. If we were to obtain an independent data set and perform forward stepwise selection on that data set, we would likely obtain a model containing a different, and perhaps even non-overlapping, set of SNPs. This does not detract from the value of the model obtained—for instance, the model might turn out to be very effective in predicting blood pressure on an independent set of patients, and might be clinically useful for physicians. But we must be careful not to overstate the results obtained, and to make it clear that what we have identified is simply *one of many possible models* for predicting blood pressure, and that it must be further validated on independent data sets.

It is also important to be particularly careful in reporting errors and measures of model fit in the high-dimensional setting. We have seen that when $p > n$, it is easy to obtain a useless model that has zero residuals. Therefore, one should *never* use sum of squared errors, p-values, R^2 statistics, or other traditional measures of model fit on the training data as evidence of a good model fit in the high-dimensional setting. For instance, as we saw in Figure 6.23, one can easily obtain a model with $R^2 = 1$ when $p > n$. Reporting this fact might mislead others into thinking that a statistically valid and useful model has been obtained, whereas in fact this provides absolutely no evidence of a compelling model. It is important to instead report results on an independent test set, or cross-validation errors. For instance, the MSE or R^2 on an independent test set is a valid measure of model fit, but the MSE on the training set certainly is not.

6.5 Lab: Linear Models and Regularization Methods

In this lab we implement many of the techniques discussed in this chapter. We import some of our libraries at this top level.

In [1]:
```
import numpy as np
import pandas as pd
from matplotlib.pyplot import subplots
from statsmodels.api import OLS
import sklearn.model_selection as skm
import sklearn.linear_model as skl
from sklearn.preprocessing import StandardScaler
from ISLP import load_data
from ISLP.models import ModelSpec as MS
from functools import partial
```

We again collect the new imports needed for this lab.

In [2]:
```
from sklearn.pipeline import Pipeline
from sklearn.decomposition import PCA
```

```
from sklearn.cross_decomposition import PLSRegression
from ISLP.models import \
     (Stepwise,
      sklearn_selected,
      sklearn_selection_path)
!pip install l0bnb
from l0bnb import fit_path
```

We have installed the package `l0bnb` on the fly. Note the escaped `!pip install` — this is run as a separate system command.

6.5.1 Subset Selection Methods

Here we implement methods that reduce the number of parameters in a model by restricting the model to a subset of the input variables.

Forward Selection

We will apply the forward-selection approach to the `Hitters` data. We wish to predict a baseball player's `Salary` on the basis of various statistics associated with performance in the previous year.

First of all, we note that the `Salary` variable is missing for some of the players. The `np.isnan()` function can be used to identify the missing observations. It returns an array of the same shape as the input vector, with a `True` for any elements that are missing, and a `False` for non-missing elements. The `sum()` method can then be used to count all of the missing elements.

`np.isnan()`

`sum()`

In [3]:
```
Hitters = load_data('Hitters')
np.isnan(Hitters['Salary']).sum()
```

Out[3]: 59

We see that `Salary` is missing for 59 players. The `dropna()` method of data frames removes all of the rows that have missing values in any variable (by default — see `Hitters.dropna?`).

In [4]:
```
Hitters = Hitters.dropna();
Hitters.shape
```

Out[4]: (263, 20)

We first choose the best model using forward selection based on C_p (6.2). This score is not built in as a metric to `sklearn`. We therefore define a function to compute it ourselves, and use it as a scorer. By default, `sklearn` tries to maximize a score, hence our scoring function computes the negative C_p statistic.

In [5]:
```
def nCp(sigma2, estimator, X, Y):
    "Negative Cp statistic"
    n, p = X.shape
    Yhat = estimator.predict(X)
    RSS = np.sum((Y - Yhat)**2)
    return -(RSS + 2 * p * sigma2) / n
```

We need to estimate the residual variance σ^2, which is the first argument in our scoring function above. We will fit the biggest model, using all the variables, and estimate σ^2 based on its MSE.

In [6]:
```
design = MS(Hitters.columns.drop('Salary')).fit(Hitters)
Y = np.array(Hitters['Salary'])
X = design.transform(Hitters)
sigma2 = OLS(Y,X).fit().scale
```

The function `sklearn_selected()` expects a scorer with just three arguments — the last three in the definition of `nCp()` above. We use the function `partial()` first seen in Section 5.3.3 to freeze the first argument with our estimate of σ^2.

In [7]:
```
neg_Cp = partial(nCp, sigma2)
```

We can now use `neg_Cp()` as a scorer for model selection.

Along with a score we need to specify the search strategy. This is done through the object `Stepwise()` in the `ISLP.models` package. The method `Stepwise.first_peak()` runs forward stepwise until any further additions to the model do not result in an improvement in the evaluation score. Similarly, the method `Stepwise.fixed_steps()` runs a fixed number of steps of stepwise search.

In [8]:
```
strategy = Stepwise.first_peak(design,
                               direction='forward',
                               max_terms=len(design.terms))
```

We now fit a linear regression model with `Salary` as outcome using forward selection. To do so, we use the function `sklearn_selected()` from the `ISLP.models` package. This takes a model from `statsmodels` along with a search strategy and selects a model with its `fit` method. Without specifying a `scoring` argument, the score defaults to MSE, and so all 19 variables will be selected (output not shown).

`sklearn_selected()`

In [9]:
```
hitters_MSE = sklearn_selected(OLS,
                               strategy)
hitters_MSE.fit(Hitters, Y)
hitters_MSE.selected_state_
```

Using `neg_Cp` results in a smaller model, as expected, with just 10 variables selected.

In [10]:
```
hitters_Cp = sklearn_selected(OLS,
                              strategy,
                              scoring=neg_Cp)
hitters_Cp.fit(Hitters, Y)
hitters_Cp.selected_state_
```

Out[10]:
```
('Assists',
 'AtBat',
 'CAtBat',
 'CRBI',
 'CRuns',
 'CWalks',
 'Division',
```

```
'Hits',
'PutOuts',
'Walks')
```

Choosing Among Models Using the Validation Set Approach and Cross-Validation

As an alternative to using C_p, we might try cross-validation to select a model in forward selection. For this, we need a method that stores the full path of models found in forward selection, and allows predictions for each of these. This can be done with the `sklearn_selection_path()` estimator from `ISLP.models`. The function `cross_val_predict()` from `ISLP.models` computes the cross-validated predictions for each of the models along the path, which we can use to evaluate the cross-validated MSE along the path.

`sklearn_selection_path()`

`cross_val_predict()`

Here we define a strategy that fits the full forward selection path. While there are various parameter choices for `sklearn_selection_path()`, we use the defaults here, which selects the model at each step based on the biggest reduction in RSS.

In [11]:
```
strategy = Stepwise.fixed_steps(design,
                                len(design.terms),
                                direction='forward')
full_path = sklearn_selection_path(OLS, strategy)
```

We now fit the full forward-selection path on the `Hitters` data and compute the fitted values.

In [12]:
```
full_path.fit(Hitters, Y)
Yhat_in = full_path.predict(Hitters)
Yhat_in.shape
```

Out[12]:
```
(263, 20)
```

This gives us an array of fitted values — 20 steps in all, including the fitted mean for the null model — which we can use to evaluate in-sample MSE. As expected, the in-sample MSE improves each step we take, indicating we must use either the validation or cross-validation approach to select the number of steps. We fix the y-axis to range from 50,000 to 250,000 to compare to the cross-validation and validation set MSE below, as well as other methods such as ridge regression, lasso and principal components regression.

In [13]:
```
mse_fig, ax = subplots(figsize=(8,8))
insample_mse = ((Yhat_in - Y[:,None])**2).mean(0)
n_steps = insample_mse.shape[0]
ax.plot(np.arange(n_steps),
        insample_mse,
        'k', # color black
        label='In-sample')
ax.set_ylabel('MSE',
              fontsize=20)
ax.set_xlabel('# steps of forward stepwise',
              fontsize=20)
ax.set_xticks(np.arange(n_steps)[::2])
ax.legend()
```

```
ax.set_ylim([50000,250000]);
```

Notice the expression None in Y[:,None] above. This adds an axis (dimension) to the one-dimensional array Y, which allows it to be recycled when subtracted from the two-dimensional Yhat_in.

We are now ready to use cross-validation to estimate test error along the model path. We must use *only the training observations* to perform all aspects of model-fitting — including variable selection. Therefore, the determination of which model of a given size is best must be made using *only the training observations* in each training fold. This point is subtle but important. If the full data set is used to select the best subset at each step, then the validation set errors and cross-validation errors that we obtain will not be accurate estimates of the test error.

We now compute the cross-validated predicted values using 5-fold cross-validation.

In [14]:
```
K = 5
kfold = skm.KFold(K,
                  random_state=0,
                  shuffle=True)
Yhat_cv = skm.cross_val_predict(full_path,
                                Hitters,
                                Y,
                                cv=kfold)
Yhat_cv.shape
```

Out[14]: (263, 20)

skm.KFold()
skm.cross_
val_predict()

The prediction matrix Yhat_cv is the same shape as Yhat_in; the difference is that the predictions in each row, corresponding to a particular sample index, were made from models fit on a training fold that did not include that row.

At each model along the path, we compute the MSE in each of the cross-validation folds. These we will average to get the mean MSE, and can also use the individual values to compute a crude estimate of the standard error of the mean.[9] Hence we must know the test indices for each cross-validation split. This can be found by using the split() method of kfold. Because we fixed the random state above, whenever we split any array with the same number of rows as Y we recover the same training and test indices, though we simply ignore the training indices below.

In [15]:
```
cv_mse = []
for train_idx, test_idx in kfold.split(Y):
    errors = (Yhat_cv[test_idx] - Y[test_idx,None])**2
    cv_mse.append(errors.mean(0)) # column means
cv_mse = np.array(cv_mse).T
cv_mse.shape
```

Out[15]: (20, 5)

[9]The estimate is crude because the five error estimates are based on overlapping training sets, and hence are not independent.

We now add the cross-validation error estimates to our MSE plot. We include the mean error across the five folds, and the estimate of the standard error of the mean.

```
In [16]: ax.errorbar(np.arange(n_steps),
                     cv_mse.mean(1),
                     cv_mse.std(1) / np.sqrt(K),
                     label='Cross-validated',
                     c='r') # color red
         ax.set_ylim([50000,250000])
         ax.legend()
         mse_fig
```

To repeat the above using the validation set approach, we simply change our `cv` argument to a validation set: one random split of the data into a test and training. We choose a test size of 20%, similar to the size of each test set in 5-fold cross-validation.

`skm.ShuffleSplit()`

```
In [17]: validation = skm.ShuffleSplit(n_splits=1,
                                       test_size=0.2,
                                       random_state=0)
         for train_idx, test_idx in validation.split(Y):
             full_path.fit(Hitters.iloc[train_idx],
                           Y[train_idx])
             Yhat_val = full_path.predict(Hitters.iloc[test_idx])
             errors = (Yhat_val - Y[test_idx,None])**2
             validation_mse = errors.mean(0)
```

As for the in-sample MSE case, the validation set approach does not provide standard errors.

```
In [18]: ax.plot(np.arange(n_steps),
                 validation_mse,
                 'b--', # color blue, broken line
                 label='Validation')
         ax.set_xticks(np.arange(n_steps)[::2])
         ax.set_ylim([50000,250000])
         ax.legend()
         mse_fig
```

Best Subset Selection

Forward stepwise is a *greedy* selection procedure; at each step it augments the current set by including one additional variable. We now apply best subset selection to the `Hitters` data, which for every subset size, searches for the best set of predictors.

We will use a package called `l0bnb` to perform best subset selection. Instead of constraining the subset to be a given size, this package produces a path of solutions using the subset size as a penalty rather than a constraint. Although the distinction is subtle, the difference comes when we cross-validate.

```
In [19]: D = design.fit_transform(Hitters)
         D = D.drop('intercept', axis=1)
         X = np.asarray(D)
```

Here we excluded the first column corresponding to the intercept, as `l0bnb` will fit the intercept separately. We can find a path using the `fit_path()` function.

```
In [20]: path = fit_path(X,
                         Y,
                         max_nonzeros=X.shape[1])
```

The function `fit_path()` returns a list whose values include the fitted coefficients as `B`, an intercept as `B0`, as well as a few other attributes related to the particular path algorithm used. Such details are beyond the scope of this book.

```
In [21]: path[3]
```

```
Out[21]:{'B': array([0.        , 3.254844, 0.        , 0.        , 0.        ,
            0.        , 0.        , 0.        , 0.        , 0.        ,
            0.        , 0.677753 , 0.        , 0.        , 0.        ,
            0.        , 0.        , 0.        , 0.        ]),
         'B0': -38.98216739555494,
         'lambda_0': 0.011416248027450194,
         'M': 0.5829861733382011,
         'Time_exceeded': False}
```

In the example above, we see that at the fourth step in the path, we have two nonzero coefficients in `'B'`, corresponding to the value 0.114 for the penalty parameter `lambda_0`. We could make predictions using this sequence of fits on a validation set as a function of `lambda_0`, or with more work using cross-validation.

6.5.2 Ridge Regression and the Lasso

We will use the `sklearn.linear_model` package (for which we use `skl` as shorthand below) to fit ridge and lasso regularized linear models on the `Hitters` data. We start with the model matrix `X` (without an intercept) that we computed in the previous section on best subset regression.

Ridge Regression

We will use the function `skl.ElasticNet()` to fit both ridge and the lasso. To fit a *path* of ridge regressions models, we use `skl.ElasticNet.path()`, which can fit both ridge and lasso, as well as a hybrid mixture; ridge regression corresponds to `l1_ratio=0`. It is good practice to standardize the columns of `X` in these applications, if the variables are measured in different units. Since `skl.ElasticNet()` does no normalization, we have to take care of that ourselves. Since we standardize first, in order to find coefficient estimates on the original scale, we must *unstandardize* the coefficient estimates. The parameter λ in (6.5) and (6.7) is called `alphas` in `sklearn`. In order to be consistent with the rest of this chapter, we use `lambdas` rather than `alphas` in what follows. [10]

`skl.ElasticNet()`
`skl.ElasticNet.path()`

[10] At the time of publication, ridge fits like the one in code chunk [22] issue unwarranted convergence warning messages; we expect these to disappear as this package matures.

```
In [22]: Xs = X - X.mean(0)[None,:]
         X_scale = X.std(0)
         Xs = Xs / X_scale[None,:]
         lambdas = 10**np.linspace(8, -2, 100) / Y.std()
         soln_array = skl.ElasticNet.path(Xs,
                                          Y,
                                          l1_ratio=0.,
                                          alphas=lambdas)[1]
         soln_array.shape
```

```
Out[22]: (19, 100)
```

Here we extract the array of coefficients corresponding to the solutions along the regularization path. By default the `skl.ElasticNet.path` method fits a path along an automatically selected range of λ values, except for the case when `l1_ratio=0`, which results in ridge regression (as is the case here).[11] So here we have chosen to implement the function over a grid of values ranging from $\lambda = 10^8$ to $\lambda = 10^{-2}$ scaled by the standard deviation of y, essentially covering the full range of scenarios from the null model containing only the intercept, to the least squares fit.

Associated with each value of λ is a vector of ridge regression coefficients, that can be accessed by a column of `soln_array`. In this case, `soln_array` is a 19×100 matrix, with 19 rows (one for each predictor) and 100 columns (one for each value of λ).

We transpose this matrix and turn it into a data frame to facilitate viewing and plotting.

```
In [23]: soln_path = pd.DataFrame(soln_array.T,
                                  columns=D.columns,
                                  index=-np.log(lambdas))
         soln_path.index.name = 'negative log(lambda)'
         soln_path
```

```
Out[23]:                AtBat      Hits     HmRun      Runs  ...
           negative
         log(lambda)
          -12.310855  0.000800  0.000889  0.000695  0.000851  ...
          -12.078271  0.001010  0.001122  0.000878  0.001074  ...
          -11.845686  0.001274  0.001416  0.001107  0.001355  ...
          -11.613102  0.001608  0.001787  0.001397  0.001710  ...
          -11.380518  0.002029  0.002255  0.001763  0.002158  ...
                 ...       ...       ...       ...       ...  ...
         100 rows × 19 columns
```

We plot the paths to get a sense of how the coefficients vary with λ. To control the location of the legend we first set `legend` to `False` in the plot method, adding it afterward with the `legend()` method of `ax`.

```
In [24]: path_fig, ax = subplots(figsize=(8,8))
         soln_path.plot(ax=ax, legend=False)
         ax.set_xlabel('$-\log(\lambda)$', fontsize=20)
```

[11]The reason is rather technical; for all models except ridge, we can find the smallest value of λ for which all coefficients are zero. For ridge this value is ∞.

```
ax.set_ylabel('Standardized coefficients', fontsize=20)
ax.legend(loc='upper left');
```

(We have used `latex` formatting in the horizontal label, in order to format the Greek λ appropriately.) We expect the coefficient estimates to be much smaller, in terms of ℓ_2 norm, when a large value of λ is used, as compared to when a small value of λ is used. (Recall that the ℓ_2 norm is the square root of the sum of squared coefficient values.) We display the coefficients at the 40th step, where λ is 25.535.

```
In [25]: beta_hat = soln_path.loc[soln_path.index[39]]
         lambdas[39], beta_hat
```

```
Out[25]: (25.535,
          AtBat        5.433750
          Hits         6.223582
          HmRun        4.585498
          Runs         5.880855
          RBI          6.195921
          Walks        6.277975
          Years        5.299767
          ...          ...
```

Let's compute the ℓ_2 norm of the standardized coefficients.

```
In [26]: np.linalg.norm(beta_hat)
```

```
Out[26]: 24.17
```

In contrast, here is the ℓ_2 norm when λ is 2.44e-01. Note the much larger ℓ_2 norm of the coefficients associated with this smaller value of λ.

```
In [27]: beta_hat = soln_path.loc[soln_path.index[59]]
         lambdas[59], np.linalg.norm(beta_hat)
```

```
Out[27]: (0.2437, 160.4237)
```

Above we normalized `X` upfront, and fit the ridge model using `Xs`. The `Pipeline()` object in `sklearn` provides a clear way to separate feature normalization from the fitting of the ridge model itself.

```
In [28]: ridge = skl.ElasticNet(alpha=lambdas[59], l1_ratio=0)
         scaler = StandardScaler(with_mean=True,  with_std=True)
         pipe = Pipeline(steps=[('scaler', scaler), ('ridge', ridge)])
         pipe.fit(X, Y)
```

We show that it gives the same ℓ_2 norm as in our previous fit on the standardized data.

```
In [29]: np.linalg.norm(ridge.coef_)
```

```
Out[29]: 160.4237
```

Notice that the operation `pipe.fit(X, Y)` above has changed the `ridge` object, and in particular has added attributes such as `coef_` that were not there before.

Estimating Test Error of Ridge Regression

Choosing an *a priori* value of λ for ridge regression is difficult if not impossible. We will want to use the validation method or cross-validation to select the tuning parameter. The reader may not be surprised that the `Pipeline()` approach can be used in `skm.cross_validate()` with either a validation method (i.e. `validation`) or k-fold cross-validation.

We fix the random state of the splitter so that the results obtained will be reproducible.

In [30]:
```
validation = skm.ShuffleSplit(n_splits=1,
                              test_size=0.5,
                              random_state=0)
ridge.alpha = 0.01
results = skm.cross_validate(ridge,
                             X,
                             Y,
                             scoring='neg_mean_squared_error',
                             cv=validation)
-results['test_score']
```

Out[30]:
```
array([134214.0])
```

The test MSE is 1.342e+05. Note that if we had instead simply fit a model with just an intercept, we would have predicted each test observation using the mean of the training observations. We can get the same result by fitting a ridge regression model with a *very* large value of λ. Note that `1e10` means 10^{10}.

In [31]:
```
ridge.alpha = 1e10
results = skm.cross_validate(ridge,
                             X,
                             Y,
                             scoring='neg_mean_squared_error',
                             cv=validation)
-results['test_score']
```

Out[31]:
```
array([231788.32])
```

Obviously choosing $\lambda = 0.01$ is arbitrary, so we will use cross-validation or the validation-set approach to choose the tuning parameter λ. The object `GridSearchCV()` allows exhaustive grid search to choose such a parameter.

`Grid SearchCV()`

We first use the validation set method to choose λ.

In [32]:
```
param_grid = {'ridge__alpha': lambdas}
grid = skm.GridSearchCV(pipe,
                        param_grid,
                        cv=validation,
                        scoring='neg_mean_squared_error')
grid.fit(X, Y)
grid.best_params_['ridge__alpha']
grid.best_estimator_
```

Out[32]:
```
Pipeline(steps=[('scaler', StandardScaler()),
                ('ridge', ElasticNet(alpha=0.005899, l1_ratio=0))])
```

Alternatively, we can use 5-fold cross-validation.

In [33]:
```
grid = skm.GridSearchCV(pipe,
                        param_grid,
                        cv=kfold,
                        scoring='neg_mean_squared_error')
grid.fit(X, Y)
grid.best_params_['ridge__alpha']
grid.best_estimator_
```

Recall we set up the `kfold` object for 5-fold cross-validation on page 271. We now plot the cross-validated MSE as a function of $-\log(\lambda)$, which has shrinkage decreasing from left to right.

In [34]:
```
ridge_fig, ax = subplots(figsize=(8,8))
ax.errorbar(-np.log(lambdas),
            -grid.cv_results_['mean_test_score'],
            yerr=grid.cv_results_['std_test_score'] / np.sqrt(K))
ax.set_ylim([50000,250000])
ax.set_xlabel('$-\log(\lambda)$', fontsize=20)
ax.set_ylabel('Cross-validated MSE', fontsize=20);
```

One can cross-validate different metrics to choose a parameter. The default metric for `skl.ElasticNet()` is test R^2. Let's compare R^2 to MSE for cross-validation here.

In [35]:
```
grid_r2 = skm.GridSearchCV(pipe,
                           param_grid,
                           cv=kfold)
grid_r2.fit(X, Y)
```

Finally, let's plot the results for cross-validated R^2.

In [36]:
```
r2_fig, ax = subplots(figsize=(8,8))
ax.errorbar(-np.log(lambdas),
            grid_r2.cv_results_['mean_test_score'],
            yerr=grid_r2.cv_results_['std_test_score'] / np.sqrt(K)
            )
ax.set_xlabel('$-\log(\lambda)$', fontsize=20)
ax.set_ylabel('Cross-validated $R^2$', fontsize=20);
```

Fast Cross-Validation for Solution Paths

The ridge, lasso, and elastic net can be efficiently fit along a sequence of λ values, creating what is known as a *solution path* or *regularization path*. Hence there is specialized code to fit such paths, and to choose a suitable value of λ using cross-validation. Even with identical splits the results will not agree *exactly* with our `grid` above because the standardization of each feature in `grid` is carried out on each fold, while in `pipeCV` below it is carried out only once. Nevertheless, the results are similar as the normalization is relatively stable across folds.

In [37]:
```
ridgeCV = skl.ElasticNetCV(alphas=lambdas,
                           l1_ratio=0,
                           cv=kfold)
pipeCV = Pipeline(steps=[('scaler', scaler),
```

```
                    ('ridge', ridgeCV)])
pipeCV.fit(X, Y)
```

Let's produce a plot again of the cross-validation error to see that it is similar to using `skm.GridSearchCV`.

```
In [38]: tuned_ridge = pipeCV.named_steps['ridge']
         ridgeCV_fig, ax = subplots(figsize=(8,8))
         ax.errorbar(-np.log(lambdas),
                     tuned_ridge.mse_path_.mean(1),
                     yerr=tuned_ridge.mse_path_.std(1) / np.sqrt(K))
         ax.axvline(-np.log(tuned_ridge.alpha_), c='k', ls='--')
         ax.set_ylim([50000,250000])
         ax.set_xlabel('$-\log(\lambda)$', fontsize=20)
         ax.set_ylabel('Cross-validated MSE', fontsize=20);
```

We see that the value of λ that results in the smallest cross-validation error is 1.19e-02, available as the value `tuned_ridge.alpha_`. What is the test MSE associated with this value of λ?

```
In [39]: np.min(tuned_ridge.mse_path_.mean(1))
```

```
Out[39]: 115526.71
```

This represents a further improvement over the test MSE that we got using $\lambda = 4$. Finally, `tuned_ridge.coef_` has the coefficients fit on the entire data set at this value of λ.

```
In [40]: tuned_ridge.coef_
```

```
Out[40]: array([-222.80877051,  238.77246614,    3.21103754,   -2.93050845,
                   3.64888723,  108.90953869,  -50.81896152, -105.15731984,
                 122.00714801,   57.1859509 ,  210.35170348,  118.05683748,
                -150.21959435,   30.36634231,  -61.62459095,   77.73832472,
                  40.07350744,  -25.02151514,  -13.68429544])
```

As expected, none of the coefficients are zero—ridge regression does not perform variable selection!

Evaluating Test Error of Cross-Validated Ridge

Choosing λ using cross-validation provides a single regression estimator, similar to fitting a linear regression model as we saw in Chapter 3. It is therefore reasonable to estimate what its test error is. We run into a problem here in that cross-validation will have *touched* all of its data in choosing λ, hence we have no further data to estimate test error. A compromise is to do an initial split of the data into two disjoint sets: a training set and a test set. We then fit a cross-validation tuned ridge regression on the training set, and evaluate its performance on the test set. We might call this cross-validation nested within the validation set approach. A priori there is no reason to use half of the data for each of the two sets in validation. Below, we use 75% for training and 25% for test, with the estimator being ridge regression tuned using 5-fold cross-validation. This can be achieved in code as follows:

In [41]:
```
outer_valid = skm.ShuffleSplit(n_splits=1,
                               test_size=0.25,
                               random_state=1)
inner_cv = skm.KFold(n_splits=5,
                     shuffle=True,
                     random_state=2)
ridgeCV = skl.ElasticNetCV(alphas=lambdas,
                           l1_ratio=0,
                           cv=inner_cv)
pipeCV = Pipeline(steps=[('scaler', scaler),
                         ('ridge', ridgeCV)]);
```

In [42]:
```
results = skm.cross_validate(pipeCV,
                             X,
                             Y,
                             cv=outer_valid,
                             scoring='neg_mean_squared_error')
-results['test_score']
```

Out[42]:
```
array([132393.84])
```

The Lasso

We saw that ridge regression with a wise choice of λ can outperform least squares as well as the null model on the `Hitters` data set. We now ask whether the lasso can yield either a more accurate or a more interpretable model than ridge regression. In order to fit a lasso model, we once again use the `ElasticNetCV()` function; however, this time we use the argument `l1_ratio=1`. Other than that change, we proceed just as we did in fitting a ridge model.

In [43]:
```
lassoCV = skl.ElasticNetCV(n_alphas=100,
                           l1_ratio=1,
                           cv=kfold)
pipeCV = Pipeline(steps=[('scaler', scaler),
                         ('lasso', lassoCV)])
pipeCV.fit(X, Y)
tuned_lasso = pipeCV.named_steps['lasso']
tuned_lasso.alpha_
```

Out[43]:
```
3.147
```

In [44]:
```
lambdas, soln_array = skl.Lasso.path(Xs,
                                     Y,
                                     l1_ratio=1,
                                     n_alphas=100)[:2]
soln_path = pd.DataFrame(soln_array.T,
                         columns=D.columns,
                         index=-np.log(lambdas))
```

We can see from the coefficient plot of the standardized coefficients that depending on the choice of tuning parameter, some of the coefficients will be exactly equal to zero.

In [45]:
```
path_fig, ax = subplots(figsize=(8,8))
soln_path.plot(ax=ax, legend=False)
ax.legend(loc='upper left')
ax.set_xlabel('$-\log(\lambda)$', fontsize=20)
ax.set_ylabel('Standardized coefficiients', fontsize=20);
```

The smallest cross-validated error is lower than the test set MSE of the null model and of least squares, and very similar to the test MSE of 115526.71 of ridge regression (page 278) with λ chosen by cross-validation.

In [46]:
```
np.min(tuned_lasso.mse_path_.mean(1))
```

Out[46]:
```
114690.73
```

Let's again produce a plot of the cross-validation error.

In [47]:
```
lassoCV_fig, ax = subplots(figsize=(8,8))
ax.errorbar(-np.log(tuned_lasso.alphas_),
            tuned_lasso.mse_path_.mean(1),
            yerr=tuned_lasso.mse_path_.std(1) / np.sqrt(K))
ax.axvline(-np.log(tuned_lasso.alpha_), c='k', ls='--')
ax.set_ylim([50000,250000])
ax.set_xlabel('$-\log(\lambda)$', fontsize=20)
ax.set_ylabel('Cross-validated MSE', fontsize=20);
```

However, the lasso has a substantial advantage over ridge regression in that the resulting coefficient estimates are sparse. Here we see that 6 of the 19 coefficient estimates are exactly zero. So the lasso model with λ chosen by cross-validation contains only 13 variables.

In [48]:
```
tuned_lasso.coef_
```

Out[48]:
```
array([-210.01008773,  243.4550306 ,    0.        ,    0.        ,
          0.        ,   97.69397357,  -41.52283116,   -0.        ,
          0.        ,   39.62298193,  205.75273856,  124.55456561,
       -126.29986768,   15.70262427,  -59.50157967,   75.24590036,
         21.62698014,  -12.04423675,   -0.        ])
```

As in ridge regression, we could evaluate the test error of cross-validated lasso by first splitting into test and training sets and internally running cross-validation on the training set. We leave this as an exercise.

6.5.3 PCR and PLS Regression

Principal Components Regression

Principal components regression (PCR) can be performed using `PCA()` from the `sklearn.decomposition` module. We now apply PCR to the `Hitters` data, in order to predict `Salary`. Again, ensure that the missing values have been removed from the data, as described in Section 6.5.1. `PCA()`

We use `LinearRegression()` to fit the regression model here. Note that it fits an intercept by default, unlike the `OLS()` function seen earlier in Section 6.5.1. `Linear Regression()`

```
In [49]: pca = PCA(n_components=2)
         linreg = skl.LinearRegression()
         pipe = Pipeline([('pca', pca),
                          ('linreg', linreg)])
         pipe.fit(X, Y)
         pipe.named_steps['linreg'].coef_
```

```
Out[49]: array([0.09846131, 0.4758765 ])
```

When performing PCA, the results vary depending on whether the data has been *standardized* or not. As in the earlier examples, this can be accomplished by including an additional step in the pipeline.

```
In [50]: pipe = Pipeline([('scaler', scaler),
                          ('pca', pca),
                          ('linreg', linreg)])
         pipe.fit(X, Y)
         pipe.named_steps['linreg'].coef_
```

```
Out[50]: array([106.36859204, -21.60350456])
```

We can of course use CV to choose the number of components, by using `skm.GridSearchCV`, in this case fixing the parameters to vary the `n_components`.

```
In [51]: param_grid = {'pca__n_components': range(1, 20)}
         grid = skm.GridSearchCV(pipe,
                                 param_grid,
                                 cv=kfold,
                                 scoring='neg_mean_squared_error')
         grid.fit(X, Y)
```

Let's plot the results as we have for other methods.

```
In [52]: pcr_fig, ax = subplots(figsize=(8,8))
         n_comp = param_grid['pca__n_components']
         ax.errorbar(n_comp,
                     -grid.cv_results_['mean_test_score'],
                     grid.cv_results_['std_test_score'] / np.sqrt(K))
         ax.set_ylabel('Cross-validated MSE', fontsize=20)
         ax.set_xlabel('# principal components', fontsize=20)
         ax.set_xticks(n_comp[::2])
         ax.set_ylim([50000,250000]);
```

We see that the smallest cross-validation error occurs when 17 components are used. However, from the plot we also see that the cross-validation error is roughly the same when only one component is included in the model. This suggests that a model that uses just a small number of components might suffice.

The CV score is provided for each possible number of components from 1 to 19 inclusive. The `PCA()` method complains if we try to fit an intercept only with `n_components=0` so we also compute the MSE for just the null model with these splits.

```
In [53]: Xn = np.zeros((X.shape[0], 1))
         cv_null = skm.cross_validate(linreg,
```

```
                         Xn,
                         Y,
                         cv=kfold,
                         scoring='neg_mean_squared_error')
-cv_null['test_score'].mean()
```

```
Out[53]: 204139.31
```

The explained_variance_ratio_ attribute of our PCA object provides the *percentage of variance explained* in the predictors and in the response using different numbers of components. This concept is discussed in greater detail in Section 12.2.

```
In [54]: pipe.named_steps['pca'].explained_variance_ratio_
```

```
Out[54]: array([0.3831424 , 0.21841076])
```

Briefly, we can think of this as the amount of information about the predictors that is captured using M principal components. For example, setting $M = 1$ only captures 38.31% of the variance, while $M = 2$ captures an additional 21.84%, for a total of 60.15% of the variance. By $M = 6$ it increases to 88.63%. Beyond this the increments continue to diminish, until we use all $M = p = 19$ components, which captures all 100% of the variance.

Partial Least Squares

Partial least squares (PLS) is implemented in the PLSRegression() function. PLS Regression()

```
In [55]: pls = PLSRegression(n_components=2,
                             scale=True)
         pls.fit(X, Y)
```

As was the case in PCR, we will want to use CV to choose the number of components.

```
In [56]: param_grid = {'n_components':range(1, 20)}
         grid = skm.GridSearchCV(pls,
                                 param_grid,
                                 cv=kfold,
                                 scoring='neg_mean_squared_error')
         grid.fit(X, Y)
```

As for our other methods, we plot the MSE.

```
In [57]: pls_fig, ax = subplots(figsize=(8,8))
         n_comp = param_grid['n_components']
         ax.errorbar(n_comp,
                     -grid.cv_results_['mean_test_score'],
                     grid.cv_results_['std_test_score'] / np.sqrt(K))
         ax.set_ylabel('Cross-validated MSE', fontsize=20)
         ax.set_xlabel('# principal components', fontsize=20)
         ax.set_xticks(n_comp[::2])
         ax.set_ylim([50000,250000]);
```

CV error is minimized at 12, though there is little noticable difference between this point and a much lower number like 2 or 3 components.

6.6 Exercises

Conceptual

1. We perform best subset, forward stepwise, and backward stepwise selection on a single data set. For each approach, we obtain $p + 1$ models, containing $0, 1, 2, \ldots, p$ predictors. Explain your answers:

   (a) Which of the three models with k predictors has the smallest *training* RSS?

   (b) Which of the three models with k predictors has the smallest *test* RSS?

   (c) True or False:

      i. The predictors in the k-variable model identified by forward stepwise are a subset of the predictors in the $(k+1)$-variable model identified by forward stepwise selection.

      ii. The predictors in the k-variable model identified by backward stepwise are a subset of the predictors in the $(k + 1)$-variable model identified by backward stepwise selection.

      iii. The predictors in the k-variable model identified by backward stepwise are a subset of the predictors in the $(k + 1)$-variable model identified by forward stepwise selection.

      iv. The predictors in the k-variable model identified by forward stepwise are a subset of the predictors in the $(k+1)$-variable model identified by backward stepwise selection.

      v. The predictors in the k-variable model identified by best subset are a subset of the predictors in the $(k + 1)$-variable model identified by best subset selection.

2. For parts (a) through (c), indicate which of i. through iv. is correct. Justify your answer.

   (a) The lasso, relative to least squares, is:

      i. More flexible and hence will give improved prediction accuracy when its increase in bias is less than its decrease in variance.

      ii. More flexible and hence will give improved prediction accuracy when its increase in variance is less than its decrease in bias.

      iii. Less flexible and hence will give improved prediction accuracy when its increase in bias is less than its decrease in variance.

      iv. Less flexible and hence will give improved prediction accuracy when its increase in variance is less than its decrease in bias.

   (b) Repeat (a) for ridge regression relative to least squares.

   (c) Repeat (a) for non-linear methods relative to least squares.

3. Suppose we estimate the regression coefficients in a linear regression model by minimizing

$$\sum_{i=1}^{n}\left(y_i - \beta_0 - \sum_{j=1}^{p}\beta_j x_{ij}\right)^2 \quad \text{subject to} \quad \sum_{j=1}^{p}|\beta_j| \leq s$$

for a particular value of s. For parts (a) through (e), indicate which of i. through v. is correct. Justify your answer.

   (a) As we increase s from 0, the training RSS will:
      i. Increase initially, and then eventually start decreasing in an inverted U shape.
      ii. Decrease initially, and then eventually start increasing in a U shape.
      iii. Steadily increase.
      iv. Steadily decrease.
      v. Remain constant.
   (b) Repeat (a) for test RSS.
   (c) Repeat (a) for variance.
   (d) Repeat (a) for (squared) bias.
   (e) Repeat (a) for the irreducible error.

4. Suppose we estimate the regression coefficients in a linear regression model by minimizing

$$\sum_{i=1}^{n}\left(y_i - \beta_0 - \sum_{j=1}^{p}\beta_j x_{ij}\right)^2 + \lambda\sum_{j=1}^{p}\beta_j^2$$

for a particular value of λ. For parts (a) through (e), indicate which of i. through v. is correct. Justify your answer.

   (a) As we increase λ from 0, the training RSS will:
      i. Increase initially, and then eventually start decreasing in an inverted U shape.
      ii. Decrease initially, and then eventually start increasing in a U shape.
      iii. Steadily increase.
      iv. Steadily decrease.
      v. Remain constant.
   (b) Repeat (a) for test RSS.
   (c) Repeat (a) for variance.
   (d) Repeat (a) for (squared) bias.
   (e) Repeat (a) for the irreducible error.

5. It is well-known that ridge regression tends to give similar coefficient values to correlated variables, whereas the lasso may give quite different coefficient values to correlated variables. We will now explore this property in a very simple setting.

   Suppose that $n = 2$, $p = 2$, $x_{11} = x_{12}$, $x_{21} = x_{22}$. Furthermore, suppose that $y_1 + y_2 = 0$ and $x_{11} + x_{21} = 0$ and $x_{12} + x_{22} = 0$, so that the estimate for the intercept in a least squares, ridge regression, or lasso model is zero: $\hat{\beta}_0 = 0$.

   (a) Write out the ridge regression optimization problem in this setting.

   (b) Argue that in this setting, the ridge coefficient estimates satisfy $\hat{\beta}_1 = \hat{\beta}_2$.

   (c) Write out the lasso optimization problem in this setting.

   (d) Argue that in this setting, the lasso coefficients $\hat{\beta}_1$ and $\hat{\beta}_2$ are not unique—in other words, there are many possible solutions to the optimization problem in (c). Describe these solutions.

6. We will now explore (6.12) and (6.13) further.

   (a) Consider (6.12) with $p = 1$. For some choice of y_1 and $\lambda > 0$, plot (6.12) as a function of β_1. Your plot should confirm that (6.12) is solved by (6.14).

   (b) Consider (6.13) with $p = 1$. For some choice of y_1 and $\lambda > 0$, plot (6.13) as a function of β_1. Your plot should confirm that (6.13) is solved by (6.15).

7. We will now derive the Bayesian connection to the lasso and ridge regression discussed in Section 6.2.2.

   (a) Suppose that $y_i = \beta_0 + \sum_{j=1}^{p} x_{ij}\beta_j + \epsilon_i$ where $\epsilon_1, \ldots, \epsilon_n$ are independent and identically distributed from a $N(0, \sigma^2)$ distribution. Write out the likelihood for the data.

   (b) Assume the following prior for β: $\beta_1, \ldots, \beta_p$ are independent and identically distributed according to a double-exponential distribution with mean 0 and common scale parameter b: i.e. $p(\beta) = \frac{1}{2b}\exp(-|\beta|/b)$. Write out the posterior for β in this setting.

   (c) Argue that the lasso estimate is the *mode* for β under this posterior distribution.

   (d) Now assume the following prior for β: $\beta_1, \ldots, \beta_p$ are independent and identically distributed according to a normal distribution with mean zero and variance c. Write out the posterior for β in this setting.

   (e) Argue that the ridge regression estimate is both the *mode* and the *mean* for β under this posterior distribution.

Applied

8. In this exercise, we will generate simulated data, and will then use this data to perform forward and backward stepwise selection.

   (a) Create a random number generator and use its `normal()` method to generate a predictor X of length $n = 100$, as well as a noise vector ϵ of length $n = 100$.

   (b) Generate a response vector Y of length $n = 100$ according to the model

   $$Y = \beta_0 + \beta_1 X + \beta_2 X^2 + \beta_3 X^3 + \epsilon,$$

   where β_0, β_1, β_2, and β_3 are constants of your choice.

   (c) Use forward stepwise selection in order to select a model containing the predictors $X, X^2, \ldots, X^{10}$. What is the model obtained according to C_p? Report the coefficients of the model obtained.

   (d) Repeat (c), using backwards stepwise selection. How does your answer compare to the results in (c)?

   (e) Now fit a lasso model to the simulated data, again using $X, X^2, \ldots, X^{10}$ as predictors. Use cross-validation to select the optimal value of λ. Create plots of the cross-validation error as a function of λ. Report the resulting coefficient estimates, and discuss the results obtained.

   (f) Now generate a response vector Y according to the model

   $$Y = \beta_0 + \beta_7 X^7 + \epsilon,$$

   and perform forward stepwise selection and the lasso. Discuss the results obtained.

9. In this exercise, we will predict the number of applications received using the other variables in the `College` data set.

   (a) Split the data set into a training set and a test set.

   (b) Fit a linear model using least squares on the training set, and report the test error obtained.

   (c) Fit a ridge regression model on the training set, with λ chosen by cross-validation. Report the test error obtained.

   (d) Fit a lasso model on the training set, with λ chosen by cross-validation. Report the test error obtained, along with the number of non-zero coefficient estimates.

   (e) Fit a PCR model on the training set, with M chosen by cross-validation. Report the test error obtained, along with the value of M selected by cross-validation.

   (f) Fit a PLS model on the training set, with M chosen by cross-validation. Report the test error obtained, along with the value of M selected by cross-validation.

(g) Comment on the results obtained. How accurately can we predict the number of college applications received? Is there much difference among the test errors resulting from these five approaches?

10. We have seen that as the number of features used in a model increases, the training error will necessarily decrease, but the test error may not. We will now explore this in a simulated data set.

    (a) Generate a data set with $p = 20$ features, $n = 1{,}000$ observations, and an associated quantitative response vector generated according to the model

    $$Y = X\beta + \epsilon,$$

    where β has some elements that are exactly equal to zero.

    (b) Split your data set into a training set containing 100 observations and a test set containing 900 observations.

    (c) Perform best subset selection on the training set, and plot the training set MSE associated with the best model of each size.

    (d) Plot the test set MSE associated with the best model of each size.

    (e) For which model size does the test set MSE take on its minimum value? Comment on your results. If it takes on its minimum value for a model containing only an intercept or a model containing all of the features, then play around with the way that you are generating the data in (a) until you come up with a scenario in which the test set MSE is minimized for an intermediate model size.

    (f) How does the model at which the test set MSE is minimized compare to the true model used to generate the data? Comment on the coefficient values.

    (g) Create a plot displaying $\sqrt{\sum_{j=1}^{p}(\beta_j - \hat{\beta}_j^r)^2}$ for a range of values of r, where $\hat{\beta}_j^r$ is the jth coefficient estimate for the best model containing r coefficients. Comment on what you observe. How does this compare to the test MSE plot from (d)?

11. We will now try to predict per capita crime rate in the `Boston` data set.

    (a) Try out some of the regression methods explored in this chapter, such as best subset selection, the lasso, ridge regression, and PCR. Present and discuss results for the approaches that you consider.

    (b) Propose a model (or set of models) that seem to perform well on this data set, and justify your answer. Make sure that you are evaluating model performance using validation set error, cross-validation, or some other reasonable alternative, as opposed to using training error.

(c) Does your chosen model involve all of the features in the data set? Why or why not?

7
Moving Beyond Linearity

So far in this book, we have mostly focused on linear models. Linear models are relatively simple to describe and implement, and have advantages over other approaches in terms of interpretation and inference. However, standard linear regression can have significant limitations in terms of predictive power. This is because the linearity assumption is almost always an approximation, and sometimes a poor one. In Chapter 6 we see that we can improve upon least squares using ridge regression, the lasso, principal components regression, and other techniques. In that setting, the improvement is obtained by reducing the complexity of the linear model, and hence the variance of the estimates. But we are still using a linear model, which can only be improved so far! In this chapter we relax the linearity assumption while still attempting to maintain as much interpretability as possible. We do this by examining very simple extensions of linear models like polynomial regression and step functions, as well as more sophisticated approaches such as splines, local regression, and generalized additive models.

- *Polynomial regression* extends the linear model by adding extra predictors, obtained by raising each of the original predictors to a power. For example, a *cubic* regression uses three variables, X, X^2, and X^3, as predictors. This approach provides a simple way to provide a nonlinear fit to data.

- *Step functions* cut the range of a variable into K distinct regions in order to produce a qualitative variable. This has the effect of fitting a piecewise constant function.

- *Regression splines* are more flexible than polynomials and step functions, and in fact are an extension of the two. They involve dividing the range of X into K distinct regions. Within each region, a polynomial function is fit to the data. However, these polynomials are

G. James et al., *An Introduction to Statistical Learning*, Springer Texts in Statistics,
https://doi.org/10.1007/978-3-031-38747-0_7

constrained so that they join smoothly at the region boundaries, or *knots*. Provided that the interval is divided into enough regions, this can produce an extremely flexible fit.

- *Smoothing splines* are similar to regression splines, but arise in a slightly different situation. Smoothing splines result from minimizing a residual sum of squares criterion subject to a smoothness penalty.
- *Local regression* is similar to splines, but differs in an important way. The regions are allowed to overlap, and indeed they do so in a very smooth way.
- *Generalized additive models* allow us to extend the methods above to deal with multiple predictors.

In Sections 7.1–7.6, we present a number of approaches for modeling the relationship between a response Y and a single predictor X in a flexible way. In Section 7.7, we show that these approaches can be seamlessly integrated in order to model a response Y as a function of several predictors $X_1, \ldots, X_p$.

7.1 Polynomial Regression

Historically, the standard way to extend linear regression to settings in which the relationship between the predictors and the response is non-linear has been to replace the standard linear model

$$y_i = \beta_0 + \beta_1 x_i + \epsilon_i$$

with a polynomial function

$$y_i = \beta_0 + \beta_1 x_i + \beta_2 x_i^2 + \beta_3 x_i^3 + \cdots + \beta_d x_i^d + \epsilon_i, \tag{7.1}$$

where ϵ_i is the error term. This approach is known as *polynomial regression*, and in fact we saw an example of this method in Section 3.3.2. For large enough degree d, a polynomial regression allows us to produce an extremely non-linear curve. Notice that the coefficients in (7.1) can be easily estimated using least squares linear regression because this is just a standard linear model with predictors $x_i, x_i^2, x_i^3, \ldots, x_i^d$. Generally speaking, it is unusual to use d greater than 3 or 4 because for large values of d, the polynomial curve can become overly flexible and can take on some very strange shapes. This is especially true near the boundary of the X variable.

polynomial regression

The left-hand panel in Figure 7.1 is a plot of `wage` against `age` for the `Wage` data set, which contains income and demographic information for males who reside in the central Atlantic region of the United States. We see the results of fitting a degree-4 polynomial using least squares (solid blue curve). Even though this is a linear regression model like any other, the individual coefficients are not of particular interest. Instead, we look at the entire fitted function across a grid of 63 values for `age` from 18 to 80 in order to understand the relationship between `age` and `wage`.

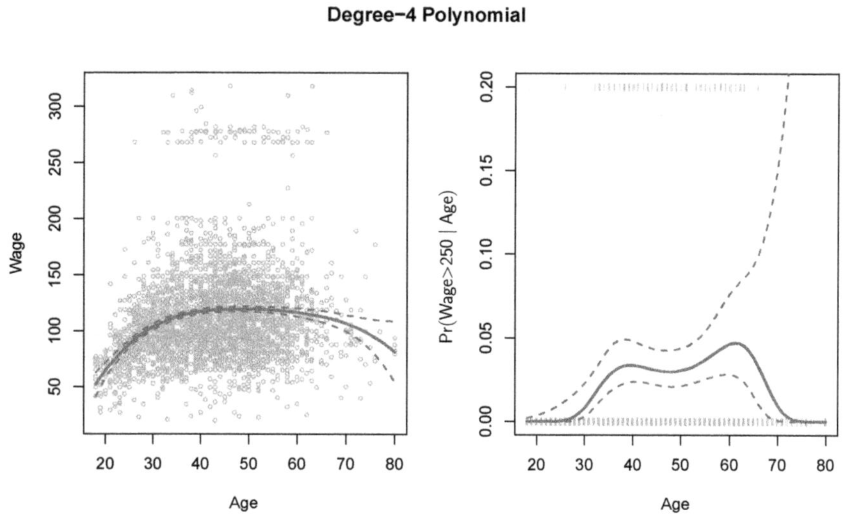

FIGURE 7.1. *The* Wage *data.* Left: *The solid blue curve is a degree-4 polynomial of* wage *(in thousands of dollars) as a function of* age, *fit by least squares. The dashed curves indicate an estimated 95 % confidence interval.* Right: *We model the binary event* wage>250 *using logistic regression, again with a degree-4 polynomial. The fitted posterior probability of* wage *exceeding* \$250,000 *is shown in blue, along with an estimated 95 % confidence interval.*

In Figure 7.1, a pair of dashed curves accompanies the fit; these are $(2\times)$ standard error curves. Let's see how these arise. Suppose we have computed the fit at a particular value of age, x_0:

$$\hat{f}(x_0) = \hat{\beta}_0 + \hat{\beta}_1 x_0 + \hat{\beta}_2 x_0^2 + \hat{\beta}_3 x_0^3 + \hat{\beta}_4 x_0^4. \tag{7.2}$$

What is the variance of the fit, i.e. $\text{Var}\hat{f}(x_0)$? Least squares returns variance estimates for each of the fitted coefficients $\hat{\beta}_j$, as well as the covariances between pairs of coefficient estimates. We can use these to compute the estimated variance of $\hat{f}(x_0)$.[1] The estimated *pointwise* standard error of $\hat{f}(x_0)$ is the square-root of this variance. This computation is repeated at each reference point x_0, and we plot the fitted curve, as well as twice the standard error on either side of the fitted curve. We plot twice the standard error because, for normally distributed error terms, this quantity corresponds to an approximate 95 % confidence interval.

It seems like the wages in Figure 7.1 are from two distinct populations: there appears to be a *high earners* group earning more than \$250,000 per annum, as well as a *low earners* group. We can treat wage as a binary variable by splitting it into these two groups. Logistic regression can then be used to predict this binary response, using polynomial functions of age

[1]If $\hat{\mathbf{C}}$ is the 5×5 covariance matrix of the $\hat{\beta}_j$, and if $\ell_0^T = (1, x_0, x_0^2, x_0^3, x_0^4)$, then $\text{Var}[\hat{f}(x_0)] = \ell_0^T \hat{\mathbf{C}} \ell_0$.

as predictors. In other words, we fit the model

$$\Pr(y_i > 250|x_i) = \frac{\exp(\beta_0 + \beta_1 x_i + \beta_2 x_i^2 + \cdots + \beta_d x_i^d)}{1 + \exp(\beta_0 + \beta_1 x_i + \beta_2 x_i^2 + \cdots + \beta_d x_i^d)}. \tag{7.3}$$

The result is shown in the right-hand panel of Figure 7.1. The gray marks on the top and bottom of the panel indicate the ages of the high earners and the low earners. The solid blue curve indicates the fitted probabilities of being a high earner, as a function of age. The estimated 95 % confidence interval is shown as well. We see that here the confidence intervals are fairly wide, especially on the right-hand side. Although the sample size for this data set is substantial ($n = 3{,}000$), there are only 79 high earners, which results in a high variance in the estimated coefficients and consequently wide confidence intervals.

7.2 Step Functions

Using polynomial functions of the features as predictors in a linear model imposes a *global* structure on the non-linear function of X. We can instead use *step functions* in order to avoid imposing such a global structure. Here we break the range of X into *bins*, and fit a different constant in each bin. This amounts to converting a continuous variable into an *ordered categorical variable.*

step function

ordered categorical variable

In greater detail, we create cutpoints $c_1, c_2, \ldots, c_K$ in the range of X, and then construct $K + 1$ new variables

$$\begin{aligned}
C_0(X) &= I(X < c_1),\\
C_1(X) &= I(c_1 \leq X < c_2),\\
C_2(X) &= I(c_2 \leq X < c_3),\\
&\vdots\\
C_{K-1}(X) &= I(c_{K-1} \leq X < c_K),\\
C_K(X) &= I(c_K \leq X),
\end{aligned} \tag{7.4}$$

where $I(\cdot)$ is an *indicator function* that returns a 1 if the condition is true, and returns a 0 otherwise. For example, $I(c_K \leq X)$ equals 1 if $c_K \leq X$, and equals 0 otherwise. These are sometimes called *dummy* variables. Notice that for any value of X, $C_0(X) + C_1(X) + \cdots + C_K(X) = 1$, since X must be in exactly one of the $K + 1$ intervals. We then use least squares to fit a linear model using $C_1(X), C_2(X), \ldots, C_K(X)$ as predictors[2]:

indicator function

$$y_i = \beta_0 + \beta_1 C_1(x_i) + \beta_2 C_2(x_i) + \cdots + \beta_K C_K(x_i) + \epsilon_i. \tag{7.5}$$

For a given value of X, at most one of $C_1, C_2, \ldots, C_K$ can be non-zero. Note that when $X < c_1$, all of the predictors in (7.5) are zero, so β_0 can

[2]We exclude $C_0(X)$ as a predictor in (7.5) because it is redundant with the intercept. This is similar to the fact that we need only two dummy variables to code a qualitative variable with three levels, provided that the model will contain an intercept. The decision to exclude $C_0(X)$ instead of some other $C_k(X)$ in (7.5) is arbitrary. Alternatively, we could include $C_0(X), C_1(X), \ldots, C_K(X)$, and exclude the intercept.

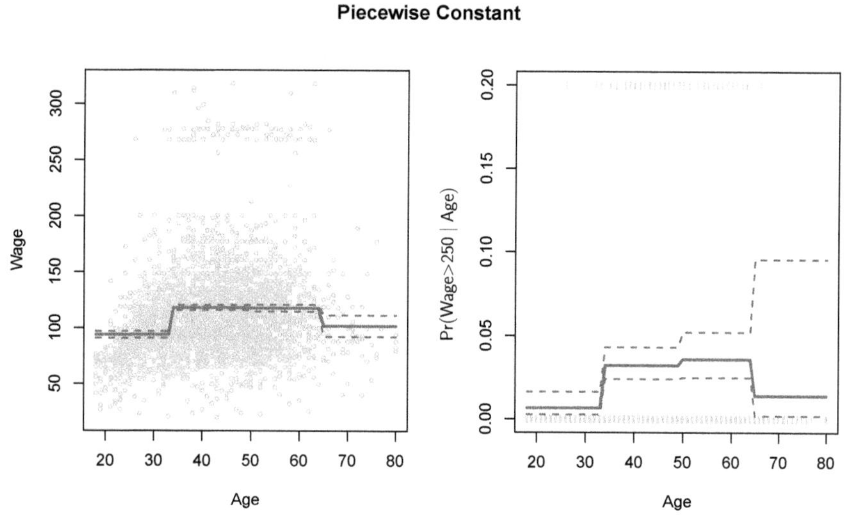

FIGURE 7.2. *The* Wage *data.* Left: *The solid curve displays the fitted value from a least squares regression of* wage *(in thousands of dollars) using step functions of* age. *The dashed curves indicate an estimated 95 % confidence interval.* Right: *We model the binary event* wage>250 *using logistic regression, again using step functions of* age. *The fitted posterior probability of* wage *exceeding* \$250,000 *is shown, along with an estimated 95 % confidence interval.*

be interpreted as the mean value of Y for $X < c_1$. By comparison, (7.5) predicts a response of $\beta_0+\beta_j$ for $c_j \leq X < c_{j+1}$, so β_j represents the average increase in the response for X in $c_j \leq X < c_{j+1}$ relative to $X < c_1$.

An example of fitting step functions to the Wage data from Figure 7.1 is shown in the left-hand panel of Figure 7.2. We also fit the logistic regression model

$$\Pr(y_i > 250|x_i) = \frac{\exp(\beta_0 + \beta_1 C_1(x_i) + \cdots + \beta_K C_K(x_i))}{1 + \exp(\beta_0 + \beta_1 C_1(x_i) + \cdots + \beta_K C_K(x_i))} \tag{7.6}$$

in order to predict the probability that an individual is a high earner on the basis of age. The right-hand panel of Figure 7.2 displays the fitted posterior probabilities obtained using this approach.

Unfortunately, unless there are natural breakpoints in the predictors, piecewise-constant functions can miss the action. For example, in the left-hand panel of Figure 7.2, the first bin clearly misses the increasing trend of wage with age. Nevertheless, step function approaches are very popular in biostatistics and epidemiology, among other disciplines. For example, 5-year age groups are often used to define the bins.

7.3 Basis Functions

Polynomial and piecewise-constant regression models are in fact special cases of a *basis function* approach. The idea is to have at hand a fam-

basis function

ily of functions or transformations that can be applied to a variable X: $b_1(X), b_2(X), \ldots, b_K(X)$. Instead of fitting a linear model in X, we fit the model

$$y_i = \beta_0 + \beta_1 b_1(x_i) + \beta_2 b_2(x_i) + \beta_3 b_3(x_i) + \cdots + \beta_K b_K(x_i) + \epsilon_i. \quad (7.7)$$

Note that the basis functions $b_1(\cdot), b_2(\cdot), \ldots, b_K(\cdot)$ are fixed and known. (In other words, we choose the functions ahead of time.) For polynomial regression, the basis functions are $b_j(x_i) = x_i^j$, and for piecewise constant functions they are $b_j(x_i) = I(c_j \leq x_i < c_{j+1})$. We can think of (7.7) as a standard linear model with predictors $b_1(x_i), b_2(x_i), \ldots, b_K(x_i)$. Hence, we can use least squares to estimate the unknown regression coefficients in (7.7). Importantly, this means that all of the inference tools for linear models that are discussed in Chapter 3, such as standard errors for the coefficient estimates and F-statistics for the model's overall significance, are available in this setting.

Thus far we have considered the use of polynomial functions and piecewise constant functions for our basis functions; however, many alternatives are possible. For instance, we can use wavelets or Fourier series to construct basis functions. In the next section, we investigate a very common choice for a basis function: *regression splines*.

regression spline

7.4 Regression Splines

Now we discuss a flexible class of basis functions that extends upon the polynomial regression and piecewise constant regression approaches that we have just seen.

7.4.1 Piecewise Polynomials

Instead of fitting a high-degree polynomial over the entire range of X, *piecewise polynomial regression* involves fitting separate low-degree polynomials over different regions of X. For example, a piecewise cubic polynomial works by fitting a cubic regression model of the form

piecewise polynomial regression

$$y_i = \beta_0 + \beta_1 x_i + \beta_2 x_i^2 + \beta_3 x_i^3 + \epsilon_i, \quad (7.8)$$

where the coefficients β_0, β_1, β_2, and β_3 differ in different parts of the range of X. The points where the coefficients change are called *knots*.

knot

For example, a piecewise cubic with no knots is just a standard cubic polynomial, as in (7.1) with $d = 3$. A piecewise cubic polynomial with a single knot at a point c takes the form

$$y_i = \begin{cases} \beta_{01} + \beta_{11} x_i + \beta_{21} x_i^2 + \beta_{31} x_i^3 + \epsilon_i & \text{if } x_i < c \\ \beta_{02} + \beta_{12} x_i + \beta_{22} x_i^2 + \beta_{32} x_i^3 + \epsilon_i & \text{if } x_i \geq c. \end{cases}$$

In other words, we fit two different polynomial functions to the data, one on the subset of the observations with $x_i < c$, and one on the subset of the observations with $x_i \geq c$. The first polynomial function has coefficients

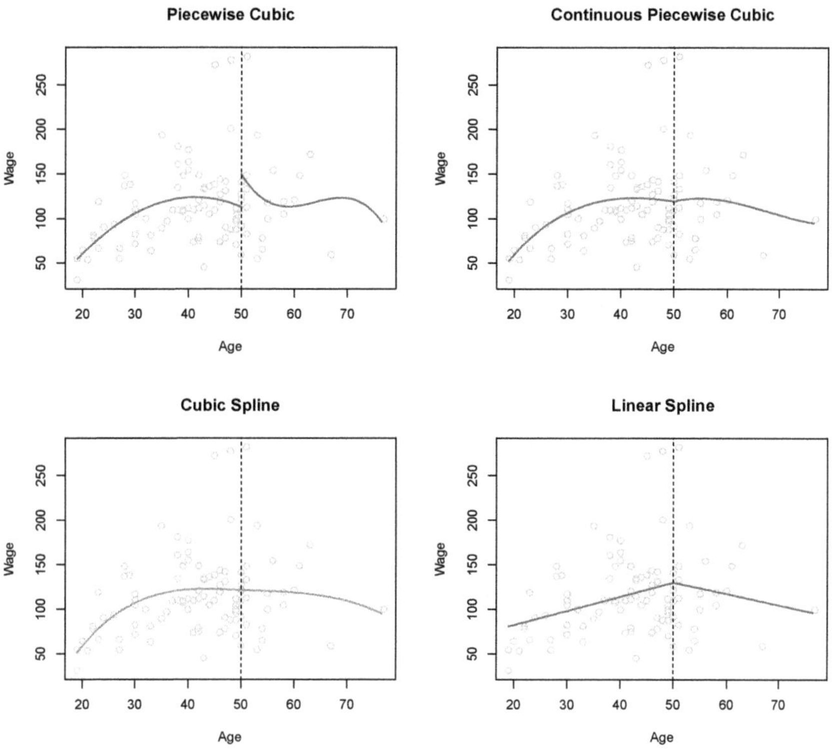

FIGURE 7.3. *Various piecewise polynomials are fit to a subset of the* `Wage` *data, with a knot at* `age=50`. Top Left: *The cubic polynomials are unconstrained.* Top Right: *The cubic polynomials are constrained to be continuous at* `age=50`. Bottom Left: *The cubic polynomials are constrained to be continuous, and to have continuous first and second derivatives.* Bottom Right: *A linear spline is shown, which is constrained to be continuous.*

$\beta_{01}, \beta_{11}, \beta_{21}$, and β_{31}, and the second has coefficients $\beta_{02}, \beta_{12}, \beta_{22}$, and β_{32}. Each of these polynomial functions can be fit using least squares applied to simple functions of the original predictor.

Using more knots leads to a more flexible piecewise polynomial. In general, if we place K different knots throughout the range of X, then we will end up fitting $K + 1$ different cubic polynomials. Note that we do not need to use a cubic polynomial. For example, we can instead fit piecewise linear functions. In fact, our piecewise constant functions of Section 7.2 are piecewise polynomials of degree 0!

The top left panel of Figure 7.3 shows a piecewise cubic polynomial fit to a subset of the `Wage` data, with a single knot at `age=50`. We immediately see a problem: the function is discontinuous and looks ridiculous! Since each polynomial has four parameters, we are using a total of eight *degrees of freedom* in fitting this piecewise polynomial model.

degrees of freedom

7.4.2 Constraints and Splines

The top left panel of Figure 7.3 looks wrong because the fitted curve is just too flexible. To remedy this problem, we can fit a piecewise polynomial under the *constraint* that the fitted curve must be continuous. In other words, there cannot be a jump when `age=50`. The top right plot in Figure 7.3 shows the resulting fit. This looks better than the top left plot, but the V-shaped join looks unnatural.

In the lower left plot, we have added two additional constraints: now both the first and second *derivatives* of the piecewise polynomials are continuous at `age=50`. In other words, we are requiring that the piecewise polynomial be not only continuous when `age=50`, but also very *smooth*. Each constraint that we impose on the piecewise cubic polynomials effectively frees up one degree of freedom, by reducing the complexity of the resulting piecewise polynomial fit. So in the top left plot, we are using eight degrees of freedom, but in the bottom left plot we imposed three constraints (continuity, continuity of the first derivative, and continuity of the second derivative) and so are left with five degrees of freedom. The curve in the bottom left plot is called a *cubic spline*.[3] In general, a cubic spline with K knots uses a total of $4 + K$ degrees of freedom.

derivative

cubic spline

In Figure 7.3, the lower right plot is a *linear spline*, which is continuous at `age=50`. The general definition of a degree-d spline is that it is a piecewise degree-d polynomial, with continuity in derivatives up to degree $d - 1$ at each knot. Therefore, a linear spline is obtained by fitting a line in each region of the predictor space defined by the knots, requiring continuity at each knot.

linear spline

In Figure 7.3, there is a single knot at `age=50`. Of course, we could add more knots, and impose continuity at each.

7.4.3 The Spline Basis Representation

The regression splines that we just saw in the previous section may have seemed somewhat complex: how can we fit a piecewise degree-d polynomial under the constraint that it (and possibly its first $d - 1$ derivatives) be continuous? It turns out that we can use the basis model (7.7) to represent a regression spline. A cubic spline with K knots can be modeled as

$$y_i = \beta_0 + \beta_1 b_1(x_i) + \beta_2 b_2(x_i) + \cdots + \beta_{K+3} b_{K+3}(x_i) + \epsilon_i, \tag{7.9}$$

for an appropriate choice of basis functions $b_1, b_2, \ldots, b_{K+3}$. The model (7.9) can then be fit using least squares.

Just as there were several ways to represent polynomials, there are also many equivalent ways to represent cubic splines using different choices of basis functions in (7.9). The most direct way to represent a cubic spline using (7.9) is to start off with a basis for a cubic polynomial—namely, x, x^2, and x^3—and then add one *truncated power basis* function per knot.

truncated power basis

[3]Cubic splines are popular because most human eyes cannot detect the discontinuity at the knots.

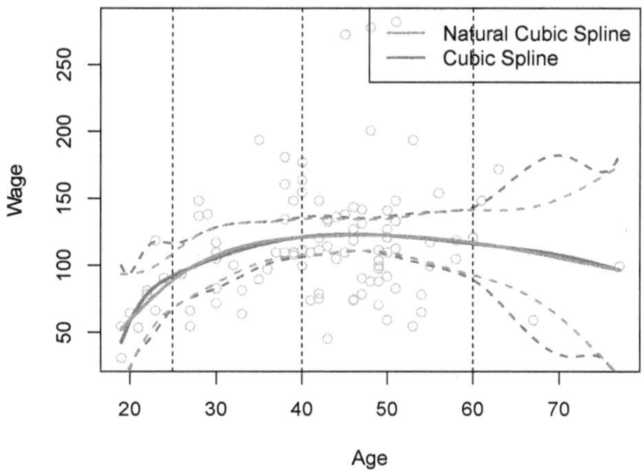

FIGURE 7.4. *A cubic spline and a natural cubic spline, with three knots, fit to a subset of the* Wage *data. The dashed lines denote the knot locations.*

A truncated power basis function is defined as

$$h(x, \xi) = (x - \xi)^3_+ = \begin{cases} (x - \xi)^3 & \text{if } x > \xi \\ 0 & \text{otherwise,} \end{cases} \tag{7.10}$$

where ξ is the knot. One can show that adding a term of the form $\beta_4 h(x, \xi)$ to the model (7.8) for a cubic polynomial will lead to a discontinuity in only the third derivative at ξ; the function will remain continuous, with continuous first and second derivatives, at each of the knots.

In other words, in order to fit a cubic spline to a data set with K knots, we perform least squares regression with an intercept and $3 + K$ predictors, of the form $X, X^2, X^3, h(X, \xi_1), h(X, \xi_2), \ldots, h(X, \xi_K)$, where $\xi_1, \ldots, \xi_K$ are the knots. This amounts to estimating a total of $K + 4$ regression coefficients; for this reason, fitting a cubic spline with K knots uses $K+4$ degrees of freedom.

Unfortunately, splines can have high variance at the outer range of the predictors—that is, when X takes on either a very small or very large value. Figure 7.4 shows a fit to the Wage data with three knots. We see that the confidence bands in the boundary region appear fairly wild. A *natural spline* is a regression spline with additional *boundary constraints*: the function is required to be linear at the boundary (in the region where X is smaller than the smallest knot, or larger than the largest knot). This additional constraint means that natural splines generally produce more stable estimates at the boundaries. In Figure 7.4, a natural cubic spline is also displayed as a red line. Note that the corresponding confidence intervals are narrower.

natural spline

7.4.4 Choosing the Number and Locations of the Knots

When we fit a spline, where should we place the knots? The regression spline is most flexible in regions that contain a lot of knots, because in those regions the polynomial coefficients can change rapidly. Hence, one

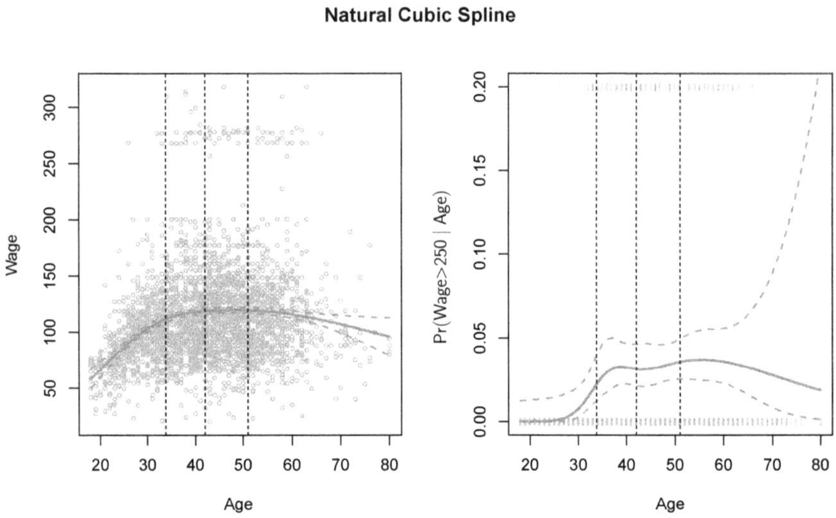

FIGURE 7.5. *A natural cubic spline function with four degrees of freedom is fit to the* `Wage` *data.* Left: *A spline is fit to* `wage` *(in thousands of dollars) as a function of* `age`. Right: *Logistic regression is used to model the binary event* `wage>250` *as a function of* `age`. *The fitted posterior probability of* `wage` *exceeding* $250,000 *is shown. The dashed lines denote the knot locations.*

option is to place more knots in places where we feel the function might vary most rapidly, and to place fewer knots where it seems more stable. While this option can work well, in practice it is common to place knots in a uniform fashion. One way to do this is to specify the desired degrees of freedom, and then have the software automatically place the corresponding number of knots at uniform quantiles of the data.

Figure 7.5 shows an example on the `Wage` data. As in Figure 7.4, we have fit a natural cubic spline with three knots, except this time the knot locations were chosen automatically as the 25th, 50th, and 75th percentiles of `age`. This was specified by requesting four degrees of freedom. The argument by which four degrees of freedom leads to three interior knots is somewhat technical.[4]

How many knots should we use, or equivalently how many degrees of freedom should our spline contain? One option is to try out different numbers of knots and see which produces the best looking curve. A somewhat more objective approach is to use cross-validation, as discussed in Chapters 5 and 6. With this method, we remove a portion of the data (say 10 %), fit a spline with a certain number of knots to the remaining data, and then use the spline to make predictions for the held-out portion. We repeat this process multiple times until each observation has been left out once, and

---

[4]There are actually five knots, including the two boundary knots. A cubic spline with five knots has nine degrees of freedom. But natural cubic splines have two additional *natural* constraints at each boundary to enforce linearity, resulting in $9 - 4 = 5$ degrees of freedom. Since this includes a constant, which is absorbed in the intercept, we count it as four degrees of freedom.

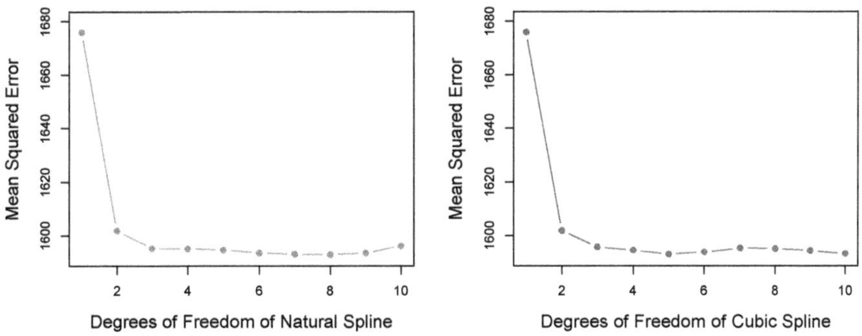

FIGURE 7.6. *Ten-fold cross-validated mean squared errors for selecting the degrees of freedom when fitting splines to the* `Wage` *data. The response is* `wage` *and the predictor* `age`. Left: *A natural cubic spline.* Right: *A cubic spline.*

then compute the overall cross-validated RSS. This procedure can be repeated for different numbers of knots K. Then the value of K giving the smallest RSS is chosen.

Figure 7.6 shows ten-fold cross-validated mean squared errors for splines with various degrees of freedom fit to the `Wage` data. The left-hand panel corresponds to a natural cubic spline and the right-hand panel to a cubic spline. The two methods produce almost identical results, with clear evidence that a one-degree fit (a linear regression) is not adequate. Both curves flatten out quickly, and it seems that three degrees of freedom for the natural spline and four degrees of freedom for the cubic spline are quite adequate.

In Section 7.7 we fit additive spline models simultaneously on several variables at a time. This could potentially require the selection of degrees of freedom for each variable. In cases like this we typically adopt a more pragmatic approach and set the degrees of freedom to a fixed number, say four, for all terms.

7.4.5 Comparison to Polynomial Regression

Figure 7.7 compares a natural cubic spline with 15 degrees of freedom to a degree-15 polynomial on the `Wage` data set. The extra flexibility in the polynomial produces undesirable results at the boundaries, while the natural cubic spline still provides a reasonable fit to the data. Regression splines often give superior results to polynomial regression. This is because unlike polynomials, which must use a high degree (exponent in the highest monomial term, e.g. X^{15}) to produce flexible fits, splines introduce flexibility by increasing the number of knots but keeping the degree fixed. Generally, this approach produces more stable estimates. Splines also allow us to place more knots, and hence flexibility, over regions where the function f seems to be changing rapidly, and fewer knots where f appears more stable.

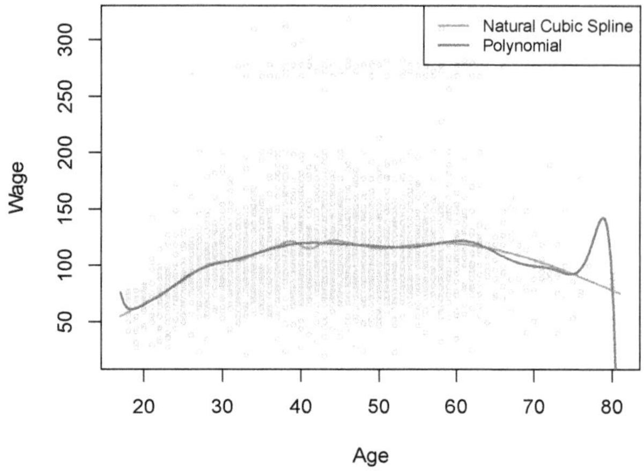

FIGURE 7.7. *On the* Wage *data set, a natural cubic spline with 15 degrees of freedom is compared to a degree-*15 *polynomial. Polynomials can show wild behavior, especially near the tails.*

7.5 Smoothing Splines

In the last section we discussed regression splines, which we create by specifying a set of knots, producing a sequence of basis functions, and then using least squares to estimate the spline coefficients. We now introduce a somewhat different approach that also produces a spline.

7.5.1 An Overview of Smoothing Splines

In fitting a smooth curve to a set of data, what we really want to do is find some function, say $g(x)$, that fits the observed data well: that is, we want $\text{RSS} = \sum_{i=1}^{n}(y_i - g(x_i))^2$ to be small. However, there is a problem with this approach. If we don't put any constraints on $g(x_i)$, then we can always make RSS zero simply by choosing g such that it *interpolates* all of the y_i. Such a function would woefully overfit the data—it would be far too flexible. What we really want is a function g that makes RSS small, but that is also *smooth*.

How might we ensure that g is smooth? There are a number of ways to do this. A natural approach is to find the function g that minimizes

$$\sum_{i=1}^{n}(y_i - g(x_i))^2 + \lambda \int g''(t)^2 dt \tag{7.11}$$

where λ is a nonnegative *tuning parameter*. The function g that minimizes (7.11) is known as a *smoothing spline*.

smoothing spline

What does (7.11) mean? Equation 7.11 takes the "Loss+Penalty" formulation that we encounter in the context of ridge regression and the lasso in Chapter 6. The term $\sum_{i=1}^{n}(y_i - g(x_i))^2$ is a *loss function* that encourages g to fit the data well, and the term $\lambda \int g''(t)^2 dt$ is a *penalty term* that penalizes the variability in g. The notation $g''(t)$ indicates the second derivative of the function g. The first derivative $g'(t)$ measures the slope

loss function

of a function at t, and the second derivative corresponds to the amount by which the slope is changing. Hence, broadly speaking, the second derivative of a function is a measure of its *roughness*: it is large in absolute value if $g(t)$ is very wiggly near t, and it is close to zero otherwise. (The second derivative of a straight line is zero; note that a line is perfectly smooth.) The $\int$ notation is an *integral*, which we can think of as a summation over the range of t. In other words, $\int g''(t)^2 dt$ is simply a measure of the total change in the function $g'(t)$, over its entire range. If g is very smooth, then $g'(t)$ will be close to constant and $\int g''(t)^2 dt$ will take on a small value. Conversely, if g is jumpy and variable then $g'(t)$ will vary significantly and $\int g''(t)^2 dt$ will take on a large value. Therefore, in (7.11), $\lambda \int g''(t)^2 dt$ encourages g to be smooth. The larger the value of λ, the smoother g will be.

When $\lambda = 0$, then the penalty term in (7.11) has no effect, and so the function g will be very jumpy and will exactly interpolate the training observations. When $\lambda \to \infty$, g will be perfectly smooth—it will just be a straight line that passes as closely as possible to the training points. In fact, in this case, g will be the linear least squares line, since the loss function in (7.11) amounts to minimizing the residual sum of squares. For an intermediate value of λ, g will approximate the training observations but will be somewhat smooth. We see that λ controls the bias-variance trade-off of the smoothing spline.

The function $g(x)$ that minimizes (7.11) can be shown to have some special properties: it is a piecewise cubic polynomial with knots at the unique values of $x_1, \ldots, x_n$, and continuous first and second derivatives at each knot. Furthermore, it is linear in the region outside of the extreme knots. In other words, *the function $g(x)$ that minimizes (7.11) is a natural cubic spline with knots at $x_1, \ldots, x_n$!* However, it is not the same natural cubic spline that one would get if one applied the basis function approach described in Section 7.4.3 with knots at $x_1, \ldots, x_n$—rather, it is a *shrunken* version of such a natural cubic spline, where the value of the tuning parameter λ in (7.11) controls the level of shrinkage.

7.5.2 Choosing the Smoothing Parameter λ

We have seen that a smoothing spline is simply a natural cubic spline with knots at every unique value of x_i. It might seem that a smoothing spline will have far too many degrees of freedom, since a knot at each data point allows a great deal of flexibility. But the tuning parameter λ controls the roughness of the smoothing spline, and hence the *effective degrees of freedom*. It is possible to show that as λ increases from 0 to ∞, the effective degrees of freedom, which we write df_λ, decrease from n to 2.

effective degrees of freedom

In the context of smoothing splines, why do we discuss *effective* degrees of freedom instead of degrees of freedom? Usually degrees of freedom refer to the number of free parameters, such as the number of coefficients fit in a polynomial or cubic spline. Although a smoothing spline has n parameters and hence n nominal degrees of freedom, these n parameters are heavily constrained or shrunk down. Hence df_λ is a measure of the flexibility of the smoothing spline—the higher it is, the more flexible (and the lower-bias but higher-variance) the smoothing spline. The definition of effective degrees of freedom is somewhat technical. We can write

$$\hat{\mathbf{g}}_\lambda = \mathbf{S}_\lambda \mathbf{y}, \tag{7.12}$$

where $\hat{\mathbf{g}}_\lambda$ is the solution to (7.11) for a particular choice of λ—that is, it is an n-vector containing the fitted values of the smoothing spline at the training points $x_1, \ldots, x_n$. Equation 7.12 indicates that the vector of fitted values when applying a smoothing spline to the data can be written as a $n \times n$ matrix $\mathbf{S}_\lambda$ (for which there is a formula) times the response vector $\mathbf{y}$. Then the effective degrees of freedom is defined to be

$$df_\lambda = \sum_{i=1}^{n} \{\mathbf{S}_\lambda\}_{ii}, \tag{7.13}$$

the sum of the diagonal elements of the matrix $\mathbf{S}_\lambda$.

In fitting a smoothing spline, we do not need to select the number or location of the knots—there will be a knot at each training observation, $x_1, \ldots, x_n$. Instead, we have another problem: we need to choose the value of λ. It should come as no surprise that one possible solution to this problem is cross-validation. In other words, we can find the value of λ that makes the cross-validated RSS as small as possible. It turns out that the *leave-one-out* cross-validation error (LOOCV) can be computed very efficiently for smoothing splines, with essentially the same cost as computing a single fit, using the following formula:

$$\text{RSS}_{cv}(\lambda) = \sum_{i=1}^{n} (y_i - \hat{g}_\lambda^{(-i)}(x_i))^2 = \sum_{i=1}^{n} \left[\frac{y_i - \hat{g}_\lambda(x_i)}{1 - \{\mathbf{S}_\lambda\}_{ii}} \right]^2 .$$

The notation $\hat{g}_\lambda^{(-i)}(x_i)$ indicates the fitted value for this smoothing spline evaluated at x_i, where the fit uses all of the training observations except for the ith observation (x_i, y_i). In contrast, $\hat{g}_\lambda(x_i)$ indicates the smoothing spline function fit to all of the training observations and evaluated at x_i. This remarkable formula says that we can compute each of these *leave-one-out* fits using only $\hat{g}_\lambda$, the original fit to *all* of the data![5] We have a very similar formula (5.2) on page 205 in Chapter 5 for least squares linear regression. Using (5.2), we can very quickly perform LOOCV for the regression splines discussed earlier in this chapter, as well as for least squares regression using arbitrary basis functions.

Figure 7.8 shows the results from fitting a smoothing spline to the `Wage` data. The red curve indicates the fit obtained from pre-specifying that we would like a smoothing spline with 16 effective degrees of freedom. The blue curve is the smoothing spline obtained when λ is chosen using LOOCV; in this case, the value of λ chosen results in 6.8 effective degrees of freedom (computed using (7.13)). For this data, there is little discernible difference between the two smoothing splines, beyond the fact that the one with 16 degrees of freedom seems slightly wigglier. Since there is little difference between the two fits, the smoothing spline fit with 6.8 degrees of freedom

[5]The exact formulas for computing $\hat{g}(x_i)$ and $\mathbf{S}_\lambda$ are very technical; however, efficient algorithms are available for computing these quantities.

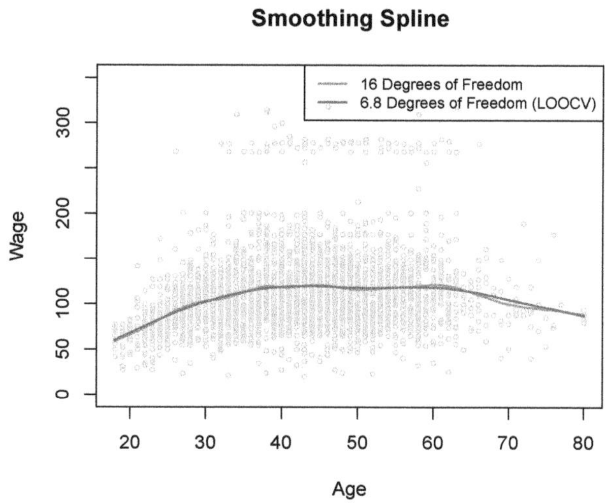

FIGURE 7.8. *Smoothing spline fits to the* Wage *data. The red curve results from specifying* 16 *effective degrees of freedom. For the blue curve,* λ *was found automatically by leave-one-out cross-validation, which resulted in* 6.8 *effective degrees of freedom.*

is preferable, since in general simpler models are better unless the data provides evidence in support of a more complex model.

7.6 Local Regression

Local regression is a different approach for fitting flexible non-linear functions, which involves computing the fit at a target point x_0 using only the nearby training observations. Figure 7.9 illustrates the idea on some simulated data, with one target point near 0.4, and another near the boundary at 0.05. In this figure the blue line represents the function $f(x)$ from which the data were generated, and the light orange line corresponds to the local regression estimate $\hat{f}(x)$. Local regression is described in Algorithm 7.1.

local regression

Note that in Step 3 of Algorithm 7.1, the weights K_{i0} will differ for each value of x_0. In other words, in order to obtain the local regression fit at a new point, we need to fit a new weighted least squares regression model by minimizing (7.14) for a new set of weights. Local regression is sometimes referred to as a *memory-based* procedure, because like nearest-neighbors, we need all the training data each time we wish to compute a prediction. We will avoid getting into the technical details of local regression here—there are books written on the topic.

In order to perform local regression, there are a number of choices to be made, such as how to define the weighting function K, and whether to fit a linear, constant, or quadratic regression in Step 3. (Equation 7.14 corresponds to a linear regression.) While all of these choices make some difference, the most important choice is the *span* s, which is the proportion of points used to compute the local regression at x_0, as defined in Step 1 above. The span plays a role like that of the tuning parameter λ in smooth-

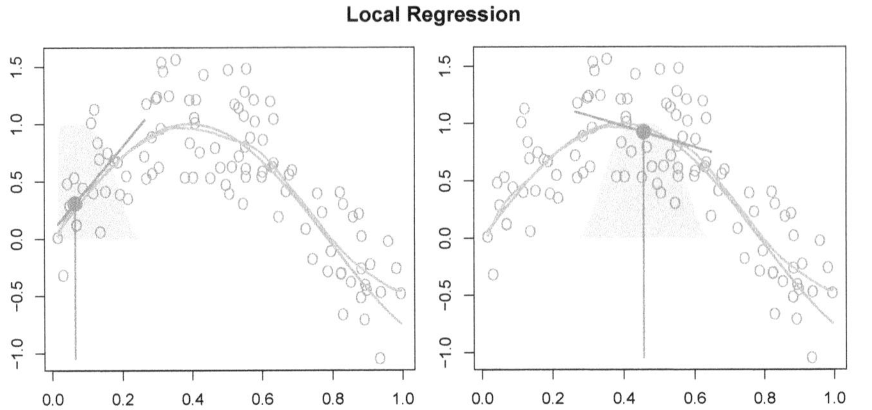

FIGURE 7.9. *Local regression illustrated on some simulated data, where the blue curve represents $f(x)$ from which the data were generated, and the light orange curve corresponds to the local regression estimate $\hat{f}(x)$. The orange colored points are local to the target point x_0, represented by the orange vertical line. The yellow bell-shape superimposed on the plot indicates weights assigned to each point, decreasing to zero with distance from the target point. The fit $\hat{f}(x_0)$ at x_0 is obtained by fitting a weighted linear regression (orange line segment), and using the fitted value at x_0 (orange solid dot) as the estimate $\hat{f}(x_0)$.*

ing splines: it controls the flexibility of the non-linear fit. The smaller the value of s, the more *local* and wiggly will be our fit; alternatively, a very large value of s will lead to a global fit to the data using all of the training observations. We can again use cross-validation to choose s, or we can specify it directly. Figure 7.10 displays local linear regression fits on the `Wage` data, using two values of s: 0.7 and 0.2. As expected, the fit obtained using $s = 0.7$ is smoother than that obtained using $s = 0.2$.

The idea of local regression can be generalized in many different ways. In a setting with multiple features $X_1, X_2, \ldots, X_p$, one very useful generalization involves fitting a multiple linear regression model that is global in some variables, but local in another, such as time. Such *varying coefficient models* are a useful way of adapting a model to the most recently gathered data. Local regression also generalizes very naturally when we want to fit models that are local in a pair of variables X_1 and X_2, rather than one. We can simply use two-dimensional neighborhoods, and fit bivariate linear regression models using the observations that are near each target point in two-dimensional space. Theoretically the same approach can be implemented in higher dimensions, using linear regressions fit to p-dimensional neighborhoods. However, local regression can perform poorly if p is much larger than about 3 or 4 because there will generally be very few training observations close to x_0. Nearest-neighbors regression, discussed in Chapter 3, suffers from a similar problem in high dimensions.

varying coefficient model

Algorithm 7.1 *Local Regression At* $X = x_0$

1. Gather the fraction $s = k/n$ of training points whose x_i are closest to x_0.

2. Assign a weight $K_{i0} = K(x_i, x_0)$ to each point in this neighborhood, so that the point furthest from x_0 has weight zero, and the closest has the highest weight. All but these k nearest neighbors get weight zero.

3. Fit a *weighted least squares regression* of the y_i on the x_i using the aforementioned weights, by finding $\hat{\beta}_0$ and $\hat{\beta}_1$ that minimize

$$\sum_{i=1}^{n} K_{i0}(y_i - \beta_0 - \beta_1 x_i)^2. \tag{7.14}$$

4. The fitted value at x_0 is given by $\hat{f}(x_0) = \hat{\beta}_0 + \hat{\beta}_1 x_0$.

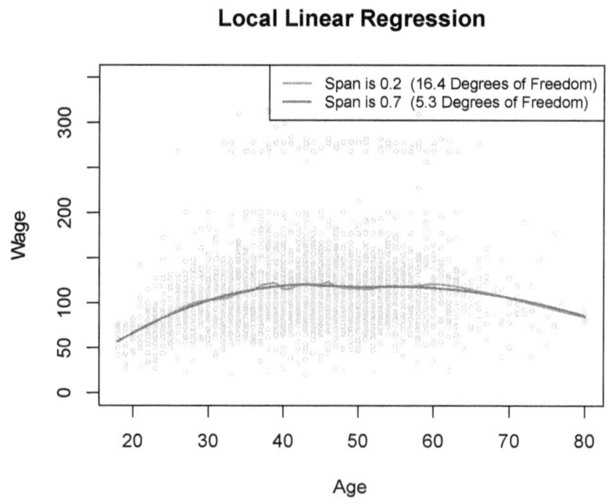

FIGURE 7.10. *Local linear fits to the* Wage *data. The span specifies the fraction of the data used to compute the fit at each target point.*

7.7 Generalized Additive Models

In Sections 7.1–7.6, we present a number of approaches for flexibly predicting a response Y on the basis of a single predictor X. These approaches can be seen as extensions of simple linear regression. Here we explore the problem of flexibly predicting Y on the basis of several predictors, $X_1, \ldots, X_p$. This amounts to an extension of multiple linear regression.

Generalized additive models (GAMs) provide a general framework for extending a standard linear model by allowing non-linear functions of each of the variables, while maintaining *additivity*. Just like linear models, GAMs can be applied with both quantitative and qualitative responses. We first

generalized additive model

additivity

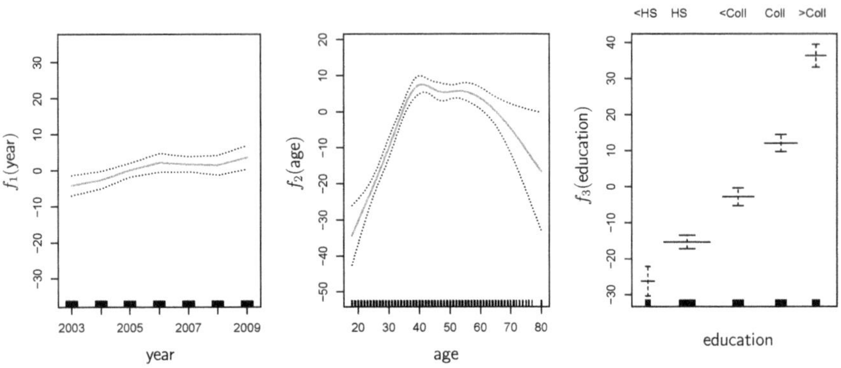

FIGURE 7.11. *For the* `Wage` *data, plots of the relationship between each feature and the response,* `wage`*, in the fitted model (7.16). Each plot displays the fitted function and pointwise standard errors. The first two functions are natural splines in* `year` *and* `age`*, with four and five degrees of freedom, respectively. The third function is a step function, fit to the qualitative variable* `education`*.*

examine GAMs for a quantitative response in Section 7.7.1, and then for a qualitative response in Section 7.7.2.

7.7.1 GAMs for Regression Problems

A natural way to extend the multiple linear regression model

$$y_i = \beta_0 + \beta_1 x_{i1} + \beta_2 x_{i2} + \cdots + \beta_p x_{ip} + \epsilon_i$$

in order to allow for non-linear relationships between each feature and the response is to replace each linear component $\beta_j x_{ij}$ with a (smooth) non-linear function $f_j(x_{ij})$. We would then write the model as

$$\begin{aligned} y_i &= \beta_0 + \sum_{j=1}^{p} f_j(x_{ij}) + \epsilon_i \\ &= \beta_0 + f_1(x_{i1}) + f_2(x_{i2}) + \cdots + f_p(x_{ip}) + \epsilon_i. \end{aligned} \tag{7.15}$$

This is an example of a GAM. It is called an *additive* model because we calculate a separate f_j for each X_j, and then add together all of their contributions.

In Sections 7.1–7.6, we discuss many methods for fitting functions to a single variable. The beauty of GAMs is that we can use these methods as building blocks for fitting an additive model. In fact, for most of the methods that we have seen so far in this chapter, this can be done fairly trivially. Take, for example, natural splines, and consider the task of fitting the model

$$\texttt{wage} = \beta_0 + f_1(\texttt{year}) + f_2(\texttt{age}) + f_3(\texttt{education}) + \epsilon \tag{7.16}$$

on the `Wage` data. Here `year` and `age` are quantitative variables, while the variable `education` is qualitative with five levels: `<HS`, `HS`, `<Coll`, `Coll`, `>Coll`, referring to the amount of high school or college education that an individual has completed. We fit the first two functions using natural splines. We

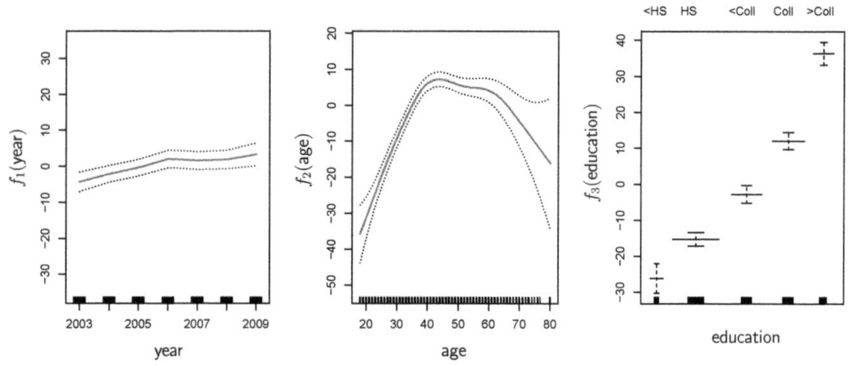

FIGURE 7.12. *Details are as in Figure 7.11, but now f_1 and f_2 are smoothing splines with four and five degrees of freedom, respectively.*

fit the third function using a separate constant for each level, via the usual dummy variable approach of Section 3.3.1.

Figure 7.11 shows the results of fitting the model (7.16) using least squares. This is easy to do, since as discussed in Section 7.4, natural splines can be constructed using an appropriately chosen set of basis functions. Hence the entire model is just a big regression onto spline basis variables and dummy variables, all packed into one big regression matrix.

Figure 7.11 can be easily interpreted. The left-hand panel indicates that holding `age` and `education` fixed, `wage` tends to increase slightly with `year`; this may be due to inflation. The center panel indicates that holding `education` and `year` fixed, `wage` tends to be highest for intermediate values of `age`, and lowest for the very young and very old. The right-hand panel indicates that holding `year` and `age` fixed, `wage` tends to increase with `education`: the more educated a person is, the higher their salary, on average. All of these findings are intuitive.

Figure 7.12 shows a similar triple of plots, but this time f_1 and f_2 are smoothing splines with four and five degrees of freedom, respectively. Fitting a GAM with a smoothing spline is not quite as simple as fitting a GAM with a natural spline, since in the case of smoothing splines, least squares cannot be used. However, standard software such as the `Python` package `pygam` can be used to fit GAMs using smoothing splines, via an approach known as *backfitting*. This method fits a model involving multiple predictors by repeatedly updating the fit for each predictor in turn, holding the others fixed. The beauty of this approach is that each time we update a function, we simply apply the fitting method for that variable to a *partial residual*.[6]

pygam

backfitting

The fitted functions in Figures 7.11 and 7.12 look rather similar. In most situations, the differences in the GAMs obtained using smoothing splines versus natural splines are small.

[6] A partial residual for X_3, for example, has the form $r_i = y_i - f_1(x_{i1}) - f_2(x_{i2})$. If we know f_1 and f_2, then we can fit f_3 by treating this residual as a response in a non-linear regression on X_3.

We do not have to use splines as the building blocks for GAMs: we can just as well use local regression, polynomial regression, or any combination of the approaches seen earlier in this chapter in order to create a GAM. GAMs are investigated in further detail in the lab at the end of this chapter.

Pros and Cons of GAMs

Before we move on, let us summarize the advantages and limitations of a GAM.

- GAMs allow us to fit a non-linear f_j to each X_j, so that we can automatically model non-linear relationships that standard linear regression will miss. This means that we do not need to manually try out many different transformations on each variable individually.
- The non-linear fits can potentially make more accurate predictions for the response Y.
- Because the model is additive, we can examine the effect of each X_j on Y individually while holding all of the other variables fixed.
- The smoothness of the function f_j for the variable X_j can be summarized via degrees of freedom.
- The main limitation of GAMs is that the model is restricted to be additive. With many variables, important interactions can be missed. However, as with linear regression, we can manually add interaction terms to the GAM model by including additional predictors of the form $X_j \times X_k$. In addition we can add low-dimensional interaction functions of the form $f_{jk}(X_j, X_k)$ into the model; such terms can be fit using two-dimensional smoothers such as local regression, or two-dimensional splines (not covered here).

For fully general models, we have to look for even more flexible approaches such as random forests and boosting, described in Chapter 8. GAMs provide a useful compromise between linear and fully nonparametric models.

7.7.2 *GAMs for Classification Problems*

GAMs can also be used in situations where Y is qualitative. For simplicity, here we assume Y takes on values 0 or 1, and let $p(X) = \Pr(Y = 1|X)$ be the conditional probability (given the predictors) that the response equals one. Recall the logistic regression model (4.6):

$$\log\left(\frac{p(X)}{1 - p(X)}\right) = \beta_0 + \beta_1 X_1 + \beta_2 X_2 + \cdots + \beta_p X_p. \qquad (7.17)$$

The left-hand side is the log of the odds of $P(Y = 1|X)$ versus $P(Y = 0|X)$, which (7.17) represents as a linear function of the predictors. A natural way to extend (7.17) to allow for non-linear relationships is to use the model

$$\log\left(\frac{p(X)}{1 - p(X)}\right) = \beta_0 + f_1(X_1) + f_2(X_2) + \cdots + f_p(X_p). \qquad (7.18)$$

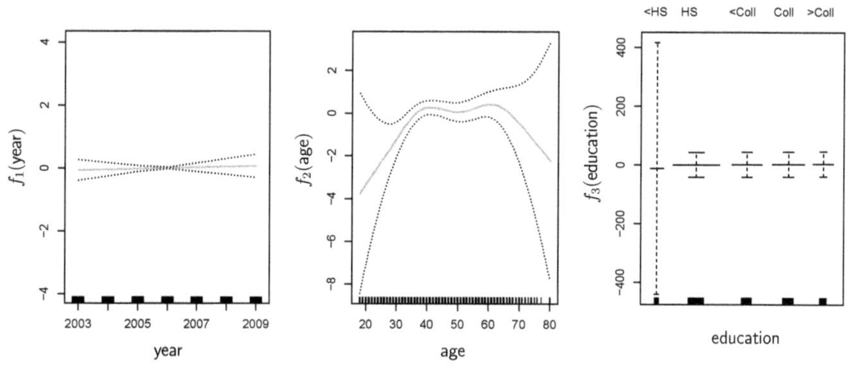

FIGURE 7.13. *For the* Wage *data, the logistic regression GAM given in (7.19) is fit to the binary response* I(wage>250). *Each plot displays the fitted function and pointwise standard errors. The first function is linear in* year, *the second function a smoothing spline with five degrees of freedom in* age, *and the third a step function for* education. *There are very wide standard errors for the first level* <HS *of* education.

Equation 7.18 is a logistic regression GAM. It has all the same pros and cons as discussed in the previous section for quantitative responses.

We fit a GAM to the Wage data in order to predict the probability that an individual's income exceeds \$250,000 per year. The GAM that we fit takes the form

$$\log\left(\frac{p(X)}{1-p(X)}\right) = \beta_0 + \beta_1 \times \texttt{year} + f_2(\texttt{age}) + f_3(\texttt{education}), \quad (7.19)$$

where

$$p(X) = \Pr(\texttt{wage} > 250|\texttt{year}, \texttt{age}, \texttt{education}).$$

Once again f_2 is fit using a smoothing spline with five degrees of freedom, and f_3 is fit as a step function, by creating dummy variables for each of the levels of education. The resulting fit is shown in Figure 7.13. The last panel looks suspicious, with very wide confidence intervals for level <HS. In fact, no response values equal one for that category: no individuals with less than a high school education make more than \$250,000 per year. Hence we refit the GAM, excluding the individuals with less than a high school education. The resulting model is shown in Figure 7.14. As in Figures 7.11 and 7.12, all three panels have similar vertical scales. This allows us to visually assess the relative contributions of each of the variables. We observe that age and education have a much larger effect than year on the probability of being a high earner.

7.8 Lab: Non-Linear Modeling

In this lab, we demonstrate some of the nonlinear models discussed in this chapter. We use the Wage data as a running example, and show that many of the complex non-linear fitting procedures discussed can easily be implemented in Python.

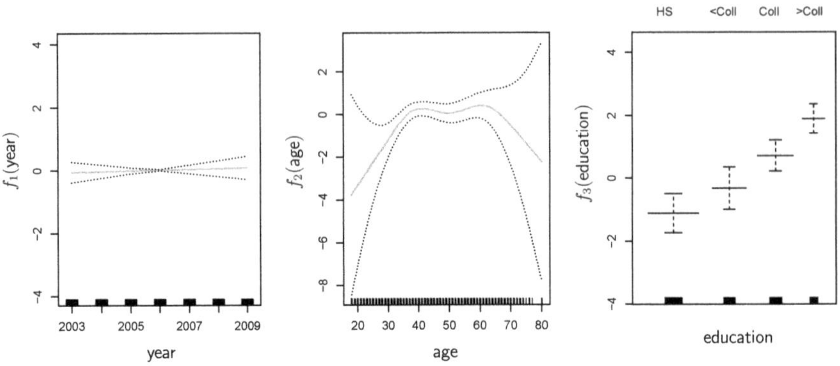

FIGURE 7.14. *The same model is fit as in Figure 7.13, this time excluding the observations for which* `education` *is* `<HS`. *Now we see that increased education tends to be associated with higher salaries.*

As usual, we start with some of our standard imports.

In [1]:
```
import numpy as np, pandas as pd
from matplotlib.pyplot import subplots
import statsmodels.api as sm
from ISLP import load_data
from ISLP.models import (summarize,
                         poly,
                         ModelSpec as MS)
from statsmodels.stats.anova import anova_lm
```

We again collect the new imports needed for this lab. Many of these are developed specifically for the `ISLP` package.

In [2]:
```
from pygam import (s as s_gam,
                   l as l_gam,
                   f as f_gam,
                   LinearGAM,
                   LogisticGAM)

from ISLP.transforms import (BSpline,
                             NaturalSpline)
from ISLP.models import bs, ns
from ISLP.pygam import (approx_lam,
                        degrees_of_freedom,
                        plot as plot_gam,
                        anova as anova_gam)
```

7.8.1 Polynomial Regression and Step Functions

We start by demonstrating how Figure 7.1 can be reproduced. Let's begin by loading the data.

In [3]:
```
Wage = load_data('Wage')
y = Wage['wage']
age = Wage['age']
```

Throughout most of this lab, our response is Wage['wage'], which we have stored as y above. As in Section 3.6.6, we will use the poly() function to create a model matrix that will fit a 4th degree polynomial in age.

In [4]:
```
poly_age = MS([poly('age', degree=4)]).fit(Wage)
M = sm.OLS(y, poly_age.transform(Wage)).fit()
summarize(M)
```

Out[4]:

	coef	std err	t	P>|t|
intercept	111.7036	0.729	153.283	0.000
poly(age, degree=4)[0]	447.0679	39.915	11.201	0.000
poly(age, degree=4)[1]	-478.3158	39.915	-11.983	0.000
poly(age, degree=4)[2]	125.5217	39.915	3.145	0.002
poly(age, degree=4)[3]	-77.9112	39.915	-1.952	0.051

This polynomial is constructed using the function poly(), which creates a special *transformer* Poly() (using sklearn terminology for feature transformations such as PCA() seen in Section 6.5.3) which allows for easy evaluation of the polynomial at new data points. Here poly() is referred to as a *helper* function, and sets up the transformation; Poly() is the actual workhorse that computes the transformation. See also the discussion of transformations on page 118.

transformer

helper

In the code above, the first line executes the fit() method using the dataframe Wage. This recomputes and stores as attributes any parameters needed by Poly() on the training data, and these will be used on all subsequent evaluations of the transform() method. For example, it is used on the second line, as well as in the plotting function developed below.

We now create a grid of values for age at which we want predictions.

In [5]:
```
age_grid = np.linspace(age.min(),
                       age.max(),
                       100)
age_df = pd.DataFrame({'age': age_grid})
```

Finally, we wish to plot the data and add the fit from the fourth-degree polynomial. As we will make several similar plots below, we first write a function to create all the ingredients and produce the plot. Our function takes in a model specification (here a basis specified by a transform), as well as a grid of age values. The function produces a fitted curve as well as 95% confidence bands. By using an argument for basis we can produce and plot the results with several different transforms, such as the splines we will see shortly.

In [6]:
```
def plot_wage_fit(age_df,
                  basis,
                  title):

    X = basis.transform(Wage)
    Xnew = basis.transform(age_df)
    M = sm.OLS(y, X).fit()
    preds = M.get_prediction(Xnew)
    bands = preds.conf_int(alpha=0.05)
    fig, ax = subplots(figsize=(8,8))
    ax.scatter(age,
               y,
```

```
                facecolor='gray',
                alpha=0.5)
    for val, ls in zip([preds.predicted_mean,
                        bands[:,0],
                        bands[:,1]],
                       ['b','r--','r--']):
        ax.plot(age_df.values, val, ls, linewidth=3)
    ax.set_title(title, fontsize=20)
    ax.set_xlabel('Age', fontsize=20)
    ax.set_ylabel('Wage', fontsize=20);
    return ax
```

We include an argument alpha to ax.scatter() to add some transparency to the points. This provides a visual indication of density. Notice the use of the zip() function in the for loop above (see Section 2.3.8). We have three lines to plot, each with different colors and line types. Here zip() conveniently bundles these together as iterators in the loop.[7] iterator

We now plot the fit of the fourth-degree polynomial using this function.

In [7]:
```
plot_wage_fit(age_df,
              poly_age,
              'Degree-4 Polynomial');
```

With polynomial regression we must decide on the degree of the polynomial to use. Sometimes we just wing it, and decide to use second or third degree polynomials, simply to obtain a nonlinear fit. But we can make such a decision in a more systematic way. One way to do this is through hypothesis tests, which we demonstrate here. We now fit a series of models ranging from linear (degree-one) to degree-five polynomials, and look to determine the simplest model that is sufficient to explain the relationship between wage and age. We use the anova_lm() function, which performs a series of ANOVA tests. An *analysis of variance* or ANOVA tests the null hypothesis that a model $\mathcal{M}_1$ is sufficient to explain the data against the alternative hypothesis that a more complex model $\mathcal{M}_2$ is required. The determination is based on an F-test. To perform the test, the models $\mathcal{M}_1$ and $\mathcal{M}_2$ must be *nested*: the space spanned by the predictors in $\mathcal{M}_1$ must be a subspace of the space spanned by the predictors in $\mathcal{M}_2$. In this case, we fit five different polynomial models and sequentially compare the simpler model to the more complex model. analysis of variance

In [8]:
```
models = [MS([poly('age', degree=d)])
          for d in range(1, 6)]
Xs = [model.fit_transform(Wage) for model in models]
anova_lm(*[sm.OLS(y, X_).fit()
           for X_ in Xs])
```

Out[8]:

	df_resid	ssr	df_diff	ss_diff	F	Pr(>F)
0	2998.0	5.022e+06	0.0	NaN	NaN	NaN
1	2997.0	4.793e+06	1.0	228786.010	143.593	2.364e-32
2	2996.0	4.778e+06	1.0	15755.694	9.889	1.679e-03
3	2995.0	4.772e+06	1.0	6070.152	3.810	5.105e-02

[7]In Python speak, an "iterator" is an object with a finite number of values, that can be iterated on, as in a loop.

```
4    2994.0  4.770e+06        1.0     1282.563     0.805  3.697e-01
```

Notice the * in the anova_lm() line above. This function takes a variable number of non-keyword arguments, in this case fitted models. When these models are provided as a list (as is done here), it must be prefixed by *.

The p-value comparing the linear models[0] to the quadratic models[1] is essentially zero, indicating that a linear fit is not sufficient.[8] Similarly the p-value comparing the quadratic models[1] to the cubic models[2] is very low (0.0017), so the quadratic fit is also insufficient. The p-value comparing the cubic and degree-four polynomials, models[2] and models[3], is approximately 5%, while the degree-five polynomial models[4] seems unnecessary because its p-value is 0.37. Hence, either a cubic or a quartic polynomial appear to provide a reasonable fit to the data, but lower- or higher-order models are not justified.

In this case, instead of using the anova() function, we could have obtained these p-values more succinctly by exploiting the fact that poly() creates orthogonal polynomials.

In [9]:
```
summarize(M)
```

Out[9]:
```
                              coef  std err        t  P>|t|
intercept                 111.7036    0.729  153.283  0.000
poly(age, degree=4)[0]    447.0679   39.915   11.201  0.000
poly(age, degree=4)[1]   -478.3158   39.915  -11.983  0.000
poly(age, degree=4)[2]    125.5217   39.915    3.145  0.002
poly(age, degree=4)[3]    -77.9112   39.915   -1.952  0.051
```

Notice that the p-values are the same, and in fact the square of the t-statistics are equal to the F-statistics from the anova_lm() function; for example:

In [10]:
```
(-11.983)**2
```

Out[10]: 143.59228

However, the ANOVA method works whether or not we used orthogonal polynomials, provided the models are nested. For example, we can use anova_lm() to compare the following three models, which all have a linear term in education and a polynomial in age of different degrees:

In [11]:
```
models = [MS(['education', poly('age', degree=d)])
              for d in range(1, 4)]
XEs = [model.fit_transform(Wage)
          for model in models]
anova_lm(*[sm.OLS(y, X_).fit() for X_ in XEs])
```

Out[11]:
```
   df_resid        ssr  df_diff     ss_diff        F     Pr(>F)
0    2997.0  3.902e+06      0.0         NaN      NaN        NaN
1    2996.0  3.759e+06      1.0  142862.701  113.992  3.838e-26
2    2995.0  3.754e+06      1.0    5926.207    4.729  2.974e-02
```

[8] Indexing starting at zero is confusing for the polynomial degree example, since models[1] is quadratic rather than linear!

As an alternative to using hypothesis tests and ANOVA, we could choose the polynomial degree using cross-validation, as discussed in Chapter 5.

Next we consider the task of predicting whether an individual earns more than $250,000 per year. We proceed much as before, except that first we create the appropriate response vector, and then apply the glm() function using the binomial family in order to fit a polynomial logistic regression model.

```
In [12]: X = poly_age.transform(Wage)
         high_earn = Wage['high_earn'] = y > 250 # shorthand
         glm = sm.GLM(y > 250,
                      X,
                      family=sm.families.Binomial())
         B = glm.fit()
         summarize(B)
```

```
Out[12]:
                                coef  std err        z  P>|z|
                   intercept -4.3012    0.345  -12.457  0.000
   poly(age, degree=4)[0]  71.9642   26.133    2.754  0.006
   poly(age, degree=4)[1] -85.7729   35.929   -2.387  0.017
   poly(age, degree=4)[2]  34.1626   19.697    1.734  0.083
   poly(age, degree=4)[3] -47.4008   24.105   -1.966  0.049
```

Once again, we make predictions using the get_prediction() method.

```
In [13]: newX = poly_age.transform(age_df)
         preds = B.get_prediction(newX)
         bands = preds.conf_int(alpha=0.05)
```

We now plot the estimated relationship.

```
In [14]: fig, ax = subplots(figsize=(8,8))
         rng = np.random.default_rng(0)
         ax.scatter(age +
                    0.2 * rng.uniform(size=y.shape[0]),
                    np.where(high_earn, 0.198, 0.002),
                    fc='gray',
                    marker='|')
         for val, ls in zip([preds.predicted_mean,
                             bands[:,0],
                             bands[:,1]],
                            ['b','r--','r--']):
             ax.plot(age_df.values, val, ls, linewidth=3)
         ax.set_title('Degree-4 Polynomial', fontsize=20)
         ax.set_xlabel('Age', fontsize=20)
         ax.set_ylim([0,0.2])
         ax.set_ylabel('P(Wage > 250)', fontsize=20);
```

We have drawn the age values corresponding to the observations with wage values above 250 as gray marks on the top of the plot, and those with wage values below 250 are shown as gray marks on the bottom of the plot. We added a small amount of noise to jitter the age values a bit so that observations with the same age value do not cover each other up. This type of plot is often called a *rug plot*. rug plot

In order to fit a step function, as discussed in Section 7.2, we first use the pd.qcut() function to discretize age based on quantiles. Then we use pd.qcut()

pd.get_dummies() to create the columns of the model matrix for this categorical variable. Note that this function will include *all* columns for a given categorical, rather than the usual approach which drops one of the levels. pd.get_dummies()

In [15]:
```
cut_age = pd.qcut(age, 4)
summarize(sm.OLS(y, pd.get_dummies(cut_age)).fit())
```

Out[15]:
```
                     coef   std err        t  P>|t|
(17.999, 33.75]   94.1584     1.478   63.692    0.0
  (33.75, 42.0]  116.6608     1.470   79.385    0.0
   (42.0, 51.0]  119.1887     1.416   84.147    0.0
   (51.0, 80.0]  116.5717     1.559   74.751    0.0
```

Here pd.qcut() automatically picked the cutpoints based on the quantiles 25%, 50% and 75%, which results in four regions. We could also have specified our own quantiles directly instead of the argument 4. For cuts not based on quantiles we would use the pd.cut() function. The function pd.qcut() (and pd.cut()) returns an ordered categorical variable. The regression model then creates a set of dummy variables for use in the regression. Since age is the only variable in the model, the value $94,158.40 is the average salary for those under 33.75 years of age, and the other coefficients are the average salary for those in the other age groups. We can produce predictions and plots just as we did in the case of the polynomial fit. pd.cut()

7.8.2 Splines

In order to fit regression splines, we use transforms from the ISLP package. The actual spline evaluation functions are in the scipy.interpolate package; we have simply wrapped them as transforms similar to Poly() and PCA().

In Section 7.4, we saw that regression splines can be fit by constructing an appropriate matrix of basis functions. The BSpline() function generates the entire matrix of basis functions for splines with the specified set of knots. By default, the B-splines produced are cubic. To change the degree, use the argument degree. BSpline()

In [16]:
```
bs_ = BSpline(internal_knots=[25,40,60], intercept=True).fit(age)
bs_age = bs_.transform(age)
bs_age.shape
```

Out[16]: (3000, 7)

This results in a seven-column matrix, which is what is expected for a cubic-spline basis with 3 interior knots. We can form this same matrix using the bs() object, which facilitates adding this to a model-matrix builder (as in poly() versus its workhorse Poly()) described in Section 7.8.1.

We now fit a cubic spline model to the Wage data.

In [17]:
```
bs_age = MS([bs('age', internal_knots=[25,40,60])])
Xbs = bs_age.fit_transform(Wage)
M = sm.OLS(y, Xbs).fit()
summarize(M)
```

```
Out[17]:                                         coef  std err  ...
                                    intercept  60.494    9.460  ...
bs(age, internal_knots=[25, 40, 60])[0]         3.980   12.538  ...
bs(age, internal_knots=[25, 40, 60])[1]        44.631    9.626  ...
bs(age, internal_knots=[25, 40, 60])[2]        62.839   10.755  ...
bs(age, internal_knots=[25, 40, 60])[3]        55.991   10.706  ...
bs(age, internal_knots=[25, 40, 60])[4]        50.688   14.402  ...
bs(age, internal_knots=[25, 40, 60])[5]        16.606   19.126  ...
```

The column names are a little cumbersome, and have caused us to truncate the printed summary. They can be set on construction using the `name` argument as follows.

```
In [18]: bs_age = MS([bs('age',
                         internal_knots=[25,40,60],
                         name='bs(age)')])
         Xbs = bs_age.fit_transform(Wage)
         M = sm.OLS(y, Xbs).fit()
         summarize(M)
```

```
Out[18]:                     coef  std err      t   P>|t|
               intercept   60.494    9.460  6.394   0.000
bs(age, knots)[0]           3.981   12.538  0.317   0.751
bs(age, knots)[1]          44.631    9.626  4.636   0.000
bs(age, knots)[2]          62.839   10.755  5.843   0.000
bs(age, knots)[3]          55.991   10.706  5.230   0.000
bs(age, knots)[4]          50.688   14.402  3.520   0.000
bs(age, knots)[5]          16.606   19.126  0.868   0.385
```

Notice that there are 6 spline coefficients rather than 7. This is because, by default, `bs()` assumes `intercept=False`, since we typically have an overall intercept in the model. So it generates the spline basis with the given knots, and then discards one of the basis functions to account for the intercept.

We could also use the `df` (degrees of freedom) option to specify the complexity of the spline. We see above that with 3 knots, the spline basis has 6 columns or degrees of freedom. When we specify `df=6` rather than the actual knots, `bs()` will produce a spline with 3 knots chosen at uniform quantiles of the training data. We can see these chosen knots most easily using `Bspline()` directly:

```
In [19]: BSpline(df=6).fit(age).internal_knots_
```

```
Out[19]: array([33.75, 42.0, 51.0])
```

When asking for six degrees of freedom, the transform chooses knots at ages 33.75, 42.0, and 51.0, which correspond to the 25th, 50th, and 75th percentiles of `age`.

When using B-splines we need not limit ourselves to cubic polynomials (i.e. `degree=3`). For instance, using `degree=0` results in piecewise constant functions, as in our example with `pd.qcut()` above.

```
In [20]: bs_age0 = MS([bs('age',
                          df=3,
                          degree=0)]).fit(Wage)
         Xbs0 = bs_age0.transform(Wage)
         summarize(sm.OLS(y, Xbs0).fit())
```

Out[20]:
```
                                coef  std err       t  P>|t|
                 intercept    94.158    1.478  63.687    0.0
bs(age, df=3, degree=0)[0]    22.349    2.152  10.388    0.0
bs(age, df=3, degree=0)[1]    24.808    2.044  12.137    0.0
bs(age, df=3, degree=0)[2]    22.781    2.087  10.917    0.0
```

This fit should be compared with cell [15] where we use `qcut()` to create four bins by cutting at the 25%, 50% and 75% quantiles of `age`. Since we specified `df=3` for degree-zero splines here, there will also be knots at the same three quantiles. Although the coefficients appear different, we see that this is a result of the different coding. For example, the first coefficient is identical in both cases, and is the mean response in the first bin. For the second coefficient, we have $94.158 + 22.349 = 116.507 \approx 116.611$, the latter being the mean in the second bin in cell [15]. Here the intercept is coded by a column of ones, so the second, third and fourth coefficients are increments for those bins. Why is the sum not exactly the same? It turns out that the `qcut()` uses $\leq$, while `bs()` uses $<$ when deciding bin membership.

In order to fit a natural spline, we use the `NaturalSpline()` transform with the corresponding helper `ns()`. Here we fit a natural spline with five degrees of freedom (excluding the intercept) and plot the results.

`Natural Spline()`

In [21]:
```
ns_age = MS([ns('age', df=5)]).fit(Wage)
M_ns = sm.OLS(y, ns_age.transform(Wage)).fit()
summarize(M_ns)
```

Out[21]:
```
                  coef  std err       t  P>|t|
       intercept  60.475    4.708  12.844  0.000
ns(age, df=5)[0]  61.527    4.709  13.065  0.000
ns(age, df=5)[1]  55.691    5.717   9.741  0.000
ns(age, df=5)[2]  46.818    4.948   9.463  0.000
ns(age, df=5)[3]  83.204   11.918   6.982  0.000
ns(age, df=5)[4]   6.877    9.484   0.725  0.468
```

We now plot the natural spline using our plotting function.

In [22]:
```
plot_wage_fit(age_df,
              ns_age,
              'Natural spline, df=5');
```

7.8.3 Smoothing Splines and GAMs

A smoothing spline is a special case of a GAM with squared-error loss and a single feature. To fit GAMs in `Python` we will use the `pygam` package which can be installed via `pip install pygam`. The estimator `LinearGAM()` uses squared-error loss. The GAM is specified by associating each column of a model matrix with a particular smoothing operation: `s` for smoothing spline; `l` for linear, and `f` for factor or categorical variables. The argument `0` passed to `s` below indicates that this smoother will apply to the first column of a feature matrix. Below, we pass it a matrix with a single column: `X_age`. The argument `lam` is the penalty parameter λ as discussed in Section 7.5.2.

`pygam`

`LinearGAM()`

In [23]:
```
X_age = np.asarray(age).reshape((-1,1))
gam = LinearGAM(s_gam(0, lam=0.6))
gam.fit(X_age, y)
```

```
Out[23]: LinearGAM(callbacks=[Deviance(), Diffs()], fit_intercept=True,
    max_iter=100, scale=None, terms=s(0) + intercept, tol=0.0001,
    verbose=False)
```

The pygam library generally expects a matrix of features so we reshape age to be a matrix (a two-dimensional array) instead of a vector (i.e. a one-dimensional array). The -1 in the call to the reshape() method tells numpy to impute the size of that dimension based on the remaining entries of the shape tuple.

Let's investigate how the fit changes with the smoothing parameter lam. The function np.logspace() is similar to np.linspace() but spaces points evenly on the log-scale. Below we vary lam from 10^{-2} to 10^6. np.logspace

```
In [24]: fig, ax = subplots(figsize=(8,8))
ax.scatter(age, y, facecolor='gray', alpha=0.5)
for lam in np.logspace(-2, 6, 5):
    gam = LinearGAM(s_gam(0, lam=lam)).fit(X_age, y)
    ax.plot(age_grid,
            gam.predict(age_grid),
            label='{:.1e}'.format(lam),
            linewidth=3)
ax.set_xlabel('Age', fontsize=20)
ax.set_ylabel('Wage', fontsize=20);
ax.legend(title='$\lambda$');
```

The pygam package can perform a search for an optimal smoothing parameter.

```
In [25]: gam_opt = gam.gridsearch(X_age, y)
ax.plot(age_grid,
        gam_opt.predict(age_grid),
        label='Grid search',
        linewidth=4)
ax.legend()
fig
```

Alternatively, we can fix the degrees of freedom of the smoothing spline using a function included in the ISLP.pygam package. Below we find a value of λ that gives us roughly four degrees of freedom. We note here that these degrees of freedom include the unpenalized intercept and linear term of the smoothing spline, hence there are at least two degrees of freedom.

```
In [26]: age_term = gam.terms[0]
lam_4 = approx_lam(X_age, age_term, 4)
age_term.lam = lam_4
degrees_of_freedom(X_age, age_term)
```

```
Out[26]: 4.000000100004728
```

Let's vary the degrees of freedom in a similar plot to above. We choose the degrees of freedom as the desired degrees of freedom plus one to account for the fact that these smoothing splines always have an intercept term. Hence, a value of one for df is just a linear fit.

```
In [27]: fig, ax = subplots(figsize=(8,8))
ax.scatter(X_age,
           y,
```

```
                facecolor='gray',
                alpha=0.3)
for df in [1,3,4,8,15]:
    lam = approx_lam(X_age, age_term, df+1)
    age_term.lam = lam
    gam.fit(X_age, y)
    ax.plot(age_grid,
            gam.predict(age_grid),
            label='{:d}'.format(df),
            linewidth=4)
ax.set_xlabel('Age', fontsize=20)
ax.set_ylabel('Wage', fontsize=20);
ax.legend(title='Degrees of freedom');
```

Additive Models with Several Terms

The strength of generalized additive models lies in their ability to fit multivariate regression models with more flexibility than linear models. We demonstrate two approaches: the first in a more manual fashion using natural splines and piecewise constant functions, and the second using the pygam package and smoothing splines.

We now fit a GAM by hand to predict wage using natural spline functions of year and age, treating education as a qualitative predictor, as in (7.16). Since this is just a big linear regression model using an appropriate choice of basis functions, we can simply do this using the sm.OLS() function.

We will build the model matrix in a more manual fashion here, since we wish to access the pieces separately when constructing partial dependence plots.

In [28]:
```
ns_age = NaturalSpline(df=4).fit(age)
ns_year = NaturalSpline(df=5).fit(Wage['year'])
Xs = [ns_age.transform(age),
      ns_year.transform(Wage['year']),
      pd.get_dummies(Wage['education']).values]
X_bh = np.hstack(Xs)
gam_bh = sm.OLS(y, X_bh).fit()
```

Here the function NaturalSpline() is the workhorse supporting the ns() helper function. We chose to use all columns of the indicator matrix for the categorical variable education, making an intercept redundant. Finally, we stacked the three component matrices horizontally to form the model matrix X_bh.

We now show how to construct partial dependence plots for each of the terms in our rudimentary GAM. We can do this by hand, given grids for age and year. We simply predict with new X matrices, fixing all but one of the features at a time.

In [29]:
```
age_grid = np.linspace(age.min(),
                       age.max(),
                       100)
X_age_bh = X_bh.copy()[:100]
X_age_bh[:] = X_bh[:].mean(0)[None,:]
X_age_bh[:,:4] = ns_age.transform(age_grid)
preds = gam_bh.get_prediction(X_age_bh)
bounds_age = preds.conf_int(alpha=0.05)
```

```
partial_age = preds.predicted_mean
center = partial_age.mean()
partial_age -= center
bounds_age -= center
fig, ax = subplots(figsize=(8,8))
ax.plot(age_grid, partial_age, 'b', linewidth=3)
ax.plot(age_grid, bounds_age[:,0], 'r--', linewidth=3)
ax.plot(age_grid, bounds_age[:,1], 'r--', linewidth=3)
ax.set_xlabel('Age')
ax.set_ylabel('Effect on wage')
ax.set_title('Partial dependence of age on wage', fontsize=20);
```

Let's explain in some detail what we did above. The idea is to create a new prediction matrix, where all but the columns belonging to `age` are constant (and set to their training-data means). The four columns for `age` are filled in with the natural spline basis evaluated at the 100 values in `age_grid`.

1. We made a grid of length 100 in `age`, and created a matrix `X_age_bh` with 100 rows and the same number of columns as `X_bh`.

2. We replaced every row of this matrix with the column means of the original.

3. We then replace just the first four columns representing `age` with the natural spline basis computed at the values in `age_grid`.

The remaining steps should by now be familiar.

We also look at the effect of `year` on `wage`; the process is the same.

In [30]:
```
year_grid = np.linspace(2003, 2009, 100)
year_grid = np.linspace(Wage['year'].min(),
                        Wage['year'].max(),
                        100)
X_year_bh = X_bh.copy()[:100]
X_year_bh[:] = X_bh[:].mean(0)[None,:]
X_year_bh[:,4:9] = ns_year.transform(year_grid)
preds = gam_bh.get_prediction(X_year_bh)
bounds_year = preds.conf_int(alpha=0.05)
partial_year = preds.predicted_mean
center = partial_year.mean()
partial_year -= center
bounds_year -= center
fig, ax = subplots(figsize=(8,8))
ax.plot(year_grid, partial_year, 'b', linewidth=3)
ax.plot(year_grid, bounds_year[:,0], 'r--', linewidth=3)
ax.plot(year_grid, bounds_year[:,1], 'r--', linewidth=3)
ax.set_xlabel('Year')
ax.set_ylabel('Effect on wage')
ax.set_title('Partial dependence of year on wage', fontsize=20);
```

We now fit the model (7.16) using smoothing splines rather than natural splines. All of the terms in (7.16) are fit simultaneously, taking each other into account to explain the response. The `pygam` package only works with matrices, so we must convert the categorical series `education` to its array representation, which can be found with the `cat.codes` attribute of `education`. As `year` only has 7 unique values, we use only seven basis functions for it.

In [31]:
```
gam_full = LinearGAM(s_gam(0) +
                     s_gam(1, n_splines=7) +
                     f_gam(2, lam=0))
Xgam = np.column_stack([age,
                        Wage['year'],
                        Wage['education'].cat.codes])
gam_full = gam_full.fit(Xgam, y)
```

The two `s_gam()` terms result in smoothing spline fits, and use a default value for λ (`lam=0.6`), which is somewhat arbitrary. For the categorical term `education`, specified using a `f_gam()` term, we specify `lam=0` to avoid any shrinkage. We produce the partial dependence plot in `age` to see the effect of these choices.

The values for the plot are generated by the `pygam` package. We provide a `plot_gam()` function for partial-dependence plots in `ISLP.pygam`, which makes this job easier than in our last example with natural splines.

plot_gam()

In [32]:
```
fig, ax = subplots(figsize=(8,8))
plot_gam(gam_full, 0, ax=ax)
ax.set_xlabel('Age')
ax.set_ylabel('Effect on wage')
ax.set_title('Partial dependence of age on wage - default lam=0.6',
     fontsize=20);
```

We see that the function is somewhat wiggly. It is more natural to specify the `df` than a value for `lam`. We refit a GAM using four degrees of freedom each for `age` and `year`. Recall that the addition of one below takes into account the intercept of the smoothing spline.

In [33]:
```
age_term = gam_full.terms[0]
age_term.lam = approx_lam(Xgam, age_term, df=4+1)
year_term = gam_full.terms[1]
year_term.lam = approx_lam(Xgam, year_term, df=4+1)
gam_full = gam_full.fit(Xgam, y)
```

Note that updating `age_term.lam` above updates it in `gam_full.terms[0]` as well! Likewise for `year_term.lam`.

Repeating the plot for `age`, we see that it is much smoother. We also produce the plot for `year`.

In [34]:
```
fig, ax = subplots(figsize=(8,8))
plot_gam(gam_full,
         1,
         ax=ax)
ax.set_xlabel('Year')
ax.set_ylabel('Effect on wage')
ax.set_title('Partial dependence of year on wage', fontsize=20)
```

Finally we plot `education`, which is categorical. The partial dependence plot is different, and more suitable for the set of fitted constants for each level of this variable.

In [35]:
```
fig, ax = subplots(figsize=(8, 8))
ax = plot_gam(gam_full, 2)
ax.set_xlabel('Education')
ax.set_ylabel('Effect on wage')
```

```
ax.set_title('Partial dependence of wage on education',
             fontsize=20);
ax.set_xticklabels(Wage['education'].cat.categories, fontsize=8);
```

ANOVA Tests for Additive Models

In all of our models, the function of `year` looks rather linear. We can perform a series of ANOVA tests in order to determine which of these three models is best: a GAM that excludes `year` ($\mathcal{M}_1$), a GAM that uses a linear function of `year` ($\mathcal{M}_2$), or a GAM that uses a spline function of `year` ($\mathcal{M}_3$).

```
In [36]: gam_0 = LinearGAM(age_term + f_gam(2, lam=0))
         gam_0.fit(Xgam, y)
         gam_linear = LinearGAM(age_term +
                                l_gam(1, lam=0) +
                                f_gam(2, lam=0))
         gam_linear.fit(Xgam, y)
```

```
Out[36]: LinearGAM(callbacks=[Deviance(), Diffs()], fit_intercept=True,
           max_iter=100, scale=None, terms=s(0) + l(1) + f(2) + intercept,
           tol=0.0001, verbose=False)
```

Notice our use of `age_term` in the expressions above. We do this because earlier we set the value for `lam` in this term to achieve four degrees of freedom.

To directly assess the effect of `year` we run an ANOVA on the three models fit above.

```
In [37]: anova_gam(gam_0, gam_linear, gam_full)
```

Out[37]:

	deviance	df	deviance_diff	df_diff	F	pvalue
0	3714362.366	2991.004	NaN	NaN	NaN	NaN
1	3696745.823	2990.005	17616.543	0.999	14.265	0.002
2	3693142.930	2987.007	3602.894	2.998	0.972	0.436

We find that there is compelling evidence that a GAM with a linear function in `year` is better than a GAM that does not include `year` at all (p-value= 0.002). However, there is no evidence that a non-linear function of `year` is needed (p-value=0.435). In other words, based on the results of this ANOVA, $\mathcal{M}_2$ is preferred.

We can repeat the same process for `age` as well. We see there is very clear evidence that a non-linear term is required for `age`.

```
In [38]: gam_0 = LinearGAM(year_term +
                           f_gam(2, lam=0))
         gam_linear = LinearGAM(l_gam(0, lam=0) +
                                year_term +
                                f_gam(2, lam=0))
         gam_0.fit(Xgam, y)
         gam_linear.fit(Xgam, y)
         anova_gam(gam_0, gam_linear, gam_full)
```

```
Out[38]:        deviance        df deviance_diff  df_diff        F  pvalue
         0  3975443.045  2991.001           NaN      NaN      NaN     NaN
         1  3850246.908  2990.001    125196.137    1.000  101.270   0.000
         2  3693142.930  2987.007    157103.978    2.993   42.448   0.000
```

There is a (verbose) `summary()` method for the GAM fit. (We do not reproduce it here.)

```
In [39]: gam_full.summary()
```

We can make predictions from `gam` objects, just like from `lm` objects, using the `predict()` method for the class `gam`. Here we make predictions on the training set.

```
In [40]: Yhat = gam_full.predict(Xgam)
```

In order to fit a logistic regression GAM, we use `LogisticGAM()` from `pygam`.

`LogisticGAM()`

```
In [41]: gam_logit = LogisticGAM(age_term +
                                 l_gam(1, lam=0) +
                                 f_gam(2, lam=0))
         gam_logit.fit(Xgam, high_earn)
```

```
Out[41]: LogisticGAM(callbacks=[Deviance(), Diffs(), Accuracy()],
             fit_intercept=True, max_iter=100,
             terms=s(0) + l(1) + f(2) + intercept, tol=0.0001, verbose=False)
```

```
In [42]: fig, ax = subplots(figsize=(8, 8))
         ax = plot_gam(gam_logit, 2)
         ax.set_xlabel('Education')
         ax.set_ylabel('Effect on wage')
         ax.set_title('Partial dependence of wage on education',
                      fontsize=20);
         ax.set_xticklabels(Wage['education'].cat.categories, fontsize=8);
```

The model seems to be very flat, with especially high error bars for the first category. Let's look at the data a bit more closely.

```
In [43]: pd.crosstab(Wage['high_earn'], Wage['education'])
```

We see that there are no high earners in the first category of education, meaning that the model will have a hard time fitting. We will fit a logistic regression GAM excluding all observations falling into this category. This provides more sensible results.

To do so, we could subset the model matrix, though this will not remove the column from `Xgam`. While we can deduce which column corresponds to this feature, for reproducibility's sake we reform the model matrix on this smaller subset.

```
In [44]: only_hs = Wage['education'] == '1. < HS Grad'
         Wage_ = Wage.loc[~only_hs]
         Xgam_ = np.column_stack([Wage_['age'],
                                  Wage_['year'],
                                  Wage_['education'].cat.codes-1])
         high_earn_ = Wage_['high_earn']
```

In the second-to-last line above, we subtract one from the codes of the category, due to a bug in pygam. It just relabels the education values and hence has no effect on the fit.

We now fit the model.

In [45]:
```
gam_logit_ = LogisticGAM(age_term +
                         year_term +
                         f_gam(2, lam=0))
gam_logit_.fit(Xgam_, high_earn_)
```

Out[45]:
```
LogisticGAM(callbacks=[Deviance(), Diffs(), Accuracy()],
    fit_intercept=True, max_iter=100,
    terms=s(0) + s(1) + f(2) + intercept, tol=0.0001, verbose=False)
```

Let's look at the effect of education, year and age on high earner status now that we've removed those observations.

In [46]:
```
fig, ax = subplots(figsize=(8, 8))
ax = plot_gam(gam_logit_, 2)
ax.set_xlabel('Education')
ax.set_ylabel('Effect on wage')
ax.set_title('Partial dependence of high earner status on education
    ', fontsize=20);
ax.set_xticklabels(Wage['education'].cat.categories[1:],
                   fontsize=8);
```

In [47]:
```
fig, ax = subplots(figsize=(8, 8))
ax = plot_gam(gam_logit_, 1)
ax.set_xlabel('Year')
ax.set_ylabel('Effect on wage')
ax.set_title('Partial dependence of high earner status on year',
             fontsize=20);
```

In [48]:
```
fig, ax = subplots(figsize=(8, 8))
ax = plot_gam(gam_logit_, 0)
ax.set_xlabel('Age')
ax.set_ylabel('Effect on wage')
ax.set_title('Partial dependence of high earner status on age',
    fontsize=20);
```

7.8.4 *Local Regression*

We illustrate the use of local regression using the lowess() function from sm.nonparametric. Some implementations of GAMs allow terms to be local regression operators; this is not the case in pygam.

lowess()

Here we fit local linear regression models using spans of 0.2 and 0.5; that is, each neighborhood consists of 20% or 50% of the observations. As expected, using a span of 0.5 is smoother than 0.2.

In [49]:
```
lowess = sm.nonparametric.lowess
fig, ax = subplots(figsize=(8,8))
ax.scatter(age, y, facecolor='gray', alpha=0.5)
for span in [0.2, 0.5]:
    fitted = lowess(y,
```

```
                    age,
                    frac=span,
                    xvals=age_grid)
    ax.plot(age_grid,
            fitted,
            label='{:.1f}'.format(span),
            linewidth=4)
ax.set_xlabel('Age', fontsize=20)
ax.set_ylabel('Wage', fontsize=20);
ax.legend(title='span', fontsize=15);
```

7.9 Exercises

Conceptual

1. It was mentioned in this chapter that a cubic regression spline with one knot at ξ can be obtained using a basis of the form x, x^2, x^3, $(x-\xi)^3_+$, where $(x-\xi)^3_+ = (x-\xi)^3$ if $x > \xi$ and equals 0 otherwise. We will now show that a function of the form

$$f(x) = \beta_0 + \beta_1 x + \beta_2 x^2 + \beta_3 x^3 + \beta_4 (x-\xi)^3_+$$

is indeed a cubic regression spline, regardless of the values of $\beta_0, \beta_1, \beta_2, \beta_3, \beta_4$.

(a) Find a cubic polynomial

$$f_1(x) = a_1 + b_1 x + c_1 x^2 + d_1 x^3$$

such that $f(x) = f_1(x)$ for all $x \leq \xi$. Express a_1, b_1, c_1, d_1 in terms of $\beta_0, \beta_1, \beta_2, \beta_3, \beta_4$.

(b) Find a cubic polynomial

$$f_2(x) = a_2 + b_2 x + c_2 x^2 + d_2 x^3$$

such that $f(x) = f_2(x)$ for all $x > \xi$. Express a_2, b_2, c_2, d_2 in terms of $\beta_0, \beta_1, \beta_2, \beta_3, \beta_4$. We have now established that $f(x)$ is a piecewise polynomial.

(c) Show that $f_1(\xi) = f_2(\xi)$. That is, $f(x)$ is continuous at ξ.

(d) Show that $f_1'(\xi) = f_2'(\xi)$. That is, $f'(x)$ is continuous at ξ.

(e) Show that $f_1''(\xi) = f_2''(\xi)$. That is, $f''(x)$ is continuous at ξ.

Therefore, $f(x)$ is indeed a cubic spline.

Hint: Parts (d) and (e) of this problem require knowledge of single-variable calculus. As a reminder, given a cubic polynomial

$$f_1(x) = a_1 + b_1 x + c_1 x^2 + d_1 x^3,$$

the first derivative takes the form

$$f_1'(x) = b_1 + 2c_1 x + 3d_1 x^2$$

and the second derivative takes the form

$$f_1''(x) = 2c_1 + 6d_1x.$$

2. Suppose that a curve $\hat{g}$ is computed to smoothly fit a set of n points using the following formula:

$$\hat{g} = \arg\min_g \left(\sum_{i=1}^n (y_i - g(x_i))^2 + \lambda \int \left[g^{(m)}(x) \right]^2 dx \right),$$

where $g^{(m)}$ represents the mth derivative of g (and $g^{(0)} = g$). Provide example sketches of $\hat{g}$ in each of the following scenarios.

(a) $\lambda = \infty, m = 0.$

(b) $\lambda = \infty, m = 1.$

(c) $\lambda = \infty, m = 2.$

(d) $\lambda = \infty, m = 3.$

(e) $\lambda = 0, m = 3.$

3. Suppose we fit a curve with basis functions $b_1(X) = X$, $b_2(X) = (X-1)^2 I(X \geq 1)$. (Note that $I(X \geq 1)$ equals 1 for $X \geq 1$ and 0 otherwise.) We fit the linear regression model

$$Y = \beta_0 + \beta_1 b_1(X) + \beta_2 b_2(X) + \epsilon,$$

and obtain coefficient estimates $\hat{\beta}_0 = 1, \hat{\beta}_1 = 1, \hat{\beta}_2 = -2$. Sketch the estimated curve between $X = -2$ and $X = 2$. Note the intercepts, slopes, and other relevant information.

4. Suppose we fit a curve with basis functions $b_1(X) = I(0 \leq X \leq 2) - (X-1)I(1 \leq X \leq 2)$, $b_2(X) = (X-3)I(3 \leq X \leq 4) + I(4 < X \leq 5)$. We fit the linear regression model

$$Y = \beta_0 + \beta_1 b_1(X) + \beta_2 b_2(X) + \epsilon,$$

and obtain coefficient estimates $\hat{\beta}_0 = 1, \hat{\beta}_1 = 1, \hat{\beta}_2 = 3$. Sketch the estimated curve between $X = -2$ and $X = 6$. Note the intercepts, slopes, and other relevant information.

5. Consider two curves, $\hat{g}_1$ and $\hat{g}_2$, defined by

$$\hat{g}_1 = \arg\min_g \left(\sum_{i=1}^n (y_i - g(x_i))^2 + \lambda \int \left[g^{(3)}(x) \right]^2 dx \right),$$

$$\hat{g}_2 = \arg\min_g \left(\sum_{i=1}^n (y_i - g(x_i))^2 + \lambda \int \left[g^{(4)}(x) \right]^2 dx \right),$$

where $g^{(m)}$ represents the mth derivative of g.

(a) As $\lambda \to \infty$, will $\hat{g}_1$ or $\hat{g}_2$ have the smaller training RSS?

(b) As $\lambda \to \infty$, will $\hat{g}_1$ or $\hat{g}_2$ have the smaller test RSS?

(c) For $\lambda = 0$, will $\hat{g}_1$ or $\hat{g}_2$ have the smaller training and test RSS?

Applied

6. In this exercise, you will further analyze the `Wage` data set considered throughout this chapter.

   (a) Perform polynomial regression to predict `wage` using `age`. Use cross-validation to select the optimal degree d for the polynomial. What degree was chosen, and how does this compare to the results of hypothesis testing using ANOVA? Make a plot of the resulting polynomial fit to the data.

   (b) Fit a step function to predict `wage` using `age`, and perform cross-validation to choose the optimal number of cuts. Make a plot of the fit obtained.

7. The `Wage` data set contains a number of other features not explored in this chapter, such as marital status (`maritl`), job class (`jobclass`), and others. Explore the relationships between some of these other predictors and `wage`, and use non-linear fitting techniques in order to fit flexible models to the data. Create plots of the results obtained, and write a summary of your findings.

8. Fit some of the non-linear models investigated in this chapter to the `Auto` data set. Is there evidence for non-linear relationships in this data set? Create some informative plots to justify your answer.

9. This question uses the variables `dis` (the weighted mean of distances to five Boston employment centers) and `nox` (nitrogen oxides concentration in parts per 10 million) from the `Boston` data. We will treat `dis` as the predictor and `nox` as the response.

   (a) Use the `poly()` function from the `ISLP.models` module to fit a cubic polynomial regression to predict `nox` using `dis`. Report the regression output, and plot the resulting data and polynomial fits.

   (b) Plot the polynomial fits for a range of different polynomial degrees (say, from 1 to 10), and report the associated residual sum of squares.

   (c) Perform cross-validation or another approach to select the optimal degree for the polynomial, and explain your results.

   (d) Use the `bs()` function from the `ISLP.models` module to fit a regression spline to predict `nox` using `dis`. Report the output for the fit using four degrees of freedom. How did you choose the knots? Plot the resulting fit.

   (e) Now fit a regression spline for a range of degrees of freedom, and plot the resulting fits and report the resulting RSS. Describe the results obtained.

   (f) Perform cross-validation or another approach in order to select the best degrees of freedom for a regression spline on this data. Describe your results.

10. This question relates to the `College` data set.

    (a) Split the data into a training set and a test set. Using out-of-state tuition as the response and the other variables as the predictors, perform forward stepwise selection on the training set in order to identify a satisfactory model that uses just a subset of the predictors.

    (b) Fit a GAM on the training data, using out-of-state tuition as the response and the features selected in the previous step as the predictors. Plot the results, and explain your findings.

    (c) Evaluate the model obtained on the test set, and explain the results obtained.

    (d) For which variables, if any, is there evidence of a non-linear relationship with the response?

11. In Section 7.7, it was mentioned that GAMs are generally fit using a *backfitting* approach. The idea behind backfitting is actually quite simple. We will now explore backfitting in the context of multiple linear regression.

    Suppose that we would like to perform multiple linear regression, but we do not have software to do so. Instead, we only have software to perform simple linear regression. Therefore, we take the following iterative approach: we repeatedly hold all but one coefficient estimate fixed at its current value, and update only that coefficient estimate using a simple linear regression. The process is continued until *convergence*—that is, until the coefficient estimates stop changing.

    We now try this out on a toy example.

    (a) Generate a response Y and two predictors X_1 and X_2, with $n = 100$.

    (b) Write a function `simple_reg()` that takes two arguments `outcome` and `feature`, fits a simple linear regression model with this outcome and feature, and returns the estimated intercept and slope.

    (c) Initialize `beta1` to take on a value of your choice. It does not matter what value you choose.

    (d) Keeping `beta1` fixed, use your function `simple_reg()` to fit the model:

    $$Y - \texttt{beta1} \cdot X_1 = \beta_0 + \beta_2 X_2 + \epsilon.$$

    Store the resulting values as `beta0` and `beta2`.

    (e) Keeping `beta2` fixed, fit the model

    $$Y - \texttt{beta2} \cdot X_2 = \beta_0 + \beta_1 X_1 + \epsilon.$$

    Store the result as `beta0` and `beta1` (overwriting their previous values).

    (f) Write a for loop to repeat (c) and (d) 1,000 times. Report the estimates of `beta0`, `beta1`, and `beta2` at each iteration of the for loop. Create a plot in which each of these values is displayed, with `beta0`, `beta1`, and `beta2`.

(g) Compare your answer in (e) to the results of simply performing multiple linear regression to predict Y using X_1 and X_2. Use `axline()` method to overlay those multiple linear regression coefficient estimates on the plot obtained in (e).

(h) On this data set, how many backfitting iterations were required in order to obtain a "good" approximation to the multiple regression coefficient estimates?

12. This problem is a continuation of the previous exercise. In a toy example with $p = 100$, show that one can approximate the multiple linear regression coefficient estimates by repeatedly performing simple linear regression in a backfitting procedure. How many backfitting iterations are required in order to obtain a "good" approximation to the multiple regression coefficient estimates? Create a plot to justify your answer.

8 Tree-Based Methods

In this chapter, we describe *tree-based* methods for regression and classification. These involve *stratifying* or *segmenting* the predictor space into a number of simple regions. In order to make a prediction for a given observation, we typically use the mean or the mode response value for the training observations in the region to which it belongs. Since the set of splitting rules used to segment the predictor space can be summarized in a tree, these types of approaches are known as *decision tree* methods.

decision tree

Tree-based methods are simple and useful for interpretation. However, they typically are not competitive with the best supervised learning approaches, such as those seen in Chapters 6 and 7, in terms of prediction accuracy. Hence in this chapter we also introduce *bagging*, *random forests*, *boosting*, and *Bayesian additive regression trees*. Each of these approaches involves producing multiple trees which are then combined to yield a single consensus prediction. We will see that combining a large number of trees can often result in dramatic improvements in prediction accuracy, at the expense of some loss in interpretation.

8.1 The Basics of Decision Trees

Decision trees can be applied to both regression and classification problems. We first consider regression problems, and then move on to classification.

8.1.1 Regression Trees

In order to motivate *regression trees*, we begin with a simple example.

regression tree

G. James et al., *An Introduction to Statistical Learning*, Springer Texts in Statistics,
https://doi.org/10.1007/978-3-031-38747-0_8

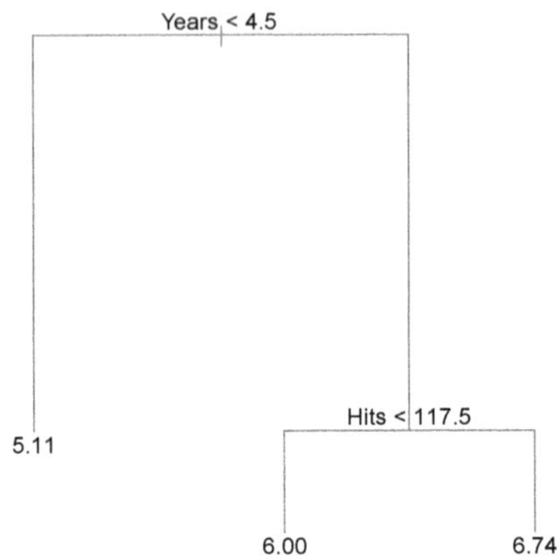

FIGURE 8.1. *For the* Hitters *data, a regression tree for predicting the log salary of a baseball player, based on the number of years that he has played in the major leagues and the number of hits that he made in the previous year. At a given internal node, the label (of the form $X_j < t_k$) indicates the left-hand branch emanating from that split, and the right-hand branch corresponds to $X_j \geq t_k$. For instance, the split at the top of the tree results in two large branches. The left-hand branch corresponds to* Years<4.5, *and the right-hand branch corresponds to* Years>=4.5. *The tree has two internal nodes and three terminal nodes, or leaves. The number in each leaf is the mean of the response for the observations that fall there.*

Predicting Baseball Players' Salaries Using Regression Trees

We use the `Hitters` data set to predict a baseball player's `Salary` based on `Years` (the number of years that he has played in the major leagues) and `Hits` (the number of hits that he made in the previous year). We first remove observations that are missing `Salary` values, and log-transform `Salary` so that its distribution has more of a typical bell-shape. (Recall that `Salary` is measured in thousands of dollars.)

Figure 8.1 shows a regression tree fit to this data. It consists of a series of splitting rules, starting at the top of the tree. The top split assigns observations having `Years<4.5` to the left branch.[1] The predicted salary for these players is given by the mean response value for the players in the data set with `Years<4.5`. For such players, the mean log salary is 5.107, and so we make a prediction of $e^{5.107}$ thousands of dollars, i.e. $165,174, for these players. Players with `Years>=4.5` are assigned to the right branch, and then that group is further subdivided by `Hits`. Overall, the tree stratifies or segments the players into three regions of predictor space: players who have played for four or fewer years, players who have played for five or more years and who made fewer than 118 hits last year, and players who have played for five or more years and who made at least 118 hits last year. These three regions can be written as R_1 ={X | `Years<4.5`}, R_2 ={X | `Years>=4.5`, `Hits<117.5`}, and R_3 ={X | `Years>=4.5`, `Hits>=117.5`}. Figure 8.2 illustrates

[1]Both `Years` and `Hits` are integers in these data; the function used to fit this tree labels the splits at the midpoint between two adjacent values.

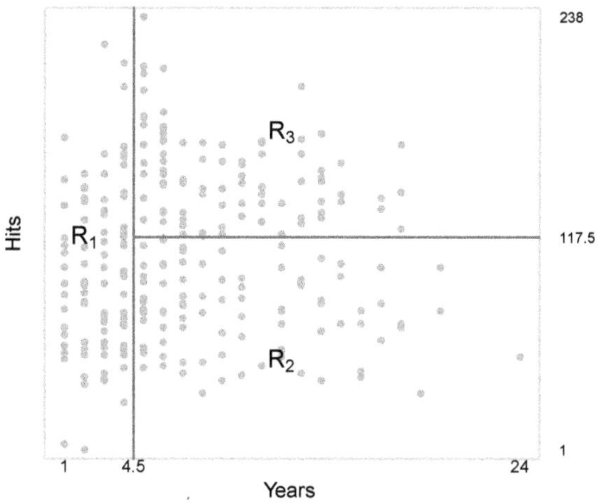

FIGURE 8.2. *The three-region partition for the* `Hitters` *data set from the regression tree illustrated in Figure 8.1.*

the regions as a function of `Years` and `Hits`. The predicted salaries for these three groups are $1,000×$e^{5.107}$ =$165,174, $1,000×$e^{5.999}$ =$402,834, and $1,000×$e^{6.740}$ =$845,346 respectively.

In keeping with the *tree* analogy, the regions R_1, R_2, and R_3 are known as *terminal nodes* or *leaves* of the tree. As is the case for Figure 8.1, decision trees are typically drawn *upside down*, in the sense that the leaves are at the bottom of the tree. The points along the tree where the predictor space is split are referred to as *internal nodes*. In Figure 8.1, the two internal nodes are indicated by the text `Years<4.5` and `Hits<117.5`. We refer to the segments of the trees that connect the nodes as *branches*.

terminal node

leaf

internal node

branch

We might interpret the regression tree displayed in Figure 8.1 as follows: `Years` is the most important factor in determining `Salary`, and players with less experience earn lower salaries than more experienced players. Given that a player is less experienced, the number of hits that he made in the previous year seems to play little role in his salary. But among players who have been in the major leagues for five or more years, the number of hits made in the previous year does affect salary, and players who made more hits last year tend to have higher salaries. The regression tree shown in Figure 8.1 is likely an over-simplification of the true relationship between `Hits`, `Years`, and `Salary`. However, it has advantages over other types of regression models (such as those seen in Chapters 3 and 6): it is easier to interpret, and has a nice graphical representation.

Prediction via Stratification of the Feature Space

We now discuss the process of building a regression tree. Roughly speaking, there are two steps.

1. We divide the predictor space — that is, the set of possible values for $X_1, X_2, \ldots, X_p$ — into J distinct and non-overlapping regions, $R_1, R_2, \ldots, R_J$.

2. For every observation that falls into the region R_j, we make the same prediction, which is simply the mean of the response values for the training observations in R_j.

For instance, suppose that in Step 1 we obtain two regions, R_1 and R_2, and that the response mean of the training observations in the first region is 10, while the response mean of the training observations in the second region is 20. Then for a given observation $X = x$, if $x \in R_1$ we will predict a value of 10, and if $x \in R_2$ we will predict a value of 20.

We now elaborate on Step 1 above. How do we construct the regions $R_1, \ldots, R_J$? In theory, the regions could have any shape. However, we choose to divide the predictor space into high-dimensional rectangles, or *boxes*, for simplicity and for ease of interpretation of the resulting predictive model. The goal is to find boxes $R_1, \ldots, R_J$ that minimize the RSS, given by

$$\sum_{j=1}^{J} \sum_{i \in R_j} (y_i - \hat{y}_{R_j})^2, \tag{8.1}$$

where $\hat{y}_{R_j}$ is the mean response for the training observations within the jth box. Unfortunately, it is computationally infeasible to consider every possible partition of the feature space into J boxes. For this reason, we take a *top-down*, *greedy* approach that is known as *recursive binary splitting*. The approach is *top-down* because it begins at the top of the tree (at which point all observations belong to a single region) and then successively splits the predictor space; each split is indicated via two new branches further down on the tree. It is *greedy* because at each step of the tree-building process, the *best* split is made at that particular step, rather than looking ahead and picking a split that will lead to a better tree in some future step.

recursive binary splitting

In order to perform recursive binary splitting, we first select the predictor X_j and the cutpoint s such that splitting the predictor space into the regions $\{X|X_j < s\}$ and $\{X|X_j \geq s\}$ leads to the greatest possible reduction in RSS. (The notation $\{X|X_j < s\}$ means *the region of predictor space in which X_j takes on a value less than s*.) That is, we consider all predictors $X_1, \ldots, X_p$, and all possible values of the cutpoint s for each of the predictors, and then choose the predictor and cutpoint such that the resulting tree has the lowest RSS. In greater detail, for any j and s, we define the pair of half-planes

$$R_1(j, s) = \{X|X_j < s\} \text{ and } R_2(j, s) = \{X|X_j \geq s\}, \tag{8.2}$$

and we seek the value of j and s that minimize the equation

$$\sum_{i:\, x_i \in R_1(j,s)} (y_i - \hat{y}_{R_1})^2 + \sum_{i:\, x_i \in R_2(j,s)} (y_i - \hat{y}_{R_2})^2, \tag{8.3}$$

where $\hat{y}_{R_1}$ is the mean response for the training observations in $R_1(j, s)$, and $\hat{y}_{R_2}$ is the mean response for the training observations in $R_2(j, s)$. Finding the values of j and s that minimize (8.3) can be done quite quickly, especially when the number of features p is not too large.

Next, we repeat the process, looking for the best predictor and best cutpoint in order to split the data further so as to minimize the RSS within

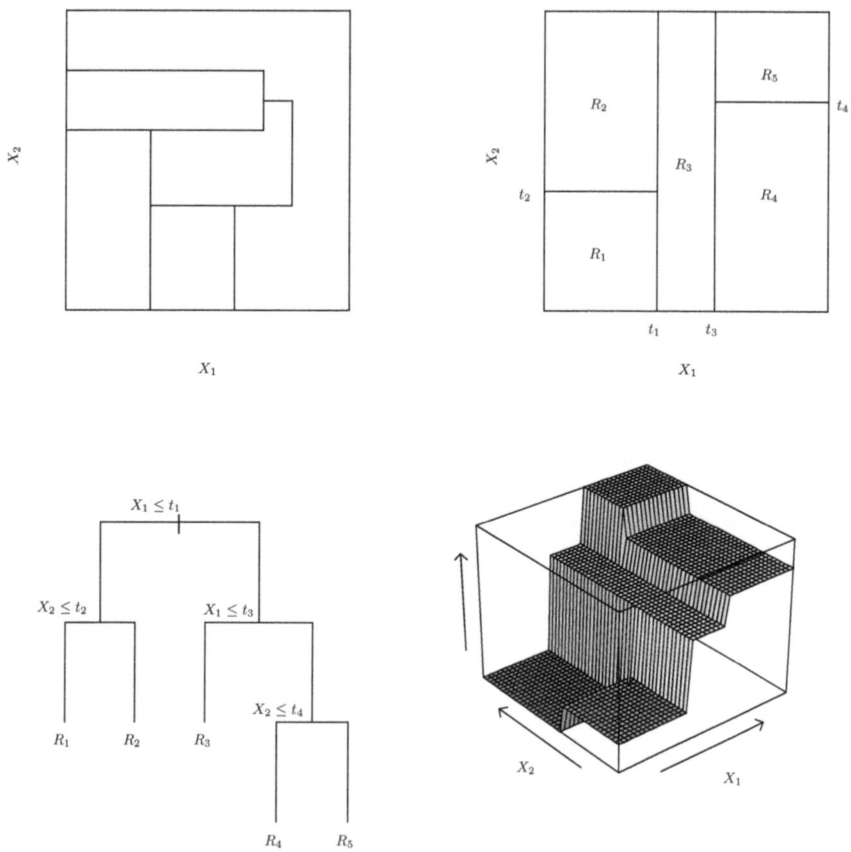

FIGURE 8.3. Top Left: *A partition of two-dimensional feature space that could not result from recursive binary splitting.* Top Right: *The output of recursive binary splitting on a two-dimensional example.* Bottom Left: *A tree corresponding to the partition in the top right panel.* Bottom Right: *A perspective plot of the prediction surface corresponding to that tree.*

each of the resulting regions. However, this time, instead of splitting the entire predictor space, we split one of the two previously identified regions. We now have three regions. Again, we look to split one of these three regions further, so as to minimize the RSS. The process continues until a stopping criterion is reached; for instance, we may continue until no region contains more than five observations.

Once the regions $R_1, \ldots, R_J$ have been created, we predict the response for a given test observation using the mean of the training observations in the region to which that test observation belongs.

A five-region example of this approach is shown in Figure 8.3.

Tree Pruning

The process described above may produce good predictions on the training set, but is likely to overfit the data, leading to poor test set performance. This is because the resulting tree might be too complex. A smaller tree with fewer splits (that is, fewer regions $R_1, \ldots, R_J$) might lead to lower variance and better interpretation at the cost of a little bias. One possible alternative to the process described above is to build the tree only so long as the decrease in the RSS due to each split exceeds some (high) threshold. This strategy will result in smaller trees, but is too short-sighted since a seemingly worthless split early on in the tree might be followed by a very good split—that is, a split that leads to a large reduction in RSS later on.

Therefore, a better strategy is to grow a very large tree T_0, and then *prune* it back in order to obtain a *subtree*. How do we determine the best way to prune the tree? Intuitively, our goal is to select a subtree that leads to the lowest test error rate. Given a subtree, we can estimate its test error using cross-validation or the validation set approach. However, estimating the cross-validation error for every possible subtree would be too cumbersome, since there is an extremely large number of possible subtrees. Instead, we need a way to select a small set of subtrees for consideration.

prune

subtree

Cost complexity pruning—also known as *weakest link pruning*—gives us a way to do just this. Rather than considering every possible subtree, we consider a sequence of trees indexed by a nonnegative tuning parameter α. For each value of α there corresponds a subtree $T \subset T_0$ such that

cost complexity pruning

weakest link pruning

$$\sum_{m=1}^{|T|} \sum_{i:\, x_i \in R_m} (y_i - \hat{y}_{R_m})^2 + \alpha|T| \tag{8.4}$$

is as small as possible. Here $|T|$ indicates the number of terminal nodes of the tree T, R_m is the rectangle (i.e. the subset of predictor space) corresponding to the mth terminal node, and $\hat{y}_{R_m}$ is the predicted response associated with R_m—that is, the mean of the training observations in R_m. The tuning parameter α controls a trade-off between the subtree's complexity and its fit to the training data. When $\alpha = 0$, then the subtree T will simply equal T_0, because then (8.4) just measures the training error. However, as α increases, there is a price to pay for having a tree with many terminal nodes, and so the quantity (8.4) will tend to be minimized for a smaller subtree. Equation 8.4 is reminiscent of the lasso (6.7) from Chapter 6, in which a similar formulation was used in order to control the complexity of a linear model.

It turns out that as we increase α from zero in (8.4), branches get pruned from the tree in a nested and predictable fashion, so obtaining the whole sequence of subtrees as a function of α is easy. We can select a value of α using a validation set or using cross-validation. We then return to the full data set and obtain the subtree corresponding to α. This process is summarized in Algorithm 8.1.

Figures 8.4 and 8.5 display the results of fitting and pruning a regression tree on the `Hitters` data, using nine of the features. First, we randomly divided the data set in half, yielding 132 observations in the training set and 131 observations in the test set. We then built a large regression tree on the training data and varied α in (8.4) in order to create subtrees with different numbers of terminal nodes. Finally, we performed six-fold cross-validation in order to estimate the cross-validated MSE of the trees as

Algorithm 8.1 *Building a Regression Tree*

1. Use recursive binary splitting to grow a large tree on the training data, stopping only when each terminal node has fewer than some minimum number of observations.

2. Apply cost complexity pruning to the large tree in order to obtain a sequence of best subtrees, as a function of α.

3. Use K-fold cross-validation to choose α. That is, divide the training observations into K folds. For each $k = 1, \ldots, K$:

   (a) Repeat Steps 1 and 2 on all but the kth fold of the training data.

   (b) Evaluate the mean squared prediction error on the data in the left-out kth fold, as a function of α.

   Average the results for each value of α, and pick α to minimize the average error.

4. Return the subtree from Step 2 that corresponds to the chosen value of α.

a function of α. (We chose to perform six-fold cross-validation because 132 is an exact multiple of six.) The unpruned regression tree is shown in Figure 8.4. The green curve in Figure 8.5 shows the CV error as a function of the number of leaves,[2] while the orange curve indicates the test error. Also shown are standard error bars around the estimated errors. For reference, the training error curve is shown in black. The CV error is a reasonable approximation of the test error: the CV error takes on its minimum for a three-node tree, while the test error also dips down at the three-node tree (though it takes on its lowest value at the ten-node tree). The pruned tree containing three terminal nodes is shown in Figure 8.1.

8.1.2 Classification Trees

A *classification tree* is very similar to a regression tree, except that it is used to predict a qualitative response rather than a quantitative one. Recall that for a regression tree, the predicted response for an observation is given by the mean response of the training observations that belong to the same terminal node. In contrast, for a classification tree, we predict that each observation belongs to the *most commonly occurring class* of training observations in the region to which it belongs. In interpreting the results of a classification tree, we are often interested not only in the class prediction corresponding to a particular terminal node region, but also in the *class proportions* among the training observations that fall into that region.

classification tree

The task of growing a classification tree is quite similar to the task of growing a regression tree. Just as in the regression setting, we use recursive

[2]Although CV error is computed as a function of α, it is convenient to display the result as a function of $|T|$, the number of leaves; this is based on the relationship between α and $|T|$ in the original tree grown to all the training data.

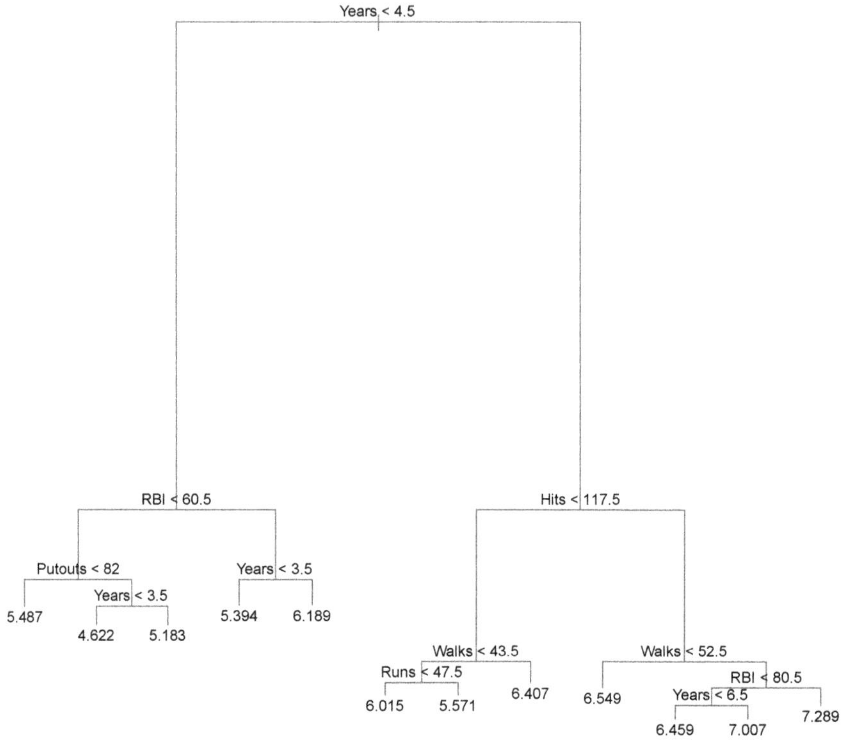

FIGURE 8.4. *Regression tree analysis for the* `Hitters` *data. The unpruned tree that results from top-down greedy splitting on the training data is shown.*

binary splitting to grow a classification tree. However, in the classification setting, RSS cannot be used as a criterion for making the binary splits. A natural alternative to RSS is the *classification error rate*. Since we plan to assign an observation in a given region to the *most commonly occurring class* of training observations in that region, the classification error rate is simply the fraction of the training observations in that region that do not belong to the most common class: classification error rate

$$E = 1 - \max_k(\hat{p}_{mk}). \tag{8.5}$$

Here $\hat{p}_{mk}$ represents the proportion of training observations in the mth region that are from the kth class. However, it turns out that classification error is not sufficiently sensitive for tree-growing, and in practice two other measures are preferable.

The *Gini index* is defined by Gini index

$$G = \sum_{k=1}^{K} \hat{p}_{mk}(1 - \hat{p}_{mk}), \tag{8.6}$$

a measure of total variance across the K classes. It is not hard to see that the Gini index takes on a small value if all of the $\hat{p}_{mk}$'s are close to zero or one. For this reason the Gini index is referred to as a measure of

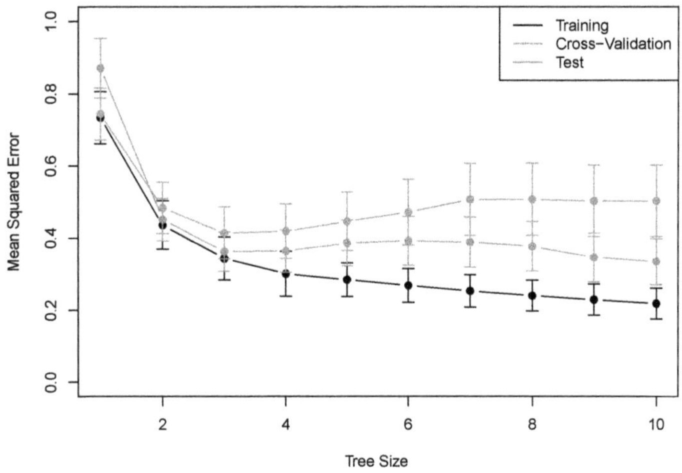

FIGURE 8.5. *Regression tree analysis for the* `Hitters` *data. The training, cross-validation, and test MSE are shown as a function of the number of terminal nodes in the pruned tree. Standard error bands are displayed. The minimum cross-validation error occurs at a tree size of three.*

node *purity*—a small value indicates that a node contains predominantly observations from a single class.

An alternative to the Gini index is *entropy*, given by entropy

$$D = -\sum_{k=1}^{K} \hat{p}_{mk} \log \hat{p}_{mk}. \tag{8.7}$$

Since $0 \leq \hat{p}_{mk} \leq 1$, it follows that $0 \leq -\hat{p}_{mk} \log \hat{p}_{mk}$. One can show that the entropy will take on a value near zero if the $\hat{p}_{mk}$'s are all near zero or near one. Therefore, like the Gini index, the entropy will take on a small value if the mth node is pure. In fact, it turns out that the Gini index and the entropy are quite similar numerically.

When building a classification tree, either the Gini index or the entropy are typically used to evaluate the quality of a particular split, since these two approaches are more sensitive to node purity than is the classification error rate. Any of these three approaches might be used when *pruning* the tree, but the classification error rate is preferable if prediction accuracy of the final pruned tree is the goal.

Figure 8.6 shows an example on the `Heart` data set. These data contain a binary outcome `HD` for 303 patients who presented with chest pain. An outcome value of `Yes` indicates the presence of heart disease based on an angiographic test, while `No` means no heart disease. There are 13 predictors including `Age`, `Sex`, `Chol` (a cholesterol measurement), and other heart and lung function measurements. Cross-validation results in a tree with six terminal nodes.

In our discussion thus far, we have assumed that the predictor variables take on continuous values. However, decision trees can be constructed even in the presence of qualitative predictor variables. For instance, in the `Heart` data, some of the predictors, such as `Sex`, `Thal` (Thallium stress test),

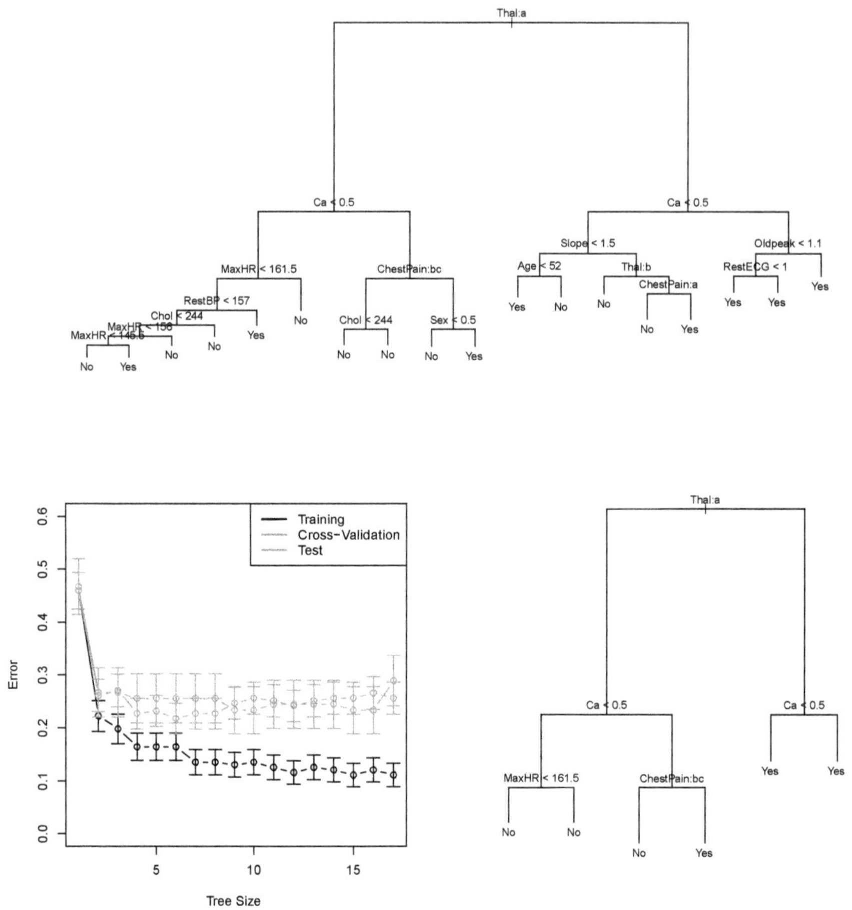

FIGURE 8.6. `Heart` *data.* Top: *The unpruned tree.* Bottom Left: *Cross-validation error, training, and test error, for different sizes of the pruned tree.* Bottom Right: *The pruned tree corresponding to the minimal cross-validation error.*

and `ChestPain`, are qualitative. Therefore, a split on one of these variables amounts to assigning some of the qualitative values to one branch and assigning the remaining to the other branch. In Figure 8.6, some of the internal nodes correspond to splitting qualitative variables. For instance, the top internal node corresponds to splitting `Thal`. The text `Thal:a` indicates that the left-hand branch coming out of that node consists of observations with the first value of the `Thal` variable (normal), and the right-hand node consists of the remaining observations (fixed or reversible defects). The text `ChestPain:bc` two splits down the tree on the left indicates that the left-hand branch coming out of that node consists of observations with the second and third values of the `ChestPain` variable, where the possible values are typical angina, atypical angina, non-anginal pain, and asymptomatic.

Figure 8.6 has a surprising characteristic: some of the splits yield two terminal nodes that have the *same predicted value.* For instance, consider the split `RestECG<1` near the bottom right of the unpruned tree. Regardless of the value of `RestECG`, a response value of `Yes` is predicted for those observations. Why, then, is the split performed at all? The split is performed because it leads to increased *node purity*. That is, all 9 of the observations corresponding to the right-hand leaf have a response value of `Yes`, whereas 7/11 of those corresponding to the left-hand leaf have a response value of `Yes`. Why is node purity important? Suppose that we have a test observation that belongs to the region given by that right-hand leaf. Then we can be pretty certain that its response value is `Yes`. In contrast, if a test observation belongs to the region given by the left-hand leaf, then its response value is probably `Yes`, but we are much less certain. Even though the split `RestECG<1` does not reduce the classification error, it improves the Gini index and the entropy, which are more sensitive to node purity.

8.1.3 Trees Versus Linear Models

Regression and classification trees have a very different flavor from the more classical approaches for regression and classification presented in Chapters 3 and 4. In particular, linear regression assumes a model of the form

$$f(X) = \beta_0 + \sum_{j=1}^{p} X_j \beta_j, \tag{8.8}$$

whereas regression trees assume a model of the form

$$f(X) = \sum_{m=1}^{M} c_m \cdot 1_{(X \in R_m)} \tag{8.9}$$

where $R_1, \ldots, R_M$ represent a partition of feature space, as in Figure 8.3.

Which model is better? It depends on the problem at hand. If the relationship between the features and the response is well approximated by a linear model as in (8.8), then an approach such as linear regression will likely work well, and will outperform a method such as a regression tree that does not exploit this linear structure. If instead there is a highly nonlinear and complex relationship between the features and the response as indicated by model (8.9), then decision trees may outperform classical approaches. An illustrative example is displayed in Figure 8.7. The relative performances of tree-based and classical approaches can be assessed by estimating the test error, using either cross-validation or the validation set approach (Chapter 5).

Of course, other considerations beyond simply test error may come into play in selecting a statistical learning method; for instance, in certain settings, prediction using a tree may be preferred for the sake of interpretability and visualization.

8.1.4 Advantages and Disadvantages of Trees

Decision trees for regression and classification have a number of advantages over the more classical approaches seen in Chapters 3 and 4:

- Trees are very easy to explain to people. In fact, they are even easier to explain than linear regression!

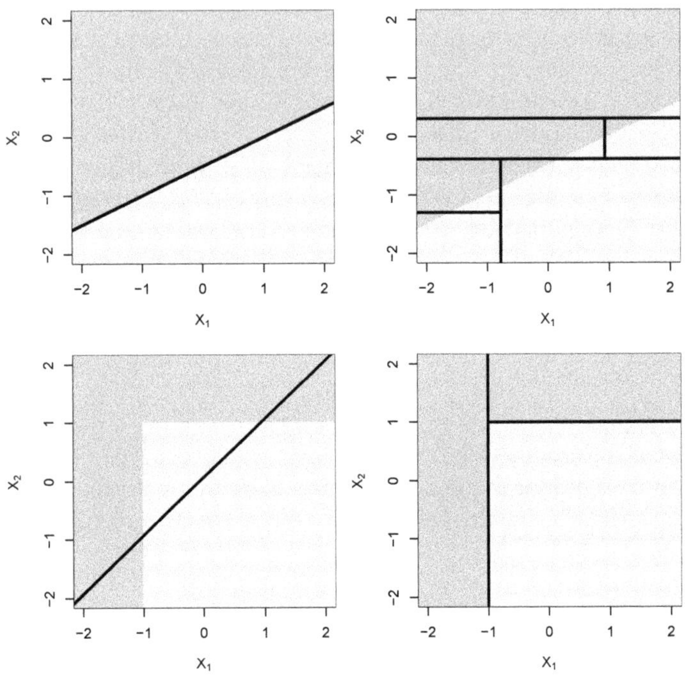

FIGURE 8.7. Top Row: *A two-dimensional classification example in which the true decision boundary is linear, and is indicated by the shaded regions. A classical approach that assumes a linear boundary (left) will outperform a decision tree that performs splits parallel to the axes (right).* Bottom Row: *Here the true decision boundary is non-linear. Here a linear model is unable to capture the true decision boundary (left), whereas a decision tree is successful (right).*

- ▲ Some people believe that decision trees more closely mirror human decision-making than do the regression and classification approaches seen in previous chapters.

- ▲ Trees can be displayed graphically, and are easily interpreted even by a non-expert (especially if they are small).

- ▲ Trees can easily handle qualitative predictors without the need to create dummy variables.

- ▼ Unfortunately, trees generally do not have the same level of predictive accuracy as some of the other regression and classification approaches seen in this book.

- ▼ Additionally, trees can be very non-robust. In other words, a small change in the data can cause a large change in the final estimated tree.

However, by aggregating many decision trees, using methods like *bagging*, *random forests*, and *boosting*, the predictive performance of trees can be substantially improved. We introduce these concepts in the next section.

8.2 Bagging, Random Forests, Boosting, and Bayesian Additive Regression Trees

An *ensemble* method is an approach that combines many simple "building block" models in order to obtain a single and potentially very powerful model. These simple building block models are sometimes known as *weak learners*, since they may lead to mediocre predictions on their own. ensemble

We will now discuss bagging, random forests, boosting, and Bayesian additive regression trees. These are ensemble methods for which the simple building block is a regression or a classification tree. weak learners

8.2.1 Bagging

The bootstrap, introduced in Chapter 5, is an extremely powerful idea. It is used in many situations in which it is hard or even impossible to directly compute the standard deviation of a quantity of interest. We see here that the bootstrap can be used in a completely different context, in order to improve statistical learning methods such as decision trees.

The decision trees discussed in Section 8.1 suffer from *high variance.* This means that if we split the training data into two parts at random, and fit a decision tree to both halves, the results that we get could be quite different. In contrast, a procedure with *low variance* will yield similar results if applied repeatedly to distinct data sets; linear regression tends to have low variance, if the ratio of n to p is moderately large. *Bootstrap aggregation*, or *bagging*, is a general-purpose procedure for reducing the variance of a statistical learning method; we introduce it here because it is particularly useful and frequently used in the context of decision trees. bagging

Recall that given a set of n independent observations $Z_1, \ldots, Z_n$, each with variance σ^2, the variance of the mean $\bar{Z}$ of the observations is given by σ^2/n. In other words, *averaging a set of observations reduces variance.* Hence a natural way to reduce the variance and increase the test set accuracy of a statistical learning method is to take many training sets from the population, build a separate prediction model using each training set, and average the resulting predictions. In other words, we could calculate $\hat{f}^1(x), \hat{f}^2(x), \ldots, \hat{f}^B(x)$ using B separate training sets, and average them in order to obtain a single low-variance statistical learning model, given by

$$\hat{f}_{\text{avg}}(x) = \frac{1}{B}\sum_{b=1}^{B}\hat{f}^b(x).$$

Of course, this is not practical because we generally do not have access to multiple training sets. Instead, we can bootstrap, by taking repeated samples from the (single) training data set. In this approach we generate B different bootstrapped training data sets. We then train our method on the bth bootstrapped training set in order to get $\hat{f}^{*b}(x)$, and finally average all the predictions, to obtain

$$\hat{f}_{\text{bag}}(x) = \frac{1}{B}\sum_{b=1}^{B}\hat{f}^{*b}(x).$$

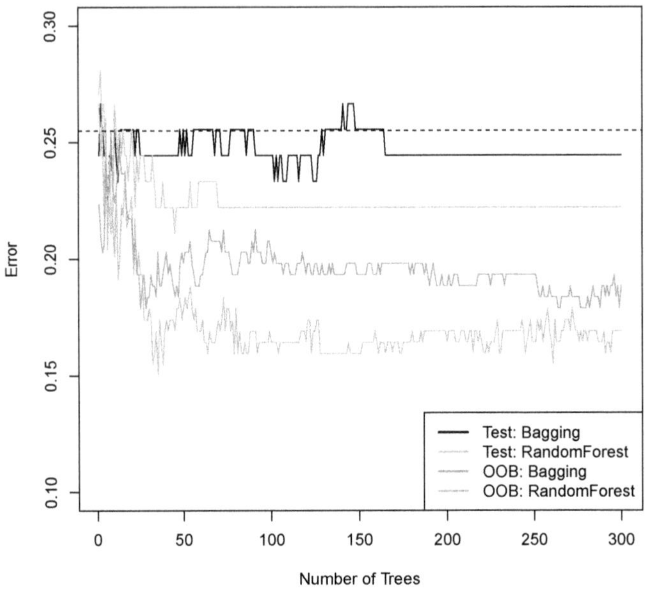

FIGURE 8.8. *Bagging and random forest results for the* Heart *data. The test error (black and orange) is shown as a function of B, the number of bootstrapped training sets used. Random forests were applied with $m = \sqrt{p}$. The dashed line indicates the test error resulting from a single classification tree. The green and blue traces show the OOB error, which in this case is — by chance — considerably lower.*

This is called bagging.

While bagging can improve predictions for many regression methods, it is particularly useful for decision trees. To apply bagging to regression trees, we simply construct B regression trees using B bootstrapped training sets, and average the resulting predictions. These trees are grown deep, and are not pruned. Hence each individual tree has high variance, but low bias. Averaging these B trees reduces the variance. Bagging has been demonstrated to give impressive improvements in accuracy by combining together hundreds or even thousands of trees into a single procedure.

Thus far, we have described the bagging procedure in the regression context, to predict a quantitative outcome Y. How can bagging be extended to a classification problem where Y is qualitative? In that situation, there are a few possible approaches, but the simplest is as follows. For a given test observation, we can record the class predicted by each of the B trees, and take a *majority vote*: the overall prediction is the most commonly occurring class among the B predictions. majority vote

Figure 8.8 shows the results from bagging trees on the Heart data. The test error rate is shown as a function of B, the number of trees constructed using bootstrapped training data sets. We see that the bagging test error rate is slightly lower in this case than the test error rate obtained from a single tree. The number of trees B is not a critical parameter with bagging; using a very large value of B will not lead to overfitting. In practice we use a value of B sufficiently large that the error has settled down. Using $B = 100$ is sufficient to achieve good performance in this example.

Out-of-Bag Error Estimation

It turns out that there is a very straightforward way to estimate the test error of a bagged model, without the need to perform cross-validation or the validation set approach. Recall that the key to bagging is that trees are repeatedly fit to bootstrapped subsets of the observations. One can show that on average, each bagged tree makes use of around two-thirds of the observations.[3] The remaining one-third of the observations not used to fit a given bagged tree are referred to as the *out-of-bag* (OOB) observations. We can predict the response for the ith observation using each of the trees in which that observation was OOB. This will yield around $B/3$ predictions for the ith observation. In order to obtain a single prediction for the ith observation, we can average these predicted responses (if regression is the goal) or can take a majority vote (if classification is the goal). This leads to a single OOB prediction for the ith observation. An OOB prediction can be obtained in this way for each of the n observations, from which the overall OOB MSE (for a regression problem) or classification error (for a classification problem) can be computed. The resulting OOB error is a valid estimate of the test error for the bagged model, since the response for each observation is predicted using only the trees that were not fit using that observation. Figure 8.8 displays the OOB error on the `Heart` data. It can be shown that with B sufficiently large, OOB error is virtually equivalent to leave-one-out cross-validation error. The OOB approach for estimating the test error is particularly convenient when performing bagging on large data sets for which cross-validation would be computationally onerous.

out-of-bag

Variable Importance Measures

As we have discussed, bagging typically results in improved accuracy over prediction using a single tree. Unfortunately, however, it can be difficult to interpret the resulting model. Recall that one of the advantages of decision trees is the attractive and easily interpreted diagram that results, such as the one displayed in Figure 8.1. However, when we bag a large number of trees, it is no longer possible to represent the resulting statistical learning procedure using a single tree, and it is no longer clear which variables are most important to the procedure. Thus, bagging improves prediction accuracy at the expense of interpretability.

Although the collection of bagged trees is much more difficult to interpret than a single tree, one can obtain an overall summary of the importance of each predictor using the RSS (for bagging regression trees) or the Gini index (for bagging classification trees). In the case of bagging regression trees, we can record the total amount that the RSS (8.1) is decreased due to splits over a given predictor, averaged over all B trees. A large value indicates an important predictor. Similarly, in the context of bagging classification

[3]This relates to Exercise 2 of Chapter 5.

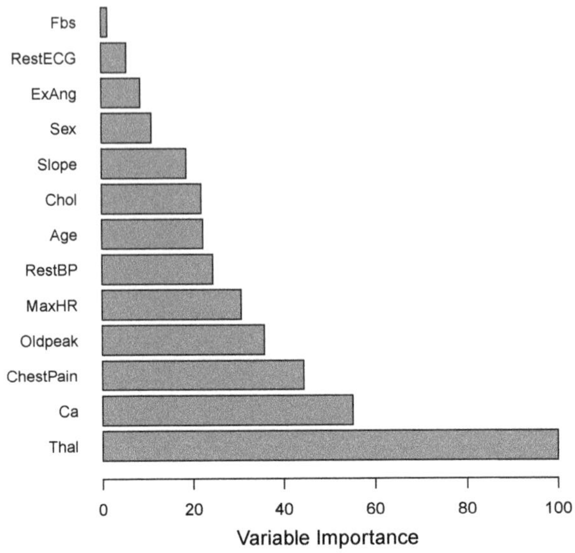

FIGURE 8.9. *A variable importance plot for the* Heart *data. Variable importance is computed using the mean decrease in Gini index, and expressed relative to the maximum.*

trees, we can add up the total amount that the Gini index (8.6) is decreased by splits over a given predictor, averaged over all B trees.

A graphical representation of the *variable importances* in the Heart data is shown in Figure 8.9. We see the mean decrease in Gini index for each variable, relative to the largest. The variables with the largest mean decrease in Gini index are Thal, Ca, and ChestPain. variable importance

8.2.2 Random Forests

Random forests provide an improvement over bagged trees by way of a small tweak that *decorrelates* the trees. As in bagging, we build a number of decision trees on bootstrapped training samples. But when building these decision trees, each time a split in a tree is considered, *a random sample of m predictors* is chosen as split candidates from the full set of p predictors. The split is allowed to use only one of those m predictors. A fresh sample of m predictors is taken at each split, and typically we choose $m \approx \sqrt{p}$—that is, the number of predictors considered at each split is approximately equal to the square root of the total number of predictors (4 out of the 13 for the Heart data). random forest

In other words, in building a random forest, at each split in the tree, the algorithm is *not even allowed to consider* a majority of the available predictors. This may sound crazy, but it has a clever rationale. Suppose that there is one very strong predictor in the data set, along with a number of other moderately strong predictors. Then in the collection of bagged trees, most or all of the trees will use this strong predictor in the top split. Consequently, all of the bagged trees will look quite similar to each other.

Hence the predictions from the bagged trees will be highly correlated. Unfortunately, averaging many highly correlated quantities does not lead to as large of a reduction in variance as averaging many uncorrelated quantities. In particular, this means that bagging will not lead to a substantial reduction in variance over a single tree in this setting.

Random forests overcome this problem by forcing each split to consider only a subset of the predictors. Therefore, on average $(p - m)/p$ of the splits will not even consider the strong predictor, and so other predictors will have more of a chance. We can think of this process as *decorrelating* the trees, thereby making the average of the resulting trees less variable and hence more reliable.

The main difference between bagging and random forests is the choice of predictor subset size m. For instance, if a random forest is built using $m = p$, then this amounts simply to bagging. On the `Heart` data, random forests using $m = \sqrt{p}$ leads to a reduction in both test error and OOB error over bagging (Figure 8.8).

Using a small value of m in building a random forest will typically be helpful when we have a large number of correlated predictors. We applied random forests to a high-dimensional biological data set consisting of expression measurements of 4,718 genes measured on tissue samples from 349 patients. There are around 20,000 genes in humans, and individual genes have different levels of activity, or expression, in particular cells, tissues, and biological conditions. In this data set, each of the patient samples has a qualitative label with 15 different levels: either normal or 1 of 14 different types of cancer. Our goal was to use random forests to predict cancer type based on the 500 genes that have the largest variance in the training set. We randomly divided the observations into a training and a test set, and applied random forests to the training set for three different values of the number of splitting variables m. The results are shown in Figure 8.10. The error rate of a single tree is 45.7 %, and the null rate is 75.4 %.[4] We see that using 400 trees is sufficient to give good performance, and that the choice $m = \sqrt{p}$ gave a small improvement in test error over bagging ($m = p$) in this example. As with bagging, random forests will not overfit if we increase B, so in practice we use a value of B sufficiently large for the error rate to have settled down.

8.2.3 Boosting

We now discuss *boosting*, yet another approach for improving the predictions resulting from a decision tree. Like bagging, boosting is a general approach that can be applied to many statistical learning methods for regression or classification. Here we restrict our discussion of boosting to the context of decision trees. boosting

Recall that bagging involves creating multiple copies of the original training data set using the bootstrap, fitting a separate decision tree to each copy, and then combining all of the trees in order to create a single predic-

[4]The null rate results from simply classifying each observation to the dominant class overall, which is in this case the normal class.

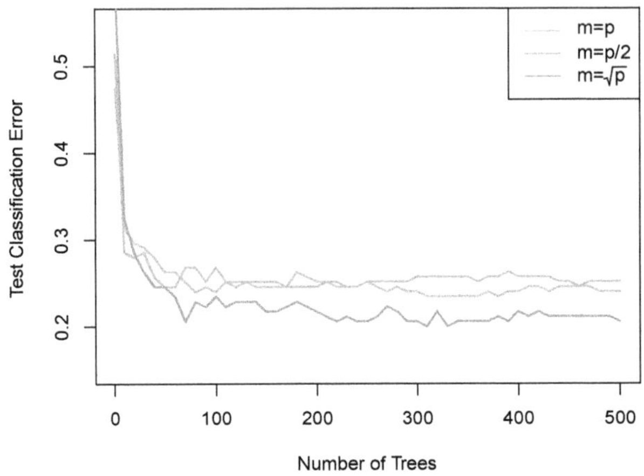

FIGURE 8.10. *Results from random forests for the 15-class gene expression data set with $p = 500$ predictors. The test error is displayed as a function of the number of trees. Each colored line corresponds to a different value of m, the number of predictors available for splitting at each interior tree node. Random forests ($m < p$) lead to a slight improvement over bagging ($m = p$). A single classification tree has an error rate of 45.7%.*

tive model. Notably, each tree is built on a bootstrap data set, independent of the other trees. Boosting works in a similar way, except that the trees are grown *sequentially*: each tree is grown using information from previously grown trees. Boosting does not involve bootstrap sampling; instead each tree is fit on a modified version of the original data set.

Consider first the regression setting. Like bagging, boosting involves combining a large number of decision trees, $\hat{f}^1, \ldots, \hat{f}^B$. Boosting is described in Algorithm 8.2.

What is the idea behind this procedure? Unlike fitting a single large decision tree to the data, which amounts to *fitting the data hard* and potentially overfitting, the boosting approach instead *learns slowly*. Given the current model, we fit a decision tree to the residuals from the model. That is, we fit a tree using the current residuals, rather than the outcome Y, as the response. We then add this new decision tree into the fitted function in order to update the residuals. Each of these trees can be rather small, with just a few terminal nodes, determined by the parameter d in the algorithm. By fitting small trees to the residuals, we slowly improve $\hat{f}$ in areas where it does not perform well. The shrinkage parameter λ slows the process down even further, allowing more and different shaped trees to attack the residuals. In general, statistical learning approaches that *learn slowly* tend to perform well. Note that in boosting, unlike in bagging, the construction of each tree depends strongly on the trees that have already been grown.

We have just described the process of boosting regression trees. Boosting classification trees proceeds in a similar but slightly more complex way, and the details are omitted here.

Algorithm 8.2 *Boosting for Regression Trees*

1. Set $\hat{f}(x) = 0$ and $r_i = y_i$ for all i in the training set.
2. For $b = 1, 2, \dots, B$, repeat:
   (a) Fit a tree $\hat{f}^b$ with d splits ($d+1$ terminal nodes) to the training data (X, r).
   (b) Update $\hat{f}$ by adding in a shrunken version of the new tree:
   $$\hat{f}(x) \leftarrow \hat{f}(x) + \lambda \hat{f}^b(x). \tag{8.10}$$
   (c) Update the residuals,
   $$r_i \leftarrow r_i - \lambda \hat{f}^b(x_i). \tag{8.11}$$
3. Output the boosted model,
$$\hat{f}(x) = \sum_{b=1}^{B} \lambda \hat{f}^b(x). \tag{8.12}$$

Boosting has three tuning parameters:

1. The number of trees B. Unlike bagging and random forests, boosting can overfit if B is too large, although this overfitting tends to occur slowly if at all. We use cross-validation to select B.
2. The shrinkage parameter λ, a small positive number. This controls the rate at which boosting learns. Typical values are 0.01 or 0.001, and the right choice can depend on the problem. Very small λ can require using a very large value of B in order to achieve good performance.
3. The number d of splits in each tree, which controls the complexity of the boosted ensemble. Often $d = 1$ works well, in which case each tree is a *stump*, consisting of a single split. In this case, the boosted ensemble is fitting an additive model, since each term involves only a single variable. More generally d is the *interaction depth*, and controls the interaction order of the boosted model, since d splits can involve at most d variables.

stump

interaction depth

In Figure 8.11, we applied boosting to the 15-class cancer gene expression data set, in order to develop a classifier that can distinguish the normal class from the 14 cancer classes. We display the test error as a function of the total number of trees and the interaction depth d. We see that simple stumps with an interaction depth of one perform well if enough of them are included. This model outperforms the depth-two model, and both outperform a random forest. This highlights one difference between boosting and random forests: in boosting, because the growth of a particular tree takes into account the other trees that have already been grown, smaller

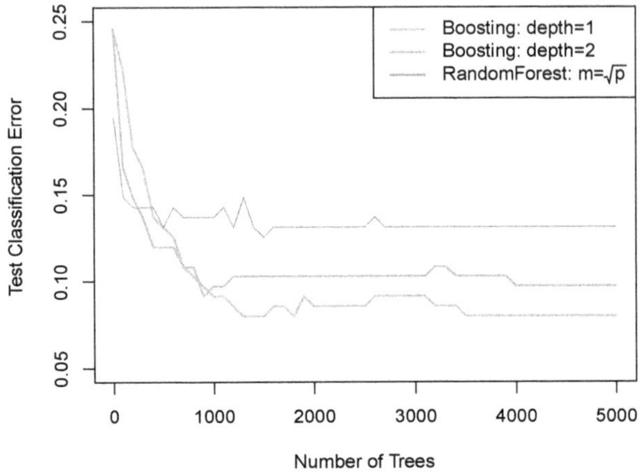

FIGURE 8.11. *Results from performing boosting and random forests on the 15-class gene expression data set in order to predict* cancer *versus* normal. *The test error is displayed as a function of the number of trees. For the two boosted models,* $\lambda = 0.01$. *Depth-1 trees slightly outperform depth-2 trees, and both outperform the random forest, although the standard errors are around 0.02, making none of these differences significant. The test error rate for a single tree is 24 %.*

trees are typically sufficient. Using smaller trees can aid in interpretability as well; for instance, using stumps leads to an additive model.

8.2.4 Bayesian Additive Regression Trees

Finally, we discuss *Bayesian additive regression trees* (BART), another ensemble method that uses decision trees as its building blocks. For simplicity, we present BART for regression (as opposed to classification). Bayesian additive regression trees

Recall that bagging and random forests make predictions from an average of regression trees, each of which is built using a random sample of data and/or predictors. Each tree is built separately from the others. By contrast, boosting uses a weighted sum of trees, each of which is constructed by fitting a tree to the residual of the current fit. Thus, each new tree attempts to capture signal that is not yet accounted for by the current set of trees. BART is related to both approaches: each tree is constructed in a random manner as in bagging and random forests, and each tree tries to capture signal not yet accounted for by the current model, as in boosting. The main novelty in BART is the way in which new trees are generated.

Before we introduce the BART algorithm, we define some notation. We let K denote the number of regression trees, and B the number of iterations for which the BART algorithm will be run. The notation $\hat{f}_k^b(x)$ represents the prediction at x for the kth regression tree used in the bth iteration. At the end of each iteration, the K trees from that iteration will be summed, i.e. $\hat{f}^b(x) = \sum_{k=1}^K \hat{f}_k^b(x)$ for $b = 1, \ldots, B$.

In the first iteration of the BART algorithm, all trees are initialized to have a single root node, with $\hat{f}_k^1(x) = \frac{1}{nK}\sum_{i=1}^n y_i$, the mean of the response

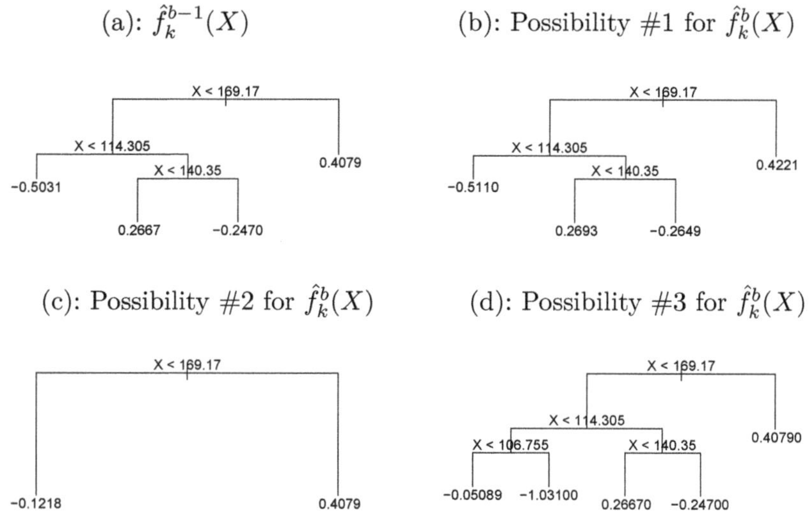

FIGURE 8.12. *A schematic of perturbed trees from the BART algorithm.* (a): *The kth tree at the $(b-1)$st iteration, $\hat{f}_k^{b-1}(X)$, is displayed. Panels (b)–(d) display three of many possibilities for $\hat{f}_k^b(X)$, given the form of $\hat{f}_k^{b-1}(X)$.* (b): *One possibility is that $\hat{f}_k^b(X)$ has the same structure as $\hat{f}_k^{b-1}(X)$, but with different predictions at the terminal nodes.* (c): *Another possibility is that $\hat{f}_k^b(X)$ results from pruning $\hat{f}_k^{b-1}(X)$.* (d): *Alternatively, $\hat{f}_k^b(X)$ may have more terminal nodes than $\hat{f}_k^{b-1}(X)$.*

values divided by the total number of trees. Thus, $\hat{f}^1(x) = \sum_{k=1}^K \hat{f}_k^1(x) = \frac{1}{n}\sum_{i=1}^n y_i$.

In subsequent iterations, BART updates each of the K trees, one at a time. In the bth iteration, to update the kth tree, we subtract from each response value the predictions from all but the kth tree, in order to obtain a *partial residual*

$$r_i = y_i - \sum_{k'<k} \hat{f}_{k'}^b(x_i) - \sum_{k'>k} \hat{f}_{k'}^{b-1}(x_i)$$

for the ith observation, $i = 1, \ldots, n$. Rather than fitting a fresh tree to this partial residual, BART randomly chooses a perturbation to the tree from the previous iteration ($\hat{f}_k^{b-1}$) from a set of possible perturbations, favoring ones that improve the fit to the partial residual. There are two components to this perturbation:

1. We may change the structure of the tree by adding or pruning branches.

2. We may change the prediction in each terminal node of the tree.

Figure 8.12 illustrates examples of possible perturbations to a tree.

The output of BART is a collection of prediction models,

$$\hat{f}^b(x) = \sum_{k=1}^K \hat{f}_k^b(x), \text{ for } b = 1, 2, \ldots, B.$$

Algorithm 8.3 *Bayesian Additive Regression Trees*

---

1. Let $\hat{f}_1^1(x) = \hat{f}_2^1(x) = \cdots = \hat{f}_K^1(x) = \frac{1}{nK}\sum_{i=1}^n y_i$.
2. Compute $\hat{f}^1(x) = \sum_{k=1}^K \hat{f}_k^1(x) = \frac{1}{n}\sum_{i=1}^n y_i$.
3. For $b = 2, \ldots, B$:
   (a) For $k = 1, 2, \ldots, K$:
      i. For $i = 1, \ldots, n$, compute the current partial residual
      $$r_i = y_i - \sum_{k'<k} \hat{f}_{k'}^b(x_i) - \sum_{k'>k} \hat{f}_{k'}^{b-1}(x_i).$$
      ii. Fit a new tree, $\hat{f}_k^b(x)$, to r_i, by randomly perturbing the kth tree from the previous iteration, $\hat{f}_k^{b-1}(x)$. Perturbations that improve the fit are favored.
   (b) Compute $\hat{f}^b(x) = \sum_{k=1}^K \hat{f}_k^b(x)$.
4. Compute the mean after L burn-in samples,
$$\hat{f}(x) = \frac{1}{B-L}\sum_{b=L+1}^{B} \hat{f}^b(x).$$

We typically throw away the first few of these prediction models, since models obtained in the earlier iterations — known as the *burn-in* period — tend not to provide very good results. We can let L denote the number of burn-in iterations; for instance, we might take $L = 200$. Then, to obtain a single prediction, we simply take the average after the burn-in iterations, $\hat{f}(x) = \frac{1}{B-L}\sum_{b=L+1}^{B} \hat{f}^b(x)$. However, it is also possible to compute quantities other than the average: for instance, the percentiles of $\hat{f}^{L+1}(x), \ldots, \hat{f}^B(x)$ provide a measure of uncertainty in the final prediction. The overall BART procedure is summarized in Algorithm 8.3.

burn-in

A key element of the BART approach is that in Step 3(a)ii., we do *not* fit a fresh tree to the current partial residual: instead, we try to improve the fit to the current partial residual by slightly modifying the tree obtained in the previous iteration (see Figure 8.12). Roughly speaking, this guards against overfitting since it limits how "hard" we fit the data in each iteration. Furthermore, the individual trees are typically quite small. We limit the tree size in order to avoid overfitting the data, which would be more likely to occur if we grew very large trees.

Figure 8.13 shows the result of applying BART to the `Heart` data, using $K = 200$ trees, as the number of iterations is increased to 10,000. During the initial iterations, the test and training errors jump around a bit. After this initial burn-in period, the error rates settle down. We note that there is only a small difference between the training error and the test error, indicating that the tree perturbation process largely avoids overfitting.

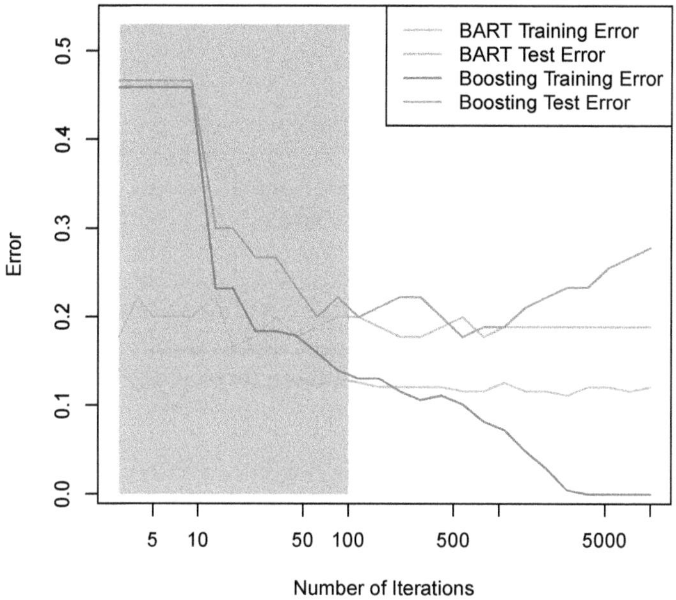

FIGURE 8.13. *BART and boosting results for the* `Heart` *data. Both training and test errors are displayed. After a burn-in period of* 100 *iterations (shown in gray), the error rates for BART settle down. Boosting begins to overfit after a few hundred iterations.*

The training and test errors for boosting are also displayed in Figure 8.13. We see that the test error for boosting approaches that of BART, but then begins to increase as the number of iterations increases. Furthermore, the training error for boosting decreases as the number of iterations increases, indicating that boosting has overfit the data.

Though the details are outside of the scope of this book, it turns out that the BART method can be viewed as a *Bayesian* approach to fitting an ensemble of trees: each time we randomly perturb a tree in order to fit the residuals, we are in fact drawing a new tree from a *posterior* distribution. (Of course, this Bayesian connection is the motivation for BART's name.) Furthermore, Algorithm 8.3 can be viewed as a *Markov chain Monte Carlo* algorithm for fitting the BART model.

Markov chain Monte Carlo

When we apply BART, we must select the number of trees K, the number of iterations B, and the number of burn-in iterations L. We typically choose large values for B and K, and a moderate value for L: for instance, $K = 200$, $B = 1{,}000$, and $L = 100$ is a reasonable choice. BART has been shown to have very impressive out-of-box performance — that is, it performs well with minimal tuning.

8.2.5 Summary of Tree Ensemble Methods

Trees are an attractive choice of weak learner for an ensemble method for a number of reasons, including their flexibility and ability to handle predictors of mixed types (i.e. qualitative as well as quantitative). We have now seen four approaches for fitting an ensemble of trees: bagging, random forests, boosting, and BART.

- In *bagging*, the trees are grown independently on random samples of the observations. Consequently, the trees tend to be quite similar to each other. Thus, bagging can get caught in local optima and can fail to thoroughly explore the model space.

- In *random forests*, the trees are once again grown independently on random samples of the observations. However, each split on each tree is performed using a random subset of the features, thereby decorrelating the trees, and leading to a more thorough exploration of model space relative to bagging.

- In *boosting*, we only use the original data, and do not draw any random samples. The trees are grown successively, using a "slow" learning approach: each new tree is fit to the signal that is left over from the earlier trees, and shrunken down before it is used.

- In *BART*, we once again only make use of the original data, and we grow the trees successively. However, each tree is perturbed in order to avoid local minima and achieve a more thorough exploration of the model space.

8.3 Lab: Tree-Based Methods

We import some of our usual libraries at this top level.

In [1]:
```
import numpy as np
import pandas as pd
from matplotlib.pyplot import subplots
from statsmodels.datasets import get_rdataset
import sklearn.model_selection as skm
from ISLP import load_data, confusion_table
from ISLP.models import ModelSpec as MS
```

We also collect the new imports needed for this lab.

In [2]:
```
from sklearn.tree import (DecisionTreeClassifier as DTC,
                          DecisionTreeRegressor as DTR,
                          plot_tree,
                          export_text)
from sklearn.metrics import (accuracy_score,
                             log_loss)
from sklearn.ensemble import \
     (RandomForestRegressor as RF,
      GradientBoostingRegressor as GBR)
from ISLP.bart import BART
```

8.3.1 Fitting Classification Trees

We first use classification trees to analyze the `Carseats` data set. In these data, `Sales` is a continuous variable, and so we begin by recoding it as a binary variable. We use the `where()` function to create a variable, called `High`, which takes on a value of `Yes` if the `Sales` variable exceeds 8, and takes on a value of `No` otherwise. `where()`

```
In [3]: Carseats = load_data('Carseats')
        High = np.where(Carseats.Sales > 8,
                        "Yes",
                        "No")
```

We now use `DecisionTreeClassifier()` to fit a classification tree in order to predict `High` using all variables but `Sales`. To do so, we must form a model matrix as we did when fitting regression models. `DecisionTree Classifier()`

```
In [4]: model = MS(Carseats.columns.drop('Sales'), intercept=False)
        D = model.fit_transform(Carseats)
        feature_names = list(D.columns)
        X = np.asarray(D)
```

We have converted `D` from a data frame to an array `X`, which is needed in some of the analysis below. We also need the `feature_names` for annotating our plots later.

There are several options needed to specify the classifier, such as `max_depth` (how deep to grow the tree), `min_samples_split` (minimum number of observations in a node to be eligible for splitting) and `criterion` (whether to use Gini or cross-entropy as the split criterion). We also set `random_state` for reproducibility; ties in the split criterion are broken at random.

```
In [5]: clf = DTC(criterion='entropy',
                  max_depth=3,
                  random_state=0)
        clf.fit(X, High)
```

```
Out[5]: DecisionTreeClassifier(criterion='entropy', max_depth=3)
```

In our discussion of qualitative features in Section 3.3, we noted that for a linear regression model such a feature could be represented by including a matrix of dummy variables (one-hot-encoding) in the model matrix, using the formula notation of `statsmodels`. As mentioned in Section 8.1, there is a more natural way to handle qualitative features when building a decision tree, that does not require such dummy variables; each split amounts to partitioning the levels into two groups. However, the `sklearn` implementation of decision trees does not take advantage of this approach; instead it simply treats the one-hot-encoded levels as separate variables.

```
In [6]: accuracy_score(High, clf.predict(X))
```

```
Out[6]: 0.7275
```

With only the default arguments, the training error rate is 21%. For classification trees, we can access the value of the deviance using `log_loss()`, `log_loss()`

$$-2 \sum_m \sum_k n_{mk} \log \hat{p}_{mk},$$

where n_{mk} is the number of observations in the mth terminal node that belong to the kth class.

In [7]:
```
resid_dev = np.sum(log_loss(High, clf.predict_proba(X)))
resid_dev
```

Out[7]: 0.4711

This is closely related to the *entropy*, defined in (8.7). A small deviance indicates a tree that provides a good fit to the (training) data.

One of the most attractive properties of trees is that they can be graphically displayed. Here we use the `plot()` function to display the tree structure (not shown here).

In [8]:
```
ax = subplots(figsize=(12,12))[1]
plot_tree(clf,
          feature_names=feature_names,
          ax=ax);
```

The most important indicator of `Sales` appears to be `ShelveLoc`.

We can see a text representation of the tree using `export_text()`, which displays the split criterion (e.g. `Price <= 92.5`) for each branch. For leaf nodes it shows the overall prediction (`Yes` or `No`). We can also see the number of observations in that leaf that take on values of `Yes` and `No` by specifying `show_weights=True`.

`export_text`

In [9]:
```
print(export_text(clf,
                  feature_names=feature_names,
                  show_weights=True))
```

Out[9]:
```
|--- ShelveLoc[Good] <= 0.50
|   |--- Price <= 92.50
|   |   |--- Income <= 57.00
|   |   |   |--- weights: [7.00, 3.00] class: No
|   |   |--- Income >  57.00
|   |   |   |--- weights: [7.00, 29.00] class: Yes
|   |--- Price >  92.50
|   |   |--- Advertising <= 13.50
|   |   |   |--- weights: [183.00, 41.00] class: No
|   |   |--- Advertising >  13.50
|   |   |   |--- weights: [20.00, 25.00] class: Yes
|--- ShelveLoc[Good] >  0.50
|   |--- Price <= 135.00
|   |   |--- US[Yes] <= 0.50
|   |   |   |--- weights: [6.00, 11.00] class: Yes
|   |   |--- US[Yes] >  0.50
|   |   |   |--- weights: [2.00, 49.00] class: Yes
|   |--- Price >  135.00
|   |   |--- Income <= 46.00
|   |   |   |--- weights: [6.00, 0.00] class: No
|   |   |--- Income >  46.00
|   |   |   |--- weights: [5.00, 6.00] class: Yes
```

In order to properly evaluate the performance of a classification tree on these data, we must estimate the test error rather than simply computing the training error. We split the observations into a training set and a test set, build the tree using the training set, and evaluate its performance on the test data. This pattern is similar to that in Chapter 6, with the linear models replaced here by decision trees — the code for validation is almost identical. This approach leads to correct predictions for 68.5% of the locations in the test data set.

```
In [10]: validation = skm.ShuffleSplit(n_splits=1,
                                       test_size=200,
                                       random_state=0)
         results = skm.cross_validate(clf,
                                      D,
                                      High,
                                      cv=validation)
         results['test_score']
```

```
Out[10]: array([0.685])
```

Next, we consider whether pruning the tree might lead to improved classification performance. We first split the data into a training and test set. We will use cross-validation to prune the tree on the training set, and then evaluate the performance of the pruned tree on the test set.

```
In [11]: (X_train,
          X_test,
          High_train,
          High_test) = skm.train_test_split(X,
                                            High,
                                            test_size=0.5,
                                            random_state=0)
```

We first refit the full tree on the training set; here we do not set a `max_depth` parameter, since we will learn that through cross-validation.

```
In [12]: clf = DTC(criterion='entropy', random_state=0)
         clf.fit(X_train, High_train)
         accuracy_score(High_test, clf.predict(X_test))
```

```
Out[12]: 0.735
```

Next we use the `cost_complexity_pruning_path()` method of `clf` to extract cost-complexity values.

`cost_complexity_pruning_path()`

```
In [13]: ccp_path = clf.cost_complexity_pruning_path(X_train, High_train)
         kfold = skm.KFold(10,
                           random_state=1,
                           shuffle=True)
```

This yields a set of impurities and α values from which we can extract an optimal one by cross-validation.

```
In [14]: grid = skm.GridSearchCV(clf,
                                 {'ccp_alpha': ccp_path.ccp_alphas},
                                 refit=True,
```

```
                        cv=kfold,
                        scoring='accuracy')
grid.fit(X_train, High_train)
grid.best_score_
```

```
Out[14]: 0.685
```

Let's take a look at the pruned true.

```
In [15]: ax = subplots(figsize=(12, 12))[1]
         best_ = grid.best_estimator_
         plot_tree(best_,
                   feature_names=feature_names,
                   ax=ax);
```

This is quite a bushy tree. We could count the leaves, or query `best_` instead.

```
In [16]: best_.tree_.n_leaves
```

```
Out[16]: 30
```

The tree with 30 terminal nodes results in the lowest cross-validation error rate, with an accuracy of 68.5%. How well does this pruned tree perform on the test data set? Once again, we apply the `predict()` function.

```
In [17]: print(accuracy_score(High_test,
                              best_.predict(X_test)))
         confusion = confusion_table(best_.predict(X_test),
                                     High_test)
         confusion
```

```
Out[17]: 0.72

     Truth    No  Yes
Predicted
       No    108   61
      Yes     10   21
```

Now 72.0% of the test observations are correctly classified, which is slightly worse than the error for the full tree (with 35 leaves). So cross-validation has not helped us much here; it only pruned off 5 leaves, at a cost of a slightly worse error. These results would change if we were to change the random number seeds above; even though cross-validation gives an unbiased approach to model selection, it does have variance.

8.3.2 Fitting Regression Trees

Here we fit a regression tree to the `Boston` data set. The steps are similar to those for classification trees.

```
In [18]: Boston = load_data("Boston")
         model = MS(Boston.columns.drop('medv'), intercept=False)
         D = model.fit_transform(Boston)
         feature_names = list(D.columns)
         X = np.asarray(D)
```

First, we split the data into training and test sets, and fit the tree to the training data. Here we use 30% of the data for the test set.

In [19]:
```
(X_train,
 X_test,
 y_train,
 y_test) = skm.train_test_split(X,
                                Boston['medv'],
                                test_size=0.3,
                                random_state=0)
```

Having formed our training and test data sets, we fit the regression tree.

In [20]:
```
reg = DTR(max_depth=3)
reg.fit(X_train, y_train)
ax = subplots(figsize=(12,12))[1]
plot_tree(reg,
          feature_names=feature_names,
          ax=ax);
```

The variable `lstat` measures the percentage of individuals with lower socioeconomic status. The tree indicates that lower values of `lstat` correspond to more expensive houses. The tree predicts a median house price of $12,042 for small-sized homes (`rm < 6.8`), in suburbs in which residents have low socioeconomic status (`lstat > 14.4`) and the crime-rate is moderate (`crim > 5.8`).

Now we use the cross-validation function to see whether pruning the tree will improve performance.

In [21]:
```
ccp_path = reg.cost_complexity_pruning_path(X_train, y_train)
kfold = skm.KFold(5,
                  shuffle=True,
                  random_state=10)
grid = skm.GridSearchCV(reg,
                        {'ccp_alpha': ccp_path.ccp_alphas},
                        refit=True,
                        cv=kfold,
                        scoring='neg_mean_squared_error')
G = grid.fit(X_train, y_train)
```

In keeping with the cross-validation results, we use the pruned tree to make predictions on the test set.

In [22]:
```
best_ = grid.best_estimator_
np.mean((y_test - best_.predict(X_test))**2)
```

Out[22]: 28.07

In other words, the test set MSE associated with the regression tree is 28.07. The square root of the MSE is therefore around 5.30, indicating that this model leads to test predictions that are within around $5300 of the true median home value for the suburb.

Let's plot the best tree to see how interpretable it is.

In [23]:
```
ax = subplots(figsize=(12,12))[1]
plot_tree(G.best_estimator_,
          feature_names=feature_names,
          ax=ax);
```

8.3.3 Bagging and Random Forests

Here we apply bagging and random forests to the Boston data, using the RandomForestRegressor() from the sklearn.ensemble package. Recall that bagging is simply a special case of a random forest with $m = p$. Therefore, the RandomForestRegressor() function can be used to perform both bagging and random forests. We start with bagging.

RandomForestRegressor()
sklearn.ensemble

```
In [24]: bag_boston = RF(max_features=X_train.shape[1], random_state=0)
         bag_boston.fit(X_train, y_train)
```

```
Out[24]: RandomForestRegressor(max_features=12, random_state=0)
```

The argument max_features indicates that all 12 predictors should be considered for each split of the tree — in other words, that bagging should be done. How well does this bagged model perform on the test set?

```
In [25]: ax = subplots(figsize=(8,8))[1]
         y_hat_bag = bag_boston.predict(X_test)
         ax.scatter(y_hat_bag, y_test)
         np.mean((y_test - y_hat_bag)**2)
```

```
Out[25]: 14.63
```

The test set MSE associated with the bagged regression tree is 14.63, about half that obtained using an optimally-pruned single tree. We could change the number of trees grown from the default of 100 by using the n_estimators argument:

```
In [26]: bag_boston = RF(max_features=X_train.shape[1],
                         n_estimators=500,
                         random_state=0).fit(X_train, y_train)
         y_hat_bag = bag_boston.predict(X_test)
         np.mean((y_test - y_hat_bag)**2)
```

```
Out[26]: 14.61
```

There is not much change. Bagging and random forests cannot overfit by increasing the number of trees, but can underfit if the number is too small.

Growing a random forest proceeds in exactly the same way, except that we use a smaller value of the max_features argument. By default, RandomForestRegressor() uses p variables when building a random forest of regression trees (i.e. it defaults to bagging), and RandomForestClassifier() uses $\sqrt{p}$ variables when building a random forest of classification trees. Here we use max_features=6.

```
In [27]: RF_boston = RF(max_features=6,
                        random_state=0).fit(X_train, y_train)
         y_hat_RF = RF_boston.predict(X_test)
         np.mean((y_test - y_hat_RF)**2)
```

```
Out[27]: 20.04
```

The test set MSE is 20.04; this indicates that random forests did somewhat worse than bagging in this case. Extracting the feature_importances_ values from the fitted model, we can view the importance of each variable.

In [28]:
```
feature_imp = pd.DataFrame(
    {'importance':RF_boston.feature_importances_},
    index=feature_names)
feature_imp.sort_values(by='importance', ascending=False)
```

Out[28]:
```
         importance
  lstat    0.368683
     rm    0.333842
ptratio    0.057306
  indus    0.053303
   crim    0.052426
    dis    0.042493
    nox    0.034410
    age    0.024327
    tax    0.022368
    rad    0.005048
     zn    0.003238
   chas    0.002557
```

This is a relative measure of the total decrease in node impurity that results from splits over that variable, averaged over all trees (this was plotted in Figure 8.9 for a model fit to the `Heart` data).

The results indicate that across all of the trees considered in the random forest, the wealth level of the community (`lstat`) and the house size (`rm`) are by far the two most important variables.

8.3.4 Boosting

Here we use `GradientBoostingRegressor()` from `sklearn.ensemble` to fit boosted regression trees to the `Boston` data set. For classification we would use `GradientBoostingClassifier()`. The argument `n_estimators=5000` indicates that we want 5000 trees, and the option `max_depth=3` limits the depth of each tree. The argument `learning_rate` is the λ mentioned earlier in the description of boosting.

`Gradient Boosting Regressor()`
`Gradient Boosting Classifier()`

In [29]:
```
boost_boston = GBR(n_estimators=5000,
                   learning_rate=0.001,
                   max_depth=3,
                   random_state=0)
boost_boston.fit(X_train, y_train)
```

We can see how the training error decreases with the `train_score_` attribute. To get an idea of how the test error decreases we can use the `staged_predict()` method to get the predicted values along the path.

In [30]:
```
test_error = np.zeros_like(boost_boston.train_score_)
for idx, y_ in enumerate(boost_boston.staged_predict(X_test)):
   test_error[idx] = np.mean((y_test - y_)**2)

plot_idx = np.arange(boost_boston.train_score_.shape[0])
ax = subplots(figsize=(8,8))[1]
ax.plot(plot_idx,
        boost_boston.train_score_,
        'b',
        label='Training')
```

```
ax.plot(plot_idx,
        test_error,
        'r',
        label='Test')
ax.legend();
```

We now use the boosted model to predict `medv` on the test set:

```
In [31]: y_hat_boost = boost_boston.predict(X_test);
         np.mean((y_test - y_hat_boost)**2)
```

```
Out[31]: 14.48
```

The test MSE obtained is 14.48, similar to the test MSE for bagging. If we want to, we can perform boosting with a different value of the shrinkage parameter λ in (8.10). The default value is 0.001, but this is easily modified. Here we take $\lambda = 0.2$.

```
In [32]: boost_boston = GBR(n_estimators=5000,
                            learning_rate=0.2,
                            max_depth=3,
                            random_state=0)
         boost_boston.fit(X_train,
                          y_train)
         y_hat_boost = boost_boston.predict(X_test);
         np.mean((y_test - y_hat_boost)**2)
```

```
Out[32]: 14.50
```

In this case, using $\lambda = 0.2$ leads to a almost the same test MSE as when using $\lambda = 0.001$.

8.3.5 Bayesian Additive Regression Trees

In this section we demonstrate a `Python` implementation of BART found in the `ISLP.bart` package. We fit a model to the `Boston` housing data set. This `BART()` estimator is designed for quantitative outcome variables, though other implementations are available for fitting logistic and probit models to categorical outcomes. `BART()`

```
In [33]: bart_boston = BART(random_state=0, burnin=5, ndraw=15)
         bart_boston.fit(X_train, y_train)
```

```
Out[33]: BART(burnin=5, ndraw=15, random_state=0)
```

On this data set, with this split into test and training, we see that the test error of BART is similar to that of random forest.

```
In [34]: yhat_test = bart_boston.predict(X_test.astype(np.float32))
         np.mean((y_test - yhat_test)**2)
```

```
Out[34]: 20.92
```

We can check how many times each variable appeared in the collection of trees. This gives a summary similar to the variable importance plot for boosting and random forests.

```
In [35]: var_inclusion = pd.Series(bart_boston.variable_inclusion_.mean(0),
                                   index=D.columns)
         var_inclusion
```

```
Out[35]:     crim     25.333333
               zn     27.000000
            indus     21.266667
             chas     20.466667
              nox     25.400000
               rm     32.400000
              age     26.133333
              dis     25.666667
              rad     24.666667
              tax     23.933333
          ptratio     25.000000
            lstat     31.866667
         dtype: float64
```

8.4 Exercises

Conceptual

1. Draw an example (of your own invention) of a partition of two-dimensional feature space that could result from recursive binary splitting. Your example should contain at least six regions. Draw a decision tree corresponding to this partition. Be sure to label all aspects of your figures, including the regions $R_1, R_2, \ldots$, the cutpoints $t_1, t_2, \ldots$, and so forth.

   Hint: Your result should look something like Figures 8.1 and 8.2.

2. It is mentioned in Section 8.2.3 that boosting using depth-one trees (or *stumps*) leads to an *additive* model: that is, a model of the form

$$f(X) = \sum_{j=1}^{p} f_j(X_j).$$

   Explain why this is the case. You can begin with (8.12) in Algorithm 8.2.

3. Consider the Gini index, classification error, and entropy in a simple classification setting with two classes. Create a single plot that displays each of these quantities as a function of $\hat{p}_{m1}$. The x-axis should display $\hat{p}_{m1}$, ranging from 0 to 1, and the y-axis should display the value of the Gini index, classification error, and entropy.

   Hint: In a setting with two classes, $\hat{p}_{m1} = 1 - \hat{p}_{m2}$. You could make this plot by hand, but it will be much easier to make in `R`.

4. This question relates to the plots in Figure 8.14.

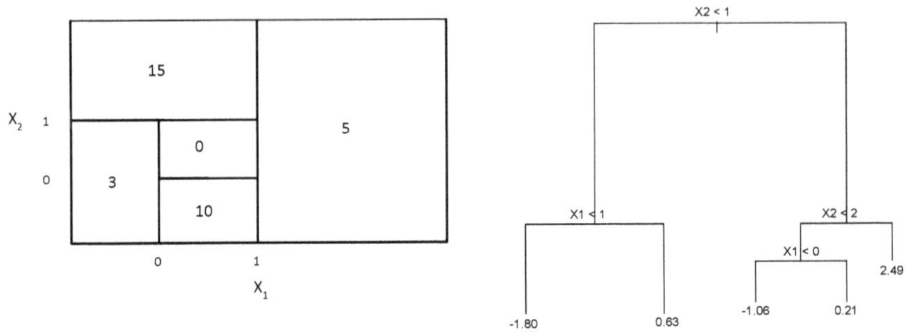

FIGURE 8.14. Left: *A partition of the predictor space corresponding to Exercise 4a.* Right: *A tree corresponding to Exercise 4b.*

(a) Sketch the tree corresponding to the partition of the predictor space illustrated in the left-hand panel of Figure 8.14. The numbers inside the boxes indicate the mean of Y within each region.

(b) Create a diagram similar to the left-hand panel of Figure 8.14, using the tree illustrated in the right-hand panel of the same figure. You should divide up the predictor space into the correct regions, and indicate the mean for each region.

5. Suppose we produce ten bootstrapped samples from a data set containing red and green classes. We then apply a classification tree to each bootstrapped sample and, for a specific value of X, produce 10 estimates of $P(\text{Class is Red}|X)$:

$$0.1, 0.15, 0.2, 0.2, 0.55, 0.6, 0.6, 0.65, 0.7, \text{ and } 0.75.$$

There are two common ways to combine these results together into a single class prediction. One is the majority vote approach discussed in this chapter. The second approach is to classify based on the average probability. In this example, what is the final classification under each of these two approaches?

6. Provide a detailed explanation of the algorithm that is used to fit a regression tree.

Applied

7. In Section 8.3.3, we applied random forests to the `Boston` data using `max_features = 6` and using `n_estimators = 100` and `n_estimators = 500`. Create a plot displaying the test error resulting from random forests on this data set for a more comprehensive range of values for `max_features` and `n_estimators`. You can model your plot after Figure 8.10. Describe the results obtained.

8. In the lab, a classification tree was applied to the `Carseats` data set after converting `Sales` into a qualitative response variable. Now we will seek to predict `Sales` using regression trees and related approaches, treating the response as a quantitative variable.

(a) Split the data set into a training set and a test set.

(b) Fit a regression tree to the training set. Plot the tree, and interpret the results. What test MSE do you obtain?

(c) Use cross-validation in order to determine the optimal level of tree complexity. Does pruning the tree improve the test MSE?

(d) Use the bagging approach in order to analyze this data. What test MSE do you obtain? Use the `feature_importance_` values to determine which variables are most important.

(e) Use random forests to analyze this data. What test MSE do you obtain? Use the `feature_importance_` values to determine which variables are most important. Describe the effect of m, the number of variables considered at each split, on the error rate obtained.

(f) Now analyze the data using BART, and report your results.

9. This problem involves the `OJ` data set which is part of the `ISLP` package.

(a) Create a training set containing a random sample of 800 observations, and a test set containing the remaining observations.

(b) Fit a tree to the training data, with `Purchase` as the response and the other variables as predictors. What is the training error rate?

(c) Create a plot of the tree, and interpret the results. How many terminal nodes does the tree have?

(d) Use the `export_tree()` function to produce a text summary of the fitted tree. Pick one of the terminal nodes, and interpret the information displayed.

(e) Predict the response on the test data, and produce a confusion matrix comparing the test labels to the predicted test labels. What is the test error rate?

(f) Use cross-validation on the training set in order to determine the optimal tree size.

(g) Produce a plot with tree size on the x-axis and cross-validated classification error rate on the y-axis.

(h) Which tree size corresponds to the lowest cross-validated classification error rate?

(i) Produce a pruned tree corresponding to the optimal tree size obtained using cross-validation. If cross-validation does not lead to selection of a pruned tree, then create a pruned tree with five terminal nodes.

(j) Compare the training error rates between the pruned and unpruned trees. Which is higher?

(k) Compare the test error rates between the pruned and unpruned trees. Which is higher?

10. We now use boosting to predict `Salary` in the `Hitters` data set.

    (a) Remove the observations for whom the salary information is unknown, and then log-transform the salaries.

    (b) Create a training set consisting of the first 200 observations, and a test set consisting of the remaining observations.

    (c) Perform boosting on the training set with 1,000 trees for a range of values of the shrinkage parameter λ. Produce a plot with different shrinkage values on the x-axis and the corresponding training set MSE on the y-axis.

    (d) Produce a plot with different shrinkage values on the x-axis and the corresponding test set MSE on the y-axis.

    (e) Compare the test MSE of boosting to the test MSE that results from applying two of the regression approaches seen in Chapters 3 and 6.

    (f) Which variables appear to be the most important predictors in the boosted model?

    (g) Now apply bagging to the training set. What is the test set MSE for this approach?

11. This question uses the `Caravan` data set.

    (a) Create a training set consisting of the first 1,000 observations, and a test set consisting of the remaining observations.

    (b) Fit a boosting model to the training set with `Purchase` as the response and the other variables as predictors. Use 1,000 trees, and a shrinkage value of 0.01. Which predictors appear to be the most important?

    (c) Use the boosting model to predict the response on the test data. Predict that a person will make a purchase if the estimated probability of purchase is greater than 20 %. Form a confusion matrix. What fraction of the people predicted to make a purchase do in fact make one? How does this compare with the results obtained from applying KNN or logistic regression to this data set?

12. Apply boosting, bagging, random forests, and BART to a data set of your choice. Be sure to fit the models on a training set and to evaluate their performance on a test set. How accurate are the results compared to simple methods like linear or logistic regression? Which of these approaches yields the best performance?

9
Support Vector Machines

In this chapter, we discuss the *support vector machine* (SVM), an approach for classification that was developed in the computer science community in the 1990s and that has grown in popularity since then. SVMs have been shown to perform well in a variety of settings, and are often considered one of the best "out of the box" classifiers.

The support vector machine is a generalization of a simple and intuitive classifier called the *maximal margin classifier*, which we introduce in Section 9.1. Though it is elegant and simple, we will see that this classifier unfortunately cannot be applied to most data sets, since it requires that the classes be separable by a linear boundary. In Section 9.2, we introduce the *support vector classifier*, an extension of the maximal margin classifier that can be applied in a broader range of cases. Section 9.3 introduces the *support vector machine*, which is a further extension of the support vector classifier in order to accommodate non-linear class boundaries. Support vector machines are intended for the binary classification setting in which there are two classes; in Section 9.4 we discuss extensions of support vector machines to the case of more than two classes. In Section 9.5 we discuss the close connections between support vector machines and other statistical methods such as logistic regression.

People often loosely refer to the maximal margin classifier, the support vector classifier, and the support vector machine as "support vector machines". To avoid confusion, we will carefully distinguish between these three notions in this chapter.

9.1 Maximal Margin Classifier

In this section, we define a hyperplane and introduce the concept of an optimal separating hyperplane.

G. James et al., *An Introduction to Statistical Learning*, Springer Texts in Statistics,
https://doi.org/10.1007/978-3-031-38747-0_9

9.1.1 What Is a Hyperplane?

In a p-dimensional space, a *hyperplane* is a flat affine subspace of dimension $p - 1$.[1] For instance, in two dimensions, a hyperplane is a flat one-dimensional subspace—in other words, a line. In three dimensions, a hyperplane is a flat two-dimensional subspace—that is, a plane. In $p > 3$ dimensions, it can be hard to visualize a hyperplane, but the notion of a $(p - 1)$-dimensional flat subspace still applies.

hyperplane

The mathematical definition of a hyperplane is quite simple. In two dimensions, a hyperplane is defined by the equation

$$\beta_0 + \beta_1 X_1 + \beta_2 X_2 = 0 \tag{9.1}$$

for parameters β_0, β_1, and β_2. When we say that (9.1) "defines" the hyperplane, we mean that any $X = (X_1, X_2)^T$ for which (9.1) holds is a point on the hyperplane. Note that (9.1) is simply the equation of a line, since indeed in two dimensions a hyperplane is a line.

Equation 9.1 can be easily extended to the p-dimensional setting:

$$\beta_0 + \beta_1 X_1 + \beta_2 X_2 + \cdots + \beta_p X_p = 0 \tag{9.2}$$

defines a p-dimensional hyperplane, again in the sense that if a point $X = (X_1, X_2, \ldots, X_p)^T$ in p-dimensional space (i.e. a vector of length p) satisfies (9.2), then X lies on the hyperplane.

Now, suppose that X does not satisfy (9.2); rather,

$$\beta_0 + \beta_1 X_1 + \beta_2 X_2 + \cdots + \beta_p X_p > 0. \tag{9.3}$$

Then this tells us that X lies to one side of the hyperplane. On the other hand, if

$$\beta_0 + \beta_1 X_1 + \beta_2 X_2 + \cdots + \beta_p X_p < 0, \tag{9.4}$$

then X lies on the other side of the hyperplane. So we can think of the hyperplane as dividing p-dimensional space into two halves. One can easily determine on which side of the hyperplane a point lies by simply calculating the sign of the left-hand side of (9.2). A hyperplane in two-dimensional space is shown in Figure 9.1.

9.1.2 Classification Using a Separating Hyperplane

Now suppose that we have an $n \times p$ data matrix $\mathbf{X}$ that consists of n training observations in p-dimensional space,

$$x_1 = \begin{pmatrix} x_{11} \\ \vdots \\ x_{1p} \end{pmatrix}, \ldots, x_n = \begin{pmatrix} x_{n1} \\ \vdots \\ x_{np} \end{pmatrix}, \tag{9.5}$$

and that these observations fall into two classes—that is, $y_1, \ldots, y_n \in \{-1, 1\}$ where -1 represents one class and 1 the other class. We also have a

[1]The word *affine* indicates that the subspace need not pass through the origin.

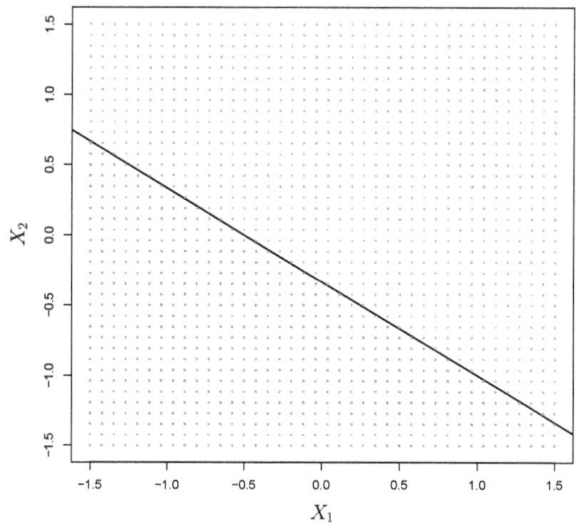

FIGURE 9.1. *The hyperplane* $1 + 2X_1 + 3X_2 = 0$ *is shown. The blue region is the set of points for which* $1 + 2X_1 + 3X_2 > 0$*, and the purple region is the set of points for which* $1 + 2X_1 + 3X_2 < 0$.

test observation, a p-vector of observed features $x^* = \begin{pmatrix} x_1^* & \ldots & x_p^* \end{pmatrix}^T$. Our goal is to develop a classifier based on the training data that will correctly classify the test observation using its feature measurements. We have seen a number of approaches for this task, such as linear discriminant analysis and logistic regression in Chapter 4, and classification trees, bagging, and boosting in Chapter 8. We will now see a new approach that is based upon the concept of a *separating hyperplane*.

separating hyperplane

Suppose that it is possible to construct a hyperplane that separates the training observations perfectly according to their class labels. Examples of three such *separating hyperplanes* are shown in the left-hand panel of Figure 9.2. We can label the observations from the blue class as $y_i = 1$ and those from the purple class as $y_i = -1$. Then a separating hyperplane has the property that

$$\beta_0 + \beta_1 x_{i1} + \beta_2 x_{i2} + \cdots + \beta_p x_{ip} > 0 \text{ if } y_i = 1, \tag{9.6}$$

and

$$\beta_0 + \beta_1 x_{i1} + \beta_2 x_{i2} + \cdots + \beta_p x_{ip} < 0 \text{ if } y_i = -1. \tag{9.7}$$

Equivalently, a separating hyperplane has the property that

$$y_i(\beta_0 + \beta_1 x_{i1} + \beta_2 x_{i2} + \cdots + \beta_p x_{ip}) > 0 \tag{9.8}$$

for all $i = 1, \ldots, n$.

If a separating hyperplane exists, we can use it to construct a very natural classifier: a test observation is assigned a class depending on which side of the hyperplane it is located. The right-hand panel of Figure 9.2 shows an example of such a classifier. That is, we classify the test observation x^* based on the sign of $f(x^*) = \beta_0 + \beta_1 x_1^* + \beta_2 x_2^* + \cdots + \beta_p x_p^*$. If $f(x^*)$ is positive, then we assign the test observation to class 1, and if $f(x^*)$ is negative, then we assign it to class -1. We can also make use of the *magnitude* of $f(x^*)$. If

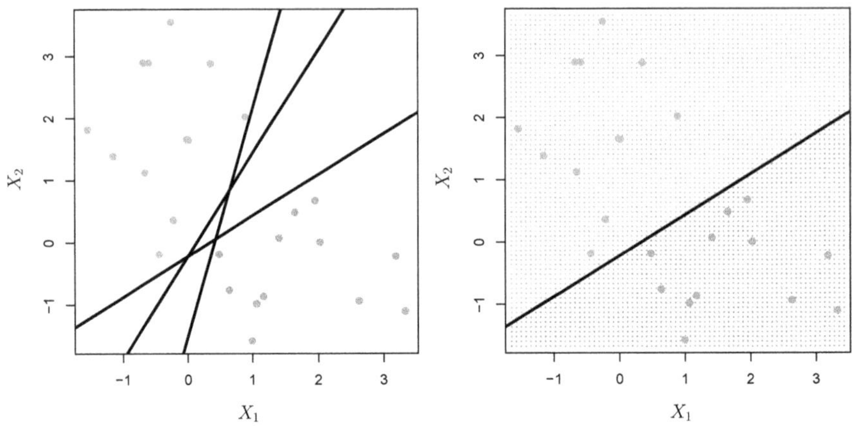

FIGURE 9.2. Left: *There are two classes of observations, shown in blue and in purple, each of which has measurements on two variables. Three separating hyperplanes, out of many possible, are shown in black.* Right: *A separating hyperplane is shown in black. The blue and purple grid indicates the decision rule made by a classifier based on this separating hyperplane: a test observation that falls in the blue portion of the grid will be assigned to the blue class, and a test observation that falls into the purple portion of the grid will be assigned to the purple class.*

$f(x^*)$ is far from zero, then this means that x^* lies far from the hyperplane, and so we can be confident about our class assignment for x^*. On the other hand, if $f(x^*)$ is close to zero, then x^* is located near the hyperplane, and so we are less certain about the class assignment for x^*. Not surprisingly, and as we see in Figure 9.2, a classifier that is based on a separating hyperplane leads to a linear decision boundary.

9.1.3 The Maximal Margin Classifier

In general, if our data can be perfectly separated using a hyperplane, then there will in fact exist an infinite number of such hyperplanes. This is because a given separating hyperplane can usually be shifted a tiny bit up or down, or rotated, without coming into contact with any of the observations. Three possible separating hyperplanes are shown in the left-hand panel of Figure 9.2. In order to construct a classifier based upon a separating hyperplane, we must have a reasonable way to decide which of the infinite possible separating hyperplanes to use.

A natural choice is the *maximal margin hyperplane* (also known as the *optimal separating hyperplane*), which is the separating hyperplane that is farthest from the training observations. That is, we can compute the (perpendicular) distance from each training observation to a given separating hyperplane; the smallest such distance is the minimal distance from the observations to the hyperplane, and is known as the *margin*. The maximal margin hyperplane is the separating hyperplane for which the margin is largest—that is, it is the hyperplane that has the farthest minimum distance to the training observations. We can then classify a test observation based on which side of the maximal margin hyperplane it lies. This is known

maximal margin hyperplane
optimal separating hyperplane
margin

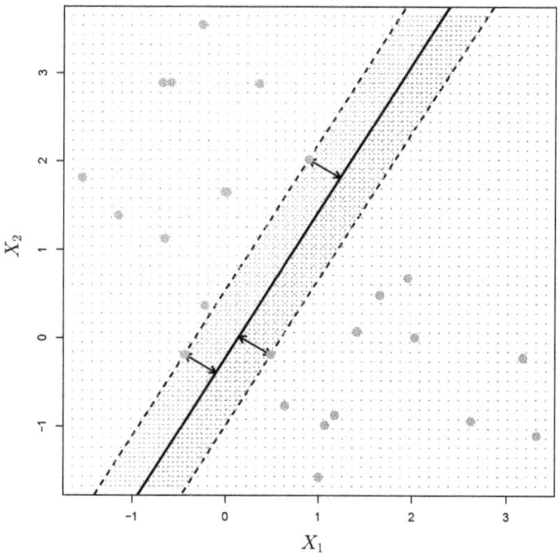

FIGURE 9.3. *There are two classes of observations, shown in blue and in purple. The maximal margin hyperplane is shown as a solid line. The margin is the distance from the solid line to either of the dashed lines. The two blue points and the purple point that lie on the dashed lines are the support vectors, and the distance from those points to the hyperplane is indicated by arrows. The purple and blue grid indicates the decision rule made by a classifier based on this separating hyperplane.*

as the *maximal margin classifier*. We hope that a classifier that has a large margin on the training data will also have a large margin on the test data, and hence will classify the test observations correctly. Although the maximal margin classifier is often successful, it can also lead to overfitting when p is large.

maximal margin classifier

If $\beta_0, \beta_1, \ldots, \beta_p$ are the coefficients of the maximal margin hyperplane, then the maximal margin classifier classifies the test observation x^* based on the sign of $f(x^*) = \beta_0 + \beta_1 x_1^* + \beta_2 x_2^* + \cdots + \beta_p x_p^*$.

Figure 9.3 shows the maximal margin hyperplane on the data set of Figure 9.2. Comparing the right-hand panel of Figure 9.2 to Figure 9.3, we see that the maximal margin hyperplane shown in Figure 9.3 does indeed result in a greater minimal distance between the observations and the separating hyperplane—that is, a larger margin. In a sense, the maximal margin hyperplane represents the mid-line of the widest "slab" that we can insert between the two classes.

Examining Figure 9.3, we see that three training observations are equidistant from the maximal margin hyperplane and lie along the dashed lines indicating the width of the margin. These three observations are known as *support vectors*, since they are vectors in p-dimensional space (in Figure 9.3, $p = 2$) and they "support" the maximal margin hyperplane in the sense that if these points were moved slightly then the maximal margin hyperplane would move as well. Interestingly, the maximal margin hyperplane depends directly on the support vectors, but not on the other observations: a movement to any of the other observations would not affect the separating hyperplane, provided that the observation's movement does not cause it to

support vector

cross the boundary set by the margin. The fact that the maximal margin hyperplane depends directly on only a small subset of the observations is an important property that will arise later in this chapter when we discuss the support vector classifier and support vector machines.

9.1.4 Construction of the Maximal Margin Classifier

We now consider the task of constructing the maximal margin hyperplane based on a set of n training observations $x_1, \ldots, x_n \in \mathbb{R}^p$ and associated class labels $y_1, \ldots, y_n \in \{-1, 1\}$. Briefly, the maximal margin hyperplane is the solution to the optimization problem

$$\underset{\beta_0,\beta_1,\ldots,\beta_p,M}{\text{maximize}} \; M \tag{9.9}$$

$$\text{subject to } \sum_{j=1}^{p} \beta_j^2 = 1, \tag{9.10}$$

$$y_i(\beta_0 + \beta_1 x_{i1} + \beta_2 x_{i2} + \cdots + \beta_p x_{ip}) \geq M \;\; \forall\, i = 1, \ldots, n. \tag{9.11}$$

This optimization problem (9.9)–(9.11) is actually simpler than it looks. First of all, the constraint in (9.11) that

$$y_i(\beta_0 + \beta_1 x_{i1} + \beta_2 x_{i2} + \cdots + \beta_p x_{ip}) \geq M \;\; \forall\, i = 1, \ldots, n$$

guarantees that each observation will be on the correct side of the hyperplane, provided that M is positive. (Actually, for each observation to be on the correct side of the hyperplane we would simply need $y_i(\beta_0 + \beta_1 x_{i1} + \beta_2 x_{i2} + \cdots + \beta_p x_{ip}) > 0$, so the constraint in (9.11) in fact requires that each observation be on the correct side of the hyperplane, with some cushion, provided that M is positive.)

Second, note that (9.10) is not really a constraint on the hyperplane, since if $\beta_0 + \beta_1 x_{i1} + \beta_2 x_{i2} + \cdots + \beta_p x_{ip} = 0$ defines a hyperplane, then so does $k(\beta_0 + \beta_1 x_{i1} + \beta_2 x_{i2} + \cdots + \beta_p x_{ip}) = 0$ for any $k \neq 0$. However, (9.10) adds meaning to (9.11); one can show that with this constraint the perpendicular distance from the ith observation to the hyperplane is given by

$$y_i(\beta_0 + \beta_1 x_{i1} + \beta_2 x_{i2} + \cdots + \beta_p x_{ip}).$$

Therefore, the constraints (9.10) and (9.11) ensure that each observation is on the correct side of the hyperplane and at least a distance M from the hyperplane. Hence, M represents the margin of our hyperplane, and the optimization problem chooses $\beta_0, \beta_1, \ldots, \beta_p$ to maximize M. This is exactly the definition of the maximal margin hyperplane! The problem (9.9)–(9.11) can be solved efficiently, but details of this optimization are outside of the scope of this book.

9.1.5 The Non-separable Case

The maximal margin classifier is a very natural way to perform classification, *if a separating hyperplane exists.* However, as we have hinted, in many cases no separating hyperplane exists, and so there is no maximal

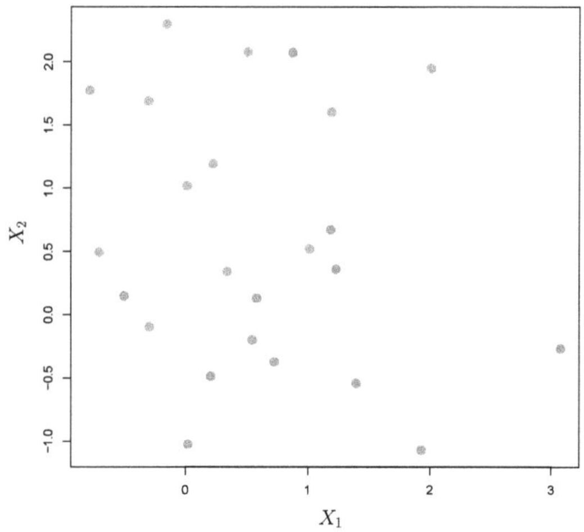

FIGURE 9.4. *There are two classes of observations, shown in blue and in purple. In this case, the two classes are not separable by a hyperplane, and so the maximal margin classifier cannot be used.*

margin classifier. In this case, the optimization problem (9.9)–(9.11) has no solution with $M > 0$. An example is shown in Figure 9.4. In this case, we cannot *exactly* separate the two classes. However, as we will see in the next section, we can extend the concept of a separating hyperplane in order to develop a hyperplane that *almost* separates the classes, using a so-called *soft margin*. The generalization of the maximal margin classifier to the non-separable case is known as the *support vector classifier*.

9.2 Support Vector Classifiers

9.2.1 Overview of the Support Vector Classifier

In Figure 9.4, we see that observations that belong to two classes are not necessarily separable by a hyperplane. In fact, even if a separating hyperplane does exist, then there are instances in which a classifier based on a separating hyperplane might not be desirable. A classifier based on a separating hyperplane will necessarily perfectly classify all of the training observations; this can lead to sensitivity to individual observations. An example is shown in Figure 9.5. The addition of a single observation in the right-hand panel of Figure 9.5 leads to a dramatic change in the maximal margin hyperplane. The resulting maximal margin hyperplane is not satisfactory—for one thing, it has only a tiny margin. This is problematic because as discussed previously, the distance of an observation from the hyperplane can be seen as a measure of our confidence that the observation was correctly classified. Moreover, the fact that the maximal margin hyperplane is extremely sensitive to a change in a single observation suggests that it may have overfit the training data.

In this case, we might be willing to consider a classifier based on a hyperplane that does *not* perfectly separate the two classes, in the interest of

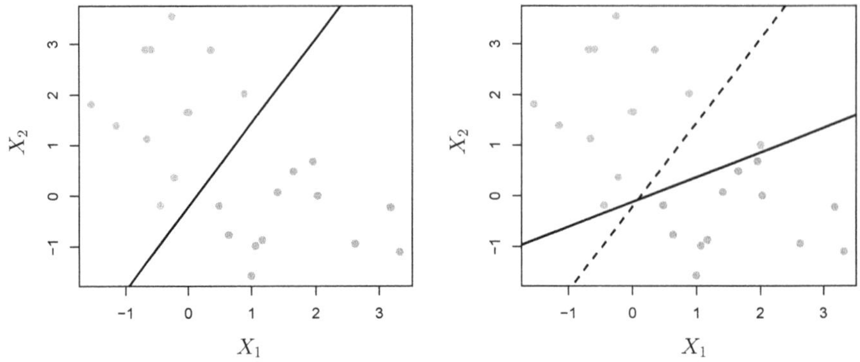

FIGURE 9.5. Left: *Two classes of observations are shown in blue and in purple, along with the maximal margin hyperplane.* Right: *An additional blue observation has been added, leading to a dramatic shift in the maximal margin hyperplane shown as a solid line. The dashed line indicates the maximal margin hyperplane that was obtained in the absence of this additional point.*

- Greater robustness to individual observations, and
- Better classification of *most* of the training observations.

That is, it could be worthwhile to misclassify a few training observations in order to do a better job in classifying the remaining observations.

The *support vector classifier*, sometimes called a *soft margin classifier*, does exactly this. Rather than seeking the largest possible margin so that every observation is not only on the correct side of the hyperplane but also on the correct side of the margin, we instead allow some observations to be on the incorrect side of the margin, or even the incorrect side of the hyperplane. (The margin is *soft* because it can be violated by some of the training observations.) An example is shown in the left-hand panel of Figure 9.6. Most of the observations are on the correct side of the margin. However, a small subset of the observations are on the wrong side of the margin.

support vector classifier
soft margin classifier

An observation can be not only on the wrong side of the margin, but also on the wrong side of the hyperplane. In fact, when there is no separating hyperplane, such a situation is inevitable. Observations on the wrong side of the hyperplane correspond to training observations that are misclassified by the support vector classifier. The right-hand panel of Figure 9.6 illustrates such a scenario.

9.2.2 Details of the Support Vector Classifier

The support vector classifier classifies a test observation depending on which side of a hyperplane it lies. The hyperplane is chosen to correctly separate most of the training observations into the two classes, but may

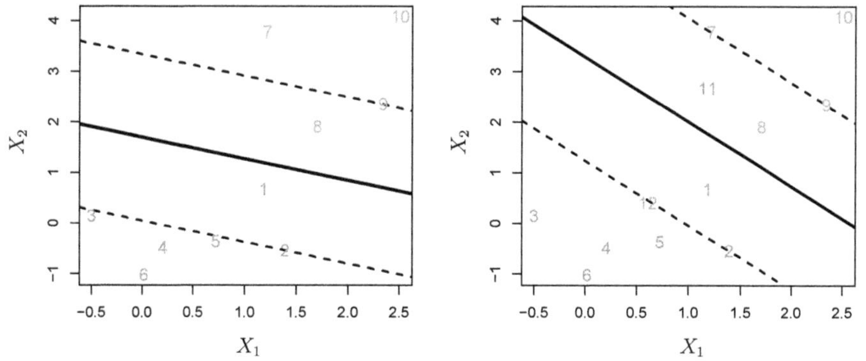

FIGURE 9.6. Left: *A support vector classifier was fit to a small data set. The hyperplane is shown as a solid line and the margins are shown as dashed lines.* Purple observations: *Observations* 3, 4, 5, *and* 6 *are on the correct side of the margin, observation* 2 *is on the margin, and observation 1 is on the wrong side of the margin.* Blue observations: *Observations* 7 *and* 10 *are on the correct side of the margin, observation* 9 *is on the margin, and observation* 8 *is on the wrong side of the margin. No observations are on the wrong side of the hyperplane.* Right: *Same as left panel with two additional points,* 11 *and* 12. *These two observations are on the wrong side of the hyperplane and the wrong side of the margin.*

misclassify a few observations. It is the solution to the optimization problem

$$\underset{\beta_0,\beta_1,\ldots,\beta_p,\epsilon_1,\ldots,\epsilon_n,\,M}{\text{maximize}} \quad M \tag{9.12}$$

$$\text{subject to } \sum_{j=1}^{p}\beta_j^2 = 1, \tag{9.13}$$

$$y_i(\beta_0 + \beta_1 x_{i1} + \beta_2 x_{i2} + \cdots + \beta_p x_{ip}) \geq M(1-\epsilon_i), \tag{9.14}$$

$$\epsilon_i \geq 0, \quad \sum_{i=1}^{n}\epsilon_i \leq C, \tag{9.15}$$

where C is a nonnegative tuning parameter. As in (9.11), M is the width of the margin; we seek to make this quantity as large as possible. In (9.14), $\epsilon_1, \ldots, \epsilon_n$ are *slack variables* that allow individual observations to be on the wrong side of the margin or the hyperplane; we will explain them in greater detail momentarily. Once we have solved (9.12)–(9.15), we classify a test observation x^* as before, by simply determining on which side of the hyperplane it lies. That is, we classify the test observation based on the sign of $f(x^*) = \beta_0 + \beta_1 x_1^* + \cdots + \beta_p x_p^*$. slack variable

The problem (9.12)–(9.15) seems complex, but insight into its behavior can be made through a series of simple observations presented below. First of all, the slack variable ϵ_i tells us where the ith observation is located, relative to the hyperplane and relative to the margin. If $\epsilon_i = 0$ then the ith observation is on the correct side of the margin, as we saw in Section 9.1.4. If $\epsilon_i > 0$ then the ith observation is on the wrong side of the margin, and we say that the ith observation has *violated* the margin. If $\epsilon_i > 1$ then it is on the wrong side of the hyperplane.

We now consider the role of the tuning parameter C. In (9.15), C bounds the sum of the ϵ_i's, and so it determines the number and severity of the violations to the margin (and to the hyperplane) that we will tolerate. We can think of C as a *budget* for the amount that the margin can be violated by the n observations. If $C = 0$ then there is no budget for violations to the margin, and it must be the case that $\epsilon_1 = \cdots = \epsilon_n = 0$, in which case (9.12)–(9.15) simply amounts to the maximal margin hyperplane optimization problem (9.9)–(9.11). (Of course, a maximal margin hyperplane exists only if the two classes are separable.) For $C > 0$ no more than C observations can be on the wrong side of the hyperplane, because if an observation is on the wrong side of the hyperplane then $\epsilon_i > 1$, and (9.15) requires that $\sum_{i=1}^{n} \epsilon_i \leq C$. As the budget C increases, we become more tolerant of violations to the margin, and so the margin will widen. Conversely, as C decreases, we become less tolerant of violations to the margin and so the margin narrows. An example is shown in Figure 9.7.

In practice, C is treated as a tuning parameter that is generally chosen via cross-validation. As with the tuning parameters that we have seen throughout this book, C controls the bias-variance trade-off of the statistical learning technique. When C is small, we seek narrow margins that are rarely violated; this amounts to a classifier that is highly fit to the data, which may have low bias but high variance. On the other hand, when C is larger, the margin is wider and we allow more violations to it; this amounts to fitting the data less hard and obtaining a classifier that is potentially more biased but may have lower variance.

The optimization problem (9.12)–(9.15) has a very interesting property: it turns out that only observations that either lie on the margin or that violate the margin will affect the hyperplane, and hence the classifier obtained. In other words, an observation that lies strictly on the correct side of the margin does not affect the support vector classifier! Changing the position of that observation would not change the classifier at all, provided that its position remains on the correct side of the margin. Observations that lie directly on the margin, or on the wrong side of the margin for their class, are known as *support vectors*. These observations do affect the support vector classifier.

The fact that only support vectors affect the classifier is in line with our previous assertion that C controls the bias-variance trade-off of the support vector classifier. When the tuning parameter C is large, then the margin is wide, many observations violate the margin, and so there are many support vectors. In this case, many observations are involved in determining the hyperplane. The top left panel in Figure 9.7 illustrates this setting: this classifier has low variance (since many observations are support vectors) but potentially high bias. In contrast, if C is small, then there will be fewer support vectors and hence the resulting classifier will have low bias but high variance. The bottom right panel in Figure 9.7 illustrates this setting, with only eight support vectors.

The fact that the support vector classifier's decision rule is based only on a potentially small subset of the training observations (the support vectors) means that it is quite robust to the behavior of observations that are far away from the hyperplane. This property is distinct from some of

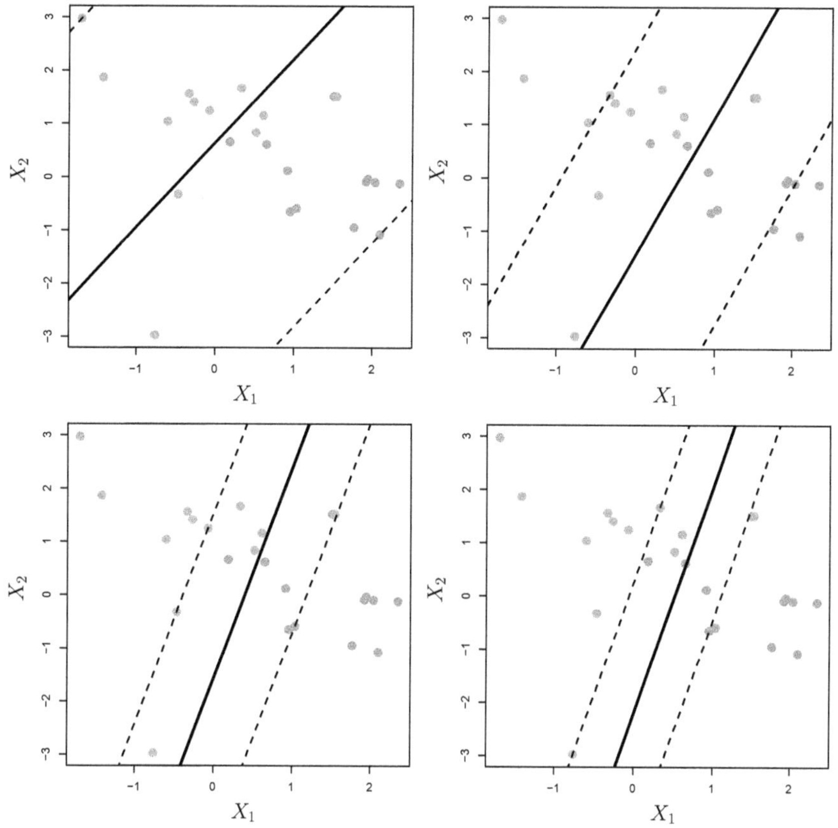

FIGURE 9.7. *A support vector classifier was fit using four different values of the tuning parameter C in (9.12)–(9.15). The largest value of C was used in the top left panel, and smaller values were used in the top right, bottom left, and bottom right panels. When C is large, then there is a high tolerance for observations being on the wrong side of the margin, and so the margin will be large. As C decreases, the tolerance for observations being on the wrong side of the margin decreases, and the margin narrows.*

the other classification methods that we have seen in preceding chapters, such as linear discriminant analysis. Recall that the LDA classification rule depends on the mean of *all* of the observations within each class, as well as the within-class covariance matrix computed using *all* of the observations. In contrast, logistic regression, unlike LDA, has very low sensitivity to observations far from the decision boundary. In fact we will see in Section 9.5 that the support vector classifier and logistic regression are closely related.

9.3 Support Vector Machines

We first discuss a general mechanism for converting a linear classifier into one that produces non-linear decision boundaries. We then introduce the support vector machine, which does this in an automatic way.

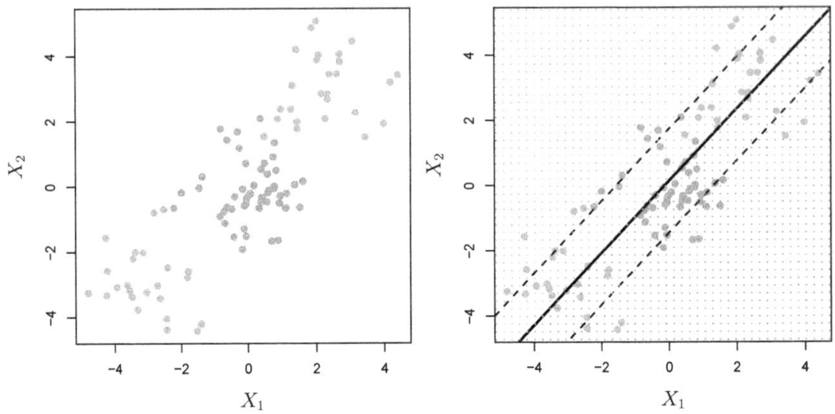

FIGURE 9.8. Left: *The observations fall into two classes, with a non-linear boundary between them.* Right: *The support vector classifier seeks a linear boundary, and consequently performs very poorly.*

9.3.1 Classification with Non-Linear Decision Boundaries

The support vector classifier is a natural approach for classification in the two-class setting, if the boundary between the two classes is linear. However, in practice we are sometimes faced with non-linear class boundaries. For instance, consider the data in the left-hand panel of Figure 9.8. It is clear that a support vector classifier or any linear classifier will perform poorly here. Indeed, the support vector classifier shown in the right-hand panel of Figure 9.8 is useless here.

In Chapter 7, we are faced with an analogous situation. We see there that the performance of linear regression can suffer when there is a non-linear relationship between the predictors and the outcome. In that case, we consider enlarging the feature space using functions of the predictors, such as quadratic and cubic terms, in order to address this non-linearity. In the case of the support vector classifier, we could address the problem of possibly non-linear boundaries between classes in a similar way, by enlarging the feature space using quadratic, cubic, and even higher-order polynomial functions of the predictors. For instance, rather than fitting a support vector classifier using p features

$$X_1, X_2, \ldots, X_p,$$

we could instead fit a support vector classifier using $2p$ features

$$X_1, X_1^2, X_2, X_2^2, \ldots, X_p, X_p^2.$$

Then (9.12)–(9.15) would become

$$\underset{\beta_0,\beta_{11},\beta_{12},\ldots,\beta_{p1},\beta_{p2},\epsilon_1,\ldots,\epsilon_n,\,M}{\text{maximize}} \quad M \tag{9.16}$$

$$\text{subject to } y_i\left(\beta_0 + \sum_{j=1}^{p}\beta_{j1}x_{ij} + \sum_{j=1}^{p}\beta_{j2}x_{ij}^2\right) \geq M(1-\epsilon_i),$$

$$\sum_{i=1}^{n}\epsilon_i \leq C, \quad \epsilon_i \geq 0, \quad \sum_{j=1}^{p}\sum_{k=1}^{2}\beta_{jk}^2 = 1.$$

Why does this lead to a non-linear decision boundary? In the enlarged feature space, the decision boundary that results from (9.16) is in fact linear. But in the original feature space, the decision boundary is of the form $q(x) = 0$, where q is a quadratic polynomial, and its solutions are generally non-linear. One might additionally want to enlarge the feature space with higher-order polynomial terms, or with interaction terms of the form $X_jX_{j'}$ for $j \neq j'$. Alternatively, other functions of the predictors could be considered rather than polynomials. It is not hard to see that there are many possible ways to enlarge the feature space, and that unless we are careful, we could end up with a huge number of features. Then computations would become unmanageable. The support vector machine, which we present next, allows us to enlarge the feature space used by the support vector classifier in a way that leads to efficient computations.

9.3.2 The Support Vector Machine

The *support vector machine* (SVM) is an extension of the support vector classifier that results from enlarging the feature space in a specific way, using *kernels*. We will now discuss this extension, the details of which are somewhat complex and beyond the scope of this book. However, the main idea is described in Section 9.3.1: we may want to enlarge our feature space in order to accommodate a non-linear boundary between the classes. The kernel approach that we describe here is simply an efficient computational approach for enacting this idea.

support vector machine

kernel

We have not discussed exactly how the support vector classifier is computed because the details become somewhat technical. However, it turns out that the solution to the support vector classifier problem (9.12)–(9.15) involves only the *inner products* of the observations (as opposed to the observations themselves). The inner product of two r-vectors a and b is defined as $\langle a, b\rangle = \sum_{i=1}^{r} a_ib_i$. Thus the inner product of two observations x_i, $x_{i'}$ is given by

$$\langle x_i, x_{i'}\rangle = \sum_{j=1}^{p} x_{ij}x_{i'j}. \tag{9.17}$$

It can be shown that

- The linear support vector classifier can be represented as

$$f(x) = \beta_0 + \sum_{i=1}^{n}\alpha_i\langle x, x_i\rangle, \tag{9.18}$$

where there are n parameters α_i, $i = 1, \ldots, n$, one per training observation.

- To estimate the parameters $\alpha_1, \ldots, \alpha_n$ and β_0, all we need are the $\binom{n}{2}$ inner products $\langle x_i, x_{i'} \rangle$ between all pairs of training observations. (The notation $\binom{n}{2}$ means $n(n-1)/2$, and gives the number of pairs among a set of n items.)

Notice that in (9.18), in order to evaluate the function $f(x)$, we need to compute the inner product between the new point x and each of the training points x_i. However, it turns out that α_i is nonzero only for the support vectors in the solution—that is, if a training observation is not a support vector, then its α_i equals zero. So if $\mathcal{S}$ is the collection of indices of these support points, we can rewrite any solution function of the form (9.18) as

$$f(x) = \beta_0 + \sum_{i \in \mathcal{S}} \alpha_i \langle x, x_i \rangle, \tag{9.19}$$

which typically involves far fewer terms than in (9.18).[2]

To summarize, in representing the linear classifier $f(x)$, and in computing its coefficients, all we need are inner products.

Now suppose that every time the inner product (9.17) appears in the representation (9.18), or in a calculation of the solution for the support vector classifier, we replace it with a *generalization* of the inner product of the form

$$K(x_i, x_{i'}), \tag{9.20}$$

where K is some function that we will refer to as a *kernel*. A kernel is a function that quantifies the similarity of two observations. For instance, we could simply take kernel

$$K(x_i, x_{i'}) = \sum_{j=1}^{p} x_{ij} x_{i'j}, \tag{9.21}$$

which would just give us back the support vector classifier. Equation 9.21 is known as a *linear* kernel because the support vector classifier is linear in the features; the linear kernel essentially quantifies the similarity of a pair of observations using Pearson (standard) correlation. But one could instead choose another form for (9.20). For instance, one could replace every instance of $\sum_{j=1}^{p} x_{ij} x_{i'j}$ with the quantity

$$K(x_i, x_{i'}) = (1 + \sum_{j=1}^{p} x_{ij} x_{i'j})^d. \tag{9.22}$$

This is known as a *polynomial kernel* of degree d, where d is a positive integer. Using such a kernel with $d > 1$, instead of the standard linear kernel (9.21), in the support vector classifier algorithm leads to a much more flexible decision boundary. It essentially amounts to fitting a support vector polynomial kernel

[2]By expanding each of the inner products in (9.19), it is easy to see that $f(x)$ is a linear function of the coordinates of x. Doing so also establishes the correspondence between the α_i and the original parameters β_j.

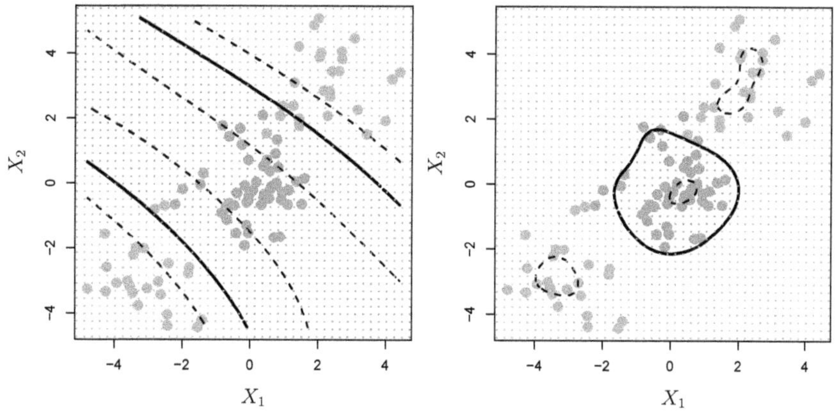

FIGURE 9.9. Left: *An SVM with a polynomial kernel of degree 3 is applied to the non-linear data from Figure 9.8, resulting in a far more appropriate decision rule.* Right: *An SVM with a radial kernel is applied. In this example, either kernel is capable of capturing the decision boundary.*

classifier in a higher-dimensional space involving polynomials of degree d, rather than in the original feature space. When the support vector classifier is combined with a non-linear kernel such as (9.22), the resulting classifier is known as a support vector machine. Note that in this case the (non-linear) function has the form

$$f(x) = \beta_0 + \sum_{i \in \mathcal{S}} \alpha_i K(x, x_i). \tag{9.23}$$

The left-hand panel of Figure 9.9 shows an example of an SVM with a polynomial kernel applied to the non-linear data from Figure 9.8. The fit is a substantial improvement over the linear support vector classifier. When $d = 1$, then the SVM reduces to the support vector classifier seen earlier in this chapter.

The polynomial kernel shown in (9.22) is one example of a possible non-linear kernel, but alternatives abound. Another popular choice is the *radial kernel*, which takes the form radial kernel

$$K(x_i, x_{i'}) = \exp(-\gamma \sum_{j=1}^{p} (x_{ij} - x_{i'j})^2). \tag{9.24}$$

In (9.24), γ is a positive constant. The right-hand panel of Figure 9.9 shows an example of an SVM with a radial kernel on this non-linear data; it also does a good job in separating the two classes.

How does the radial kernel (9.24) actually work? If a given test observation $x^* = (x_1^*, \ldots, x_p^*)^T$ is far from a training observation x_i in terms of Euclidean distance, then $\sum_{j=1}^{p}(x_j^* - x_{ij})^2$ will be large, and so $K(x^*, x_i) = \exp(-\gamma \sum_{j=1}^{p}(x_j^* - x_{ij})^2)$ will be tiny. This means that in (9.23), x_i will play virtually no role in $f(x^*)$. Recall that the predicted class label for the test observation x^* is based on the sign of $f(x^*)$. In other words, training observations that are far from x^* will play essentially no role in the predicted class label for x^*. This means that the radial kernel has very *local*

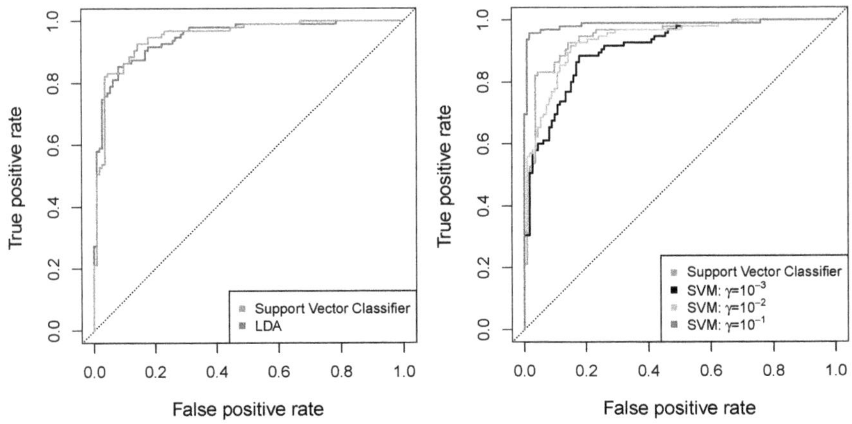

FIGURE 9.10. *ROC curves for the* `Heart` *data training set.* Left: *The support vector classifier and LDA are compared.* Right: *The support vector classifier is compared to an SVM using a radial basis kernel with* $\gamma = 10^{-3}$, 10^{-2}, *and* 10^{-1}.

behavior, in the sense that only nearby training observations have an effect on the class label of a test observation.

What is the advantage of using a kernel rather than simply enlarging the feature space using functions of the original features, as in (9.16)? One advantage is computational, and it amounts to the fact that using kernels, one need only compute $K(x_i, x'_i)$ for all $\binom{n}{2}$ distinct pairs i, i'. This can be done without explicitly working in the enlarged feature space. This is important because in many applications of SVMs, the enlarged feature space is so large that computations are intractable. For some kernels, such as the radial kernel (9.24), the feature space is *implicit* and infinite-dimensional, so we could never do the computations there anyway!

9.3.3 An Application to the Heart Disease Data

In Chapter 8 we apply decision trees and related methods to the `Heart` data. The aim is to use 13 predictors such as `Age`, `Sex`, and `Chol` in order to predict whether an individual has heart disease. We now investigate how an SVM compares to LDA on this data. After removing 6 missing observations, the data consist of 297 subjects, which we randomly split into 207 training and 90 test observations.

We first fit LDA and the support vector classifier to the training data. Note that the support vector classifier is equivalent to an SVM using a polynomial kernel of degree $d = 1$. The left-hand panel of Figure 9.10 displays ROC curves (described in Section 4.4.2) for the training set predictions for both LDA and the support vector classifier. Both classifiers compute scores of the form $\hat{f}(X) = \hat{\beta}_0 + \hat{\beta}_1 X_1 + \hat{\beta}_2 X_2 + \cdots + \hat{\beta}_p X_p$ for each observation. For any given cutoff t, we classify observations into the *heart disease* or *no heart disease* categories depending on whether $\hat{f}(X) < t$ or $\hat{f}(X) \geq t$. The ROC curve is obtained by forming these predictions and computing the false positive and true positive rates for a range of values of t. An optimal classifier will hug the top left corner of the ROC plot. In this instance

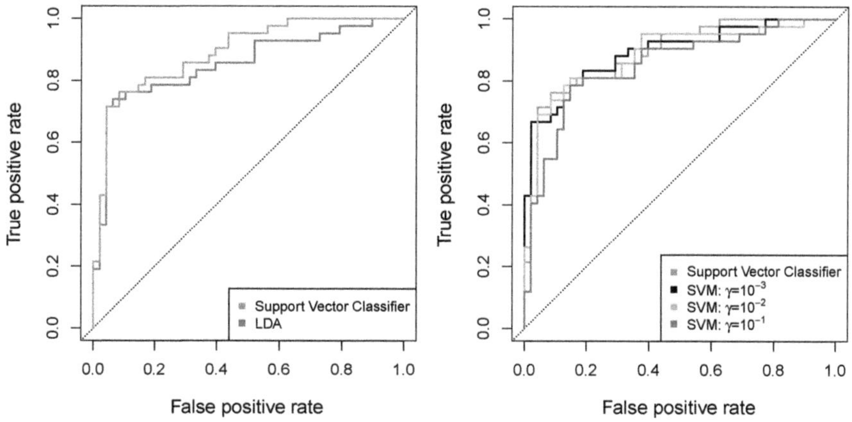

FIGURE 9.11. *ROC curves for the test set of the* `Heart` *data.* Left: *The support vector classifier and LDA are compared.* Right: *The support vector classifier is compared to an SVM using a radial basis kernel with* $\gamma = 10^{-3}$, 10^{-2}, *and* 10^{-1}.

LDA and the support vector classifier both perform well, though there is a suggestion that the support vector classifier may be slightly superior.

The right-hand panel of Figure 9.10 displays ROC curves for SVMs using a radial kernel, with various values of γ. As γ increases and the fit becomes more non-linear, the ROC curves improve. Using $\gamma = 10^{-1}$ appears to give an almost perfect ROC curve. However, these curves represent training error rates, which can be misleading in terms of performance on new test data. Figure 9.11 displays ROC curves computed on the 90 test observations. We observe some differences from the training ROC curves. In the left-hand panel of Figure 9.11, the support vector classifier appears to have a small advantage over LDA (although these differences are not statistically significant). In the right-hand panel, the SVM using $\gamma = 10^{-1}$, which showed the best results on the training data, produces the worst estimates on the test data. This is once again evidence that while a more flexible method will often produce lower training error rates, this does not necessarily lead to improved performance on test data. The SVMs with $\gamma = 10^{-2}$ and $\gamma = 10^{-3}$ perform comparably to the support vector classifier, and all three outperform the SVM with $\gamma = 10^{-1}$.

9.4 SVMs with More than Two Classes

So far, our discussion has been limited to the case of binary classification: that is, classification in the two-class setting. How can we extend SVMs to the more general case where we have some arbitrary number of classes? It turns out that the concept of separating hyperplanes upon which SVMs are based does not lend itself naturally to more than two classes. Though a number of proposals for extending SVMs to the K-class case have been made, the two most popular are the *one-versus-one* and *one-versus-all* approaches. We briefly discuss those two approaches here.

9.4.1 One-Versus-One Classification

Suppose that we would like to perform classification using SVMs, and there are $K > 2$ classes. A *one-versus-one* or *all-pairs* approach constructs $\binom{K}{2}$ SVMs, each of which compares a pair of classes. For example, one such SVM might compare the kth class, coded as $+1$, to the k'th class, coded as -1. We classify a test observation using each of the $\binom{K}{2}$ classifiers, and we tally the number of times that the test observation is assigned to each of the K classes. The final classification is performed by assigning the test observation to the class to which it was most frequently assigned in these $\binom{K}{2}$ pairwise classifications.

one-versus-one

9.4.2 One-Versus-All Classification

The *one-versus-all* approach (also referred to as *one-versus-rest*) is an alternative procedure for applying SVMs in the case of $K > 2$ classes. We fit K SVMs, each time comparing one of the K classes to the remaining $K-1$ classes. Let $\beta_{0k}, \beta_{1k}, \ldots, \beta_{pk}$ denote the parameters that result from fitting an SVM comparing the kth class (coded as $+1$) to the others (coded as -1). Let x^* denote a test observation. We assign the observation to the class for which $\beta_{0k} + \beta_{1k}x_1^* + \beta_{2k}x_2^* + \cdots + \beta_{pk}x_p^*$ is largest, as this amounts to a high level of confidence that the test observation belongs to the kth class rather than to any of the other classes.

one-versus-all
one-versus-rest

9.5 Relationship to Logistic Regression

When SVMs were first introduced in the mid-1990s, they made quite a splash in the statistical and machine learning communities. This was due in part to their good performance, good marketing, and also to the fact that the underlying approach seemed both novel and mysterious. The idea of finding a hyperplane that separates the data as well as possible, while allowing some violations to this separation, seemed distinctly different from classical approaches for classification, such as logistic regression and linear discriminant analysis. Moreover, the idea of using a kernel to expand the feature space in order to accommodate non-linear class boundaries appeared to be a unique and valuable characteristic.

However, since that time, deep connections between SVMs and other more classical statistical methods have emerged. It turns out that one can rewrite the criterion (9.12)–(9.15) for fitting the support vector classifier $f(X) = \beta_0 + \beta_1 X_1 + \cdots + \beta_p X_p$ as

$$\underset{\beta_0,\beta_1,\ldots,\beta_p}{\text{minimize}} \left\{ \sum_{i=1}^{n} \max\left[0, 1 - y_i f(x_i)\right] + \lambda \sum_{j=1}^{p} \beta_j^2 \right\}, \tag{9.25}$$

where λ is a nonnegative tuning parameter. When λ is large then $\beta_1, \ldots, \beta_p$ are small, more violations to the margin are tolerated, and a low-variance but high-bias classifier will result. When λ is small then few violations to the margin will occur; this amounts to a high-variance but low-bias classifier. Thus, a small value of λ in (9.25) amounts to a small value of C in (9.15). Note that the $\lambda \sum_{j=1}^{p} \beta_j^2$ term in (9.25) is the ridge penalty term from Section 6.2.1, and plays a similar role in controlling the bias-variance trade-off for the support vector classifier.

Now (9.25) takes the "Loss + Penalty" form that we have seen repeatedly throughout this book:

$$\underset{\beta_0,\beta_1,\ldots,\beta_p}{\text{minimize}} \left\{ L(\mathbf{X}, \mathbf{y}, \beta) + \lambda P(\beta) \right\}. \tag{9.26}$$

In (9.26), $L(\mathbf{X}, \mathbf{y}, \beta)$ is some loss function quantifying the extent to which the model, parametrized by β, fits the data $(\mathbf{X}, \mathbf{y})$, and $P(\beta)$ is a penalty function on the parameter vector β whose effect is controlled by a nonnegative tuning parameter λ. For instance, ridge regression and the lasso both take this form with

$$L(\mathbf{X}, \mathbf{y}, \beta) = \sum_{i=1}^{n} \left(y_i - \beta_0 - \sum_{j=1}^{p} x_{ij}\beta_j \right)^2$$

and with $P(\beta) = \sum_{j=1}^{p} \beta_j^2$ for ridge regression and $P(\beta) = \sum_{j=1}^{p} |\beta_j|$ for the lasso. In the case of (9.25) the loss function instead takes the form

$$L(\mathbf{X}, \mathbf{y}, \beta) = \sum_{i=1}^{n} \max\left[0, 1 - y_i(\beta_0 + \beta_1 x_{i1} + \cdots + \beta_p x_{ip})\right].$$

This is known as *hinge loss*, and is depicted in Figure 9.12. However, it turns out that the hinge loss function is closely related to the loss function used in logistic regression, also shown in Figure 9.12.

hinge loss

An interesting characteristic of the support vector classifier is that only support vectors play a role in the classifier obtained; observations on the correct side of the margin do not affect it. This is due to the fact that the loss function shown in Figure 9.12 is exactly zero for observations for which $y_i(\beta_0 + \beta_1 x_{i1} + \cdots + \beta_p x_{ip}) \geq 1$; these correspond to observations that are on the correct side of the margin.[3] In contrast, the loss function for logistic regression shown in Figure 9.12 is not exactly zero anywhere. But it is very small for observations that are far from the decision boundary. Due to the similarities between their loss functions, logistic regression and the support vector classifier often give very similar results. When the classes are well separated, SVMs tend to behave better than logistic regression; in more overlapping regimes, logistic regression is often preferred.

When the support vector classifier and SVM were first introduced, it was thought that the tuning parameter C in (9.15) was an unimportant "nuisance" parameter that could be set to some default value, like 1. However, the "Loss + Penalty" formulation (9.25) for the support vector classifier indicates that this is not the case. The choice of tuning parameter is very important and determines the extent to which the model underfits or overfits the data, as illustrated, for example, in Figure 9.7.

---

[3] With this hinge-loss + penalty representation, the margin corresponds to the value one, and the width of the margin is determined by $\sum \beta_j^2$.

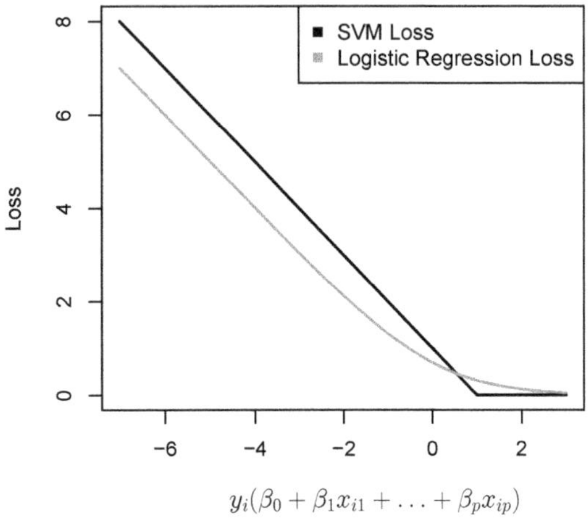

FIGURE 9.12. *The SVM and logistic regression loss functions are compared, as a function of* $y_i(\beta_0+\beta_1 x_{i1}+\cdots+\beta_p x_{ip})$. *When* $y_i(\beta_0+\beta_1 x_{i1}+\cdots+\beta_p x_{ip})$ *is greater than 1, then the SVM loss is zero, since this corresponds to an observation that is on the correct side of the margin. Overall, the two loss functions have quite similar behavior.*

We have established that the support vector classifier is closely related to logistic regression and other preexisting statistical methods. Is the SVM unique in its use of kernels to enlarge the feature space to accommodate non-linear class boundaries? The answer to this question is "no". We could just as well perform logistic regression or many of the other classification methods seen in this book using non-linear kernels; this is closely related to some of the non-linear approaches seen in Chapter 7. However, for historical reasons, the use of non-linear kernels is much more widespread in the context of SVMs than in the context of logistic regression or other methods.

Though we have not addressed it here, there is in fact an extension of the SVM for regression (i.e. for a quantitative rather than a qualitative response), called *support vector regression*. In Chapter 3, we saw that least squares regression seeks coefficients $\beta_0, \beta_1, \ldots, \beta_p$ such that the sum of squared residuals is as small as possible. (Recall from Chapter 3 that residuals are defined as $y_i - \beta_0 - \beta_1 x_{i1} - \cdots - \beta_p x_{ip}$.) Support vector regression instead seeks coefficients that minimize a different type of loss, where only residuals larger in absolute value than some positive constant contribute to the loss function. This is an extension of the margin used in support vector classifiers to the regression setting.

support vector regression

9.6 Lab: Support Vector Machines

In this lab, we use the `sklearn.svm` library to demonstrate the support vector classifier and the support vector machine.

We import some of our usual libraries.

In [1]:
```
import numpy as np
from matplotlib.pyplot import subplots, cm
import sklearn.model_selection as skm
from ISLP import load_data, confusion_table
```

We also collect the new imports needed for this lab.

In [2]:
```
from sklearn.svm import SVC
from ISLP.svm import plot as plot_svm
from sklearn.metrics import RocCurveDisplay
```

We will use the function `RocCurveDisplay.from_estimator()` to produce several ROC plots, using a shorthand `roc_curve`.

`RocCurveDisplay.from_estimator()`

In [3]:
```
roc_curve = RocCurveDisplay.from_estimator # shorthand
```

9.6.1 *Support Vector Classifier*

We now use the `SupportVectorClassifier()` function (abbreviated `SVC()`) from `sklearn` to fit the support vector classifier for a given value of the parameter `C`. The `C` argument allows us to specify the cost of a violation to the margin. When the `cost` argument is small, then the margins will be wide and many support vectors will be on the margin or will violate the margin. When the `C` argument is large, then the margins will be narrow and there will be few support vectors on the margin or violating the margin.

`SupportVectorClassifier()`

Here we demonstrate the use of `SVC()` on a two-dimensional example, so that we can plot the resulting decision boundary. We begin by generating the observations, which belong to two classes, and checking whether the classes are linearly separable.

In [4]:
```
rng = np.random.default_rng(1)
X = rng.standard_normal((50, 2))
y = np.array([-1]*25+[1]*25)
X[y==1] += 1
fig, ax = subplots(figsize=(8,8))
ax.scatter(X[:,0],
           X[:,1],
           c=y,
           cmap=cm.coolwarm);
```

They are not. We now fit the classifier.

In [5]:
```
svm_linear = SVC(C=10, kernel='linear')
svm_linear.fit(X, y)
```

Out[5]:
```
SVC(C=10, kernel='linear')
```

The support vector classifier with two features can be visualized by plotting values of its *decision function*. We have included a function for this in the `ISLP` package (inspired by a similar example in the `sklearn` docs).

decision function

```
In [6]: fig, ax = subplots(figsize=(8,8))
        plot_svm(X,
                 y,
                 svm_linear,
                 ax=ax)
```

The decision boundary between the two classes is linear (because we used the argument `kernel='linear'`). The support vectors are marked with + and the remaining observations are plotted as circles.

What if we instead used a smaller value of the cost parameter?

```
In [7]: svm_linear_small = SVC(C=0.1, kernel='linear')
        svm_linear_small.fit(X, y)
        fig, ax = subplots(figsize=(8,8))
        plot_svm(X,
                 y,
                 svm_linear_small,
                 ax=ax)
```

With a smaller value of the cost parameter, we obtain a larger number of support vectors, because the margin is now wider. For linear kernels, we can extract the coefficients of the linear decision boundary as follows:

```
In [8]: svm_linear.coef_
```

```
Out[8]: array([[1.173   , 0.7734]])
```

Since the support vector machine is an estimator in `sklearn`, we can use the usual machinery to tune it.

```
In [9]: kfold = skm.KFold(5,
                          random_state=0,
                          shuffle=True)
        grid = skm.GridSearchCV(svm_linear,
                                {'C':[0.001,0.01,0.1,1,5,10,100]},
                                refit=True,
                                cv=kfold,
                                scoring='accuracy')
        grid.fit(X, y)
        grid.best_params_
```

```
Out[9]: {'C': 1}
```

We can easily access the cross-validation errors for each of these models in `grid.cv_results_`. This prints out a lot of detail, so we extract the accuracy results only.

```
In [10]: grid.cv_results_[('mean_test_score')]
```

```
Out[10]: array([0.46, 0.46, 0.72, 0.74, 0.74, 0.74, 0.74])
```

We see that `C=1` results in the highest cross-validation accuracy of 0.74, though the accuracy is the same for several values of `C`. The classifier `grid.best_estimator_` can be used to predict the class label on a set of test observations. Let's generate a test data set.

In [11]:
```
X_test = rng.standard_normal((20, 2))
y_test = np.array([-1]*10+[1]*10)
X_test[y_test==1] += 1
```

Now we predict the class labels of these test observations. Here we use the best model selected by cross-validation in order to make the predictions.

In [12]:
```
best_ = grid.best_estimator_
y_test_hat = best_.predict(X_test)
confusion_table(y_test_hat, y_test)
```

Out[12]:
```
      Truth  -1   1
Predicted
         -1   8   4
          1   2   6
```

Thus, with this value of `C`, 70% of the test observations are correctly classified. What if we had instead used `C=0.001`?

In [13]:
```
svm_ = SVC(C=0.001,
           kernel='linear').fit(X, y)
y_test_hat = svm_.predict(X_test)
confusion_table(y_test_hat, y_test)
```

Out[13]:
```
      Truth  -1   1
Predicted
         -1   2   0
          1   8  10
```

In this case 60% of test observations are correctly classified.

We now consider a situation in which the two classes are linearly separable. Then we can find an optimal separating hyperplane using the `SVC()` estimator. We first further separate the two classes in our simulated data so that they are linearly separable:

In [14]:
```
X[y==1] += 1.9;
fig, ax = subplots(figsize=(8,8))
ax.scatter(X[:,0], X[:,1], c=y, cmap=cm.coolwarm);
```

Now the observations are just barely linearly separable.

In [15]:
```
svm_ = SVC(C=1e5, kernel='linear').fit(X, y)
y_hat = svm_.predict(X)
confusion_table(y_hat, y)
```

Out[15]:
```
      Truth  -1   1
Predicted
         -1  25   0
          1   0  25
```

We fit the support vector classifier and plot the resulting hyperplane, using a very large value of `C` so that no observations are misclassified.

In [16]:
```
fig, ax = subplots(figsize=(8,8))
plot_svm(X,
         y,
         svm_,
         ax=ax)
```

Indeed no training errors were made and only three support vectors were used. In fact, the large value of `C` also means that these three support points are *on the margin*, and define it. One may wonder how good the classifier could be on test data that depends on only three data points! We now try a smaller value of `C`.

```
In [17]: svm_ = SVC(C=0.1, kernel='linear').fit(X, y)
         y_hat = svm_.predict(X)
         confusion_table(y_hat, y)
```

```
Out[17]:     Truth   -1   1
         Predicted
                -1   25   0
                 1    0  25
```

Using `C=0.1`, we again do not misclassify any training observations, but we also obtain a much wider margin and make use of twelve support vectors. These jointly define the orientation of the decision boundary, and since there are more of them, it is more stable. It seems possible that this model will perform better on test data than the model with `C=1e5` (and indeed, a simple experiment with a large test set would bear this out).

```
In [18]: fig, ax = subplots(figsize=(8,8))
         plot_svm(X,
                  y,
                  svm_,
                  ax=ax)
```

9.6.2 Support Vector Machine

In order to fit an SVM using a non-linear kernel, we once again use the `SVC()` estimator. However, now we use a different value of the parameter `kernel`. To fit an SVM with a polynomial kernel we use `kernel="poly"`, and to fit an SVM with a radial kernel we use `kernel="rbf"`. In the former case we also use the `degree` argument to specify a degree for the polynomial kernel (this is d in (9.22)), and in the latter case we use `gamma` to specify a value of γ for the radial basis kernel (9.24).

We first generate some data with a non-linear class boundary, as follows:

```
In [19]: X = rng.standard_normal((200, 2))
         X[:100] += 2
         X[100:150] -= 2
         y = np.array([1]*150+[2]*50)
```

Plotting the data makes it clear that the class boundary is indeed non-linear.

```
In [20]: fig, ax = subplots(figsize=(8,8))
         ax.scatter(X[:,0],
                    X[:,1],
                    c=y,
                    cmap=cm.coolwarm)
```

```
Out[20]: <matplotlib.collections.PathCollection at 0x7faa9ba52eb0>
```

The data is randomly split into training and testing groups. We then fit the training data using the `SVC()` estimator with a radial kernel and $\gamma = 1$:

```
In [21]: (X_train,
          X_test,
          y_train,
          y_test) = skm.train_test_split(X,
                                         y,
                                         test_size=0.5,
                                         random_state=0)
         svm_rbf = SVC(kernel="rbf", gamma=1, C=1)
         svm_rbf.fit(X_train, y_train)
```

The plot shows that the resulting SVM has a decidedly non-linear boundary.

```
In [22]: fig, ax = subplots(figsize=(8,8))
         plot_svm(X_train,
                  y_train,
                  svm_rbf,
                  ax=ax)
```

We can see from the figure that there are a fair number of training errors in this SVM fit. If we increase the value of `C`, we can reduce the number of training errors. However, this comes at the price of a more irregular decision boundary that seems to be at risk of overfitting the data.

```
In [23]: svm_rbf = SVC(kernel="rbf", gamma=1, C=1e5)
         svm_rbf.fit(X_train, y_train)
         fig, ax = subplots(figsize=(8,8))
         plot_svm(X_train,
                  y_train,
                  svm_rbf,
                  ax=ax)
```

We can perform cross-validation using `skm.GridSearchCV()` to select the best choice of γ and `C` for an SVM with a radial kernel:

```
In [24]: kfold = skm.KFold(5,
                           random_state=0,
                           shuffle=True)
         grid = skm.GridSearchCV(svm_rbf,
                                 {'C':[0.1,1,10,100,1000],
                                  'gamma':[0.5,1,2,3,4]},
                                 refit=True,
                                 cv=kfold,
                                 scoring='accuracy');
         grid.fit(X_train, y_train)
         grid.best_params_

Out[24]: {'C': 100, 'gamma': 1}
```

The best choice of parameters under five-fold CV is achieved at `C=1` and `gamma=0.5`, though several other values also achieve the same value.

```
In [25]: best_svm = grid.best_estimator_
         fig, ax = subplots(figsize=(8,8))
         plot_svm(X_train,
```

```
              y_train,
              best_svm,
              ax=ax)

y_hat_test = best_svm.predict(X_test)
confusion_table(y_hat_test, y_test)
```

Out[25]:
```
Truth      1    2
Predicted
        1  69    6
        2   6   19
```

With these parameters, 12% of test observations are misclassified by this SVM.

9.6.3 ROC Curves

SVMs and support vector classifiers output class labels for each observation. However, it is also possible to obtain *fitted values* for each observation, which are the numerical scores used to obtain the class labels. For instance, in the case of a support vector classifier, the fitted value for an observation $X = (X_1, X_2, \ldots, X_p)^T$ takes the form $\hat{\beta}_0 + \hat{\beta}_1 X_1 + \hat{\beta}_2 X_2 + \ldots + \hat{\beta}_p X_p$. For an SVM with a non-linear kernel, the equation that yields the fitted value is given in (9.23). The sign of the fitted value determines on which side of the decision boundary the observation lies. Therefore, the relationship between the fitted value and the class prediction for a given observation is simple: if the fitted value exceeds zero then the observation is assigned to one class, and if it is less than zero then it is assigned to the other. By changing this threshold from zero to some positive value, we skew the classifications in favor of one class versus the other. By considering a range of these thresholds, positive and negative, we produce the ingredients for a ROC plot. We can access these values by calling the `decision_function()` method of a fitted SVM estimator.

`.function_decision()`

The function `ROCCurveDisplay.from_estimator()` (which we have abbreviated to `roc_curve()`) will produce a plot of a ROC curve. It takes a fitted estimator as its first argument, followed by a model matrix X and labels y. The argument `name` is used in the legend, while `color` is used for the color of the line. Results are plotted on our axis object `ax`.

`roc_curve()`

In [26]:
```
fig, ax = subplots(figsize=(8,8))
roc_curve(best_svm,
          X_train,
          y_train,
          name='Training',
          color='r',
          ax=ax);
```

In this example, the SVM appears to provide accurate predictions. By increasing γ we can produce a more flexible fit and generate further improvements in accuracy.

In [27]:
```
svm_flex = SVC(kernel="rbf",
               gamma=50,
```

```
                  C=1)
svm_flex.fit(X_train, y_train)
fig, ax = subplots(figsize=(8,8))
roc_curve(svm_flex,
          X_train,
          y_train,
          name='Training $\gamma=50$',
          color='r',
          ax=ax);
```

However, these ROC curves are all on the training data. We are really more interested in the level of prediction accuracy on the test data. When we compute the ROC curves on the test data, the model with $\gamma = 0.5$ appears to provide the most accurate results.

In [28]:
```
roc_curve(svm_flex,
          X_test,
          y_test,
          name='Test $\gamma=50$',
          color='b',
          ax=ax)
fig;
```

Let's look at our tuned SVM.

In [29]:
```
fig, ax = subplots(figsize=(8,8))
for (X_, y_, c, name) in zip(
     (X_train, X_test),
     (y_train, y_test),
     ('r', 'b'),
     ('CV tuned on training',
      'CV tuned on test')):
    roc_curve(best_svm,
              X_,
              y_,
              name=name,
              ax=ax,
              color=c)
```

9.6.4 SVM with Multiple Classes

If the response is a factor containing more than two levels, then the `SVC()` function will perform multi-class classification using either the one-versus-one approach (when `decision_function_shape=='ovo'`) or one-versus-rest[4] (when `decision_function_shape=='ovr'`). We explore that setting briefly here by generating a third class of observations.

In [30]:
```
rng = np.random.default_rng(123)
X = np.vstack([X, rng.standard_normal((50, 2))])
y = np.hstack([y, [0]*50])
X[y==0,1] += 2
fig, ax = subplots(figsize=(8,8))
ax.scatter(X[:,0], X[:,1], c=y, cmap=cm.coolwarm);
```

[4]One-versus-rest is also known as one-versus-all.

We now fit an SVM to the data:

```
In [31]: svm_rbf_3 = SVC(kernel="rbf",
                          C=10,
                          gamma=1,
                          decision_function_shape='ovo');
         svm_rbf_3.fit(X, y)
         fig, ax = subplots(figsize=(8,8))
         plot_svm(X,
                  y,
                  svm_rbf_3,
                  scatter_cmap=cm.tab10,
                  ax=ax)
```

The `sklearn.svm` library can also be used to perform support vector regression with a numerical response using the estimator `SupportVector-Regression()`.

SupportVect
Regression(

9.6.5 Application to Gene Expression Data

We now examine the `Khan` data set, which consists of a number of tissue samples corresponding to four distinct types of small round blue cell tumors. For each tissue sample, gene expression measurements are available. The data set consists of training data, `xtrain` and `ytrain`, and testing data, `xtest` and `ytest`.

We examine the dimension of the data:

```
In [32]: Khan = load_data('Khan')
         Khan['xtrain'].shape, Khan['xtest'].shape
```

```
Out[32]: ((63, 2308), (20, 2308))
```

This data set consists of expression measurements for 2,308 genes. The training and test sets consist of 63 and 20 observations, respectively.

We will use a support vector approach to predict cancer subtype using gene expression measurements. In this data set, there is a very large number of features relative to the number of observations. This suggests that we should use a linear kernel, because the additional flexibility that will result from using a polynomial or radial kernel is unnecessary.

```
In [33]: khan_linear = SVC(kernel='linear', C=10)
         khan_linear.fit(Khan['xtrain'], Khan['ytrain'])
         confusion_table(khan_linear.predict(Khan['xtrain']),
                         Khan['ytrain'])
```

```
Out[33]:      Truth    1   2   3   4
         Predicted
                 1    8   0   0   0
                 2    0  23   0   0
                 3    0   0  12   0
                 4    0   0   0  20
```

We see that there are *no* training errors. In fact, this is not surprising, because the large number of variables relative to the number of observations implies that it is easy to find hyperplanes that fully separate the classes.

We are more interested in the support vector classifier's performance on the test observations.

```
In [34]: confusion_table(khan_linear.predict(Khan['xtest']),
                         Khan['ytest'])
```

```
Out[34]:     Truth   1  2  3  4
         Predicted
                 1   3  0  0  0
                 2   0  6  2  0
                 3   0  0  4  0
                 4   0  0  0  5
```

We see that using `C=10` yields two test set errors on these data.

9.7 Exercises

Conceptual

1. This problem involves hyperplanes in two dimensions.

   (a) Sketch the hyperplane $1 + 3X_1 - X_2 = 0$. Indicate the set of points for which $1 + 3X_1 - X_2 > 0$, as well as the set of points for which $1 + 3X_1 - X_2 < 0$.

   (b) On the same plot, sketch the hyperplane $-2 + X_1 + 2X_2 = 0$. Indicate the set of points for which $-2 + X_1 + 2X_2 > 0$, as well as the set of points for which $-2 + X_1 + 2X_2 < 0$.

2. We have seen that in $p = 2$ dimensions, a linear decision boundary takes the form $\beta_0 + \beta_1 X_1 + \beta_2 X_2 = 0$. We now investigate a non-linear decision boundary.

   (a) Sketch the curve

   $$(1 + X_1)^2 + (2 - X_2)^2 = 4.$$

   (b) On your sketch, indicate the set of points for which

   $$(1 + X_1)^2 + (2 - X_2)^2 > 4,$$

   as well as the set of points for which

   $$(1 + X_1)^2 + (2 - X_2)^2 \leq 4.$$

   (c) Suppose that a classifier assigns an observation to the blue class if

   $$(1 + X_1)^2 + (2 - X_2)^2 > 4,$$

   and to the red class otherwise. To what class is the observation $(0, 0)$ classified? $(-1, 1)$? $(2, 2)$? $(3, 8)$?

   (d) Argue that while the decision boundary in (c) is not linear in terms of X_1 and X_2, it is linear in terms of X_1, X_1^2, X_2, and X_2^2.

3. Here we explore the maximal margin classifier on a toy data set.

   (a) We are given $n = 7$ observations in $p = 2$ dimensions. For each observation, there is an associated class label.

Obs.	X_1	X_2	Y
1	3	4	Red
2	2	2	Red
3	4	4	Red
4	1	4	Red
5	2	1	Blue
6	4	3	Blue
7	4	1	Blue

   Sketch the observations.

   (b) Sketch the optimal separating hyperplane, and provide the equation for this hyperplane (of the form (9.1)).

   (c) Describe the classification rule for the maximal margin classifier. It should be something along the lines of "Classify to Red if $\beta_0 + \beta_1 X_1 + \beta_2 X_2 > 0$, and classify to Blue otherwise." Provide the values for β_0, β_1, and β_2.

   (d) On your sketch, indicate the margin for the maximal margin hyperplane.

   (e) Indicate the support vectors for the maximal margin classifier.

   (f) Argue that a slight movement of the seventh observation would not affect the maximal margin hyperplane.

   (g) Sketch a hyperplane that is *not* the optimal separating hyperplane, and provide the equation for this hyperplane.

   (h) Draw an additional observation on the plot so that the two classes are no longer separable by a hyperplane.

Applied

4. Generate a simulated two-class data set with 100 observations and two features in which there is a visible but non-linear separation between the two classes. Show that in this setting, a support vector machine with a polynomial kernel (with degree greater than 1) or a radial kernel will outperform a support vector classifier on the training data. Which technique performs best on the test data? Make plots and report training and test error rates in order to back up your assertions.

5. We have seen that we can fit an SVM with a non-linear kernel in order to perform classification using a non-linear decision boundary. We will now see that we can also obtain a non-linear decision boundary by performing logistic regression using non-linear transformations of the features.

(a) Generate a data set with $n = 500$ and $p = 2$, such that the observations belong to two classes with a quadratic decision boundary between them. For instance, you can do this as follows:

```
rng = np.random.default_rng(5)
x1 = rng.uniform(size=500) - 0.5
x2 = rng.uniform(size=500) - 0.5
y = x1**2 - x2**2 > 0
```

(b) Plot the observations, colored according to their class labels. Your plot should display X_1 on the x-axis, and X_2 on the y-axis.

(c) Fit a logistic regression model to the data, using X_1 and X_2 as predictors.

(d) Apply this model to the *training data* in order to obtain a predicted class label for each training observation. Plot the observations, colored according to the *predicted* class labels. The decision boundary should be linear.

(e) Now fit a logistic regression model to the data using non-linear functions of X_1 and X_2 as predictors (e.g. X_1^2, $X_1 \times X_2$, $\log(X_2)$, and so forth).

(f) Apply this model to the *training data* in order to obtain a predicted class label for each training observation. Plot the observations, colored according to the *predicted* class labels. The decision boundary should be obviously non-linear. If it is not, then repeat (a)–(e) until you come up with an example in which the predicted class labels are obviously non-linear.

(g) Fit a support vector classifier to the data with X_1 and X_2 as predictors. Obtain a class prediction for each training observation. Plot the observations, colored according to the *predicted class labels.*

(h) Fit a SVM using a non-linear kernel to the data. Obtain a class prediction for each training observation. Plot the observations, colored according to the *predicted class labels.*

(i) Comment on your results.

6. At the end of Section 9.6.1, it is claimed that in the case of data that is just barely linearly separable, a support vector classifier with a small value of `C` that misclassifies a couple of training observations may perform better on test data than one with a huge value of `C` that does not misclassify any training observations. You will now investigate this claim.

(a) Generate two-class data with $p = 2$ in such a way that the classes are just barely linearly separable.

(b) Compute the cross-validation error rates for support vector classifiers with a range of `C` values. How many training observations are misclassified for each value of `C` considered, and how does this relate to the cross-validation errors obtained?

(c) Generate an appropriate test data set, and compute the test errors corresponding to each of the values of `C` considered. Which value of `C` leads to the fewest test errors, and how does this compare to the values of `C` that yield the fewest training errors and the fewest cross-validation errors?

(d) Discuss your results.

7. In this problem, you will use support vector approaches in order to predict whether a given car gets high or low gas mileage based on the `Auto` data set.

   (a) Create a binary variable that takes on a 1 for cars with gas mileage above the median, and a 0 for cars with gas mileage below the median.

   (b) Fit a support vector classifier to the data with various values of `C`, in order to predict whether a car gets high or low gas mileage. Report the cross-validation errors associated with different values of this parameter. Comment on your results. Note you will need to fit the classifier without the gas mileage variable to produce sensible results.

   (c) Now repeat (b), this time using SVMs with radial and polynomial basis kernels, with different values of `gamma` and `degree` and `C`. Comment on your results.

   (d) Make some plots to back up your assertions in (b) and (c).

   Hint: In the lab, we used the `plot_svm()` *function for fitted SVMs. When $p > 2$, you can use the keyword argument* `features` *to create plots displaying pairs of variables at a time.*

8. This problem involves the `OJ` data set which is part of the `ISLP` package.

   (a) Create a training set containing a random sample of 800 observations, and a test set containing the remaining observations.

   (b) Fit a support vector classifier to the training data using `C = 0.01`, with `Purchase` as the response and the other variables as predictors. How many support points are there?

   (c) What are the training and test error rates?

   (d) Use cross-validation to select an optimal `C`. Consider values in the range 0.01 to 10.

   (e) Compute the training and test error rates using this new value for `C`.

   (f) Repeat parts (b) through (e) using a support vector machine with a radial kernel. Use the default value for `gamma`.

   (g) Repeat parts (b) through (e) using a support vector machine with a polynomial kernel. Set `degree = 2`.

   (h) Overall, which approach seems to give the best results on this data?

10
Deep Learning

This chapter covers the important topic of *deep learning*. At the time of writing (2020), deep learning is a very active area of research in the machine learning and artificial intelligence communities. The cornerstone of deep learning is the *neural network*.

deep learning

neural network

Neural networks rose to fame in the late 1980s. There was a lot of excitement and a certain amount of hype associated with this approach, and they were the impetus for the popular *Neural Information Processing Systems* meetings (NeurIPS, formerly NIPS) held every year, typically in exotic places like ski resorts. This was followed by a synthesis stage, where the properties of neural networks were analyzed by machine learners, mathematicians and statisticians; algorithms were improved, and the methodology stabilized. Then along came SVMs, boosting, and random forests, and neural networks fell somewhat from favor. Part of the reason was that neural networks required a lot of tinkering, while the new methods were more automatic. Also, on many problems the new methods outperformed poorly-trained neural networks. This was the *status quo* for the first decade in the new millennium.

All the while, though, a core group of neural-network enthusiasts were pushing their technology harder on ever-larger computing architectures and data sets. Neural networks resurfaced after 2010 with the new name *deep learning*, with new architectures, additional bells and whistles, and a string of success stories on some niche problems such as image and video classification, speech and text modeling. Many in the field believe that the major reason for these successes is the availability of ever-larger training datasets, made possible by the wide-scale use of digitization in science and industry.

In this chapter we discuss the basics of neural networks and deep learning, and then go into some of the specializations for specific problems, such as convolutional neural networks (CNNs) for image classification, and recurrent neural networks (RNNs) for time series and other sequences. We

G. James et al., *An Introduction to Statistical Learning*, Springer Texts in Statistics,
https://doi.org/10.1007/978-3-031-38747-0_10

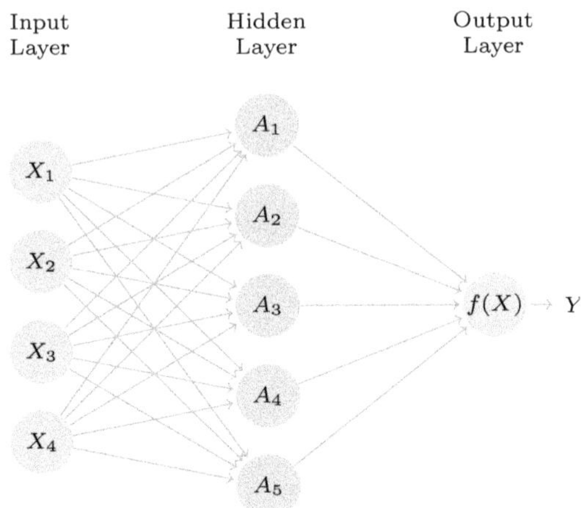

FIGURE 10.1. *Neural network with a single hidden layer. The hidden layer computes activations $A_k = h_k(X)$ that are nonlinear transformations of linear combinations of the inputs $X_1, X_2, \ldots, X_p$. Hence these A_k are not directly observed. The functions $h_k(\cdot)$ are not fixed in advance, but are learned during the training of the network. The output layer is a linear model that uses these activations A_k as inputs, resulting in a function $f(X)$.*

will also demonstrate these models using the `Python` `torch` package, along with a number of helper packages.

The material in this chapter is slightly more challenging than elsewhere in this book.

10.1 Single Layer Neural Networks

A neural network takes an input vector of p variables $X = (X_1, X_2, \ldots, X_p)$ and builds a nonlinear function $f(X)$ to predict the response Y. We have built nonlinear prediction models in earlier chapters, using trees, boosting and generalized additive models. What distinguishes neural networks from these methods is the particular *structure* of the model. Figure 10.1 shows a simple *feed-forward neural network* for modeling a quantitative response using $p = 4$ predictors. In the terminology of neural networks, the four features $X_1, \ldots, X_4$ make up the units in the *input layer*. The arrows indicate that each of the inputs from the input layer feeds into each of the K *hidden units* (we get to pick K; here we chose 5). The neural network model has the form

feed-forward neural network

input layer

hidden units

$$\begin{aligned} f(X) &= \beta_0 + \textstyle\sum_{k=1}^{K} \beta_k h_k(X) \\ &= \beta_0 + \textstyle\sum_{k=1}^{K} \beta_k g(w_{k0} + \sum_{j=1}^{p} w_{kj} X_j). \end{aligned} \quad (10.1)$$

It is built up here in two steps. First the K *activations* A_k, $k = 1, \ldots, K$, in the hidden layer are computed as functions of the input features $X_1, \ldots, X_p$,

activations

$$A_k = h_k(X) = g(w_{k0} + \textstyle\sum_{j=1}^{p} w_{kj} X_j), \quad (10.2)$$

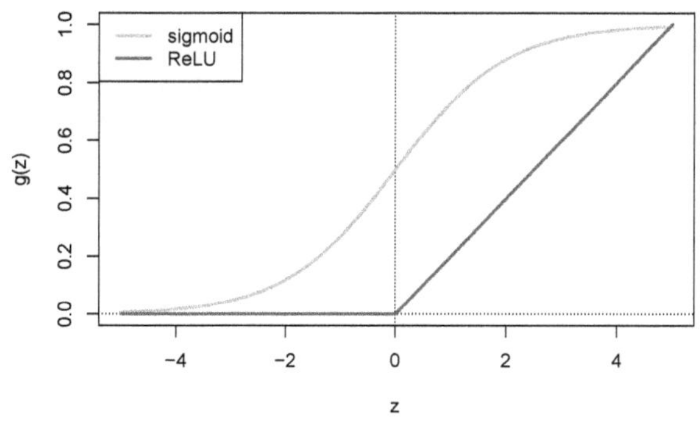

FIGURE 10.2. *Activation functions. The piecewise-linear* **ReLU** *function is popular for its efficiency and computability. We have scaled it down by a factor of five for ease of comparison.*

where $g(z)$ is a nonlinear *activation function* that is specified in advance. We can think of each A_k as a different transformation $h_k(X)$ of the original features, much like the basis functions of Chapter 7. These K activations from the hidden layer then feed into the output layer, resulting in

activation function

$$f(X) = \beta_0 + \sum_{k=1}^{K} \beta_k A_k, \tag{10.3}$$

a linear regression model in the $K = 5$ activations. All the parameters $\beta_0, \ldots, \beta_K$ and $w_{10}, \ldots, w_{Kp}$ need to be estimated from data. In the early instances of neural networks, the *sigmoid* activation function was favored,

sigmoid

$$g(z) = \frac{e^z}{1+e^z} = \frac{1}{1+e^{-z}}, \tag{10.4}$$

which is the same function used in logistic regression to convert a linear function into probabilities between zero and one (see Figure 10.2). The preferred choice in modern neural networks is the *ReLU* (*rectified linear unit*) activation function, which takes the form

ReLU

rectified linear unit

$$g(z) = (z)_+ = \begin{cases} 0 & \text{if } z < 0 \\ z & \text{otherwise.} \end{cases} \tag{10.5}$$

A ReLU activation can be computed and stored more efficiently than a sigmoid activation. Although it thresholds at zero, because we apply it to a linear function (10.2) the constant term w_{k0} will shift this inflection point.

So in words, the model depicted in Figure 10.1 derives five new features by computing five different linear combinations of X, and then squashes each through an activation function $g(\cdot)$ to transform it. The final model is linear in these derived variables.

The name *neural network* originally derived from thinking of these hidden units as analogous to neurons in the brain — values of the activations $A_k = h_k(X)$ close to one are *firing*, while those close to zero are *silent* (using the sigmoid activation function).

The nonlinearity in the activation function $g(\cdot)$ is essential, since without it the model $f(X)$ in (10.1) would collapse into a simple linear model in

$X_1, \ldots, X_p$. Moreover, having a nonlinear activation function allows the model to capture complex nonlinearities and interaction effects. Consider a very simple example with $p = 2$ input variables $X = (X_1, X_2)$, and $K = 2$ hidden units $h_1(X)$ and $h_2(X)$ with $g(z) = z^2$. We specify the other parameters as

$$\begin{array}{lll} \beta_0 = 0, & \beta_1 = \frac{1}{4}, & \beta_2 = -\frac{1}{4}, \\ w_{10} = 0, & w_{11} = 1, & w_{12} = \;\;1, \\ w_{20} = 0, & w_{21} = 1, & w_{22} = -1. \end{array} \tag{10.6}$$

From (10.2), this means that

$$\begin{array}{rcl} h_1(X) & = & (0 + X_1 + X_2)^2, \\ h_2(X) & = & (0 + X_1 - X_2)^2. \end{array} \tag{10.7}$$

Then plugging (10.7) into (10.1), we get

$$\begin{array}{rcl} f(X) & = & 0 + \frac{1}{4} \cdot (0 + X_1 + X_2)^2 - \frac{1}{4} \cdot (0 + X_1 - X_2)^2 \\ & = & \frac{1}{4}\left[(X_1 + X_2)^2 - (X_1 - X_2)^2\right] \\ & = & X_1 X_2. \end{array} \tag{10.8}$$

So the sum of two nonlinear transformations of linear functions can give us an interaction! In practice we would not use a quadratic function for $g(z)$, since we would always get a second-degree polynomial in the original coordinates $X_1, \ldots, X_p$. The sigmoid or ReLU activations do not have such a limitation.

Fitting a neural network requires estimating the unknown parameters in (10.1). For a quantitative response, typically squared-error loss is used, so that the parameters are chosen to minimize

$$\sum_{i=1}^{n} (y_i - f(x_i))^2. \tag{10.9}$$

Details about how to perform this minimization are provided in Section 10.7.

10.2 Multilayer Neural Networks

Modern neural networks typically have more than one hidden layer, and often many units per layer. In theory a single hidden layer with a large number of units has the ability to approximate most functions. However, the learning task of discovering a good solution is made much easier with multiple layers each of modest size.

We will illustrate a large dense network on the famous and publicly available `MNIST` handwritten digit dataset.[1] Figure 10.3 shows examples of these digits. The idea is to build a model to classify the images into their correct digit class 0–9. Every image has $p = 28 \times 28 = 784$ pixels, each of which is an eight-bit grayscale value between 0 and 255 representing

[1]See LeCun, Cortes, and Burges (2010) "The MNIST database of handwritten digits", available at `http://yann.lecun.com/exdb/mnist`.

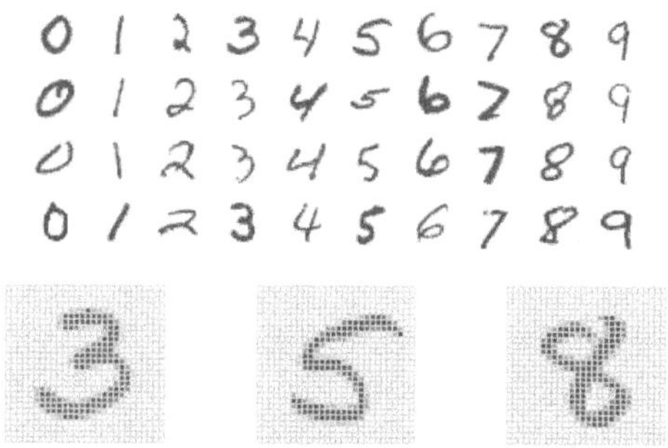

FIGURE 10.3. *Examples of handwritten digits from the* MNIST *corpus. Each grayscale image has* 28×28 *pixels, each of which is an eight-bit number (0–255) which represents how dark that pixel is. The first 3, 5, and 8 are enlarged to show their 784 individual pixel values.*

the relative amount of the written digit in that tiny square.[2] These pixels are stored in the input vector X (in, say, column order). The output is the class label, represented by a vector $Y = (Y_0, Y_1, \ldots, Y_9)$ of 10 dummy variables, with a one in the position corresponding to the label, and zeros elsewhere. In the machine learning community, this is known as *one-hot encoding*. There are 60,000 training images, and 10,000 test images.

one-hot encoding

On a historical note, digit recognition problems were the catalyst that accelerated the development of neural network technology in the late 1980s at AT&T Bell Laboratories and elsewhere. Pattern recognition tasks of this kind are relatively simple for humans. Our visual system occupies a large fraction of our brains, and good recognition is an evolutionary force for survival. These tasks are not so simple for machines, and it has taken more than 30 years to refine the neural-network architectures to match human performance.

Figure 10.4 shows a multilayer network architecture that works well for solving the digit-classification task. It differs from Figure 10.1 in several ways:

- It has two hidden layers L_1 (256 units) and L_2 (128 units) rather than one. Later we will see a network with seven hidden layers.

- It has ten output variables, rather than one. In this case the ten variables really represent a single qualitative variable and so are quite dependent. (We have indexed them by the digit class 0–9 rather than 1–10, for clarity.) More generally, in *multi-task learning* one can predict different responses simultaneously with a single network; they all have a say in the formation of the hidden layers.

multi-task learning

- The loss function used for training the network is tailored for the multiclass classification task.

[2]In the analog-to-digital conversion process, only part of the written numeral may fall in the square representing a particular pixel.

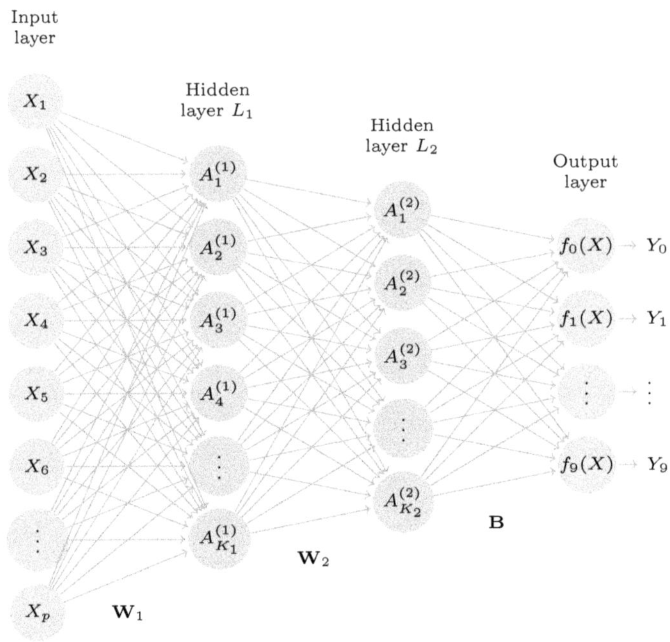

FIGURE 10.4. *Neural network diagram with two hidden layers and multiple outputs, suitable for the* MNIST *handwritten-digit problem. The input layer has* $p = 784$ *units, the two hidden layers* $K_1 = 256$ *and* $K_2 = 128$ *units respectively, and the output layer* 10 *units. Along with intercepts (referred to as* biases *in the deep-learning community) this network has 235,146 parameters (referred to as weights).*

The first hidden layer is as in (10.2), with

$$\begin{aligned} A_k^{(1)} &= h_k^{(1)}(X) \\ &= g(w_{k0}^{(1)} + \textstyle\sum_{j=1}^{p} w_{kj}^{(1)} X_j) \end{aligned} \tag{10.10}$$

for $k = 1, \ldots, K_1$. The second hidden layer treats the activations $A_k^{(1)}$ of the first hidden layer as inputs and computes new activations

$$\begin{aligned} A_\ell^{(2)} &= h_\ell^{(2)}(X) \\ &= g(w_{\ell 0}^{(2)} + \textstyle\sum_{k=1}^{K_1} w_{\ell k}^{(2)} A_k^{(1)}) \end{aligned} \tag{10.11}$$

for $\ell = 1, \ldots, K_2$. Notice that each of the activations in the second layer $A_\ell^{(2)} = h_\ell^{(2)}(X)$ is a function of the input vector X. This is the case because while they are explicitly a function of the activations $A_k^{(1)}$ from layer L_1, these in turn are functions of X. This would also be the case with more hidden layers. Thus, through a chain of transformations, the network is able to build up fairly complex transformations of X that ultimately feed into the output layer as features.

We have introduced additional superscript notation such as $h_\ell^{(2)}(X)$ and $w_{\ell j}^{(2)}$ in (10.10) and (10.11) to indicate to which layer the activations and *weights* (coefficients) belong, in this case layer 2. The notation $\mathbf{W}_1$ in Fig- weights ure 10.4 represents the entire matrix of weights that feed from the input layer to the first hidden layer L_1. This matrix will have $785 \times 256 = 200{,}960$ elements; there are 785 rather than 784 because we must account for the intercept or *bias* term.[3]

bias

Each element $A_k^{(1)}$ feeds to the second hidden layer L_2 via the matrix of weights $\mathbf{W}_2$ of dimension $257 \times 128 = 32{,}896$.

We now get to the output layer, where we now have ten responses rather than one. The first step is to compute ten different linear models similar to our single model (10.1),

$$\begin{aligned} Z_m &= \beta_{m0} + \sum_{\ell=1}^{K_2} \beta_{m\ell} h_\ell^{(2)}(X) \\ &= \beta_{m0} + \sum_{\ell=1}^{K_2} \beta_{m\ell} A_\ell^{(2)}, \end{aligned} \tag{10.12}$$

for $m = 0, 1, \ldots, 9$. The matrix $\mathbf{B}$ stores all $129 \times 10 = 1{,}290$ of these weights.

If these were all separate quantitative responses, we would simply set each $f_m(X) = Z_m$ and be done. However, we would like our estimates to represent class probabilities $f_m(X) = \Pr(Y = m|X)$, just like in multinomial logistic regression in Section 4.3.5. So we use the special *softmax* activation function (see (4.13) on page 145),

softmax

$$f_m(X) = \Pr(Y = m|X) = \frac{e^{Z_m}}{\sum_{\ell=0}^{9} e^{Z_\ell}}, \tag{10.13}$$

for $m = 0, 1, \ldots, 9$. This ensures that the 10 numbers behave like probabilities (non-negative and sum to one). Even though the goal is to build a classifier, our model actually estimates a probability for each of the 10 classes. The classifier then assigns the image to the class with the highest probability.

To train this network, since the response is qualitative, we look for coefficient estimates that minimize the negative multinomial log-likelihood

$$-\sum_{i=1}^{n} \sum_{m=0}^{9} y_{im} \log(f_m(x_i)), \tag{10.14}$$

also known as the *cross-entropy*. This is a generalization of the criterion (4.5) for two-class logistic regression. Details on how to minimize this objective are given in Section 10.7. If the response were quantitative, we would instead minimize squared-error loss as in (10.9).

cross-entropy

Table 10.1 compares the test performance of the neural network with two simple models presented in Chapter 4 that make use of linear decision boundaries: multinomial logistic regression and linear discriminant analysis. The improvement of neural networks over both of these linear methods is dramatic: the network with dropout regularization achieves a test error rate below 2% on the 10,000 test images. (We describe dropout regularization in Section 10.7.3.) In Section 10.9.2 of the lab, we present the code for fitting this model, which runs in just over two minutes on a laptop computer.

---

[3]The use of "weights" for coefficients and "bias" for the intercepts w_{k0} in (10.2) is popular in the machine learning community; this use of bias is not to be confused with the "bias-variance" usage elsewhere in this book.

Method	Test Error
Neural Network + Ridge Regularization	2.3%
Neural Network + Dropout Regularization	1.8%
Multinomial Logistic Regression	7.2%
Linear Discriminant Analysis	12.7%

TABLE 10.1. *Test error rate on the* MNIST *data, for neural networks with two forms of regularization, as well as multinomial logistic regression and linear discriminant analysis. In this example, the extra complexity of the neural network leads to a marked improvement in test error.*

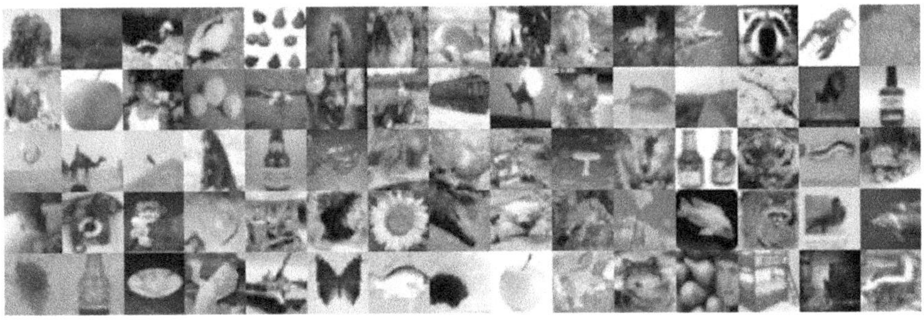

FIGURE 10.5. *A sample of images from the* CIFAR100 *database: a collection of natural images from everyday life, with 100 different classes represented.*

Adding the number of coefficients in $\mathbf{W}_1$, $\mathbf{W}_2$ and $\mathbf{B}$, we get 235,146 in all, more than 33 times the number $785 \times 9 = 7{,}065$ needed for multinomial logistic regression. Recall that there are 60,000 images in the training set. While this might seem like a large training set, there are almost four times as many coefficients in the neural network model as there are observations in the training set! To avoid overfitting, some regularization is needed. In this example, we used two forms of regularization: ridge regularization, which is similar to ridge regression from Chapter 6, and *dropout* regularization. We discuss both forms of regularization in Section 10.7. dropout

10.3 Convolutional Neural Networks

Neural networks rebounded around 2010 with big successes in image classification. Around that time, massive databases of labeled images were being accumulated, with ever-increasing numbers of classes. Figure 10.5 shows 75 images drawn from the CIFAR100 database.[4] This database consists of 60,000 images labeled according to 20 superclasses (e.g. aquatic mammals), with five classes per superclass (beaver, dolphin, otter, seal, whale). Each image has a resolution of 32×32 pixels, with three eight-bit numbers per pixel representing red, green and blue. The numbers for each image are organized in a three-dimensional array called a *feature map*. The first two feature map

[4]See Chapter 3 of Krizhevsky (2009) "Learning multiple layers of features from tiny images", available at https://www.cs.toronto.edu/~kriz/learning-features-2009-TR.pdf.

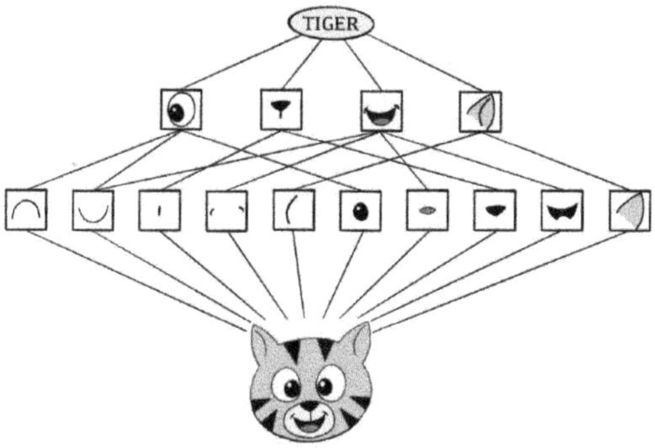

FIGURE 10.6. *Schematic showing how a convolutional neural network classifies an image of a tiger. The network takes in the image and identifies local features. It then combines the local features in order to create compound features, which in this example include eyes and ears. These compound features are used to output the label "tiger".*

axes are spatial (both are 32-dimensional), and the third is the *channel* axis,[5] representing the three colors. There is a designated training set of 50,000 images, and a test set of 10,000.

channel

A special family of *convolutional neural networks* (CNNs) has evolved for classifying images such as these, and has shown spectacular success on a wide range of problems. CNNs mimic to some degree how humans classify images, by recognizing specific features or patterns anywhere in the image that distinguish each particular object class. In this section we give a brief overview of how they work.

convolutional neural networks

Figure 10.6 illustrates the idea behind a convolutional neural network on a cartoon image of a tiger.[6]

The network first identifies low-level features in the input image, such as small edges, patches of color, and the like. These low-level features are then combined to form higher-level features, such as parts of ears, eyes, and so on. Eventually, the presence or absence of these higher-level features contributes to the probability of any given output class.

How does a convolutional neural network build up this hierarchy? It combines two specialized types of hidden layers, called *convolution* layers and *pooling* layers. Convolution layers search for instances of small patterns in the image, whereas pooling layers downsample these to select a prominent subset. In order to achieve state-of-the-art results, contemporary neural-network architectures make use of many convolution and pooling layers. We describe convolution and pooling layers next.

10.3.1 Convolution Layers

A *convolution layer* is made up of a large number of *convolution filters*, each

convolution layer

convolution filter

[5]The term *channel* is taken from the signal-processing literature. Each channel is a distinct source of information.

[6] Thanks to Elena Tuzhilina for producing the diagram and https://www.cartooning4kids.com/ for permission to use the cartoon tiger.

of which is a template that determines whether a particular local feature is present in an image. A convolution filter relies on a very simple operation, called a *convolution*, which basically amounts to repeatedly multiplying matrix elements and then adding the results.

To understand how a convolution filter works, consider a very simple example of a 4×3 image:

$$\text{Original Image} = \begin{bmatrix} a & b & c \\ d & e & f \\ g & h & i \\ j & k & l \end{bmatrix}.$$

Now consider a 2×2 filter of the form

$$\text{Convolution Filter} = \begin{bmatrix} \alpha & \beta \\ \gamma & \delta \end{bmatrix}.$$

When we *convolve* the image with the filter, we get the result[7]

$$\text{Convolved Image} = \begin{bmatrix} a\alpha + b\beta + d\gamma + e\delta & b\alpha + c\beta + e\gamma + f\delta \\ d\alpha + e\beta + g\gamma + h\delta & e\alpha + f\beta + h\gamma + i\delta \\ g\alpha + h\beta + j\gamma + k\delta & h\alpha + i\beta + k\gamma + l\delta \end{bmatrix}.$$

For instance, the top-left element comes from multiplying each element in the 2×2 filter by the corresponding element in the top left 2×2 portion of the image, and adding the results. The other elements are obtained in a similar way: the convolution filter is applied to every 2×2 submatrix of the original image in order to obtain the convolved image. If a 2×2 submatrix of the original image resembles the convolution filter, then it will have a *large* value in the convolved image; otherwise, it will have a *small* value. Thus, *the convolved image highlights regions of the original image that resemble the convolution filter.* We have used 2×2 as an example; in general convolution filters are small $\ell_1 \times \ell_2$ arrays, with ℓ_1 and ℓ_2 small positive integers that are not necessarily equal.

Figure 10.7 illustrates the application of two convolution filters to a 192×179 image of a tiger, shown on the left-hand side.[8] Each convolution filter is a 15×15 image containing mostly zeros (black), with a narrow strip of ones (white) oriented either vertically or horizontally within the image. When each filter is convolved with the image of the tiger, areas of the tiger that resemble the filter (i.e. that have either horizontal or vertical stripes or edges) are given large values, and areas of the tiger that do not resemble the feature are given small values. The convolved images are displayed on the right-hand side. We see that the horizontal stripe filter picks out horizontal stripes and edges in the original image, whereas the vertical stripe filter picks out vertical stripes and edges in the original image.

[7]The convolved image is smaller than the original image because its dimension is given by the number of 2×2 submatrices in the original image. Note that 2×2 is the dimension of the convolution filter. If we want the convolved image to have the same dimension as the original image, then padding can be applied.

[8]The tiger image used in Figures 10.7–10.9 was obtained from the public domain image resource https://www.needpix.com/.

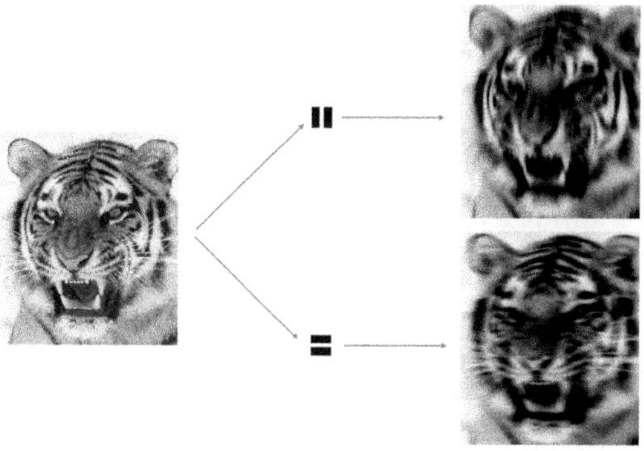

FIGURE 10.7. *Convolution filters find local features in an image, such as edges and small shapes. We begin with the image of the tiger shown on the left, and apply the two small convolution filters in the middle. The convolved images highlight areas in the original image where details similar to the filters are found. Specifically, the top convolved image highlights the tiger's vertical stripes, whereas the bottom convolved image highlights the tiger's horizontal stripes. We can think of the original image as the input layer in a convolutional neural network, and the convolved images as the units in the first hidden layer.*

We have used a large image and two large filters in Figure 10.7 for illustration. For the `CIFAR100` database there are 32×32 color pixels per image, and we use 3×3 convolution filters.

In a convolution layer, we use a whole bank of filters to pick out a variety of differently-oriented edges and shapes in the image. Using predefined filters in this way is standard practice in image processing. By contrast, with CNNs the filters are *learned* for the specific classification task. We can think of the filter weights as the parameters going from an input layer to a hidden layer, with one hidden unit for each pixel in the convolved image. This is in fact the case, though the parameters are highly structured and constrained (see Exercise 4 for more details). They operate on localized patches in the input image (so there are many structural zeros), and the same weights in a given filter are reused for all possible patches in the image (so the weights are constrained).[9]

We now give some additional details.

- Since the input image is in color, it has three channels represented by a three-dimensional feature map (array). Each channel is a two-dimensional (32×32) feature map — one for red, one for green, and one for blue. A single convolution filter will also have three channels, one per color, each of dimension 3×3, with potentially different filter weights. The results of the three convolutions are summed to form a two-dimensional output feature map. Note that at this point the color information has been used, and is not passed on to subsequent layers except through its role in the convolution.

[9]This used to be called *weight sharing* in the early years of neural networks.

- If we use K different convolution filters at this first hidden layer, we get K two-dimensional output feature maps, which together are treated as a single three-dimensional feature map. We view each of the K output feature maps as a separate channel of information, so now we have K channels in contrast to the three color channels of the original input feature map. The three-dimensional feature map is just like the activations in a hidden layer of a simple neural network, except organized and produced in a spatially structured way.

- We typically apply the ReLU activation function (10.5) to the convolved image. This step is sometimes viewed as a separate layer in the convolutional neural network, in which case it is referred to as a *detector layer*. detector layer

10.3.2 Pooling Layers

A *pooling* layer provides a way to condense a large image into a smaller summary image. While there are a number of possible ways to perform pooling, the *max pooling* operation summarizes each non-overlapping 2×2 block of pixels in an image using the maximum value in the block. This reduces the size of the image by a factor of two in each direction, and it also provides some *location invariance*: i.e. as long as there is a large value in one of the four pixels in the block, the whole block registers as a large value in the reduced image. pooling

Here is a simple example of max pooling:

$$\text{Max pool} \begin{bmatrix} 1 & 2 & 5 & 3 \\ 3 & 0 & 1 & 2 \\ 2 & 1 & 3 & 4 \\ 1 & 1 & 2 & 0 \end{bmatrix} \rightarrow \begin{bmatrix} 3 & 5 \\ 2 & 4 \end{bmatrix}.$$

10.3.3 Architecture of a Convolutional Neural Network

So far we have defined a single convolution layer — each filter produces a new two-dimensional feature map. The number of convolution filters in a convolution layer is akin to the number of units at a particular hidden layer in a fully-connected neural network of the type we saw in Section 10.2. This number also defines the number of channels in the resulting three-dimensional feature map. We have also described a pooling layer, which reduces the first two dimensions of each three-dimensional feature map. Deep CNNs have many such layers. Figure 10.8 shows a typical architecture for a CNN for the `CIFAR100` image classification task.

At the input layer, we see the three-dimensional feature map of a color image, where the channel axis represents each color by a 32×32 two-dimensional feature map of pixels. Each convolution filter produces a new channel at the first hidden layer, each of which is a 32×32 feature map (after some padding at the edges). After this first round of convolutions, we now have a new "image"; a feature map with considerably more channels than the three color input channels (six in the figure, since we used six convolution filters).

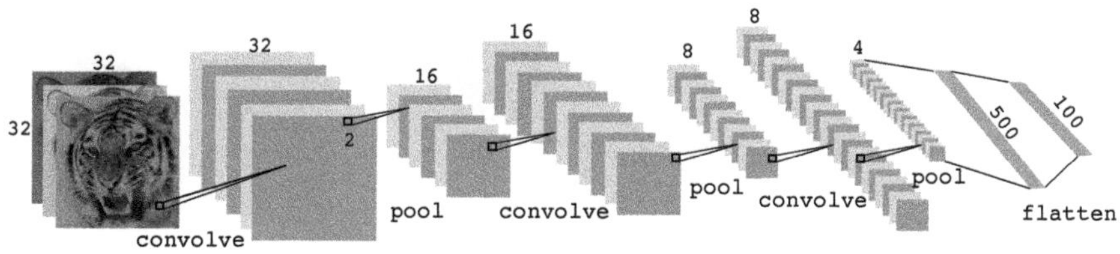

FIGURE 10.8. *Architecture of a deep CNN for the* `CIFAR100` *classification task. Convolution layers are interspersed with* 2×2 *max-pool layers, which reduce the size by a factor of 2 in both dimensions.*

This is followed by a max-pool layer, which reduces the size of the feature map in each channel by a factor of four: two in each dimension.

This convolve-then-pool sequence is now repeated for the next two layers. Some details are as follows:

- Each subsequent convolve layer is similar to the first. It takes as input the three-dimensional feature map from the previous layer and treats it like a single multi-channel image. Each convolution filter learned has as many channels as this feature map.

- Since the channel feature maps are reduced in size after each pool layer, we usually increase the number of filters in the next convolve layer to compensate.

- Sometimes we repeat several convolve layers before a pool layer. This effectively increases the dimension of the filter.

These operations are repeated until the pooling has reduced each channel feature map down to just a few pixels in each dimension. At this point the three-dimensional feature maps are *flattened* — the pixels are treated as separate units — and fed into one or more fully-connected layers before reaching the output layer, which is a *softmax activation* for the 100 classes (as in (10.13)).

There are many tuning parameters to be selected in constructing such a network, apart from the number, nature, and sizes of each layer. Dropout learning can be used at each layer, as well as lasso or ridge regularization (see Section 10.7). The details of constructing a convolutional neural network can seem daunting. Fortunately, terrific software is available, with extensive examples and vignettes that provide guidance on sensible choices for the parameters. For the `CIFAR100` official test set, the best accuracy as of this writing is just above 75%, but undoubtedly this performance will continue to improve.

10.3.4 Data Augmentation

An additional important trick used with image modeling is *data augmentation*. Essentially, each training image is replicated many times, with each replicate randomly distorted in a natural way such that human recognition is unaffected. Figure 10.9 shows some examples. Typical distortions are

data augmentation

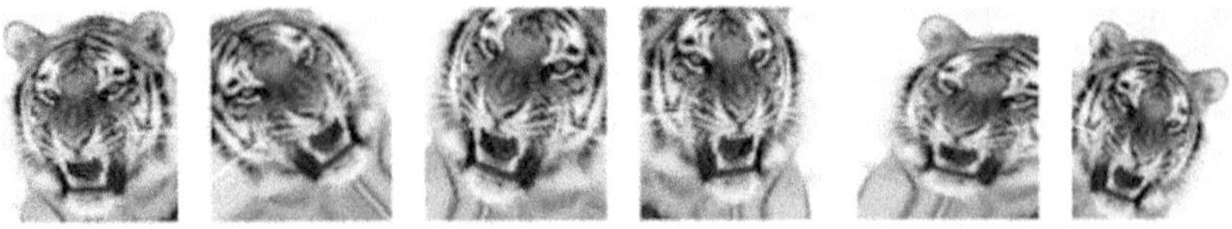

FIGURE 10.9. *Data augmentation. The original image (leftmost) is distorted in natural ways to produce different images with the same class label. These distortions do not fool humans, and act as a form of regularization when fitting the CNN.*

zoom, horizontal and vertical shift, shear, small rotations, and in this case horizontal flips. At face value this is a way of increasing the training set considerably with somewhat different examples, and thus protects against overfitting. In fact we can see this as a form of regularization: we build a cloud of images around each original image, all with the same label. This kind of fattening of the data is similar in spirit to ridge regularization.

We will see in Section 10.7.2 that the stochastic gradient descent algorithms for fitting deep learning models repeatedly process randomly-selected batches of, say, 128 training images at a time. This works hand-in-glove with augmentation, because we can distort each image in the batch on the fly, and hence do not have to store all the new images.

10.3.5 Results Using a Pretrained Classifier

Here we use an industry-level pretrained classifier to predict the class of some new images. The `resnet50` classifier is a convolutional neural network that was trained using the `imagenet` data set, which consists of millions of images that belong to an ever-growing number of categories.[10] Figure 10.10 demonstrates the performance of `resnet50` on six photographs (private collection of one of the authors).[11] The CNN does a reasonable job classifying the hawk in the second image. If we zoom out as in the third image, it gets confused and chooses the fountain rather than the hawk. In the final image a "jacamar" is a tropical bird from South and Central America with similar coloring to the South African Cape Weaver. We give more details on this example in Section 10.9.4.

Much of the work in fitting a CNN is in learning the convolution filters at the hidden layers; these are the coefficients of a CNN. For models fit to massive corpora such as `imagenet` with many classes, the output of these filters can serve as features for general natural-image classification problems. One can use these pretrained hidden layers for new problems with much smaller training sets (a process referred to as *weight freezing*), and just train the last few layers of the network, which requires much less data. weight freezing

[10]For more information about `resnet50`, see He, Zhang, Ren, and Sun (2015) "Deep residual learning for image recognition", `https://arxiv.org/abs/1512.03385`. For details about `imagenet`, see Russakovsky, Deng, et al. (2015) "ImageNet Large Scale Visual Recognition Challenge", in *International Journal of Computer Vision.*

[11]These `resnet` results can change with time, since the publicly-trained model gets updated periodically.

flamingo		Cooper's hawk		Cooper's hawk	
flamingo	0.83	kite	0.60	fountain	0.35
spoonbill	0.17	great grey owl	0.09	nail	0.12
white stork	0.00	robin	0.06	hook	0.07
Lhasa Apso		**cat**		**Cape weaver**	
Tibetan terrier	0.56	Old English sheepdog	0.82	jacamar	0.28
Lhasa	0.32	Shih-Tzu	0.04	macaw	0.12
cocker spaniel	0.03	Persian cat	0.04	robin	0.12

FIGURE 10.10. *Classification of six photographs using the* `resnet50` *CNN trained on the* `imagenet` *corpus. The table below the images displays the true (intended) label at the top of each panel, and the top three choices of the classifier (out of 100). The numbers are the estimated probabilities for each choice. (A kite is a raptor, but not a hawk.)*

The vignettes and book[12] that accompany the `keras` package give more details on such applications.

10.4 Document Classification

In this section we introduce a new type of example that has important applications in industry and science: predicting attributes of documents. Examples of documents include articles in medical journals, Reuters news feeds, emails, tweets, and so on. Our example will be `IMDb` (Internet Movie Database) ratings — short documents where viewers have written critiques of movies.[13] The response in this case is the `sentiment` of the review, which will be *positive* or *negative*.

[12] *Deep Learning with R* by F. Chollet and J.J. Allaire, 2018, Manning Publications.

[13] For details, see Maas et al. (2011) "Learning word vectors for sentiment analysis", in *Proceedings of the 49th Annual Meeting of the Association for Computational Linguistics: Human Language Technologies*, pages 142–150.

Here is the beginning of a rather amusing negative review:

> *This has to be one of the worst films of the 1990s. When my friends & I were watching this film (being the target audience it was aimed at) we just sat & watched the first half an hour with our jaws touching the floor at how bad it really was. The rest of the time, everyone else in the theater just started talking to each other, leaving or generally crying into their popcorn ...*

Each review can be a different length, include slang or non-words, have spelling errors, etc. We need to find a way to *featurize* such a document. This is modern parlance for defining a set of predictors.

featurize

The simplest and most common featurization is the ***bag-of-words*** model. We score each document for the presence or absence of each of the words in a language dictionary — in this case an English dictionary. If the dictionary contains M words, that means for each document we create a binary feature vector of length M, and score a 1 for every word present, and 0 otherwise. That can be a very wide feature vector, so we limit the dictionary — in this case to the 10,000 most frequently occurring words in the training corpus of 25,000 reviews. Fortunately there are nice tools for doing this automatically. Here is the beginning of a positive review that has been redacted in this way:

bag-of-words

> *⟨START⟩ this film was just brilliant casting location scenery story direction everyone's really suited the part they played and you could just imagine being there robert ⟨UNK⟩ is an amazing actor and now the same being director ⟨UNK⟩ father came from the same scottish island as myself so i loved ...*

Here we can see many words have been omitted, and some unknown words (UNK) have been marked as such. With this reduction the binary feature vector has length 10,000, and consists mostly of 0's and a smattering of 1's in the positions corresponding to words that are present in the document. We have a training set and test set, each with 25,000 examples, and each balanced with regard to `sentiment`. The resulting training feature matrix $\mathbf{X}$ has dimension $25{,}000 \times 10{,}000$, but only 1.3% of the binary entries are nonzero. We call such a matrix sparse, because most of the values are the same (zero in this case); it can be stored efficiently in *sparse matrix format*.[14] There are a variety of ways to account for the document length; here we only score a word as in or out of the document, but for example one could instead record the relative frequency of words. We split off a validation set of size 2,000 from the 25,000 training observations (for model tuning), and fit two model sequences:

sparse matrix format

- A lasso logistic regression using the `glmnet` package;
- A two-class neural network with two hidden layers, each with 16 ReLU units.

---

[14]Rather than store the whole matrix, we can store instead the location and values for the nonzero entries. In this case, since the nonzero entries are all 1, just the locations are stored.

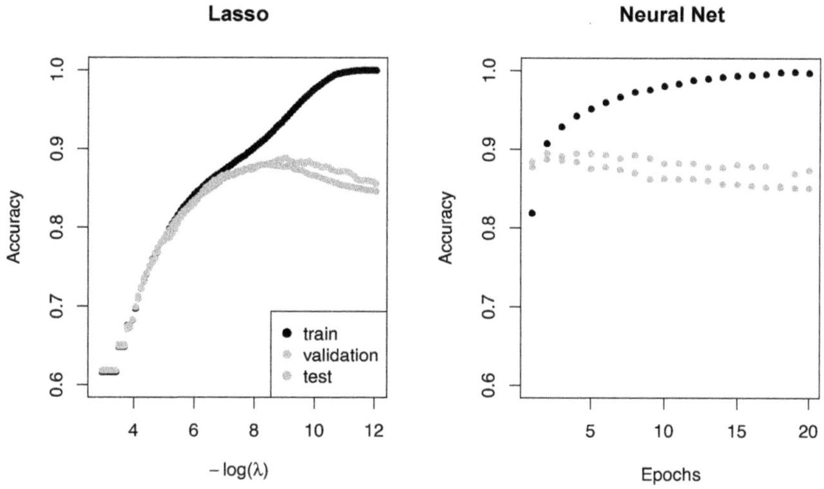

FIGURE 10.11. *Accuracy of the lasso and a two-hidden-layer neural network on the* IMDb *data. For the lasso, the x-axis displays* $-\log(\lambda)$*, while for the neural network it displays epochs (number of times the fitting algorithm passes through the training set). Both show a tendency to overfit, and achieve approximately the same test accuracy.*

Both methods produce a sequence of solutions. The lasso sequence is indexed by the regularization parameter λ. The neural-net sequence is indexed by the number of gradient-descent iterations used in the fitting, as measured by training epochs or passes through the training set (Section 10.7). Notice that the training accuracy in Figure 10.11 (black points) increases monotonically in both cases. We can use the validation error to pick a good solution from each sequence (blue points in the plots), which would then be used to make predictions on the test data set.

Note that a two-class neural network amounts to a nonlinear logistic regression model. From (10.12) and (10.13) we can see that

$$\begin{aligned} \log\left(\frac{\Pr(Y=1|X)}{\Pr(Y=0|X)}\right) &= Z_1 - Z_0 \qquad (10.15) \\ &= (\beta_{10}-\beta_{00}) + \sum_{\ell=1}^{K_2}(\beta_{1\ell}-\beta_{0\ell})A_\ell^{(2)}. \end{aligned}$$

(This shows the redundancy in the softmax function; for K classes we really only need to estimate $K-1$ sets of coefficients. See Section 4.3.5.) In Figure 10.11 we show *accuracy* (fraction correct) rather than classification error (fraction incorrect), the former being more popular in the machine learning community. Both models achieve a test-set accuracy of about 88%.

accuracy

The bag-of-words model summarizes a document by the words present, and ignores their context. There are at least two popular ways to take the context into account:

- The *bag-of-n-grams* model. For example, a bag of 2-grams records

bag-of-n-grams

the consecutive co-occurrence of every distinct pair of words. "Blissfully long" can be seen as a positive phrase in a movie review, while "blissfully short" a negative.

- Treat the document as a sequence, taking account of all the words in the context of those that preceded and those that follow.

In the next section we explore models for sequences of data, which have applications in weather forecasting, speech recognition, language translation, and time-series prediction, to name a few. We continue with this `IMDb` example there.

10.5 Recurrent Neural Networks

Many data sources are sequential in nature, and call for special treatment when building predictive models. Examples include:

- Documents such as book and movie reviews, newspaper articles, and tweets. The sequence and relative positions of words in a document capture the narrative, theme and tone, and can be exploited in tasks such as topic classification, sentiment analysis, and language translation.
- Time series of temperature, rainfall, wind speed, air quality, and so on. We may want to forecast the weather several days ahead, or climate several decades ahead.
- Financial time series, where we track market indices, trading volumes, stock and bond prices, and exchange rates. Here prediction is often difficult, but as we will see, certain indices can be predicted with reasonable accuracy.
- Recorded speech, musical recordings, and other sound recordings. We may want to give a text transcription of a speech, or perhaps a language translation. We may want to assess the quality of a piece of music, or assign certain attributes.
- Handwriting, such as doctor's notes, and handwritten digits such as zip codes. Here we want to turn the handwriting into digital text, or read the digits (optical character recognition).

In a *recurrent neural network* (RNN), the input object X is a *sequence.* Consider a corpus of documents, such as the collection of `IMDb` movie reviews. Each document can be represented as a sequence of L words, so $X = \{X_1, X_2, \ldots, X_L\}$, where each X_ℓ represents a word. The order of the words, and closeness of certain words in a sentence, convey semantic meaning. RNNs are designed to accommodate and take advantage of the sequential nature of such input objects, much like convolutional neural networks accommodate the spatial structure of image inputs. The output Y can also be a sequence (such as in language translation), but often is a scalar, like the binary sentiment label of a movie review document.

recurrent neural network

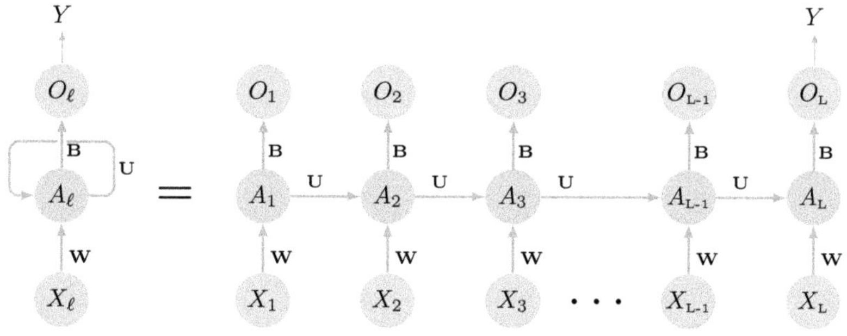

FIGURE 10.12. *Schematic of a simple recurrent neural network. The input is a sequence of vectors* $\{X_\ell\}_1^L$, *and here the target is a single response. The network processes the input sequence* X *sequentially; each* X_ℓ *feeds into the hidden layer, which also has as input the activation vector* $A_{\ell-1}$ *from the previous element in the sequence, and produces the current activation vector* A_ℓ. *The same collections of weights* **W**, **U** *and* **B** *are used as each element of the sequence is processed. The output layer produces a sequence of predictions* O_ℓ *from the current activation* A_ℓ, *but typically only the last of these,* O_L, *is of relevance. To the left of the equal sign is a concise representation of the network, which is* unrolled *into a more explicit version on the right.*

Figure 10.12 illustrates the structure of a very basic RNN with a sequence $X = \{X_1, X_2, \ldots, X_L\}$ as input, a simple output Y, and a hidden-layer sequence $\{A_\ell\}_1^L = \{A_1, A_2, \ldots, A_L\}$. Each X_ℓ is a vector; in the document example X_ℓ could represent a one-hot encoding for the ℓth word based on the language dictionary for the corpus (see the top panel in Figure 10.13 for a simple example). As the sequence is processed one vector X_ℓ at a time, the network updates the activations A_ℓ in the hidden layer, taking as input the vector X_ℓ and the activation vector $A_{\ell-1}$ from the previous step in the sequence. Each A_ℓ feeds into the output layer and produces a prediction O_ℓ for Y. O_L, the last of these, is the most relevant.

In detail, suppose each vector X_ℓ of the input sequence has p components $X_\ell^T = (X_{\ell 1}, X_{\ell 2}, \ldots, X_{\ell p})$, and the hidden layer consists of K units $A_\ell^T = (A_{\ell 1}, A_{\ell 2}, \ldots, A_{\ell K})$. As in Figure 10.4, we represent the collection of $K \times (p+1)$ shared weights w_{kj} for the input layer by a matrix **W**, and similarly **U** is a $K \times K$ matrix of the weights u_{ks} for the hidden-to-hidden layers, and **B** is a $K+1$ vector of weights β_k for the output layer. Then

$$A_{\ell k} = g\Big(w_{k0} + \sum_{j=1}^{p} w_{kj} X_{\ell j} + \sum_{s=1}^{K} u_{ks} A_{\ell-1,s}\Big), \tag{10.16}$$

and the output O_ℓ is computed as

$$O_\ell = \beta_0 + \sum_{k=1}^{K} \beta_k A_{\ell k} \tag{10.17}$$

for a quantitative response, or with an additional sigmoid activation function for a binary response, for example. Here $g(\cdot)$ is an activation function such as ReLU. Notice that the same weights **W**, **U** and **B** are used as we process each element in the sequence, i.e. they are not functions of ℓ. This is a form of *weight sharing* used by RNNs, and similar to the use of filters in convolutional neural networks (Section 10.3.1.) As we proceed from beginning to end, the activations A_ℓ accumulate a history of what has been seen before, so that the learned context can be used for prediction.

weight sharing

For regression problems the loss function for an observation (X, Y) is

$$(Y - O_L)^2, \tag{10.18}$$

which only references the final output $O_L = \beta_0 + \sum_{k=1}^{K} \beta_k A_{Lk}$. Thus $O_1, O_2, \ldots, O_{L-1}$ are not used. When we fit the model, each element X_ℓ of the input sequence X contributes to O_L via the chain (10.16), and hence contributes indirectly to learning the shared parameters $\mathbf{W}$, $\mathbf{U}$ and $\mathbf{B}$ via the loss (10.18). With n input sequence/response pairs (x_i, y_i), the parameters are found by minimizing the sum of squares

$$\sum_{i=1}^{n}(y_i - o_{iL})^2 = \sum_{i=1}^{n}\Big(y_i - \big(\beta_0 + \sum_{k=1}^{K}\beta_k g\big(w_{k0} + \sum_{j=1}^{p} w_{kj}x_{iLj} + \sum_{s=1}^{K} u_{ks}a_{i,L-1,s}\big)\big)\Big)^2. \tag{10.19}$$

Here we use lowercase letters for the observed y_i and vector sequences $x_i = \{x_{i1}, x_{i2}, \ldots, x_{iL}\}$,[15] as well as the derived activations.

Since the intermediate outputs O_ℓ are not used, one may well ask why they are there at all. First of all, they come for free, since they use the same output weights $\mathbf{B}$ needed to produce O_L, and provide an evolving prediction for the output. Furthermore, for some learning tasks the response is also a sequence, and so the output sequence $\{O_1, O_2, \ldots, O_L\}$ is explicitly needed.

When used at full strength, recurrent neural networks can be quite complex. We illustrate their use in two simple applications. In the first, we continue with the `IMDb` sentiment analysis of the previous section, where we process the words in the reviews sequentially. In the second application, we illustrate their use in a financial time series forecasting problem.

10.5.1 Sequential Models for Document Classification

Here we return to our classification task with the `IMDb` reviews. Our approach in Section 10.4 was to use the bag-of-words model. Here the plan is to use instead the sequence of words occurring in a document to make predictions about the label for the entire document.

We have, however, a dimensionality problem: each word in our document is represented by a one-hot-encoded vector (dummy variable) with 10,000 elements (one per word in the dictionary)! An approach that has become popular is to represent each word in a much lower-dimensional *embedding* space. This means that rather than representing each word by a binary vector with 9,999 zeros and a single one in some position, we will represent it instead by a set of m real numbers, none of which are typically zero. Here m is the embedding dimension, and can be in the low 100s, or even less. This means (in our case) that we need a matrix $\mathbf{E}$ of dimension $m \times 10{,}000$,

embedding

[15]This is a sequence of vectors; each element $x_{i\ell}$ is a p-vector.

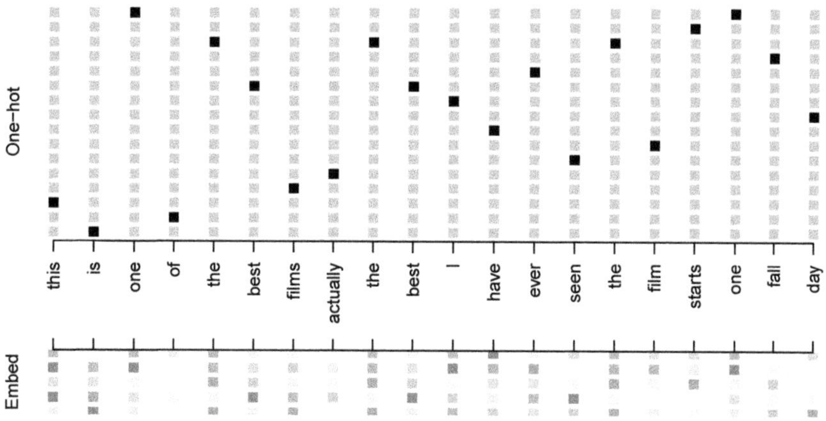

FIGURE 10.13. *Depiction of a sequence of* 20 *words representing a single document: one-hot encoded using a dictionary of* 16 *words (top panel) and embedded in an* m*-dimensional space with* $m = 5$ *(bottom panel).*

where each column is indexed by one of the 10,000 words in our dictionary, and the values in that column give the m coordinates for that word in the embedding space.

Figure 10.13 illustrates the idea (with a dictionary of 16 rather than 10,000, and $m = 5$). Where does $\mathbf{E}$ come from? If we have a large corpus of labeled documents, we can have the neural network *learn* $\mathbf{E}$ as part of the optimization. In this case $\mathbf{E}$ is referred to as an *embedding layer*, and a specialized $\mathbf{E}$ is learned for the task at hand. Otherwise we can insert a precomputed matrix $\mathbf{E}$ in the embedding layer, a process known as *weight freezing*. Two pretrained embeddings, `word2vec` and `GloVe`, are widely used.[16] These are built from a very large corpus of documents by a variant of principal components analysis (Section 12.2). The idea is that the positions of words in the embedding space preserve semantic meaning; e.g. synonyms should appear near each other.

embedding layer

weight freezing

`word2vec`
`GloVe`

So far, so good. Each document is now represented as a sequence of m-vectors that represents the sequence of words. The next step is to limit each document to the last L words. Documents that are shorter than L get padded with zeros upfront. So now each document is represented by a series consisting of L vectors $X = \{X_1, X_2, \ldots, X_L\}$, and each X_ℓ in the sequence has m components.

We now use the RNN structure in Figure 10.12. The training corpus consists of n separate series (documents) of length L, each of which gets processed sequentially from left to right. In the process, a parallel series of hidden activation vectors A_ℓ, $\ell = 1, \ldots, L$ is created as in (10.16) for each document. A_ℓ feeds into the output layer to produce the evolving prediction O_ℓ. We use the final value O_L to predict the response: the sentiment of the review.

[16] `word2vec` is described in Mikolov, Chen, Corrado, and Dean (2013), available at `https://code.google.com/archive/p/word2vec`. `GloVe` is described in Pennington, Socher, and Manning (2014), available at `https://nlp.stanford.edu/projects/glove`.

This is a simple RNN, and has relatively few parameters. If there are K hidden units, the common weight matrix $\mathbf{W}$ has $K \times (m+1)$ parameters, the matrix $\mathbf{U}$ has $K \times K$ parameters, and $\mathbf{B}$ has $2(K+1)$ for the two-class logistic regression as in (10.15). These are used repeatedly as we process the sequence $X = \{X_\ell\}_1^L$ from left to right, much like we use a single convolution filter to process each patch in an image (Section 10.3.1). If the embedding layer $\mathbf{E}$ is learned, that adds an additional $m \times D$ parameters ($D = 10{,}000$ here), and is by far the biggest cost.

We fit the RNN as described in Figure 10.12 and the accompaying text to the `IMDb` data. The model had an embedding matrix $\mathbf{E}$ with $m = 32$ (which was learned in training as opposed to precomputed), followed by a single recurrent layer with $K = 32$ hidden units. The model was trained with dropout regularization on the 25,000 reviews in the designated training set, and achieved a disappointing 76% accuracy on the `IMDb` test data. A network using the `GloVe` pretrained embedding matrix $\mathbf{E}$ performed slightly worse.

For ease of exposition we have presented a very simple RNN. More elaborate versions use *long term* and *short term* memory (LSTM). Two tracks of hidden-layer activations are maintained, so that when the activation A_ℓ is computed, it gets input from hidden units both further back in time, and closer in time — a so-called *LSTM RNN*. With long sequences, this overcomes the problem of early signals being washed out by the time they get propagated through the chain to the final activation vector A_L.

LSTM RNN

When we refit our model using the LSTM architecture for the hidden layer, the performance improved to 87% on the `IMDb` test data. This is comparable with the 88% achieved by the bag-of-words model in Section 10.4. We give details on fitting these models in Section 10.9.6.

Despite this added LSTM complexity, our RNN is still somewhat "entry level". We could probably achieve slightly better results by changing the size of the model, changing the regularization, and including additional hidden layers. However, LSTM models take a long time to train, which makes exploring many architectures and parameter optimization tedious.

RNNs provide a rich framework for modeling data sequences, and they continue to evolve. There have been many advances in the development of RNNs — in architecture, data augmentation, and in the learning algorithms. At the time of this writing (early 2020) the leading RNN configurations report accuracy above 95% on the `IMDb` data. The details are beyond the scope of this book.[17]

10.5.2 Time Series Forecasting

Figure 10.14 shows historical trading statistics from the New York Stock Exchange. Shown are three daily time series covering the period December 3, 1962 to December 31, 1986:[18]

---

[17] An `IMDb` leaderboard can be found at https://paperswithcode.com/sota/sentiment-analysis-on-imdb.

[18] These data were assembled by LeBaron and Weigend (1998) *IEEE Transactions on Neural Networks*, 9(1): 213–220.

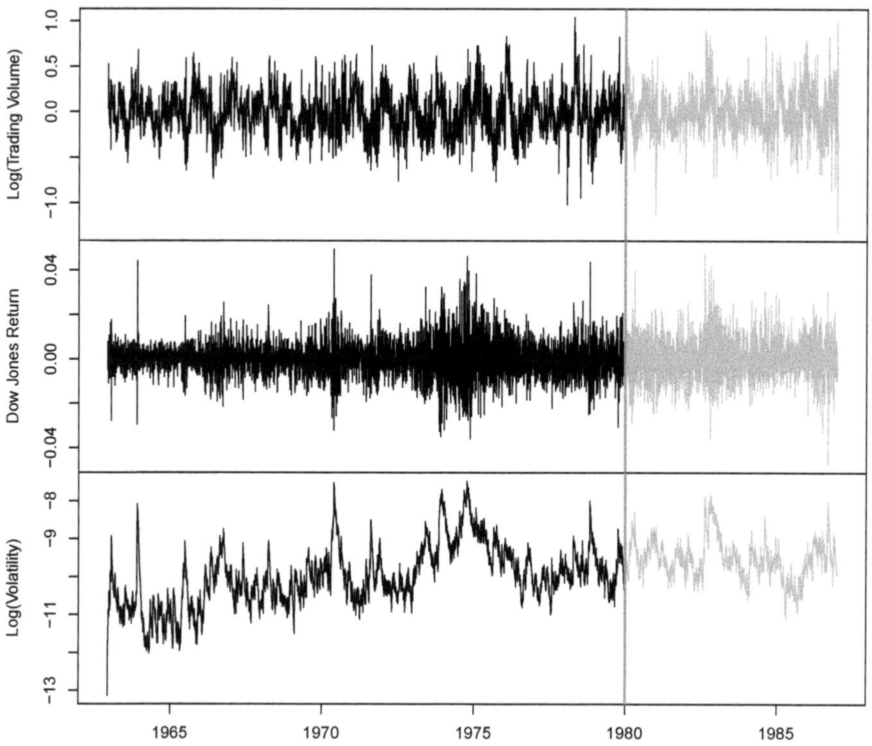

FIGURE 10.14. *Historical trading statistics from the New York Stock Exchange. Daily values of the normalized log trading volume, DJIA return, and log volatility are shown for a 24-year period from 1962–1986. We wish to predict trading volume on any day, given the history on all earlier days. To the left of the red bar (January 2, 1980) is training data, and to the right test data.*

- `Log trading volume`. This is the fraction of all outstanding shares that are traded on that day, relative to a 100-day moving average of past turnover, on the log scale.
- `Dow Jones return`. This is the difference between the log of the Dow Jones Industrial Index on consecutive trading days.
- `Log volatility`. This is based on the absolute values of daily price movements.

Predicting stock prices is a notoriously hard problem, but it turns out that predicting trading volume based on recent past history is more manageable (and is useful for planning trading strategies).

An observation here consists of the measurements (v_t, r_t, z_t) on day t, in this case the values for `log_volume`, `DJ_return` and `log_volatility`. There are a total of $T = 6{,}051$ such triples, each of which is plotted as a time series in Figure 10.14. One feature that strikes us immediately is that the day-to-day observations are not independent of each other. The series exhibit *auto-correlation* — in this case values nearby in time tend to be similar to each other. This distinguishes time series from other data sets we have encountered, in which observations can be assumed to be independent of

auto-correlation

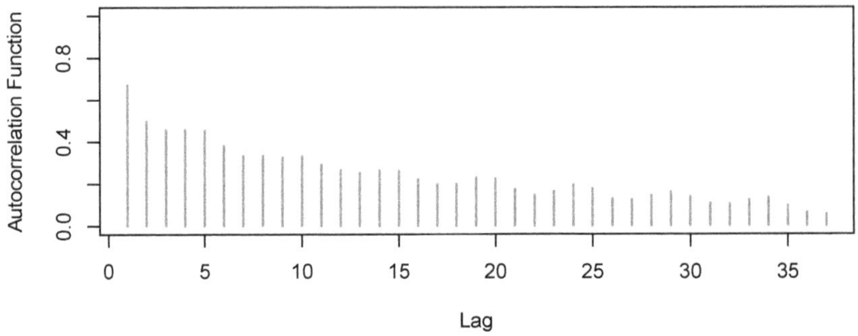

FIGURE 10.15. *The autocorrelation function for* `log_volume`. *We see that nearby values are fairly strongly correlated, with correlations above* 0.2 *as far as* 20 *days apart.*

each other. To be clear, consider pairs of observations $(v_t, v_{t-\ell})$, a *lag* of ℓ days apart. If we take all such pairs in the v_t series and compute their correlation coefficient, this gives the autocorrelation at lag ℓ. Figure 10.15 shows the autocorrelation function for all lags up to 37, and we see considerable correlation.

lag

Another interesting characteristic of this forecasting problem is that the response variable v_t — `log_volume` — is also a predictor! In particular, we will use the past values of `log_volume` to predict values in the future.

RNN forecaster

We wish to predict a value v_t from past values $v_{t-1}, v_{t-2}, \ldots$, and also to make use of past values of the other series $r_{t-1}, r_{t-2}, \ldots$ and $z_{t-1}, z_{t-2}, \ldots$. Although our combined data is quite a long series with 6,051 trading days, the structure of the problem is different from the previous document-classification example.

- We only have one series of data, not 25,000.
- We have an entire *series* of targets v_t, and the inputs include past values of this series.

How do we represent this problem in terms of the structure displayed in Figure 10.12? The idea is to extract many short mini-series of input sequences $X = \{X_1, X_2, \ldots, X_L\}$ with a predefined length L (called the *lag* in this context), and a corresponding target Y. They have the form

lag

$$X_1 = \begin{pmatrix} v_{t-L} \\ r_{t-L} \\ z_{t-L} \end{pmatrix}, \; X_2 = \begin{pmatrix} v_{t-L+1} \\ r_{t-L+1} \\ z_{t-L+1} \end{pmatrix}, \cdots, X_L = \begin{pmatrix} v_{t-1} \\ r_{t-1} \\ z_{t-1} \end{pmatrix}, \quad \text{and } Y = v_t. \tag{10.20}$$

So here the target Y is the value of `log_volume` v_t at a single timepoint t, and the input sequence X is the series of 3-vectors $\{X_\ell\}_1^L$ each consisting of the three measurements `log_volume`, `DJ_return` and `log_volatility` from day $t-L$, $t-L+1$, up to $t-1$. Each value of t makes a separate (X, Y) pair, for t running from $L+1$ to T. For the `NYSE` data we will use the past

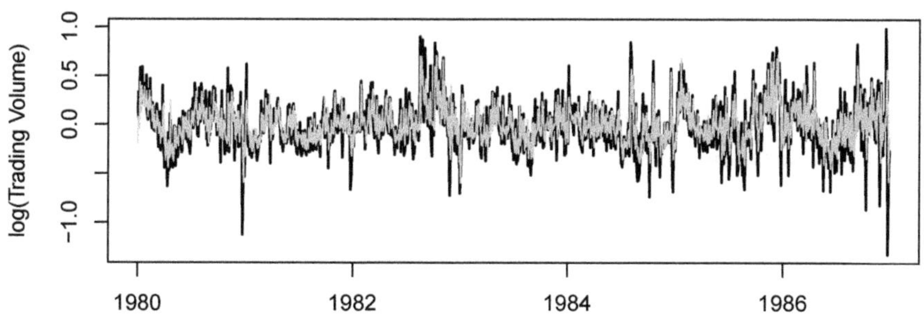

FIGURE 10.16. *RNN forecast of* `log_volume` *on the* `NYSE` *test data. The black lines are the true volumes, and the superimposed orange the forecasts. The forecasted series accounts for 42% of the variance of* `log_volume`.

five trading days to predict the next day's trading volume. Hence, we use $L = 5$. Since $T =$ 6,051, we can create 6,046 such (X, Y) pairs. Clearly L is a parameter that should be chosen with care, perhaps using validation data.

We fit this model with $K = 12$ hidden units using the 4,281 training sequences derived from the data before January 2, 1980 (see Figure 10.14), and then used it to forecast the 1,770 values of `log_volume` after this date. We achieve an $R^2 = 0.42$ on the test data. Details are given in Section 10.9.6. As a *straw man*,[19] using yesterday's value for `log_volume` as the prediction for today has $R^2 = 0.18$. Figure 10.16 shows the forecast results. We have plotted the observed values of the daily `log_volume` for the test period 1980–1986 in black, and superimposed the predicted series in orange. The correspondence seems rather good.

In forecasting the value of `log_volume` in the test period, we have to use the test data itself in forming the input sequences X. This may feel like cheating, but in fact it is not; we are always using past data to predict the future.

Autoregression

The RNN we just fit has much in common with a traditional *autoregression* (AR) linear model, which we present now for comparison. We first consider the response sequence v_t alone, and construct a response vector $\mathbf{y}$ and a matrix $\mathbf{M}$ of predictors for least squares regression as follows:

auto-regression

$$\mathbf{y} = \begin{bmatrix} v_{L+1} \\ v_{L+2} \\ v_{L+3} \\ \vdots \\ v_T \end{bmatrix} \qquad \mathbf{M} = \begin{bmatrix} 1 & v_L & v_{L-1} & \cdots & v_1 \\ 1 & v_{L+1} & v_L & \cdots & v_2 \\ 1 & v_{L+2} & v_{L+1} & \cdots & v_3 \\ \vdots & \vdots & \vdots & \ddots & \vdots \\ 1 & v_{T-1} & v_{T-2} & \cdots & v_{T-L} \end{bmatrix}. \qquad (10.21)$$

$\mathbf{M}$ and $\mathbf{y}$ each have $T - L$ rows, one per observation. We see that the predictors for any given response v_t on day t are the previous L values

[19]A straw man here refers to a simple and sensible prediction that can be used as a baseline for comparison.

of the same series. Fitting a regression of $\mathbf{y}$ on $\mathbf{M}$ amounts to fitting the model

$$\hat{v}_t = \hat{\beta}_0 + \hat{\beta}_1 v_{t-1} + \hat{\beta}_2 v_{t-2} + \cdots + \hat{\beta}_L v_{t-L}, \qquad (10.22)$$

and is called an order-L autoregressive model, or simply AR(L). For the `NYSE` data we can include lagged versions of `DJ_return` and `log_volatility`, r_t and z_t, in the predictor matrix $\mathbf{M}$, resulting in $3L + 1$ columns. An AR model with $L = 5$ achieves a test R^2 of 0.41, slightly inferior to the 0.42 achieved by the RNN.

Of course the RNN and AR models are very similar. They both use the same response Y and input sequences X of length $L = 5$ and dimension $p = 3$ in this case. The RNN processes this sequence from left to right with the same weights $\mathbf{W}$ (for the input layer), while the AR model simply treats all L elements of the sequence equally as a vector of $L \times p$ predictors — a process called *flattening* in the neural network literature. Of course the RNN also includes the hidden layer activations A_ℓ which transfer information along the sequence, and introduces additional nonlinearity. From (10.19) with $K = 12$ hidden units, we see that the RNN has $13 + 12 \times (1 + 3 + 12) = 205$ parameters, compared to the 16 for the AR(5) model.

flattening

An obvious extension of the AR model is to use the set of lagged predictors as the input vector to an ordinary feedforward neural network (10.1), and hence add more flexibility. This achieved a test $R^2 = 0.42$, slightly better than the linear AR, and the same as the RNN.

All the models can be improved by including the variable `day_of_week` corresponding to the day t of the target v_t (which can be learned from the calendar dates supplied with the data); trading volume is often higher on Mondays and Fridays. Since there are five trading days, this one-hot encodes to five binary variables. The performance of the AR model improved to $R^2 = 0.46$ as did the RNN, and the nonlinear AR model improved to $R^2 = 0.47$.

We used the most simple version of the RNN in our examples here. Additional experiments with the LSTM extension of the RNN yielded small improvements, typically of up to 1% in R^2 in these examples.

We give details of how we fit all three models in Section 10.9.6.

10.5.3 Summary of RNNs

We have illustrated RNNs through two simple use cases, and have only scratched the surface.

There are many variations and enhancements of the simple RNN we used for sequence modeling. One approach we did not discuss uses a one-dimensional convolutional neural network, treating the sequence of vectors (say words, as represented in the embedding space) as an image. The convolution filter slides along the sequence in a one-dimensional fashion, with the potential to learn particular phrases or short subsequences relevant to the learning task.

One can also have additional hidden layers in an RNN. For example, with two hidden layers, the sequence A_ℓ is treated as an input sequence to the next hidden layer in an obvious fashion.

The RNN we used scanned the document from beginning to end; alternative *bidirectional* RNNs scan the sequences in both directions.

bidirectional

In language translation the target is also a sequence of words, in a language different from that of the input sequence. Both the input sequence and the target sequence are represented by a structure similar to Figure 10.12, and they share the hidden units. In this so-called *Seq2Seq* learning, the hidden units are thought to capture the semantic meaning of the sentences. Some of the big breakthroughs in language modeling and translation resulted from the relatively recent improvements in such RNNs.

Seq2Seq

Algorithms used to fit RNNs can be complex and computationally costly. Fortunately, good software protects users somewhat from these complexities, and makes specifying and fitting these models relatively painless. Many of the models that we enjoy in daily life (like *Google Translate*) use state-of-the-art architectures developed by teams of highly skilled engineers, and have been trained using massive computational and data resources.

10.6 When to Use Deep Learning

The performance of deep learning in this chapter has been rather impressive. It nailed the digit classification problem, and deep CNNs have really revolutionized image classification. We see daily reports of new success stories for deep learning. Many of these are related to image classification tasks, such as machine diagnosis of mammograms or digital X-ray images, ophthalmology eye scans, annotations of MRI scans, and so on. Likewise there are numerous successes of RNNs in speech and language translation, forecasting, and document modeling. The question that then begs an answer is: *should we discard all our older tools, and use deep learning on every problem with data?* To address this question, we revisit our `Hitters` dataset from Chapter 6.

This is a regression problem, where the goal is to predict the `Salary` of a baseball player in 1987 using his performance statistics from 1986. After removing players with missing responses, we are left with 263 players and 19 variables. We randomly split the data into a training set of 176 players (two thirds), and a test set of 87 players (one third). We used three methods for fitting a regression model to these data.

- A linear model was used to fit the training data, and make predictions on the test data. The model has 20 parameters.
- The same linear model was fit with lasso regularization. The tuning parameter was selected by 10-fold cross-validation on the training data. It selected a model with 12 variables having nonzero coefficients.
- A neural network with one hidden layer consisting of 64 `ReLU` units was fit to the data. This model has 1,345 parameters.[20]

[20]The model was fit by stochastic gradient descent with a batch size of 32 for 1,000 epochs, and 10% dropout regularization. The test error performance flattened out and started to slowly increase after 1,000 epochs. These fitting details are discussed in Section 10.7.

Model	# Parameters	Mean Abs. Error	Test Set R^2
Linear Regression	20	254.7	0.56
Lasso	12	252.3	0.51
Neural Network	1345	257.4	0.54

TABLE 10.2. *Prediction results on the* `Hitters` *test data for linear models fit by ordinary least squares and lasso, compared to a neural network fit by stochastic gradient descent with dropout regularization.*

	Coefficient	Std. error	t-statistic	p-value
`Intercept`	-226.67	86.26	-2.63	0.0103
`Hits`	3.06	1.02	3.00	0.0036
`Walks`	0.181	2.04	0.09	0.9294
`CRuns`	0.859	0.12	7.09	< 0.0001
`PutOuts`	0.465	0.13	3.60	0.0005

TABLE 10.3. *Least squares coefficient estimates associated with the regression of* `Salary` *on four variables chosen by lasso on the* `Hitters` *data set. This model achieved the best performance on the test data, with a mean absolute error of 224.8. The results reported here were obtained from a regression on the test data, which was not used in fitting the lasso model.*

Table 10.2 compares the results. We see similar performance for all three models. We report the mean absolute error on the test data, as well as the test R^2 for each method, which are all respectable (see Exercise 5). We spent a fair bit of time fiddling with the configuration parameters of the neural network to achieve these results. It is possible that if we were to spend more time, and got the form and amount of regularization just right, that we might be able to match or even outperform linear regression and the lasso. But with great ease we obtained linear models that work well. Linear models are much easier to present and understand than the neural network, which is essentially a black box. The lasso selected 12 of the 19 variables in making its prediction. So in cases like this we are much better off following the *Occam's razor* principle: when faced with several methods that give roughly equivalent performance, pick the simplest. Occam's razor

After a bit more exploration with the lasso model, we identified an even simpler model with four variables. We then refit the linear model with these four variables to the training data (the so-called *relaxed lasso*), and achieved a test mean absolute error of 224.8, the overall winner! It is tempting to present the summary table from this fit, so we can see coefficients and p-values; however, since the model was selected on the training data, there would be *selection bias*. Instead, we refit the model on the test data, which was not used in the selection. Table 10.3 shows the results.

We have a number of very powerful tools at our disposal, including neural networks, random forests and boosting, support vector machines and generalized additive models, to name a few. And then we have linear models, and simple variants of these. When faced with new data modeling and prediction problems, it's tempting to always go for the trendy new methods. Often they give extremely impressive results, especially when the datasets are very large and can support the fitting of high-dimensional nonlinear models. However, *if* we can produce models with the simpler tools that perform as well, they are likely to be easier to fit and understand, and potentially less fragile than the more complex approaches. Wherever possible, it makes sense to try the simpler models as well, and then make a choice based on the performance/complexity tradeoff.

Typically we expect deep learning to be an attractive choice when the sample size of the training set is extremely large, and when interpretability of the model is not a high priority.

10.7 Fitting a Neural Network

Fitting neural networks is somewhat complex, and we give a brief overview here. The ideas generalize to much more complex networks. Readers who find this material challenging can safely skip it. Fortunately, as we see in the lab at the end of this chapter, good software is available to fit neural network models in a relatively automated way, without worrying about the technical details of the model-fitting procedure.

We start with the simple network depicted in Figure 10.1 in Section 10.1. In model (10.1) the parameters are $\beta = (\beta_0, \beta_1, \dots, \beta_K)$, as well as each of the $w_k = (w_{k0}, w_{k1}, \dots, w_{kp})$, $k = 1, \dots, K$. Given observations (x_i, y_i), $i = 1, \dots, n$, we could fit the model by solving a nonlinear least squares problem

$$\underset{\{w_k\}_1^K,\ \beta}{\text{minimize}} \frac{1}{2} \sum_{i=1}^{n} (y_i - f(x_i))^2, \tag{10.23}$$

where

$$f(x_i) = \beta_0 + \sum_{k=1}^{K} \beta_k g\Big(w_{k0} + \sum_{j=1}^{p} w_{kj} x_{ij}\Big). \tag{10.24}$$

The objective in (10.23) looks simple enough, but because of the nested arrangement of the parameters and the symmetry of the hidden units, it is not straightforward to minimize. The problem is nonconvex in the parameters, and hence there are multiple solutions. As an example, Figure 10.17 shows a simple nonconvex function of a single variable θ; there are two solutions: one is a *local minimum* and the other is a *global minimum*. Furthermore, (10.1) is the very simplest of neural networks; in this chapter we have presented much more complex ones where these problems are compounded. To overcome some of these issues and to protect from overfitting, two general strategies are employed when fitting neural networks.

local minimum

global minimum

- *Slow Learning:* the model is fit in a somewhat slow iterative fashion, using *gradient descent*. The fitting process is then stopped when overfitting is detected.

gradient descent

- *Regularization:* penalties are imposed on the parameters, usually lasso or ridge as discussed in Section 6.2.

Suppose we represent all the parameters in one long vector θ. Then we can rewrite the objective in (10.23) as

$$R(\theta) = \frac{1}{2} \sum_{i=1}^{n} (y_i - f_\theta(x_i))^2, \tag{10.25}$$

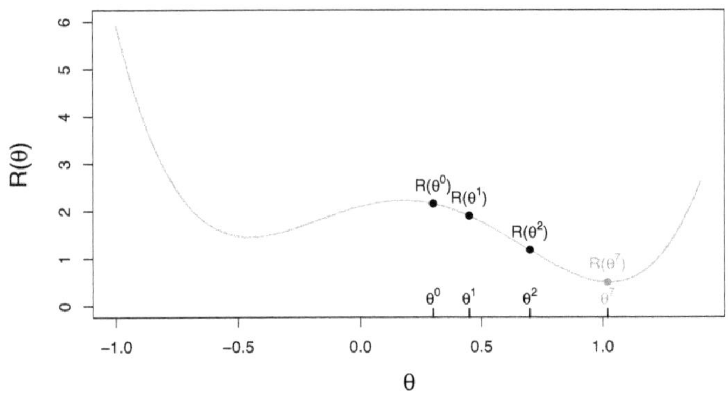

FIGURE 10.17. *Illustration of gradient descent for one-dimensional θ. The objective function $R(\theta)$ is not convex, and has two minima, one at $\theta = -0.46$ (local), the other at $\theta = 1.02$ (global). Starting at some value θ^0 (typically randomly chosen), each step in θ moves downhill — against the gradient — until it cannot go down any further. Here gradient descent reached the global minimum in 7 steps.*

where we make explicit the dependence of f on the parameters. The idea of gradient descent is very simple.

1. Start with a guess θ^0 for all the parameters in θ, and set $t = 0$.
2. Iterate until the objective (10.25) fails to decrease:
   (a) Find a vector δ that reflects a small change in θ, such that $\theta^{t+1} = \theta^t + \delta$ *reduces* the objective; i.e. such that $R(\theta^{t+1}) < R(\theta^t)$.
   (b) Set $t \leftarrow t + 1$.

One can visualize (Figure 10.17) standing in a mountainous terrain, and the goal is to get to the bottom through a series of steps. As long as each step goes downhill, we must eventually get to the bottom. In this case we were lucky, because with our starting guess θ^0 we end up at the global minimum. In general we can hope to end up at a (good) local minimum.

10.7.1 Backpropagation

How do we find the directions to move θ so as to decrease the objective $R(\theta)$ in (10.25)? The *gradient* of $R(\theta)$, evaluated at some current value $\theta = \theta^m$, is the vector of partial derivatives at that point: gradient

$$\nabla R(\theta^m) = \left.\frac{\partial R(\theta)}{\partial \theta}\right|_{\theta=\theta^m}. \tag{10.26}$$

The subscript $\theta = \theta^m$ means that after computing the vector of derivatives, we evaluate it at the current guess, θ^m. This gives the direction in θ-space in which $R(\theta)$ *increases* most rapidly. The idea of gradient descent is to move θ a little in the *opposite* direction (since we wish to go downhill):

$$\theta^{m+1} \leftarrow \theta^m - \rho \nabla R(\theta^m). \tag{10.27}$$

For a small enough value of the *learning rate* ρ, this step will decrease the objective $R(\theta)$; i.e. $R(\theta^{m+1}) \leq R(\theta^m)$. If the gradient vector is zero, then we may have arrived at a minimum of the objective.

learning rate

How complicated is the calculation (10.26)? It turns out that it is quite simple here, and remains simple even for much more complex networks, because of the *chain rule* of differentiation.

chain rule

Since $R(\theta) = \sum_{i=1}^n R_i(\theta) = \frac{1}{2}\sum_{i=1}^n (y_i - f_\theta(x_i))^2$ is a sum, its gradient is also a sum over the n observations, so we will just examine one of these terms,

$$R_i(\theta) = \frac{1}{2}\Big(y_i - \beta_0 - \sum_{k=1}^K \beta_k g\big(w_{k0} + \sum_{j=1}^p w_{kj}x_{ij}\big)\Big)^2. \tag{10.28}$$

To simplify the expressions to follow, we write $z_{ik} = w_{k0} + \sum_{j=1}^p w_{kj}x_{ij}$. First we take the derivative with respect to β_k:

$$\begin{aligned} \frac{\partial R_i(\theta)}{\partial \beta_k} &= \frac{\partial R_i(\theta)}{\partial f_\theta(x_i)} \cdot \frac{\partial f_\theta(x_i)}{\partial \beta_k} \\ &= -(y_i - f_\theta(x_i)) \cdot g(z_{ik}). \end{aligned} \tag{10.29}$$

And now we take the derivative with respect to w_{kj}:

$$\begin{aligned} \frac{\partial R_i(\theta)}{\partial w_{kj}} &= \frac{\partial R_i(\theta)}{\partial f_\theta(x_i)} \cdot \frac{\partial f_\theta(x_i)}{\partial g(z_{ik})} \cdot \frac{\partial g(z_{ik})}{\partial z_{ik}} \cdot \frac{\partial z_{ik}}{\partial w_{kj}} \\ &= -(y_i - f_\theta(x_i)) \cdot \beta_k \cdot g'(z_{ik}) \cdot x_{ij}. \end{aligned} \tag{10.30}$$

Notice that both these expressions contain the residual $y_i - f_\theta(x_i)$. In (10.29) we see that a fraction of that residual gets attributed to each of the hidden units according to the value of $g(z_{ik})$. Then in (10.30) we see a similar attribution to input j via hidden unit k. So the act of differentiation assigns a fraction of the residual to each of the parameters via the chain rule — a process known as *backpropagation* in the neural network literature. Although these calculations are straightforward, it takes careful bookkeeping to keep track of all the pieces.

backpropagation

10.7.2 Regularization and Stochastic Gradient Descent

Gradient descent usually takes many steps to reach a local minimum. In practice, there are a number of approaches for accelerating the process. Also, when n is large, instead of summing (10.29)–(10.30) over all n observations, we can sample a small fraction or *minibatch* of them each time we compute a gradient step. This process is known as *stochastic gradient descent* (SGD) and is the state of the art for learning deep neural networks. Fortunately, there is very good software for setting up deep learning models, and for fitting them to data, so most of the technicalities are hidden from the user.

minibatch

stochastic gradient descent

We now turn to the multilayer network (Figure 10.4) used in the digit recognition problem. The network has over 235,000 weights, which is around four times the number of training examples. Regularization is essential here

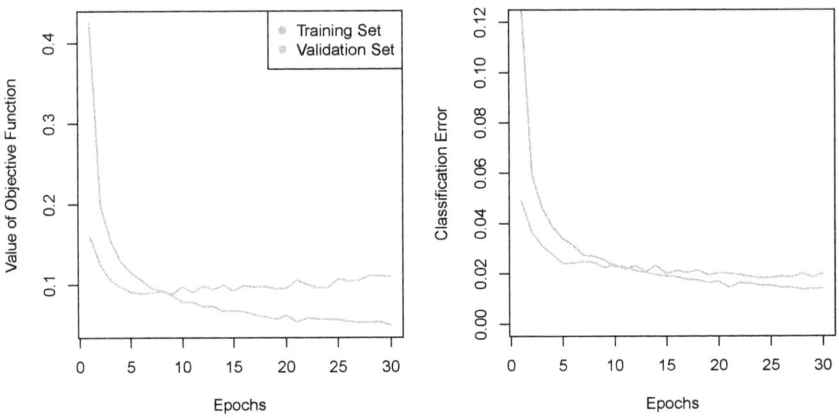

FIGURE 10.18. *Evolution of training and validation errors for the* `MNIST` *neural network depicted in Figure 10.4, as a function of training epochs. The objective refers to the log-likelihood (10.14).*

to avoid overfitting. The first row in Table 10.1 uses ridge regularization on the weights. This is achieved by augmenting the objective function (10.14) with a penalty term:

$$R(\theta; \lambda) = -\sum_{i=1}^{n} \sum_{m=0}^{9} y_{im} \log(f_m(x_i)) + \lambda \sum_j \theta_j^2. \tag{10.31}$$

The parameter λ is often preset at a small value, or else it is found using the validation-set approach of Section 5.3.1. We can also use different values of λ for the groups of weights from different layers; in this case $\mathbf{W}_1$ and $\mathbf{W}_2$ were penalized, while the relatively few weights $\mathbf{B}$ of the output layer were not penalized at all. Lasso regularization is also popular as an additional form of regularization, or as an alternative to ridge.

Figure 10.18 shows some metrics that evolve during the training of the network on the `MNIST` data. It turns out that SGD naturally enforces its own form of approximately quadratic regularization.[21] Here the minibatch size was 128 observations per gradient update. The term *epochs* labeling the horizontal axis in Figure 10.18 counts the number of times an equivalent of the full training set has been processed. For this network, 20% of the 60,000 training observations were used as a validation set in order to determine when training should stop. So in fact 48,000 observations were used for training, and hence there are 48,000/128 $\approx$ 375 minibatch gradient updates per epoch. We see that the value of the validation objective actually starts to increase by 30 epochs, so *early stopping* can also be used as an additional form of regularization.

epochs

early stopping

[21]This and other properties of SGD for deep learning are the subject of much research in the machine learning literature at the time of writing.

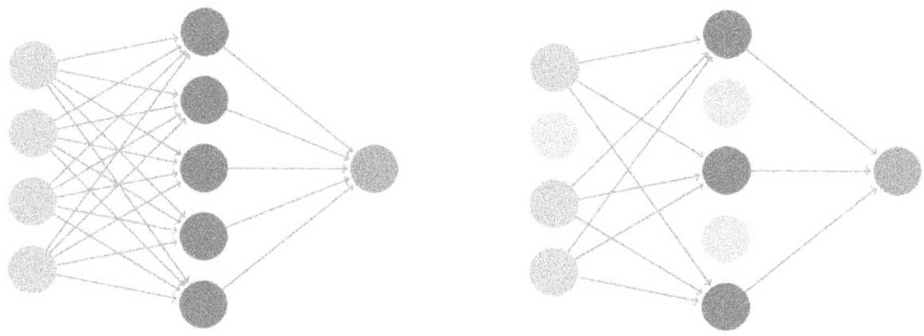

FIGURE 10.19. *Dropout Learning. Left: a fully connected network. Right: network with dropout in the input and hidden layer. The nodes in grey are selected at random, and ignored in an instance of training.*

10.7.3 Dropout Learning

The second row in Table 10.1 is labeled *dropout.* This is a relatively new and efficient form of regularization, similar in some respects to ridge regularization. Inspired by random forests (Section 8.2), the idea is to randomly remove a fraction ϕ of the units in a layer when fitting the model. Figure 10.19 illustrates this. This is done separately each time a training observation is processed. The surviving units stand in for those missing, and their weights are scaled up by a factor of $1/(1-\phi)$ to compensate. This prevents nodes from becoming over-specialized, and can be seen as a form of regularization. In practice dropout is achieved by randomly setting the activations for the "dropped out" units to zero, while keeping the architecture intact.

dropout

10.7.4 Network Tuning

The network in Figure 10.4 is considered to be relatively straightforward; it nevertheless requires a number of choices that all have an effect on the performance:

- *The number of hidden layers, and the number of units per layer.* Modern thinking is that the number of units per hidden layer can be large, and overfitting can be controlled via the various forms of regularization.

- *Regularization tuning parameters.* These include the dropout rate ϕ and the strength λ of lasso and ridge regularization, and are typically set separately at each layer.

- *Details of stochastic gradient descent.* These include the batch size, the number of epochs, and if used, details of data augmentation (Section 10.3.4.)

Choices such as these can make a difference. In preparing this `MNIST` example, we achieved a respectable 1.8% misclassification error after some trial and error. Finer tuning and training of a similar network can get under 1% error on these data, but the tinkering process can be tedious, and can result in overfitting if done carelessly.

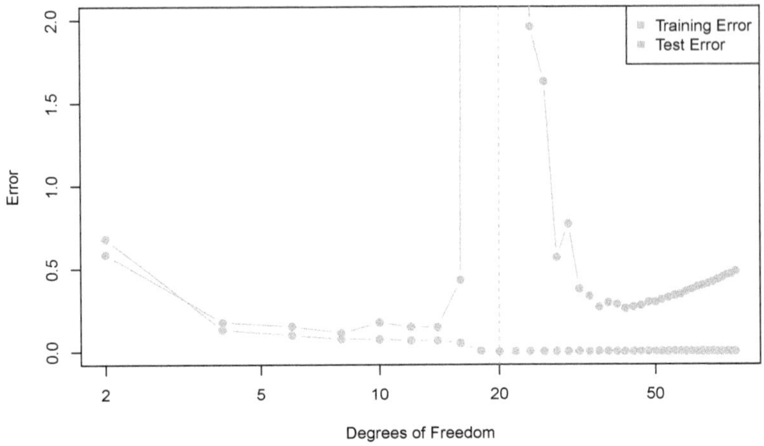

FIGURE 10.20. *Double descent phenomenon, illustrated using error plots for a one-dimensional natural spline example. The horizontal axis refers to the number of spline basis functions on the log scale. The training error hits zero when the degrees of freedom coincides with the sample size $n = 20$, the "interpolation threshold", and remains zero thereafter. The test error increases dramatically at this threshold, but then descends again to a reasonable value before finally increasing again.*

10.8 Interpolation and Double Descent

Throughout this book, we have repeatedly discussed the bias-variance trade-off, first presented in Section 2.2.2. This trade-off indicates that statistical learning methods tend to perform the best, in terms of test-set error, for an intermediate level of model complexity. In particular, if we plot "flexibility" on the x-axis and error on the y-axis, then we generally expect to see that test error has a U-shape, whereas training error decreases monotonically. Two "typical" examples of this behavior can be seen in the right-hand panel of Figure 2.9 on page 29, and in Figure 2.17 on page 39. One implication of the bias-variance trade-off is that it is generally not a good idea to *interpolate* the training data — that is, to get zero training error — since that will often result in very high test error. interpolate

However, it turns out that in certain specific settings it can be possible for a statistical learning method that interpolates the training data to perform well — or at least, better than a slightly less complex model that does not quite interpolate the data. This phenomenon is known as *double descent*, and is displayed in Figure 10.20. "Double descent" gets its name from the fact that the test error has a U-shape before the interpolation threshold is reached, and then it descends again (for a while, at least) as an increasingly flexible model is fit.

We now describe the set-up that resulted in Figure 10.20. We simulated $n = 20$ observations from the model

$$Y = \sin(X) + \epsilon,$$

where $X \sim U[-5, 5]$ (uniform distribution), and $\epsilon \sim N(0, \sigma^2)$ with $\sigma = 0.3$. We then fit a natural spline to the data, as described in Section 7.4, with d

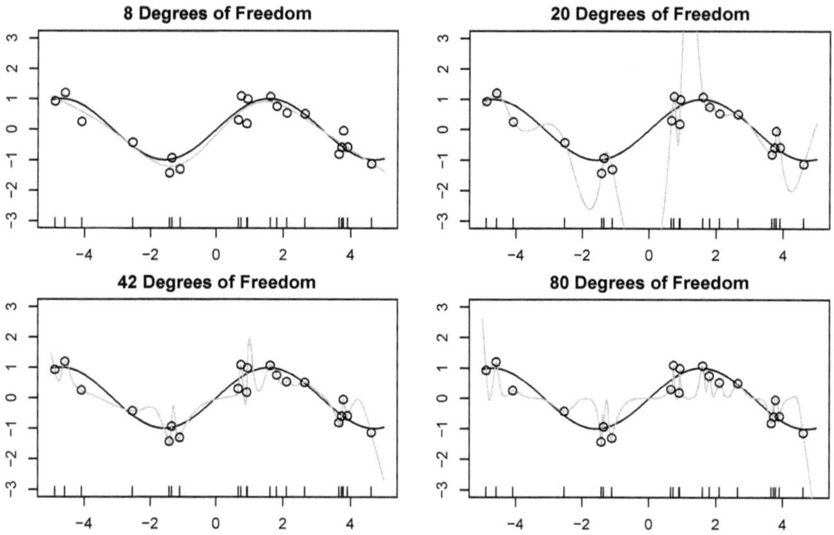

FIGURE 10.21. *Fitted functions* $\hat{f}_d(X)$ *(orange), true function* $f(X)$ *(black) and the observed* 20 *training data points. A different value of* d *(degrees of freedom) is used in each panel. For* $d \geq 20$ *the orange curves all interpolate the training points, and hence the training error is zero.*

degrees of freedom.[22] Recall from Section 7.4 that fitting a natural spline with d degrees of freedom amounts to fitting a least-squares regression of the response onto a set of d basis functions. The upper-left panel of Figure 10.21 shows the data, the true function $f(X)$, and $\hat{f}_8(X)$, the fitted natural spline with $d = 8$ degrees of freedom.

Next, we fit a natural spline with $d = 20$ degrees of freedom. Since $n = 20$, this means that $n = d$, and we have zero training error; in other words, we have interpolated the training data! We can see from the top-right panel of Figure 10.21 that $\hat{f}_{20}(X)$ makes wild excursions, and hence the test error will be large.

We now continue to fit natural splines to the data, with increasing values of d. For $d > 20$, the least squares regression of Y onto d basis functions is not unique: there are an infinite number of least squares coefficient estimates that achieve zero error. To select among them, we choose the one with the smallest sum of squared coefficients, $\sum_{j=1}^{d} \hat{\beta}_j^2$. This is known as the *minimum-norm* solution.

The two lower panels of Figure 10.21 show the minimum-norm natural spline fits with $d = 42$ and $d = 80$ degrees of freedom. Incredibly, $\hat{f}_{42}(X)$ is quite a bit *less* less wild than $\hat{f}_{20}(X)$, *even though it makes use of more degrees of freedom.* And $\hat{f}_{80}(X)$ is not much different. How can this be? Essentially, $\hat{f}_{20}(X)$ is very wild because there is just a single way to interpolate $n = 20$ observations using $d = 20$ basis functions, and that single way results in a somewhat extreme fitted function. By contrast, there are an

[22]This implies the choice of d knots, here chosen at d equi-probability quantiles of the training data. When $d > n$, the quantiles are found by interpolation.

infinite number of ways to interpolate $n = 20$ observations using $d = 42$ or $d = 80$ basis functions, and the smoothest of them — that is, the minimum norm solution — is much less wild than $\hat{f}_{20}(X)$!

In Figure 10.20, we display the training error and test error associated with $\hat{f}_d(X)$, for a range of values of the degrees of freedom d. We see that the training error drops to zero once $d = 20$ and beyond; i.e. once the interpolation threshold is reached. By contrast, the test error shows a U-shape for $d \leq 20$, grows extremely large around $d = 20$, and then shows a second region of descent for $d > 20$. For this example the signal-to-noise ratio — $\text{Var}(f(X))/\sigma^2$ — is 5.9, which is quite high (the data points are close to the true curve). So an estimate that interpolates the data and does not wander too far inbetween the observed data points will likely do well.

In Figures 10.20 and 10.21, we have illustrated the double descent phenomenon in a simple one-dimensional setting using natural splines. However, it turns out that the same phenomenon can arise for deep learning. Basically, when we fit neural networks with a huge number of parameters, we are sometimes able to get good results with zero training error. This is particularly true in problems with high signal-to-noise ratio, such as natural image recognition and language translation, for example. This is because the techniques used to fit neural networks, including stochastic gradient descent, naturally lend themselves to selecting a "smooth" interpolating model that has good test-set performance on these kinds of problems.

Some points are worth emphasizing:

- *The double-descent phenomenon does not contradict the bias-variance trade-off, as presented in Section 2.2.2.* Rather, the double-descent curve seen in the right-hand side of Figure 10.20 is a consequence of the fact that the x-axis displays the number of spline basis functions used, which does not properly capture the true "flexibility" of models that interpolate the training data. Stated another way, in this example, the minimum-norm natural spline with $d = 42$ has lower variance than the natural spline with $d = 20$.

- *Most of the statistical learning methods seen in this book do not exhibit double descent.* For instance, regularization approaches typically do not interpolate the training data, and thus double descent does not occur. This is not a drawback of regularized methods: they can give great results *without interpolating the data*!

  In particular, in the examples here, if we had fit the natural splines using ridge regression with an appropriately-chosen penalty rather than least squares, then we would not have seen double descent, and in fact would have obtained better test error results.

- *In Chapter 9, we saw that maximal margin classifiers and SVMs that have zero training error nonetheless often achieve very good test error.* This is in part because those methods seek smooth minimum norm solutions. This is similar to the fact that the minimum-norm natural spline can give good results with zero training error.

- *The double-descent phenomenon has been used by the machine learning community to explain the successful practice of using an over-*

parametrized neural network (many layers, and many hidden units), and then fitting all the way to zero training error. However, fitting to zero error is not always optimal, and whether it is advisable depends on the signal-to-noise ratio. For instance, we may use ridge regularization to avoid overfitting a neural network, as in (10.31). In this case, provided that we use an appropriate choice for the tuning parameter λ, we will never interpolate the training data, and thus will not see the double descent phenomenon. Nonetheless we can get very good test-set performance, likely much better than we would have achieved had we interpolated the training data. Early stopping during stochastic gradient descent can also serve as a form of regularization that prevents us from interpolating the training data, while still getting very good results on test data.

To summarize: though double descent can sometimes occur in neural networks, we typically do not want to rely on this behavior. Moreover, it is important to remember that the bias-variance trade-off always holds (though it is possible that test error as a function of flexibility may not exhibit a U-shape, depending on how we have parametrized the notion of "flexibility" on the x-axis).

10.9 Lab: Deep Learning

In this section we demonstrate how to fit the examples discussed in the text. We use the `Python` `torch` package, along with the `pytorch_lightning` package which provides utilities to simplify fitting and evaluating models. This code can be impressively fast with certain special processors, such as Apple's new M1 chip. The package is well-structured, flexible, and will feel comfortable to `Python` users. A good companion is the site pytorch.org/tutorials. Much of our code is adapted from there, as well as the `pytorch_lightning` documentation.[23]

torch

pytorch_lightning

We start with several standard imports that we have seen before.

In [1]:
```
import numpy as np, pandas as pd
from matplotlib.pyplot import subplots
from sklearn.linear_model import \
     (LinearRegression,
      LogisticRegression,
      Lasso)
from sklearn.preprocessing import StandardScaler
from sklearn.model_selection import KFold
from sklearn.pipeline import Pipeline
from ISLP import load_data
from ISLP.models import ModelSpec as MS
from sklearn.model_selection import \
     (train_test_split,
      GridSearchCV)
```

[23]The precise URLs at the time of writing are https://pytorch.org/tutorials/beginner/basics/intro.html and https://pytorch-lightning.readthedocs.io/en/latest/.

Torch-Specific Imports

There are a number of imports for torch. (These are not included with ISLP, so must be installed separately.) First we import the main library and essential tools used to specify sequentially-structured networks.

In [2]:
```
import torch
from torch import nn
from torch.optim import RMSprop
from torch.utils.data import TensorDataset
```

There are several other helper packages for torch. For instance, the torchmetrics package has utilities to compute various metrics to evaluate performance when fitting a model. The torchinfo package provides a useful summary of the layers of a model. We use the read_image() function when loading test images in Section 10.9.4.

torchmetrics
torchinfo
read_image()

In [3]:
```
from torchmetrics import (MeanAbsoluteError,
                          R2Score)
from torchinfo import summary
from torchvision.io import read_image
```

The package pytorch_lightning is a somewhat higher-level interface to torch that simplifies the specification and fitting of models by reducing the amount of boilerplate code needed (compared to using torch alone).

In [4]:
```
from pytorch_lightning import Trainer
from pytorch_lightning.loggers import CSVLogger
```

In order to reproduce results we use seed_everything(). We will also instruct torch to use deterministic algorithms where possible.

seed_everything()

In [5]:
```
from pytorch_lightning.utilities.seed import seed_everything
seed_everything(0, workers=True)
torch.use_deterministic_algorithms(True, warn_only=True)
```

We will use several datasets shipped with torchvision for our examples: a pretrained network for image classification, as well as some transforms used for preprocessing.

torchvision

In [6]:
```
from torchvision.datasets import MNIST, CIFAR100
from torchvision.models import (resnet50,
                                ResNet50_Weights)
from torchvision.transforms import (Resize,
                                    Normalize,
                                    CenterCrop,
                                    ToTensor)
```

We have provided a few utilities in ISLP specifically for this lab. The SimpleDataModule and SimpleModule are simple versions of objects used in pytorch_lightning, the high-level module for fitting torch models. Although more advanced uses such as computing on graphical processing units (GPUs) and parallel data processing are possible in this module, we will not be focusing much on these in this lab. The ErrorTracker handles collections of targets and predictions over each mini-batch in the validation or test stage, allowing computation of the metric over the entire validation or test data set.

In [7]:
```
from ISLP.torch import (SimpleDataModule,
                        SimpleModule,
                        ErrorTracker,
                        rec_num_workers)
```

In addition we have included some helper functions to load the IMDb database, as well as a lookup that maps integers to particular keys in the database. We've included a slightly modified copy of the preprocessed IMDb data from keras, a separate package for fitting deep learning models. This saves us significant preprocessing and allows us to focus on specifying and fitting the models themselves.

keras

In [8]:
```
from ISLP.torch.imdb import (load_lookup,
                             load_tensor,
                             load_sparse,
                             load_sequential)
```

Finally, we introduce some utility imports not directly related to torch. The glob() function from the glob module is used to find all files matching wildcard characters, which we will use in our example applying the ResNet50 model to some of our own images. The json module will be used to load a JSON file for looking up classes to identify the labels of the pictures in the ResNet50 example.

glob()

json

In [9]:
```
from glob import glob
import json
```

10.9.1 Single Layer Network on Hitters Data

We start by fitting the models in Section 10.6 on the Hitters data.

In [10]:
```
Hitters = load_data('Hitters').dropna()
n = Hitters.shape[0]
```

We will fit two linear models (least squares and lasso) and compare their performance to that of a neural network. For this comparison we will use mean absolute error on a validation dataset.

$$\text{MAE}(y, \hat{y}) = \frac{1}{n}\sum_{i=1}^{n} |y_i - \hat{y}_i|.$$

We set up the model matrix and the response.

In [11]:
```
model = MS(Hitters.columns.drop('Salary'), intercept=False)
X = model.fit_transform(Hitters).to_numpy()
Y = Hitters['Salary'].to_numpy()
```

The to_numpy() method above converts pandas data frames or series to numpy arrays. We do this because we will need to use sklearn to fit the lasso model, and it requires this conversion. We also use a linear regression method from sklearn, rather than the method in Chapter 3 from statsmodels, to facilitate the comparisons.

to_numpy()

We now split the data into test and training, fixing the random state used by sklearn to do the split.

In [12]:
```
(X_train,
 X_test,
 Y_train,
 Y_test) = train_test_split(X,
                            Y,
                            test_size=1/3,
                            random_state=1)
```

Linear Models

We fit the linear model and evaluate the test error directly.

In [13]:
```
hit_lm = LinearRegression().fit(X_train, Y_train)
Yhat_test = hit_lm.predict(X_test)
np.abs(Yhat_test - Y_test).mean()
```

Out[13]: 259.7153

Next we fit the lasso using `sklearn`. We are using mean absolute error to select and evaluate a model, rather than mean squared error. The specialized solver we used in Section 6.5.2 uses only mean squared error. So here, with a bit more work, we create a cross-validation grid and perform the cross-validation directly.

We encode a pipeline with two steps: we first normalize the features using a `StandardScaler()` transform, and then fit the lasso without further normalization.

In [14]:
```
scaler = StandardScaler(with_mean=True, with_std=True)
lasso = Lasso(warm_start=True, max_iter=30000)
standard_lasso = Pipeline(steps=[('scaler', scaler),
                                 ('lasso', lasso)])
```

We need to create a grid of values for λ. As is common practice, we choose a grid of 100 values of λ, uniform on the log scale from `lam_max` down to `0.01*lam_max`. Here `lam_max` is the smallest value of λ with an all-zero solution. This value equals the largest absolute inner-product between any predictor and the (centered) response.[24]

In [15]:
```
X_s = scaler.fit_transform(X_train)
n = X_s.shape[0]
lam_max = np.fabs(X_s.T.dot(Y_train - Y_train.mean())).max() / n
param_grid = {'alpha': np.exp(np.linspace(0, np.log(0.01), 100))
             * lam_max}
```

Note that we had to transform the data first, since the scale of the variables impacts the choice of λ. We now perform cross-validation using this sequence of λ values.

In [16]:
```
cv = KFold(10,
           shuffle=True,
           random_state=1)
grid = GridSearchCV(lasso,
```

[24]The derivation of this result is beyond the scope of this book.

```
                       param_grid,
                       cv=cv,
                       scoring='neg_mean_absolute_error')
grid.fit(X_train, Y_train);
```

We extract the lasso model with best cross-validated mean absolute error, and evaluate its performance on X_test and Y_test, which were not used in cross-validation.

In [17]:
```
trained_lasso = grid.best_estimator_
Yhat_test = trained_lasso.predict(X_test)
np.fabs(Yhat_test - Y_test).mean()
```

Out[17]: 257.2382

This is similar to the results we got for the linear model fit by least squares. However, these results can vary a lot for different train/test splits; we encourage the reader to try a different seed in code block 12 and rerun the subsequent code up to this point.

Specifying a Network: Classes and Inheritance

To fit the neural network, we first set up a model structure that describes the network. Doing so requires us to define new classes specific to the model we wish to fit. Typically this is done in pytorch by sub-classing a generic representation of a network, which is the approach we take here. Although this example is simple, we will go through the steps in some detail, since it will serve us well for the more complex examples to follow.

In [18]:
```
class HittersModel(nn.Module):

    def __init__(self, input_size):
        super(HittersModel, self).__init__()
        self.flatten = nn.Flatten()
        self.sequential = nn.Sequential(
            nn.Linear(input_size, 50),
            nn.ReLU(),
            nn.Dropout(0.4),
            nn.Linear(50, 1))

    def forward(self, x):
        x = self.flatten(x)
        return torch.flatten(self.sequential(x))
```

The class statement identifies the code chunk as a declaration for a class HittersModel that inherits from the base class nn.Module. This base class is ubiquitous in torch and represents the mappings in the neural networks.

Indented beneath the class statement are the methods of this class: in this case __init__ and forward. The __init__ method is called when an instance of the class is created as in the cell below. In the methods, self always refers to an instance of the class. In the __init__ method, we have attached two objects to self as attributes: flatten and sequential. These are used in the forward method to describe the map that this module implements.

There is one additional line in the `__init__` method, which is a call to `super()`. This function allows subclasses (i.e. `HittersModel`) to access methods of the class they inherit from. For example, the class `nn.Module` has its own `__init__` method, which is different from the `HittersModel.__init__()` method we've written above. Using `super()` allows us to call the method of the base class. For `torch` models, we will always be making this `super()` call as it is necessary for the model to be properly interpreted by `torch`.

super()

The object `nn.Module` has more methods than simply `__init__` and `forward`. These methods are directly accessible to `HittersModel` instances because of this inheritance. One such method we will see shortly is the `eval()` method, used to disable dropout for when we want to evaluate the model on test data.

In [19]:
```
hit_model = HittersModel(X.shape[1])
```

The object `self.sequential` is a composition of four maps. The first maps the 19 features of `Hitters` to 50 dimensions, introducing $50 \times 19 + 50$ parameters for the weights and *intercept* of the map (often called the *bias*). This layer is then mapped to a ReLU layer followed by a 40% dropout layer, and finally a linear map down to 1 dimension, again with a bias. The total number of trainable parameters is therefore $50 \times 19 + 50 + 50 + 1 = 1051$.

The package `torchinfo` provides a `summary()` function that neatly summarizes this information. We specify the size of the input and see the size of each tensor as it passes through layers of the network.

In [20]:
```
summary(hit_model,
        input_size=X_train.shape,
        col_names=['input_size',
                   'output_size',
                   'num_params'])
```

Out[20]:
```
===================================================================
Layer (type:depth-idx)        Input Shape     Output Shape    Param #
===================================================================
HittersModel                  [175, 19]       [175]           --
  Flatten: 1-1                [175, 19]       [175, 19]       --
  Sequential: 1-2             [175, 19]       [175, 1]        --
       Linear: 2-1            [175, 19]       [175, 50]       1,000
       ReLU: 2-2              [175, 50]       [175, 50]       --
       Dropout: 2-3           [175, 50]       [175, 50]       --
       Linear: 2-4            [175, 50]       [175, 1]        51
===================================================================
Total params: 1,051
Trainable params: 1,051
```

We have truncated the end of the output slightly, here and in subsequent uses.

We now need to transform our training data into a form accessible to `torch`. The basic datatype in `torch` is a `tensor`, which is very similar to an `ndarray` from early chapters. We also note here that `torch` typically works with 32-bit (*single precision*) rather than 64-bit (*double precision*) floating point numbers. We therefore convert our data to `np.float32` before forming the tensor. The X and Y tensors are then arranged into a `Dataset`

Dataset

recognized by torch using TensorDataset().

Tensor Dataset()

In [21]:
```
X_train_t = torch.tensor(X_train.astype(np.float32))
Y_train_t = torch.tensor(Y_train.astype(np.float32))
hit_train = TensorDataset(X_train_t, Y_train_t)
```

We do the same for the test data.

In [22]:
```
X_test_t = torch.tensor(X_test.astype(np.float32))
Y_test_t = torch.tensor(Y_test.astype(np.float32))
hit_test = TensorDataset(X_test_t, Y_test_t)
```

Finally, this dataset is passed to a DataLoader() which ultimately passes data into our network. While this may seem like a lot of overhead, this structure is helpful for more complex tasks where data may live on different machines, or where data must be passed to a GPU. We provide a helper function SimpleDataModule() in ISLP to make this task easier for standard usage. One of its arguments is num_workers, which indicates how many processes we will use for loading the data. For small data like Hitters this will have little effect, but it does provide an advantage for the MNIST and CIFAR100 examples below. The torch package will inspect the process running and determine a maximum number of workers.[25] We've included a function rec_num_workers() to compute this so we know how many workers might be reasonable (here the max was 16).

SimpleData Module()

In [23]:
```
max_num_workers = rec_num_workers()
```

The general training setup in pytorch_lightning involves training, validation and test data. These are each represented by different data loaders. During each epoch, we run a training step to learn the model and a validation step to track the error. The test data is typically used at the end of training to evaluate the model.

In this case, as we had split only into test and training, we'll use the test data as validation data with the argument validation=hit_test. The validation argument can be a float between 0 and 1, an integer, or a Dataset. If a float (respectively, integer), it is interpreted as a percentage (respectively number) of the *training* observations to be used for validation. If it is a Dataset, it is passed directly to a data loader.

In [24]:
```
hit_dm = SimpleDataModule(hit_train,
                          hit_test,
                          batch_size=32,
                          num_workers=min(4, max_num_workers),
                          validation=hit_test)
```

Next we must provide a pytorch_lightning module that controls the steps performed during the training process. We provide methods for our SimpleModule() that simply record the value of the loss function and any additional metrics at the end of each epoch. These operations are controlled by the methods SimpleModule.[training/test/validation]_step(), though we will not be modifying these in our examples.

[25]This depends on the computing hardware and the number of cores available.

```
In [25]: hit_module = SimpleModule.regression(hit_model,
                              metrics={'mae':MeanAbsoluteError()})
```

By using the SimpleModule.regression() method, we indicate that we will use squared-error loss as in (10.23). We have also asked for mean absolute error to be tracked as well in the metrics that are logged.

SimpleModule.
regression()

We log our results via CSVLogger(), which in this case stores the results in a CSV file within a directory logs/hitters. After the fitting is complete, this allows us to load the results as a pd.DataFrame() and visualize them below. There are several ways to log the results within pytorch_lightning, though we will not cover those here in detail.

```
In [26]: hit_logger = CSVLogger('logs', name='hitters')
```

Finally we are ready to train our model and log the results. We use the Trainer() object from pytorch_lightning to do this work. The argument datamodule=hit_dm tells the trainer how training/validation/test logs are produced, while the first argument hit_module specifies the network architecture as well as the training/validation/test steps. The callbacks argument allows for several tasks to be carried out at various points while training a model. Here our ErrorTracker() callback will enable us to compute validation error while training and, finally, the test error. We now fit the model for 50 epochs.

```
In [27]: hit_trainer = Trainer(deterministic=True,
                               max_epochs=50,
                               log_every_n_steps=5,
                               logger=hit_logger,
                               callbacks=[ErrorTracker()])
         hit_trainer.fit(hit_module, datamodule=hit_dm)
```

At each step of SGD, the algorithm randomly selects 32 training observations for the computation of the gradient. Recall from Section 10.7 that an epoch amounts to the number of SGD steps required to process n observations. Since the training set has $n = 175$, and we specified a batch_size of 32 in the construction of hit_dm, an epoch is $175/32 = 5.5$ SGD steps.

After having fit the model, we can evaluate performance on our test data using the test() method of our trainer.

```
In [28]: hit_trainer.test(hit_module, datamodule=hit_dm)
```

```
Out[28]: [{'test_loss': 104098.5469, 'test_mae': 229.5012}]
```

The results of the fit have been logged into a CSV file. We can find the results specific to this run in the experiment.metrics_file_path attribute of our logger. Note that each time the model is fit, the logger will output results into a new subdirectory of our directory logs/hitters.

We now create a plot of the MAE (mean absolute error) as a function of the number of epochs. First we retrieve the logged summaries.

```
hit_results = pd.read_csv(hit_logger.experiment.metrics_file_path)
```

Since we will produce similar plots in later examples, we write a simple generic function to produce this plot.

```
In [29]: def summary_plot(results,
                          ax,
                          col='loss',
                          valid_legend='Validation',
                          training_legend='Training',
                          ylabel='Loss',
                          fontsize=20):
             for (column,
                  color,
                  label) in zip([f'train_{col}_epoch',
                                 f'valid_{col}'],
                                ['black',
                                 'red'],
                                [training_legend,
                                 valid_legend]):
                 results.plot(x='epoch',
                              y=column,
                              label=label,
                              marker='o',
                              color=color,
                              ax=ax)
             ax.set_xlabel('Epoch')
             ax.set_ylabel(ylabel)
             return ax
```

We now set up our axes, and use our function to produce the MAE plot.

```
In [30]: fig, ax = subplots(1, 1, figsize=(6, 6))
         ax = summary_plot(hit_results,
                           ax,
                           col='mae',
                           ylabel='MAE',
                           valid_legend='Validation (=Test)')
         ax.set_ylim([0, 400])
         ax.set_xticks(np.linspace(0, 50, 11).astype(int));
```

We can predict directly from the final model, and evaluate its performance on the test data. Before fitting, we call the `eval()` method of `hit_model`. This tells `torch` to effectively consider this model to be fitted, so that we can use it to predict on new data. For our model here, the biggest change is that the dropout layers will be turned off, i.e. no weights will be randomly dropped in predicting on new data.

```
In [31]: hit_model.eval()
         preds = hit_module(X_test_t)
         torch.abs(Y_test_t - preds).mean()
```

```
Out[31]: tensor(229.5012, grad_fn=<MeanBackward0>)
```

Cleanup

In setting up our data module, we had initiated several worker processes that will remain running. We delete all references to the torch objects to ensure these processes will be killed.

In [32]:
```
del(Hitters,
    hit_model, hit_dm,
    hit_logger,
    hit_test, hit_train,
    X, Y,
    X_test, X_train,
    Y_test, Y_train,
    X_test_t, Y_test_t,
    hit_trainer, hit_module)
```

10.9.2 Multilayer Network on the MNIST Digit Data

The `torchvision` package comes with a number of example datasets, including the `MNIST` digit data. Our first step is to retrieve the training and test data sets; the `MNIST()` function within `torchvision.datasets` is provided for this purpose. The data will be downloaded the first time this function is executed, and stored in the directory `data/MNIST`. `MNIST()`

In [33]:
```
(mnist_train,
 mnist_test) = [MNIST(root='data',
                      train=train,
                      download=True,
                      transform=ToTensor())
                for train in [True, False]]
mnist_train
```

Out[33]:
```
Dataset MNIST
    Number of datapoints: 60000
    Root location: data
    Split: Train
    StandardTransform
Transform: ToTensor()
```

There are 60,000 images in the training data and 10,000 in the test data. The images are 28 × 28, and stored as a matrix of pixels. We need to transform each one into a vector.

Neural networks are somewhat sensitive to the scale of the inputs, much as ridge and lasso regularization are affected by scaling. Here the inputs are eight-bit grayscale values between 0 and 255, so we rescale to the unit interval.[26] This transformation, along with some reordering of the axes, is performed by the `ToTensor()` transform from the `torchvision.transforms` package.

As in our `Hitters` example, we form a data module from the training and test datasets, setting aside 20% of the training images for validation.

In [34]:
```
mnist_dm = SimpleDataModule(mnist_train,
                            mnist_test,
                            validation=0.2,
                            num_workers=max_num_workers,
                            batch_size=256)
```

[26]Note: eight bits means 2^8, which equals 256. Since the convention is to start at 0, the possible values range from 0 to 255.

Let's take a look at the data that will get fed into our network. We loop through the first few chunks of the test dataset, breaking after 2 batches:

```
In [35]: for idx, (X_ ,Y_) in enumerate(mnist_dm.train_dataloader()):
             print('X: ', X_.shape)
             print('Y: ', Y_.shape)
             if idx >= 1:
                 break
```

```
X:  torch.Size([256, 1, 28, 28])
Y:  torch.Size([256])
X:  torch.Size([256, 1, 28, 28])
Y:  torch.Size([256])
```

We see that the X for each batch consists of 256 images of size `1x28x28`. Here the `1` indicates a single channel (greyscale). For RGB images such as `CIFAR100` below, we will see that the `1` in the size will be replaced by `3` for the three RGB channels.

Now we are ready to specify our neural network.

```
In [36]: class MNISTModel(nn.Module):
             def __init__(self):
                 super(MNISTModel, self).__init__()
                 self.layer1 = nn.Sequential(
                     nn.Flatten(),
                     nn.Linear(28*28, 256),
                     nn.ReLU(),
                     nn.Dropout(0.4))
                 self.layer2 = nn.Sequential(
                     nn.Linear(256, 128),
                     nn.ReLU(),
                     nn.Dropout(0.3))
                 self._forward = nn.Sequential(
                     self.layer1,
                     self.layer2,
                     nn.Linear(128, 10))
             def forward(self, x):
                 return self._forward(x)
```

We see that in the first layer, each `1x28x28` image is flattened, then mapped to 256 dimensions where we apply a ReLU activation with 40% dropout. A second layer maps the first layer's output down to 128 dimensions, applying a ReLU activation with 30% dropout. Finally, the 128 dimensions are mapped down to 10, the number of classes in the `MNIST` data.

```
In [37]: mnist_model = MNISTModel()
```

We can check that the model produces output of expected size based on our existing batch `X_` above.

```
In [38]: mnist_model(X_).size()
```

```
Out[38]: torch.Size([256, 10])
```

Let's take a look at the summary of the model. Instead of an `input_size` we can pass a tensor of correct shape. In this case, we pass through the final batched `X_` from above.

In [39]:
```
summary(mnist_model,
        input_data=X_,
        col_names=['input_size',
                   'output_size',
                   'num_params'])
```

Out[39]:
```
=====================================================================
Layer (type:depth-idx)          Input Shape        Output Shape  Param #
=====================================================================
MNISTModel                      [256, 1, 28, 28]   [256, 10]     --
  Sequential: 1-1               [256, 1, 28, 28]   [256, 10]     --
      Sequential: 2-1           [256, 1, 28, 28]   [256, 256]    --
          Flatten: 3-1          [256, 1, 28, 28]   [256, 784]    --
          Linear: 3-2           [256, 784]         [256, 256]    200,960
          ReLU: 3-3             [256, 256]         [256, 256]    --
          Dropout: 3-4          [256, 256]         [256, 256]    --
      Sequential: 2-2           [256, 256]         [256, 128]    --
          Linear: 3-5           [256, 256]         [256, 128]    32,896
          ReLU: 3-6             [256, 128]         [256, 128]    --
          Dropout: 3-7          [256, 128]         [256, 128]    --
      Linear: 2-3               [256, 128]         [256, 10]     1,290
=====================================================================
Total params: 235,146
Trainable params: 235,146
```

Having set up both the model and the data module, fitting this model is now almost identical to the `Hitters` example. In contrast to our regression model, here we will use the `SimpleModule.classification()` method which uses the cross-entropy loss function instead of mean squared error.

SimpleModul classifi-cation()

In [40]:
```
mnist_module = SimpleModule.classification(mnist_model)
mnist_logger = CSVLogger('logs', name='MNIST')
```

Now we are ready to go. The final step is to supply training data, and fit the model.

In [41]:
```
mnist_trainer = Trainer(deterministic=True,
                        max_epochs=30,
                        logger=mnist_logger,
                        callbacks=[ErrorTracker()])
mnist_trainer.fit(mnist_module,
                  datamodule=mnist_dm)
```

We have suppressed the output here, which is a progress report on the fitting of the model, grouped by epoch. This is very useful, since on large datasets fitting can take time. Fitting this model took 245 seconds on a MacBook Pro with an Apple M1 Pro chip with 10 cores and 16 GB of RAM. Here we specified a validation split of 20%, so training is actually performed on 80% of the 60,000 observations in the training set. This is an alternative to actually supplying validation data, like we did for the `Hitters` data. SGD uses batches of 256 observations in computing the gradient, and doing the arithmetic, we see that an epoch corresponds to 188 gradient steps.

`SimpleModule.classification()` includes an accuracy metric by default. Other classification metrics can be added from `torchmetrics`. We will use our `summary_plot()` function to display accuracy across epochs.

```
In [42]: mnist_results = pd.read_csv(mnist_logger.experiment.
             metrics_file_path)
         fig, ax = subplots(1, 1, figsize=(6, 6))
         summary_plot(mnist_results,
                      ax,
                      col='accuracy',
                      ylabel='Accuracy')
         ax.set_ylim([0.5, 1])
         ax.set_ylabel('Accuracy')
         ax.set_xticks(np.linspace(0, 30, 7).astype(int));
```

Once again we evaluate the accuracy using the `test()` method of our trainer. This model achieves 97% accuracy on the test data.

```
In [43]: mnist_trainer.test(mnist_module,
                            datamodule=mnist_dm)
```

```
Out[43]: [{'test_loss': 0.1471, 'test_accuracy': 0.9681}]
```

Table 10.1 also reports the error rates resulting from LDA (Chapter 4) and multiclass logistic regression. For LDA we refer the reader to Section 4.7.3. Although we could use the `sklearn` function `LogisticRegression()` to fit multiclass logistic regression, we are set up here to fit such a model with `torch`. We just have an input layer and an output layer, and omit the hidden layers!

```
In [44]: class MNIST_MLR(nn.Module):
             def __init__(self):
                 super(MNIST_MLR, self).__init__()
                 self.linear = nn.Sequential(nn.Flatten(),
                                             nn.Linear(784, 10))
             def forward(self, x):
                 return self.linear(x)

         mlr_model = MNIST_MLR()
         mlr_module = SimpleModule.classification(mlr_model)
         mlr_logger = CSVLogger('logs', name='MNIST_MLR')
```

```
In [45]: mlr_trainer = Trainer(deterministic=True,
                               max_epochs=30,
                               callbacks=[ErrorTracker()])
         mlr_trainer.fit(mlr_module, datamodule=mnist_dm)
```

We fit the model just as before and compute the test results.

```
In [46]: mlr_trainer.test(mlr_module,
                          datamodule=mnist_dm)
```

```
Out[46]: [{'test_loss': 0.3187, 'test_accuracy': 0.9241}]
```

The accuracy is above 90% even for this pretty simple model.

As in the `Hitters` example, we delete some of the objects we created above.

```
In [47]: del(mnist_test,
             mnist_train,
```

```
    mnist_model,
    mnist_dm,
    mnist_trainer,
    mnist_module,
    mnist_results,
    mlr_model,
    mlr_module,
    mlr_trainer)
```

10.9.3 Convolutional Neural Networks

In this section we fit a CNN to the `CIFAR100` data, which is available in the `torchvision` package. It is arranged in a similar fashion as the `MNIST` data.

In [48]:
```
(cifar_train,
 cifar_test) = [CIFAR100(root="data",
                         train=train,
                         download=True)
             for train in [True, False]]
```

In [49]:
```
transform = ToTensor()
cifar_train_X = torch.stack([transform(x) for x in
                            cifar_train.data])
cifar_test_X = torch.stack([transform(x) for x in
                            cifar_test.data])
cifar_train = TensorDataset(cifar_train_X,
                            torch.tensor(cifar_train.targets))
cifar_test = TensorDataset(cifar_test_X,
                            torch.tensor(cifar_test.targets))
```

The `CIFAR100` dataset consists of 50,000 training images, each represented by a three-dimensional tensor: each three-color image is represented as a set of three channels, each of which consists of 32×32 eight-bit pixels. We standardize as we did for the digits, but keep the array structure. This is accomplished with the `ToTensor()` transform.

Creating the data module is similar to the `MNIST` example.

In [50]:
```
cifar_dm = SimpleDataModule(cifar_train,
                            cifar_test,
                            validation=0.2,
                            num_workers=max_num_workers,
                            batch_size=128)
```

We again look at the shape of typical batches in our data loaders.

In [51]:
```
for idx, (X_ ,Y_) in enumerate(cifar_dm.train_dataloader()):
    print('X: ', X_.shape)
    print('Y: ', Y_.shape)
    if idx >= 1:
        break
```

```
X:  torch.Size([128, 3, 32, 32])
Y:  torch.Size([128])
X:  torch.Size([128, 3, 32, 32])
Y:  torch.Size([128])
```

Before we start, we look at some of the training images; similar code produced Figure 10.5 on page 406. The example below also illustrates that `TensorDataset` objects can be indexed with integers — we are choosing random images from the training data by indexing `cifar_train`. In order to display correctly, we must reorder the dimensions by a call to `np.transpose()`.

In [52]:
```
fig, axes = subplots(5, 5, figsize=(10,10))
rng = np.random.default_rng(4)
indices = rng.choice(np.arange(len(cifar_train)), 25,
                     replace=False).reshape((5,5))
for i in range(5):
    for j in range(5):
        idx = indices[i,j]
        axes[i,j].imshow(np.transpose(cifar_train[idx][0],
                                      [1,2,0]),
                                      interpolation=None)
        axes[i,j].set_xticks([])
        axes[i,j].set_yticks([])
```

Here the `imshow()` method recognizes from the shape of its argument that it is a 3-dimensional array, with the last dimension indexing the three RGB color channels. `.imshow()`

We specify a moderately-sized CNN for demonstration purposes, similar in structure to Figure 10.8. We use several layers, each consisting of convolution, ReLU, and max-pooling steps. We first define a module that defines one of these layers. As in our previous examples, we overwrite the `__init__()` and `forward()` methods of `nn.Module`. This user-defined module can now be used in ways just like `nn.Linear()` or `nn.Dropout()`.

In [53]:
```
class BuildingBlock(nn.Module):

    def __init__(self,
                 in_channels,
                 out_channels):

        super(BuildingBlock, self).__init__()
        self.conv = nn.Conv2d(in_channels=in_channels,
                              out_channels=out_channels,
                              kernel_size=(3,3),
                              padding='same')
        self.activation = nn.ReLU()
        self.pool = nn.MaxPool2d(kernel_size=(2,2))

    def forward(self, x):
        return self.pool(self.activation(self.conv(x)))
```

Notice that we used the `padding = "same"` argument to `nn.Conv2d()`, which ensures that the output channels have the same dimension as the input channels. There are 32 channels in the first hidden layer, in contrast to the three channels in the input layer. We use a 3×3 convolution filter for each channel in all the layers. Each convolution is followed by a max-pooling layer over 2×2 blocks.

In forming our deep learning model for the `CIFAR100` data, we use several of our `BuildingBlock()` modules sequentially. This simple example illustrates some of the power of `torch`. Users can define modules of their own, which can be combined in other modules. Ultimately, everything is fit by a generic trainer.

In [54]:
```
class CIFARModel(nn.Module):

    def __init__(self):
        super(CIFARModel, self).__init__()
        sizes = [(3,32),
                 (32,64),
                 (64,128),
                 (128,256)]
        self.conv = nn.Sequential(*[BuildingBlock(in_, out_)
                                    for in_, out_ in sizes])

        self.output = nn.Sequential(nn.Dropout(0.5),
                                    nn.Linear(2*2*256, 512),
                                    nn.ReLU(),
                                    nn.Linear(512, 100))
    def forward(self, x):
        val = self.conv(x)
        val = torch.flatten(val, start_dim=1)
        return self.output(val)
```

We build the model and look at the summary. (We had created examples of `X_` earlier.)

In [55]:
```
cifar_model = CIFARModel()
summary(cifar_model,
        input_data=X_,
        col_names=['input_size',
                   'output_size',
                   'num_params'])
```

Out[55]:
```
=========================================================================
Layer (type:depth-idx)  Input Shape         Output Shape         Param #
=========================================================================
CIFARModel              [128, 3, 32, 32]    [128, 100]           --
  Sequential: 1-1       [128, 3, 32, 32]    [128, 256, 2, 2]     --
    BuildingBlock: 2-1  [128, 3, 32, 32]    [128, 32, 16, 16]    --
        Conv2d: 3-1     [128, 3, 32, 32]    [128, 32, 32, 32]    896
        ReLU: 3-2       [128, 32, 32, 32]   [128, 32, 32, 32]    --
        MaxPool2d: 3-3  [128, 32, 32, 32]   [128, 32, 16, 16]    --
    BuildingBlock: 2-2  [128, 32, 16, 16]   [128, 64, 8, 8]      --
        Conv2d: 3-4     [128, 32, 16, 16]   [128, 64, 16, 16]    18,496
        ReLU: 3-5       [128, 64, 16, 16]   [128, 64, 16, 16]    --
        MaxPool2d: 3-6  [128, 64, 16, 16]   [128, 64, 8, 8]      --
    BuildingBlock: 2-3  [128, 64, 8, 8]     [128, 128, 4, 4]     --
        Conv2d: 3-7     [128, 64, 8, 8]     [128, 128, 8, 8]     73,856
        ReLU: 3-8       [128, 128, 8, 8]    [128, 128, 8, 8]     --
        MaxPool2d: 3-9  [128, 128, 8, 8]    [128, 128, 4, 4]     --
    BuildingBlock: 2-4  [128, 128, 4, 4]    [128, 256, 2, 2]     --
        Conv2d: 3-10    [128, 128, 4, 4]    [128, 256, 4, 4]     295,168
        ReLU: 3-11      [128, 256, 4, 4]    [128, 256, 4, 4]     --
        MaxPool2d: 3-12 [128, 256, 4, 4]    [128, 256, 2, 2]     --
  Sequential: 1-2       [128, 1024]         [128, 100]           --
      Dropout: 2-5      [128, 1024]         [128, 1024]          --
      Linear: 2-6       [128, 1024]         [128, 512]           524,800
```

```
        ReLU: 2-7           [128, 512]          [128, 512]          --
        Linear: 2-8         [128, 512]          [128, 100]          51,300
======================================================================
Total params: 964,516
Trainable params: 964,516
```

The total number of trainable parameters is 964,516. By studying the size of the parameters, we can see that the channels halve in both dimensions after each of these max-pooling operations. After the last of these we have a layer with 256 channels of dimension 2×2. These are then flattened to a dense layer of size 1,024; in other words, each of the 2×2 matrices is turned into a 4-vector, and put side-by-side in one layer. This is followed by a dropout regularization layer, then another dense layer of size 512, and finally, the output layer.

Up to now, we have been using a default optimizer in `SimpleModule()`. For these data, experiments show that a smaller learning rate performs better than the default 0.01. We use a custom optimizer here with a learning rate of 0.001. Besides this, the logging and training follow a similar pattern to our previous examples. The optimizer takes an argument `params` that informs the optimizer which parameters are involved in SGD (stochastic gradient descent).

We saw earlier that entries of a module's parameters are tensors. In passing the parameters to the optimizer we are doing more than simply passing arrays; part of the structure of the graph is encoded in the tensors themselves.

In [56]:
```
cifar_optimizer = RMSprop(cifar_model.parameters(), lr=0.001)
cifar_module = SimpleModule.classification(cifar_model,
                                optimizer=cifar_optimizer)
cifar_logger = CSVLogger('logs', name='CIFAR100')
```

In [57]:
```
cifar_trainer = Trainer(deterministic=True,
                        max_epochs=30,
                        logger=cifar_logger,
                        callbacks=[ErrorTracker()])
cifar_trainer.fit(cifar_module,
                  datamodule=cifar_dm)
```

This model takes 10 minutes or more to run and achieves about 42% accuracy on the test data. Although this is not terrible for 100-class data (a random classifier gets 1% accuracy), searching the web we see results around 75%. Typically it takes a lot of architecture carpentry, fiddling with regularization, and time, to achieve such results.

Let's take a look at the validation and training accuracy across epochs.

In [58]:
```
log_path = cifar_logger.experiment.metrics_file_path
cifar_results = pd.read_csv(log_path)
fig, ax = subplots(1, 1, figsize=(6, 6))
summary_plot(cifar_results,
             ax,
             col='accuracy',
             ylabel='Accuracy')
ax.set_xticks(np.linspace(0, 10, 6).astype(int))
ax.set_ylabel('Accuracy')
ax.set_ylim([0, 1]);
```

Finally, we evaluate our model on our test data.

In [59]:
```
cifar_trainer.test(cifar_module,
                   datamodule=cifar_dm)
```

Out[59]:
```
[{'test_loss': 2.4238 'test_accuracy': 0.4206}]
```

Hardware Acceleration

As deep learning has become ubiquitous in machine learning, hardware manufacturers have produced special libraries that can often speed up the gradient-descent steps.

For instance, Mac OS devices with the M1 chip may have the *Metal* programming framework enabled, which can speed up the `torch` computations. We present an example of how to use this acceleration.

The main changes are to the `Trainer()` call as well as to the metrics that will be evaluated on the data. These metrics must be told where the data will be located at evaluation time. This is accomplished with a call to the `to()` method of the metrics.

In [60]:
```
try:
    for name, metric in cifar_module.metrics.items():
        cifar_module.metrics[name] = metric.to('mps')
    cifar_trainer_mps = Trainer(accelerator='mps',
                                deterministic=True,
                                max_epochs=30)
    cifar_trainer_mps.fit(cifar_module,
                          datamodule=cifar_dm)
    cifar_trainer_mps.test(cifar_module,
                          datamodule=cifar_dm)
except:
    pass
```

This yields approximately two- or three-fold acceleration for each epoch. We have protected this code block using `try:` and `except:` clauses; if it works, we get the speedup, if it fails, nothing happens.

10.9.4 Using Pretrained CNN Models

We now show how to use a CNN pretrained on the `imagenet` database to classify natural images, and demonstrate how we produced Figure 10.10. We copied six JPEG images from a digital photo album into the directory `book_images`. These images are available from the data section of `www.statlearning.com`, the ISLP book website. Download `book_images.zip`; when clicked it creates the `book_images` directory.

The pretrained network we use is called `resnet50`; specification details can be found on the web. We will read in the images, and convert them into the array format expected by the `torch` software to match the specifications in `resnet50`. The conversion involves a resize, a crop and then a predefined standardization for each of the three channels. We now read in the images and preprocess them.

```
In [61]: resize = Resize((232,232))
         crop = CenterCrop(224)
         normalize = Normalize([0.485,0.456,0.406],
                               [0.229,0.224,0.225])
         imgfiles = sorted([f for f in glob('book_images/*')])
         imgs = torch.stack([torch.div(crop(resize(read_image(f))), 255)
                             for f in imgfiles])
         imgs = normalize(imgs)
         imgs.size()
```

```
Out[61]: torch.Size([6, 3, 224, 224])
```

We now set up the trained network with the weights we read in code block 6. The model has 50 layers, with a fair bit of complexity.

```
In [62]: resnet_model = resnet50(weights=ResNet50_Weights.DEFAULT)
         summary(resnet_model,
                 input_data=imgs,
                 col_names=['input_size',
                            'output_size',
                            'num_params'])
```

We set the mode to `eval()` to ensure that the model is ready to predict on new data.

```
In [63]: resnet_model.eval()
```

Inspecting the output above, we see that when setting up the `resnet_model`, the authors defined a `Bottleneck`, much like our `BuildingBlock` module.

We now feed our six images through the fitted network.

```
In [64]: img_preds = resnet_model(imgs)
```

Let's look at the predicted probabilities for each of the top 3 choices. First we compute the probabilities by applying the softmax to the logits in `img_preds`. Note that we have had to call the `detach()` method on the tensor `img_preds` in order to convert it to our a more familiar `ndarray`.

```
In [65]: img_probs = np.exp(np.asarray(img_preds.detach()))
         img_probs /= img_probs.sum(1)[:,None]
```

In order to see the class labels, we must download the index file associated with `imagenet`.[27]

```
In [66]: labs = json.load(open('imagenet_class_index.json'))
         class_labels = pd.DataFrame([(int(k), v[1]) for k, v in
                                      labs.items()],
                                      columns=['idx', 'label'])
         class_labels = class_labels.set_index('idx')
         class_labels = class_labels.sort_index()
```

We'll now construct a data frame for each image file with the labels with the three highest probabilities as estimated by the model above.

[27]This is avalable from the book website and s3.amazonaws.com/deep-learning-models/image-models/imagenet_class_index.json.

In [67]:
```
for i, imgfile in enumerate(imgfiles):
    img_df = class_labels.copy()
    img_df['prob'] = img_probs[i]
    img_df = img_df.sort_values(by='prob', ascending=False)[:3]
    print(f'Image: {imgfile}')
    print(img_df.reset_index().drop(columns=['idx']))
```

```
Image: book_images/Cape_Weaver.jpg
      label      prob
0    jacamar  0.287283
1  bee_eater  0.046768
2     bulbul  0.037507
Image: book_images/Flamingo.jpg
             label      prob
0         flamingo  0.591761
1        spoonbill  0.012386
2  American_egret  0.002105
Image: book_images/Hawk_Fountain.jpg
             label      prob
0  great_grey_owl  0.287959
1            kite  0.039478
2        fountain  0.029384
Image: book_images/Hawk_cropped.jpg
    label      prob
0    kite  0.301830
1     jay  0.121674
2  magpie  0.015513
Image: book_images/Lhasa_Apso.jpg
             label      prob
0            Lhasa  0.151143
1         Shih-Tzu  0.129850
2  Tibetan_terrier  0.102358
Image: book_images/Sleeping_Cat.jpg
       label      prob
0      tabby  0.173627
1  tiger_cat  0.110414
2    doormat  0.093447
```

We see that the model is quite confident about `Flamingo.jpg`, but a little less so for the other images.

We end this section with our usual cleanup.

In [68]:
```
del(cifar_test,
    cifar_train,
    cifar_dm,
    cifar_module,
    cifar_logger,
    cifar_optimizer,
    cifar_trainer)
```

10.9.5 IMDB Document Classification

We now implement models for sentiment classification (Section 10.4) on the `IMDB` dataset. As mentioned above code block 8, we are using a preprocessed version of the `IMDB` dataset found in the `keras` package. As `keras` uses tensorflow, a different tensor and deep learning library, we have converted the data to be suitable for torch. The code used to convert from keras is available in the module ISLP.torch._make_imdb. It requires some of the keras packages to run. These data use a dictionary of size 10,000.

We have stored three different representations of the review data for this lab:

- load_tensor(), a sparse tensor version usable by torch;
- load_sparse(), a sparse matrix version usable by sklearn, since we will compare with a lasso fit;
- load_sequential(), a padded version of the original sequence representation, limited to the last 500 words of each review.

In [69]:
```
(imdb_seq_train,
 imdb_seq_test) = load_sequential(root='data/IMDB')
padded_sample = np.asarray(imdb_seq_train.tensors[0][0])
sample_review = padded_sample[padded_sample > 0][:12]
sample_review[:12]
```

Out[69]:
```
array([   1,    14,    22,    16,    43,   530,   973,  1622,  1385,
          65,   458,  4468], dtype=int32)
```

The datasets imdb_seq_train and imdb_seq_test are both instances of the class TensorDataset. The tensors used to construct them can be found in the tensors attribute, with the first tensor the features X and the second the outcome Y. We have taken the first row of features and stored it as padded_sample. In the preprocessing used to form these data, sequences were padded with 0s in the beginning if they were not long enough, hence we remove this padding by restricting to entries where padded_sample > 0. We then provide the first 12 words of the sample review.

We can find these words in the lookup dictionary from the ISLP.torch.imdb module.

In [70]:
```
lookup = load_lookup(root='data/IMDB')
' '.join(lookup[i] for i in sample_review)
```

Out[70]:
```
"<START> this film was just brilliant casting location scenery
    story direction everyone's"
```

For our first model, we have created a binary feature for each of the 10,000 possible words in the dataset, with an entry of one in the i, j entry if word j appears in review i. As most reviews are quite short, such a feature matrix has over 98% zeros. These data are accessed using load_tensor() from the ISLP library.

In [71]:
```
max_num_workers=10
(imdb_train,
 imdb_test) = load_tensor(root='data/IMDB')
imdb_dm = SimpleDataModule(imdb_train,
                           imdb_test,
                           validation=2000,
                           num_workers=min(6, max_num_workers),
                           batch_size=512)
```

We'll use a two-layer model for our first model.

In [72]:
```
class IMDBModel(nn.Module):

    def __init__(self, input_size):
        super(IMDBModel, self).__init__()
        self.dense1 = nn.Linear(input_size, 16)
        self.activation = nn.ReLU()
        self.dense2 = nn.Linear(16, 16)
        self.output = nn.Linear(16, 1)

    def forward(self, x):
        val = x
        for _map in [self.dense1,
                     self.activation,
                     self.dense2,
                     self.activation,
                     self.output]:
            val = _map(val)
        return torch.flatten(val)
```

We now instantiate our model and look at a summary (not shown).

In [73]:
```
imdb_model = IMDBModel(imdb_test.tensors[0].size()[1])
summary(imdb_model,
        input_size=imdb_test.tensors[0].size(),
        col_names=['input_size',
                   'output_size',
                   'num_params'])
```

We'll again use a smaller learning rate for these data, hence we pass an `optimizer` to the `SimpleModule`. Since the reviews are classified into positive or negative sentiment, we use `SimpleModule.binary_classification()`.[28]

In [74]:
```
imdb_optimizer = RMSprop(imdb_model.parameters(), lr=0.001)
imdb_module = SimpleModule.binary_classification(
                         imdb_model,
                         optimizer=imdb_optimizer)
```

Having loaded the datasets into a data module and created a `SimpleModule`, the remaining steps are familiar.

In [75]:
```
imdb_logger = CSVLogger('logs', name='IMDB')
imdb_trainer = Trainer(deterministic=True,
                       max_epochs=30,
                       logger=imdb_logger,
                       callbacks=[ErrorTracker()])
imdb_trainer.fit(imdb_module,
                 datamodule=imdb_dm)
```

Evaluating the test error yields roughly 86% accuracy.

In [76]:
```
test_results = imdb_trainer.test(imdb_module, datamodule=imdb_dm)
test_results
```

[28]Our use of `binary_classification()` instead of `classification()` is due to some subtlety in how `torchmetrics.Accuracy()` works, as well as the data type of the targets.

```
Out[76]: [{'test_loss': 1.0863, 'test_accuracy': 0.8550}]
```

Comparison to Lasso

We now fit a lasso logistic regression model using `LogisticRegression()` from `sklearn`. Since `sklearn` does not recognize the sparse tensors of `torch`, we use a sparse matrix that is recognized by `sklearn`.

```
In [77]: ((X_train, Y_train),
          (X_valid, Y_valid),
          (X_test, Y_test)) = load_sparse(validation=2000,
                                          random_state=0,
                                          root='data/IMDB')
```

Similar to what we did in Section 10.9.1, we construct a series of 50 values for the lasso reguralization parameter λ.

```
In [78]: lam_max = np.abs(X_train.T * (Y_train - Y_train.mean())).max()
         lam_val = lam_max * np.exp(np.linspace(np.log(1),
                                                np.log(1e-4), 50))
```

With `LogisticRegression()` the regularization parameter C is specified as the inverse of λ. There are several solvers for logistic regression; here we use `liblinear` which works well with the sparse input format.

```
In [79]: logit = LogisticRegression(penalty='l1',
                                    C=1/lam_max,
                                    solver='liblinear',
                                    warm_start=True,
                                    fit_intercept=True)
```

The path of 50 values takes approximately 40 seconds to run.

```
In [80]: coefs = []
         intercepts = []

         for l in lam_val:
             logit.C = 1/l
             logit.fit(X_train, Y_train)
             coefs.append(logit.coef_.copy())
             intercepts.append(logit.intercept_)
```

The coefficient and intercepts have an extraneous dimension which can be removed by the `np.squeeze()` function.

```
In [81]: coefs = np.squeeze(coefs)
         intercepts = np.squeeze(intercepts)
```

We'll now make a plot to compare our neural network results with the lasso.

```
In [82]: %%capture
         fig, axes = subplots(1, 2, figsize=(16, 8), sharey=True)
         for ((X_, Y_),
              data_,
              color) in zip([(X_train, Y_train),
                             (X_valid, Y_valid),
                             (X_test, Y_test)],
```

```
                       ['Training', 'Validation', 'Test'],
                       ['black', 'red', 'blue']):
    linpred_ = X_ * coefs.T + intercepts[None,:]
    label_ = np.array(linpred_ > 0)
    accuracy_ = np.array([np.mean(Y_ == l) for l in label_.T])
    axes[0].plot(-np.log(lam_val / X_train.shape[0]),
                 accuracy_,
                 '.--',
                 color=color,
                 markersize=13,
                 linewidth=2,
                 label=data_)
axes[0].legend()
axes[0].set_xlabel(r'$-\log(\lambda)$', fontsize=20)
axes[0].set_ylabel('Accuracy', fontsize=20)
```

Notice the use of %%capture, which suppresses the displaying of the partially completed figure. This is useful when making a complex figure, since the steps can be spread across two or more cells. We now add a plot of the lasso accuracy, and display the composed figure by simply entering its name at the end of the cell. %%capture

```
In [83]: imdb_results = pd.read_csv(imdb_logger.experiment.metrics_file_path)
summary_plot(imdb_results,
             axes[1],
             col='accuracy',
             ylabel='Accuracy')
axes[1].set_xticks(np.linspace(0, 30, 7).astype(int))
axes[1].set_ylabel('Accuracy', fontsize=20)
axes[1].set_xlabel('Epoch', fontsize=20)
axes[1].set_ylim([0.5, 1]);
axes[1].axhline(test_results[0]['test_accuracy'],
                color='blue',
                linestyle='--',
                linewidth=3)
fig
```

From the graphs we see that the accuracy of the lasso logistic regression peaks at about 0.88, as it does for the neural network.

Once again, we end with a cleanup.

```
In [84]: del(imdb_model,
    imdb_trainer,
    imdb_logger,
    imdb_dm,
    imdb_train,
    imdb_test)
```

10.9.6 Recurrent Neural Networks

In this lab we fit the models illustrated in Section 10.5.

Sequential Models for Document Classification

Here we fit a simple LSTM RNN for sentiment prediction to the `IMDb` movie-review data, as discussed in Section 10.5.1. For an RNN we use the sequence of words in a document, taking their order into account. We loaded the preprocessed data at the beginning of Section 10.9.5. A script that details the preprocessing can be found in the ISLP library. Notably, since more than 90% of the documents had fewer than 500 words, we set the document length to 500. For longer documents, we used the last 500 words, and for shorter documents, we padded the front with blanks.

In [85]:
```
imdb_seq_dm = SimpleDataModule(imdb_seq_train,
                               imdb_seq_test,
                               validation=2000,
                               batch_size=300,
                               num_workers=min(6, max_num_workers)
                               )
```

The first layer of the RNN is an embedding layer of size 32, which will be learned during training. This layer one-hot encodes each document as a matrix of dimension $500 \times 10,003$, and then maps these $10,003$ dimensions down to 32.[29] Since each word is represented by an integer, this is effectively achieved by the creation of an embedding matrix of size $10,003 \times 32$; each of the 500 integers in the document are then mapped to the appropriate 32 real numbers by indexing the appropriate rows of this matrix.

The second layer is an LSTM with 32 units, and the output layer is a single logit for the binary classification task. In the last line of the forward() method below, we take the last 32-dimensional output of the LSTM and map it to our response.

In [86]:
```
class LSTMModel(nn.Module):
    def __init__(self, input_size):
        super(LSTMModel, self).__init__()
        self.embedding = nn.Embedding(input_size, 32)
        self.lstm = nn.LSTM(input_size=32,
                            hidden_size=32,
                            batch_first=True)
        self.dense = nn.Linear(32, 1)
    def forward(self, x):
        val, (h_n, c_n) = self.lstm(self.embedding(x))
        return torch.flatten(self.dense(val[:,-1]))
```

We instantiate and take a look at the summary of the model, using the first 10 documents in the corpus.

In [87]:
```
lstm_model = LSTMModel(X_test.shape[-1])
summary(lstm_model,
        input_data=imdb_seq_train.tensors[0][:10],
        col_names=['input_size',
                   'output_size',
                   'num_params'])
```

Out[87]:
```
===================================================================
Layer (type:depth-idx)     Input Shape      Output Shape     Param #
===================================================================
LSTMModel                  [10, 500]        [10]             --
```

[29]The extra 3 dimensions correspond to commonly occurring non-word entries in the reviews.

```
 Embedding: 1-1            [10, 500]         [10, 500, 32]     320,096
 LSTM: 1-2                 [10, 500, 32]     [10, 500, 32]     8,448
 Linear: 1-3               [10, 32]          [10, 1]           33
=====================================================================
Total params: 328,577
Trainable params: 328,577
```

The 10,003 is suppressed in the summary, but we see it in the parameter count, since $10,003 \times 32 = 320,096$.

In [88]:
```
lstm_module = SimpleModule.binary_classification(lstm_model)
lstm_logger = CSVLogger('logs', name='IMDB_LSTM')
```

In [89]:
```
lstm_trainer = Trainer(deterministic=True,
                       max_epochs=20,
                       logger=lstm_logger,
                       callbacks=[ErrorTracker()])
lstm_trainer.fit(lstm_module,
                 datamodule=imdb_seq_dm)
```

The rest is now similar to other networks we have fit. We track the test performance as the network is fit, and see that it attains 85% accuracy.

In [90]:
```
lstm_trainer.test(lstm_module, datamodule=imdb_seq_dm)
```

Out[90]:
```
[{'test_loss': 0.8178, 'test_accuracy': 0.8476}]
```

We once again show the learning progress, followed by cleanup.

In [91]:
```
lstm_results = pd.read_csv(lstm_logger.experiment.metrics_file_path)
fig, ax = subplots(1, 1, figsize=(6, 6))
summary_plot(lstm_results,
             ax,
             col='accuracy',
             ylabel='Accuracy')
ax.set_xticks(np.linspace(0, 20, 5).astype(int))
ax.set_ylabel('Accuracy')
ax.set_ylim([0.5, 1])
```

In [92]:
```
del(lstm_model,
    lstm_trainer,
    lstm_logger,
    imdb_seq_dm,
    imdb_seq_train,
    imdb_seq_test)
```

Time Series Prediction

We now show how to fit the models in Section 10.5.2 for time series prediction. We first load and standardize the data.

In [93]:
```
NYSE = load_data('NYSE')
cols = ['DJ_return', 'log_volume', 'log_volatility']
X = pd.DataFrame(StandardScaler(
                     with_mean=True,
                     with_std=True).fit_transform(NYSE[cols]),
                 columns=NYSE[cols].columns,
                 index=NYSE.index)
```

Next we set up the lagged versions of the data, dropping any rows with missing values using the `dropna()` method.

```
In [94]: for lag in range(1, 6):
             for col in cols:
                 newcol = np.zeros(X.shape[0]) * np.nan
                 newcol[lag:] = X[col].values[:-lag]
                 X.insert(len(X.columns), "{0}_{1}".format(col, lag), newcol)
         X.insert(len(X.columns), 'train', NYSE['train'])
         X = X.dropna()
```

Finally, we extract the response, training indicator, and drop the current day's `DJ_return` and `log_volatility` to predict only from previous day's data.

```
In [95]: Y, train = X['log_volume'], X['train']
         X = X.drop(columns=['train'] + cols)
         X.columns
```

```
Out[95]: Index(['DJ_return_1', 'log_volume_1', 'log_volatility_1',
                'DJ_return_2', 'log_volume_2', 'log_volatility_2',
                'DJ_return_3', 'log_volume_3', 'log_volatility_3',
                'DJ_return_4', 'log_volume_4', 'log_volatility_4',
                'DJ_return_5', 'log_volume_5', 'log_volatility_5'],
               dtype='object')
```

We first fit a simple linear model and compute the R^2 on the test data using the `score()` method.

```
In [96]: M = LinearRegression()
         M.fit(X[train], Y[train])
         M.score(X[~train], Y[~train])
```

```
Out[96]: 0.4129
```

We refit this model, including the factor variable `day_of_week`. For a categorical series in `pandas`, we can form the indicators using the `get_dummies()` method.

```
In [97]: X_day = pd.merge(X,
                          pd.get_dummies(NYSE['day_of_week']),
                          on='date')
```

Note that we do not have to reinstantiate the linear regression model as its `fit()` method accepts a design matrix and a response directly.

```
In [98]: M.fit(X_day[train], Y[train])
         M.score(X_day[~train], Y[~train])
```

```
Out[98]: 0.4595
```

This model achieves an R^2 of about 46%.

To fit the RNN, we must reshape the data, as it will expect 5 lagged versions of each feature as indicated by the `input_shape` argument to the layer `nn.RNN()` below. We first ensure the columns of our data frame are such that a reshaped matrix will have the variables correctly lagged. We use the `reindex()` method to do this.

For an input shape (5,3), each row represents a lagged version of the three variables. The nn.RNN() layer also expects the first row of each observation to be earliest in time, so we must reverse the current order. Hence we loop over range(5,0,-1) below, which is an example of using a slice() to index iterable objects. The general notation is start:end:step.

```
In [99]: ordered_cols = []
         for lag in range(5,0,-1):
             for col in cols:
                 ordered_cols.append('{0}_{1}'.format(col, lag))
         X = X.reindex(columns=ordered_cols)
         X.columns
```

```
Out[99]: Index(['DJ_return_5', 'log_volume_5', 'log_volatility_5',
                'DJ_return_4', 'log_volume_4', 'log_volatility_4',
                'DJ_return_3', 'log_volume_3', 'log_volatility_3',
                'DJ_return_2', 'log_volume_2', 'log_volatility_2',
                'DJ_return_1', 'log_volume_1', 'log_volatility_1'],
               dtype='object')
```

We now reshape the data.

```
In [100]: X_rnn = X.to_numpy().reshape((-1,5,3))
          X_rnn.shape
```

```
Out[100]: (6046, 5, 3)
```

By specifying the first size as -1, numpy.reshape() deduces its size based on the remaining arguments.

Now we are ready to proceed with the RNN, which uses 12 hidden units, and 10% dropout. After passing through the RNN, we extract the final time point as val[:,-1] in forward() below. This gets passed through a 10% dropout and then flattened through a linear layer.

```
In [101]: class NYSEModel(nn.Module):
              def __init__(self):
                  super(NYSEModel, self).__init__()
                  self.rnn = nn.RNN(3,
                                    12,
                                    batch_first=True)
                  self.dense = nn.Linear(12, 1)
                  self.dropout = nn.Dropout(0.1)
              def forward(self, x):
                  val, h_n = self.rnn(x)
                  val = self.dense(self.dropout(val[:,-1]))
                  return torch.flatten(val)
          nyse_model = NYSEModel()
```

We fit the model in a similar fashion to previous networks. We supply the fit function with test data as validation data, so that when we monitor its progress and plot the history function we can see the progress on the test data. Of course we should not use this as a basis for early stopping, since then the test performance would be biased.

We form the training dataset similar to our Hitters example.

In [102]:
```
datasets = []
for mask in [train, ~train]:
    X_rnn_t = torch.tensor(X_rnn[mask].astype(np.float32))
    Y_t = torch.tensor(Y[mask].astype(np.float32))
    datasets.append(TensorDataset(X_rnn_t, Y_t))
nyse_train, nyse_test = datasets
```

Following our usual pattern, we inspect the summary.

In [103]:
```
summary(nyse_model,
        input_data=X_rnn_t,
        col_names=['input_size',
                   'output_size',
                   'num_params'])
```

Out[103]:
```
=========================================================================
Layer (type:depth-idx)     Input Shape      Output Shape      Param #
=========================================================================
NYSEModel                  [1770, 5, 3]     [1770]            --
  RNN: 1-1                 [1770, 5, 3]     [1770, 5, 12]     204
  Dropout: 1-2             [1770, 12]       [1770, 12]        --
  Linear: 1-3              [1770, 12]       [1770, 1]         13
=========================================================================
Total params: 217
Trainable params: 217
```

We again put the two datasets into a data module, with a batch size of 64.

In [104]:
```
nyse_dm = SimpleDataModule(nyse_train,
                           nyse_test,
                           num_workers=min(4, max_num_workers),
                           validation=nyse_test,
                           batch_size=64)
```

We run some data through our model to be sure the sizes match up correctly.

In [105]:
```
for idx, (x, y) in enumerate(nyse_dm.train_dataloader()):
    out = nyse_model(x)
    print(y.size(), out.size())
    if idx >= 2:
        break
```

```
torch.Size([64]) torch.Size([64])
torch.Size([64]) torch.Size([64])
torch.Size([64]) torch.Size([64])
```

We follow our previous example for setting up a trainer for a regression problem, requesting the R^2 metric to be be computed at each epoch.

In [106]:
```
nyse_optimizer = RMSprop(nyse_model.parameters(),
                         lr=0.001)
nyse_module = SimpleModule.regression(nyse_model,
                                      optimizer=nyse_optimizer,
                                      metrics={'r2':R2Score()})
```

Fitting the model should by now be familiar. The results on the test data are very similar to the linear AR model.

In[107]:
```
nyse_trainer = Trainer(deterministic=True,
                       max_epochs=200,
                       callbacks=[ErrorTracker()])
nyse_trainer.fit(nyse_module,
                 datamodule=nyse_dm)
nyse_trainer.test(nyse_module,
                  datamodule=nyse_dm)
```

Out[107]:
```
[{'test_loss': 0.6141, 'test_r2': 0.4172}]
```

We could also fit a model without the `nn.RNN()` layer by just using a `nn.Flatten()` layer instead. This would be a nonlinear AR model. If in addition we excluded the hidden layer, this would be equivalent to our earlier linear AR model.

Instead we will fit a nonlinear AR model using the feature set `X_day` that includes the `day_of_week` indicators. To do so, we must first create our test and training datasets and a corresponding data module. This may seem a little burdensome, but is part of the general pipeline for `torch`.

In[108]:
```
datasets = []
for mask in [train, ~train]:
    X_day_t = torch.tensor(
                   np.asarray(X_day[mask]).astype(np.float32))
    Y_t = torch.tensor(np.asarray(Y[mask]).astype(np.float32))
    datasets.append(TensorDataset(X_day_t, Y_t))
day_train, day_test = datasets
```

Creating a data module follows a familiar pattern.

In[109]:
```
day_dm = SimpleDataModule(day_train,
                          day_test,
                          num_workers=min(4, max_num_workers),
                          validation=day_test,
                          batch_size=64)
```

We build a `NonLinearARModel()` that takes as input the 20 features and a hidden layer with 32 units. The remaining steps are familiar.

In[110]:
```
class NonLinearARModel(nn.Module):
    def __init__(self):
        super(NonLinearARModel, self).__init__()
        self._forward = nn.Sequential(nn.Flatten(),
                                      nn.Linear(20, 32),
                                      nn.ReLU(),
                                      nn.Dropout(0.5),
                                      nn.Linear(32, 1))
    def forward(self, x):
        return torch.flatten(self._forward(x))
```

In[111]:
```
nl_model = NonLinearARModel()
nl_optimizer = RMSprop(nl_model.parameters(),
                       lr=0.001)
nl_module = SimpleModule.regression(nl_model,
                                    optimizer=nl_optimizer,
                                    metrics={'r2':R2Score()})
```

We continue with the usual training steps, fit the model, and evaluate the test error. We see the test R^2 is a slight improvement over the linear AR model that also includes day_of_week.

In [112]:
```
nl_trainer = Trainer(deterministic=True,
                     max_epochs=20,
                     callbacks=[ErrorTracker()])
nl_trainer.fit(nl_module, datamodule=day_dm)
nl_trainer.test(nl_module, datamodule=day_dm)
```

Out[112]:
```
[{'test_loss': 0.5625, 'test_r2': 0.4662}]
```

10.10 Exercises

Conceptual

1. Consider a neural network with two hidden layers: $p = 4$ input units, 2 units in the first hidden layer, 3 units in the second hidden layer, and a single output.

   (a) Draw a picture of the network, similar to Figures 10.1 or 10.4.

   (b) Write out an expression for $f(X)$, assuming ReLU activation functions. Be as explicit as you can!

   (c) Now plug in some values for the coefficients and write out the value of $f(X)$.

   (d) How many parameters are there?

2. Consider the *softmax* function in (10.13) (see also (4.13) on page 145) for modeling multinomial probabilities.

   (a) In (10.13), show that if we add a constant c to each of the z_ℓ, then the probability is unchanged.

   (b) In (4.13), show that if we add constants c_j, $j = 0, 1, \ldots, p$, to each of the corresponding coefficients for each of the classes, then the predictions at any new point x are unchanged.

   This shows that the softmax function is *over-parametrized*. However, regularization and SGD typically constrain the solutions so that this is not a problem.

   over-parametrized

3. Show that the negative multinomial log-likelihood (10.14) is equivalent to the negative log of the likelihood expression (4.5) when there are $M = 2$ classes.

4. Consider a CNN that takes in 32×32 grayscale images and has a single convolution layer with three 5×5 convolution filters (without boundary padding).

   (a) Draw a sketch of the input and first hidden layer similar to Figure 10.8.

(b) How many parameters are in this model?

(c) Explain how this model can be thought of as an ordinary feed-forward neural network with the individual pixels as inputs, and with constraints on the weights in the hidden units. What are the constraints?

(d) If there were no constraints, then how many weights would there be in the ordinary feed-forward neural network in (c)?

5. In Table 10.2 on page 426, we see that the ordering of the three methods with respect to mean absolute error is different from the ordering with respect to test set R^2. How can this be?

Applied

6. Consider the simple function $R(\beta) = \sin(\beta) + \beta/10$.

   (a) Draw a graph of this function over the range $\beta \in [-6, 6]$.

   (b) What is the derivative of this function?

   (c) Given $\beta^0 = 2.3$, run gradient descent to find a local minimum of $R(\beta)$ using a learning rate of $\rho = 0.1$. Show each of $\beta^0, \beta^1, \ldots$ in your plot, as well as the final answer.

   (d) Repeat with $\beta^0 = 1.4$.

7. Fit a neural network to the `Default` data. Use a single hidden layer with 10 units, and dropout regularization. Have a look at Labs 10.9.1–10.9.2 for guidance. Compare the classification performance of your model with that of linear logistic regression.

8. From your collection of personal photographs, pick 10 images of animals (such as dogs, cats, birds, farm animals, etc.). If the subject does not occupy a reasonable part of the image, then crop the image. Now use a pretrained image classification CNN as in Lab 10.9.4 to predict the class of each of your images, and report the probabilities for the top five predicted classes for each image.

9. Fit a lag-5 autoregressive model to the `NYSE` data, as described in the text and Lab 10.9.6. Refit the model with a 12-level factor representing the month. Does this factor improve the performance of the model?

10. In Section 10.9.6, we showed how to fit a linear AR model to the `NYSE` data using the `LinearRegression()` function. However, we also mentioned that we can "flatten" the short sequences produced for the RNN model in order to fit a linear AR model. Use this latter approach to fit a linear AR model to the `NYSE` data. Compare the test R^2 of this linear AR model to that of the linear AR model that we fit in the lab. What are the advantages/disadvantages of each approach?

11. Repeat the previous exercise, but now fit a nonlinear AR model by "flattening" the short sequences produced for the RNN model.

12. Consider the RNN fit to the NYSE data in Section 10.9.6. Modify the code to allow inclusion of the variable day_of_week, and fit the RNN. Compute the test R^2.

13. Repeat the analysis of Lab 10.9.5 on the IMDb data using a similarly structured neural network. We used 16 hidden units at each of two hidden layers. Explore the effect of increasing this to 32 and 64 units per layer, with and without 30% dropout regularization.

11
Survival Analysis and Censored Data

In this chapter, we will consider the topics of *survival analysis* and *censored data*. These arise in the analysis of a unique kind of outcome variable: the *time until an event occurs.*

survival analysis

censored data

For example, suppose that we have conducted a five-year medical study, in which patients have been treated for cancer. We would like to fit a model to predict patient survival time, using features such as baseline health measurements or type of treatment. At first pass, this may sound like a regression problem of the kind discussed in Chapter 3. But there is an important complication: hopefully some or many of the patients have survived until the end of the study. Such a patient's survival time is said to be *censored*: we know that it is at least five years, but we do not know its true value. We do not want to discard this subset of surviving patients, as the fact that they survived at least five years amounts to valuable information. However, it is not clear how to make use of this information using the techniques covered thus far in this textbook.

Though the phrase "survival analysis" evokes a medical study, the applications of survival analysis extend far beyond medicine. For example, consider a company that wishes to model *churn*, the process by which customers cancel subscription to a service. The company might collect data on customers over some time period, in order to model each customer's time to cancellation as a function of demographics or other predictors. However, presumably not all customers will have canceled their subscription by the end of this time period; for such customers, the time to cancellation is censored.

In fact, survival analysis is relevant even in application areas that are unrelated to time. For instance, suppose we wish to model a person's weight as a function of some covariates, using a dataset with measurements for a large number of people. Unfortunately, the scale used to weigh those people is unable to report weights above a certain number. Then, any weights that

G. James et al., *An Introduction to Statistical Learning*, Springer Texts in Statistics,
https://doi.org/10.1007/978-3-031-38747-0_11

exceed that number are censored. The survival analysis methods presented in this chapter could be used to analyze this dataset.

Survival analysis is a very well-studied topic within statistics, due to its critical importance in a variety of applications, both in and out of medicine. However, it has received relatively little attention in the machine learning community.

11.1 Survival and Censoring Times

For each individual, we suppose that there is a true *survival time*, T, as well as a true *censoring time*, C. (The survival time is also known as the *failure time* or the *event time*.) The survival time represents the time at which the event of interest occurs: for instance, the time at which the patient dies, or the customer cancels his or her subscription. By contrast, the censoring time is the time at which censoring occurs: for example, the time at which the patient drops out of the study or the study ends.

survival time

censoring time

failure time

event time

We observe either the survival time T or else the censoring time C. Specifically, we observe the random variable

$$Y = \min(T, C). \tag{11.1}$$

In other words, if the event occurs before censoring (i.e. $T < C$) then we observe the true survival time T; however, if censoring occurs before the event ($T > C$) then we observe the censoring time. We also observe a status indicator,

$$\delta = \begin{cases} 1 & \text{if } T \leq C \\ 0 & \text{if } T > C. \end{cases}$$

Thus, $\delta = 1$ if we observe the true survival time, and $\delta = 0$ if we instead observe the censoring time.

Now, suppose we observe n (Y, δ) pairs, which we denote as $(y_1, \delta_1), \ldots,$ (y_n, δ_n). Figure 11.1 displays an example from a (fictitious) medical study in which we observe $n = 4$ patients for a 365-day follow-up period. For patients 1 and 3, we observe the time to event (such as death or disease relapse) $T = t_i$. Patient 2 was alive when the study ended, and patient 4 dropped out of the study, or was "lost to follow-up"; for these patients we observe $C = c_i$. Therefore, $y_1 = t_1$, $y_3 = t_3$, $y_2 = c_2$, $y_4 = c_4$, $\delta_1 = \delta_3 = 1$, and $\delta_2 = \delta_4 = 0$.

11.2 A Closer Look at Censoring

In order to analyze survival data, we need to make some assumptions about *why* censoring has occurred. For instance, suppose that a number of patients drop out of a cancer study early because they are very sick. An analysis that does not take into consideration the reason why the patients dropped out will likely overestimate the true average survival time. Similarly, suppose that males who are very sick are more likely to drop out of the study than

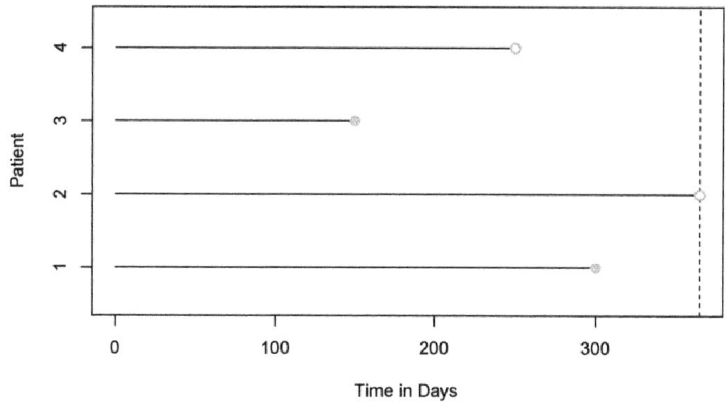

FIGURE 11.1. *Illustration of censored survival data. For patients 1 and 3, the event was observed. Patient 2 was alive when the study ended. Patient 4 dropped out of the study.*

females who are very sick. Then a comparison of male and female survival times may wrongly suggest that males survive longer than females.

In general, we need to assume that the censoring mechanism is *independent*: conditional on the features, the event time T is independent of the censoring time C. The two examples above violate the assumption of independent censoring. Typically, it is not possible to determine from the data itself whether the censoring mechanism is independent. Instead, one has to carefully consider the data collection process in order to determine whether independent censoring is a reasonable assumption. In the remainder of this chapter, we will assume that the censoring mechanism is independent.[1]

In this chapter, we focus on *right censoring*, which occurs when $T \geq Y$, i.e. the true event time T is at least as large as the observed time Y. (Notice that $T \geq Y$ is a consequence of (11.1). Right censoring derives its name from the fact that time is typically displayed from left to right, as in Figure 11.1.) However, other types of censoring are possible. For instance, in *left censoring*, the true event time T is less than or equal to the observed time Y. For example, in a study of pregnancy duration, suppose that we survey patients 250 days after conception, when some have already had their babies. Then we know that for those patients, pregnancy duration is less than 250 days. More generally, *interval censoring* refers to the setting in which we do not know the exact event time, but we know that it falls in some interval. For instance, this setting arises if we survey patients once per week in order to determine whether the event has occurred. While left censoring and interval censoring can be accommodated using variants of the ideas presented in this chapter, in what follows we focus specifically on right censoring.

---

[1]The assumption of independent censoring can be relaxed somewhat using the notion of *non-informative censoring*; however, the definition of non-informative censoring is too technical for this book.

11.3 The Kaplan–Meier Survival Curve

The *survival curve*, or *survival function*, is defined as

survival curve survival function

$$S(t) = \Pr(T > t). \tag{11.2}$$

This decreasing function quantifies the probability of surviving past time t. For example, suppose that a company is interested in modeling customer churn. Let T represent the time that a customer cancels a subscription to the company's service. Then $S(t)$ represents the probability that a customer cancels later than time t. The larger the value of $S(t)$, the less likely that the customer will cancel before time t.

In this section, we will consider the task of estimating the survival curve. Our investigation is motivated by the `BrainCancer` dataset, which contains the survival times for patients with primary brain tumors undergoing treatment with stereotactic radiation methods.[2] The predictors are `gtv` (gross tumor volume, in cubic centimeters); `sex` (male or female); `diagnosis` (meningioma, LG glioma, HG glioma, or other); `loc` (the tumor location: either infratentorial or supratentorial); `ki` (Karnofsky index); and `stereo` (stereotactic method: either stereotactic radiosurgery or fractionated stereotactic radiotherapy, abbreviated as SRS and SRT, respectively). Only 53 of the 88 patients were still alive at the end of the study.

Now, we consider the task of estimating the survival curve (11.2) for these data. To estimate $S(20) = \Pr(T > 20)$, the probability that a patient survives for at least $t = 20$ months, it is tempting to simply compute the proportion of patients who are known to have survived past 20 months, i.e. the proportion of patients for whom $Y > 20$. This turns out to be 48/88, or approximately 55%. However, this does not seem quite right, since Y and T represent different quantities. In particular, 17 of the 40 patients who did not survive to 20 months were actually censored, and this analysis implicitly assumes that $T < 20$ for all of those censored patients; of course, we do not know whether that is true.

Alternatively, to estimate $S(20)$, we could consider computing the proportion of patients for whom $Y > 20$, out of the 71 patients who were *not* censored by time $t = 20$; this comes out to 48/71, or approximately 68%. However, this is not quite right either, since it amounts to completely ignoring the patients who were censored before time $t = 20$, even though the *time* at which they are censored is potentially informative. For instance, a patient who was censored at time $t = 19.9$ likely would have survived past $t = 20$ had he or she not been censored.

We have seen that estimating $S(t)$ is complicated by the presence of censoring. We now present an approach to overcome these challenges. We let $d_1 < d_2 < \cdots < d_K$ denote the K unique death times among the non-censored patients, and we let q_k denote the number of patients who died at time d_k. For $k = 1, \ldots, K$, we let r_k denote the number of patients alive

[2]This dataset is described in the following paper: Selingerová et al. (2016) Survival of patients with primary brain tumors: Comparison of two statistical approaches. PLoS One, 11(2):e0148733.

and in the study just before d_k; these are the *at risk* patients. The set of patients that are at risk at a given time are referred to as the *risk set.*

risk set

By the law of total probability,[3]

$$\Pr(T > d_k) = \Pr(T > d_k|T > d_{k-1})\Pr(T > d_{k-1}) + \Pr(T > d_k|T \leq d_{k-1})\Pr(T \leq d_{k-1}).$$

The fact that $d_{k-1} < d_k$ implies that $\Pr(T > d_k|T \leq d_{k-1}) = 0$ (it is impossible for a patient to survive past time d_k if he or she did not survive until an earlier time d_{k-1}). Therefore,

$$S(d_k) = \Pr(T > d_k) = \Pr(T > d_k|T > d_{k-1})\Pr(T > d_{k-1}).$$

Plugging in (11.2) again, we see that

$$S(d_k) = \Pr(T > d_k|T > d_{k-1})S(d_{k-1}).$$

This implies that

$$S(d_k) = \Pr(T > d_k|T > d_{k-1}) \times \cdots \times \Pr(T > d_2|T > d_1)\Pr(T > d_1).$$

We now must simply plug in estimates of each of the terms on the right-hand side of the previous equation. It is natural to use the estimator

$$\widehat{\Pr}(T > d_j|T > d_{j-1}) = (r_j - q_j)/r_j,$$

which is the fraction of the risk set at time d_j who survived past time d_j. This leads to the *Kaplan–Meier estimator* of the survival curve:

Kaplan–Meier estimator

$$\widehat{S}(d_k) = \prod_{j=1}^{k}\left(\frac{r_j - q_j}{r_j}\right). \tag{11.3}$$

For times t between d_k and d_{k+1}, we set $\widehat{S}(t) = \widehat{S}(d_k)$. Consequently, the Kaplan–Meier survival curve has a step-like shape.

The Kaplan–Meier survival curve for the `BrainCancer` data is displayed in Figure 11.2. Each point in the solid step-like curve shows the estimated probability of surviving past the time indicated on the horizontal axis. The estimated probability of survival past 20 months is 71%, which is quite a bit higher than the naive estimates of 55% and 68% presented earlier.

The sequential construction of the Kaplan–Meier estimator — starting at time zero and mapping out the observed events as they unfold in time — is fundamental to many of the key techniques in survival analysis. These include the log-rank test of Section 11.4, and Cox's proportional hazard model of Section 11.5.2.

---

[3]The law of total probability states that for any two events A and B, $\Pr(A) = \Pr(A|B)\Pr(B) + \Pr(A|B^c)\Pr(B^c)$, where B^c is the complement of the event B, i.e. it is the event that B does not hold.

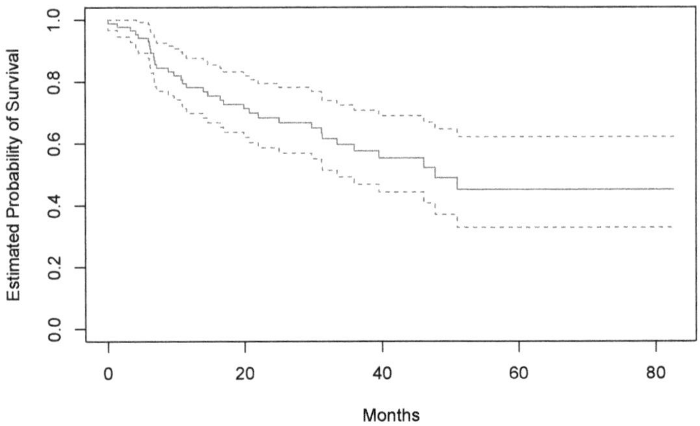

FIGURE 11.2. *For the* `BrainCancer` *data, we display the Kaplan–Meier survival curve (solid curve), along with standard error bands (dashed curves).*

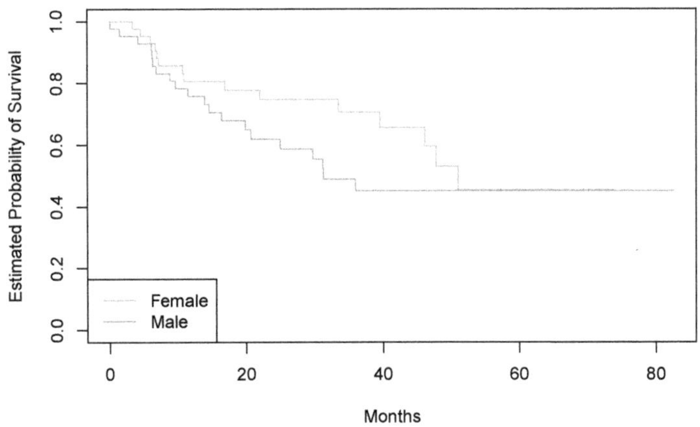

FIGURE 11.3. *For the* `BrainCancer` *data, Kaplan–Meier survival curves for males and females are displayed.*

11.4 The Log-Rank Test

We now continue our analysis of the `BrainCancer` data introduced in Section 11.3. We wish to compare the survival of males to that of females. Figure 11.3 shows the Kaplan–Meier survival curves for the two groups. Females seem to fare a little better up to about 50 months, but then the two curves both level off to about 50%. How can we carry out a formal test of equality of the two survival curves?

At first glance, a two-sample t-test seems like an obvious choice: we could test whether the mean survival time among the females equals the mean survival time among the males. But the presence of censoring again creates a complication. To overcome this challenge, we will conduct a *log-rank test*,[4] log-rank tes

	Group 1	Group 2	Total
Died	q_{1k}	q_{2k}	q_k
Survived	$r_{1k} - q_{1k}$	$r_{2k} - q_{2k}$	$r_k - q_k$
Total	r_{1k}	r_{2k}	r_k

TABLE 11.1. *Among the set of patients at risk at time d_k, the number of patients who died and survived in each of two groups is reported.*

which examines how the events in each group unfold sequentially in time.

Recall from Section 11.3 that $d_1 < d_2 < \cdots < d_K$ are the unique death times among the non-censored patients, r_k is the number of patients at risk at time d_k, and q_k is the number of patients who died at time d_k. We further define r_{1k} and r_{2k} to be the number of patients in groups 1 and 2, respectively, who are at risk at time d_k. Similarly, we define q_{1k} and q_{2k} to be the number of patients in groups 1 and 2, respectively, who died at time d_k. Note that $r_{1k} + r_{2k} = r_k$ and $q_{1k} + q_{2k} = q_k$.

At each death time d_k, we construct a 2×2 table of counts of the form shown in Table 11.1. Note that if the death times are unique (i.e. no two individuals die at the same time), then one of q_{1k} and q_{2k} equals one, and the other equals zero.

The main idea behind the log-rank test statistic is as follows. In order to test $H_0 : \mathrm{E}(X) = \mu$ for some random variable X, one approach is to construct a test statistic of the form

$$W = \frac{X - \mu}{\sqrt{\mathrm{Var}(X)}}. \tag{11.4}$$

To construct the log-rank test statistic, we compute a quantity that takes exactly the form (11.4), with $X = \sum_{k=1}^{K} q_{1k}$, where q_{1k} is given in the top left of Table 11.1.

In greater detail, if there is no difference in survival between the two groups, and conditioning on the row and column totals in Table 11.1, the expected value of q_{1k} is

$$\mu_k = \frac{r_{1k}}{r_k} q_k. \tag{11.5}$$

So the expected value of $X = \sum_{k=1}^{K} q_{1k}$ is $\mu = \sum_{k=1}^{K} \frac{r_{1k}}{r_k} q_k$. Furthermore, it can be shown[5] that the variance of q_{1k} is

$$\mathrm{Var}\left(q_{1k}\right) = \frac{q_k (r_{1k}/r_k)(1 - r_{1k}/r_k)(r_k - q_k)}{r_k - 1}. \tag{11.6}$$

Though $q_{11}, \ldots, q_{1K}$ may be correlated, we nonetheless estimate

$$\mathrm{Var}\left(\sum_{k=1}^{K} q_{1k}\right) \approx \sum_{k=1}^{K} \mathrm{Var}\left(q_{1k}\right) = \sum_{k=1}^{K} \frac{q_k (r_{1k}/r_k)(1 - r_{1k}/r_k)(r_k - q_k)}{r_k - 1}. \tag{11.7}$$

[4] The log-rank test is also known as the *Mantel–Haenszel test* or *Cochran–Mantel–Haenszel test*.

[5] For details, see Exercise 7 at the end of this chapter.

Therefore, to compute the log-rank test statistic, we simply proceed as in (11.4), with $X = \sum_{k=1}^{K} q_{1k}$, making use of (11.5) and (11.7). That is, we calculate

$$W = \frac{\sum_{k=1}^{K} (q_{1k} - \mu_k)}{\sqrt{\sum_{k=1}^{K} \text{Var}(q_{1k})}} = \frac{\sum_{k=1}^{K} \left(q_{1k} - \frac{q_k}{r_k} r_{1k}\right)}{\sqrt{\sum_{k=1}^{K} \frac{q_k (r_{1k}/r_k)(1 - r_{1k}/r_k)(r_k - q_k)}{r_k - 1}}}. \quad (11.8)$$

When the sample size is large, the log-rank test statistic W has approximately a standard normal distribution; this can be used to compute a p-value for the null hypothesis that there is no difference between the survival curves in the two groups.[6]

Comparing the survival times of females and males on the `BrainCancer` data gives a log-rank test statistic of $W = 1.2$, which corresponds to a two-sided p-value of 0.2 using the theoretical null distribution, and a p-value of 0.25 using the permutation null distribution with 1,000 permutations. Thus, we cannot reject the null hypothesis of no difference in survival curves between females and males.

The log-rank test is closely related to Cox's proportional hazards model, which we discuss in Section 11.5.2.

11.5 Regression Models With a Survival Response

We now consider the task of fitting a regression model to survival data. As in Section 11.1, the observations are of the form (Y, δ), where $Y = \min(T, C)$ is the (possibly censored) survival time, and δ is an indicator variable that equals 1 if $T \leq C$. Furthermore, $X \in \mathbb{R}^p$ is a vector of p features. We wish to predict the true survival time T.

Since the observed quantity Y is positive and may have a long right tail, we might be tempted to fit a linear regression of $\log(Y)$ on X. But as the reader will surely guess, censoring again creates a problem since we are actually interested in predicting T and not Y. To overcome this difficulty, we instead make use of a sequential construction, similar to the constructions of the Kaplan–Meier survival curve in Section 11.3 and the log-rank test in Section 11.4.

11.5.1 The Hazard Function

The *hazard function* or *hazard rate* — also known as the *force of mortality* — is formally defined as

hazard function

$$h(t) = \lim_{\Delta t \to 0} \frac{\Pr(t < T \leq t + \Delta t | T > t)}{\Delta t}, \quad (11.9)$$

[6] Alternatively, we can estimate the p-value via permutations, using ideas that will be presented in Section 13.5. The permutation distribution is obtained by randomly swapping the labels for the observations in the two groups.

where T is the (unobserved) survival time. It is the death rate in the instant after time t, given survival past that time.[7] In (11.9), we take the limit as Δt approaches zero, so we can think of Δt as being an extremely tiny number. Thus, more informally, (11.9) implies that

$$h(t) \approx \frac{\Pr(t < T \le t + \Delta t | T > t)}{\Delta t}$$

for some arbitrarily small Δt.

Why should we care about the hazard function? First of all, it is closely related to the survival curve (11.2), as we will see next. Second, it turns out that a key approach for modeling survival data as a function of covariates relies heavily on the hazard function; we will introduce this approach — Cox's proportional hazards model — in Section 11.5.2.

We now consider the hazard function $h(t)$ in a bit more detail. Recall that for two events A and B, the probability of A given B can be expressed as $\Pr(A \mid B) = \Pr(A \cap B)/\Pr(B)$, i.e. the probability that A and B both occur divided by the probability that B occurs. Furthermore, recall from (11.2) that $S(t) = \Pr(T > t)$. Thus,

$$\begin{aligned} h(t) &= \lim_{\Delta t \to 0} \frac{\Pr\left((t < T \le t + \Delta t) \cap (T > t)\right)/\Delta t}{\Pr(T > t)} \\ &= \lim_{\Delta t \to 0} \frac{\Pr(t < T \le t + \Delta t)/\Delta t}{\Pr(T > t)} \\ &= \frac{f(t)}{S(t)}, \end{aligned} \tag{11.10}$$

where

$$f(t) = \lim_{\Delta t \to 0} \frac{\Pr(t < T \le t + \Delta t)}{\Delta t} \tag{11.11}$$

is the *probability density function* associated with T, i.e. it is the instantaneous rate of death at time t. The second equality in (11.10) made use of the fact that if $t < T \le t + \Delta t$, then it must be the case that $T > t$.

probability density function

Equation 11.10 implies a relationship between the hazard function $h(t)$, the survival function $S(t)$, and the probability density function $f(t)$. In fact, these are three equivalent ways[8] of describing the distribution of T.

The likelihood associated with the ith observation is

$$\begin{aligned} L_i &= \begin{cases} f(y_i) & \text{if the } i\text{th observation is not censored} \\ S(y_i) & \text{if the } i\text{th observation is censored} \end{cases} \\ &= f(y_i)^{\delta_i} S(y_i)^{1-\delta_i}. \end{aligned} \tag{11.12}$$

The intuition behind (11.12) is as follows: if $Y = y_i$ and the ith observation is not censored, then the likelihood is the probability of dying in a tiny interval around time y_i. If the ith observation is censored, then the likelihood

[7]Due to the Δt in the denominator of (11.9), the hazard function is a rate of death, rather than a probability of death. However, higher values of $h(t)$ directly correspond to a higher probability of death, just as higher values of a probability density function correspond to more likely outcomes for a random variable. In fact, $h(t)$ is the probability density function for T conditional on $T > t$.

[8]See Exercise 8.

is the probability of surviving at least until time y_i. Assuming that the n observations are independent, the likelihood for the data takes the form

$$L = \prod_{i=1}^{n} f(y_i)^{\delta_i} S(y_i)^{1-\delta_i} = \prod_{i=1}^{n} h(y_i)^{\delta_i} S(y_i), \tag{11.13}$$

where the second equality follows from (11.10).

We now consider the task of modeling the survival times. If we assume exponential survival, i.e. that the probability density function of the survival time T takes the form $f(t) = \lambda \exp(-\lambda t)$, then estimating the parameter λ by maximizing the likelihood in (11.13) is straightforward.[9] Alternatively, we could assume that the survival times are drawn from a more flexible family of distributions, such as the Gamma or Weibull family. Another possibility is to model the survival times non-parametrically, as was done in Section 11.3 using the Kaplan–Meier estimator.

However, what we would really like to do is model the survival time *as a function of the covariates.* To do this, it is convenient to work directly with the hazard function, instead of the probability density function.[10] One possible approach is to assume a functional form for the hazard function $h(t|x_i)$, such as $h(t|x_i) = \exp\left(\beta_0 + \sum_{j=1}^{p} \beta_j x_{ij}\right)$, where the exponent function guarantees that the hazard function is non-negative. Note that the exponential hazard function is special, in that it does not vary with time.[11] Given $h(t|x_i)$, we could calculate $S(t|x_i)$. Plugging these equations into (11.13), we could then maximize the likelihood in order to estimate the parameter $\beta = (\beta_0, \beta_1, \ldots, \beta_p)^T$. However, this approach is quite restrictive, in the sense that it requires us to make a very stringent assumption on the form of the hazard function $h(t|x_i)$. In the next section, we will consider a much more flexible approach.

11.5.2 Proportional Hazards

The Proportional Hazards Assumption

The *proportional hazards assumption* states that

proportional hazards assumption

$$h(t|x_i) = h_0(t) \exp\left(\sum_{j=1}^{p} x_{ij}\beta_j\right), \tag{11.14}$$

where $h_0(t) \geq 0$ is an unspecified function, known as the *baseline hazard.* It is the hazard function for an individual with features $x_{i1} = \cdots = x_{ip} = 0$. The name "proportional hazards" arises from the fact that the hazard function for an individual with feature vector x_i is some unknown function

baseline hazard

[9]See Exercise 9.

[10]Given the close relationship between the hazard function $h(t)$ and the density function $f(t)$ explored in Exercise 8, posing an assumption about the form of the hazard function is closely related to posing an assumption about the form of the density function, as was done in the previous paragraph.

[11]The notation $h(t|x_i)$ indicates that we are now considering the hazard function for the ith observation conditional on the values of the covariates, x_i.

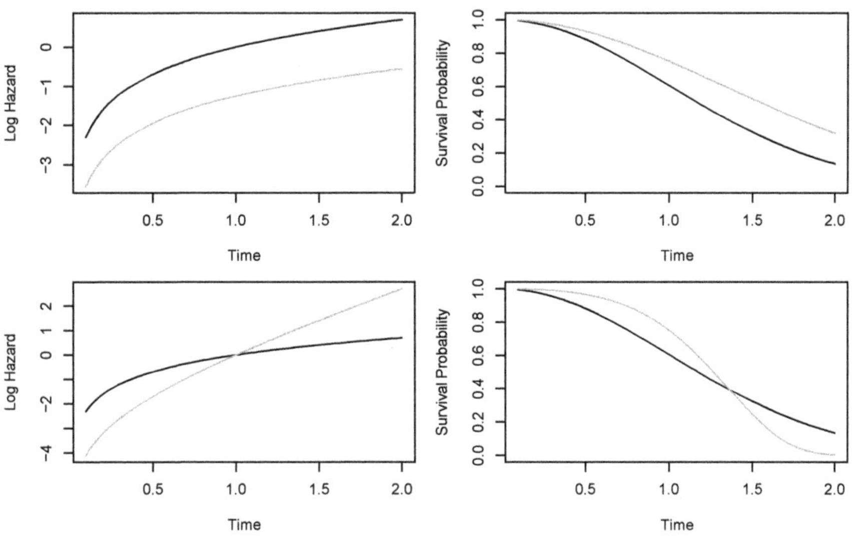

FIGURE 11.4. Top: *In a simple example with* $p = 1$ *and a binary covariate* $x_i \in \{0, 1\}$*, the log hazard and the survival function under the model* (11.14) *are shown (green for* $x_i = 0$ *and black for* $x_i = 1$*). Because of the proportional hazards assumption* (11.14)*, the log hazard functions differ by a constant, and the survival functions do not cross.* Bottom: *Again we have a single binary covariate* $x_i \in \{0, 1\}$*. However, the proportional hazards assumption* (11.14) *does not hold. The log hazard functions cross, as do the survival functions.*

$h_0(t)$ times the factor $\exp\left(\sum_{j=1}^p x_{ij}\beta_j\right)$. The quantity $\exp\left(\sum_{j=1}^p x_{ij}\beta_j\right)$ is called the *relative risk* for the feature vector $x_i = (x_{i1}, \ldots, x_{ip})^T$, relative to that for the feature vector $x_i = (0, \ldots, 0)^T$.

What does it mean that the baseline hazard function $h_0(t)$ in (11.14) is unspecified? Basically, we make no assumptions about its functional form. We allow the instantaneous probability of death at time t, given that one has survived at least until time t, to take any form. This means that the hazard function is very flexible and can model a wide range of relationships between the covariates and survival time. Our only assumption is that a one-unit increase in x_{ij} corresponds to an increase in $h(t|x_i)$ by a factor of $\exp(\beta_j)$.

An illustration of the proportional hazards assumption (11.14) is given in Figure 11.4, in a simple setting with a single binary covariate $x_i \in \{0, 1\}$ (so that $p = 1$). In the top row, the proportional hazards assumption (11.14) holds. Thus, the hazard functions of the two groups are a constant multiple of each other, so that on the log scale, the gap between them is constant. Furthermore, the survival curves never cross, and in fact the gap between the survival curves tends to (initially) increase over time. By contrast, in the bottom row, (11.14) does not hold. We see that the log hazard functions for the two groups cross, as do the survival curves.

Cox's Proportional Hazards Model

Because the form of $h_0(t)$ in the proportional hazards assumption (11.14) is unknown, we cannot simply plug $h(t|x_i)$ into the likelihood (11.13) and then estimate $\beta = (\beta_1, \ldots, \beta_p)^T$ by maximum likelihood. The magic of *Cox's proportional hazards model* lies in the fact that it is in fact possible to estimate β *without having to specify the form of* $h_0(t)$.

Cox's proportional hazards model

To accomplish this, we make use of the same "sequential in time" logic that we used to derive the Kaplan–Meier survival curve and the log-rank test. For simplicity, assume that there are no ties among the failure, or death, times: i.e. each failure occurs at a distinct time. Assume that $\delta_i = 1$, i.e. the ith observation is uncensored, and thus y_i is its failure time. Then the hazard function for the ith observation at time y_i is $h(y_i|x_i) = h_0(y_i)\exp\left(\sum_{j=1}^p x_{ij}\beta_j\right)$, and the total hazard at time y_i for the at risk observations[12] is

$$\sum_{i':y_{i'}\geq y_i} h_0(y_i)\exp\left(\sum_{j=1}^p x_{i'j}\beta_j\right).$$

Therefore, the probability that the ith observation is the one to fail at time y_i (as opposed to one of the other observations in the risk set) is

$$\frac{h_0(y_i)\exp\left(\sum_{j=1}^p x_{ij}\beta_j\right)}{\sum_{i':y_{i'}\geq y_i} h_0(y_i)\exp\left(\sum_{j=1}^p x_{i'j}\beta_j\right)} = \frac{\exp\left(\sum_{j=1}^p x_{ij}\beta_j\right)}{\sum_{i':y_{i'}\geq y_i} \exp\left(\sum_{j=1}^p x_{i'j}\beta_j\right)}. \tag{11.15}$$

Notice that the unspecified baseline hazard function $h_0(y_i)$ cancels out of the numerator and denominator!

The *partial likelihood* is simply the product of these probabilities over all of the uncensored observations,

partial likelihood

$$PL(\beta) = \prod_{i:\delta_i=1} \frac{\exp\left(\sum_{j=1}^p x_{ij}\beta_j\right)}{\sum_{i':y_{i'}\geq y_i} \exp\left(\sum_{j=1}^p x_{i'j}\beta_j\right)}. \tag{11.16}$$

Critically, the partial likelihood is valid regardless of the true value of $h_0(t)$, making the model very flexible and robust.[13]

To estimate β, we simply maximize the partial likelihood (11.16) with respect to β. As was the case for logistic regression in Chapter 4, no closed-form solution is available, and so iterative algorithms are required.

In addition to estimating β, we can also obtain other model outputs that we saw in the context of least squares regression in Chapter 3 and logistic regression in Chapter 4. For example, we can obtain p-values corresponding

---

[12]Recall that the "at risk" observations at time y_i are those that are still at risk of failure, i.e. those that have not yet failed or been censored before time y_i.

[13]In general, the partial likelihood is used in settings where it is difficult to compute the full likelihood for all of the parameters. Instead, we compute a likelihood for just the parameters of primary interest: in this case, $\beta_1, \ldots, \beta_p$. It can be shown that maximizing (11.16) provides good estimates for these parameters.

to particular null hypotheses (e.g. $H_0 : \beta_j = 0$), as well as confidence intervals associated with the coefficients.

Connection With The Log-Rank Test

Suppose we have just a single predictor ($p = 1$), which we assume to be binary, i.e. $x_i \in \{0, 1\}$. In order to determine whether there is a difference between the survival times of the observations in the group $\{i : x_i = 0\}$ and those in the group $\{i : x_i = 1\}$, we can consider taking two possible approaches:

Approach #1: Fit a Cox proportional hazards model, and test the null hypothesis $H_0 : \beta = 0$. (Since $p = 1$, β is a scalar.)

Approach #2: Perform a log-rank test to compare the two groups, as in Section 11.4.

Which one should we prefer?

In fact, there is a close relationship between these two approaches. In particular, when taking Approach #1, there are a number of possible ways to test H_0. One way is known as a score test. It turns out that in the case of a single binary covariate, the score test for $H_0 : \beta = 0$ in Cox's proportional hazards model is exactly equal to the log-rank test. In other words, it does not matter whether we take Approach #1 or Approach #2!

Additional Details

The discussion of Cox's proportional hazards model glossed over a few subtleties:

- There is no intercept in (11.14) nor in the equations that follow, because an intercept can be absorbed into the baseline hazard $h_0(t)$.

- We have assumed that there are no tied failure times. In the case of ties, the exact form of the partial likelihood (11.16) is a bit more complicated, and a number of computational approximations must be used.

- (11.16) is known as the *partial* likelihood because it is not exactly a likelihood. That is, it does not correspond exactly to the probability of the data under the assumption (11.14). However, it is a very good approximation.

- We have focused only on estimation of the coefficients $\beta = (\beta_1, \ldots, \beta_p)^T$. However, at times we may also wish to estimate the baseline hazard $h_0(t)$, for instance so that we can estimate the survival curve $S(t|x)$ for an individual with feature vector x. The details are beyond the scope of this book. Estimation of $h_0(t)$ is implemented in the `lifelines` package in `Python`, which we will see in Section 11.8.

11.5.3 Example: Brain Cancer Data

Table 11.2 shows the result of fitting the proportional hazards model to the `BrainCancer` data, which was originally described in Section 11.3. The coefficient column displays $\hat{\beta}_j$. The results indicate, for instance, that the estimated hazard for a male patient is $e^{0.18} = 1.2$ times greater than for a female patient: in other words, with all other features held fixed, males have a 1.2 times greater chance of dying than females, at any point in time. However, the p-value is 0.61, which indicates that this difference between males and females is not significant.

As another example, we also see that each one-unit increase in the Karnofsky index corresponds to a multiplier of $\exp(-0.05) = 0.95$ in the instantaneous chance of dying. In other words, the higher the Karnofsky index, the lower the chance of dying at any given point in time. This effect is highly significant, with a p-value of 0.0027.

	Coefficient	Std. error	z-statistic	p-value
`sex[Male]`	0.18	0.36	0.51	0.61
`diagnosis[LG Glioma]`	0.92	0.64	1.43	0.15
`diagnosis[HG Glioma]`	2.15	0.45	4.78	0.00
`diagnosis[Other]`	0.89	0.66	1.35	0.18
`loc[Supratentorial]`	0.44	0.70	0.63	0.53
`ki`	-0.05	0.02	-3.00	<0.01
`gtv`	0.03	0.02	1.54	0.12
`stereo[SRT]`	0.18	0.60	0.30	0.77

TABLE 11.2. *Results for Cox's proportional hazards model fit to the* `BrainCancer` *data, which was first described in Section 11.3. The variable* `diagnosis` *is qualitative with four levels: meningioma, LG glioma, HG glioma, or other. The variables* `sex`, `loc`, *and* `stereo` *are binary.*

11.5.4 Example: Publication Data

Next, we consider the dataset `Publication` involving the time to publication of journal papers reporting the results of clinical trials funded by the National Heart, Lung, and Blood Institute.[14] For 244 trials, the time in months until publication is recorded. Of the 244 trials, only 156 were published during the study period; the remaining studies were censored. The covariates include whether the trial focused on a clinical endpoint (`clinend`), whether the trial involved multiple centers (`multi`), the funding mechanism within the National Institutes of Health (`mech`), trial sample size (`sampsize`), budget (`budget`), impact (`impact`, related to the number of citations), and whether the trial produced a positive (significant) result (`posres`). The last covariate is particularly interesting, as a number of studies have suggested that positive trials have a higher publication rate.

[14]This dataset is described in the following paper: Gordon et al. (2013) Publication of trials funded by the National Heart, Lung, and Blood Institute. New England Journal of Medicine, 369(20):1926–1934.

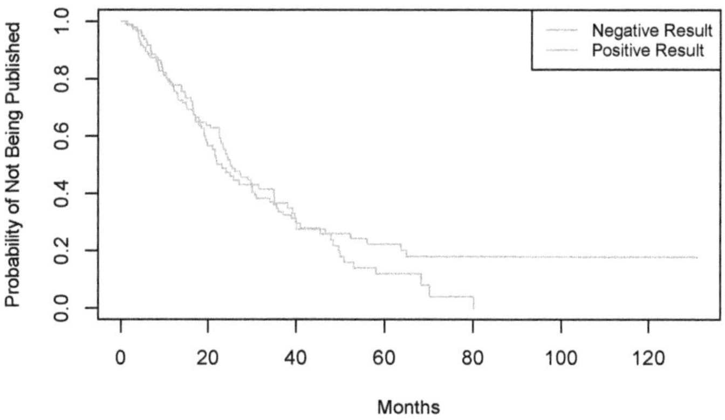

FIGURE 11.5. *Survival curves for time until publication for the* `Publication` *data described in Section 11.5.4, stratified by whether or not the study produced a positive result.*

Figure 11.5 shows the Kaplan–Meier curves for the time until publication, stratified by whether or not the study produced a positive result. We see slight evidence that time until publication is lower for studies with a positive result. However, the log-rank test yields a very unimpressive p-value of 0.36.

We now consider a more careful analysis that makes use of all of the available predictors. The results of fitting Cox's proportional hazards model using all of the available features are shown in Table 11.3. We find that the chance of publication of a study with a positive result is $e^{0.55} = 1.74$ times higher than the chance of publication of a study with a negative result at any point in time, holding all other covariates fixed. The very small p-value associated with `posres` in Table 11.3 indicates that this result is highly significant. This is striking, especially in light of our earlier finding that a log-rank test comparing time to publication for studies with positive versus negative results yielded a p-value of 0.36. How can we explain this discrepancy? The answer stems from the fact that the log-rank test did not consider any other covariates, whereas the results in Table 11.3 are based on a Cox model using all of the available covariates. In other words, after we adjust for all of the other covariates, then whether or not the study yielded a positive result is highly predictive of the time to publication.

In order to gain more insight into this result, in Figure 11.6 we display estimates of the survival curves associated with positive and negative results, adjusting for the other predictors. To produce these survival curves, we estimated the underlying baseline hazard $h_0(t)$. We also needed to select representative values for the other predictors; we used the mean value for each predictor, except for the categorical predictor `mech`, for which we used the most prevalent category (`R01`). Adjusting for the other predictors, we now see a clear difference in the survival curves between studies with positive versus negative results.

Other interesting insights can be gleaned from Table 11.3. For example, studies with a clinical endpoint are more likely to be published at any given point in time than those with a non-clinical endpoint. The funding

	Coefficient	Std. error	z-statistic	p-value
posres[Yes]	0.55	0.18	3.02	0.00
multi[Yes]	0.15	0.31	0.47	0.64
clinend[Yes]	0.51	0.27	1.89	0.06
mech[K01]	1.05	1.06	1.00	0.32
mech[K23]	-0.48	1.05	-0.45	0.65
mech[P01]	-0.31	0.78	-0.40	0.69
mech[P50]	0.60	1.06	0.57	0.57
mech[R01]	0.10	0.32	0.30	0.76
mech[R18]	1.05	1.05	0.99	0.32
mech[R21]	-0.05	1.06	-0.04	0.97
mech[R24,K24]	0.81	1.05	0.77	0.44
mech[R42]	-14.78	3414.38	-0.00	1.00
mech[R44]	-0.57	0.77	-0.73	0.46
mech[RC2]	-14.92	2243.60	-0.01	0.99
mech[U01]	-0.22	0.32	-0.70	0.48
mech[U54]	0.47	1.07	0.44	0.66
sampsize	0.00	0.00	0.19	0.85
budget	0.00	0.00	1.67	0.09
impact	0.06	0.01	8.23	0.00

TABLE 11.3. *Results for Cox's proportional hazards model fit to the* Publication *data, using all of the available features. The features* posres, multi, *and* clinend *are binary. The feature* mech *is qualitative with 14 levels; it is coded so that the baseline level is* Contract.

mechanism did not appear to be significantly associated with time until publication.

11.6 Shrinkage for the Cox Model

In this section, we illustrate that the shrinkage methods of Section 6.2 can be applied to the survival data setting. In particular, motivated by the "loss+penalty" formulation of Section 6.2, we consider minimizing a penalized version of the negative log partial likelihood in (11.16),

$$-\log\left(\prod_{i:\delta_i=1}\frac{\exp\left(\sum_{j=1}^p x_{ij}\beta_j\right)}{\sum_{i':y_{i'}\geq y_i}\exp\left(\sum_{j=1}^p x_{i'j}\beta_j\right)}\right)+\lambda P(\beta), \tag{11.17}$$

with respect to $\beta = (\beta_1, \ldots, \beta_p)^T$. We might take $P(\beta) = \sum_{j=1}^p \beta_j^2$, which corresponds to a ridge penalty, or $P(\beta) = \sum_{j=1}^p |\beta_j|$, which corresponds to a lasso penalty.

In (11.17), λ is a non-negative tuning parameter; typically we will minimize it over a range of values of λ. When $\lambda = 0$, then minimizing (11.17) is equivalent to simply maximizing the usual Cox partial likelihood (11.16). However, when $\lambda > 0$, then minimizing (11.17) yields a shrunken version of the coefficient estimates. When λ is large, then using a ridge penalty will give small coefficients that are not exactly equal to zero. By contrast, for a

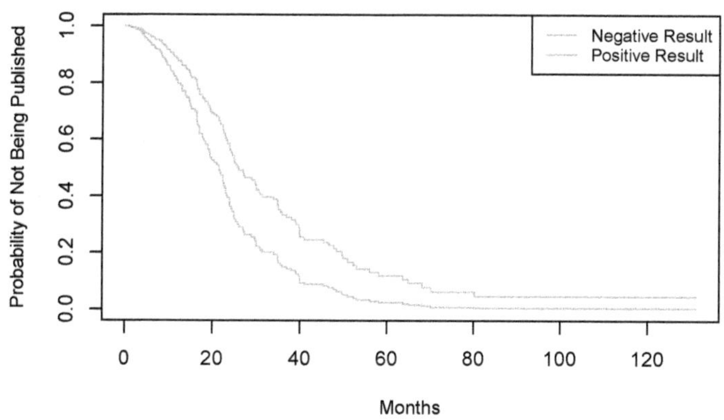

FIGURE 11.6. *For the* Publication *data, we display survival curves for time until publication, stratified by whether or not the study produced a positive result, after adjusting for all other covariates.*

sufficiently large value of λ, using a lasso penalty will give some coefficients that are exactly equal to zero.

We now apply the lasso-penalized Cox model to the Publication data, described in Section 11.5.4. We first randomly split the 244 trials into equally-sized training and test sets. The cross-validation results from the training set are shown in Figure 11.7. The "partial likelihood deviance", shown on the y-axis, is twice the cross-validated negative log partial likelihood; it plays the role of the cross-validation error.[15] Note the "U-shape" of the partial likelihood deviance: just as we saw in previous chapters, the cross-validation error is minimized for an intermediate level of model complexity. Specifically, this occurs when just two predictors, budget and impact, have non-zero estimated coefficients.

Now, how do we apply this model to the test set? This brings up an important conceptual point: in essence, there is no simple way to compare predicted survival times and true survival times on the test set. The first problem is that some of the observations are censored, and so the true survival times for those observations are unobserved. The second issue arises from the fact that in the Cox model, rather than predicting a single survival time given a covariate vector x, we instead estimate an entire survival curve, $S(t|x)$, as a function of t.

Therefore, to assess the model fit, we must take a different approach, which involves stratifying the observations using the coefficient estimates. In particular, for each test observation, we compute the "risk" score

$$\texttt{budget}_i \cdot \hat{\beta}_{\texttt{budget}} + \texttt{impact}_i \cdot \hat{\beta}_{\texttt{impact}},$$

where $\hat{\beta}_{\texttt{budget}}$ and $\hat{\beta}_{\texttt{impact}}$ are the coefficient estimates for these two features from the training set. We then use these risk scores to categorize the observations based on their "risk". For instance, the high risk group consists of the observations for which $\texttt{budget}_i \cdot \hat{\beta}_{\texttt{budget}} + \texttt{impact}_i \cdot \hat{\beta}_{\texttt{impact}}$ is largest; by

[15] Cross-validation for the Cox model is more involved than for linear or logistic regression, because the objective function is not a sum over the observations.

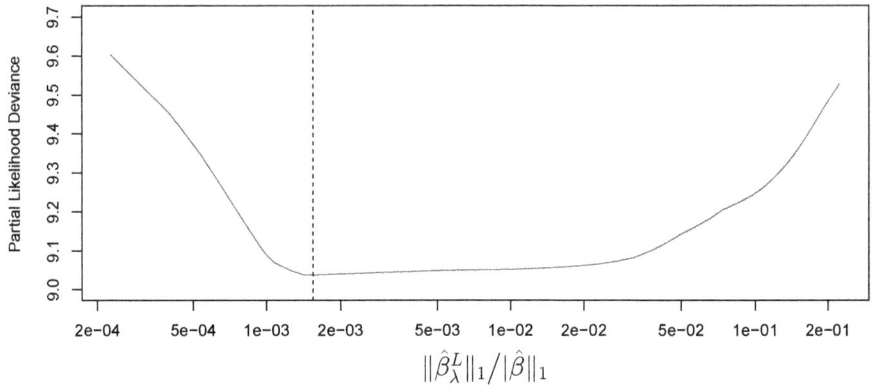

FIGURE 11.7. *For the* Publication *data described in Section 11.5.4, cross-validation results for the lasso-penalized Cox model are shown. The y-axis displays the partial likelihood deviance, which plays the role of the cross-validation error. The x-axis displays the ℓ_1 norm (that is, the sum of the absolute values) of the coefficients of the lasso-penalized Cox model with tuning parameter λ, divided by the ℓ_1 norm of the coefficients of the unpenalized Cox model. The dashed line indicates the minimum cross-validation error.*

(11.14), we see that these are the observations for which the instantaneous probability of being published at any moment in time is largest. In other words, the high risk group consists of the trials that are likely to be published sooner. On the Publication data, we stratify the observations into tertiles of low, medium, and high risk. The resulting survival curves for each of the three strata are displayed in Figure 11.8. We see that there is clear separation between the three strata, and that the strata are correctly ordered in terms of low, medium, and high risk of publication.

11.7 Additional Topics

11.7.1 Area Under the Curve for Survival Analysis

In Chapter 4, we introduced the area under the ROC curve — often referred to as the "AUC" — as a way to quantify the performance of a two-class classifier. Define the *score* for the ith observation to be the classifier's estimate of $\Pr(Y = 1|X = x_i)$. It turns out that if we consider all pairs consisting of one observation in Class 1 and one observation in Class 2, then the AUC is the fraction of pairs for which the score for the observation in Class 1 exceeds the score for the observation in Class 2.

This suggests a way to generalize the notion of AUC to survival analysis. We calculate an estimated risk score, $\hat{\eta}_i = \hat{\beta}_1 x_{i1} + \cdots + \hat{\beta}_p x_{ip}$, for $i = 1, \ldots, n$, using the Cox model coefficients. If $\hat{\eta}_{i'} > \hat{\eta}_i$, then the model predicts that the i'th observation has a larger hazard than the ith observation, and thus that the survival time t_i will be *greater* than $t_{i'}$. Thus, it is tempting to try to generalize AUC by computing the proportion of observations for which $t_i > t_{i'}$ and $\hat{\eta}_{i'} > \hat{\eta}_i$. However, things are not quite so easy, because recall that we do not observe $t_1, \ldots, t_n$; instead, we observe

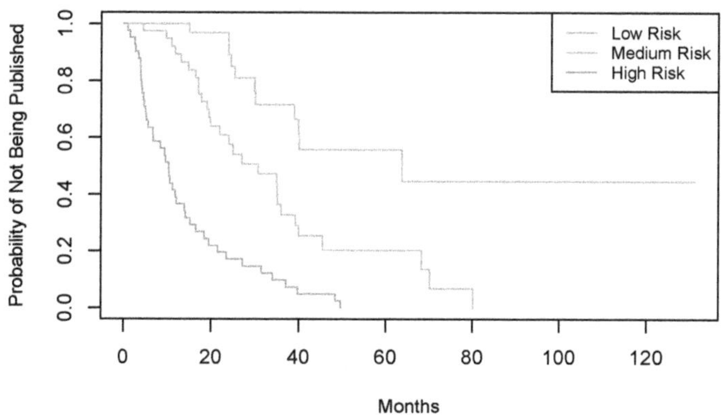

FIGURE 11.8. *For the* `Publication` *data introduced in Section 11.5.4, we compute tertiles of "risk" in the test set using coefficients estimated on the training set. There is clear separation between the resulting survival curves.*

the (possibly-censored) times $y_1, \ldots, y_n$, as well as the censoring indicators $\delta_1, \ldots, \delta_n$.

Therefore, *Harrell's concordance index* (or *C-index*) computes the proportion of observation pairs for which $\hat{\eta}_{i'} > \hat{\eta}_i$ and $y_i > y_{i'}$:

Harrell's concordance index

$$C = \frac{\sum_{i,i':y_i>y_{i'}} I(\hat{\eta}_{i'} > \hat{\eta}_i)\delta_{i'}}{\sum_{i,i':y_i>y_{i'}} \delta_{i'}},$$

where the indicator variable $I(\hat{\eta}_{i'} > \hat{\eta}_i)$ equals one if $\hat{\eta}_{i'} > \hat{\eta}_i$, and equals zero otherwise. The numerator and denominator are multiplied by the status indicator $\delta_{i'}$, since if the i'th observation is uncensored (i.e. if $\delta_{i'} = 1$), then $y_i > y_{i'}$ implies that $t_i > t_{i'}$. By contrast, if $\delta_{i'} = 0$, then $y_i > y_{i'}$ does not imply that $t_i > t_{i'}$.

We fit a Cox proportional hazards model on the training set of the `Publication` data, and computed the C-index on the test set. This yielded $C = 0.733$. Roughly speaking, given two random papers from the test set, the model can predict with 73.3% accuracy which will be published first.

11.7.2 Choice of Time Scale

In the examples considered thus far in this chapter, it has been fairly clear how to define *time*. For example, in the `Publication` example, *time zero* for each paper was defined to be the calendar time at the end of the study, and the failure time was defined to be the number of months that elapsed from the end of the study until the paper was published.

However, in other settings, the definitions of time zero and failure time may be more subtle. For example, when examining the association between risk factors and disease occurrence in an epidemiological study, one might use the patient's age to define time, so that time zero is the patient's date of birth. With this choice, the association between age and survival cannot be measured; however, there is no need to adjust for age in the analysis. When examining covariates associated with disease-free survival (i.e. the amount of time elapsed between treatment and disease recurrence), one might use the date of treatment as time zero.

11.7.3 Time-Dependent Covariates

A powerful feature of the proportional hazards model is its ability to handle *time-dependent covariates*, predictors whose value may change over time. For example, suppose we measure a patient's blood pressure every week over the course of a medical study. In this case, we can think of the blood pressure for the ith observation not as x_i, but rather as $x_i(t)$ at time t.

Because the partial likelihood in (11.16) is constructed sequentially in time, dealing with time-dependent covariates is straightforward. In particular, we simply replace x_{ij} and $x_{i'j}$ in (11.16) with $x_{ij}(y_i)$ and $x_{i'j}(y_i)$, respectively; these are the current values of the predictors at time y_i. By contrast, time-dependent covariates would pose a much greater challenge within the context of a traditional parametric approach, such as (11.13).

One example of time-dependent covariates appears in the analysis of data from the Stanford Heart Transplant Program. Patients in need of a heart transplant were put on a waiting list. Some patients received a transplant, but others died while still on the waiting list. The primary objective of the analysis was to determine whether a transplant was associated with longer patient survival.

A naïve approach would use a fixed covariate to represent transplant status: that is, $x_i = 1$ if the ith patient ever received a transplant, and $x_i = 0$ otherwise. But this approach overlooks the fact that patients had to live long enough to get a transplant, and hence, on average, healthier patients received transplants. This problem can be solved by using a time-dependent covariate for transplant: $x_i(t) = 1$ if the patient received a transplant by time t, and $x_i(t) = 0$ otherwise.

11.7.4 Checking the Proportional Hazards Assumption

We have seen that Cox's proportional hazards model relies on the proportional hazards assumption (11.14). While results from the Cox model tend to be fairly robust to violations of this assumption, it is still a good idea to check whether it holds. In the case of a qualitative feature, we can plot the log hazard function for each level of the feature. If (11.14) holds, then the log hazard functions should just differ by a constant, as seen in the top-left panel of Figure 11.4. In the case of a quantitative feature, we can take a similar approach by stratifying the feature.

11.7.5 Survival Trees

In Chapter 8, we discussed flexible and adaptive learning procedures such as trees, random forests, and boosting, which we applied in both the regression and classification settings. Most of these approaches can be generalized to the survival analysis setting. For example, *survival trees* are a modification of classification and regression trees that use a split criterion that maximizes survival trees the difference between the survival curves in the resulting daughter nodes. Survival trees can then be used to create random survival forests.

11.8 Lab: Survival Analysis

In this lab, we perform survival analyses on three separate data sets. In Section 11.8.1 we analyze the `BrainCancer` data that was first described in Section 11.3. In Section 11.8.2, we examine the `Publication` data from Section 11.5.4. Finally, Section 11.8.3 explores a simulated call-center data set.

We begin by importing some of our libraries at this top level. This makes the code more readable, as scanning the first few lines of the notebook tell us what libraries are used in this notebook.

In [1]:
```
from matplotlib.pyplot import subplots
import numpy as np
import pandas as pd
from ISLP.models import ModelSpec as MS
from ISLP import load_data
```

We also collect the new imports needed for this lab.

In [2]:
```
from lifelines import \
     (KaplanMeierFitter,
      CoxPHFitter)
from lifelines.statistics import \
     (logrank_test,
      multivariate_logrank_test)
from ISLP.survival import sim_time
```

11.8.1 Brain Cancer Data

We begin with the `BrainCancer` data set, contained in the `ISLP` package.

In [3]:
```
BrainCancer = load_data('BrainCancer')
BrainCancer.columns
```

Out[3]:
```
Index(['sex', 'diagnosis', 'loc', 'ki', 'gtv', 'stereo',
       'status', 'time'],
       dtype='object')
```

The rows index the 88 patients, while the 8 columns contain the predictors and outcome variables. We first briefly examine the data.

In [4]:
```
BrainCancer['sex'].value_counts()
```

Out[4]:
```
Female    45
Male      43
Name: sex, dtype: int64
```

In [5]:
```
BrainCancer['diagnosis'].value_counts()
```

```
Out[5]: Meningioma    42
        HG glioma     22
        Other         14
        LG glioma      9
        Name: diagnosis, dtype: int64
```

```
In [6]: BrainCancer['status'].value_counts()
```

```
Out[6]: 0    53
        1    35
        Name: status, dtype: int64
```

Before beginning an analysis, it is important to know how the `status` variable has been coded. Most software uses the convention that a `status` of 1 indicates an uncensored observation (often death), and a `status` of 0 indicates a censored observation. But some scientists might use the opposite coding. For the `BrainCancer` data set 35 patients died before the end of the study, so we are using the conventional coding.

To begin the analysis, we re-create the Kaplan-Meier survival curve shown in Figure 11.2. The main package we will use for survival analysis is `lifelines`. The variable `time` corresponds to y_i, the time to the ith event (either censoring or death). The first argument to `km.fit` is the event time, and the second argument is the censoring variable, with a 1 indicating an observed failure time. The `plot()` method produces a survival curve with pointwise confidence intervals. By default, these are 90% confidence intervals, but this can be changed by setting the `alpha` argument to one minus the desired confidence level.

lifelines

.plot()

```
In [7]: fig, ax = subplots(figsize=(8,8))
        km = KaplanMeierFitter()
        km_brain = km.fit(BrainCancer['time'], BrainCancer['status'])
        km_brain.plot(label='Kaplan Meier estimate', ax=ax)
```

Next we create Kaplan-Meier survival curves that are stratified by `sex`, in order to reproduce Figure 11.3. We do this using the `groupby()` method of a dataframe. This method returns a generator that can be iterated over in the `for` loop. In this case, the items in the `for` loop are 2-tuples representing the groups: the first entry is the value of the grouping column `sex` while the second value is the dataframe consisting of all rows in the dataframe matching that value of `sex`. We will want to use this data below in the log-rank test, hence we store this information in the dictionary `by_sex`. Finally, we have also used the notion of *string interpolation* to automatically label the different lines in the plot. String interpolation is a powerful technique to format strings — `Python` has many ways to facilitate such operations.

.groupby()

string interpolation

```
In [8]: fig, ax = subplots(figsize=(8,8))
        by_sex = {}
        for sex, df in BrainCancer.groupby('sex'):
            by_sex[sex] = df
            km_sex = km.fit(df['time'], df['status'])
            km_sex.plot(label='Sex=%s' % sex, ax=ax)
```

As discussed in Section 11.4, we can perform a log-rank test to compare the survival of males to females. We use the `logrank_test()` function from

logrank_test()

the `lifelines.statistics` module. The first two arguments are the event times, with the second denoting the corresponding (optional) censoring indicators.

```
In [9]: logrank_test(by_sex['Male']['time'],
                     by_sex['Female']['time'],
                     by_sex['Male']['status'],
                     by_sex['Female']['status'])
```

```
Out[9]:                  t_0            -1
         null_distribution   chi squared
        degrees_of_freedom             1
                 test_name  logrank_test


         test_statistic    p  -log2(p)
                   1.44 0.23      2.12
```

The resulting p-value is 0.23, indicating no evidence of a difference in survival between the two sexes.

Next, we use the `CoxPHFitter()` estimator from `lifelines` to fit Cox proportional hazards models. To begin, we consider a model that uses `sex` as the only predictor.

`CoxPHFitter()`

```
In [10]: coxph = CoxPHFitter # shorthand
         sex_df = BrainCancer[['time', 'status', 'sex']]
         model_df = MS(['time', 'status', 'sex'],
                       intercept=False).fit_transform(sex_df)
         cox_fit = coxph().fit(model_df,
                               'time',
                               'status')
         cox_fit.summary[['coef', 'se(coef)', 'p']]
```

```
Out[10]:                  coef  se(coef)         p
         covariate
         sex[Male]    0.407667  0.342004  0.233263
```

The first argument to `fit` should be a data frame containing at least the event time (the second argument `time` in this case), as well as an optional censoring variable (the argument `status` in this case). Note also that the Cox model does not include an intercept, which is why we used the `intercept=False` argument to `ModelSpec` above. The `summary()` method delivers many columns; we chose to abbreviate its output here. It is possible to obtain the likelihood ratio test comparing this model to the one with no features as follows:

```
In [11]: cox_fit.log_likelihood_ratio_test()
```

```
Out[11]: null_distribution                      chi squared
           degrees_freedom                                1
                 test_name    log-likelihood ratio test

          test_statistic    p  -log2(p)
                    1.44 0.23      2.12
```

Regardless of which test we use, we see that there is no clear evidence for a difference in survival between males and females. As we learned in this chapter, the score test from the Cox model is exactly equal to the log rank test statistic!

Now we fit a model that makes use of additional predictors. We first note that one of our diagnosis values is missing, hence we drop that observation before continuing.

In [12]:
```
cleaned = BrainCancer.dropna()
all_MS = MS(cleaned.columns, intercept=False)
all_df = all_MS.fit_transform(cleaned)
fit_all = coxph().fit(all_df,
                      'time',
                      'status')
fit_all.summary[['coef', 'se(coef)', 'p']]
```

Out[12]:

covariate	coef	se(coef)	p
sex[Male]	0.183748	0.360358	0.610119
diagnosis[LG glioma]	-1.239541	0.579557	0.032454
diagnosis[Meningioma]	-2.154566	0.450524	0.000002
diagnosis[Other]	-1.268870	0.617672	0.039949
loc[Supratentorial]	0.441195	0.703669	0.530664
ki	-0.054955	0.018314	0.002693
gtv	0.034293	0.022333	0.124660
stereo[SRT]	0.177778	0.601578	0.767597

The diagnosis variable has been coded so that the baseline corresponds to HG glioma. The results indicate that the risk associated with HG glioma is more than eight times (i.e. $e^{2.15} = 8.62$) the risk associated with meningioma. In other words, after adjusting for the other predictors, patients with HG glioma have much worse survival compared to those with meningioma. In addition, larger values of the Karnofsky index, ki, are associated with lower risk, i.e. longer survival.

Finally, we plot estimated survival curves for each diagnosis category, adjusting for the other predictors. To make these plots, we set the values of the other predictors equal to the mean for quantitative variables and equal to the mode for categorical. To do this, we use the apply() method across rows (i.e. axis=0) with a function representative that checks if a column is categorical or not.

In [13]:
```
levels = cleaned['diagnosis'].unique()
def representative(series):
    if hasattr(series.dtype, 'categories'):
        return pd.Series.mode(series)
    else:
        return series.mean()
modal_data = cleaned.apply(representative, axis=0)
```

We make four copies of the column means and assign the diagnosis column to be the four different diagnoses.

In [14]:
```
modal_df = pd.DataFrame(
              [modal_data.iloc[0] for _ in range(len(levels))])
modal_df['diagnosis'] = levels
modal_df
```

```
Out[14]:    sex   diagnosis               loc      ki     gtv  stereo  ...
         Female  Meningioma  Supratentorial  80.920  8.687     SRT  ...
         Female   HG glioma  Supratentorial  80.920  8.687     SRT  ...
         Female   LG glioma  Supratentorial  80.920  8.687     SRT  ...
         Female       Other  Supratentorial  80.920  8.687     SRT  ...
```

We then construct the model matrix based on the model specification `all_MS` used to fit the model, and name the rows according to the levels of `diagnosis`.

```
In [15]: modal_X = all_MS.transform(modal_df)
         modal_X.index = levels
         modal_X
```

We can use the `predict_survival_function()` method to obtain the estimated survival function.

`.predict_survival_function()`

```
In [16]: predicted_survival = fit_all.predict_survival_function(modal_X)
         predicted_survival
```

```
Out[16]:     Meningioma  HG glioma  LG glioma  Other
          0.070    0.998      0.982      0.995  0.995
          1.180    0.998      0.982      0.995  0.995
          1.410    0.996      0.963      0.989  0.990
          1.540    0.996      0.963      0.989  0.990
            ...      ...        ...        ...    ...
         67.380    0.689      0.040      0.394  0.405
         73.740    0.689      0.040      0.394  0.405
         78.750    0.689      0.040      0.394  0.405
         82.560    0.689      0.040      0.394  0.405
         85 rows × 4 columns
```

This returns a data frame, whose plot methods yields the different survival curves. To avoid clutter in the plots, we do not display confidence intervals.

```
In [17]: fig, ax = subplots(figsize=(8, 8))
         predicted_survival.plot(ax=ax);
```

11.8.2 Publication Data

The `Publication` data presented in Section 11.5.4 can be found in the `ISLP` package. We first reproduce Figure 11.5 by plotting the Kaplan-Meier curves stratified on the `posres` variable, which records whether the study had a positive or negative result.

```
In [18]: fig, ax = subplots(figsize=(8,8))
         Publication = load_data('Publication')
         by_result = {}
         for result, df in Publication.groupby('posres'):
             by_result[result] = df
             km_result = km.fit(df['time'], df['status'])
             km_result.plot(label='Result=%d' % result, ax=ax)
```

As discussed previously, the p-values from fitting Cox's proportional hazards model to the `posres` variable are quite large, providing no evidence of a difference in time-to-publication between studies with positive versus negative results.

In [19]:
```
posres_df = MS(['posres',
                'time',
                'status'],
               intercept=False).fit_transform(Publication)
posres_fit = coxph().fit(posres_df,
                         'time',
                         'status')
posres_fit.summary[['coef', 'se(coef)', 'p']]
```

Out[19]:
```
                coef  se(coef)         p
covariate
posres      0.148076  0.161625  0.359578
```

However, the results change dramatically when we include other predictors in the model. Here we exclude the funding mechanism variable.

In [20]:
```
model = MS(Publication.columns.drop('mech'),
           intercept=False)
coxph().fit(model.fit_transform(Publication),
            'time',
            'status').summary[['coef', 'se(coef)', 'p']]
```

Out[20]:
```
               coef  se(coef)             p
covariate
posres     0.570774  0.175960  1.179606e-03
multi     -0.040863  0.251194  8.707727e-01
clinend    0.546180  0.262001  3.710099e-02
sampsize   0.000005  0.000015  7.506978e-01
budget     0.004386  0.002464  7.511276e-02
impact     0.058318  0.006676  2.426779e-18
```

We see that there are a number of statistically significant variables, including whether the trial focused on a clinical endpoint, the impact of the study, and whether the study had positive or negative results.

11.8.3 Call Center Data

In this section, we will simulate survival data using the relationship between cumulative hazard and the survival function explored in Exercise 8. Our simulated data will represent the observed wait times (in seconds) for 2,000 customers who have phoned a call center. In this context, censoring occurs if a customer hangs up before his or her call is answered.

There are three covariates: `Operators` (the number of call center operators available at the time of the call, which can range from 5 to 15), `Center` (either A, B, or C), and `Time` of day (Morning, Afternoon, or Evening). We generate data for these covariates so that all possibilities are equally likely: for instance, morning, afternoon and evening calls are equally likely, and any number of operators from 5 to 15 is equally likely.

In [21]:
```
rng = np.random.default_rng(10)
N = 2000
Operators = rng.choice(np.arange(5, 16),
                       N,
                       replace=True)
```

```
Center = rng.choice(['A', 'B', 'C'],
                    N,
                    replace=True)
Time = rng.choice(['Morn.', 'After.', 'Even.'],
                  N,
                  replace=True)
D = pd.DataFrame({'Operators': Operators,
                  'Center': pd.Categorical(Center),
                  'Time': pd.Categorical(Time)})
```

We then build a model matrix (omitting the intercept)

In [22]:
```
model = MS(['Operators',
            'Center',
            'Time'],
           intercept=False)
X = model.fit_transform(D)
```

It is worthwhile to take a peek at the model matrix X, so that we can be sure that we understand how the variables have been coded. By default, the levels of categorical variables are sorted and, as usual, the first column of the one-hot encoding of the variable is dropped.

In [23]:
```
X[:5]
```

Out[23]:

	Operators	Center[B]	Center[C]	Time[Even.]	Time[Morn.]
0	13	0.0	1.0	0.0	0.0
1	15	0.0	0.0	1.0	0.0
2	7	1.0	0.0	0.0	1.0
3	7	0.0	1.0	0.0	1.0
4	13	0.0	1.0	1.0	0.0

Next, we specify the coefficients and the hazard function.

In [24]:
```
true_beta = np.array([0.04, -0.3, 0, 0.2, -0.2])
true_linpred = X.dot(true_beta)
hazard = lambda t: 1e-5 * t
```

Here, we have set the coefficient associated with Operators to equal 0.04; in other words, each additional operator leads to a $e^{0.04} = 1.041$-fold increase in the "risk" that the call will be answered, given the Center and Time covariates. This makes sense: the greater the number of operators at hand, the shorter the wait time! The coefficient associated with Center == B is -0.3, and Center == A is treated as the baseline. This means that the risk of a call being answered at Center B is 0.74 times the risk that it will be answered at Center A; in other words, the wait times are a bit longer at Center B.

Recall from Section 2.3.7 the use of lambda for creating short functions on the fly. We use the function sim_time() from the ISLP.survival package. This function uses the relationship between the survival function and cumulative hazard $S(t) = \exp(-H(t))$ and the specific form of the cumulative hazard function in the Cox model to simulate data based on values of the linear predictor true_linpred and the cumulative hazard. We need to provide the cumulative hazard function, which we do here.

sim_time()

In [25]:
```
cum_hazard = lambda t: 1e-5 * t**2 / 2
```

We are now ready to generate data under the Cox proportional hazards model. We truncate the maximum time to 1000 seconds to keep simulated wait times reasonable. The function `sim_time()` takes a linear predictor, a cumulative hazard function and a random number generator.

In [26]:
```
W = np.array([sim_time(l, cum_hazard, rng)
              for l in true_linpred])
D['Wait time'] = np.clip(W, 0, 1000)
```

We now simulate our censoring variable, for which we assume 90% of calls were answered (`Failed==1`) before the customer hung up (`Failed==0`).

In [27]:
```
D['Failed'] = rng.choice([1, 0],
                         N,
                         p=[0.9, 0.1])
D[:5]
```

Out[27]:

	Operators	Center	Time	Wait time	Failed
0	13	C	After.	525.064979	1
1	15	A	Even.	254.677835	1
2	7	B	Morn.	487.739224	1
3	7	C	Morn.	308.580292	1
4	13	C	Even.	154.174608	1

In [28]:
```
D['Failed'].mean()
```

Out[28]: 0.8985

We now plot Kaplan-Meier survival curves. First, we stratify by `Center`.

In [29]:
```
fig, ax = subplots(figsize=(8,8))
by_center = {}
for center, df in D.groupby('Center'):
    by_center[center] = df
    km_center = km.fit(df['Wait time'], df['Failed'])
    km_center.plot(label='Center=%s' % center, ax=ax)
ax.set_title("Probability of Still Being on Hold")
```

Next, we stratify by `Time`.

In [30]:
```
fig, ax = subplots(figsize=(8,8))
by_time = {}
for time, df in D.groupby('Time'):
    by_time[time] = df
    km_time = km.fit(df['Wait time'], df['Failed'])
    km_time.plot(label='Time=%s' % time, ax=ax)
ax.set_title("Probability of Still Being on Hold")
```

It seems that calls at Call Center B take longer to be answered than calls at Centers A and C. Similarly, it appears that wait times are longest in the morning and shortest in the evening hours. We can use a log-rank test to determine whether these differences are statistically significant using the function `multivariate_logrank_test()`.

In [31]:
```
multivariate_logrank_test(D['Wait time'],
                          D['Center'],
                          D['Failed'])
```

```
Out[31]:               t_0                             -1
          null_distribution                   chi squared
         degrees_of_freedom                             2
                  test_name   multivariate_logrank_test

           test_statistic       p  -log2(p)
                    20.30  <0.005     14.65
```

Next, we consider the effect of `Time`.

```
In [32]: multivariate_logrank_test(D['Wait time'],
                                   D['Time'],
                                   D['Failed'])
```

```
Out[32]:               t_0                             -1
          null_distribution                   chi squared
         degrees_of_freedom                             2
                  test_name   multivariate_logrank_test

           test_statistic       p  -log2(p)
                    49.90  <0.005     35.99
```

As in the case of a categorical variable with 2 levels, these results are similar to the likelihood ratio test from the Cox proportional hazards model. First, we look at the results for `Center`.

```
In [33]: X = MS(['Wait time',
                 'Failed',
                 'Center'],
                 intercept=False).fit_transform(D)
         F = coxph().fit(X, 'Wait time', 'Failed')
         F.log_likelihood_ratio_test()
```

```
Out[33]: null_distribution                   chi squared
           degrees_freedom                             2
                 test_name   log-likelihood ratio test

           test_statistic       p  -log2(p)
                    20.58  <0.005     14.85
```

Next, we look at the results for `Time`.

```
In [34]: X = MS(['Wait time',
                 'Failed',
                 'Time'],
                intercept=False).fit_transform(D)
         F = coxph().fit(X, 'Wait time', 'Failed')
         F.log_likelihood_ratio_test()
```

```
Out[34]: null_distribution                   chi squared
           degrees_freedom                             2
                 test_name   log-likelihood ratio test

           test_statistic       p  -log2(p)
                    48.12  <0.005     34.71
```

We find that differences between centers are highly significant, as are differences between times of day.

Finally, we fit Cox's proportional hazards model to the data.

In [35]:
```
X = MS(D.columns,
       intercept=False).fit_transform(D)
fit_queuing = coxph().fit(
                  X,
                  'Wait time',
                  'Failed')
fit_queuing.summary[['coef', 'se(coef)', 'p']]
```

Out[35]:
```
                    coef  se(coef)             p
covariate
Operators       0.043934  0.007520  5.143677e-09
Center[B]      -0.236059  0.058113  4.864734e-05
Center[C]       0.012231  0.057518  8.316083e-01
Time[Even.]     0.268845  0.057797  3.294914e-06
Time[Morn.]    -0.148215  0.057334  9.734378e-03
```

The p-values for Center B and evening time are very small. It is also clear that the hazard — that is, the instantaneous risk that a call will be answered — increases with the number of operators. Since we generated the data ourselves, we know that the true coefficients for `Operators`, `Center = B`, `Center = C`, `Time = Even.` and `Time = Morn.` are 0.04, −0.3, 0, 0.2, and −0.2, respectively. The coefficient estimates from the fitted Cox model are fairly accurate.

11.9 Exercises

Conceptual

1. For each example, state whether or not the censoring mechanism is independent. Justify your answer.

   (a) In a study of disease relapse, due to a careless research scientist, all patients whose phone numbers begin with the number "2" are lost to follow up.

   (b) In a study of longevity, a formatting error causes all patient ages that exceed 99 years to be lost (i.e. we know that those patients are more than 99 years old, but we do not know their exact ages).

   (c) Hospital A conducts a study of longevity. However, very sick patients tend to be transferred to Hospital B, and are lost to follow up.

   (d) In a study of unemployment duration, the people who find work earlier are less motivated to stay in touch with study investigators, and therefore are more likely to be lost to follow up.

   (e) In a study of pregnancy duration, women who deliver their babies pre-term are more likely to do so away from their usual hospital, and thus are more likely to be censored, relative to women who deliver full-term babies.

(f) A researcher wishes to model the number of years of education of the residents of a small town. Residents who enroll in college out of town are more likely to be lost to follow up, and are also more likely to attend graduate school, relative to those who attend college in town.

(g) Researchers conduct a study of disease-free survival (i.e. time until disease relapse following treatment). Patients who have not relapsed within five years are considered to be cured, and thus their survival time is censored at five years.

(h) We wish to model the failure time for some electrical component. This component can be manufactured in Iowa or in Pittsburgh, with no difference in quality. The Iowa factory opened five years ago, and so components manufactured in Iowa are censored at five years. The Pittsburgh factory opened two years ago, so those components are censored at two years.

(i) We wish to model the failure time of an electrical component made in two different factories, one of which opened before the other. We have reason to believe that the components manufactured in the factory that opened earlier are of higher quality.

2. We conduct a study with $n = 4$ participants who have just purchased cell phones, in order to model the time until phone replacement. The first participant replaces her phone after 1.2 years. The second participant still has not replaced her phone at the end of the two-year study period. The third participant changes her phone number and is lost to follow up (but has not yet replaced her phone) 1.5 years into the study. The fourth participant replaces her phone after 0.2 years.

   For each of the four participants ($i = 1, \ldots, 4$), answer the following questions using the notation introduced in Section 11.1:

   (a) Is the participant's cell phone replacement time censored?

   (b) Is the value of c_i known, and if so, then what is it?

   (c) Is the value of t_i known, and if so, then what is it?

   (d) Is the value of y_i known, and if so, then what is it?

   (e) Is the value of δ_i known, and if so, then what is it?

3. For the example in Exercise 2, report the values of K, $d_1, \ldots, d_K$, $r_1, \ldots, r_K$, and $q_1, \ldots, q_K$, where this notation was defined in Section 11.3.

4. This problem makes use of the Kaplan-Meier survival curve displayed in Figure 11.9. The raw data that went into plotting this survival curve is given in Table 11.4. The covariate column of that table is not needed for this problem.

   (a) What is the estimated probability of survival past 50 days?

Observation (Y)	Censoring Indicator (δ)	Covariate (X)
26.5	1	0.1
37.2	1	11
57.3	1	-0.3
90.8	0	2.8
20.2	0	1.8
89.8	0	0.4

TABLE 11.4. *Data used in Exercise 4.*

(b) Write out an analytical expression for the estimated survival function. For instance, your answer might be something along the lines of

$$\widehat{S}(t) = \begin{cases} 0.8 & \text{if } t < 31 \\ 0.5 & \text{if } 31 \leq t < 77 \\ 0.22 & \text{if } 77 \leq t. \end{cases}$$

(The previous equation is for illustration only: it is not the correct answer!)

5. Sketch the survival function given by the equation

$$\widehat{S}(t) = \begin{cases} 0.8 & \text{if } t < 31 \\ 0.5 & \text{if } 31 \leq t < 77 \\ 0.22 & \text{if } 77 \leq t. \end{cases}$$

Your answer should look something like Figure 11.9.

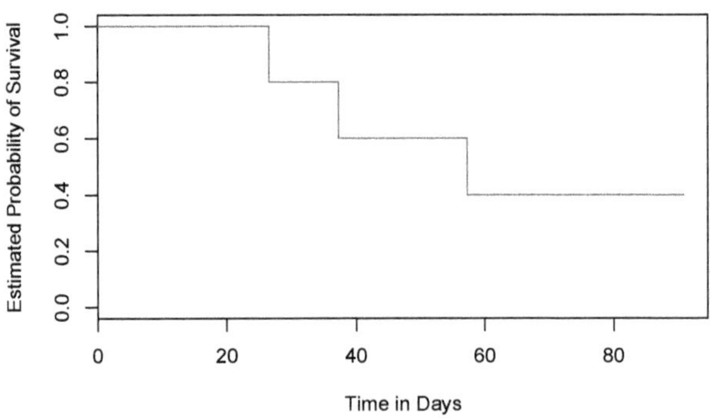

FIGURE 11.9. *A Kaplan-Meier survival curve used in Exercise 4.*

6. This problem makes use of the data displayed in Figure 11.1. In completing this problem, you can refer to the observation times as $y_1, \ldots, y_4$. The ordering of these observation times can be seen from Figure 11.1; their exact values are not required.

(a) Report the values of $\delta_1, \ldots, \delta_4$, K, $d_1, \ldots, d_K$, $r_1, \ldots, r_K$, and $q_1, \ldots, q_K$. The relevant notation is defined in Sections 11.1 and 11.3.

(b) Sketch the Kaplan-Meier survival curve corresponding to this data set. (You do not need to use any software to do this — you can sketch it by hand using the results obtained in (a).)

(c) Based on the survival curve estimated in (b), what is the probability that the event occurs within 200 days? What is the probability that the event does not occur within 310 days?

(d) Write out an expression for the estimated survival curve from (b).

7. In this problem, we will derive (11.5) and (11.6), which are needed for the construction of the log-rank test statistic (11.8). Recall the notation in Table 11.1.

(a) Assume that there is no difference between the survival functions of the two groups. Then we can think of q_{1k} as the number of failures if we draw r_{1k} observations, without replacement, from a risk set of r_k observations that contains a total of q_k failures. Argue that q_{1k} follows a *hypergeometric distribution*. Write the parameters of this distribution in terms of r_{1k}, r_k, and q_k.

hyper-geometric distribution

(b) Given your previous answer, and the properties of the hypergeometric distribution, what are the mean and variance of q_{1k}? Compare your answer to (11.5) and (11.6).

8. Recall that the survival function $S(t)$, the hazard function $h(t)$, and the density function $f(t)$ are defined in (11.2), (11.9), and (11.11), respectively. Furthermore, define $F(t) = 1 - S(t)$. Show that the following relationships hold:

$$\begin{aligned} f(t) &= dF(t)/dt \\ S(t) &= \exp\left(-\int_0^t h(u)du\right). \end{aligned}$$

9. In this exercise, we will explore the consequences of assuming that the survival times follow an exponential distribution.

(a) Suppose that a survival time follows an $\text{Exp}(\lambda)$ distribution, so that its density function is $f(t) = \lambda \exp(-\lambda t)$. Using the relationships provided in Exercise 8, show that $S(t) = \exp(-\lambda t)$.

(b) Now suppose that each of n independent survival times follows an $\text{Exp}(\lambda)$ distribution. Write out an expression for the likelihood function (11.13).

(c) Show that the maximum likelihood estimator for λ is

$$\hat{\lambda} = \sum_{i=1}^{n} \delta_i / \sum_{i=1}^{n} y_i.$$

(d) Use your answer to (c) to derive an estimator of the mean survival time.

Hint: For (d), recall that the mean of an $\text{Exp}(\lambda)$ *random variable is* $1/\lambda$.

Applied

10. This exercise focuses on the brain tumor data, which is included in the `ISLP` library.

    (a) Plot the Kaplan-Meier survival curve with ± 1 standard error bands, using the `KaplanMeierFitter()` estimator in the `lifelines` package.

    (b) Draw a bootstrap sample of size $n = 88$ from the pairs (y_i, δ_i), and compute the resulting Kaplan-Meier survival curve. Repeat this process $B = 200$ times. Use the results to obtain an estimate of the standard error of the Kaplan-Meier survival curve at each timepoint. Compare this to the standard errors obtained in (a).

    (c) Fit a Cox proportional hazards model that uses all of the predictors to predict survival. Summarize the main findings.

    (d) Stratify the data by the value of `ki`. (Since only one observation has `ki==40`, you can group that observation together with the observations that have `ki==60`.) Plot Kaplan-Meier survival curves for each of the five strata, adjusted for the other predictors.

11. This exercise makes use of the data in Table 11.4.

    (a) Create two groups of observations. In Group 1, $X < 2$, whereas in Group 2, $X \geq 2$. Plot the Kaplan-Meier survival curves corresponding to the two groups. Be sure to label the curves so that it is clear which curve corresponds to which group. By eye, does there appear to be a difference between the two groups' survival curves?

    (b) Fit Cox's proportional hazards model, using the group indicator as a covariate. What is the estimated coefficient? Write a sentence providing the interpretation of this coefficient, in terms of the hazard or the instantaneous probability of the event. Is there evidence that the true coefficient value is non-zero?

    (c) Recall from Section 11.5.2 that in the case of a single binary covariate, the log-rank test statistic should be identical to the score statistic for the Cox model. Conduct a log-rank test to determine whether there is a difference between the survival curves for the two groups. How does the p-value for the log-rank test statistic compare to the p-value for the score statistic for the Cox model from (b)?

12 Unsupervised Learning

Most of this book concerns *supervised learning* methods such as regression and classification. In the supervised learning setting, we typically have access to a set of p features $X_1, X_2, \ldots, X_p$, measured on n observations, and a response Y also measured on those same n observations. The goal is then to predict Y using $X_1, X_2, \ldots, X_p$.

This chapter will instead focus on *unsupervised learning*, a set of statistical tools intended for the setting in which we have only a set of features $X_1, X_2, \ldots, X_p$ measured on n observations. We are not interested in prediction, because we do not have an associated response variable Y. Rather, the goal is to discover interesting things about the measurements on $X_1, X_2, \ldots, X_p$. Is there an informative way to visualize the data? Can we discover subgroups among the variables or among the observations? Unsupervised learning refers to a diverse set of techniques for answering questions such as these. In this chapter, we will focus on two particular types of unsupervised learning: *principal components analysis*, a tool used for data visualization or data pre-processing before supervised techniques are applied, and *clustering*, a broad class of methods for discovering unknown subgroups in data.

12.1 The Challenge of Unsupervised Learning

Supervised learning is a well-understood area. In fact, if you have read the preceding chapters in this book, then you should by now have a good grasp of supervised learning. For instance, if you are asked to predict a binary outcome from a data set, you have a very well developed set of tools at your disposal (such as logistic regression, linear discriminant analysis, classification trees, support vector machines, and more) as well as a clear

G. James et al., *An Introduction to Statistical Learning*, Springer Texts in Statistics,
https://doi.org/10.1007/978-3-031-38747-0_12

understanding of how to assess the quality of the results obtained (using cross-validation, validation on an independent test set, and so forth).

In contrast, unsupervised learning is often much more challenging. The exercise tends to be more subjective, and there is no simple goal for the analysis, such as prediction of a response. Unsupervised learning is often performed as part of an *exploratory data analysis*. Furthermore, it can be hard to assess the results obtained from unsupervised learning methods, since there is no universally accepted mechanism for performing cross-validation or validating results on an independent data set. The reason for this difference is simple. If we fit a predictive model using a supervised learning technique, then it is possible to *check our work* by seeing how well our model predicts the response Y on observations not used in fitting the model. However, in unsupervised learning, there is no way to check our work because we don't know the true answer—the problem is unsupervised.

exploratory data analysis

Techniques for unsupervised learning are of growing importance in a number of fields. A cancer researcher might assay gene expression levels in 100 patients with breast cancer. He or she might then look for subgroups among the breast cancer samples, or among the genes, in order to obtain a better understanding of the disease. An online shopping site might try to identify groups of shoppers with similar browsing and purchase histories, as well as items that are of particular interest to the shoppers within each group. Then an individual shopper can be preferentially shown the items in which he or she is particularly likely to be interested, based on the purchase histories of similar shoppers. A search engine might choose which search results to display to a particular individual based on the click histories of other individuals with similar search patterns. These statistical learning tasks, and many more, can be performed via unsupervised learning techniques.

12.2 Principal Components Analysis

Principal components are discussed in Section 6.3.1 in the context of principal components regression. When faced with a large set of correlated variables, principal components allow us to summarize this set with a smaller number of representative variables that collectively explain most of the variability in the original set. The principal component directions are presented in Section 6.3.1 as directions in feature space along which the original data are *highly variable*. These directions also define lines and subspaces that are *as close as possible* to the data cloud. To perform principal components regression, we simply use principal components as predictors in a regression model in place of the original larger set of variables.

Principal components analysis (PCA) refers to the process by which principal components are computed, and the subsequent use of these components in understanding the data. PCA is an unsupervised approach, since it involves only a set of features $X_1, X_2, \ldots, X_p$, and no associated response Y. Apart from producing derived variables for use in supervised learning problems, PCA also serves as a tool for data visualization (visualization of

principal components analysis

the observations or visualization of the variables). It can also be used as a tool for data imputation — that is, for filling in missing values in a data matrix.

We now discuss PCA in greater detail, focusing on the use of PCA as a tool for unsupervised data exploration, in keeping with the topic of this chapter.

12.2.1 What Are Principal Components?

Suppose that we wish to visualize n observations with measurements on a set of p features, $X_1, X_2, \ldots, X_p$, as part of an exploratory data analysis. We could do this by examining two-dimensional scatterplots of the data, each of which contains the n observations' measurements on two of the features. However, there are $\binom{p}{2} = p(p-1)/2$ such scatterplots; for example, with $p = 10$ there are 45 plots! If p is large, then it will certainly not be possible to look at all of them; moreover, most likely none of them will be informative since they each contain just a small fraction of the total information present in the data set. Clearly, a better method is required to visualize the n observations when p is large. In particular, we would like to find a low-dimensional representation of the data that captures as much of the information as possible. For instance, if we can obtain a two-dimensional representation of the data that captures most of the information, then we can plot the observations in this low-dimensional space.

PCA provides a tool to do just this. It finds a low-dimensional representation of a data set that contains as much as possible of the variation. The idea is that each of the n observations lives in p-dimensional space, but not all of these dimensions are equally interesting. PCA seeks a small number of dimensions that are as interesting as possible, where the concept of *interesting* is measured by the amount that the observations vary along each dimension. Each of the dimensions found by PCA is a linear combination of the p features. We now explain the manner in which these dimensions, or *principal components*, are found.

The *first principal component* of a set of features $X_1, X_2, \ldots, X_p$ is the normalized linear combination of the features

$$Z_1 = \phi_{11}X_1 + \phi_{21}X_2 + \cdots + \phi_{p1}X_p \tag{12.1}$$

that has the largest variance. By *normalized*, we mean that $\sum_{j=1}^{p} \phi_{j1}^2 = 1$. We refer to the elements $\phi_{11}, \ldots, \phi_{p1}$ as the *loadings* of the first principal component; together, the loadings make up the principal component loading vector, $\phi_1 = (\phi_{11}\ \phi_{21}\ \ldots\ \phi_{p1})^T$. We constrain the loadings so that their sum of squares is equal to one, since otherwise setting these elements to be arbitrarily large in absolute value could result in an arbitrarily large variance. loading

Given an $n \times p$ data set $\mathbf{X}$, how do we compute the first principal component? Since we are only interested in variance, we assume that each of the variables in $\mathbf{X}$ has been centered to have mean zero (that is, the column means of $\mathbf{X}$ are zero). We then look for the linear combination of the sample feature values of the form

$$z_{i1} = \phi_{11}x_{i1} + \phi_{21}x_{i2} + \cdots + \phi_{p1}x_{ip} \tag{12.2}$$

that has largest sample variance, subject to the constraint that $\sum_{j=1}^{p} \phi_{j1}^2 = 1$. In other words, the first principal component loading vector solves the optimization problem

$$\underset{\phi_{11},\ldots,\phi_{p1}}{\text{maximize}} \left\{ \frac{1}{n} \sum_{i=1}^{n} \left(\sum_{j=1}^{p} \phi_{j1} x_{ij} \right)^2 \right\} \text{ subject to } \sum_{j=1}^{p} \phi_{j1}^2 = 1. \tag{12.3}$$

From (12.2) we can write the objective in (12.3) as $\frac{1}{n}\sum_{i=1}^{n} z_{i1}^2$. Since $\frac{1}{n}\sum_{i=1}^{n} x_{ij} = 0$, the average of the $z_{11}, \ldots, z_{n1}$ will be zero as well. Hence the objective that we are maximizing in (12.3) is just the sample variance of the n values of z_{i1}. We refer to $z_{11}, \ldots, z_{n1}$ as the *scores* of the first principal component. Problem (12.3) can be solved via an *eigen decomposition*, a standard technique in linear algebra, but the details are outside of the scope of this book.[1]

score

eigen decomposition

There is a nice geometric interpretation of the first principal component. The loading vector ϕ_1 with elements $\phi_{11}, \phi_{21}, \ldots, \phi_{p1}$ defines a direction in feature space along which the data vary the most. If we project the n data points $x_1, \ldots, x_n$ onto this direction, the projected values are the principal component scores $z_{11}, \ldots, z_{n1}$ themselves. For instance, Figure 6.14 on page 254 displays the first principal component loading vector (green solid line) on an advertising data set. In these data, there are only two features, and so the observations as well as the first principal component loading vector can be easily displayed. As can be seen from (6.19), in that data set $\phi_{11} = 0.839$ and $\phi_{21} = 0.544$.

After the first principal component Z_1 of the features has been determined, we can find the second principal component Z_2. The second principal component is the linear combination of $X_1, \ldots, X_p$ that has maximal variance out of all linear combinations that are *uncorrelated* with Z_1. The second principal component scores $z_{12}, z_{22}, \ldots, z_{n2}$ take the form

$$z_{i2} = \phi_{12} x_{i1} + \phi_{22} x_{i2} + \cdots + \phi_{p2} x_{ip}, \tag{12.4}$$

where ϕ_2 is the second principal component loading vector, with elements $\phi_{12}, \phi_{22}, \ldots, \phi_{p2}$. It turns out that constraining Z_2 to be uncorrelated with Z_1 is equivalent to constraining the direction ϕ_2 to be orthogonal (perpendicular) to the direction ϕ_1. In the example in Figure 6.14, the observations lie in two-dimensional space (since $p = 2$), and so once we have found ϕ_1, there is only one possibility for ϕ_2, which is shown as a blue dashed line. (From Section 6.3.1, we know that $\phi_{12} = 0.544$ and $\phi_{22} = -0.839$.) But in a larger data set with $p > 2$ variables, there are multiple distinct principal components, and they are defined in a similar manner. To find ϕ_2, we solve a problem similar to (12.3) with ϕ_2 replacing ϕ_1, and with the additional constraint that ϕ_2 is orthogonal to ϕ_1.[2]

[1] As an alternative to the eigen decomposition, a related technique called the singular value decomposition can be used. This will be explored in the lab at the end of this chapter.

[2] On a technical note, the principal component directions ϕ_1, ϕ_2, $\phi_3, \ldots$ are given by the ordered sequence of eigenvectors of the matrix $\mathbf{X}^T\mathbf{X}$, and the variances of the components are the eigenvalues. There are at most $\min(n-1, p)$ principal components.

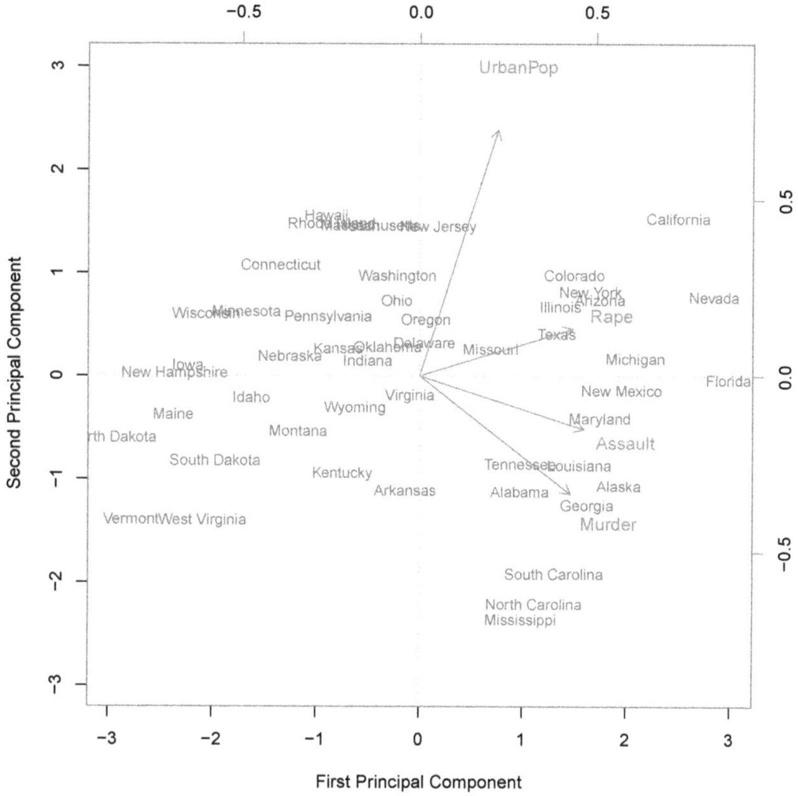

FIGURE 12.1. *The first two principal components for the* `USArrests` *data. The blue state names represent the scores for the first two principal components. The orange arrows indicate the first two principal component loading vectors (with axes on the top and right). For example, the loading for* `Rape` *on the first component is* 0.54*, and its loading on the second principal component* 0.17 *(the word* `Rape` *is centered at the point* $(0.54, 0.17)$*). This figure is known as a biplot, because it displays both the principal component scores and the principal component loadings.*

Once we have computed the principal components, we can plot them against each other in order to produce low-dimensional views of the data. For instance, we can plot the score vector Z_1 against Z_2, Z_1 against Z_3, Z_2 against Z_3, and so forth. Geometrically, this amounts to projecting the original data down onto the subspace spanned by ϕ_1, ϕ_2, and ϕ_3, and plotting the projected points.

We illustrate the use of PCA on the `USArrests` data set. For each of the 50 states in the United States, the data set contains the number of arrests per 100,000 residents for each of three crimes: `Assault`, `Murder`, and `Rape`. We also record `UrbanPop` (the percent of the population in each state living in urban areas). The principal component score vectors have length $n = 50$, and the principal component loading vectors have length $p = 4$. PCA was performed after standardizing each variable to have mean zero and standard

	PC1	PC2
`Murder`	0.5358995	−0.4181809
`Assault`	0.5831836	−0.1879856
`UrbanPop`	0.2781909	0.8728062
`Rape`	0.5434321	0.1673186

TABLE 12.1. *The principal component loading vectors, ϕ_1 and ϕ_2, for the* `USArrests` *data. These are also displayed in Figure 12.1.*

deviation one. Figure 12.1 plots the first two principal components of these data. The figure represents both the principal component scores and the loading vectors in a single *biplot* display. The loadings are also given in Table 12.2.1. biplot

In Figure 12.1, we see that the first loading vector places approximately equal weight on `Assault`, `Murder`, and `Rape`, but with much less weight on `UrbanPop`. Hence this component roughly corresponds to a measure of overall rates of serious crimes. The second loading vector places most of its weight on `UrbanPop` and much less weight on the other three features. Hence, this component roughly corresponds to the level of urbanization of the state. Overall, we see that the crime-related variables (`Murder`, `Assault`, and `Rape`) are located close to each other, and that the `UrbanPop` variable is far from the other three. This indicates that the crime-related variables are correlated with each other—states with high murder rates tend to have high assault and rape rates—and that the `UrbanPop` variable is less correlated with the other three.

We can examine differences between the states via the two principal component score vectors shown in Figure 12.1. Our discussion of the loading vectors suggests that states with large positive scores on the first component, such as California, Nevada and Florida, have high crime rates, while states like North Dakota, with negative scores on the first component, have low crime rates. California also has a high score on the second component, indicating a high level of urbanization, while the opposite is true for states like Mississippi. States close to zero on both components, such as Indiana, have approximately average levels of both crime and urbanization.

12.2.2 Another Interpretation of Principal Components

The first two principal component loading vectors in a simulated three-dimensional data set are shown in the left-hand panel of Figure 12.2; these two loading vectors span a plane along which the observations have the highest variance.

In the previous section, we describe the principal component loading vectors as the directions in feature space along which the data vary the most, and the principal component scores as projections along these directions. However, an alternative interpretation of principal components can also be

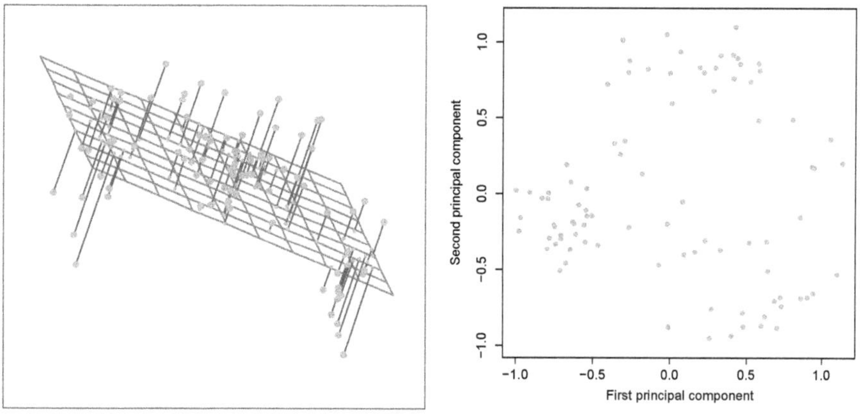

FIGURE 12.2. *Ninety observations simulated in three dimensions. The observations are displayed in color for ease of visualization.* Left: *the first two principal component directions span the plane that best fits the data. The plane is positioned to minimize the sum of squared distances to each point.* Right: *the first two principal component score vectors give the coordinates of the projection of the 90 observations onto the plane.*

useful: principal components provide low-dimensional linear surfaces that are *closest* to the observations. We expand upon that interpretation here.[3]

The first principal component loading vector has a very special property: it is the line in p-dimensional space that is *closest* to the n observations (using average squared Euclidean distance as a measure of closeness). This interpretation can be seen in the left-hand panel of Figure 6.15; the dashed lines indicate the distance between each observation and the line defined by the first principal component loading vector. The appeal of this interpretation is clear: we seek a single dimension of the data that lies as close as possible to all of the data points, since such a line will likely provide a good summary of the data.

The notion of principal components as the dimensions that are closest to the n observations extends beyond just the first principal component. For instance, the first two principal components of a data set span the plane that is closest to the n observations, in terms of average squared Euclidean distance. An example is shown in the left-hand panel of Figure 12.2. The first three principal components of a data set span the three-dimensional hyperplane that is closest to the n observations, and so forth.

Using this interpretation, together the first M principal component score vectors and the first M principal component loading vectors provide the best M-dimensional approximation (in terms of Euclidean distance) to

[3]In this section, we continue to assume that each column of the data matrix $\mathbf{X}$ has been centered to have mean zero—that is, the column mean has been subtracted from each column.

the ith observation x_{ij}. This representation can be written as

$$x_{ij} \approx \sum_{m=1}^{M} z_{im}\phi_{jm}. \tag{12.5}$$

We can state this more formally by writing down an optimization problem. Suppose the data matrix $\mathbf{X}$ is column-centered. Out of all approximations of the form $x_{ij} \approx \sum_{m=1}^{M} a_{im}b_{jm}$, we could ask for the one with the smallest residual sum of squares:

$$\underset{\mathbf{A}\in\mathbb{R}^{n\times M},\mathbf{B}\in\mathbb{R}^{p\times M}}{\text{minimize}} \left\{ \sum_{j=1}^{p}\sum_{i=1}^{n}\left(x_{ij} - \sum_{m=1}^{M} a_{im}b_{jm}\right)^2 \right\}. \tag{12.6}$$

Here, $\mathbf{A}$ is an $n \times M$ matrix whose (i, m) element is a_{im}, and $\mathbf{B}$ is a $p \times M$ element whose (j, m) element is b_{jm}.

It can be shown that for any value of M, the columns of the matrices $\hat{\mathbf{A}}$ and $\hat{\mathbf{B}}$ that solve (12.6) are in fact the first M principal components score and loading vectors. In other words, if $\hat{\mathbf{A}}$ and $\hat{\mathbf{B}}$ solve (12.6), then $\hat{a}_{im} = z_{im}$ and $\hat{b}_{jm} = \phi_{jm}$.[4] This means that the smallest possible value of the objective in (12.6) is

$$\sum_{j=1}^{p}\sum_{i=1}^{n}\left(x_{ij} - \sum_{m=1}^{M} z_{im}\phi_{jm}\right)^2. \tag{12.7}$$

In summary, together the M principal component score vectors and M principal component loading vectors can give a good approximation to the data when M is sufficiently large. When $M = \min(n-1, p)$, then the representation is exact: $x_{ij} = \sum_{m=1}^{M} z_{im}\phi_{jm}$.

12.2.3 The Proportion of Variance Explained

In Figure 12.2, we performed PCA on a three-dimensional data set (left-hand panel) and projected the data onto the first two principal component loading vectors in order to obtain a two-dimensional view of the data (i.e. the principal component score vectors; right-hand panel). We see that this two-dimensional representation of the three-dimensional data does successfully capture the major pattern in the data: the orange, green, and cyan observations that are near each other in three-dimensional space remain nearby in the two-dimensional representation. Similarly, we have seen on the `USArrests` data set that we can summarize the 50 observations and 4 variables using just the first two principal component score vectors and the first two principal component loading vectors.

We can now ask a natural question: how much of the information in a given data set is lost by projecting the observations onto the first few principal components? That is, how much of the variance in the data is *not* contained in the first few principal components? More generally, we are interested in knowing the *proportion of variance explained* (PVE) by each

proportion of variance explained

[4]Technically, the solution to (12.6) is not unique. Thus, it is more precise to state that any solution to (12.6) can be easily transformed to yield the principal components.

principal component. The *total variance* present in a data set (assuming that the variables have been centered to have mean zero) is defined as

$$\sum_{j=1}^{p} \text{Var}(X_j) = \sum_{j=1}^{p} \frac{1}{n} \sum_{i=1}^{n} x_{ij}^2, \tag{12.8}$$

and the variance explained by the mth principal component is

$$\frac{1}{n} \sum_{i=1}^{n} z_{im}^2 = \frac{1}{n} \sum_{i=1}^{n} \left(\sum_{j=1}^{p} \phi_{jm} x_{ij} \right)^2 . \tag{12.9}$$

Therefore, the PVE of the mth principal component is given by

$$\frac{\sum_{i=1}^{n} z_{im}^2}{\sum_{j=1}^{p} \sum_{i=1}^{n} x_{ij}^2} = \frac{\sum_{i=1}^{n} \left(\sum_{j=1}^{p} \phi_{jm} x_{ij} \right)^2}{\sum_{j=1}^{p} \sum_{i=1}^{n} x_{ij}^2}. \tag{12.10}$$

The PVE of each principal component is a positive quantity. In order to compute the cumulative PVE of the first M principal components, we can simply sum (12.10) over each of the first M PVEs. In total, there are $\min(n-1, p)$ principal components, and their PVEs sum to one.

In Section 12.2.2, we showed that the first M principal component loading and score vectors can be interpreted as the best M-dimensional approximation to the data, in terms of residual sum of squares. It turns out that the variance of the data can be decomposed into the variance of the first M principal components plus the mean squared error of this M-dimensional approximation, as follows:

$$\underbrace{\sum_{j=1}^{p} \frac{1}{n} \sum_{i=1}^{n} x_{ij}^2}_{\text{Var. of data}} = \underbrace{\sum_{m=1}^{M} \frac{1}{n} \sum_{i=1}^{n} z_{im}^2}_{\text{Var. of first } M \text{ PCs}} + \underbrace{\frac{1}{n} \sum_{j=1}^{p} \sum_{i=1}^{n} \left(x_{ij} - \sum_{m=1}^{M} z_{im} \phi_{jm} \right)^2}_{\text{MSE of } M\text{-dimensional approximation}} \tag{12.11}$$

The three terms in this decomposition are discussed in (12.8), (12.9), and (12.7), respectively. Since the first term is fixed, we see that by maximizing the variance of the first M principal components, we minimize the mean squared error of the M-dimensional approximation, and vice versa. This explains why principal components can be equivalently viewed as minimizing the approximation error (as in Section 12.2.2) or maximizing the variance (as in Section 12.2.1).

Moreover, we can use (12.11) to see that the PVE defined in (12.10) equals

$$1 - \frac{\sum_{j=1}^{p} \sum_{i=1}^{n} \left(x_{ij} - \sum_{m=1}^{M} z_{im} \phi_{jm} \right)^2}{\sum_{j=1}^{p} \sum_{i=1}^{n} x_{ij}^2} = 1 - \frac{\text{RSS}}{\text{TSS}},$$

where TSS represents the total sum of squared elements of $\mathbf{X}$, and RSS represents the residual sum of squares of the M-dimensional approximation given by the principal components. Recalling the definition of R^2 from (3.17), this means that we can interpret the PVE as the R^2 of the approximation for $\mathbf{X}$ given by the first M principal components.

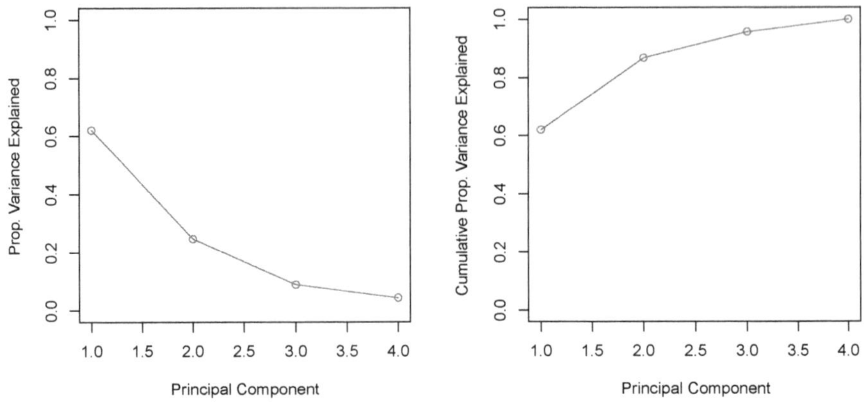

FIGURE 12.3. Left: *a scree plot depicting the proportion of variance explained by each of the four principal components in the* `USArrests` *data.* Right: *the cumulative proportion of variance explained by the four principal components in the* `USArrests` *data.*

In the `USArrests` data, the first principal component explains 62.0 % of the variance in the data, and the next principal component explains 24.7 % of the variance. Together, the first two principal components explain almost 87 % of the variance in the data, and the last two principal components explain only 13 % of the variance. This means that Figure 12.1 provides a pretty accurate summary of the data using just two dimensions. The PVE of each principal component, as well as the cumulative PVE, is shown in Figure 12.3. The left-hand panel is known as a *scree plot*, and will be discussed later in this chapter. scree plot

12.2.4 More on PCA

Scaling the Variables

We have already mentioned that before PCA is performed, the variables should be centered to have mean zero. Furthermore, *the results obtained when we perform PCA will also depend on whether the variables have been individually scaled* (each multiplied by a different constant). This is in contrast to some other supervised and unsupervised learning techniques, such as linear regression, in which scaling the variables has no effect. (In linear regression, multiplying a variable by a factor of c will simply lead to multiplication of the corresponding coefficient estimate by a factor of $1/c$, and thus will have no substantive effect on the model obtained.)

For instance, Figure 12.1 was obtained after scaling each of the variables to have standard deviation one. This is reproduced in the left-hand plot in Figure 12.4. Why does it matter that we scaled the variables? In these data, the variables are measured in different units; `Murder`, `Rape`, and `Assault` are reported as the number of occurrences per 100,000 people, and `UrbanPop` is the percentage of the state's population that lives in an urban area. These four variables have variances of 18.97, 87.73, 6945.16, and 209.5, respectively. Consequently, if we perform PCA on the unscaled variables, then

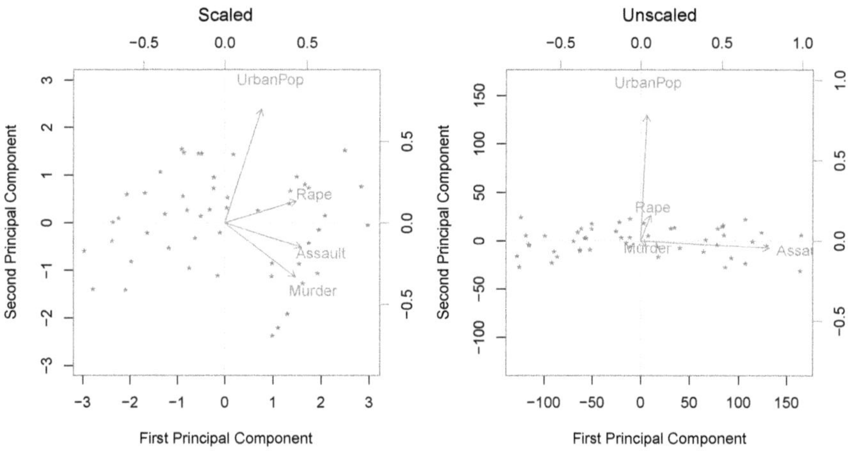

FIGURE 12.4. *Two principal component biplots for the* `USArrests` *data.* Left: *the same as Figure 12.1, with the variables scaled to have unit standard deviations.* Right: *principal components using unscaled data.* `Assault` *has by far the largest loading on the first principal component because it has the highest variance among the four variables. In general, scaling the variables to have standard deviation one is recommended.*

the first principal component loading vector will have a very large loading for `Assault`, since that variable has by far the highest variance. The right-hand plot in Figure 12.4 displays the first two principal components for the `USArrests` data set, without scaling the variables to have standard deviation one. As predicted, the first principal component loading vector places almost all of its weight on `Assault`, while the second principal component loading vector places almost all of its weight on `UrbanPop`. Comparing this to the left-hand plot, we see that scaling does indeed have a substantial effect on the results obtained.

However, this result is simply a consequence of the scales on which the variables were measured. For instance, if `Assault` were measured in units of the number of occurrences per 100 people (rather than number of occurrences per $100,000$ people), then this would amount to dividing all of the elements of that variable by $1,000$. Then the variance of the variable would be tiny, and so the first principal component loading vector would have a very small value for that variable. Because it is undesirable for the principal components obtained to depend on an arbitrary choice of scaling, we typically scale each variable to have standard deviation one before we perform PCA.

In certain settings, however, the variables may be measured in the same units. In this case, we might not wish to scale the variables to have standard deviation one before performing PCA. For instance, suppose that the variables in a given data set correspond to expression levels for p genes. Then since expression is measured in the same "units" for each gene, we might choose not to scale the genes to each have standard deviation one.

Uniqueness of the Principal Components

While in theory the principal components need not be unique, in almost all practical settings they are (up to sign flips). This means that two different software packages will yield the same principal component loading vectors, although the signs of those loading vectors may differ. The signs may differ because each principal component loading vector specifies a direction in p-dimensional space: flipping the sign has no effect as the direction does not change. (Consider Figure 6.14—the principal component loading vector is a line that extends in either direction, and flipping its sign would have no effect.) Similarly, the score vectors are unique up to a sign flip, since the variance of Z is the same as the variance of $-Z$. It is worth noting that when we use (12.5) to approximate x_{ij} we multiply z_{im} by ϕ_{jm}. Hence, if the sign is flipped on both the loading and score vectors, the final product of the two quantities is unchanged.

Deciding How Many Principal Components to Use

In general, an $n \times p$ data matrix $\mathbf{X}$ has $\min(n-1, p)$ distinct principal components. However, we usually are not interested in all of them; rather, we would like to use just the first few principal components in order to visualize or interpret the data. In fact, we would like to use the smallest number of principal components required to get a *good* understanding of the data. How many principal components are needed? Unfortunately, there is no single (or simple!) answer to this question.

We typically decide on the number of principal components required to visualize the data by examining a *scree plot*, such as the one shown in the left-hand panel of Figure 12.3. We choose the smallest number of principal components that are required in order to explain a sizable amount of the variation in the data. This is done by eyeballing the scree plot, and looking for a point at which the proportion of variance explained by each subsequent principal component drops off. This drop is often referred to as an *elbow* in the scree plot. For instance, by inspection of Figure 12.3, one might conclude that a fair amount of variance is explained by the first two principal components, and that there is an elbow after the second component. After all, the third principal component explains less than ten percent of the variance in the data, and the fourth principal component explains less than half that and so is essentially worthless.

However, this type of visual analysis is inherently *ad hoc*. Unfortunately, there is no well-accepted objective way to decide how many principal components are *enough*. In fact, the question of how many principal components are enough is inherently ill-defined, and will depend on the specific area of application and the specific data set. In practice, we tend to look at the first few principal components in order to find interesting patterns in the data. If no interesting patterns are found in the first few principal components, then further principal components are unlikely to be of interest. Conversely, if the first few principal components are interesting, then we typically continue to look at subsequent principal components until no further interesting patterns are found. This is admittedly a subjective approach, and is reflective of the fact that PCA is generally used as a tool for exploratory data analysis.

On the other hand, if we compute principal components for use in a supervised analysis, such as the principal components regression presented in Section 6.3.1, then there is a simple and objective way to determine how many principal components to use: we can treat the number of principal component score vectors to be used in the regression as a tuning parameter to be selected via cross-validation or a related approach. The comparative simplicity of selecting the number of principal components for a supervised analysis is one manifestation of the fact that supervised analyses tend to be more clearly defined and more objectively evaluated than unsupervised analyses.

12.2.5 Other Uses for Principal Components

We saw in Section 6.3.1 that we can perform regression using the principal component score vectors as features. In fact, many statistical techniques, such as regression, classification, and clustering, can be easily adapted to use the $n \times M$ matrix whose columns are the first $M \ll p$ principal component score vectors, rather than using the full $n \times p$ data matrix. This can lead to *less noisy* results, since it is often the case that the signal (as opposed to the noise) in a data set is concentrated in its first few principal components.

12.3 Missing Values and Matrix Completion

Often datasets have missing values, which can be a nuisance. For example, suppose that we wish to analyze the `USArrests` data, and discover that 20 of the 200 values have been randomly corrupted and marked as missing. Unfortunately, the statistical learning methods that we have seen in this book cannot handle missing values. How should we proceed?

We could remove the rows that contain missing observations and perform our data analysis on the complete rows. But this seems wasteful, and depending on the fraction missing, unrealistic. Alternatively, if x_{ij} is missing, then we could replace it by the mean of the jth column (using the non-missing entries to compute the mean). Although this is a common and convenient strategy, often we can do better by exploiting the correlation between the variables.

In this section we show how principal components can be used to *impute* the missing values, through a process known as *matrix completion*. The completed matrix can then be used in a statistical learning method, such as linear regression or LDA.

impute
imputation
matrix completion

This approach for imputing missing data is appropriate if the missingness is random. For example, it is suitable if a patient's weight is missing because the battery of the electronic scale was flat at the time of his exam. By contrast, if the weight is missing because the patient was too heavy to climb on the scale, then this is not missing at random; the missingness is

missing at random

informative, and the approach described here for handling missing data is not suitable.

Sometimes data is missing by necessity. For example, if we form a matrix of the ratings (on a scale from 1 to 5) that n customers have given to the entire Netflix catalog of p movies, then most of the matrix will be missing, since no customer will have seen and rated more than a tiny fraction of the catalog. If we can impute the missing values well, then we will have an idea of what each customer will think of movies they have not yet seen. Hence matrix completion can be used to power *recommender systems.* recommender systems

Principal Components with Missing Values

In Section 12.2.2, we showed that the first M principal component score and loading vectors provide the "best" approximation to the data matrix $\mathbf{X}$, in the sense of (12.6). Suppose that some of the observations x_{ij} are missing. We now show how one can both impute the missing values and solve the principal component problem at the same time. We return to a modified form of the optimization problem (12.6),

$$\underset{\mathbf{A}\in\mathbb{R}^{n\times M},\mathbf{B}\in\mathbb{R}^{p\times M}}{\text{minimize}} \left\{ \sum_{(i,j)\in\mathcal{O}} \left(x_{ij} - \sum_{m=1}^{M} a_{im}b_{jm} \right)^2 \right\}, \tag{12.12}$$

where $\mathcal{O}$ is the set of all *observed* pairs of indices (i, j), a subset of the possible $n \times p$ pairs.

Once we solve this problem:

- we can estimate a missing observation x_{ij} using $\hat{x}_{ij} = \sum_{m=1}^{M} \hat{a}_{im}\hat{b}_{jm}$, where $\hat{a}_{im}$ and $\hat{b}_{jm}$ are the (i, m) and (j, m) elements, respectively, of the matrices $\hat{\mathbf{A}}$ and $\hat{\mathbf{B}}$ that solve (12.12); and
- we can (approximately) recover the M principal component scores and loadings, as we did when the data were complete.

It turns out that solving (12.12) exactly is difficult, unlike in the case of complete data: the eigen decomposition no longer applies. But the simple iterative approach in Algorithm 12.1, which is demonstrated in Section 12.5.2, typically provides a good solution.[5][6]

We illustrate Algorithm 12.1 on the `USArrests` data. There are $p = 4$ variables and $n = 50$ observations (states). We first standardized the data so each variable has mean zero and standard deviation one. We then randomly selected 20 of the 50 states, and then for each of these we randomly set one of the four variables to be missing. Thus, 10% of the elements of the data matrix were missing. We applied Algorithm 12.1 with $M = 1$ principal component. Figure 12.5 shows that the recovery of the missing elements

---

[5] This algorithm is referred to as "Hard-Impute" in Mazumder, Hastie, and Tibshirani (2010) "Spectral regularization algorithms for learning large incomplete matrices", published in *Journal of Machine Learning Research*, pages 2287–2322.

[6] Each iteration of Step 2 of this algorithm decreases the objective (12.14). However, the algorithm is not guaranteed to achieve the global optimum of (12.12).

Algorithm 12.1 *Iterative Algorithm for Matrix Completion*

1. Create a complete data matrix $\tilde{\mathbf{X}}$ of dimension $n \times p$ of which the (i, j) element equals

$$\tilde{x}_{ij} = \begin{cases} x_{ij} & \text{if } (i,j) \in \mathcal{O} \\ \bar{x}_j & \text{if } (i,j) \notin \mathcal{O}, \end{cases}$$

where $\bar{x}_j$ is the average of the observed values for the jth variable in the incomplete data matrix $\mathbf{X}$. Here, $\mathcal{O}$ indexes the observations that are observed in $\mathbf{X}$.

2. Repeat steps (a)–(c) until the objective (12.14) fails to decrease:

(a) Solve

$$\underset{\mathbf{A}\in\mathbb{R}^{n\times M},\mathbf{B}\in\mathbb{R}^{p\times M}}{\text{minimize}} \left\{ \sum_{j=1}^{p}\sum_{i=1}^{n} \left(\tilde{x}_{ij} - \sum_{m=1}^{M} a_{im} b_{jm} \right)^2 \right\} \tag{12.13}$$

by computing the principal components of $\tilde{\mathbf{X}}$.

(b) For each element $(i, j) \notin \mathcal{O}$, set $\tilde{x}_{ij} \leftarrow \sum_{m=1}^{M} \hat{a}_{im}\hat{b}_{jm}$.

(c) Compute the objective

$$\sum_{(i,j)\in\mathcal{O}} \left(x_{ij} - \sum_{m=1}^{M} \hat{a}_{im}\hat{b}_{jm} \right)^2 . \tag{12.14}$$

3. Return the estimated missing entries $\tilde{x}_{ij}$, $(i, j) \notin \mathcal{O}$.

---

is pretty accurate. Over 100 random runs of this experiment, the average correlation between the true and imputed values of the missing elements is 0.63, with a standard deviation of 0.11. Is this good performance? To answer this question, we can compare this correlation to what we would have gotten if we had estimated these 20 values using the *complete* data — that is, if we had simply computed $\hat{x}_{ij} = z_{i1}\phi_{j1}$, where z_{i1} and ϕ_{j1} are elements of the first principal component score and loading vectors of the complete data.[7] Using the complete data in this way results in an average correlation of 0.79 between the true and estimated values for these 20 elements, with a standard deviation of 0.08. Thus, our imputation method does worse than the method that uses all of the data (0.63 ± 0.11 versus 0.79 ± 0.08), but its performance is still pretty good. (And of course, the method that uses all of the data cannot be applied in a real-world setting with missing data.)

Figure 12.6 further indicates that Algorithm 12.1 performs fairly well on this dataset.

---

[7]This is an unattainable gold standard, in the sense that with missing data, we of course cannot compute the principal components of the complete data.

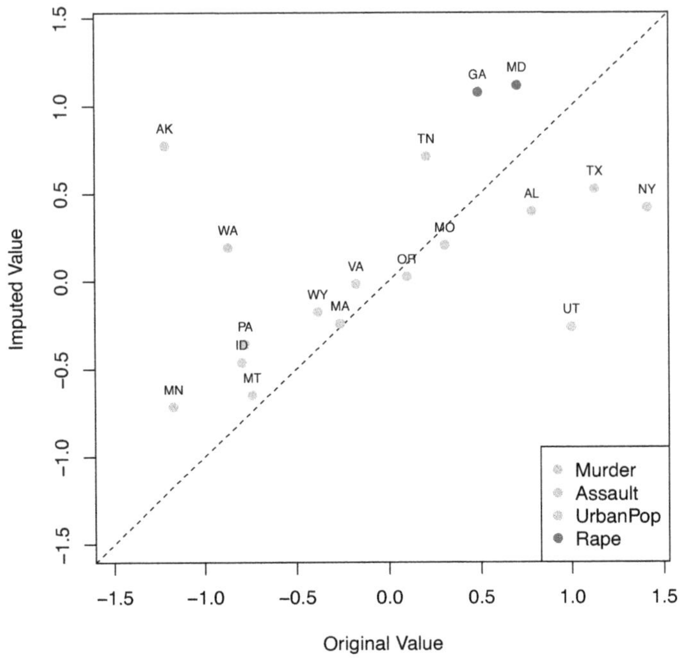

FIGURE 12.5. *Missing value imputation on the* USArrests *data. Twenty values (10% of the total number of matrix elements) were artificially set to be missing, and then imputed via Algorithm 12.1 with* $M = 1$. *The figure displays the true value* x_{ij} *and the imputed value* $\hat{x}_{ij}$ *for all twenty missing values. For each of the twenty missing values, the color indicates the variable, and the label indicates the state. The correlation between the true and imputed values is around* 0.63.

We close with a few observations:

- The USArrests data has only four variables, which is on the low end for methods like Algorithm 12.1 to work well. For this reason, for this demonstration we randomly set at most one variable per state to be missing, and only used $M = 1$ principal component.
- In general, in order to apply Algorithm 12.1, we must select M, the number of principal components to use for the imputation. One approach is to randomly leave out a few additional elements from the matrix, and select M based on how well those known values are recovered. This is closely related to the validation-set approach seen in Chapter 5.

Recommender Systems

Digital streaming services like Netflix and Amazon use data about the content that a customer has viewed in the past, as well as data from other customers, to suggest other content for the customer. As a concrete example, some years back, Netflix had customers rate each movie that they had seen with a score from 1–5. This resulted in a very big $n \times p$ matrix for which the (i, j) element is the rating given by the ith customer to the

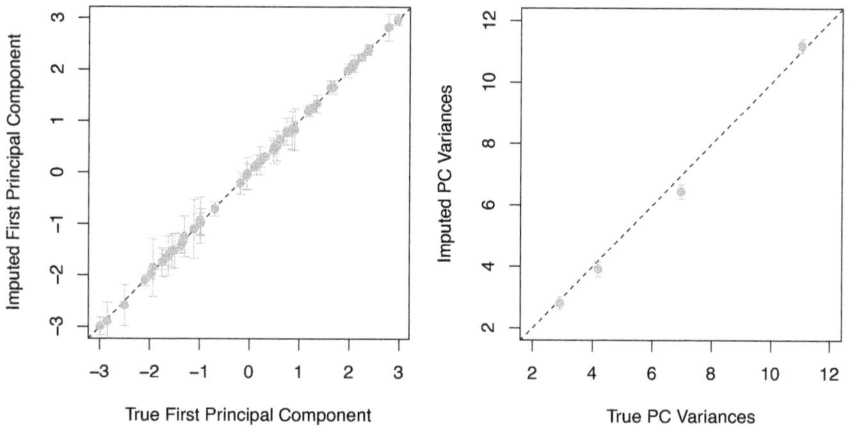

FIGURE 12.6. *As described in the text, in each of 100 trials, we left out 20 elements of the* `USArrests` *dataset. In each trial, we applied Algorithm 12.1 with* $M = 1$ *to impute the missing elements and compute the principal components.* Left: *For each of the 50 states, the imputed first principal component scores (averaged over 100 trials, and displayed with a standard deviation bar) are plotted against the first principal component scores computed using all the data.* Right: *The imputed principal component loadings (averaged over 100 trials, and displayed with a standard deviation bar) are plotted against the true principal component loadings.*

jth movie. One specific early example of this matrix had $n = 480{,}189$ customers and $p = 17{,}770$ movies. However, on average each customer had seen around 200 movies, so 99% of the matrix had missing elements. Table 12.2 illustrates the setup.

In order to suggest a movie that a particular customer might like, Netflix needed a way to impute the missing values of this data matrix. The key idea is as follows: the set of movies that the ith customer has seen will overlap with those that other customers have seen. Furthermore, some of those other customers will have similar movie preferences to the ith customer. Thus, it should be possible to use similar customers' ratings of movies that the ith customer has not seen to predict whether the ith customer will like those movies.

More concretely, by applying Algorithm 12.1, we can predict the ith customer's rating for the jth movie using $\hat{x}_{ij} = \sum_{m=1}^{M} \hat{a}_{im}\hat{b}_{jm}$. Furthermore, we can interpret the M components in terms of "cliques" and "genres":

- $\hat{a}_{im}$ represents the strength with which the ith user belongs to the mth clique, where a *clique* is a group of customers that enjoys movies of the mth genre;
- $\hat{b}_{jm}$ represents the strength with which the jth movie belongs to the mth *genre*.

Examples of genres include Romance, Western, and Action.

Principal component models similar to Algorithm 12.1 are at the heart of many recommender systems. Although the data matrices involved are

	Jerry Maguire	Oceans	Road to Perdition	A Fortunate Man	Catch Me If You Can	Driving Miss Daisy	The Two Popes	The Laundromat	Code 8	The Social Network	...
Customer 1					4						
Customer 2			3				3			3	
Customer 3		2		4					2		
Customer 4	3										
Customer 5	5	1			4						
Customer 6						2	4				
Customer 7			5					3			
Customer 8											
Customer 9	3				5			1			
⋮											

TABLE 12.2. *Excerpt of the Netflix movie rating data. The movies are rated from 1 (worst) to 5 (best). The symbol represents a missing value: a movie that was not rated by the corresponding customer.*

typically massive, algorithms have been developed that can exploit the high level of missingness in order to perform efficient computations.

12.4 Clustering Methods

Clustering refers to a very broad set of techniques for finding *subgroups*, or *clusters*, in a data set. When we cluster the observations of a data set, we seek to partition them into distinct groups so that the observations within each group are quite similar to each other, while observations in different groups are quite different from each other. Of course, to make this concrete, we must define what it means for two or more observations to be *similar* or *different*. Indeed, this is often a domain-specific consideration that must be made based on knowledge of the data being studied. clustering

For instance, suppose that we have a set of n observations, each with p features. The n observations could correspond to tissue samples for patients with breast cancer, and the p features could correspond to measurements collected for each tissue sample; these could be clinical measurements, such as tumor stage or grade, or they could be gene expression measurements. We may have a reason to believe that there is some heterogeneity among the n tissue samples; for instance, perhaps there are a few different *unknown* subtypes of breast cancer. Clustering could be used to find these subgroups. This is an unsupervised problem because we are trying to discover structure—in this case, distinct clusters—on the basis of a data set. The goal in supervised problems, on the other hand, is to try to predict some outcome vector such as survival time or response to drug treatment.

Both clustering and PCA seek to simplify the data via a small number of summaries, but their mechanisms are different:

- PCA looks to find a low-dimensional representation of the observations that explain a good fraction of the variance;
- Clustering looks to find homogeneous subgroups among the observations.

Another application of clustering arises in marketing. We may have access to a large number of measurements (e.g. median household income, occupation, distance from nearest urban area, and so forth) for a large number of people. Our goal is to perform *market segmentation* by identifying subgroups of people who might be more receptive to a particular form of advertising, or more likely to purchase a particular product. The task of performing market segmentation amounts to clustering the people in the data set.

Since clustering is popular in many fields, there exist a great number of clustering methods. In this section we focus on perhaps the two best-known clustering approaches: *K-means clustering* and *hierarchical clustering*. In K-means clustering, we seek to partition the observations into a pre-specified number of clusters. On the other hand, in hierarchical clustering, we do not know in advance how many clusters we want; in fact, we end up with a tree-like visual representation of the observations, called a *dendrogram*, that allows us to view at once the clusterings obtained for each possible number of clusters, from 1 to n. There are advantages and disadvantages to each of these clustering approaches, which we highlight in this chapter.

K-means clustering

hierarchical clustering

dendrogram

In general, we can cluster observations on the basis of the features in order to identify subgroups among the observations, or we can cluster features on the basis of the observations in order to discover subgroups among the features. In what follows, for simplicity we will discuss clustering observations on the basis of the features, though the converse can be performed by simply transposing the data matrix.

12.4.1 K-Means Clustering

K-means clustering is a simple and elegant approach for partitioning a data set into K distinct, non-overlapping clusters. To perform K-means clustering, we must first specify the desired number of clusters K; then the K-means algorithm will assign each observation to exactly one of the K clusters. Figure 12.7 shows the results obtained from performing K-means clustering on a simulated example consisting of 150 observations in two dimensions, using three different values of K.

The K-means clustering procedure results from a simple and intuitive mathematical problem. We begin by defining some notation. Let $C_1, \ldots, C_K$ denote sets containing the indices of the observations in each cluster. These sets satisfy two properties:

1. $C_1 \cup C_2 \cup \cdots \cup C_K = \{1, \ldots, n\}$. In other words, each observation belongs to at least one of the K clusters.
2. $C_k \cap C_{k'} = \emptyset$ for all $k \neq k'$. In other words, the clusters are non-overlapping: no observation belongs to more than one cluster.

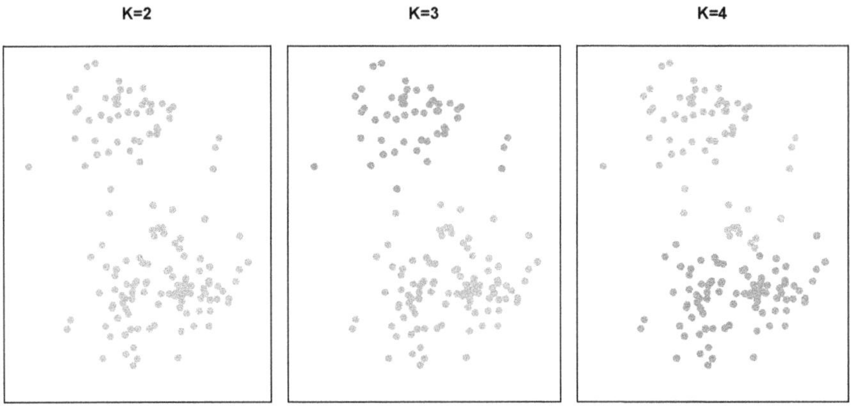

FIGURE 12.7. *A simulated data set with 150 observations in two-dimensional space. Panels show the results of applying K-means clustering with different values of K, the number of clusters. The color of each observation indicates the cluster to which it was assigned using the K-means clustering algorithm. Note that there is no ordering of the clusters, so the cluster coloring is arbitrary. These cluster labels were not used in clustering; instead, they are the outputs of the clustering procedure.*

For instance, if the ith observation is in the kth cluster, then $i \in C_k$. The idea behind K-means clustering is that a *good* clustering is one for which the *within-cluster variation* is as small as possible. The within-cluster variation for cluster C_k is a measure $W(C_k)$ of the amount by which the observations within a cluster differ from each other. Hence we want to solve the problem

$$\underset{C_1,\ldots,C_K}{\text{minimize}} \left\{ \sum_{k=1}^{K} W(C_k) \right\}. \tag{12.15}$$

In words, this formula says that we want to partition the observations into K clusters such that the total within-cluster variation, summed over all K clusters, is as small as possible.

Solving (12.15) seems like a reasonable idea, but in order to make it actionable we need to define the within-cluster variation. There are many possible ways to define this concept, but by far the most common choice involves *squared Euclidean distance.* That is, we define

$$W(C_k) = \frac{1}{|C_k|} \sum_{i,i' \in C_k} \sum_{j=1}^{p} (x_{ij} - x_{i'j})^2, \tag{12.16}$$

where $|C_k|$ denotes the number of observations in the kth cluster. In other words, the within-cluster variation for the kth cluster is the sum of all of the pairwise squared Euclidean distances between the observations in the kth cluster, divided by the total number of observations in the kth cluster. Combining (12.15) and (12.16) gives the optimization problem that defines

K-means clustering,

$$\underset{C_1,\ldots,C_K}{\text{minimize}}\left\{\sum_{k=1}^{K}\frac{1}{|C_k|}\sum_{i,i'\in C_k}\sum_{j=1}^{p}(x_{ij}-x_{i'j})^2\right\}. \tag{12.17}$$

Now, we would like to find an algorithm to solve (12.17)—that is, a method to partition the observations into K clusters such that the objective of (12.17) is minimized. This is in fact a very difficult problem to solve precisely, since there are almost K^n ways to partition n observations into K clusters. This is a huge number unless K and n are tiny! Fortunately, a very simple algorithm can be shown to provide a local optimum—a *pretty good solution*—to the K-means optimization problem (12.17). This approach is laid out in Algorithm 12.2.

Algorithm 12.2 *K-Means Clustering*

1. Randomly assign a number, from 1 to K, to each of the observations. These serve as initial cluster assignments for the observations.

2. Iterate until the cluster assignments stop changing:

   (a) For each of the K clusters, compute the cluster *centroid.* The kth cluster centroid is the vector of the p feature means for the observations in the kth cluster.

   (b) Assign each observation to the cluster whose centroid is closest (where *closest* is defined using Euclidean distance).

Algorithm 12.2 is guaranteed to decrease the value of the objective (12.17) at each step. To understand why, the following identity is illuminating:

$$\frac{1}{|C_k|}\sum_{i,i'\in C_k}\sum_{j=1}^{p}(x_{ij}-x_{i'j})^2 = 2\sum_{i\in C_k}\sum_{j=1}^{p}(x_{ij}-\bar{x}_{kj})^2, \tag{12.18}$$

where $\bar{x}_{kj} = \frac{1}{|C_k|}\sum_{i\in C_k} x_{ij}$ is the mean for feature j in cluster C_k. In Step 2(a) the cluster means for each feature are the constants that minimize the sum-of-squared deviations, and in Step 2(b), reallocating the observations can only improve (12.18). This means that as the algorithm is run, the clustering obtained will continually improve until the result no longer changes; the objective of (12.17) will never increase. When the result no longer changes, a *local optimum* has been reached. Figure 12.8 shows the progression of the algorithm on the toy example from Figure 12.7. K-means clustering derives its name from the fact that in Step 2(a), the cluster centroids are computed as the mean of the observations assigned to each cluster.

Because the K-means algorithm finds a local rather than a global optimum, the results obtained will depend on the initial (random) cluster assignment of each observation in Step 1 of Algorithm 12.2. For this reason, it is important to run the algorithm multiple times from different random

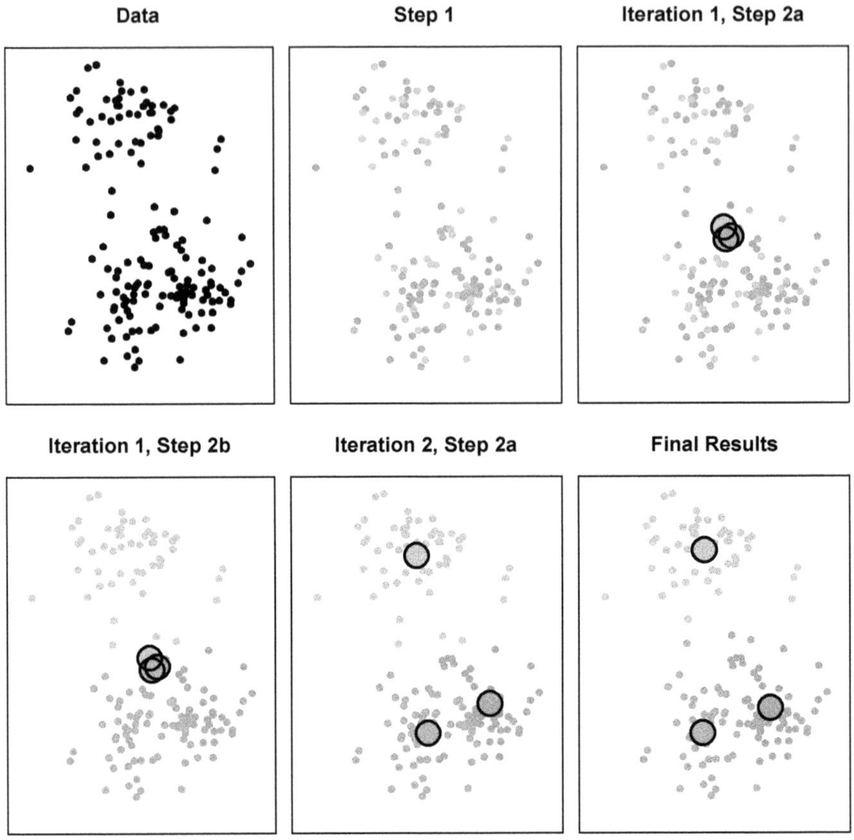

FIGURE 12.8. *The progress of the K-means algorithm on the example of Figure 12.7 with $K=3$.* Top left: *the observations are shown.* Top center: *in Step 1 of the algorithm, each observation is randomly assigned to a cluster.* Top right: *in Step 2(a), the cluster centroids are computed. These are shown as large colored disks. Initially the centroids are almost completely overlapping because the initial cluster assignments were chosen at random.* Bottom left: *in Step 2(b), each observation is assigned to the nearest centroid.* Bottom center: *Step 2(a) is once again performed, leading to new cluster centroids.* Bottom right: *the results obtained after ten iterations.*

initial configurations. Then one selects the *best* solution, i.e. that for which the objective (12.17) is smallest. Figure 12.9 shows the local optima obtained by running K-means clustering six times using six different initial cluster assignments, using the toy data from Figure 12.7. In this case, the best clustering is the one with an objective value of 235.8.

As we have seen, to perform K-means clustering, we must decide how many clusters we expect in the data. The problem of selecting K is far from simple. This issue, along with other practical considerations that arise in performing K-means clustering, is addressed in Section 12.4.3.

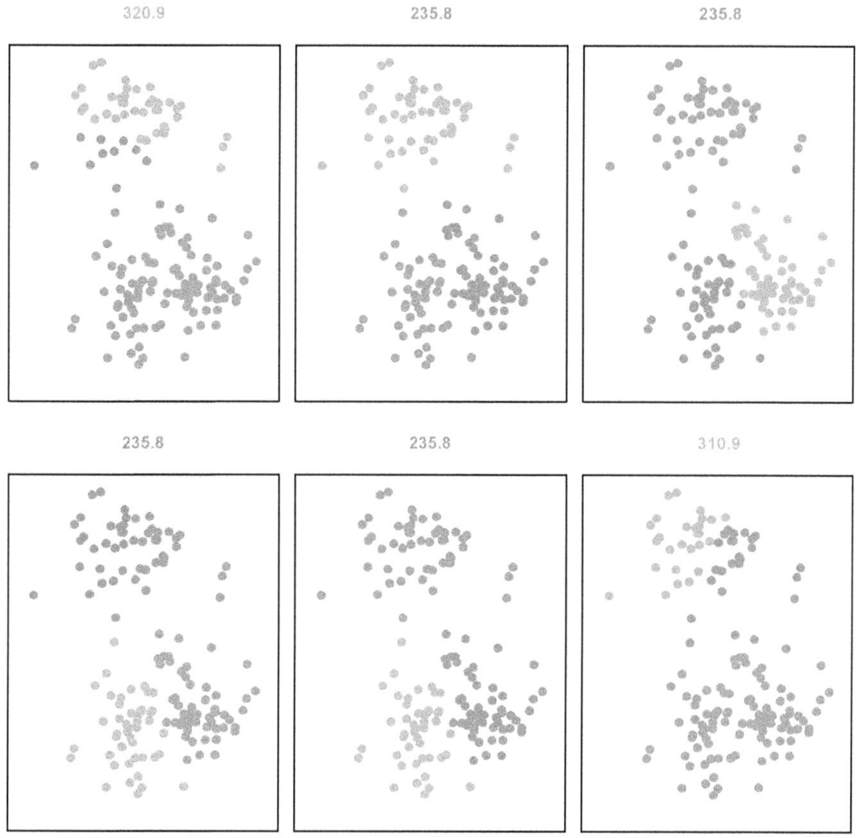

FIGURE 12.9. *K-means clustering performed six times on the data from Figure 12.7 with $K = 3$, each time with a different random assignment of the observations in Step 1 of the K-means algorithm. Above each plot is the value of the objective (12.17). Three different local optima were obtained, one of which resulted in a smaller value of the objective and provides better separation between the clusters. Those labeled in red all achieved the same best solution, with an objective value of 235.8.*

12.4.2 Hierarchical Clustering

One potential disadvantage of K-means clustering is that it requires us to pre-specify the number of clusters K. *Hierarchical clustering* is an alternative approach which does not require that we commit to a particular choice of K. Hierarchical clustering has an added advantage over K-means clustering in that it results in an attractive tree-based representation of the observations, called a *dendrogram*.

In this section, we describe *bottom-up* or *agglomerative* clustering. This is the most common type of hierarchical clustering, and refers to the fact that a dendrogram (generally depicted as an upside-down tree; see Figure 12.11) is built starting from the leaves and combining clusters up to the trunk. We will begin with a discussion of how to interpret a dendrogram

bottom-up
agglomerative

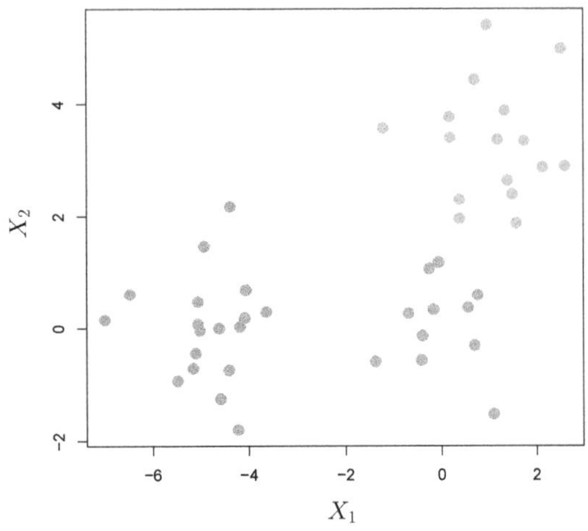

FIGURE 12.10. *Forty-five observations generated in two-dimensional space. In reality there are three distinct classes, shown in separate colors. However, we will treat these class labels as unknown and will seek to cluster the observations in order to discover the classes from the data.*

and then discuss how hierarchical clustering is actually performed—that is, how the dendrogram is built.

Interpreting a Dendrogram

We begin with the simulated data set shown in Figure 12.10, consisting of 45 observations in two-dimensional space. The data were generated from a three-class model; the true class labels for each observation are shown in distinct colors. However, suppose that the data were observed without the class labels, and that we wanted to perform hierarchical clustering of the data. Hierarchical clustering (with complete linkage, to be discussed later) yields the result shown in the left-hand panel of Figure 12.11. How can we interpret this dendrogram?

In the left-hand panel of Figure 12.11, each *leaf* of the dendrogram represents one of the 45 observations in Figure 12.10. However, as we move up the tree, some leaves begin to *fuse* into branches. These correspond to observations that are similar to each other. As we move higher up the tree, branches themselves fuse, either with leaves or other branches. The earlier (lower in the tree) fusions occur, the more similar the groups of observations are to each other. On the other hand, observations that fuse later (near the top of the tree) can be quite different. In fact, this statement can be made precise: for any two observations, we can look for the point in the tree where branches containing those two observations are first fused. The height of this fusion, as measured on the vertical axis, indicates how different the two observations are. Thus, observations that fuse at the very bottom of the tree are quite similar to each other, whereas observations that fuse close to the top of the tree will tend to be quite different.

This highlights a very important point in interpreting dendrograms that is often misunderstood. Consider the left-hand panel of Figure 12.12, which shows a simple dendrogram obtained from hierarchically clustering nine

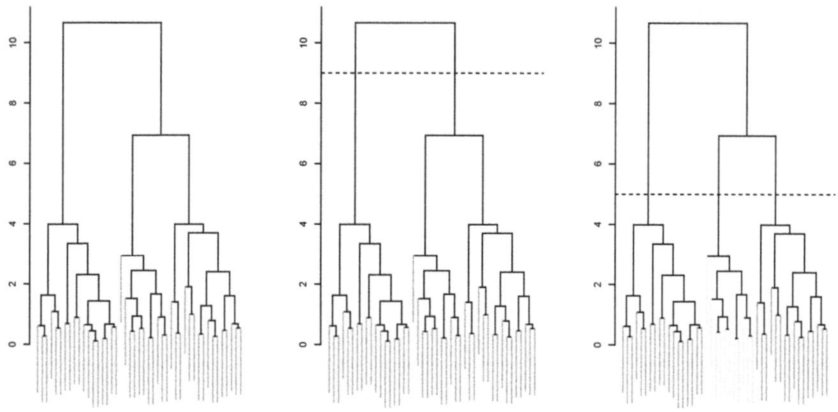

FIGURE 12.11. Left: *dendrogram obtained from hierarchically clustering the data from Figure 12.10 with complete linkage and Euclidean distance.* Center: *the dendrogram from the left-hand panel, cut at a height of nine (indicated by the dashed line). This cut results in two distinct clusters, shown in different colors.* Right: *the dendrogram from the left-hand panel, now cut at a height of five. This cut results in three distinct clusters, shown in different colors. Note that the colors were not used in clustering, but are simply used for display purposes in this figure.*

observations. One can see that observations 5 and 7 are quite similar to each other, since they fuse at the lowest point on the dendrogram. Observations 1 and 6 are also quite similar to each other. However, it is tempting but incorrect to conclude from the figure that observations 9 and 2 are quite similar to each other on the basis that they are located near each other on the dendrogram. In fact, based on the information contained in the dendrogram, observation 9 is no more similar to observation 2 than it is to observations $8, 5$, and 7. (This can be seen from the right-hand panel of Figure 12.12, in which the raw data are displayed.) To put it mathematically, there are 2^{n-1} possible reorderings of the dendrogram, where n is the number of leaves. This is because at each of the $n-1$ points where fusions occur, the positions of the two fused branches could be swapped without affecting the meaning of the dendrogram. Therefore, we cannot draw conclusions about the similarity of two observations based on their proximity along the *horizontal axis*. Rather, we draw conclusions about the similarity of two observations based on the location on the *vertical axis* where branches containing those two observations first are fused.

Now that we understand how to interpret the left-hand panel of Figure 12.11, we can move on to the issue of identifying clusters on the basis of a dendrogram. In order to do this, we make a horizontal cut across the dendrogram, as shown in the center and right-hand panels of Figure 12.11. The distinct sets of observations beneath the cut can be interpreted as clusters. In the center panel of Figure 12.11, cutting the dendrogram at a height of nine results in two clusters, shown in distinct colors. In the right-hand panel, cutting the dendrogram at a height of five results in three clusters. Further cuts can be made as one descends the dendrogram in order to obtain any number of clusters, between 1 (corresponding to no cut) and n

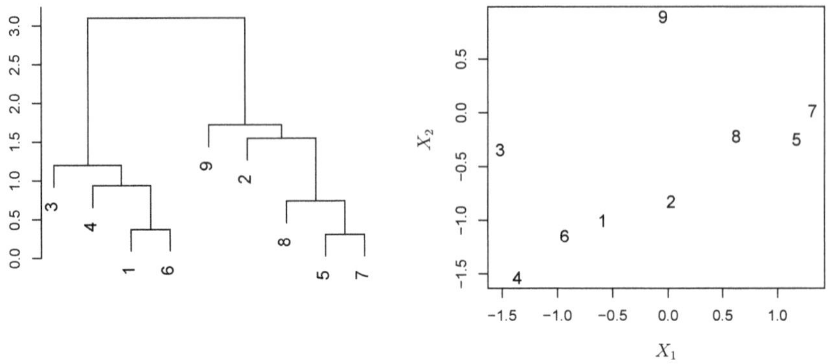

FIGURE 12.12. *An illustration of how to properly interpret a dendrogram with nine observations in two-dimensional space.* Left: *a dendrogram generated using Euclidean distance and complete linkage. Observations* 5 *and* 7 *are quite similar to each other, as are observations* 1 *and* 6. *However, observation* 9 *is* no more similar to *observation* 2 *than it is to observations* 8, 5, *and* 7, *even though observations* 9 *and* 2 *are close together in terms of horizontal distance. This is because observations* 2, 8, 5, *and* 7 *all fuse with observation* 9 *at the same height, approximately* 1.8. Right: *the raw data used to generate the dendrogram can be used to confirm that indeed, observation* 9 *is no more similar to observation* 2 *than it is to observations* 8, 5, *and* 7.

(corresponding to a cut at height 0, so that each observation is in its own cluster). In other words, the height of the cut to the dendrogram serves the same role as the K in K-means clustering: it controls the number of clusters obtained.

Figure 12.11 therefore highlights a very attractive aspect of hierarchical clustering: one single dendrogram can be used to obtain any number of clusters. In practice, people often look at the dendrogram and select by eye a sensible number of clusters, based on the heights of the fusion and the number of clusters desired. In the case of Figure 12.11, one might choose to select either two or three clusters. However, often the choice of where to cut the dendrogram is not so clear.

The term *hierarchical* refers to the fact that clusters obtained by cutting the dendrogram at a given height are necessarily nested within the clusters obtained by cutting the dendrogram at any greater height. However, on an arbitrary data set, this assumption of hierarchical structure might be unrealistic. For instance, suppose that our observations correspond to a group of men and women, evenly split among Americans, Japanese, and French. We can imagine a scenario in which the best division into two groups might split these people by gender, and the best division into three groups might split them by nationality. In this case, the true clusters are not nested, in the sense that the best division into three groups does not result from taking the best division into two groups and splitting up one of those groups. Consequently, this situation could not be well-represented by hierarchical clustering. Due to situations such as this one, hierarchical clustering can sometimes yield *worse* (i.e. less accurate) results than K-means clustering for a given number of clusters.

Algorithm 12.3 *Hierarchical Clustering*

1. Begin with n observations and a measure (such as Euclidean distance) of all the $\binom{n}{2} = n(n-1)/2$ pairwise dissimilarities. Treat each observation as its own cluster.
2. For $i = n, n-1, \ldots, 2$:
   (a) Examine all pairwise inter-cluster dissimilarities among the i clusters and identify the pair of clusters that are least dissimilar (that is, most similar). Fuse these two clusters. The dissimilarity between these two clusters indicates the height in the dendrogram at which the fusion should be placed.
   (b) Compute the new pairwise inter-cluster dissimilarities among the $i-1$ remaining clusters.

The Hierarchical Clustering Algorithm

The hierarchical clustering dendrogram is obtained via an extremely simple algorithm. We begin by defining some sort of *dissimilarity* measure between each pair of observations. Most often, Euclidean distance is used; we will discuss the choice of dissimilarity measure later in this chapter. The algorithm proceeds iteratively. Starting out at the bottom of the dendrogram, each of the n observations is treated as its own cluster. The two clusters that are most similar to each other are then *fused* so that there now are $n-1$ clusters. Next the two clusters that are most similar to each other are fused again, so that there now are $n-2$ clusters. The algorithm proceeds in this fashion until all of the observations belong to one single cluster, and the dendrogram is complete. Figure 12.13 depicts the first few steps of the algorithm, for the data from Figure 12.12. To summarize, the hierarchical clustering algorithm is given in Algorithm 12.3.

This algorithm seems simple enough, but one issue has not been addressed. Consider the bottom right panel in Figure 12.13. How did we determine that the cluster $\{5, 7\}$ should be fused with the cluster $\{8\}$? We have a concept of the dissimilarity between pairs of observations, but how do we define the dissimilarity between two clusters if one or both of the clusters contains multiple observations? The concept of dissimilarity between a pair of observations needs to be extended to a pair of *groups of observations*. This extension is achieved by developing the notion of *linkage*, which defines the dissimilarity between two groups of observations. The four most common types of linkage—*complete*, *average*, *single*, and *centroid*—are briefly described in Table 12.3. Average, complete, and single linkage are most popular among statisticians. Average and complete linkage are generally preferred over single linkage, as they tend to yield more balanced dendrograms. Centroid linkage is often used in genomics, but suffers from a major drawback in that an *inversion* can occur, whereby two clusters are fused at a height *below* either of the individual clusters in the dendrogram. This can lead to difficulties in visualization as well as in interpretation of the dendrogram. The dissimilarities computed in Step 2(b)

linkage

inversion

Linkage	*Description*
Complete	Maximal intercluster dissimilarity. Compute all pairwise dissimilarities between the observations in cluster A and the observations in cluster B, and record the *largest* of these dissimilarities.
Single	Minimal intercluster dissimilarity. Compute all pairwise dissimilarities between the observations in cluster A and the observations in cluster B, and record the *smallest* of these dissimilarities. Single linkage can result in extended, trailing clusters in which single observations are fused one-at-a-time.
Average	Mean intercluster dissimilarity. Compute all pairwise dissimilarities between the observations in cluster A and the observations in cluster B, and record the *average* of these dissimilarities.
Centroid	Dissimilarity between the centroid for cluster A (a mean vector of length p) and the centroid for cluster B. Centroid linkage can result in undesirable *inversions*.

TABLE 12.3. *A summary of the four most commonly-used types of linkage in hierarchical clustering.*

of the hierarchical clustering algorithm will depend on the type of linkage used, as well as on the choice of dissimilarity measure. Hence, the resulting dendrogram typically depends quite strongly on the type of linkage used, as is shown in Figure 12.14.

Choice of Dissimilarity Measure

Thus far, the examples in this chapter have used Euclidean distance as the dissimilarity measure. But sometimes other dissimilarity measures might be preferred. For example, *correlation-based distance* considers two observations to be similar if their features are highly correlated, even though the observed values may be far apart in terms of Euclidean distance. This is an unusual use of correlation, which is normally computed between variables; here it is computed between the observation profiles for each pair of observations. Figure 12.15 illustrates the difference between Euclidean and correlation-based distance. Correlation-based distance focuses on the shapes of observation profiles rather than their magnitudes.

The choice of dissimilarity measure is very important, as it has a strong effect on the resulting dendrogram. In general, careful attention should be paid to the type of data being clustered and the scientific question at hand. These considerations should determine what type of dissimilarity measure is used for hierarchical clustering.

For instance, consider an online retailer interested in clustering shoppers based on their past shopping histories. The goal is to identify subgroups of *similar* shoppers, so that shoppers within each subgroup can be shown items and advertisements that are particularly likely to interest them. Suppose the data takes the form of a matrix where the rows are the shoppers and the columns are the items available for purchase; the elements of the data matrix indicate the number of times a given shopper has purchased a

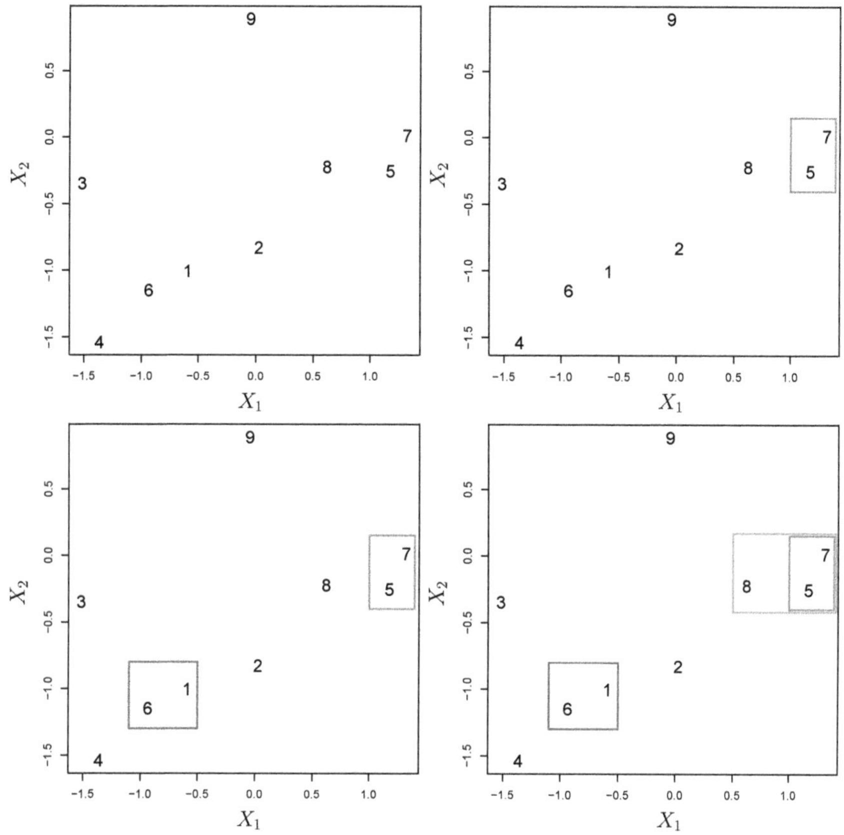

FIGURE 12.13. *An illustration of the first few steps of the hierarchical clustering algorithm, using the data from Figure 12.12, with complete linkage and Euclidean distance.* Top Left: *initially, there are nine distinct clusters,* $\{1\}, \{2\}, \ldots, \{9\}$. Top Right: *the two clusters that are closest together,* $\{5\}$ *and* $\{7\}$*, are fused into a single cluster.* Bottom Left: *the two clusters that are closest together,* $\{6\}$ *and* $\{1\}$*, are fused into a single cluster.* Bottom Right: *the two clusters that are closest together using* complete linkage, $\{8\}$ *and the cluster* $\{5, 7\}$*, are fused into a single cluster.*

given item (i.e. a 0 if the shopper has never purchased this item, a 1 if the shopper has purchased it once, etc.) What type of dissimilarity measure should be used to cluster the shoppers? If Euclidean distance is used, then shoppers who have bought very few items overall (i.e. infrequent users of the online shopping site) will be clustered together. This may not be desirable. On the other hand, if correlation-based distance is used, then shoppers with similar preferences (e.g. shoppers who have bought items A and B but never items C or D) will be clustered together, even if some shoppers with these preferences are higher-volume shoppers than others. Therefore, for this application, correlation-based distance may be a better choice.

In addition to carefully selecting the dissimilarity measure used, one must also consider whether or not the variables should be scaled to have standard deviation one before the dissimilarity between the observations is computed. To illustrate this point, we continue with the online shopping ex-

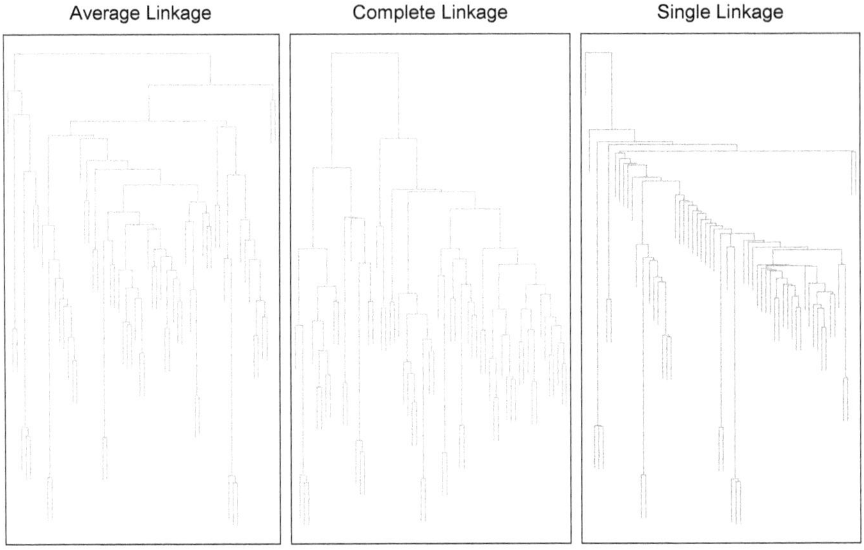

FIGURE 12.14. *Average, complete, and single linkage applied to an example data set. Average and complete linkage tend to yield more balanced clusters.*

ample just described. Some items may be purchased more frequently than others; for instance, a shopper might buy ten pairs of socks a year, but a computer very rarely. High-frequency purchases like socks therefore tend to have a much larger effect on the inter-shopper dissimilarities, and hence on the clustering ultimately obtained, than rare purchases like computers. This may not be desirable. If the variables are scaled to have standard deviation one before the inter-observation dissimilarities are computed, then each variable will in effect be given equal importance in the hierarchical clustering performed. We might also want to scale the variables to have standard deviation one if they are measured on different scales; otherwise, the choice of units (e.g. centimeters versus kilometers) for a particular variable will greatly affect the dissimilarity measure obtained. It should come as no surprise that whether or not it is a good decision to scale the variables before computing the dissimilarity measure depends on the application at hand. An example is shown in Figure 12.16. We note that the issue of whether or not to scale the variables before performing clustering applies to K-means clustering as well.

12.4.3 Practical Issues in Clustering

Clustering can be a very useful tool for data analysis in the unsupervised setting. However, there are a number of issues that arise in performing clustering. We describe some of these issues here.

Small Decisions with Big Consequences

In order to perform clustering, some decisions must be made.

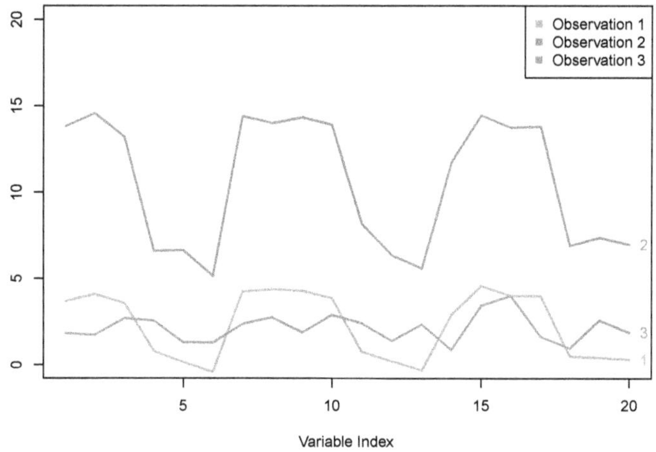

FIGURE 12.15. *Three observations with measurements on 20 variables are shown. Observations 1 and 3 have similar values for each variable and so there is a small Euclidean distance between them. But they are very weakly correlated, so they have a large correlation-based distance. On the other hand, observations 1 and 2 have quite different values for each variable, and so there is a large Euclidean distance between them. But they are highly correlated, so there is a small correlation-based distance between them.*

- Should the observations or features first be standardized in some way? For instance, maybe the variables should be scaled to have standard deviation one.
- In the case of hierarchical clustering,
  - What dissimilarity measure should be used?
  - What type of linkage should be used?
  - Where should we cut the dendrogram in order to obtain clusters?
- In the case of K-means clustering, how many clusters should we look for in the data?

Each of these decisions can have a strong impact on the results obtained. In practice, we try several different choices, and look for the one with the most useful or interpretable solution. With these methods, there is no single right answer—any solution that exposes some interesting aspects of the data should be considered.

Validating the Clusters Obtained

Any time clustering is performed on a data set we will find clusters. But we really want to know whether the clusters that have been found represent true subgroups in the data, or whether they are simply a result of *clustering the noise*. For instance, if we were to obtain an independent set of observations, then would those observations also display the same set of clusters? This is a hard question to answer. There exist a number of techniques for assigning a p-value to a cluster in order to assess whether there is more

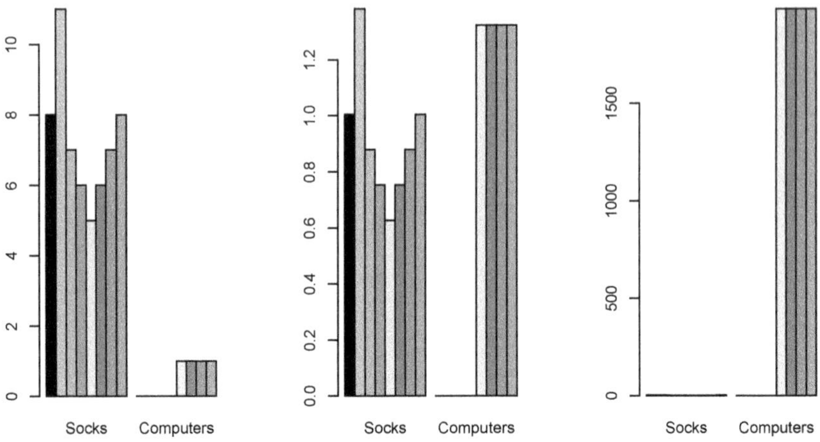

FIGURE 12.16. *An eclectic online retailer sells two items: socks and computers.* Left: *the number of pairs of socks, and computers, purchased by eight online shoppers is displayed. Each shopper is shown in a different color. If inter-observation dissimilarities are computed using Euclidean distance on the raw variables, then the number of socks purchased by an individual will drive the dissimilarities obtained, and the number of computers purchased will have little effect. This might be undesirable, since (1) computers are more expensive than socks and so the online retailer may be more interested in encouraging shoppers to buy computers than socks, and (2) a large difference in the number of socks purchased by two shoppers may be less informative about the shoppers' overall shopping preferences than a small difference in the number of computers purchased.* Center: *the same data are shown, after scaling each variable by its standard deviation. Now the two products will have a comparable effect on the inter-observation dissimilarities obtained.* Right: *the same data are displayed, but now the y-axis represents the number of dollars spent by each online shopper on socks and on computers. Since computers are much more expensive than socks, now computer purchase history will drive the inter-observation dissimilarities obtained.*

evidence for the cluster than one would expect due to chance. However, there has been no consensus on a single best approach. More details can be found in ESL.[8]

Other Considerations in Clustering

Both K-means and hierarchical clustering will assign each observation to a cluster. However, sometimes this might not be appropriate. For instance, suppose that most of the observations truly belong to a small number of (unknown) subgroups, and a small subset of the observations are quite different from each other and from all other observations. Then since K-means and hierarchical clustering force *every* observation into a cluster, the clusters found may be heavily distorted due to the presence of outliers that do not belong to any cluster. Mixture models are an attractive approach for accommodating the presence of such outliers. These amount to a *soft* version of K-means clustering, and are described in ESL.

[8]ESL: *The Elements of Statistical Learning* by Hastie, Tibshirani and Friedman.

In addition, clustering methods generally are not very robust to perturbations to the data. For instance, suppose that we cluster n observations, and then cluster the observations again after removing a subset of the n observations at random. One would hope that the two sets of clusters obtained would be quite similar, but often this is not the case!

A Tempered Approach to Interpreting the Results of Clustering

We have described some of the issues associated with clustering. However, clustering can be a very useful and valid statistical tool if used properly. We mentioned that small decisions in how clustering is performed, such as how the data are standardized and what type of linkage is used, can have a large effect on the results. Therefore, we recommend performing clustering with different choices of these parameters, and looking at the full set of results in order to see what patterns consistently emerge. Since clustering can be non-robust, we recommend clustering subsets of the data in order to get a sense of the robustness of the clusters obtained. Most importantly, we must be careful about how the results of a clustering analysis are reported. These results should not be taken as the absolute truth about a data set. Rather, they should constitute a starting point for the development of a scientific hypothesis and further study, preferably on an independent data set.

12.5 Lab: Unsupervised Learning

In this lab we demonstrate PCA and clustering on several datasets. As in other labs, we import some of our libraries at this top level. This makes the code more readable, as scanning the first few lines of the notebook tell us what libraries are used in this notebook.

In [1]:
```
import numpy as np
import pandas as pd
import matplotlib.pyplot as plt
from statsmodels.datasets import get_rdataset
from sklearn.decomposition import PCA
from sklearn.preprocessing import StandardScaler
from ISLP import load_data
```

We also collect the new imports needed for this lab.

In [2]:
```
from sklearn.cluster import \
     (KMeans,
      AgglomerativeClustering)
from scipy.cluster.hierarchy import \
     (dendrogram,
      cut_tree)
from ISLP.cluster import compute_linkage
```

12.5.1 *Principal Components Analysis*

In this lab, we perform PCA on `USArrests`, a data set in the `R` computing environment. We retrieve the data using `get_rdataset()`, which can fetch

get_
rdataset()

data from many standard R packages.

The rows of the data set contain the 50 states, in alphabetical order.

In [3]:
```
USArrests = get_rdataset('USArrests').data
USArrests
```

Out[3]:
```
            Murder   Assault   UrbanPop   Rape
Alabama       13.2       236         58   21.2
Alaska        10.0       263         48   44.5
Arizona        8.1       294         80   31.0
...            ...       ...        ...    ...
Wisconsin      2.6        53         66   10.8
Wyoming        6.8       161         60   15.6
```

The columns of the data set contain the four variables.

In [4]:
```
USArrests.columns
```

Out[4]:
```
Index(['Murder', 'Assault', 'UrbanPop', 'Rape'],
      dtype='object')
```

We first briefly examine the data. We notice that the variables have vastly different means.

In [5]:
```
USArrests.mean()
```

Out[5]:
```
Murder        7.788
Assault     170.760
UrbanPop     65.540
Rape         21.232
dtype: float64
```

Dataframes have several useful methods for computing column-wise summaries. We can also examine the variance of the four variables using the `var()` method.

In [6]:
```
USArrests.var()
```

Out[6]:
```
Murder        18.970465
Assault     6945.165714
UrbanPop     209.518776
Rape          87.729159
dtype: float64
```

Not surprisingly, the variables also have vastly different variances. The `UrbanPop` variable measures the percentage of the population in each state living in an urban area, which is not a comparable number to the number of rapes in each state per 100,000 individuals. PCA looks for derived variables that account for most of the variance in the data set. If we do not scale the variables before performing PCA, then the principal components would mostly be driven by the `Assault` variable, since it has by far the largest variance. So if the variables are measured in different units or vary widely in scale, it is recommended to standardize the variables to have standard deviation one before performing PCA. Typically we set the means to zero as well.

This scaling can be done via the `StandardScaler()` transform imported above. We first `fit` the scaler, which computes the necessary means and standard deviations and then apply it to our data using the `transform` method. As before, we combine these steps using the `fit_transform()` method.

In [7]:
```
scaler = StandardScaler(with_std=True,
                        with_mean=True)
USArrests_scaled = scaler.fit_transform(USArrests)
```

Having scaled the data, we can then perform principal components analysis using the `PCA()` transform from the `sklearn.decomposition` package. PCA()

In [8]:
```
pcaUS = PCA()
```

(By default, the `PCA()` transform centers the variables to have mean zero though it does not scale them.) The transform `pcaUS` can be used to find the PCA `scores` returned by `fit()`. Once the `fit` method has been called, the `pcaUS` object also contains a number of useful quantities.

In [9]:
```
pcaUS.fit(USArrests_scaled)
```

After fitting, the `mean_` attribute corresponds to the means of the variables. In this case, since we centered and scaled the data with `scaler()` the means will all be 0.

In [10]:
```
pcaUS.mean_
```

Out[10]:
```
array([-0.,  0., -0.,  0.])
```

The scores can be computed using the `transform()` method of `pcaUS` after it has been fit.

In [11]:
```
scores = pcaUS.transform(USArrests_scaled)
```

We will plot these scores a bit further down. The `components_` attribute provides the principal component loadings: each row of `pcaUS.components_` contains the corresponding principal component loading vector.

In [12]:
```
pcaUS.components_
```

Out[12]:
```
array([[ 0.53589947,  0.58318363,  0.27819087,  0.54343209],
       [ 0.41818087,  0.1879856 , -0.87280619, -0.16731864],
       [-0.34123273, -0.26814843, -0.37801579,  0.81777791],
       [ 0.6492278 , -0.74340748,  0.13387773,  0.08902432]])
```

The `biplot` is a common visualization method used with PCA. It is not built in as a standard part of `sklearn`, though there are python packages that do produce such plots. Here we make a simple biplot manually.

In [13]:
```
i, j = 0, 1 # which components
fig, ax = plt.subplots(1, 1, figsize=(8, 8))
ax.scatter(scores[:,0], scores[:,1])
ax.set_xlabel('PC%d' % (i+1))
ax.set_ylabel('PC%d' % (j+1))
for k in range(pcaUS.components_.shape[1]):
```

```
    ax.arrow(0, 0, pcaUS.components_[i,k], pcaUS.components_[j,k])
    ax.text(pcaUS.components_[i,k],
            pcaUS.components_[j,k],
            USArrests.columns[k])
```

Notice that this figure is a reflection of Figure 12.1 through the y-axis. Recall that the principal components are only unique up to a sign change, so we can reproduce that figure by flipping the signs of the second set of scores and loadings. We also increase the length of the arrows to emphasize the loadings.

```
In [14]: scale_arrow = s_ = 2
         scores[:,1] *= -1
         pcaUS.components_[1] *= -1 # flip the y-axis
         fig, ax = plt.subplots(1, 1, figsize=(8, 8))
         ax.scatter(scores[:,0], scores[:,1])
         ax.set_xlabel('PC%d' % (i+1))
         ax.set_ylabel('PC%d' % (j+1))
         for k in range(pcaUS.components_.shape[1]):
             ax.arrow(0, 0, s_*pcaUS.components_[i,k], s_*pcaUS.components_[
                 j,k])
             ax.text(s_*pcaUS.components_[i,k],
                     s_*pcaUS.components_[j,k],
                     USArrests.columns[k])
```

The standard deviations of the principal component scores are as follows:

```
In [15]: scores.std(0, ddof=1)

Out[15]: array([1.5909, 1.0050, 0.6032, 0.4207])
```

The variance of each score can be extracted directly from the `pcaUS` object via the `explained_variance_` attribute.

```
In [16]: pcaUS.explained_variance_

Out[16]: array([2.5309, 1.01  , 0.3638, 0.177 ])
```

The proportion of variance explained by each principal component (PVE) is stored as `explained_variance_ratio_`:

```
In [17]: pcaUS.explained_variance_ratio_

Out[17]: array([0.6201, 0.2474, 0.0891, 0.0434])
```

We see that the first principal component explains 62.0% of the variance in the data, the next principal component explains 24.7% of the variance, and so forth. We can plot the PVE explained by each component, as well as the cumulative PVE. We first plot the proportion of variance explained.

```
In [18]: %%capture
         fig, axes = plt.subplots(1, 2, figsize=(15, 6))
         ticks = np.arange(pcaUS.n_components_)+1
         ax = axes[0]
         ax.plot(ticks,
                 pcaUS.explained_variance_ratio_,
                 marker='o')
```

```
ax.set_xlabel('Principal Component');
ax.set_ylabel('Proportion of Variance Explained')
ax.set_ylim([0,1])
ax.set_xticks(ticks)
```

Notice the use of `%%capture`, which suppresses the displaying of the partially completed figure.

```
In [19]: ax = axes[1]
         ax.plot(ticks,
                 pcaUS.explained_variance_ratio_.cumsum(),
                 marker='o')
         ax.set_xlabel('Principal Component')
         ax.set_ylabel('Cumulative Proportion of Variance Explained')
         ax.set_ylim([0, 1])
         ax.set_xticks(ticks)
         fig
```

The result is similar to that shown in Figure 12.3. Note that the method `cumsum()` computes the cumulative sum of the elements of a numeric vector. For instance:

`cumsum()`

```
In [20]: a = np.array([1,2,8,-3])
         np.cumsum(a)
```

```
Out[20]: array([ 1,  3, 11,  8])
```

12.5.2 Matrix Completion

We now re-create the analysis carried out on the `USArrests` data in Section 12.3.

We saw in Section 12.2.2 that solving the optimization problem (12.6) on a centered data matrix $\mathbf{X}$ is equivalent to computing the first M principal components of the data. We use our scaled and centered `USArrests` data as $\mathbf{X}$ below. The *singular value decomposition* (SVD) is a general algorithm for solving (12.6).

singular value decomposition

`svd()`

```
In [21]: X = USArrests_scaled
         U, D, V = np.linalg.svd(X, full_matrices=False)
         U.shape, D.shape, V.shape
```

```
Out[21]: ((50, 4), (4,), (4, 4))
```

The `np.linalg.svd()` function returns three components, `U`, `D` and `V`. The matrix `V` is equivalent to the loading matrix from principal components (up to an unimportant sign flip). Using the `full_matrices=False` option ensures that for a tall matrix the shape of `U` is the same as the shape of `X`.

`np.linalg.svd()`

```
In [22]: V
```

```
Out[22]: array([[-0.53589947, -0.58318363, -0.27819087, -0.54343209],
                [ 0.41818087,  0.1879856 , -0.87280619, -0.16731864],
                [-0.34123273, -0.26814843, -0.37801579,  0.81777791],
                [ 0.6492278 , -0.74340748,  0.13387773,  0.08902432]])
```

```
In [23]: pcaUS.components_
```

```
Out[23]: array([[ 0.53589947,  0.58318363,  0.27819087,  0.54343209],
                [ 0.41818087,  0.1879856 , -0.87280619, -0.16731864],
                [-0.34123273, -0.26814843, -0.37801579,  0.81777791],
                [ 0.6492278 , -0.74340748,  0.13387773,  0.08902432]])
```

The matrix `U` corresponds to a *standardized* version of the PCA score matrix (each column standardized to have sum-of-squares one). If we multiply each column of `U` by the corresponding element of `D`, we recover the PCA scores exactly (up to a meaningless sign flip).

```
In [24]: (U * D[None,:])[:3]
```

```
Out[24]: array([[-0.9856,  1.1334, -0.4443,  0.1563],
                [-1.9501,  1.0732,  2.04  , -0.4386],
                [-1.7632, -0.746 ,  0.0548, -0.8347]])
```

```
In [25]: scores[:3]
```

```
Out[25]: array([[ 0.9856, -1.1334, -0.4443,  0.1563],
                [ 1.9501, -1.0732,  2.04  , -0.4386],
                [ 1.7632,  0.746 ,  0.0548, -0.8347]])
```

While it would be possible to carry out this lab using the `PCA()` estimator, here we use the `np.linalg.svd()` function in order to illustrate its use.

We now omit 20 entries in the 50×4 data matrix at random. We do so by first selecting 20 rows (states) at random, and then selecting one of the four entries in each row at random. This ensures that every row has at least three observed values.

```
In [26]: n_omit = 20
         np.random.seed(15)
         r_idx = np.random.choice(np.arange(X.shape[0]),
                                  n_omit,
                                  replace=False)
         c_idx = np.random.choice(np.arange(X.shape[1]),
                                  n_omit,
                                  replace=True)
         Xna = X.copy()
         Xna[r_idx, c_idx] = np.nan
```

Here the array `r_idx` contains 20 integers from 0 to 49; this represents the states (rows of `X`) that are selected to contain missing values. And `c_idx` contains 20 integers from 0 to 3, representing the features (columns in `X`) that contain the missing values for each of the selected states.

We now write some code to implement Algorithm 12.1. We first write a function that takes in a matrix, and returns an approximation to the matrix using the `svd()` function. This will be needed in Step 2 of Algorithm 12.1.

```
In [27]: def low_rank(X, M=1):
             U, D, V = np.linalg.svd(X)
             L = U[:,:M] * D[None,:M]
             return L.dot(V[:M])
```

To conduct Step 1 of the algorithm, we initialize Xhat — this is $\tilde{\mathbf{X}}$ in Algorithm 12.1 — by replacing the missing values with the column means of the non-missing entries. These are stored in Xbar below after running np.nanmean() over the row axis. We make a copy so that when we assign values to Xhat below we do not also overwrite the values in Xna.

np.nanmean()

In [28]:
```
Xhat = Xna.copy()
Xbar = np.nanmean(Xhat, axis=0)
Xhat[r_idx, c_idx] = Xbar[c_idx]
```

Before we begin Step 2, we set ourselves up to measure the progress of our iterations:

In [29]:
```
thresh = 1e-7
rel_err = 1
count = 0
ismiss = np.isnan(Xna)
mssold = np.mean(Xhat[~ismiss]**2)
mss0 = np.mean(Xna[~ismiss]**2)
```

Here ismiss is a logical matrix with the same dimensions as Xna; a given element is True if the corresponding matrix element is missing. The notation ~ismiss negates this boolean vector. This is useful because it allows us to access both the missing and non-missing entries. We store the mean of the squared non-missing elements in mss0. We store the mean squared error of the non-missing elements of the old version of Xhat in mssold (which currently agrees with mss0). We plan to store the mean squared error of the non-missing elements of the current version of Xhat in mss, and will then iterate Step 2 of Algorithm 12.1 until the *relative error*, defined as (mssold - mss) / mss0, falls below thresh = 1e-7. [9]

In Step 2(a) of Algorithm 12.1, we approximate Xhat using low_rank(); we call this Xapp. In Step 2(b), we use Xapp to update the estimates for elements in Xhat that are missing in Xna. Finally, in Step 2(c), we compute the relative error. These three steps are contained in the following while loop:

In [30]:
```
while rel_err > thresh:
    count += 1
    # Step 2(a)
    Xapp = low_rank(Xhat, M=1)
    # Step 2(b)
    Xhat[ismiss] = Xapp[ismiss]
    # Step 2(c)
    mss = np.mean(((Xna - Xapp)[~ismiss])**2)
    rel_err = (mssold - mss) / mss0
    mssold = mss
    print("Iteration: {0}, MSS:{1:.3f}, Rel.Err {2:.2e}"
          .format(count, mss, rel_err))
```

[9]Algorithm 12.1 tells us to iterate Step 2 until (12.14) is no longer decreasing. Determining whether (12.14) is decreasing requires us only to keep track of mssold - mss. However, in practice, we keep track of (mssold - mss) / mss0 instead: this makes it so that the number of iterations required for Algorithm 12.1 to converge does not depend on whether we multiplied the raw data **X** by a constant factor.

```
Iteration: 1, MSS:0.395, Rel.Err 5.99e-01
Iteration: 2, MSS:0.382, Rel.Err 1.33e-02
Iteration: 3, MSS:0.381, Rel.Err 1.44e-03
Iteration: 4, MSS:0.381, Rel.Err 1.79e-04
Iteration: 5, MSS:0.381, Rel.Err 2.58e-05
Iteration: 6, MSS:0.381, Rel.Err 4.22e-06
Iteration: 7, MSS:0.381, Rel.Err 7.65e-07
Iteration: 8, MSS:0.381, Rel.Err 1.48e-07
Iteration: 9, MSS:0.381, Rel.Err 2.95e-08
```

We see that after eight iterations, the relative error has fallen below `thresh = 1e-7`, and so the algorithm terminates. When this happens, the mean squared error of the non-missing elements equals 0.381.

Finally, we compute the correlation between the 20 imputed values and the actual values:

```
In [31]: np.corrcoef(Xapp[ismiss], X[ismiss])[0,1]
```

```
Out[31]: 0.711
```

In this lab, we implemented Algorithm 12.1 ourselves for didactic purposes. However, a reader who wishes to apply matrix completion to their data might look to more specialized `Python` implementations.

12.5.3 Clustering

K-Means Clustering

The estimator `sklearn.cluster.KMeans()` performs K-means clustering in `Python`. We begin with a simple simulated example in which there truly are two clusters in the data: the first 25 observations have a mean shift relative to the next 25 observations.

`Kmeans()`

```
In [32]: np.random.seed(0);
         X = np.random.standard_normal((50,2));
         X[:25,0] += 3;
         X[:25,1] -= 4;
```

We now perform K-means clustering with $K = 2$.

```
In [33]: kmeans = KMeans(n_clusters=2,
                         random_state=2,
                         n_init=20).fit(X)
```

We specify `random_state` to make the results reproducible. The cluster assignments of the 50 observations are contained in `kmeans.labels_`.

```
In [34]: kmeans.labels_
```

```
Out[34]: array([1, 1, 1, 1, 1, 1, 1, 1, 1, 1, 1, 1, 1, 1, 1, 1, 1, 1, 1,
                1, 1, 0, 1, 1, 1, 0, 0, 0, 0, 0, 0, 0, 0, 0, 0, 0, 0, 0,
                0, 0, 0, 0, 0, 0, 0, 0, 0, 0, 0], dtype=int32)
```

The K-means clustering perfectly separated the observations into two clusters even though we did not supply any group information to `KMeans()`. We can plot the data, with each observation colored according to its cluster assignment.

```
In [35]: fig, ax = plt.subplots(1, 1, figsize=(8,8))
         ax.scatter(X[:,0], X[:,1], c=kmeans.labels_)
         ax.set_title("K-Means Clustering Results with K=2");
```

Here the observations can be easily plotted because they are two-dimensional. If there were more than two variables then we could instead perform PCA and plot the first two principal component score vectors to represent the clusters.

In this example, we knew that there really were two clusters because we generated the data. However, for real data, we do not know the true number of clusters, nor whether they exist in any precise way. We could instead have performed K-means clustering on this example with $K = 3$.

```
In [36]: kmeans = KMeans(n_clusters=3,
                         random_state=3,
                         n_init=20).fit(X)
         fig, ax = plt.subplots(figsize=(8,8))
         ax.scatter(X[:,0], X[:,1], c=kmeans.labels_)
         ax.set_title("K-Means Clustering Results with K=3");
```

When $K = 3$, K-means clustering splits up the two clusters. We have used the `n_init` argument to run the K-means with 20 initial cluster assignments (the default is 10). If a value of `n_init` greater than one is used, then K-means clustering will be performed using multiple random assignments in Step 1 of Algorithm 12.2, and the `KMeans()` function will report only the best results. Here we compare using `n_init=1` to `n_init=20`.

```
In [37]: kmeans1 = KMeans(n_clusters=3,
                          random_state=3,
                          n_init=1).fit(X)
         kmeans20 = KMeans(n_clusters=3,
                           random_state=3,
                           n_init=20).fit(X);
         kmeans1.inertia_, kmeans20.inertia_
```

```
Out[37]: (78.06, 75.04)
```

Note that `kmeans.inertia_` is the total within-cluster sum of squares, which we seek to minimize by performing K-means clustering (12.17).

We *strongly* recommend always running K-means clustering with a large value of `n_init`, such as 20 or 50, since otherwise an undesirable local optimum may be obtained.

When performing K-means clustering, in addition to using multiple initial cluster assignments, it is also important to set a random seed using the `random_state` argument to `KMeans()`. This way, the initial cluster assignments in Step 1 can be replicated, and the K-means output will be fully reproducible.

Hierarchical Clustering

The `AgglomerativeClustering()` class from the `sklearn.clustering` package implements hierarchical clustering. As its name is long, we use the short hand `HClust` for *hierarchical clustering*. Note that this will not change

`Agglomerative Clustering()`

the return type when using this method, so instances will still be of class AgglomerativeClustering. In the following example we use the data from the previous lab to plot the hierarchical clustering dendrogram using complete, single, and average linkage clustering with Euclidean distance as the dissimilarity measure. We begin by clustering observations using complete linkage.

In [38]:
```
HClust = AgglomerativeClustering
hc_comp = HClust(distance_threshold=0,
                 n_clusters=None,
                 linkage='complete')
hc_comp.fit(X)
```

This computes the entire dendrogram. We could just as easily perform hierarchical clustering with average or single linkage instead:

In [39]:
```
hc_avg = HClust(distance_threshold=0,
                n_clusters=None,
                linkage='average');
hc_avg.fit(X)
hc_sing = HClust(distance_threshold=0,
                 n_clusters=None,
                 linkage='single');
hc_sing.fit(X);
```

To use a precomputed distance matrix, we provide an additional argument metric="precomputed". In the code below, the first four lines computes the 50×50 pairwise-distance matrix.

In [40]:
```
D = np.zeros((X.shape[0], X.shape[0]));
for i in range(X.shape[0]):
    x_ = np.multiply.outer(np.ones(X.shape[0]), X[i])
    D[i] = np.sqrt(np.sum((X - x_)**2, 1));
hc_sing_pre = HClust(distance_threshold=0,
                     n_clusters=None,
                     metric='precomputed',
                     linkage='single')
hc_sing_pre.fit(D)
```

We use dendrogram() from scipy.cluster.hierarchy to plot the dendrogram. However, dendrogram() expects a so-called *linkage-matrix representation* of the clustering, which is not provided by AgglomerativeClustering(), but can be computed. The function compute_linkage() in the ISLP.cluster package is provided for this purpose. dendrogram() compute_linkage() ISLP.cluster

We can now plot the dendrograms. The numbers at the bottom of the plot identify each observation. The dendrogram() function has a default method to color different branches of the tree that suggests a pre-defined cut of the tree at a particular depth. We prefer to overwrite this default by setting this threshold to be infinite. Since we want this behavior for many dendrograms, we store these values in a dictionary cargs and pass this as keyword arguments using the notation **cargs.

In [41]:
```
cargs = {'color_threshold':-np.inf,
         'above_threshold_color':'black'}
linkage_comp = compute_linkage(hc_comp)
fig, ax = plt.subplots(1, 1, figsize=(8, 8))
```

```
dendrogram(linkage_comp,
           ax=ax,
           **cargs);
```

We may want to color branches of the tree above and below a cut-threshold differently. This can be achieved by changing the `color_threshold`. Let's cut the tree at a height of 4, coloring links that merge above 4 in black.

In [42]:
```
fig, ax = plt.subplots(1, 1, figsize=(8, 8))
dendrogram(linkage_comp,
           ax=ax,
           color_threshold=4,
           above_threshold_color='black');
```

To determine the cluster labels for each observation associated with a given cut of the dendrogram, we can use the `cut_tree()` function from `scipy.cluster.hierarchy`:

`cut_tree()`

In [43]:
```
cut_tree(linkage_comp, n_clusters=4).T
```

Out[43]:
```
array([[0, 1, 0, 0, 1, 1, 0, 1, 0, 0, 2, 0, 0, 0, 1, 1, 0, 0, 1,
        0, 0, 2, 0, 2, 2, 3, 2, 3, 3, 3, 3, 2, 3, 3, 3, 3, 2, 3,
        3, 3, 3, 2, 3, 3, 3, 3, 3, 3, 3, 3]])
```

This can also be achieved by providing an argument `n_clusters` to `HClust()`; however each cut would require recomputing the clustering. Similarly, trees may be cut by distance threshold with an argument of `distance_threshold` to `HClust()` or `height` to `cut_tree()`.

In [44]:
```
cut_tree(linkage_comp, height=5)
```

Out[44]:
```
array([[0, 0, 0, 0, 0, 0, 0, 0, 0, 0, 1, 0, 0, 0, 0, 0, 0, 0, 0,
        0, 0, 1, 0, 1, 1, 2, 1, 2, 2, 2, 2, 1, 2, 2, 2, 2, 1, 2,
        2, 2, 2, 1, 2, 2, 2, 2, 2, 2, 2, 2]])
```

To scale the variables before performing hierarchical clustering of the observations, we use `StandardScaler()` as in our PCA example:

In [45]:
```
scaler = StandardScaler()
X_scale = scaler.fit_transform(X)
hc_comp_scale = HClust(distance_threshold=0,
                       n_clusters=None,
                       linkage='complete').fit(X_scale)
linkage_comp_scale = compute_linkage(hc_comp_scale)
fig, ax = plt.subplots(1, 1, figsize=(8, 8))
dendrogram(linkage_comp_scale, ax=ax, **cargs)
ax.set_title("Hierarchical Clustering with Scaled Features");
```

Correlation-based distances between observations can be used for clustering. The correlation between two observations measures the similarity of their feature values.[10] With n observations, the $n \times n$ correlation matrix

[10]Suppose each observation has p features, each a single numerical value. We measure the similarity of two such observations by computing the correlation of these p pairs of numbers.

can then be used as a similarity (or affinity) matrix, i.e. so that one minus the correlation matrix is the dissimilarity matrix used for clustering.

Note that using correlation only makes sense for data with at least three features since the absolute correlation between any two observations with measurements on two features is always one. Hence, we will cluster a three-dimensional data set.

In [46]:
```
X = np.random.standard_normal((30, 3))
corD = 1 - np.corrcoef(X)
hc_cor = HClust(linkage='complete',
                distance_threshold=0,
                n_clusters=None,
                metric='precomputed')
hc_cor.fit(corD)
linkage_cor = compute_linkage(hc_cor)
fig, ax = plt.subplots(1, 1, figsize=(8, 8))
dendrogram(linkage_cor, ax=ax, **cargs)
ax.set_title("Complete Linkage with Correlation-Based Dissimilarity
    ");
```

12.5.4 NCI60 Data Example

Unsupervised techniques are often used in the analysis of genomic data. In particular, PCA and hierarchical clustering are popular tools. We illustrate these techniques on the NCI60 cancer cell line microarray data, which consists of 6830 gene expression measurements on 64 cancer cell lines.

In [47]:
```
NCI60 = load_data('NCI60')
nci_labs = NCI60['labels']
nci_data = NCI60['data']
```

Each cell line is labeled with a cancer type. We do not make use of the cancer types in performing PCA and clustering, as these are unsupervised techniques. But after performing PCA and clustering, we will check to see the extent to which these cancer types agree with the results of these unsupervised techniques.

The data has 64 rows and 6830 columns.

In [48]:
```
nci_data.shape
```

Out[48]:
```
(64, 6830)
```

We begin by examining the cancer types for the cell lines.

In [49]:
```
nci_labs.value_counts()
```

Out[49]:
```
label
NSCLC        9
RENAL        9
MELANOMA     8
BREAST       7
COLON        7
LEUKEMIA     6
OVARIAN      6
```

```
CNS              5
PROSTATE         2
K562A-repro      1
K562B-repro      1
MCF7A-repro      1
MCF7D-repro      1
UNKNOWN          1
dtype: int64
```

PCA on the NCI60 Data

We first perform PCA on the data after scaling the variables (genes) to have standard deviation one, although here one could reasonably argue that it is better not to scale the genes as they are measured in the same units.

In [50]:
```
scaler = StandardScaler()
nci_scaled = scaler.fit_transform(nci_data)
nci_pca = PCA()
nci_scores = nci_pca.fit_transform(nci_scaled)
```

We now plot the first few principal component score vectors, in order to visualize the data. The observations (cell lines) corresponding to a given cancer type will be plotted in the same color, so that we can see to what extent the observations within a cancer type are similar to each other.

In [51]:
```
cancer_types = list(np.unique(nci_labs))
nci_groups = np.array([cancer_types.index(lab)
                       for lab in nci_labs.values])
fig, axes = plt.subplots(1, 2, figsize=(15,6))
ax = axes[0]
ax.scatter(nci_scores[:,0],
           nci_scores[:,1],
           c=nci_groups,
           marker='o',
           s=50)
ax.set_xlabel('PC1'); ax.set_ylabel('PC2')
ax = axes[1]
ax.scatter(nci_scores[:,0],
           nci_scores[:,2],
           c=nci_groups,
           marker='o',
           s=50)
ax.set_xlabel('PC1'); ax.set_ylabel('PC3');
```

The resulting plots are shown in Figure 12.17. On the whole, cell lines corresponding to a single cancer type do tend to have similar values on the first few principal component score vectors. This indicates that cell lines from the same cancer type tend to have pretty similar gene expression levels.

We can also plot the percent variance explained by the principal components as well as the cumulative percent variance explained. This is similar to the plots we made earlier for the `USArrests` data.

In [52]:
```
fig, axes = plt.subplots(1, 2, figsize=(15,6))
ax = axes[0]
ticks = np.arange(nci_pca.n_components_)+1
```

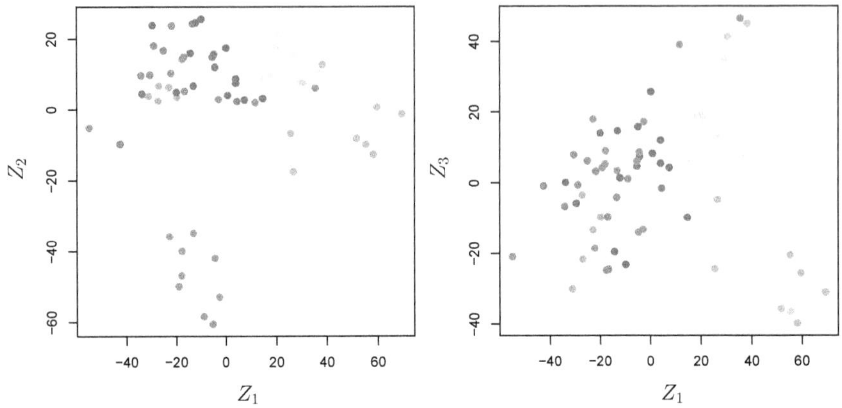

FIGURE 12.17. *Projections of the* NCI60 *cancer cell lines onto the first three principal components (in other words, the scores for the first three principal components). On the whole, observations belonging to a single cancer type tend to lie near each other in this low-dimensional space. It would not have been possible to visualize the data without using a dimension reduction method such as PCA, since based on the full data set there are* $\binom{6,830}{2}$ *possible scatterplots, none of which would have been particularly informative.*

```
ax.plot(ticks,
        nci_pca.explained_variance_ratio_,
        marker='o')
ax.set_xlabel('Principal Component');
ax.set_ylabel('PVE')
ax = axes[1]
ax.plot(ticks,
        nci_pca.explained_variance_ratio_.cumsum(),
        marker='o');
ax.set_xlabel('Principal Component')
ax.set_ylabel('Cumulative PVE');
```

The resulting plots are shown in Figure 12.18.

We see that together, the first seven principal components explain around 40% of the variance in the data. This is not a huge amount of the variance. However, looking at the scree plot, we see that while each of the first seven principal components explain a substantial amount of variance, there is a marked decrease in the variance explained by further principal components. That is, there is an *elbow* in the plot after approximately the seventh principal component. This suggests that there may be little benefit to examining more than seven or so principal components (though even examining seven principal components may be difficult).

Clustering the Observations of the NCI60 Data

We now perform hierarchical clustering of the cell lines in the `NCI60` data using complete, single, and average linkage. Once again, the goal is to find out whether or not the observations cluster into distinct types of cancer. Euclidean distance is used as the dissimilarity measure. We first write a short function to produce the three dendrograms.

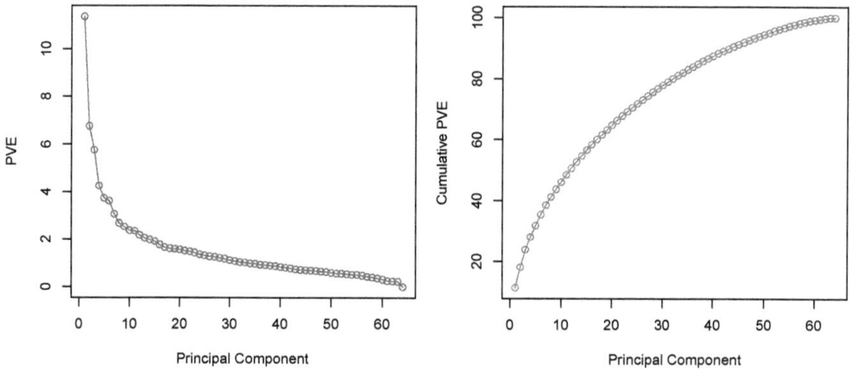

FIGURE 12.18. *The PVE of the principal components of the* `NCI60` *cancer cell line microarray data set.* Left: *the PVE of each principal component is shown.* Right: *the cumulative PVE of the principal components is shown. Together, all principal components explain 100,% of the variance.*

In [53]:
```
def plot_nci(linkage, ax, cut=-np.inf):
    cargs = {'above_threshold_color':'black',
             'color_threshold':cut}
    hc = HClust(n_clusters=None,
                distance_threshold=0,
                linkage=linkage.lower()).fit(nci_scaled)
    linkage_ = compute_linkage(hc)
    dendrogram(linkage_,
               ax=ax,
               labels=np.asarray(nci_labs),
               leaf_font_size=10,
               **cargs)
    ax.set_title('%s Linkage' % linkage)
    return hc
```

Let's plot our results.

In [54]:
```
fig, axes = plt.subplots(3, 1, figsize=(15,30))
ax = axes[0]; hc_comp = plot_nci('Complete', ax)
ax = axes[1]; hc_avg = plot_nci('Average', ax)
ax = axes[2]; hc_sing = plot_nci('Single', ax)
```

The results are shown in Figure 12.19. We see that the choice of linkage certainly does affect the results obtained. Typically, single linkage will tend to yield *trailing* clusters: very large clusters onto which individual observations attach one-by-one. On the other hand, complete and average linkage tend to yield more balanced, attractive clusters. For this reason, complete and average linkage are generally preferred to single linkage. Clearly cell lines within a single cancer type do tend to cluster together, although the clustering is not perfect. We will use complete linkage hierarchical clustering for the analysis that follows.

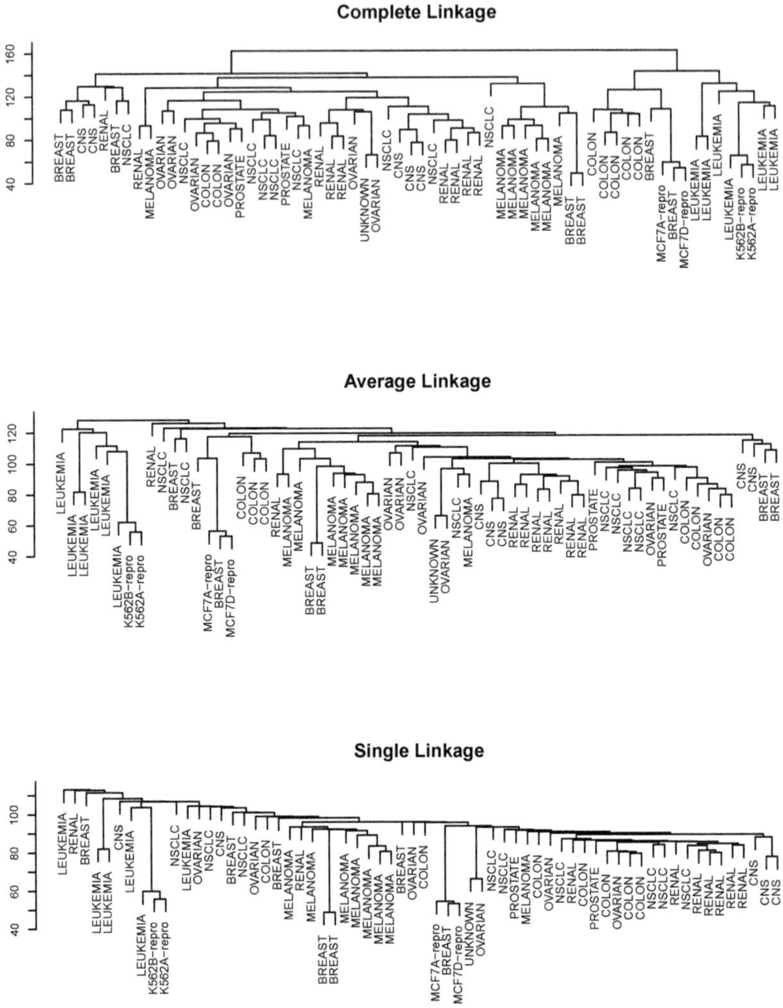

FIGURE 12.19. *The* NCI60 *cancer cell line microarray data, clustered with average, complete, and single linkage, and using Euclidean distance as the dissimilarity measure. Complete and average linkage tend to yield evenly sized clusters whereas single linkage tends to yield extended clusters to which single leaves are fused one by one.*

We can cut the dendrogram at the height that will yield a particular number of clusters, say four:

In [55]:
```
linkage_comp = compute_linkage(hc_comp)
comp_cut = cut_tree(linkage_comp, n_clusters=4).reshape(-1)
pd.crosstab(nci_labs['label'],
            pd.Series(comp_cut.reshape(-1), name='Complete'))
```

There are some clear patterns. All the leukemia cell lines fall in one cluster, while the breast cancer cell lines are spread out over three different clusters.

We can plot a cut on the dendrogram that produces these four clusters:

In [56]:
```
fig, ax = plt.subplots(figsize=(10,10))
plot_nci('Complete', ax, cut=140)
ax.axhline(140, c='r', linewidth=4);
```

The `axhline()` function draws a horizontal line line on top of any existing set of axes. The argument `140` plots a horizontal line at height 140 on the dendrogram; this is a height that results in four distinct clusters. It is easy to verify that the resulting clusters are the same as the ones we obtained in `comp_cut`.

We claimed earlier in Section 12.4.2 that K-means clustering and hierarchical clustering with the dendrogram cut to obtain the same number of clusters can yield very different results. How do these `NCI60` hierarchical clustering results compare to what we get if we perform K-means clustering with $K = 4$?

In [57]:
```
nci_kmeans = KMeans(n_clusters=4,
                    random_state=0,
                    n_init=20).fit(nci_scaled)
pd.crosstab(pd.Series(comp_cut, name='HClust'),
            pd.Series(nci_kmeans.labels_, name='K-means'))
```

Out[57]:

K-means HClust	0	1	2	3
0	28	3	9	0
1	7	0	0	0
2	0	0	0	8
3	0	9	0	0

We see that the four clusters obtained using hierarchical clustering and K-means clustering are somewhat different. First we note that the labels in the two clusterings are arbitrary. That is, swapping the identifier of the cluster does not change the clustering. We see here Cluster 3 in K-means clustering is identical to cluster 2 in hierarchical clustering. However, the other clusters differ: for instance, cluster 0 in K-means clustering contains a portion of the observations assigned to cluster 0 by hierarchical clustering, as well as all of the observations assigned to cluster 1 by hierarchical clustering.

Rather than performing hierarchical clustering on the entire data matrix, we can also perform hierarchical clustering on the first few principal component score vectors, regarding these first few components as a less noisy version of the data.

In [58]:
```
hc_pca = HClust(n_clusters=None,
                distance_threshold=0,
                linkage='complete'
                ).fit(nci_scores[:,:5])
linkage_pca = compute_linkage(hc_pca)
fig, ax = plt.subplots(figsize=(8,8))
dendrogram(linkage_pca,
           labels=np.asarray(nci_labs),
           leaf_font_size=10,
           ax=ax,
           **cargs)
ax.set_title("Hier. Clust. on First Five Score Vectors")
pca_labels = pd.Series(cut_tree(linkage_pca,
                                n_clusters=4).reshape(-1),
                       name='Complete-PCA')
pd.crosstab(nci_labs['label'], pca_labels)
```

12.6 Exercises

Conceptual

1. This problem involves the K-means clustering algorithm.

   (a) Prove (12.18).

   (b) On the basis of this identity, argue that the K-means clustering algorithm (Algorithm 12.2) decreases the objective (12.17) at each iteration.

2. Suppose that we have four observations, for which we compute a dissimilarity matrix, given by

$$\begin{bmatrix} & 0.3 & 0.4 & 0.7 \\ 0.3 & & 0.5 & 0.8 \\ 0.4 & 0.5 & & 0.45 \\ 0.7 & 0.8 & 0.45 & \end{bmatrix}.$$

   For instance, the dissimilarity between the first and second observations is 0.3, and the dissimilarity between the second and fourth observations is 0.8.

   (a) On the basis of this dissimilarity matrix, sketch the dendrogram that results from hierarchically clustering these four observations using complete linkage. Be sure to indicate on the plot the height at which each fusion occurs, as well as the observations corresponding to each leaf in the dendrogram.

   (b) Repeat (a), this time using single linkage clustering.

   (c) Suppose that we cut the dendrogram obtained in (a) such that two clusters result. Which observations are in each cluster?

   (d) Suppose that we cut the dendrogram obtained in (b) such that two clusters result. Which observations are in each cluster?

(e) It is mentioned in this chapter that at each fusion in the dendrogram, the position of the two clusters being fused can be swapped without changing the meaning of the dendrogram. Draw a dendrogram that is equivalent to the dendrogram in (a), for which two or more of the leaves are repositioned, but for which the meaning of the dendrogram is the same.

3. In this problem, you will perform K-means clustering manually, with $K = 2$, on a small example with $n = 6$ observations and $p = 2$ features. The observations are as follows.

Obs.	X_1	X_2
1	1	4
2	1	3
3	0	4
4	5	1
5	6	2
6	4	0

(a) Plot the observations.

(b) Randomly assign a cluster label to each observation. You can use the `np.random.choice()` function to do this. Report the cluster labels for each observation.

(c) Compute the centroid for each cluster.

(d) Assign each observation to the centroid to which it is closest, in terms of Euclidean distance. Report the cluster labels for each observation.

(e) Repeat (c) and (d) until the answers obtained stop changing.

(f) In your plot from (a), color the observations according to the cluster labels obtained.

4. Suppose that for a particular data set, we perform hierarchical clustering using single linkage and using complete linkage. We obtain two dendrograms.

(a) At a certain point on the single linkage dendrogram, the clusters $\{1, 2, 3\}$ and $\{4, 5\}$ fuse. On the complete linkage dendrogram, the clusters $\{1, 2, 3\}$ and $\{4, 5\}$ also fuse at a certain point. Which fusion will occur higher on the tree, or will they fuse at the same height, or is there not enough information to tell?

(b) At a certain point on the single linkage dendrogram, the clusters $\{5\}$ and $\{6\}$ fuse. On the complete linkage dendrogram, the clusters $\{5\}$ and $\{6\}$ also fuse at a certain point. Which fusion will occur higher on the tree, or will they fuse at the same height, or is there not enough information to tell?

5. In words, describe the results that you would expect if you performed K-means clustering of the eight shoppers in Figure 12.16, on the basis of their sock and computer purchases, with $K = 2$. Give three answers, one for each of the variable scalings displayed. Explain.

6. We saw in Section 12.2.2 that the principal component loading and score vectors provide an approximation to a matrix, in the sense of (12.5). Specifically, the principal component score and loading vectors solve the optimization problem given in (12.6).

   Now, suppose that the M principal component score vectors z_{im}, $m = 1, \ldots, M$, are known. Using (12.6), explain that each of the first M principal component loading vectors ϕ_{jm}, $m = 1, \ldots, M$, can be obtained by performing p separate least squares linear regressions. In each regression, the principal component score vectors are the predictors, and one of the features of the data matrix is the response.

Applied

7. In this chapter, we mentioned the use of correlation-based distance and Euclidean distance as dissimilarity measures for hierarchical clustering. It turns out that these two measures are almost equivalent: if each observation has been centered to have mean zero and standard deviation one, and if we let r_{ij} denote the correlation between the ith and jth observations, then the quantity $1 - r_{ij}$ is proportional to the squared Euclidean distance between the ith and jth observations.

   On the `USArrests` data, show that this proportionality holds.

   Hint: The Euclidean distance can be calculated using the `pairwise_distances()` *function from the* `sklearn.metrics` *module, and correlations can be calculated using the* `np.corrcoef()` *function.*

   `pairwise_distances()`

8. In Section 12.2.3, a formula for calculating PVE was given in Equation 12.10. We also saw that the PVE can be obtained using the `explained_variance_ratio_` attribute of a fitted `PCA()` estimator.

   On the `USArrests` data, calculate PVE in two ways:

   (a) Using the `explained_variance_ratio_` output of the fitted `PCA()` estimator, as was done in Section 12.2.3.

   (b) By applying Equation 12.10 directly. The loadings are stored as the `components_` attribute of the fitted `PCA()` estimator. Use those loadings in Equation 12.10 to obtain the PVE.

   These two approaches should give the same results.

   Hint: You will only obtain the same results in (a) and (b) if the same data is used in both cases. For instance, if in (a) you performed `PCA()` *using centered and scaled variables, then you must center and scale the variables before applying Equation 12.10 in (b).*

9. Consider the `USArrests` data. We will now perform hierarchical clustering on the states.

   (a) Using hierarchical clustering with complete linkage and Euclidean distance, cluster the states.

   (b) Cut the dendrogram at a height that results in three distinct clusters. Which states belong to which clusters?

(c) Hierarchically cluster the states using complete linkage and Euclidean distance, *after scaling the variables to have standard deviation one.*

(d) What effect does scaling the variables have on the hierarchical clustering obtained? In your opinion, should the variables be scaled before the inter-observation dissimilarities are computed? Provide a justification for your answer.

10. In this problem, you will generate simulated data, and then perform PCA and K-means clustering on the data.

(a) Generate a simulated data set with 20 observations in each of three classes (i.e. 60 observations total), and 50 variables.

Hint: There are a number of functions in `Python` *that you can use to generate data. One example is the* `normal()` *method of the* `random()` *function in* `numpy`*; the* `uniform()` *method is another option. Be sure to add a mean shift to the observations in each class so that there are three distinct classes.*

(b) Perform PCA on the 60 observations and plot the first two principal component score vectors. Use a different color to indicate the observations in each of the three classes. If the three classes appear separated in this plot, then continue on to part (c). If not, then return to part (a) and modify the simulation so that there is greater separation between the three classes. Do not continue to part (c) until the three classes show at least some separation in the first two principal component score vectors.

(c) Perform K-means clustering of the observations with $K = 3$. How well do the clusters that you obtained in K-means clustering compare to the true class labels?

Hint: You can use the `pd.crosstab()` *function in* `Python` *to compare the true class labels to the class labels obtained by clustering. Be careful how you interpret the results: K-means clustering will arbitrarily number the clusters, so you cannot simply check whether the true class labels and clustering labels are the same.*

(d) Perform K-means clustering with $K = 2$. Describe your results.

(e) Now perform K-means clustering with $K = 4$, and describe your results.

(f) Now perform K-means clustering with $K = 3$ on the first two principal component score vectors, rather than on the raw data. That is, perform K-means clustering on the 60×2 matrix of which the first column is the first principal component score vector, and the second column is the second principal component score vector. Comment on the results.

(g) Using the `StandardScaler()` estimator, perform K-means clustering with $K = 3$ on the data *after scaling each variable to have standard deviation one.* How do these results compare to those obtained in (b)? Explain.

11. Write a `Python` function to perform matrix completion as in Algorithm 12.1, and as outlined in Section 12.5.2. In each iteration, the function should keep track of the relative error, as well as the iteration count. Iterations should continue until the relative error is small enough or until some maximum number of iterations is reached (set a default value for this maximum number). Furthermore, there should be an option to print out the progress in each iteration.

    Test your function on the `Boston` data. First, standardize the features to have mean zero and standard deviation one using the `StandardScaler()` function. Run an experiment where you randomly leave out an increasing (and nested) number of observations from 5% to 30%, in steps of 5%. Apply Algorithm 12.1 with $M = 1, 2, \ldots, 8$. Display the approximation error as a function of the fraction of observations that are missing, and the value of M, averaged over 10 repetitions of the experiment.

12. In Section 12.5.2, Algorithm 12.1 was implemented using the `svd()` function from the `np.linalg` module. However, given the connection between the `svd()` function and the `PCA()` estimator highlighted in the lab, we could have instead implemented the algorithm using `PCA()`.

    Write a function to implement Algorithm 12.1 that makes use of `PCA()` rather than `svd()`.

13. On the book website, `www.statlearning.com`, there is a gene expression data set (`Ch12Ex13.csv`) that consists of 40 tissue samples with measurements on 1,000 genes. The first 20 samples are from healthy patients, while the second 20 are from a diseased group.

    (a) Load in the data using `pd.read_csv()`. You will need to select `header = None`.

    (b) Apply hierarchical clustering to the samples using correlation-based distance, and plot the dendrogram. Do the genes separate the samples into the two groups? Do your results depend on the type of linkage used?

    (c) Your collaborator wants to know which genes differ the most across the two groups. Suggest a way to answer this question, and apply it here.

13
Multiple Testing

Thus far, this textbook has mostly focused on *estimation* and its close cousin, *prediction*. In this chapter, we instead focus on hypothesis testing, which is key to conducting *inference*. We remind the reader that inference was briefly discussed in Chapter 2.

While Section 13.1 provides a brief review of null hypotheses, p-values, test statistics, and other key ideas in hypothesis testing, this chapter assumes that the reader has had previous exposure to these topics. In particular, we will not focus on *why* or *how* to conduct a hypothesis test — a topic on which entire books can be (and have been) written! Instead, we will assume that the reader is interested in testing some particular set of null hypotheses, and has a specific plan in mind for how to conduct the tests and obtain p-values.

Much of the emphasis in classical statistics focuses on testing a single null hypothesis, such as H_0*: the expected blood pressure of mice in the control group equals the expected blood pressure of mice in the treatment group.* Of course, we would probably like to discover that there *is* a difference between the mean blood pressure in the two groups. But for reasons that will become clear, we construct a null hypothesis corresponding to no difference.

In contemporary settings, we are often faced with huge amounts of data, and consequently may wish to test a great many null hypotheses. For instance, rather than simply testing H_0, we might want to test m null hypotheses, $H_{01}, \ldots, H_{0m}$, where H_{0j}*: the expected value of the* j^{th} *biomarker among mice in the control group equals the expected value of the* j^{th} *biomarker among mice in the treatment group.* When conducting *multiple testing*, we need to be very careful about how we interpret the results, in order to avoid erroneously rejecting far too many null hypotheses.

This chapter discusses classical as well as more contemporary ways to conduct multiple testing in a big-data setting. In Section 13.2, we highlight the challenges associated with multiple testing. Classical solutions to these

G. James et al., *An Introduction to Statistical Learning*, Springer Texts in Statistics,
https://doi.org/10.1007/978-3-031-38747-0_13

challenges are presented in Section 13.3, and more contemporary solutions in Sections 13.4 and 13.5.

In particular, Section 13.4 focuses on the false discovery rate. The notion of the false discovery rate dates back to the 1990s. It quickly rose in popularity in the early 2000s, when large-scale data sets began to come out of genomics. These datasets were unique not only because of their large size,[1] but also because they were typically collected for *exploratory* purposes: researchers collected these datasets in order to test a huge number of null hypotheses, rather than just a very small number of pre-specified null hypotheses. Today, of course, huge datasets are collected without a pre-specified null hypothesis across virtually all fields. As we will see, the false discovery rate is perfectly-suited for this modern-day reality.

This chapter naturally centers upon the classical statistical technique of p-values, used to quantify the results of hypothesis tests. At the time of writing of this book (2020), p-values have recently been the topic of extensive commentary in the social science research community, to the extent that some social science journals have gone so far as to ban the use of p-values altogether! We will simply comment that when properly understood and applied, p-values provide a powerful tool for drawing inferential conclusions from our data.

13.1 A Quick Review of Hypothesis Testing

Hypothesis tests provide a rigorous statistical framework for answering simple "yes-or-no" questions about data, such as the following:

1. Is the true coefficient β_j in a linear regression of Y onto $X_1, \ldots, X_p$ equal to zero?[2]

2. Is there a difference in the expected blood pressure of laboratory mice in the control group and laboratory mice in the treatment group?[3]

In Section 13.1.1, we briefly review the steps involved in hypothesis testing. Section 13.1.2 discusses the different types of mistakes, or errors, that can occur in hypothesis testing.

13.1.1 Testing a Hypothesis

Conducting a hypothesis test typically proceeds in four steps. First, we define the null and alternative hypotheses. Next, we construct a test statistic that summarizes the strength of evidence against the null hypothesis. We then compute a p-value that quantifies the probability of having obtained

---

[1] Microarray data was viewed as "big data" at the time, although by today's standards, this label seems quaint: a microarray dataset can be (and typically was) stored in a Microsoft Excel spreadsheet!

[2] This hypothesis test was discussed on page 76 of Chapter 3.

[3] The "treatment group" refers to the set of mice that receive an experimental treatment, and the "control group" refers to those that do not.

a comparable or more extreme value of the test statistic under the null hypothesis. Finally, based on the p-value, we decide whether to reject the null hypothesis. We now briefly discuss each of these steps in turn.

Step 1: Define the Null and Alternative Hypotheses

In hypothesis testing, we divide the world into two possibilities: the *null hypothesis* and the *alternative hypothesis*. The null hypothesis, denoted H_0, is the default state of belief about the world.[4] For instance, null hypotheses associated with the two questions posed earlier in this chapter are as follows:

null hypothesis

alternative hypothesis

1. The true coefficient β_j in a linear regression of Y onto $X_1, \ldots, X_p$ equals zero.

2. There is no difference between the expected blood pressure of mice in the control and treatment groups.

The null hypothesis is boring by construction: it may well be true, but we might hope that our data will tell us otherwise.

The alternative hypothesis, denoted H_a, represents something different and unexpected: for instance, that there *is* a difference between the expected blood pressure of the mice in the two groups. Typically, the alternative hypothesis simply posits that the null hypothesis does not hold: if the null hypothesis states that *there is no difference between A and B*, then the alternative hypothesis states that *there is a difference between A and B*.

It is important to note that the treatment of H_0 and H_a is asymmetric. H_0 is treated as the default state of the world, and we focus on using data to reject H_0. If we reject H_0, then this provides evidence in favor of H_a. We can think of rejecting H_0 as making a *discovery* about our data: namely, we are discovering that H_0 does not hold! By contrast, if we fail to reject H_0, then our findings are more nebulous: we will not know whether we failed to reject H_0 because our sample size was too small (in which case testing H_0 again on a larger or higher-quality dataset might lead to rejection), or whether we failed to reject H_0 because H_0 really holds.

Step 2: Construct the Test Statistic

Next, we wish to use our data in order to find evidence for or against the null hypothesis. In order to do this, we must compute a *test statistic*, denoted T, which summarizes the extent to which our data are consistent with H_0. The way in which we construct T depends on the nature of the null hypothesis that we are testing.

test statistic

To make things concrete, let $x_1^t, \ldots, x_{n_t}^t$ denote the blood pressure measurements for the n_t mice in the treatment group, and let $x_1^c, \ldots, x_{n_c}^c$ denote the blood pressure measurements for the n_c mice in the control group, and $\mu_t = \mathrm{E}(X^t)$, $\mu_c = \mathrm{E}(X^c)$. To test $H_0 : \mu_t = \mu_c$, we make use of a *two-sample t-statistic*,[5] defined as

two-sample t-statistic

[4] H_0 is pronounced "H naught" or "H zero".

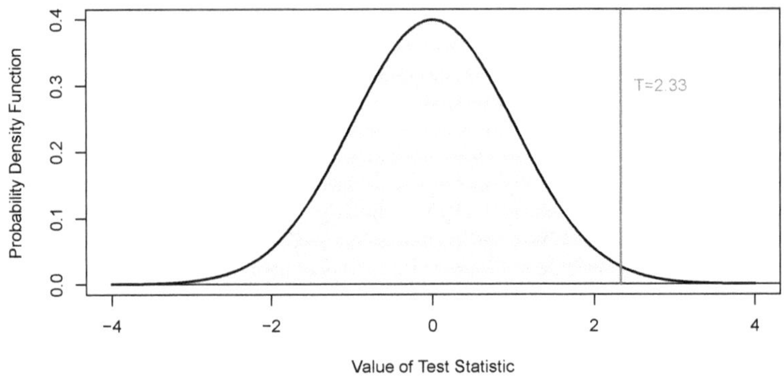

FIGURE 13.1. *The density function for the* $N(0,1)$ *distribution, with the vertical line indicating a value of* 2.33. *1% of the area under the curve falls to the right of the vertical line, so there is only a 2% chance of observing a* $N(0,1)$ *value that is greater than* 2.33 *or less than* -2.33. *Therefore, if a test statistic has a* $N(0,1)$ *null distribution, then an observed test statistic of* $T = 2.33$ *leads to a p-value of 0.02.*

$$T = \frac{\hat{\mu}_t - \hat{\mu}_c}{s\sqrt{\frac{1}{n_t} + \frac{1}{n_c}}} \tag{13.1}$$

where $\hat{\mu}_t = \frac{1}{n_t}\sum_{i=1}^{n_t} x_i^t$, $\hat{\mu}_c = \frac{1}{n_c}\sum_{i=1}^{n_c} x_i^c$, and

$$s = \sqrt{\frac{(n_t - 1)s_t^2 + (n_c - 1)s_c^2}{n_t + n_c - 2}} \tag{13.2}$$

is an estimator of the pooled standard deviation of the two samples.[6] Here, s_t^2 and s_c^2 are unbiased estimators of the variance of the blood pressure in the treatment and control groups, respectively. A large (absolute) value of T provides evidence against $H_0 : \mu_t = \mu_c$, and hence evidence in support of $H_a : \mu_t \neq \mu_c$.

Step 3: Compute the p-Value

In the previous section, we noted that a large (absolute) value of a two-sample t-statistic provides evidence against H_0. This begs the question: *how large is large?* In other words, how much evidence against H_0 is provided by a given value of the test statistic?

The notion of a *p-value* provides us with a way to formalize as well as answer this question. The p-value is defined as the probability of observing a test statistic equal to or more extreme than the observed statistic, *under the assumption that* H_0 *is in fact true.* Therefore, a small p-value provides evidence *against* H_0. p-value

[5]The t-statistic derives its name from the fact that, under H_0, it follows a t-distribution.

[6]Note that (13.2) assumes that the control and treatment groups have equal variance. Without this assumption, (13.2) would take a slightly different form.

To make this concrete, suppose that $T = 2.33$ for the test statistic in (13.1). Then, we can ask: what is the probability of having observed such a large value of T, if indeed H_0 holds? It turns out that under H_0, the distribution of T in (13.1) follows approximately a $N(0, 1)$ distribution[7] — that is, a normal distribution with mean 0 and variance 1. This distribution is displayed in Figure 13.1. We see that the vast majority — 98% — of the $N(0, 1)$ distribution falls between -2.33 and 2.33. This means that under H_0, we would expect to see such a large value of $|T|$ only 2% of the time. Therefore, the p-value corresponding to $T = 2.33$ is 0.02.

The distribution of the test statistic under H_0 (also known as the test statistic's *null distribution*) will depend on the details of what type of null hypothesis is being tested, and what type of test statistic is used. In general, most commonly-used test statistics follow a well-known statistical distribution under the null hypothesis — such as a normal distribution, a t-distribution, a χ^2-distribution, or an F-distribution — provided that the sample size is sufficiently large and that some other assumptions hold. Typically, the R function that is used to compute a test statistic will make use of this null distribution in order to output a p-value. In Section 13.5, we will see an approach to estimate the null distribution of a test statistic using re-sampling; in many contemporary settings, this is a very attractive option, as it exploits the availability of fast computers in order to avoid having to make potentially problematic assumptions about the data.

null distribution

The p-value is perhaps one of the most used and abused notions in all of statistics. In particular, it is sometimes said that the p-value is the probability that H_0 holds, i.e., that the null hypothesis is true. This is not correct! The one and only correct interpretation of the p-value is as the fraction of the time that we would expect to see such an extreme value of the test statistic[8] if we repeated the experiment many many times, *provided H_0 holds.*

In Step 2 we computed a test statistic, and noted that a large (absolute) value of the test statistic provides evidence against H_0. In Step 3 the test statistic was converted to a p-value, with small p-values providing evidence against H_0. What, then, did we accomplish by converting the test statistic from Step 2 into a p-value in Step 3? To answer this question, suppose a data analyst conducts a statistical test, and reports a test statistic of $T = 17.3$. Does this provide strong evidence against H_0? It's impossible to know, without more information: in particular, we would need to know

[7]More precisely, assuming that the observations are drawn from a normal distribution, then T follows a t-distribution with $n_t + n_c - 2$ degrees of freedom. Provided that $n_t + n_c - 2$ is larger than around 40, this is very well-approximated by a $N(0, 1)$ distribution. In Section 13.5, we will see an alternative and often more attractive way to approximate the null distribution of T, which avoids making stringent assumptions about the data.

[8]A *one-sided* p-value is the probability of seeing such an extreme value of the test statistic; e.g. the probability of seeing a test statistic greater than or equal to $T = 2.33$. A *two-sided* p-value is the probability of seeing such an extreme value of the *absolute* test statistic; e.g. the probability of seeing a test statistic greater than or equal to 2.33 or less than or equal to -2.33. The default recommendation is to report a two-sided p-value rather than a one-sided p-value, unless there is a clear and compelling reason that only one direction of the test statistic is of scientific interest.

		Truth	
		H_0	H_a
Decision	Reject H_0	Type I Error	Correct
	Do Not Reject H_0	Correct	Type II Error

TABLE 13.1. *A summary of the possible scenarios associated with testing the null hypothesis H_0. Type I errors are also known as false positives, and Type II errors as false negatives.*

what value of the test statistic should be expected, under H_0. This is exactly what a p-value gives us. In other words, a p-value allows us to transform our test statistic, which is measured on some arbitrary and uninterpretable scale, into a number between 0 and 1 that can be more easily interpreted.

Step 4: Decide Whether to Reject the Null Hypothesis

Once we have computed a p-value corresponding to H_0, it remains for us to decide whether or not to reject H_0. (We do not usually talk about "accepting" H_0: instead, we talk about "failing to reject" H_0.) A small p-value indicates that such a large value of the test statistic is unlikely to occur under H_0, and thereby provides evidence against H_0. If the p-value is sufficiently small, then we will want to reject H_0 (and, therefore, make a "discovery"). But how small is small enough to reject H_0?

It turns out that the answer to this question is very much in the eyes of the beholder, or more specifically, the data analyst. The smaller the p-value, the stronger the evidence against H_0. In some fields, it is typical to reject H_0 if the p-value is below 0.05; this means that, if H_0 holds, we would expect to see such a small p-value no more than 5% of the time.[9] However, in other fields, a much higher burden of proof is required: for example, in some areas of physics, it is typical to reject H_0 only if the p-value is below 10^{-9}!

In the example displayed in Figure 13.1, if we use a threshold of 0.05 as our cut-off for rejecting the null hypothesis, then we will reject the null. By contrast, if we use a threshold of 0.01, then we will fail to reject the null. These ideas are formalized in the next section.

13.1.2 Type I and Type II Errors

If the null hypothesis holds, then we say that it is a *true null hypothesis*; otherwise, it is a *false null hypothesis*. For instance, if we test $H_0 : \mu_t = \mu_c$ as in Section 13.1.1, and there is indeed no difference in the *population* mean blood pressure for mice in the treatment group and mice in the control group, then H_0 is true; otherwise, it is false. Of course, we do not know *a priori* whether H_0 is true or whether it is false: this is why we need to conduct a hypothesis test!

true null hypothesis

false null hypothesis

[9]Though a threshold of 0.05 to reject H_0 is ubiquitous in some areas of science, we advise against blind adherence to this arbitrary choice. Furthermore, a data analyst should typically report the p-value itself, rather than just whether or not it exceeds a specified threshold value.

Table 13.1 summarizes the possible scenarios associated with testing the null hypothesis H_0.[10] Once the hypothesis test is performed, the *row* of the table is known (based on whether or not we have rejected H_0); however, it is impossible for us to know which *column* we are in. If we reject H_0 when H_0 is false (i.e., when H_a is true), or if we do not reject H_0 when it is true, then we arrived at the correct result. However, if we erroneously reject H_0 when H_0 is in fact true, then we have committed a *Type I error*. The *Type I error rate* is defined as the probability of making a Type I error given that H_0 holds, i.e., the probability of incorrectly rejecting H_0. Alternatively, if we do not reject H_0 when H_0 is in fact false, then we have committed a *Type II error*. The *power* of the hypothesis test is defined as the probability of not making a Type II error given that H_a holds, i.e., the probability of correctly rejecting H_0.

Type I error

Type I error rate

Type II error

power

Ideally we would like both the Type I and Type II error rates to be small. But in practice, this is hard to achieve! There typically is a trade-off: we can make the Type I error small by only rejecting H_0 if we are quite sure that it doesn't hold; however, this will result in an increase in the Type II error. Alternatively, we can make the Type II error small by rejecting H_0 in the presence of even modest evidence that it does not hold, but this will cause the Type I error to be large. In practice, we typically view Type I errors as more "serious" than Type II errors, because the former involves declaring a scientific finding that is not correct. Hence, when we perform hypothesis testing, we typically require a low Type I error rate — e.g., at most $\alpha = 0.05$ — while trying to make the Type II error small (or, equivalently, the power large).

It turns out that there is a direct correspondence between the p-value threshold that causes us to reject H_0, and the Type I error rate. By only rejecting H_0 when the p-value is below α, we ensure that the Type I error rate will be less than or equal to α.

13.2 The Challenge of Multiple Testing

In the previous section, we saw that rejecting H_0 if the p-value is below (say) 0.01 provides us with a simple way to control the Type I error for H_0 at level 0.01: if H_0 is true, then there is no more than a 1% probability that we will reject it. But now suppose that we wish to test m null hypotheses, $H_{01}, \ldots, H_{0m}$. Will it do to simply reject all null hypotheses for which the corresponding p-value falls below (say) 0.01? Stated another way, if we reject all null hypotheses for which the p-value falls below 0.01, then how many Type I errors should we expect to make?

As a first step towards answering this question, consider a stockbroker who wishes to drum up new clients by convincing them of her trading

[10]There are parallels between Table 13.1 and Table 4.6, which has to do with the output of a binary classifier. In particular, recall from Table 4.6 that a false positive results from predicting a positive (non-null) label when the true label is in fact negative (null). This is closely related to a Type I error, which results from rejecting the null hypothesis when in fact the null hypothesis holds.

acumen. She tells 1,024 ($1{,}024 = 2^{10}$) potential new clients that she can correctly predict whether Apple's stock price will increase or decrease for 10 days running. There are 2^{10} possibilities for how Apple's stock price might change over the course of these 10 days. Therefore, she emails each client one of these 2^{10} possibilities. The vast majority of her potential clients will find that the stockbroker's predictions are no better than chance (and many will find them to be even worse than chance). But a broken clock is right twice a day, and one of her potential clients will be really impressed to find that her predictions were correct for all 10 of the days! And so the stockbroker gains a new client.

What happened here? Does the stockbroker have any actual insight into whether Apple's stock price will increase or decrease? No. How, then, did she manage to predict Apple's stock price perfectly for 10 days running? The answer is that she made a lot of guesses, and one of them happened to be exactly right.

How does this relate to multiple testing? Suppose that we flip 1,024 fair coins[11] ten times each. Then we would expect (on average) one coin to come up all tails. (There's a $1/2^{10} = 1/1{,}024$ chance that any single coin will come up all tails. So if we flip 1,024 coins, then we expect one coin to come up all tails, on average.) If one of our coins comes up all tails, then we might therefore conclude that this particular coin is not fair. In fact, a standard hypothesis test for the null hypothesis that this particular coin is fair would lead to a p-value below 0.002![12] But it would be incorrect to conclude that the coin is not fair: in fact, the null hypothesis holds, and we just happen to have gotten ten tails in a row by chance.

These examples illustrate the main challenge of *multiple testing*: when testing a huge number of null hypotheses, we are bound to get some very small p-values by chance. If we make a decision about whether to reject each null hypothesis without accounting for the fact that we have performed a very large number of tests, then we may end up rejecting a great number of true null hypotheses — that is, making a large number of Type I errors.

multiple testing

How severe is the problem? Recall from the previous section that if we reject a single null hypothesis, H_0, if its p-value is less than, say, $\alpha = 0.01$, then there is a 1% chance of making a false rejection if H_0 is in fact true. Now what if we test m null hypotheses, $H_{01}, \ldots, H_{0m}$, all of which are true? There's a 1% chance of rejecting any individual null hypothesis; therefore, we expect to falsely reject approximately $0.01 \times m$ null hypotheses. If $m =$ 10,000, then that means that we expect to falsely reject 100 null hypotheses by chance! That is a *lot* of Type I errors.

The crux of the issue is as follows: rejecting a null hypothesis if the p-value is below α controls the probability of falsely rejecting *that null hypothesis* at level α. However, if we do this for m null hypotheses, then the chance of falsely rejecting *at least one of the m null hypotheses* is quite a bit higher!

---

[11]A *fair coin* is one that has an equal chance of landing heads or tails.

[12]Recall that the p-value is the probability of observing data at least this extreme, under the null hypothesis. If the coin is fair, then the probability of observing at least ten tails is $(1/2)^{10} = 1/1{,}024 < 0.001$. The p-value is therefore $2/1{,}024 < 0.002$, since this is the probability of observing ten heads or ten tails.

	H_0 is True	H_0 is False	Total
Reject H_0	V	S	R
Do Not Reject H_0	U	W	$m - R$
Total	m_0	$m - m_0$	m

TABLE 13.2. *A summary of the results of testing m null hypotheses. A given null hypothesis is either true or false, and a test of that null hypothesis can either reject or fail to reject it. In practice, the individual values of V, S, U, and W are unknown. However, we do have access to $V + S = R$ and $U + W = m - R$, which are the numbers of null hypotheses rejected and not rejected, respectively.*

We will investigate this issue in greater detail, and pose a solution to it, in Section 13.3.

13.3 The Family-Wise Error Rate

In the following sections, we will discuss testing multiple hypotheses while controlling the probability of making at least one Type I error.

13.3.1 What is the Family-Wise Error Rate?

Recall that the Type I error rate is the probability of rejecting H_0 if H_0 is true. The *family-wise error rate* (FWER) generalizes this notion to the setting of m null hypotheses, $H_{01}, \ldots, H_{0m}$, and is defined as the probability of making *at least one* Type I error. To state this idea more formally, consider Table 13.2, which summarizes the possible outcomes when performing m hypothesis tests. Here, V represents the number of Type I errors (also known as false positives or false discoveries), S the number of true positives, U the number of true negatives, and W the number of Type II errors (also known as false negatives). Then the family-wise error rate is given by

family-wise error rate

$$\text{FWER} = \Pr(V \geq 1). \tag{13.3}$$

A strategy of rejecting any null hypothesis for which the p-value is below α (i.e. controlling the Type I error for each null hypothesis at level α) leads to a FWER of

$$\begin{aligned} \text{FWER}(\alpha) &= 1 - \Pr(V = 0) \\ &= 1 - \Pr(\text{do not falsely reject any null hypotheses}) \\ &= 1 - \Pr\Big(\textstyle\bigcap_{j=1}^{m} \{\text{do not falsely reject } H_{0j}\}\Big). \end{aligned} \tag{13.4}$$

Recall from basic probability that if two events A and B are independent, then $\Pr(A \cap B) = \Pr(A)\Pr(B)$. Therefore, if we make the additional rather strong assumptions that the m tests are independent and that all m null hypotheses are true, then

$$\text{FWER}(\alpha) = 1 - \prod_{j=1}^{m} (1 - \alpha) = 1 - (1 - \alpha)^m. \tag{13.5}$$

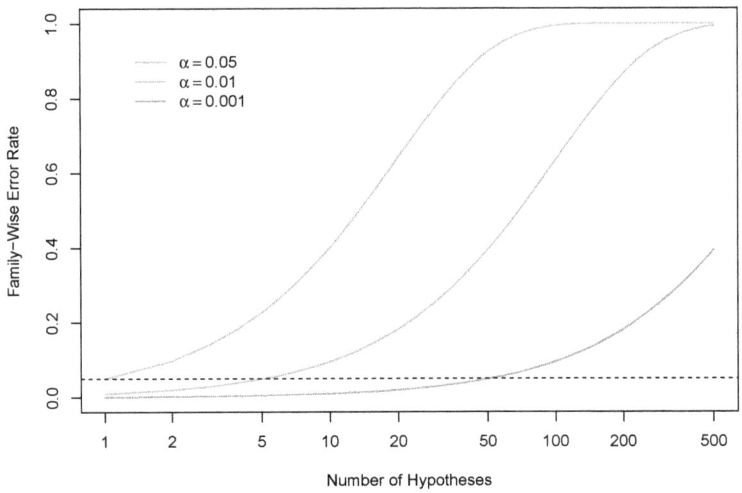

FIGURE 13.2. *The family-wise error rate, as a function of the number of hypotheses tested (displayed on the log scale), for three values of* α*:* $\alpha = 0.05$ *(orange),* $\alpha = 0.01$ *(blue), and* $\alpha = 0.001$ *(purple). The dashed line indicates* 0.05*. For example, in order to control the FWER at* 0.05 *when testing* $m = 50$ *null hypotheses, we must control the Type I error for each null hypothesis at level* $\alpha = 0.001$.

Hence, if we test only one null hypothesis, then $\text{FWER}(\alpha) = 1-(1-\alpha)^1 = \alpha$, so the Type I error rate and the FWER are equal. However, if we perform $m = 100$ independent tests, then $\text{FWER}(\alpha) = 1-(1-\alpha)^{100}$. For instance, taking $\alpha = 0.05$ leads to a FWER of $1-(1-0.05)^{100} = 0.994$. In other words, we are virtually guaranteed to make at least one Type I error!

Figure 13.2 displays (13.5) for various values of m, the number of hypotheses, and α, the Type I error. We see that setting $\alpha = 0.05$ results in a high FWER even for moderate m. With $\alpha = 0.01$, we can test no more than five null hypotheses before the FWER exceeds 0.05. Only for very small values, such as $\alpha = 0.001$, do we manage to ensure a small FWER, at least for moderately-sized m.

We now briefly return to the example in Section 13.1.1, in which we consider testing a single null hypothesis of the form $H_0 : \mu_t = \mu_c$ using a two-sample t-statistic. Recall from Figure 13.1 that in order to guarantee that the Type I error does not exceed 0.02, we decide whether or not to reject H_0 using a cutpoint of 2.33 (i.e. we reject H_0 if $|T| \geq 2.33$). Now, what if we wish to test 10 null hypotheses using two-sample t-statistics, instead of just one? We will see in Section 13.3.2 that we can guarantee that the FWER does not exceed 0.02 by rejecting only null hypotheses for which the p-value falls below 0.002. This corresponds to a much more stringent cutpoint of 3.09 (i.e. we should reject H_{0j} only if its test statistic $|T_j| \geq 3.09$, for $j = 1, \ldots, 10$). In other words, controlling the FWER at level α amounts to a much higher bar, in terms of evidence required to reject any given null hypothesis, than simply controlling the Type I error for each null hypothesis at level α.

Manager	Mean, $\bar{x}$	Standard Deviation, s	t-statistic	p-value
One	3.0	7.4	2.86	0.006
Two	-0.1	6.9	-0.10	0.918
Three	2.8	7.5	2.62	0.012
Four	0.5	6.7	0.53	0.601
Five	0.3	6.8	0.31	0.756

TABLE 13.3. *The first two columns correspond to the sample mean and sample standard deviation of the percentage excess return, over $n = 50$ months, for the first five managers in the* Fund *dataset. The last two columns provide the t-statistic ($\sqrt{n} \cdot \bar{X}/S$) and associated p-value for testing $H_{0j} : \mu_j = 0$, the null hypothesis that the (population) mean return for the jth hedge fund manager equals zero.*

13.3.2 Approaches to Control the Family-Wise Error Rate

In this section, we briefly survey some approaches to control the FWER. We will illustrate these approaches on the Fund dataset, which records the monthly percentage excess returns for 2,000 fund managers over $n = 50$ months.[13] Table 13.3 provides relevant summary statistics for the first five managers.

We first present the Bonferroni method and Holm's step-down procedure, which are very general-purpose approaches for controlling the FWER that can be applied whenever m p-values have been computed, regardless of the form of the null hypotheses, the choice of test statistics, or the (in)dependence of the p-values. We then briefly discuss Tukey's method and Scheffé's method in order to illustrate the fact that, in certain situations, more specialized approaches for controlling the FWER may be preferable.

The Bonferroni Method

As in the previous section, suppose we wish to test $H_{01}, \ldots, H_{0m}$. Let A_j denote the event that we make a Type I error for the jth null hypothesis, for $j = 1, \ldots, m$. Then

$$\begin{aligned} \text{FWER} &= \Pr(\text{falsely reject at least one null hypothesis}) \\ &= \Pr(\cup_{j=1}^{m} A_j) \\ &\leq \sum_{j=1}^{m} \Pr(A_j). \end{aligned} \tag{13.6}$$

In (13.6), the inequality results from the fact that for any two events A and B, $\Pr(A \cup B) \leq \Pr(A) + \Pr(B)$, regardless of whether A and B are independent. The *Bonferroni method*, or *Bonferroni correction*, sets the threshold for rejecting each hypothesis test to α/m, so that $\Pr(A_j) \leq \alpha/m$. Equation 13.6 implies that

$$\text{FWER}(\alpha/m) \leq m \times \frac{\alpha}{m} = \alpha,$$

[13] Excess returns correspond to the additional return the fund manager achieves beyond the market's overall return. So if the market increases by 5% during a given period and the fund manager achieves a 7% return, their *excess return* would be 7% − 5% = 2%.

so this procedure controls the FWER at level α. For instance, in order to control the FWER at level 0.1 while testing $m = 100$ null hypotheses, the Bonferroni procedure requires us to control the Type I error for each null hypothesis at level $0.1/100 = 0.001$, i.e. to reject all null hypotheses for which the p-value is below 0.001.

We now consider the `Fund` dataset in Table 13.3. If we control the Type I error at level $\alpha = 0.05$ for each fund manager separately, then we will conclude that the first and third managers have significantly non-zero excess returns; in other words, we will reject $H_{01} : \mu_1 = 0$ and $H_{03} : \mu_3 = 0$. However, as discussed in previous sections, this procedure does not account for the fact that we have tested multiple hypotheses, and therefore it will lead to a FWER greater than 0.05. If we instead wish to control the FWER at level 0.05, then, using a Bonferroni correction, we must control the Type I error for each individual manager at level $\alpha/m = 0.05/5 = 0.01$. Consequently, we will reject the null hypothesis only for the first manager, since the p-values for all other managers exceed 0.01. The Bonferroni correction gives us peace of mind that we have not falsely rejected too many null hypotheses, but for a price: we reject few null hypotheses, and thus will typically make quite a few Type II errors.

The Bonferroni correction is by far the best-known and most commonly-used multiplicity correction in all of statistics. Its ubiquity is due in large part to the fact that it is very easy to understand and simple to implement, and also from the fact that it successfully controls Type I error regardless of whether the m hypothesis tests are independent. However, as we will see, it is typically neither the most powerful nor the best approach for multiple testing correction. In particular, the Bonferroni correction can be quite conservative, in the sense that the true FWER is often quite a bit lower than the nominal (or target) FWER; this results from the inequality in (13.6). By contrast, a less conservative procedure might allow us to control the FWER while rejecting more null hypotheses, and therefore making fewer Type II errors.

Holm's Step-Down Procedure

Holm's method, also known as Holm's step-down procedure or the Holm–Bonferroni method, is an alternative to the Bonferroni procedure. Holm's method controls the FWER, but it is less conservative than Bonferroni, in the sense that it will reject more null hypotheses, typically resulting in fewer Type II errors and hence greater power. The procedure is summarized in Algorithm 13.1. The proof that this method controls the FWER is similar to, but slightly more complicated than, the argument in (13.6) that the Bonferroni method controls the FWER. It is worth noting that in Holm's procedure, the threshold that we use to reject each null hypothesis — $p_{(L)}$ in Step 5 — actually depends on the values of *all* m of the p-values. (See the definition of L in (13.7).) This is in contrast to the Bonferroni procedure, in which to control the FWER at level α, we reject any null hypotheses for which the p-value is below α/m, regardless of the other p-values. Holm's method makes no independence assumptions about the m hypothesis tests, and is uniformly more powerful than the Bonferroni method — it will

Holm's method

Algorithm 13.1 *Holm's Step-Down Procedure to Control the FWER*

1. Specify α, the level at which to control the FWER.
2. Compute p-values, $p_1, \ldots, p_m$, for the m null hypotheses $H_{01}, \ldots, H_{0m}$.
3. Order the m p-values so that $p_{(1)} \leq p_{(2)} \leq \cdots \leq p_{(m)}$.
4. Define
$$L = \min\left\{j : p_{(j)} > \frac{\alpha}{m+1-j}\right\}. \tag{13.7}$$
5. Reject all null hypotheses H_{0j} for which $p_j < p_{(L)}$.

always reject at least as many null hypotheses as Bonferroni — and so it should always be preferred.

We now consider applying Holm's method to the first five fund managers in the `Fund` dataset in Table 13.3, while controlling the FWER at level 0.05. The ordered p-values are $p_{(1)} = 0.006, p_{(2)} = 0.012, p_{(3)} = 0.601, p_{(4)} = 0.756$ and $p_{(5)} = 0.918$. The Holm procedure rejects the first two null hypotheses, because $p_{(1)} = 0.006 < 0.05/(5+1-1) = 0.01$ and $p_{(2)} = 0.012 < 0.05/(5+1-2) = 0.0125$, but $p_{(3)} = 0.601 > 0.05/(5+1-3) = 0.0167$, which implies that $L = 3$. We note that, in this setting, Holm is more powerful than Bonferroni: the former rejects the null hypotheses for the first and third managers, whereas the latter rejects the null hypothesis only for the first manager.

Figure 13.3 provides an illustration of the Bonferroni and Holm methods on three simulated data sets in a setting involving $m = 10$ hypothesis tests, of which $m_0 = 2$ of the null hypotheses are true. Each panel displays the ten corresponding p-values, ordered from smallest to largest, and plotted on a log scale. The eight red points represent the false null hypotheses, and the two black points represent the true null hypotheses. We wish to control the FWER at level 0.05. The Bonferroni procedure requires us to reject all null hypotheses for which the p-value is below 0.005; this is represented by the black horizontal line. The Holm procedure requires us to reject all null hypotheses that fall below the blue line. The blue line always lies above the black line, so Holm will always reject more tests than Bonferroni; the region between the two lines corresponds to the hypotheses that are only rejected by Holm. In the left-hand panel, both Bonferroni and Holm successfully reject seven of the eight false null hypotheses. In the center panel, Holm successfully rejects all eight of the false null hypotheses, while Bonferroni fails to reject one. In the right-hand panel, Bonferroni only rejects three of the false null hypotheses, while Holm rejects all eight. Neither Bonferroni nor Holm makes any Type I errors in these examples.

Two Special Cases: Tukey's Method and Scheffé's Method

Bonferroni's method and Holm's method can be used in virtually any setting in which we wish to control the FWER for m null hypotheses: they

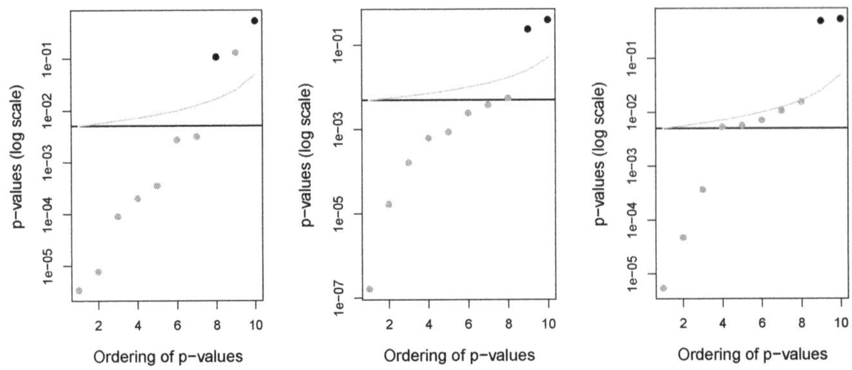

FIGURE 13.3. *Each panel displays, for a separate simulation, the sorted p-values for tests of $m = 10$ null hypotheses. The p-values corresponding to the $m_0 = 2$ true null hypotheses are displayed in black, and the rest are in red. When controlling the FWER at level 0.05, the Bonferroni procedure rejects all null hypotheses that fall below the black line, and the Holm procedure rejects all null hypotheses that fall below the blue line. The region between the blue and black lines indicates null hypotheses that are rejected using the Holm procedure but not using the Bonferroni procedure. In the center panel, the Holm procedure rejects one more null hypothesis than the Bonferroni procedure. In the right-hand panel, it rejects five more null hypotheses.*

make no assumptions about the nature of the null hypotheses, the type of test statistic used, or the (in)dependence of the p-values. However, in certain very specific settings, we can achieve higher power by controlling the FWER using approaches that are more tailored to the task at hand. Tukey's method and Scheffé's method provide two such examples.

Table 13.3 indicates that for the `Fund` dataset, Managers One and Two have the greatest difference in their sample mean returns. This finding might motivate us to test the null hypothesis $H_0 : \mu_1 = \mu_2$, where μ_j is the (population) mean return for the jth fund manager. A two-sample t-test (13.1) for H_0 yields a p-value of 0.0349, suggesting modest evidence against H_0. However, this p-value is misleading, since we decided to compare the average returns of Managers One and Two only after having examined the returns for all five managers; this essentially amounts to having performed $m = 5 \times (5 - 1)/2 = 10$ hypothesis tests, and selecting the one with the smallest p-value. This suggests that in order to control the FWER at level 0.05, we should make a Bonferroni correction for $m = 10$ hypothesis tests, and therefore should only reject a null hypothesis for which the p-value is below 0.005. If we do this, then we will be unable to reject the null hypothesis that Managers One and Two have identical performance.

However, in this setting, a Bonferroni correction is actually a bit too stringent, since it fails to consider the fact that the $m = 10$ hypothesis tests are all somewhat related: for instance, Managers Two and Five have similar mean returns, as do Managers Two and Four; this guarantees that the mean returns of Managers Four and Five are similar. Stated another way, the m p-values for the m pairwise comparisons are *not* independent. Therefore, it should be possible to control the FWER in a way that is

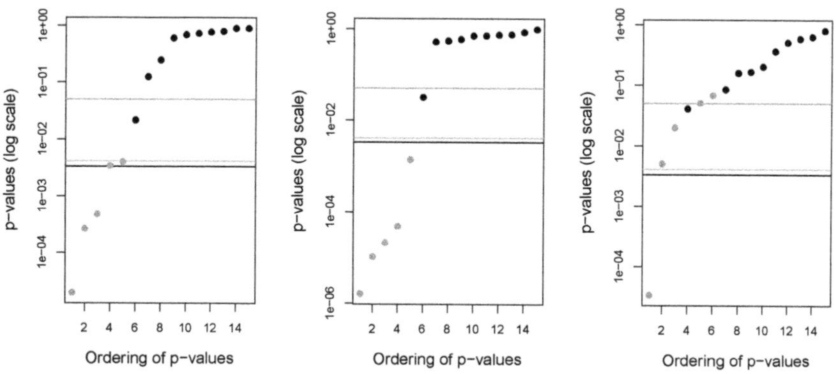

FIGURE 13.4. *Each panel displays, for a separate simulation, the sorted p-values for tests of* $m = 15$ *hypotheses, corresponding to pairwise tests for the equality of* $G = 6$ *means. The* $m_0 = 10$ *true null hypotheses are displayed in black, and the rest are in red. When controlling the FWER at level* 0.05*, the Bonferroni procedure rejects all null hypotheses that fall below the black line, whereas Tukey rejects all those that fall below the blue line. Thus, Tukey's method has slightly higher power than Bonferroni's method. Controlling the Type I error* without *adjusting for multiple testing involves rejecting all those that fall below the green line.*

less conservative. This is exactly the idea behind *Tukey's method*: when performing $m = G(G-1)/2$ pairwise comparisons of G means, it allows us to control the FWER at level α while rejecting all null hypotheses for which the p-value falls below α_T, for some $\alpha_T > \alpha/m$. Tukey's method

Figure 13.4 illustrates Tukey's method on three simulated data sets in a setting with $G = 6$ means, with $\mu_1 = \mu_2 = \mu_3 = \mu_4 = \mu_5 \neq \mu_6$. Therefore, of the $m = G(G-1)/2 = 15$ null hypotheses of the form $H_0 : \mu_j = \mu_k$, ten are true and five are false. In each panel, the true null hypotheses are displayed in black, and the false ones are in red. The horizontal lines indicate that Tukey's method always results in at least as many rejections as Bonferroni's method. In the left-hand panel, Tukey correctly rejects two more null hypotheses than Bonferroni.

Now, suppose that we once again examine the data in Table 13.3, and notice that Managers One and Three have higher mean returns than Managers Two, Four, and Five. This might motivate us to test the null hypothesis

$$H_0 : \frac{1}{2}(\mu_1 + \mu_3) = \frac{1}{3}(\mu_2 + \mu_4 + \mu_5). \tag{13.8}$$

(Recall that μ_j is the population mean return for the jth hedge fund manager.) It turns out that we could test (13.8) using a variant of the two-sample t-test presented in (13.1), leading to a p-value of 0.004. This suggests strong evidence of a difference between Managers One and Three compared to Managers Two, Four, and Five. However, there is a problem: we decided to test the null hypothesis in (13.8) only after peeking at the data in Table 13.3. In a sense, this means that we have conducted multiple testing. In this setting, using Bonferroni to control the FWER at level α

would require a p-value threshold of α/m, for an extremely large value of m[14].

Scheffé's method is designed for exactly this setting. It allows us to compute a value α_S such that rejecting the null hypothesis H_0 in (13.8) if the p-value is below α_S will control the Type I error at level α. It turns out that for the Fund example, in order to control the Type I error at level $\alpha = 0.05$, we must set $\alpha_S = 0.002$. Therefore, we are unable to reject H_0 in (13.8), despite the apparently very small p-value of 0.004. An important advantage of Scheffé's method is that we can use this same threshold of $\alpha_S = 0.002$ in order to perform a pairwise comparison of any split of the managers into two groups: for instance, we could also test $H_0 : \frac{1}{3}(\mu_1 + \mu_2 + \mu_3) = \frac{1}{2}(\mu_4 + \mu_5)$ and $H_0 : \frac{1}{4}(\mu_1 + \mu_2 + \mu_3 + \mu_4) = \mu_5$ using the same threshold of 0.002, without needing to further adjust for multiple testing.

Scheffé's method

To summarize, Holm's procedure and Bonferroni's procedure are very general approaches for multiple testing correction that can be applied under all circumstances. However, in certain special cases, more powerful procedures for multiple testing correction may be available, in order to control the FWER while achieving higher power (i.e. committing fewer Type II errors) than would be possible using Holm or Bonferroni. In this section, we have illustrated two such examples.

13.3.3 Trade-Off Between the FWER and Power

In general, there is a trade-off between the FWER threshold that we choose, and our *power* to reject the null hypotheses. Recall that power is defined as the number of false null hypotheses that we reject divided by the total number of false null hypotheses, i.e. $S/(m - m_0)$ using the notation of Table 13.2. Figure 13.5 illustrates the results of a simulation setting involving m null hypotheses, of which 90% are true and the remaining 10% are false; power is displayed as a function of the FWER. In this particular simulation setting, when $m = 10$, a FWER of 0.05 corresponds to power of approximately 60%. However, as m increases, the power decreases. With $m = 500$, the power is below 0.2 at a FWER of 0.05, so that we successfully reject only 20% of the false null hypotheses.

Figure 13.5 indicates that it is reasonable to control the FWER when m takes on a small value, like 5 or 10. However, for $m = 100$ or $m = 1{,}000$, attempting to control the FWER will make it almost impossible to reject any of the false null hypotheses. In other words, the power will be extremely low.

Why is this the case? Recall that, using the notation in Table 13.2, the FWER is defined as $\Pr(V \geq 1)$ (13.3). In other other words, controlling the FWER at level α guarantees that the data analyst is *very unlikely* (with probability no more than α) to reject *any* true null hypotheses, i.e. to have any false positives. In order to make good on this guarantee when m is large, the data analyst may be forced to reject very few null hypotheses, or perhaps even none at all (since if $R = 0$ then also $V = 0$; see Table 13.2).

---

[14]In fact, calculating the "correct" value of m is quite technical, and outside the scope of this book.

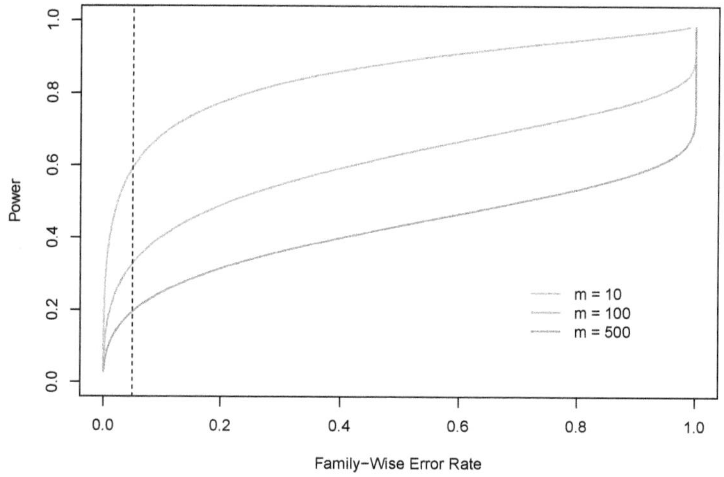

FIGURE 13.5. *In a simulation setting in which 90% of the m null hypotheses are true, we display the power (the fraction of false null hypotheses that we successfully reject) as a function of the family-wise error rate. The curves correspond to* $m = 10$ (orange), $m = 100$ (blue), *and* $m = 500$ (purple). *As the value of m increases, the power decreases. The vertical dashed line indicates a FWER of* 0.05.

This is scientifically uninteresting, and typically results in very low power, as in Figure 13.5.

In practice, when m is large, we may be willing to tolerate a few false positives, in the interest of making more discoveries, i.e. more rejections of the null hypothesis. This is the motivation behind the false discovery rate, which we present next.

13.4 The False Discovery Rate

13.4.1 Intuition for the False Discovery Rate

As we just discussed, when m is large, then trying to prevent *any* false positives (as in FWER control) is simply too stringent. Instead, we might try to make sure that the ratio of false positives (V) to total positives ($V + S = R$) is sufficiently low, so that most of the rejected null hypotheses are not false positives. The ratio V/R is known as the *false discovery proportion* (FDP). false discovery proportion

It might be tempting to ask the data analyst to control the FDP: to make sure that no more than, say, 20% of the rejected null hypotheses are false positives. However, in practice, controlling the FDP is an impossible task for the data analyst, since she has no way to be certain, on any particular dataset, which hypotheses are true and which are false. This is very similar to the fact that the data analyst can control the FWER, i.e. she can guarantee that $\Pr(V \geq 1) \leq \alpha$ for any pre-specified α, but she cannot guarantee that $V = 0$ on any particular dataset (short of failing to reject any null hypotheses, i.e. setting $R = 0$).

Therefore, we instead control the *false discovery rate* (FDR)[15], defined as

false discovery rate

$$\mathrm{FDR} = \mathrm{E}(\mathrm{FDP}) = \mathrm{E}(V/R). \tag{13.9}$$

When we control the FDR at (say) level $q = 20\%$, we are rejecting as many null hypotheses as possible while guaranteeing that no more than 20% of those rejected null hypotheses are false positives, *on average.*

In the definition of the FDR in (13.9), the expectation is taken over the population from which the data are generated. For instance, suppose we control the FDR for m null hypotheses at $q = 0.2$. This means that if we repeat this experiment a huge number of times, and each time control the FDR at $q = 0.2$, then we should expect that, on average, 20% of the rejected null hypotheses will be false positives. On a given dataset, the fraction of false positives among the rejected hypotheses may be greater than or less than 20%.

Thus far, we have motivated the use of the FDR from a pragmatic perspective, by arguing that when m is large, controlling the FWER is simply too stringent, and will not lead to "enough" discoveries. An additional motivation for the use of the FDR is that it aligns well with the way that data are often collected in contemporary applications. As datasets continue to grow in size across a variety of fields, it is increasingly common to conduct a huge number of hypothesis tests for exploratory, rather than confirmatory, purposes. For instance, a genomic researcher might sequence the genomes of individuals with and without some particular medical condition, and then, for each of 20,000 genes, test whether sequence variants in that gene are associated with the medical condition of interest. This amounts to performing $m = 20{,}000$ hypothesis tests. The analysis is exploratory in nature, in the sense that the researcher does not have any particular hypothesis in mind; instead she wishes to see whether there is modest evidence for the association between each gene and the disease, with a plan to further investigate any genes for which there is such evidence. She is likely willing to tolerate some number of false positives in the set of genes that she will investigate further; thus, the FWER is not an appropriate choice. However, some correction for multiple testing is required: it would not be a good idea for her to simply investigate *all* genes with p-values less than (say) 0.05, since we would expect 1,000 genes to have such small p-values simply by chance, even if no genes are associated with the disease (since $0.05 \times 20{,}000 = 1{,}000$). Controlling the FDR for her exploratory analysis at 20% guarantees that — on average — no more than 20% of the genes that she investigates further are false positives.

It is worth noting that unlike p-values, for which a threshold of 0.05 is typically viewed as the minimum standard of evidence for a "positive" result, and a threshold of 0.01 or even 0.001 is viewed as much more compelling, there is no standard accepted threshold for FDR control. Instead, the choice of FDR threshold is typically context-dependent, or even dataset-dependent. For instance, the genomic researcher in the previous example might seek to control the FDR at a threshold of 10% if the planned follow-

[15] If $R = 0$, then we replace the ratio V/R with 0, to avoid computing 0/0. Formally, $\mathrm{FDR} = \mathrm{E}(V/R|R > 0)\Pr(R > 0)$.

up analysis is time-consuming or expensive. Alternatively, a much larger threshold of 30% might be suitable if she plans an inexpensive follow-up analysis.

13.4.2 The Benjamini–Hochberg Procedure

We now focus on the task of controlling the FDR: that is, deciding which null hypotheses to reject while guaranteeing that the FDR, $\mathrm{E}(V/R)$, is less than or equal to some pre-specified value q. In order to do this, we need some way to connect the p-values, $p_1, \ldots, p_m$, from the m null hypotheses to the desired FDR value, q. It turns out that a very simple procedure, outlined in Algorithm 13.2, can be used to control the FDR.

Algorithm 13.2 *Benjamini–Hochberg Procedure to Control the FDR*

1. Specify q, the level at which to control the FDR.
2. Compute p-values, $p_1, \ldots, p_m$, for the m null hypotheses $H_{01}, \ldots, H_{0m}$.
3. Order the m p-values so that $p_{(1)} \leq p_{(2)} \leq \cdots \leq p_{(m)}$.
4. Define
$$L = \max\{j : p_{(j)} < qj/m\}. \tag{13.10}$$
5. Reject all null hypotheses H_{0j} for which $p_j \leq p_{(L)}$.

Algorithm 13.2 is known as the *Benjamini–Hochberg procedure*. The crux of this procedure lies in (13.10). For example, consider again the first five managers in the `Fund` dataset, presented in Table 13.3. (In this example, $m = 5$, although typically we control the FDR in settings involving a much greater number of null hypotheses.) We see that $p_{(1)} = 0.006 < 0.05 \times 1/5$, $p_{(2)} = 0.012 < 0.05 \times 2/5$, $p_{(3)} = 0.601 > 0.05 \times 3/5$, $p_{(4)} = 0.756 > 0.05 \times 4/5$, and $p_{(5)} = 0.918 > 0.05 \times 5/5$. Therefore, to control the FDR at 5%, we reject the null hypotheses that the first and third fund managers perform no better than chance.

Benjamini–Hochberg procedure

As long as the m p-values are independent or only mildly dependent, then the Benjamini–Hochberg procedure guarantees[16] that

$$\mathrm{FDR} \leq q.$$

In other words, this procedure ensures that, on average, no more than a fraction q of the rejected null hypotheses are false positives. Remarkably, this holds regardless of how many null hypotheses are true, and regardless of the distribution of the p-values for the null hypotheses that are false. Therefore, the Benjamini–Hochberg procedure gives us a very easy way to determine, given a set of m p-values, which null hypotheses to reject in order to control the FDR at any pre-specified level q.

---

[16]However, the proof is well beyond the scope of this book.

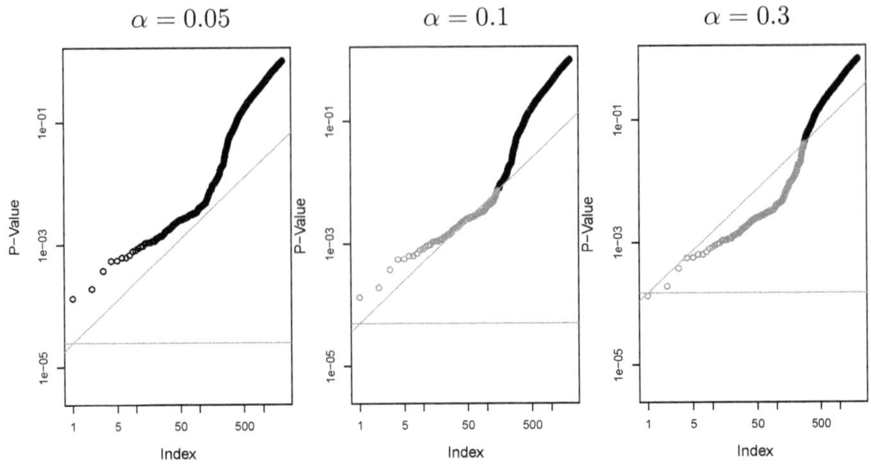

FIGURE 13.6. *Each panel displays the same set of $m = 2{,}000$ ordered p-values for the* Fund *data. The green lines indicate the p-value thresholds corresponding to FWER control, via the Bonferroni procedure, at levels $\alpha = 0.05$ (left), $\alpha = 0.1$ (center), and $\alpha = 0.3$ (right). The orange lines indicate the p-value thresholds corresponding to FDR control, via Benjamini–Hochberg, at levels $q = 0.05$ (left), $q = 0.1$ (center), and $q = 0.3$ (right). When the FDR is controlled at level $q = 0.1$, 146 null hypotheses are rejected* (center)*; the corresponding p-values are shown in blue. When the FDR is controlled at level $q = 0.3$, 279 null hypotheses are rejected* (right)*; the corresponding p-values are shown in blue.*

There is a fundamental difference between the Bonferroni procedure of Section 13.3.2 and the Benjamini–Hochberg procedure. In the Bonferroni procedure, in order to control the FWER for m null hypotheses at level α, we must simply reject null hypotheses for which the p-value is below α/m. This threshold of α/m does not depend on anything about the data (beyond the value of m), and certainly does not depend on the p-values themselves. By contrast, the rejection threshold used in the Benjamini–Hochberg procedure is more complicated: we reject all null hypotheses for which the p-value is less than or equal to the Lth smallest p-value, where L is itself a function of all m p-values, as in (13.10). Therefore, when conducting the Benjamini–Hochberg procedure, we cannot plan out in advance what threshold we will use to reject p-values; we need to first see our data. For instance, in the abstract, there is no way to know whether we will reject a null hypothesis corresponding to a p-value of 0.01 when using an FDR threshold of 0.1 with $m = 100$; the answer depends on the values of the other $m - 1$ p-values. This property of the Benjamini–Hochberg procedure is shared by the Holm procedure, which also involves a data-dependent p-value threshold.

Figure 13.6 displays the results of applying the Bonferroni and Benjamini–Hochberg procedures on the Fund data set, using the full set of $m = 2{,}000$ fund managers, of which the first five were displayed in Table 13.3. When the FWER is controlled at level 0.3 using Bonferroni, only one null hypothesis is rejected; that is, we can conclude only that a single fund manager is beating the market. This is despite the fact that a substantial portion of the $m = 2{,}000$ fund managers appear to have beaten the market without performing correction for multiple testing — for instance, 13 of them have p-values below 0.001. By contrast, when the FDR is controlled at level 0.3, we can conclude that 279 fund managers are beating the market: we expect that no more than around $279 \times 0.3 = 83.7$ of these fund managers had good performance only due to chance. Thus, we see that FDR control is much milder — and more powerful — than FWER control, in the sense that it allows us to reject many more null hypotheses, with a cost of substantially more false positives.

The Benjamini–Hochberg procedure has been around since the mid-1990s. While a great many papers have been published since then proposing alternative approaches for FDR control that can perform better in particular scenarios, the Benjamini–Hochberg procedure remains a very useful and widely-applicable approach.

13.5 A Re-Sampling Approach to p-Values and False Discovery Rates

Thus far, the discussion in this chapter has assumed that we are interested in testing a particular null hypothesis H_0 using a test statistic T, which has some known (or assumed) distribution under H_0, such as a normal distribution, a t-distribution, a χ^2-distribution, or an F-distribution. This is referred to as the *theoretical null distribution*. We typically rely upon the availability of a theoretical null distribution in order to obtain a p-value associated with our test statistic. Indeed, for most of the types of null hypotheses that we might be interested in testing, a theoretical null distribution is available, provided that we are willing to make stringent assumptions about our data.

theoretical null distribution

However, if our null hypothesis H_0 or test statistic T is somewhat unusual, then it may be the case that no theoretical null distribution is available. Alternatively, even if a theoretical null distribution exists, then we may be wary of relying upon it, perhaps because some assumption that is required for it to hold is violated. For instance, maybe the sample size is too small.

In this section, we present a framework for performing inference in this setting, which exploits the availability of fast computers in order to approximate the null distribution of T, and thereby to obtain a p-value. While this framework is very general, it must be carefully instantiated for a specific problem of interest. Therefore, in what follows, we consider a specific example in which we wish to test whether the means of two random variables are equal, using a two-sample t-test.

The discussion in this section is more challenging than the preceding sections in this chapter, and can be safely skipped by a reader who is content to use the theoretical null distribution to compute p-values for his or her test statistics.

13.5.1 A Re-Sampling Approach to the p-Value

We return to the example of Section 13.1.1, in which we wish to test whether the mean of a random variable X equals the mean of a random variable Y, i.e. $H_0 : \text{E}(X) = \text{E}(Y)$, against the alternative $H_a : \text{E}(X) \neq \text{E}(Y)$. Given n_X independent observations from X and n_Y independent observations from Y, the two-sample t-statistic takes the form

$$T = \frac{\hat{\mu}_X - \hat{\mu}_Y}{s\sqrt{\frac{1}{n_X} + \frac{1}{n_Y}}} \tag{13.11}$$

where $\hat{\mu}_X = \frac{1}{n_X}\sum_{i=1}^{n_X} x_i$, $\hat{\mu}_Y = \frac{1}{n_Y}\sum_{i=1}^{n_Y} y_i$, $s = \sqrt{\frac{(n_X-1)s_X^2+(n_Y-1)s_Y^2}{n_X+n_Y-2}}$, and s_X^2 and s_Y^2 are unbiased estimators of the variances in the two groups. A large (absolute) value of T provides evidence against H_0.

If n_X and n_Y are large, then T in (13.11) approximately follows a $N(0, 1)$ distribution. But if n_X and n_Y are small, then in the absence of a strong assumption about the distribution of X and Y, we do not know the theoretical null distribution of T.[17] In this case, it turns out that we can approximate the null distribution of T using a *re-sampling* approach, or more specifically, a *permutation* approach.

re-sampling
permutation

To do this, we conduct a thought experiment. If H_0 holds, so that $\text{E}(X) = \text{E}(Y)$, and we make the stronger assumption that the distributions of X and Y are the same, then the distribution of T is invariant under swapping observations of X with observations of Y. That is, if we randomly swap some of the observations in X with the observations in Y, then *the test statistic T in* (13.11) *computed based on this swapped data has the same distribution as T based on the original data.* This is true only if H_0 holds, and the distributions of X and Y are the same.

This suggests that in order to approximate the null distribution of T, we can take the following approach. We randomly permute the $n_X + n_Y$ observations B times, for some large value of B, and each time we compute (13.11). We let $T^{*1}, \ldots, T^{*B}$ denote the values of (13.11) on the permuted data. These can be viewed as an approximation of the null distribution of T under H_0. Recall that by definition, a p-value is the probability of observing a test statistic at least this extreme under H_0. Therefore, to compute a p-value for T, we can simply compute

$$p\text{-value} = \frac{\sum_{b=1}^{B} 1_{(|T^{*b}| \geq |T|)}}{B}, \tag{13.12}$$

the fraction of permuted datasets for which the value of the test statistic is at least as extreme as the value observed on the original data. This procedure is summarized in Algorithm 13.3.

---

[17]If we assume that X and Y are normally distributed, then T in (13.11) follows a t-distribution with $n_X + n_Y - 2$ degrees of freedom under H_0. However, in practice, the distribution of random variables is rarely known, and so it can be preferable to perform a re-sampling approach instead of making strong and unjustified assumptions. If the results of the re-sampling approach disagree with the results of assuming a theoretical null distribution, then the results of the re-sampling approach are more trustworthy.

Algorithm 13.3 *Re-Sampling p-Value for a Two-Sample t-Test*

1. Compute T, defined in (13.11), on the original data $x_1, \ldots, x_{n_X}$ and $y_1, \ldots, y_{n_Y}$.
2. For $b = 1, \ldots, B$, where B is a large number (e.g. $B = 10{,}000$):
   (a) Permute the $n_X + n_Y$ observations at random. Call the first n_X permuted observations $x_1^*, \ldots, x_{n_X}^*$, and call the remaining n_Y observations $y_1^*, \ldots, y_{n_Y}^*$.
   (b) Compute (13.11) on the permuted data $x_1^*, \ldots, x_{n_X}^*$ and $y_1^*, \ldots, y_{n_Y}^*$, and call the result T^{*b}.
3. The p-value is given by $\frac{\sum_{b=1}^{B} 1_{(|T^{*b}| \geq |T|)}}{B}$.

We try out this procedure on the `Khan` dataset, which consists of expression measurements for 2,308 genes in four sub-types of small round blood cell tumors, a type of cancer typically seen in children. This dataset is part of the `ISLR2` package. We restrict our attention to the two sub-types for which the most observations are available: rhabdomyosarcoma ($n_X = 29$) and Burkitt's lymphoma ($n_Y = 25$).

A two-sample t-test for the null hypothesis that the 11th gene's mean expression values are equal in the two groups yields $T = -2.09$. Using the theoretical null distribution, which is a t_{52} distribution (since $n_X + n_Y - 2 = 52$), we obtain a p-value of 0.041. (Note that a t_{52} distribution is virtually indistinguishable from a $N(0, 1)$ distribution.) If we instead apply Algorithm 13.3 with $B = 10{,}000$, then we obtain a p-value of 0.042. Figure 13.7 displays the theoretical null distribution, the re-sampling null distribution, and the actual value of the test statistic ($T = -2.09$) for this gene. In this example, we see very little difference between the p-values obtained using the theoretical null distribution and the re-sampling null distribution.

By contrast, Figure 13.8 shows an analogous set of results for the 877th gene. In this case, there is a substantial difference between the theoretical and re-sampling null distributions, which results in a difference between their p-values.

In general, in settings with a smaller sample size or a more skewed data distribution (so that the theoretical null distribution is less accurate), the difference between the re-sampling and theoretical p-values will tend to be more pronounced. In fact, the substantial difference between the re-sampling and theoretical null distributions in Figure 13.8 is due to the fact that a single observation in the 877th gene is very far from the other observations, leading to a very skewed distribution.

13.5.2 A Re-Sampling Approach to the False Discovery Rate

Now, suppose that we wish to control the FDR for m null hypotheses, $H_{01}, \ldots, H_{0m}$, in a setting in which either no theoretical null distribution is available, or else we simply prefer to avoid the use of a theoretical null

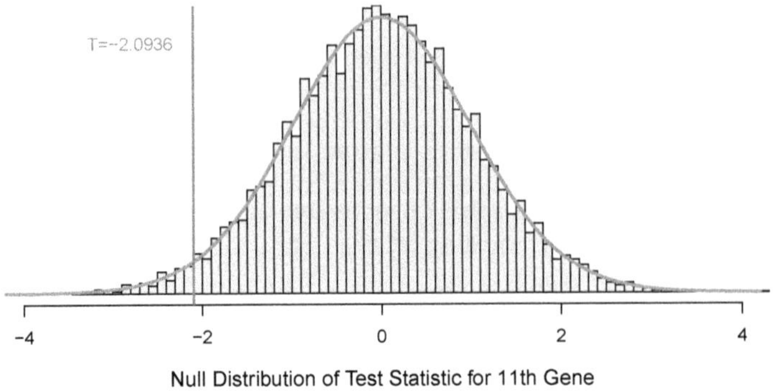

FIGURE 13.7. *The* 11*th gene in the* Khan *dataset has a test statistic of* $T = -2.09$. *Its theoretical and re-sampling null distributions are almost identical. The theoretical p-value equals* 0.041 *and the re-sampling p-value equals* 0.042.

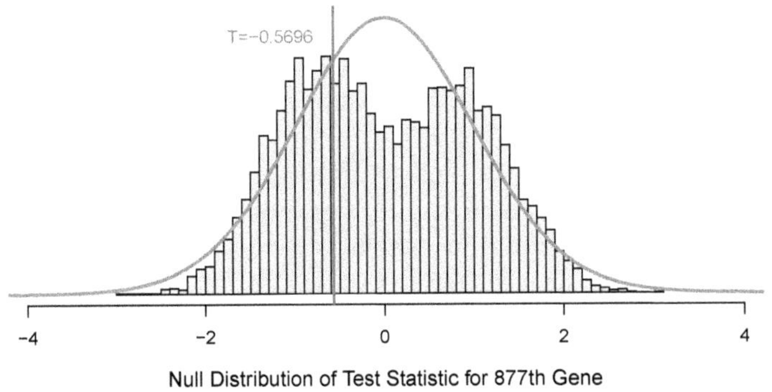

FIGURE 13.8. *The* 877*th gene in the* Khan *dataset has a test statistic of* $T = -0.57$. *Its theoretical and re-sampling null distributions are quite different. The theoretical p-value equals* 0.571, *and the re-sampling p-value equals* 0.673.

distribution. As in Section 13.5.1, we make use of a two-sample t-statistic for each hypothesis, leading to the test statistics $T_1, \ldots, T_m$. We could simply compute a p-value for each of the m null hypotheses, as in Section 13.5.1, and then apply the Benjamini–Hochberg procedure of Section 13.4.2 to these p-values. However, it turns out that we can do this in a more direct way, without even needing to compute p-values.

Recall from Section 13.4 that the FDR is defined as $\mathrm{E}(V/R)$, using the notation in Table 13.2. In order to estimate the FDR via re-sampling, we first make the following approximation:

$$\mathrm{FDR} = E\left(\frac{V}{R}\right) \approx \frac{\mathrm{E}(V)}{R}. \tag{13.13}$$

Now suppose we reject any null hypothesis for which the test statistic exceeds c in absolute value. Then computing R in the denominator on the right-hand side of (13.13) is straightforward: $R = \sum_{j=1}^{m} 1_{(|T_j| \geq c)}$.

However, the numerator $\mathrm{E}(V)$ on the right-hand side of (13.13) is more challenging. This is the expected number of false positives associated with rejecting any null hypothesis for which the test statistic exceeds c in absolute value. At the risk of stating the obvious, estimating V is challenging because we do not know which of $H_{01}, \ldots, H_{0m}$ are really true, and so we do not know which rejected hypotheses are false positives. To overcome this problem, we take a re-sampling approach, in which we simulate data under $H_{01}, \ldots, H_{0m}$, and then compute the resulting test statistics. The number of re-sampled test statistics that exceed c provides an estimate of V.

In greater detail, in the case of a two-sample t-statistic (13.11) for each of the null hypotheses $H_{01}, \ldots, H_{0m}$, we can estimate $\mathrm{E}(V)$ as follows. Let $x_1^{(j)}, \ldots, x_{n_X}^{(j)}$ and $y_1^{(j)}, \ldots, y_{n_Y}^{(j)}$ denote the data associated with the jth null hypothesis, $j = 1, \ldots, m$. We permute these $n_X + n_Y$ observations at random, and then compute the t-statistic on the permuted data. For this permuted data, we know that all of the null hypotheses $H_{01}, \ldots, H_{0m}$ hold; therefore, the number of permuted t-statistics that exceed the threshold c in absolute value provides an estimate for $\mathrm{E}(V)$. This estimate can be further improved by repeating the permutation process B times, for a large value of B, and averaging the results.

Algorithm 13.4 details this procedure.[18] It provides what is known as a *plug-in estimate* of the FDR, because the approximation in (13.13) allows us to estimate the FDR by plugging R into the denominator and an estimate for $\mathrm{E}(V)$ into the numerator.

We apply the re-sampling approach to the FDR from Algorithm 13.4, as well as the Benjamini–Hochberg approach from Algorithm 13.2 using theoretical p-values, to the $m = 2{,}308$ genes in the `Khan` dataset. Results are shown in Figure 13.9. We see that for a given number of rejected hypotheses, the estimated FDRs are almost identical for the two methods.

We began this section by noting that in order to control the FDR for m hypothesis tests using a re-sampling approach, we could simply compute m re-sampling p-values as in Section 13.5.1, and then apply the Benjamini–Hochberg procedure of Section 13.4.2 to these p-values. It turns out that if we define the jth re-sampling p-value as

$$p_j = \frac{\sum_{j'=1}^{m} \sum_{b=1}^{B} 1_{(|T_{j'}^{*b}| \geq |T_j|)}}{Bm} \tag{13.14}$$

for $j = 1, \ldots, m$, instead of as in (13.12), then applying the Benjamini–Hochberg procedure to these re-sampled p-values is *exactly* equivalent to Algorithm 13.4. Note that (13.14) is an alternative to (13.12) that pools the information across all m hypothesis tests in approximating the null distribution.

13.5.3 When Are Re-Sampling Approaches Useful?

In Sections 13.5.1 and 13.5.2, we considered testing null hypotheses of the form $H_0 : \mathrm{E}(X) = \mathrm{E}(Y)$ using a two-sample t-statistic (13.11), for which we

---

[18]To implement Algorithm 13.4 efficiently, the same set of permutations in Step 2(b)i. should be used for all m null hypotheses.

Algorithm 13.4 *Plug-In FDR for a Two-Sample T-Test*

1. Select a threshold c, where $c > 0$.
2. For $j = 1, \ldots, m$:
   (a) Compute $T^{(j)}$, the two-sample t-statistic (13.11) for the null hypothesis H_{0j} on the basis of the original data, $x_1^{(j)}, \ldots, x_{n_X}^{(j)}$ and $y_1^{(j)}, \ldots, y_{n_Y}^{(j)}$.
   (b) For $b = 1, \ldots, B$, where B is a large number (e.g. $B = 10{,}000$):
      i. Permute the $n_X + n_Y$ observations at random. Call the first n_X observations $x_1^{*(j)}, \ldots, x_{n_X}^{*(j)}$, and call the remaining observations $y_1^{*(j)}, \ldots, y_{n_Y}^{*(j)}$.
      ii. Compute (13.11) on the permuted data $x_1^{*(j)}, \ldots, x_{n_X}^{*(j)}$ and $y_1^{*(j)}, \ldots, y_{n_Y}^{*(j)}$, and call the result $T^{(j),*b}$.
3. Compute $R = \sum_{j=1}^{m} 1_{(|T^{(j)}| \geq c)}$.
4. Compute $\widehat{V} = \frac{\sum_{b=1}^{B} \sum_{j=1}^{m} 1_{(|T^{(j),*b}| \geq c)}}{B}$.
5. The estimated FDR associated with the threshold c is $\widehat{V}/R$.

---

approximated the null distribution via a re-sampling approach. We saw that using the re-sampling approach gave us substantially different results from using the theoretical p-value approach in Figure 13.8, but not in Figure 13.7.

In general, there are two settings in which a re-sampling approach is particularly useful:

1. Perhaps no theoretical null distribution is available. This may be the case if you are testing an unusual null hypothesis H_0, or using an unsual test statistic T.

2. Perhaps a theoretical null distribution *is* available, but the assumptions required for its validity do not hold. For instance, the two-sample t-statistic in (13.11) follows a $t_{n_X+n_Y-2}$ distribution only if the observations are normally distributed. Furthermore, it follows a $N(0, 1)$ distribution only if n_X and n_Y are quite large. If the data are non-normal and n_X and n_Y are small, then p-values that make use of the theoretical null distribution will not be valid (i.e. they will not properly control the Type I error).

In general, if you can come up with a way to re-sample or permute your observations in order to generate data that follow the null distribution, then you can compute p-values or estimate the FDR using variants of Algorithms 13.3 and 13.4. In many real-world settings, this provides a powerful tool for hypothesis testing when no out-of-box hypothesis tests are available, or when the key assumptions underlying those out-of-box tests are violated.

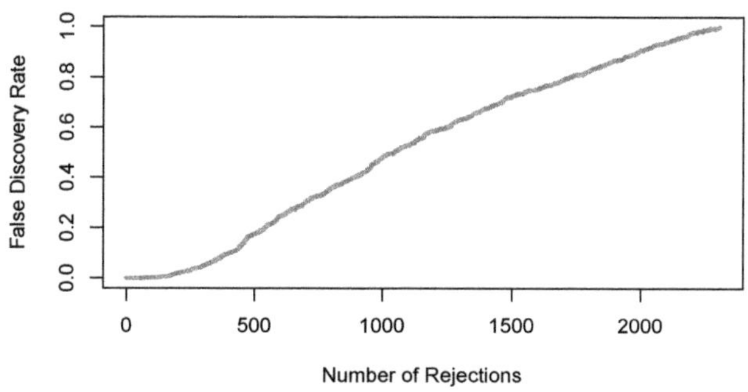

FIGURE 13.9. *For $j = 1, \ldots, m = 2{,}308$, we tested the null hypothesis that for the jth gene in the* `Khan` *dataset, the mean expression in Burkitt's lymphoma equals the mean expression in rhabdomyosarcoma. For each value of k from 1 to 2,308, the y-axis displays the estimated FDR associated with rejecting the null hypotheses corresponding to the k smallest p-values. The orange dashed curve shows the FDR obtained using the Benjamini–Hochberg procedure, whereas the blue solid curve shows the FDR obtained using the re-sampling approach of Algorithm 13.4, with $B = 10{,}000$. There is very little difference between the two FDR estimates. According to either estimate, rejecting the null hypothesis for the 500 genes with the smallest p-values corresponds to an FDR of around 17.7%.*

13.6 Lab: Multiple Testing

We include our usual imports seen in earlier labs.

In [1]:
```
import numpy as np
import pandas as pd
import matplotlib.pyplot as plt
import statsmodels.api as sm
from ISLP import load_data
```

We also collect the new imports needed for this lab.

In [2]:
```
from scipy.stats import \
   (ttest_1samp,
    ttest_rel,
    ttest_ind,
    t as t_dbn)
from statsmodels.stats.multicomp import \
    pairwise_tukeyhsd
from statsmodels.stats.multitest import \
    multipletests as mult_test
```

13.6.1 Review of Hypothesis Tests

We begin by performing some one-sample t-tests. First we create 100 variables, each consisting of 10 observations. The first 50 variables have mean 0.5 and variance 1, while the others have mean 0 and variance 1.

In [3]:
```
rng = np.random.default_rng(12)
X = rng.standard_normal((10, 100))
true_mean = np.array([0.5]*50 + [0]*50)
X += true_mean[None,:]
```

To begin, we use `ttest_1samp()` from the `scipy.stats` module to test $H_0 : \mu_1 = 0$, the null hypothesis that the first variable has mean zero. ttest_1samp

In [4]:
```
result = ttest_1samp(X[:,0], 0)
result.pvalue
```

Out[4]: 0.931

The p-value comes out to 0.931, which is not low enough to reject the null hypothesis at level $\alpha = 0.05$. In this case, $\mu_1 = 0.5$, so the null hypothesis is false. Therefore, we have made a Type II error by failing to reject the null hypothesis when the null hypothesis is false.

We now test $H_{0,j} : \mu_j = 0$ for $j = 1, \ldots, 100$. We compute the 100 p-values, and then construct a vector recording whether the jth p-value is less than or equal to 0.05, in which case we reject H_{0j}, or greater than 0.05, in which case we do not reject H_{0j}, for $j = 1, \ldots, 100$.

In [5]:
```
p_values = np.empty(100)
for i in range(100):
    p_values[i] = ttest_1samp(X[:,i], 0).pvalue
decision = pd.cut(p_values,
                  [0, 0.05, 1],
                  labels=['Reject H0',
                          'Do not reject H0'])
truth = pd.Categorical(true_mean == 0,
                       categories=[True, False],
                       ordered=True)
```

Since this is a simulated data set, we can create a 2×2 table similar to Table 13.2.

In [6]:
```
pd.crosstab(decision,
            truth,
     rownames=['Decision'],
     colnames=['H0'])
```

Out[6]:
```
                 H0   True  False
          Decision
         Reject H0      5     15
  Do not reject H0     45     35
```

Therefore, at level $\alpha = 0.05$, we reject 15 of the 50 false null hypotheses, and we incorrectly reject 5 of the true null hypotheses. Using the notation from Section 13.3, we have $V = 5$, $S = 15$, $U = 45$ and $W = 35$. We have set $\alpha = 0.05$, which means that we expect to reject around 5% of the true null hypotheses. This is in line with the 2×2 table above, which indicates that we rejected $V = 5$ of the 50 true null hypotheses.

In the simulation above, for the false null hypotheses, the ratio of the mean to the standard deviation was only $0.5/1 = 0.5$. This amounts to quite a weak signal, and it resulted in a high number of Type II errors. Let's instead simulate data with a stronger signal, so that the ratio of the mean to the standard deviation for the false null hypotheses equals 1. We make only 10 Type II errors.

In [7]:
```
true_mean = np.array([1]*50 + [0]*50)
X = rng.standard_normal((10, 100))
X += true_mean[None,:]
for i in range(100):
    p_values[i] = ttest_1samp(X[:,i], 0).pvalue
decision = pd.cut(p_values,
                  [0, 0.05, 1],
                  labels=['Reject H0',
                          'Do not reject H0'])
truth = pd.Categorical(true_mean == 0,
                       categories=[True, False],
                       ordered=True)
pd.crosstab(decision,
            truth,
            rownames=['Decision'],
            colnames=['H0'])
```

Out[7]:
```
                H0   True  False
          Decision
         Reject H0      2     40
  Do not reject H0     48     10
```

13.6.2 Family-Wise Error Rate

Recall from (13.5) that if the null hypothesis is true for each of m independent hypothesis tests, then the FWER is equal to $1 - (1 - \alpha)^m$. We can use this expression to compute the FWER for $m = 1, \ldots, 500$ and $\alpha = 0.05$, 0.01, and 0.001. We plot the FWER for these values of α in order to reproduce Figure 13.2.

In [8]:
```
m = np.linspace(1, 501)
fig, ax = plt.subplots()
[ax.plot(m,
         1 - (1 - alpha)**m,
         label=r'$\alpha=%s$' % str(alpha))
         for alpha in [0.05, 0.01, 0.001]]
ax.set_xscale('log')
ax.set_xlabel('Number of Hypotheses')
ax.set_ylabel('Family-Wise Error Rate')
ax.legend()
ax.axhline(0.05, c='k', ls='--');
```

As discussed previously, even for moderate values of m such as 50, the FWER exceeds 0.05 unless α is set to a very low value, such as 0.001. Of course, the problem with setting α to such a low value is that we are likely to make a number of Type II errors: in other words, our power is very low.

We now conduct a one-sample t-test for each of the first five managers in the `Fund` dataset, in order to test the null hypothesis that the jth fund manager's mean return equals zero, $H_{0,j} : \mu_j = 0$.

In [9]:
```
Fund = load_data('Fund')
fund_mini = Fund.iloc[:,:5]
fund_mini_pvals = np.empty(5)
for i in range(5):
```

```
    fund_mini_pvals[i] = ttest_1samp(fund_mini.iloc[:,i], 0).pvalue
fund_mini_pvals
```

```
Out[9]: array([0.006, 0.918, 0.012, 0.601, 0.756])
```

The p-values are low for Managers One and Three, and high for the other three managers. However, we cannot simply reject $H_{0,1}$ and $H_{0,3}$, since this would fail to account for the multiple testing that we have performed. Instead, we will conduct Bonferroni's method and Holm's method to control the FWER.

To do this, we use the `multipletests()` function from the `statsmodels` module (abbreviated to `mult_test()`). Given the p-values, for methods like Holm and Bonferroni the function outputs *adjusted p-values*, which can be thought of as a new set of p-values that have been corrected for multiple testing. If the adjusted p-value for a given hypothesis is less than or equal to α, then that hypothesis can be rejected while maintaining a FWER of no more than α. In other words, for such methods, the adjusted p-values resulting from the `multipletests()` function can simply be compared to the desired FWER in order to determine whether or not to reject each hypothesis. We will later see that we can use the same function to control FDR as well.

multiple-tests()

adjusted p-values

The `mult_test()` function takes p-values and a `method` argument, as well as an optional `alpha` argument. It returns the decisions (`reject` below) as well as the adjusted p-values (`bonf`).

```
In [10]: reject, bonf = mult_test(fund_mini_pvals, method = "bonferroni")[:2]
         reject
```

```
Out[10]: array([ True, False, False, False, False])
```

The p-values `bonf` are simply the `fund_mini_pvalues` multiplied by 5 and truncated to be less than or equal to 1.

```
In [11]: bonf, np.minimum(fund_mini_pvals * 5, 1)
```

```
Out[11]: (array([0.03, 1.  , 0.06, 1.  , 1.  ]),
          array([0.03, 1.  , 0.06, 1.  , 1.  ]))
```

Therefore, using Bonferroni's method, we are able to reject the null hypothesis only for Manager One while controlling FWER at 0.05.

By contrast, using Holm's method, the adjusted p-values indicate that we can reject the null hypotheses for Managers One and Three at a FWER of 0.05.

```
In [12]: mult_test(fund_mini_pvals, method = "holm", alpha=0.05)[:2]
```

```
Out[12]: (array([ True, False,  True, False, False]),
          array([0.03, 1.  , 0.05, 1.  , 1.  ]))
```

As discussed previously, Manager One seems to perform particularly well, whereas Manager Two has poor performance.

```
In [13]: fund_mini.mean()
```

```
Out[13]: Manager1    3.0
         Manager2   -0.1
         Manager3    2.8
         Manager4    0.5
         Manager5    0.3
         dtype: float64
```

Is there evidence of a meaningful difference in performance between these two managers? We can check this by performing a *paired t-test* using the `ttest_rel()` function from `scipy.stats`:

paired t-test
`ttest_rel()`

```
In [14]: ttest_rel(fund_mini['Manager1'],
                   fund_mini['Manager2']).pvalue
```

```
Out[14]: 0.038
```

The test results in a p-value of 0.038, suggesting a statistically significant difference.

However, we decided to perform this test only after examining the data and noting that Managers One and Two had the highest and lowest mean performances. In a sense, this means that we have implicitly performed $\binom{5}{2} = 5(5-1)/2 = 10$ hypothesis tests, rather than just one, as discussed in Section 13.3.2. Hence, we use the `pairwise_tukeyhsd()` function from `statsmodels.stats.multicomp` to apply Tukey's method in order to adjust for multiple testing. This function takes as input a fitted *ANOVA* regression model, which is essentially just a linear regression in which all of the predictors are qualitative. In this case, the response consists of the monthly excess returns achieved by each manager, and the predictor indicates the manager to which each return corresponds.

`pairwise_tukeyhsd()`
ANOVA

```
In [15]: returns = np.hstack([fund_mini.iloc[:,i] for i in range(5)])
         managers = np.hstack([[i+1]*50 for i in range(5)])
         tukey = pairwise_tukeyhsd(returns, managers)
         print(tukey.summary())
```

```
Multiple Comparison of Means - Tukey HSD, FWER=0.05
===================================================
group1 group2 meandiff p-adj   lower  upper  reject
---------------------------------------------------
     1      2     -3.1 0.1862 -6.9865 0.7865  False
     1      3     -0.2 0.9999 -4.0865 3.6865  False
     1      4     -2.5 0.3948 -6.3865 1.3865  False
     1      5     -2.7 0.3152 -6.5865 1.1865  False
     2      3      2.9 0.2453 -0.9865 6.7865  False
     2      4      0.6 0.9932 -3.2865 4.4865  False
     2      5      0.4 0.9986 -3.4865 4.2865  False
     3      4     -2.3  0.482 -6.1865 1.5865  False
     3      5     -2.5 0.3948 -6.3865 1.3865  False
     4      5     -0.2 0.9999 -4.0865 3.6865  False
---------------------------------------------------
```

The `pairwise_tukeyhsd()` function provides confidence intervals for the difference between each pair of managers (`lower` and `upper`), as well as a

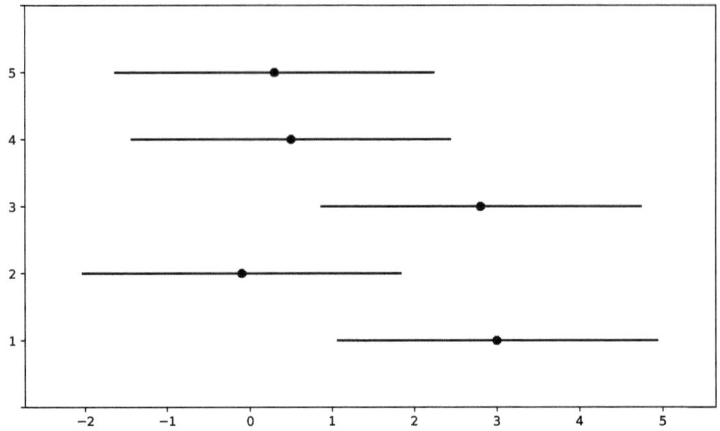

FIGURE 13.10. *95% confidence intervals for each manager on the* `Fund` *data, using Tukey's method to adjust for multiple testing. All of the confidence intervals overlap, so none of the differences among managers are statistically significant when controlling FWER at level* 0.05.

p-value. All of these quantities have been adjusted for multiple testing. Notice that the p-value for the difference between Managers One and Two has increased from 0.038 to 0.186, so there is no longer clear evidence of a difference between the managers' performances. We can plot the confidence intervals for the pairwise comparisons using the `plot_simultaneous()` method of `tukey`. Any pair of intervals that don't overlap indicates a significant difference at the nominal level of 0.05. In this case, no differences are considered significant as reported in the table above.

In [16]:
```
fig, ax = plt.subplots(figsize=(8,8))
tukey.plot_simultaneous(ax=ax);
```

The result can be seen[19] in Figure 13.10.

13.6.3 False Discovery Rate

Now we perform hypothesis tests for all 2,000 fund managers in the `Fund` dataset. We perform a one-sample t-test of $H_{0,j} : \mu_j = 0$, which states that the jth fund manager's mean return is zero.

In [17]:
```
fund_pvalues = np.empty(2000)
for i, manager in enumerate(Fund.columns):
    fund_pvalues[i] = ttest_1samp(Fund[manager], 0).pvalue
```

There are far too many managers to consider trying to control the FWER. Instead, we focus on controlling the FDR: that is, the expected fraction of rejected null hypotheses that are actually false positives. The

[19]Traditionally this plot shows intervals for each paired difference. With many groups it is more convenient and equivalent to display one interval per group, as is done here. By "differencing" all pairs of intervals displayed here you recover the traditional plot.

multipletests() function (abbreviated mult_test()) can be used to carry out the Benjamini–Hochberg procedure.

```
In [18]: fund_qvalues = mult_test(fund_pvalues, method = "fdr_bh")[1]
         fund_qvalues[:10]
```

```
Out[18]: array([0.09, 0.99, 0.12, 0.92, 0.96, 0.08, 0.08, 0.08, 0.08,
                0.08])
```

The *q-values* output by the Benjamini–Hochberg procedure can be interpreted as the smallest FDR threshold at which we would reject a particular null hypothesis. For instance, a q-value of 0.1 indicates that we can reject the corresponding null hypothesis at an FDR of 10% or greater, but that we cannot reject the null hypothesis at an FDR below 10%. q-values

If we control the FDR at 10%, then for how many of the fund managers can we reject $H_{0,j} : \mu_j = 0$?

```
In [19]: (fund_qvalues <= 0.1).sum()
```

```
Out[19]: 146
```

We find that 146 of the 2,000 fund managers have a q-value below 0.1; therefore, we are able to conclude that 146 of the fund managers beat the market at an FDR of 10%. Only about 15 (10% of 146) of these fund managers are likely to be false discoveries.

By contrast, if we had instead used Bonferroni's method to control the FWER at level $\alpha = 0.1$, then we would have failed to reject any null hypotheses!

```
In [20]: (fund_pvalues <= 0.1 / 2000).sum()
```

```
Out[20]: 0
```

Figure 13.6 displays the ordered p-values, $p_{(1)} \leq p_{(2)} \leq \cdots \leq p_{(2000)}$, for the Fund dataset, as well as the threshold for rejection by the Benjamini–Hochberg procedure. Recall that the Benjamini–Hochberg procedure identifies the largest p-value such that $p_{(j)} < qj/m$, and rejects all hypotheses for which the p-value is less than or equal to $p_{(j)}$. In the code below, we implement the Benjamini–Hochberg procedure ourselves, in order to illustrate how it works. We first order the p-values. We then identify all p-values that satisfy $p_{(j)} < qj/m$ (sorted_set_). Finally, selected_ is a boolean array indicating which p-values are less than or equal to the largest p-value in sorted_[sorted_set_]. Therefore, selected_ indexes the p-values rejected by the Benjamini–Hochberg procedure.

```
In [21]: sorted_ = np.sort(fund_pvalues)
         m = fund_pvalues.shape[0]
         q = 0.1
         sorted_set_ = np.where(sorted_ < q * np.linspace(1, m, m) / m)[0]
         if sorted_set_.shape[0] > 0:
             selected_ = fund_pvalues < sorted_[sorted_set_].max()
             sorted_set_ = np.arange(sorted_set_.max())
         else:
             selected_ = []
             sorted_set_ = []
```

We now reproduce the middle panel of Figure 13.6.

```
In [22]: fig, ax = plt.subplots()
         ax.scatter(np.arange(0, sorted_.shape[0]) + 1,
                    sorted_, s=10)
         ax.set_yscale('log')
         ax.set_xscale('log')
         ax.set_ylabel('P-Value')
         ax.set_xlabel('Index')
         ax.scatter(sorted_set_+1, sorted_[sorted_set_], c='r', s=20)
         ax.axline((0, 0), (1,q/m), c='k', ls='--', linewidth=3);
```

13.6.4 A Re-Sampling Approach

Here, we implement the re-sampling approach to hypothesis testing using the `Khan` dataset, which we investigated in Section 13.5. First, we merge the training and testing data, which results in observations on 83 patients for 2,308 genes.

```
In [23]: Khan = load_data('Khan')
         D = pd.concat([Khan['xtrain'], Khan['xtest']])
         D['Y'] = pd.concat([Khan['ytrain'], Khan['ytest']])
         D['Y'].value_counts()
```

```
Out[23]: 2    29
         4    25
         3    18
         1    11
         Name: Y, dtype: int64
```

There are four classes of cancer. For each gene, we compare the mean expression in the second class (rhabdomyosarcoma) to the mean expression in the fourth class (Burkitt's lymphoma). Performing a standard two-sample t-test using `ttest_ind()` from `scipy.stats` on the 11th gene produces a test-statistic of -2.09 and an associated p-value of 0.0412, suggesting modest evidence of a difference in mean expression levels between the two cancer types. `ttest_ind()`

```
In [24]: D2 = D[lambda df:df['Y'] == 2]
         D4 = D[lambda df:df['Y'] == 4]
         gene_11 = 'G0011'
         observedT, pvalue = ttest_ind(D2[gene_11],
                                       D4[gene_11],
                                       equal_var=True)
         observedT, pvalue
```

```
Out[24]: (-2.094, 0.041)
```

However, this p-value relies on the assumption that under the null hypothesis of no difference between the two groups, the test statistic follows a t-distribution with $29 + 25 - 2 = 52$ degrees of freedom. Instead of using this theoretical null distribution, we can randomly split the 54 patients into two groups of 29 and 25, and compute a new test statistic. Under the null hypothesis of no difference between the groups, this new test statistic should have the same distribution as our original one. Repeating this process 10,000 times allows us to approximate the null distribution of the test statistic. We compute the fraction of the time that our observed test statistic exceeds the test statistics obtained via re-sampling.

In [25]:
```
B = 10000
Tnull = np.empty(B)
D_ = np.hstack([D2[gene_11], D4[gene_11]])
n_ = D2[gene_11].shape[0]
D_null = D_.copy()
for b in range(B):
    rng.shuffle(D_null)
    ttest_ = ttest_ind(D_null[:n_],
                       D_null[n_:],
                       equal_var=True)
    Tnull[b] = ttest_.statistic
(np.abs(Tnull) > np.abs(observedT)).mean()
```

Out[25]: 0.0398

This fraction, 0.0398, is our re-sampling-based p-value. It is almost identical to the p-value of 0.0412 obtained using the theoretical null distribution. We can plot a histogram of the re-sampling-based test statistics in order to reproduce Figure 13.7.

In [26]:
```
fig, ax = plt.subplots(figsize=(8,8))
ax.hist(Tnull,
        bins=100,
        density=True,
        facecolor='y',
        label='Null')
xval = np.linspace(-4.2, 4.2, 1001)
ax.plot(xval,
        t_dbn.pdf(xval, D_.shape[0]-2),
        c='r')
ax.axvline(observedT,
           c='b',
           label='Observed')
ax.legend()
ax.set_xlabel("Null Distribution of Test Statistic");
```

The re-sampling-based null distribution is almost identical to the theoretical null distribution, which is displayed in red.

Finally, we implement the plug-in re-sampling FDR approach outlined in Algorithm 13.4. Depending on the speed of your computer, calculating the FDR for all 2,308 genes in the `Khan` dataset may take a while. Hence, we will illustrate the approach on a random subset of 100 genes. For each gene, we first compute the observed test statistic, and then produce 10,000 re-sampled test statistics. This may take a few minutes to run. If you are in a rush, then you could set `B` equal to a smaller value (e.g. `B=500`).

In [27]:
```
m, B = 100, 10000
idx = rng.choice(Khan['xtest'].columns, m, replace=False)
T_vals = np.empty(m)
Tnull_vals = np.empty((m, B))

for j in range(m):
    col = idx[j]
```

```
    T_vals[j] = ttest_ind(D2[col],
                          D4[col],
                          equal_var=True).statistic
    D_ = np.hstack([D2[col], D4[col]])
    D_null = D_.copy()
    for b in range(B):
        rng.shuffle(D_null)
        ttest_ = ttest_ind(D_null[:n_],
                           D_null[n_:],
                           equal_var=True)
        Tnull_vals[j,b] = ttest_.statistic
```

Next, we compute the number of rejected null hypotheses R, the estimated number of false positives $\widehat{V}$, and the estimated FDR, for a range of threshold values c in Algorithm 13.4. The threshold values are chosen using the absolute values of the test statistics from the 100 genes.

```
In [28]: cutoffs = np.sort(np.abs(T_vals))
         FDRs, Rs, Vs = np.empty((3, m))
         for j in range(m):
            R = np.sum(np.abs(T_vals) >= cutoffs[j])
            V = np.sum(np.abs(Tnull_vals) >= cutoffs[j]) / B
            Rs[j] = R
            Vs[j] = V
            FDRs[j] = V / R
```

Now, for any given FDR, we can find the genes that will be rejected. For example, with FDR controlled at 0.1, we reject 15 of the 100 null hypotheses. On average, we would expect about one or two of these genes (i.e. 10% of 15) to be false discoveries. At an FDR of 0.2, we can reject the null hypothesis for 28 genes, of which we expect around six to be false discoveries.

The variable `idx` stores which genes were included in our 100 randomly-selected genes. Let's look at the genes whose estimated FDR is less than 0.1.

```
In [29]: sorted(idx[np.abs(T_vals) >= cutoffs[FDRs < 0.1].min()])
```

At an FDR threshold of 0.2, more genes are selected, at the cost of having a higher expected proportion of false discoveries.

```
In [30]: sorted(idx[np.abs(T_vals) >= cutoffs[FDRs < 0.2].min()])
```

The next line generates Figure 13.11, which is similar to Figure 13.9, except that it is based on only a subset of the genes.

```
In [31]: fig, ax = plt.subplots()
         ax.plot(Rs, FDRs, 'b', linewidth=3)
         ax.set_xlabel("Number of Rejections")
         ax.set_ylabel("False Discovery Rate");
```

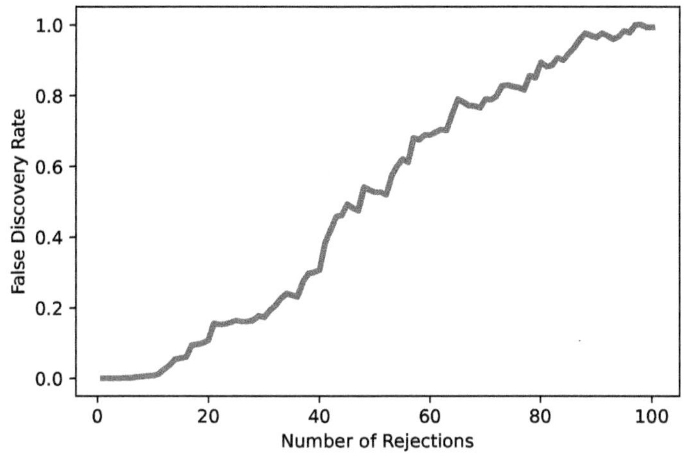

FIGURE 13.11. *The estimated false discovery rate versus the number of rejected null hypotheses, for 100 genes randomly selected from the* `Khan` *dataset.*

13.7 Exercises

Conceptual

1. Suppose we test m null hypotheses, all of which are true. We control the Type I error for each null hypothesis at level α. For each sub-problem, justify your answer.

   (a) In total, how many Type I errors do we expect to make?

   (b) Suppose that the m tests that we perform are independent. What is the family-wise error rate associated with these m tests?

   Hint: If two events A and B are independent, then $\Pr(A \cap B) = \Pr(A)\Pr(B)$.

   (c) Suppose that $m = 2$, and that the p-values for the two tests are positively correlated, so that if one is small then the other will tend to be small as well, and if one is large then the other will tend to be large. How does the family-wise error rate associated with these $m = 2$ tests qualitatively compare to the answer in (b) with $m = 2$?

   Hint: First, suppose that the two p-values are perfectly correlated.

   (d) Suppose again that $m = 2$, but that now the p-values for the two tests are negatively correlated, so that if one is large then the other will tend to be small. How does the family-wise error rate associated with these $m = 2$ tests qualitatively compare to the answer in (b) with $m = 2$?

   Hint: First, suppose that whenever one p-value is less than α*, then the other will be greater than* α*. In other words, we can never reject both null hypotheses.*

2. Suppose that we test m hypotheses, and control the Type I error for each hypothesis at level α. Assume that all m p-values are independent, and that all null hypotheses are true.

   (a) Let the random variable A_j equal 1 if the jth null hypothesis is rejected, and 0 otherwise. What is the distribution of A_j?

   (b) What is the distribution of $\sum_{j=1}^{m} A_j$?

   (c) What is the standard deviation of the number of Type I errors that we will make?

3. Suppose we test m null hypotheses, and control the Type I error for the jth null hypothesis at level α_j, for $j = 1, \ldots, m$. Argue that the family-wise error rate is no greater than $\sum_{j=1}^{m} \alpha_j$.

Null Hypothesis	p-value
H_{01}	0.0011
H_{02}	0.031
H_{03}	0.017
H_{04}	0.32
H_{05}	0.11
H_{06}	0.90
H_{07}	0.07
H_{08}	0.006
H_{09}	0.004
H_{10}	0.0009

TABLE 13.4. *p-values for Exercise 4.*

4. Suppose we test $m = 10$ hypotheses, and obtain the p-values shown in Table 13.4.

   (a) Suppose that we wish to control the Type I error for each null hypothesis at level $\alpha = 0.05$. Which null hypotheses will we reject?

   (b) Now suppose that we wish to control the FWER at level $\alpha = 0.05$. Which null hypotheses will we reject? Justify your answer.

   (c) Now suppose that we wish to control the FDR at level $q = 0.05$. Which null hypotheses will we reject? Justify your answer.

   (d) Now suppose that we wish to control the FDR at level $q = 0.2$. Which null hypotheses will we reject? Justify your answer.

   (e) Of the null hypotheses rejected at FDR level $q = 0.2$, approximately how many are false positives? Justify your answer.

5. For this problem, you will make up p-values that lead to a certain number of rejections using the Bonferroni and Holm procedures.

   (a) Give an example of five p-values (i.e. five numbers between 0 and 1 which, for the purpose of this problem, we will interpret as p-values) for which both Bonferroni's method and Holm's method reject exactly one null hypothesis when controlling the FWER at level 0.1.

(b) Now give an example of five p-values for which Bonferroni rejects one null hypothesis and Holm rejects more than one null hypothesis at level 0.1.

6. For each of the three panels in Figure 13.3, answer the following questions:

(a) How many false positives, false negatives, true positives, true negatives, Type I errors, and Type II errors result from applying the Bonferroni procedure to control the FWER at level $\alpha = 0.05$?

(b) How many false positives, false negatives, true positives, true negatives, Type I errors, and Type II errors result from applying the Holm procedure to control the FWER at level $\alpha = 0.05$?

(c) What is the false discovery proportion associated with using the Bonferroni procedure to control the FWER at level $\alpha = 0.05$?

(d) What is the false discovery proportion associated with using the Holm procedure to control the FWER at level $\alpha = 0.05$?

(e) How would the answers to (a) and (c) change if we instead used the Bonferroni procedure to control the FWER at level $\alpha = 0.001$?

Applied

7. This problem makes use of the `Carseats` dataset in the `ISLP` package.

(a) For each quantitative variable in the dataset besides `Sales`, fit a linear model to predict `Sales` using that quantitative variable. Report the p-values associated with the coefficients for the variables. That is, for each model of the form $Y = \beta_0 + \beta_1 X + \epsilon$, report the p-value associated with the coefficient β_1. Here, Y represents `Sales` and X represents one of the other quantitative variables.

(b) Suppose we control the Type I error at level $\alpha = 0.05$ for the p-values obtained in (a). Which null hypotheses do we reject?

(c) Now suppose we control the FWER at level 0.05 for the p-values. Which null hypotheses do we reject?

(d) Finally, suppose we control the FDR at level 0.2 for the p-values. Which null hypotheses do we reject?

8. In this problem, we will simulate data from $m = 100$ fund managers.

```
rng = np.random.default_rng(1)
n, m = 20, 100
X = rng.normal(size=(n, m))
```

These data represent each fund manager's percentage returns for each of $n = 20$ months. We wish to test the null hypothesis that each fund manager's percentage returns have population mean equal to zero. Notice that we simulated the data in such a way that each fund manager's percentage returns do have population mean zero; in other words, all m null hypotheses are true.

(a) Conduct a one-sample t-test for each fund manager, and plot a histogram of the p-values obtained.

(b) If we control Type I error for each null hypothesis at level $\alpha = 0.05$, then how many null hypotheses do we reject?

(c) If we control the FWER at level 0.05, then how many null hypotheses do we reject?

(d) If we control the FDR at level 0.05, then how many null hypotheses do we reject?

(e) Now suppose we "cherry-pick" the 10 fund managers who perform the best in our data. If we control the FWER for just these 10 fund managers at level 0.05, then how many null hypotheses do we reject? If we control the FDR for just these 10 fund managers at level 0.05, then how many null hypotheses do we reject?

(f) Explain why the analysis in (e) is misleading.
Hint: The standard approaches for controlling the FWER and FDR assume that all *tested null hypotheses are adjusted for multiplicity, and that no "cherry-picking" of the smallest p-values has occurred. What goes wrong if we cherry-pick?*

Index

G. James et al., *An Introduction to Statistical Learning*, Springer Texts in Statistics,
https://doi.org/10.1007/978-3-031-38747-0

www.ingramcontent.com/pod-product-compliance
Ingram Content Group UK Ltd.
Pitfield, Milton Keynes, MK11 3LW, UK
UKHW051641031026
15588UKWH00007B/1255
9783031387487